# GOOD
# BOOKS

# GOOD BOOKS

## A BOOK LOVER'S COMPANION

### STEVEN GILBAR

TICKNOR & FIELDS

NEW HAVEN AND NEW YORK

1982

*Library of Congress Cataloging in Publication Data*
Gilbar, Steven.
Good books.

Includes indexes.
1. Bibliography — Best books. I. Title.
Z1035.G54    011′.7    82-5554
ISBN 0-89919-127-4    AACR2
ISBN 0-89919-132-0 (pbk.)

Printed in the United States of America

V 10 9 8 7 6 5 4 3 2 1

*To my parents*

# Acknowledgments

I would like to thank the following people for their help at a very early stage in the preparation of this book — when I was thinking what categories to include and what sort of books to include in certain categories. Their ideas kept me on the right track. But as for the outcome, these kind people are innocent.

Robert Martin Adams, John Bowers, John Goldthwaite, Stanley Kauffmann, Helen Rogan, David Ehrenfeld, Paul Fussell, Dorothy James, Tom Settle, Paula Glatzer, Neal Goldman, Karin Goldman, David Wax, Elaine Cali, Charles Dumas, David Dubal, William Pritchard, A. D. Coleman, Robert Cornfield, Patrick Carr, Robert Duncan, Robert Christgau, Parke Puterbaugh, Alfred Gingold, Matthew Holtzman, A. Walton Litz, Stanley Karnow, Terence O'-Donnell, Michael Wood, Roger Sale, Maureen Mylander, Alex Szogyi, Kay Rees, Calvin Trillin, Alice Trillin, Michael Apstein, Don Cutler, Gillian Darley, Joan Kahn, Meira Chand, Barbara Apstein, Anthony Dias Blue

A special thank-you to my agent, Maria Carvainis, who has been helpful in many ways. And finally, James Raimes, Amy Mantell, and Floyd Tomkins have been remarkable in the care and patience they have extended to the editing of this book.

# Contents

# Foreword

BENJAMIN FRANKLIN was a guest at a dinner in Paris when the question was posed: What condition of man most deserves pity? Franklin's offering: "A lonesome man on a rainy day who does not know how to read."

You who hold this volume in your hands can never be in this pitiable state. You belong to a happy and privileged class. If you did not already love books, you would not have bought, borrowed, or stolen this one. You at once recognized that it offers you a choice among several thousand possible companions. You know that they will visit you at your convenience, whether you are lonesome or not, on rainy days or fair. They propose themselves as either transient acquaintances or permanent friends. They will stay as long as you like, departing or returning as you wish. Their friendship entails no obligation. Best of all, and not always true of our merely human friends, they have Cleopatra's infinite variety.

Well, perhaps not infinite. Naturally enough, I at once searched the subject index for the kitchen sink. It is not there. Still, the table of contents gives me Cooking, also Baking. Near enough, Mr. Gilbar. I must be content with only 500 subjects, with only 9,000 books, and with a dragnet that scoops up, among other matter, the Cosmos, the Future, and Philadelphia.

To ask for more than Mr. Gilbar gives us is to require the Library of Congress catalogue to collapse and then re-establish itself in our living rooms. He gives enough. Here are thousands of good books, ranging from the merely readable to the merely immortal, all departmentalized so as to satisfy most mutations of human interest and curiosity. Furthermore, this guide also addresses itself to the book junkie's recurrent plaint: "But I've got nothing to *read!*" Would Mallarmé have written his wistful

> *La chair est triste, hélas! et j'ai lu tous les livres*

with Mr. Gilbar's listings ready to hand?

The pleasures of this impressive compilation involve more than the immense quantity of bibliographic information it contains. It would be absurd to ask for more than the editor gives us, for of the listing of books there is no end. Yet one gets a certain all-too-human satisfaction from making mental additions. Where, one asks complacently, checking New Hampshire, is Thomas Bailey Aldrich's minor classic, *The Story of a Bad Boy?* Should not Louis Bromfield's best book, *The Farm,* show up under Ohio? G. H. Hardy's *A Mathematician's Apology* under Mathematics? Virginia Woolf's *Flush* under Dogs? Jack London's *John Barleycorn* under Alcoholism? All bibliomanes have a little list of books that never should be missed. Yet it takes but a moment to realize how silly is such petty snobbery. Besides, there is the reverse pleasure of recognizing that Mr. Gilbar's taste and knowledge are quite as superior as one's own. What a smart fellow he must be to include under New York City one of *my* favorites, *The Pushcart War* by Jean Merrill!

More positive pleasures offer themselves. To the compiler's catholicity we owe the tiny and delightful surprise of noting that he includes *As You Like It* under Forests. There is the Bard, cheek by jowl with a solemn work of scholarship called *Rain Forests and Cloud Forests.* How seemingly odd, yet, on reflection, quite logical to find under France the inimitable Castang detective stories of Nicolas Freeling. And suppose you are suddenly seized by a furious desire to read about aunts. I know of no way to sate such a lust if not with Mr. Gilbar's assistance.

But perhaps the chief attraction of *Good Books* lies in its retrieval value. I have been a professional reader for sixty years. Yet as I turn these pages I come upon hundreds of titles vaguely familiar and immediately attractive. They are guideposts to books I have always wanted to read but, as we always say, never got around to.

Mr. Gilbar can only list, arrange, index, and briefly comment on his titles. He cannot tell you how to get hold of them, though he assures us that "they exist and can be found." True enough, but it's getting harder. How many of us systematically use our local libraries after we've left high school? The resources of the library system remain truly astonishing. Should you be a buyer rather than a borrower, do not overlook either the small, independent bookshop or the second-hand bookstore. They may not have what you want, but the chances are good that the owner will understand what you want and either supply it or know how to get it for you. If American book buyers as a whole would demand more of all of their bookstores, the level of American culture would rise appreciably.

Meanwhile, *Good Books* should help toward that desirable consummation.

— Clifton Fadiman

# GOOD BOOKS

# Introduction

> Read the best books first, or you may not have a chance
> to read them at all                                    — Thoreau

Excellent advice, but who's to say which books are the best? Certainly not I. Hearing about and suggesting good books of all sorts, though, is my pleasure, and that's what I am doing in this book. What do I mean by good? Not morally good, and not academically good, and not simply popular, although the books I recommend may have one or all of those qualities. "Rewarding and pleasurable" — those terms I think characterize the books I am recommending.

Most books have subjects, and I believe most good books aim to treat well at least one subject of human interest — even novels. *War and Peace* at least concerns its title, and so does *Crime and Punishment,* and so does *Middlemarch* (subtitled *A Novel of Provincial Life*). So I have used a great many general headings to classify the books I have to recommend, and I hope the result is not only fascinating and happily surprising (Charles Lamb lies down with Tom Wolfe) to browse in, but of value in helping readers seek out rewarding and pleasurable books on wine, babies, India, the nineteenth century, and so on.

I assume readers will look first at the subjects they know something about. They may not agree completely with my choices or my characterizations of their favorite books or my omissions; but I hope they'll be reassured enough to trust my recommendations in subjects they don't know about but want to. Readers who agree with me that the novels of E. M. Forster, Paul Scott, and Salman Rushdie are good books about India, and that Thomas Carlyle, Charles Dickens, and George Lefebvre are worth reading on the French Revolution will I hope be encouraged to sample Ernest Schweibert and Ray Bergman if they're taking up fishing or Calvin Trillin and M. F. K. Fisher if they want to give someone a book about food. Sly Stone's immortal words hold true: "Different strokes for different folks." People take their reading pleasure in different ways. Some take it in being challenged, others in being lulled, but I hope all will find pleasure here.

All sorts of books appear here: novels, memoirs, studies, essays, biographies, picture books, children's books, thrillers, how-to books, old books and new, thick books and thin. You will find books by Bertrand Russell and Bill Russell; Edward Arlington Robinson and Sugar Ray Robinson; William Burroughs and Edgar Rice Burroughs. No book, I hope, is so abstruse as to be inaccessible to readers unfamiliar with its subject matter; none is so poorly written as to annoy readers; none so tedious as to numb readers' minds. Many are important books; some are great literature.

Many good books have been left out, from ignorance and from prejudice; many, many more because of space. If only every good book ever written could have been listed! I will be disappointed if I am not reproached for omissions as well as suggestions for substitution.

Remember, I'm recommending books with subjects. Many books of poetry are slighted here because though poems often have easily describable subjects, not so many books of poetry do. That may be their glory, but as far as this book is concerned it's their problem. So Wordsworth's *Prelude* gets in, and Anne Sexton's *Live or Die* gets in, but the *Collected Poems* of Pope doesn't.

Many books, especially the really great ones like *Emma* and *Ulysses,* are "about" several or many subjects, so I could have placed them in categories other than the ones I chose. I must plead that at least they fit where they are. If I then describe them as masterpieces, readers can infer that they may transcend their categories in any number of ways.

There are many categories I have not included. My guiding principle has been generality of interest: there must be at least five (preferably twenty-five) rather than one or two pleasurable general books on a subject to justify the inclusion of that subject as a category. Hence television, but not lasers; wine, but not vodka; fishing, but not bowling.

I should describe my own prejudices. I am a pleasure reader. I don't read a particular book because it has been assigned or because it should be read or because it appears on a best-seller list. I am fortunate in being free to read as inclination leads. But I've found that time is too precious to waste on unrewarding reading. That is not to say that I only read books that are "important." Far from it, I enjoy the most whimsical of writings, provided they have wit or charm. I like "dippable" books (to use R. L. Stevenson's expression) for bedside reading, and some nonbooks, and have found guilty pleasure in trashy books. I just don't like inaccessible, ponderous, pompous, or boring books.

In the period just before I embarked on compiling *Good Books* I read and enjoyed the following:

Siegfried Sassoon, *Memoirs of an Infantry Officer*
John Gregory Dunne, *True Confessions*
James Thurber, *The Years with Ross*
Mark DeW. Howe, *John Jay Chapman and His Letters*
R. L. Stevenson, *The Amateur Emigrant*
George Santayana, *Persons and Places*

Maureen Howard, *Facts of Life*
Baba Ram Dass, *Grist for the Mill*
Wendell Berry, *The Memory of Old Jack*
Edmund Wilson, *The Twenties*
Charles Dickens, *Martin Chuzzlewit*
John Cheever, *The Wapshot Chronicle*
Jessica Mitford, *Daughters and Rebels*
Ruth Jhabvala, *Heat and Dust*
Peter Matthiessen, *The Snow Leopard*
Evelyn Waugh, *When the Going Was Good*
Ford Madox Ford, *Portraits from Life*
J. Christopher Herald, *Mistress of an Age*
Anthony Trollope, *An Autobiography*
*The Diary of Alice James*
Jan Morris, *Oxford*
Mysteries: Dashiel Hammett, Raymond Chandler, Ross McDonald
Thrillers: Ross Thomas, Eric Ambler
Selma M. Fraiberg, *The Magic Years*
Lawrence Clark Powell, *Southwest Classics*
S. J. Perelman, *The Rising Gorge*
Farley Mowat, *The Snow Walker*
*The Goncourt Journals*
Theodore H. White, *In Search of History*
Irving Howe, *World of Our Fathers*
Paul Dickson, *The Official Rules*
Frederick Franck, *Pilgrimage to Now/Here*
Richard Brickner, *My Second Twenty Years*
John Updike, *The Maples Stories*
Philip Roth, *The Ghost Writer*
Joan Didion, *The White Album*
Bruce Chatwin, *In Patagonia*
Paul Scott, *The Raj Quartet*
Laurie Lee, *Cider with Rosie*
John McPhee, *Coming into the Country*
Edward Field (ed.), *A Geography of Poets*
Eric Partridge, *Dictionary of Cliches*
John Simon, *Paradigms Lost*
*The Oxford Book of Literary Anecdotes*
Edward Abbey, *Desert Solitaire*
Susan Sontag, *On Photography*
*The Whole Earth Catalog*
C. Woodham-Smith, *The Great Hunger*
Lawrence Durrell, *The Greek Islands*
James Clavell, *Shogun*
Hesketh Pearson, *The Smith of Smiths*

George Orwell, *Burmese Days*
Studs Terkel, *American Dreams*
H. L. Mencken, *Selections*
Michael J. Arlen, *Passage to Ararat*

There are plenty of old books on that list. In fact, I seldom read new books now, as I have become conscious of how many really good old ones I have to catch up with. Like a lot of people I find that my pleasure-reading time has diminished with such responsibilities as work, a wife, and a child, as well as with competing media (I like to see movies and good TV, and I am a magazine junkie as well). Then there is real life, like maintaining friendships, being outdoors, morbid introspection, and so on. Really not much time to read anymore; so I guess I'm a little picky. But then, there are times when I don't want a stimulating book, I want the pure escapism of a good mystery.

While I was working on *Good Books,* I had no time left to read for myself. I didn't read a single book during that time unless to decide whether to include it. My time was entirely taken up with consulting hundreds of people and sources: experts in special fields, specialist bibliographies, historical associations, librarians, the people next door. My quest: good *general* books. I asked my consultants to comment on my suggestions, and to make their own recommendations. Then I checked each recommendation against several other opinions and, wherever possible, against the books themselves. No, I could not personally read every book I wanted to list. But I listed no book that I couldn't double-check, triple-check, or cross-check, and I listed no book that didn't fit my idea of good.

A word about the entries within lists. Books are listed alphabetically by author. After a brief description of the book, there may be a reference to another book. If it has only a title, that means it was written by the same author. I have not given the name of the publisher, and sorry, some of the books may not be in print or readily available at your local bookstore. But I assure you they exist and they can be found.

PART I

# THE WORLD

# THE COSMOS

**Adams, Douglas, *The Hitchhiker's Guide to the Galaxy*** (1980). An interstellar jaunt provides the action in this hilarious science fiction novel. Its sequel is *The Restaurant at the End of the Universe* (1981).

**Anderson, Poul, *Tau Zero*** (1970). Continuous acceleration of space ship to near speed of light has incredible consequences in this "hard" science fiction classic. See *The Many Worlds of Poul Anderson* (1974).

**Asimov, Isaac, *The Foundation Trilogy*** (1951–53). A galactic empire far in the future on the brink of collapse; a bold conceptual framework with an imaginative feel for cosmic existence. Asimov, prolific polymath and master explainer, has written many books of science fact about the solar system as well.

**Boeke, Kees, *Cosmic View: The Universe in 40 Jumps*** (1957). "A graphic journey through the universe, to the edge of infinity in one direction and to the nucleus of the atom in the other." A mind-boggling tour de force.

**Calvino, Italo, *Cosmicomics*** (1968). Stories from the Italian master fabulist, narrated by Qfwfq and about his life, that range back to the beginning of the universe. "Metaphysical science fiction." See *t zero* (1969).

**Clement, Hal, *Mission of Gravity*** (1954). About a planet with dramatic variations of gravity, by a writer who takes the trouble to explain the basis in physics and astronomy for his imaginative extrapolations. See *Starlight* (1971), a sequel.

**Cloud, Preston, *Cosmos, Earth, and Man: A Short History of the Universe*** (1978). The whole story since the big bang, unfolded by a learned and graceful writer.

**Ferris, Timothy, *Galaxies*** (1980). Lavishly produced large-format volume of remarkable photographs which attempts to make unimaginable distances imaginable.

**Heppenheimer, T. A., *Toward Distant Suns*** (1979). Provocative enquiry into space colonization. See Gerald K. O'-Neill, *The High Frontier* (1976).

**Hoyle, Fred and Chandra Wickramasinghe, *Lifecloud: The Origin of Life in the Universe*** (1979). As an alternative to the "primeval soup" theory of the origin of life on earth, the authors theorize that earth was bombarded by comets and meteorites laden with living cells. Hoyle, a noted English astronomer, is also a re-

nowned science fiction writer; see *The
Black Cloud* (1957).

**Jastrow, Robert,** *Red Giants and White
Dwarfs* (rev. 1979). Physics and metaphysics join in what is probably the most lucid
account yet published for the layperson
of our descent from the stars. See *Until
the Sun Dies* (1977) and *The Enchanted
Loom: The Mind of the Universe* (1981).

**Mitton, Simon,** *Daytime Star: The Story
of Our Sun* (1981). All about the sun, from
ancient solar worship to the most ad-
vanced knowledge. See *Prentice-Hall
Concise Book of Astronomy* (1979) and *Exploring the Galaxies* (1978).

**Moore, Patrick (ed.),** *Rand McNally New
Concise Atlas of the Universe* (rev. 1978).
A perfect *vade mecum* for the armchair
space traveler. See Joseph H. Jackson and
John Baumert, *Pictorial Guide to the Pla-
nets* (rev. 1981).

**Niven, Larry,** *Ringworld* (1970). One
novel in a "future history" series, it can be
enjoyed for its inventiveness and technological extrapolations. See *The Ringworld
Engineers* (1980) and *Tales of Known
Space: The Universe of Larry Niven* (1975).

**Rey, H. A.,** *The Stars: A New Way to See
Them* (1952). For teenage readers: how to
locate the constellations. *Find the Constellations* (1954) is a simplified version for
younger children. For everyone, *Whitney's Star Finder* (rev. 1982) is a recommended field guide to the heavens.

**Sagan, Carl and I. S. Shklovskii,** *Intelligent Life in the Universe* (rev. 1978). The
popular American astronomer and a Russian scientist speculate on the question of
extraterrestrial intelligence. See Gerald
Feinberg and Robert Shapiro, *Life Beyond Earth: The Intelligent Earthling's
Guide to Life in the Universe* (1981).

**Silk, Joseph,** *The Big Bang: The Creation
and Evolution of the Universe* (1980). Cosmology surveyed by a leading expert, with
helpful diagrams.

**Stapledon, Olaf,** *Starmaker* (1937). A
mind-expanding novel that chronicles the
universe. Perhaps the most expansive
science-fiction novel ever written. See
*Sirius* (1944).

**Sullivan, Walter,** *Black Holes: The Edge
of Space, the Edge of Time* (1979). Lucid
survey of a cosmic mystery by the science
reporter of the *New York Times.*

**Whipple, Fred J.,** *Orbiting the Sun* (1981).
A standard guide to the solar system.

## The Moon

**Budrys, Algis,** *Rogue Moon* (1960). Already a modern classic of science fiction,
it is the tale of an alien labyrinth found on
the moon and humans' attempts at exploring it.

**Collins, Michael,** *Carrying The Fire: An
Astronaut's Journeys* (1974). In 1969, when
Neil Armstrong took the first giant step
for mankind, Collins found his own lunar
experience high above, alone in the command module. This is his vivid account of
that experience.

**Heinlein, Robert A.,** *The Moon Is a Harsh
Mistress* (1967). This novel about the revolution of earth's lunar colonies is one of
Heinlein's best. Other good lunar sci-fi
novels are Ben Bova, *Millennium* (1976)
and Arthur C. Clarke, *A Fall of Moondust*
(1961).

**Katzeff, Paul,** *Full Moons* (1981). Miscel-
lanea luniana; informal fascinating collection of facts regarding the moon.

**Thurber, James,** *Many Moons* (1943).
Charming tale of a little princess who
wanted the moon and how she got it. The
illustrations by Louis Slobodkin won the
Caldecott Medal.

## Mars

**Bradbury, Ray,** *The Martian Chronicles*
(1950). Not so much "hard" science

fiction as a collection of short stories — a mix of horror, satire, and nostalgia — that happen to take place on Mars. A classic.

**Compton, D. G.,** *Farewell Earth's Bliss* (rev. 1971). The story of a Kafkaesque martian penal colony and the attempt of the settlers to adjust themselves to its harshness. Unusually well written.

**Dick, Philip K.,** *Martian Time-Slip* (1964). Deftly juggling shifts in reality and psychotic delusion, Dick wittily challenges the reader. See *The Three Stigmata of Palmer Eldritch* (1965).

**Pohl, Frederik,** *Man Plus* (1976). In order to survive on the surface of Mars, our hero must undergo severe biological engineering and yet maintain his sanity until he arrives at his destination. Other interesting modern novels about Mars include Ludek Pesek, *The Earth Is Near* (1974) and Ian Watson, *The Martian Inca* (1976).

**Washburn, Mark,** *Mars at Last* (1977). Comprehensive, post-Viking guide to the red planet. Don't leave home without it. See Michael H. Carr, *The Surface of Mars* (1981).

## Imaginary Worlds

**Alexander, Lloyd,** *Chronicles of Prydain* (1964–68). Five-volume Newbery Award–winning series of young adult novels set in an imaginary land that blends the rich elements of Welsh legend and universal mythology.

**Carroll, Lewis,** *Alice's Adventures in Wonderland* (1865). Not only do children continue to be intrigued by Alice's wanderings through a strange and hostile world of grownups and animals (modeled on Victorian Oxford), but its imaginative texture and conundrums entrance adult readers as well. *Through the Looking-Glass* (1872) is its sequel.

**Eddison, E. R.,** *The Worm Ouroboros* (1922). Classic heroic fantasy set in a medieval world, written by a scholar of Old Norse.

**Garner, Alan,** *The Weirdstone of Brisingamen* (1960). Swift-paced fantasy about two children caught up in clashes of magic forces and such creatures as witches, wizards, goblins, elves, and dwarves. See *The Moon of Gomrath* (1963) and *Elidor* (1965) in which good and evil continue to battle.

**Le Guin, Ursula K.,** *The Wizard of Earthsea* (1968). The opening book of the Earthsea trilogy for young readers. Wizards, dragons, and Jungian archetypes interact in a world of numberless islands and vast oceans where magi wandered, looking for adventure and working magic.

**L'Engle, Madeline,** *A Wrinkle in Time* (1962). Newberry Award–winning novel about the Murry children's search in the fifth dimension for their father. Teaches about the nature of good and evil. See *A Wind in the Door* (1973), a sequel.

**Lewis, C. S.,** *The Narnia Series* (1950–56). Four children enter the land of Narnia through the back of a wardrobe and are caught up in events that frighten, excite, and enchant young readers, most of whom do not realize its profound Christian analogies. *The Perelandra Trilogy* (1938–56) is a science fiction allegory of combat between the forces of light and darkness.

**Lindsay, David,** *A Voyage to Arcturus* (1963). An Everyman journeys "through the wilds of the Arcturian planet Tormance, seeking from its strange inhabitants the meaning of the universe, some word of its creator. . . . This is not a common story of adventure. Rather, it is a story of the most dangerous journey in the world, the journey into the self and beyond the self" (Loren Eiseley).

**Swift, Jonathan,** *Gulliver's Travels* (1726). Bitter and devastating satire in the form of a fantastic tale of the four voyages of an honest, blunt English ship's surgeon to such places as Lilliput, Brobdingnag, and the country of the Houyhnhnms. As a tale of marvelous travels and as a model of English prose it appeals to old and young.

**Tolkien, J. R. R.,** *The Lord of the Rings* (1954–55). Epic fantasy about three hobbits of Middle Earth who must return the evil ring to Mordor, which is ruled over by the Dark Lord. In an earlier children's book, *The Hobbit* (1937), the fat and furry creatures are introduced. See *The Silmarillion* (1977).

## The Planet

**Atkinson, Brooks,** *Cingalese Prince* (1934). Witty, keenly observed account of an around-the-world trip on the freighter, *Cingalese Prince,* by the former drama critic of the *New York Times.* A similar trip was made by Aldous Huxley and recorded in *Jesting Pilate* (1926).

**Bodechtel, Johann and Hans-Gunter Gierloff-Emden,** *The Earth from Space* (1974). Spectacular color photographs of our planet taken from satellites. See Charles Sheffield, *Earthwatch: A Survey of the World from Space* (1981).

**Darwin, Charles,** *The Voyage of the Beagle* (1830). The young naturalist's account of his five-year around-the-world surveying expedition aboard H.M.S. *Beagle,* on which he began the observations that led to his formulation of the theory of evolution. See Alan Moorehead's beautifully illustrated *Darwin and the Beagle* (1969).

**Dinely, David,** *Earth's Voyage Through Space* (1974). Authoritative recapitulation of the earth's geological history, from how mountain chains are formed to earthquake patterns.

**Gerster, Georg,** *Grand Design: The Earth from Above* (1976). "The best book of aerial photographs ever. I've seen no other book — not even the space satellite ones — with perspective like this" (Stewart Brand).

**Morris, Richard,** *The End of the World* (1980). For anyone even mildly curious about possible scenarios for doomsday, this is the book. From earthquakes to collision with comets, from climate change to collapse into a black hole, the whole depressing picture. See *The Fate of the Universe* (1982).

*The New York Times Atlas of the World* (1980). Prepared from the same sources as the *Times of London Atlas* (the finest, but too large and expensive for the average home), it entices as it informs.

*The Next Whole Earth Catalog* (rev. 1982). Stewart Brand and Company's marvelous guide to the tools of the planet.

**Perelman, S. J.,** *Westward Ha! or Around the World in Eighty Cliches* (1948). A global amble by the master humorist and the caricaturist Hirschfeld.

**Wilford, John Noble,** *The Mapmakers* (1981). Account of man's efforts to map the surface of the earth is "thoroughly absorbing science and history, the work of an author who not only knows his subject, but enjoys sharing it" (David McCullough).

# CONTINENTS & REGIONS

## North America

*The Complete Field Guide to North American Wildlife* (1981). Handsome, well-indexed, pocket-sized book in two volumes: an Eastern edition assembled by Henry Hill Collins, Jr. and a Western edition by Jay Ellis Ransom. See William Burt, *A Field Guide to the Mammals* (rev. 1976).

**Farb, Peter,** *Man's Rise to Civilization: The Cultural Ascent of the Indian of North America* (rev. 1978). "A mind stretching book . . . crammed with ideas about the past, present, and future of mankind" (Clifton Fadiman). See the National Geographic Society's beautifully illustrated *The World of the American Indian* (1974).

*Our Continent: A Natural History of North America* (1978). Clearly written, nontechnical account of four billion years of natural history; superb photos and drawings. A National Geographic Society production. See Peter Farb's fine continental history, *The Face of North America* (1963).

**Parkman, Francis,** *France and England in North America* (1849–84). The struggles of England and France for North America recounted by "a grand, exciting, old-fashioned writer, florid and free without any self-consciousness, saturated in his subject" (Elizabeth Spencer). Samuel Eliot Morison has distilled its seven volumes into one, *The Parkman Reader* (1955). For precolonial exploration, see Farley Mowat, *Westviking: The Ancient Norse in Greenland and North America* (1965).

**Stout, Gardner D. (ed.),** *The Shorebirds of North America* (1967). With text by Peter Matthiessen and paintings by Robert Verity Clem, this modern classic "transcends its subject for it is high achievement both as literature and as art as well as first-class ornithology" (Hal Borland). A fine companion is Ann Sutton and Myron Sutton's *The Wild Shores of North America* (1977).

## Central America

**McCullough, David,** *The Path Between the Seas: The Creation of the Panama Canal, 1870–1914* (1977). Exciting, spacious story of the incredible project.

**Skutch, Alexander F.,** *A Naturalist on a Tropical Farm* (1980). The observations of a sensitive writer who has spent forty years on his farm in southern Costa Rica. See *A Birdwatcher's Adventures in Tropical America* (1977).

**Stephens, John L.,** *Incidents of Travel in Central America, Chiapas and Yucatan* (1841). Travel classic by the American diplomat and archaeologist whose expeditions in the period 1839–41 brought to light the accomplishments of the Mayan culture. See *Incidents of Travel in Yucatan* (1843). A fascinating synthesis of what anthropologists have learned about modern descendants of the Mayans is Eric Wolf, *Sons of the Shaking Earth* (1959).

**Stone, Robert,** *A Flag for Sunrise* (1981). Powerful novel about a group of Americans drawn into the maelstrom of revolution in a small Central American republic. Other political novels about the region include Norman Lewis, *Volcanoes Above Us* (1958) and Tad Szulc, *Diplomatic Immunity* (1981).

**Theroux, Paul,** *The Mosquito Coast* (1981). Picaresque novel about a New Englander who is convinced that American society is on the brink of collapse, so transplants his family to the primitive Central American jungle.

## The Caribbean

**Carr, Archie,** *The Windward Road: Adventures of a Naturalist on Remote Caribbean Shores* (1955). Delightful collection of essays. See his *High Jungles and Low* (1957) and *Ulendo: Travels of a Naturalist in and out of Africa* (1964).

**Fermor, Patrick L.,** *The Traveller's Tree: A Journey Through the Caribbean* (1950). Refreshing account of island meanderings by a writer of wit and charm.

**Harris, Wilson,** *Black Marsden* (1972). Poetic, visionary novel about author's native Guyana. Another Guyanese novelist of note is Edgar Mittelholzer; see *Children of Kaywana* (1952).

**Hearn, Lafcadio,** *Two Years in the French West Indies* (1890). Highly satisfying account of his stay in the Caribbean. His novel *Chita* (1887) takes place on a small island threatened by a tidal wave.

**Lamming, George,** *In the Castle of My Skin* (1953). Eloquent autobiographical novel of peasant childhood in Barbados which seems really to be about his village and its emergence from colonialism. See *Season of Adventure* (1960).

**MacInnes, Colin,** *Westward to Laughter* (1970). This energetic novel about a West Indian slave revolt of the eighteenth century is a literary sendup of the English adventure novel of that period.

**McKay, Claude,** *Banana Bottom* (1933). Vivid novel about Jamaican life, with memorable characters. *My Green Hills of Jamaica* (1975) is a memoir written in the forties describing his village boyhood around the turn of the century. See *Songs of Jamaica* (1912), a collection of poems.

**Marshall, Paule,** *The Chosen Place, The Timeless People* (1969). Novel about the effects of the invasion of an island by a team of social scientists. Rich in the texture of West Indian life.

**Matthiessen, Peter,** *Far Tortuga* (1975). Highly charged, original sea novel shimmering with the colors and sounds of the Caribbean, "a masterfully spun yarn, a little other-worldly, a dreamlike momentum. . . . Like everything of his, it's also a deep declaration of love for the planet" (Thomas Pynchon).

**Naipaul, V. S.,** *The Loss of El Dorado* (1970). Exotic and original history of Trinidad under Spanish and English rule by the greatest of West Indian writers. His novels of Trinidadian life include *The Mystic Masseur* (1957) and *The Mimic Men* (1967).

**Reid, V. S.,** *New Day* (1949). This first novel in which an old man recalls events of his lifetime in Jamaica, though based on historical fact, is "a liquid, lyrical thing of wondrous beauty. Homer himself might have sung it as he wandered from court to court in ancient Greece. The book has something of the flavor of the venerable Bede" (Zora Neale Hurston).

**Rhys, Jean,** *Wide Sargasso Sea* (1966). Set in Jamaica and Dominica of the 1830s and permeated with a Caribbean gothic atmosphere, it is the story of a mad Creole heiress, based on the first Mrs. Rochester, the insane wife in *Jane Eyre*. Many of the stories in *Sleep It Off, Lady* (1976) are set against the West Indian background of Rhys's childhood.

**Salkey, Andrew,** *A Quality of Violence* (1959). Historical novel depicting superstition in a Jamaican village in 1900. Salkey has also written poignantly about the plight of the West Indian emigrant in *Escape to an Autumn Pavement* (1960).

**Sanchez, Luis Rafael,** *Macho Camacho's Beat* (1981). Translated by Gregory Rabassa, this funny, poetic novel throbs with the latin beat of life in San Juan, Puerto Rico. See María Teresa Babín and Stan Steiner, *Borinquen: An Anthology of Puerto Rican Literature* (1974).

**Schwarz-Bart, Simone,** *The Bridge of Beyond* (1974). Low-keyed novel about the life of a black woman of Guadaloupe that captures the pastoral, languid feeling of the island. See *Between Two Worlds* (1981).

**Selvon, Samuel,** *Ways of Light* (1958). Collection of polished, light short stories by a writer who, like Naipaul, is an East Indian Trinidadian. His work, however, is more proletarian, often using native dialect.

**Thelwell, Michael,** *The Harder They Come* (1980). Inspired by the reggae movie of the same title, Thelwell's novel explores the life of the slums of Kingston, Jamaica. Roger Mais's novels of the fifties also dealt with the impoverished of Kingston; see *Three Novels* (1966).

**Walcott, Derek,** *The Star-apple Kingdom* (1979). Collection of sensual, musical poetry about the kingdom of the Caribbean by one of the best poets writing in English. See *The Gulf* (1969). His dramas include *Remembrance & Pantomine: Two Plays* (1980).

**Waugh, Alec,** *A Family of Islands* (1964). Well-researched, revealing history of the region from 1493 to the end of Spanish rule in 1898 by an English writer who has spent many years in the Caribbean. See *Love and the Caribbean* (1959).

## South America

**Alegría, Ciro,** *The Golden Serpent* (1935). The boat people of the Amazon and the Indian villagers who live beside the great river are the subjects of this sympathetic novel by the gifted Peruvian writer. A South American classic.

**Bates, Marston,** *The Land and Wildlife of South America* (1964). Part of the Life Nature Library, with text by the eminent biologist and a rich lode of photographic illustrations.

**Donoso, Jose,** *The Obscene Bird of Night* (1972). Densely written novel of the grotesque and surreal by a Chilean author of the "magical realism" school. See *Sacred Families* (1977) and *The Boom in Spanish American Literature: A Personal History* (1977).

*Fodor's South America* (curr. rev.). The best standard guide to the continent. *The Budget Travelers' Guide to Latin America* (curr. rev.) is the best for on-the-cheap traveling.

**García Márquez, Gabriel,** *One Hundred Years of Solitude* (1970). One of the great novels of our time. The history of the Buendía families, written as a hearsay report on the growth of a little Colombian town, blends realism and fantasy. The town is also the scene of *Leaf Storm and Other Stories* (1972) and *No One Writes to the Colonel* (1971).

**Greene, Graham,** *The Honorary Consul* (1973). Political kidnapping of a British

functionary supplies the framework for the classic Greene mixture of violent action and religious speculation.

**Matthiessen, Peter,** *The Cloud Forest: A Chronicle of the South American Wilderness* (1961). Extraordinarily honest and perceptive journal of his 20,000-mile trek from the Amazon to Tierra del Fuego. See his novel of the Amazon *At Play in the Fields of the Lord* (1965).

**Parry, J. H.,** *The Discovery of South America* (1979). Dramatic, vividly illustrated story of European exploration based on eyewitness accounts.

*Pre-Columbian Art of South America* (1976). Large-format photographic survey of archaeological specimens, principally ceramics, many of them from private collections not otherwise available for viewing.

**Quiroga, Horacio,** *South American Jungle Tales* (1950). Collection of tales by the Uruguayan master of the short story, who died in 1937. See *The Decapitated Chicken and Other Stories* (1976). The leading contemporary Uruguayan novelist is Juan Carlos Onetti whose *The Shipyard* (1968), like many of his works, takes place in the mythic town of Santa Maria.

**Sitwell, Sacheverell,** *Golden Wall and Mirador: Travels and Observations in Peru* (1961). The great cathedrals of several South American countries receive primary attention in this eloquent and perceptive volume by the English poet-critic.

**Sylvester, Hans (p) and Jacques Soustelle (t),** *The Route of the Incas* (1977). Magnificent photographic album of the Andes and inhabitants of the region.

**Vargas Llosa, Mario,** *Captain Pantoja and the Special Service* (1978). Politics and sex are the targets of this hilarious farce about a militarized brothel, fashioned out of a montage of documents, letters, radio broadcasts, dialogue, and dream sequences by the talented Peruvian novelist. See *Aunt Julia and the Scriptwriter* (1982).

**Waterton, Charles,** *Wanderings in South America* (1825). "A most entertaining and vivacious record of adventures and unconventional travel. One may open this book at any page and be sure of entertainment" *(Cambridge History of English Literature).*

**Waugh, Evelyn,** *Ninety-two Days* (1934). The English novelist's humorous account of his tropical journey through British Guiana and part of Brazil. Other amusing English travel pieces are Alan Pryce-Jones, *People in the South* (1932) and Christopher Isherwood, *The Condor and the Cows* (1949).

## The Arctic

**Bruemmer, Fred,** *Seasons of the Eskimo* (1971). Astounding photographs that capture the harsh beauty of a disappearing way of life. See *Encounters with Arctic Animals* (1972).

**Freuchen, Peter,** *The Peter Freuchen Reader* (1965). Posthumous selection of work spanning Freuchen's long career as polar explorer, fiction writer, journalist, resistance fighter, and TV entertainer. A blend of knowledge, wonder, truth, and artistry. See *Book of the Eskimos* (1961).

**Frison-Roche, Roger,** *The Raid* (1964). Novel about the winter life of a clan in the far north of Lapland. *The Last Migration* (1967) is a sequel.

**Giddings, James Louis,** *Ancient Men of the Arctic* (1967). Exciting account of American archaeologist's search for evidence of ancient arctic culture in Alaska.

**Herbert, Marie,** *Snow People* (1973). Vivid account of her two years among polar Eskimos in northwestern Greenland. See *Great Polar Adventures* (1975) and *The Reindeer People* (1976).

**Houston, James,** *The White Dawn* (1971). Novel based on an incident in 1896: three New England whalers were rescued by Eskimos and tragedy ensued. See *The Spirit Wrestler* (1980) and Katherine Scherman's novel, *The Long White Night* (1964).

**Kent, Rockwell,** *Greenland Journal* (1963). The artist's long-forgotten diary of being shipwrecked there in 1928; accompanied by his drawings. See *Salamina* (1935).

**Mowat, Farley,** *The Snow Walker* (1975). Tales of survival in the Arctic, ranging in time from the earliest life to the most contemporary, about a people now threatened with extinction by civilization. See *The Top of the World Trilogy* (1973) and *The Great Betrayal: Arctic Canada Now* (1977).

**Poncins, Gontran de,** *Kabloona* (1941). Arctic classic by a French aristocrat. His encounters with the Eskimos of the Canadian Arctic become a vision of how our Stone Age ancestors lived and thought.

**Ruesch, Hans,** *Top of the World* (1950). Survival novel that depicts the stark lives of Eskimos. See *Back to the Top of the World* (1973), about the same people.

## Antarctica

**Billings, Graham,** *Forbush and the Penguins* (1966). Warm, observant novel, mostly autobiographical, about a young ornithologist's five months alone observing penguins. Another novel about a man alone — this time with seals — is Marie Herbert's *Winter of the White Seal* (1982).

**Cameron, Ian,** *Antarctica: The Last Continent* (1974). Excellent narrative and photo history, principally about antarctic exploration. See *The White Ship* (1975), a novel.

**Halle, Louis I.,** *The Sea and The Ice: A Naturalist in Antarctica* (1973). Illustrated guide to the continent.

Langone, John, *Life at the Bottom: The People of Antarctica* (1977). Journalist's description of work and life of the National Science Foundation research teams on the isolated, forbidding continent.

Porter, Eliot, *Antarctica* (1978). The photographer went there in his seventies: large, seductive pictures of remote vistas and wildlife.

## *Europe*

Belloc, Hilaire, *The Path to Rome* (1902). This record of his pilgrimage on foot from Lorraine to Rome is one of his most felicitous books.

*Blue Guides* (curr. rev.). Considered to be the finest guidebook series extant, rich in historical background and with superb maps. The guides to the British Isles are especially noteworthy.

*Companion Guides* (curr. rev.). The most intelligently and stylishly written guides available. Primarily descriptive, the volumes on the south of France, Venice, Paris, and London are particularly good. For armchair traveler and tourist.

Horizon Magazine Editors, *A Horizon Guide: Great Historic Places of Europe* (1974). More than a thousand places. Can be happily pored over by people planning a trip to Europe and people remembering one.

*Let's Go; Europe* (curr. rev.). Prepared by Harvard Student Agencies, it is the best budget guide to the Continent.

*Michelin Guides* (curr. rev.). The great French series of guide books, noted for their thoroughness. The guide for France as a whole, as well as the ones for each province and for Paris, are *nonpareil*. There are also guides in English for such other countries as Switzerland, Spain, and Germany. The "Red" guides rank hotels and restaurants, while the "Green" guides describe the sights.

Smollett, Tobias, *Travels Through France and Italy* (1766). This memorable record of the English comic novelist's extensive excursions on the Continent is a classic of nastiness. Laurence Sterne's *A Sentimental Journey Through France and Italy* (1768) was written in response to Smollett's offensive book and steers a course between sentiment and irony.

Waugh, Evelyn, *Labels: A Mediterranean Journal* (1930). Spain, Italy, Monte Carlo, Palestine, Egypt, and Algiers visited by Waugh's cruise ship in 1929. This is the nice Waugh, the witty and charming guide.

## *North Africa*

Bowles, Paul, *The Sheltering Sky* (1949). One of several works of fiction by the American novelist and composer long resident in Morocco that are gothic in mood, often symbolic, usually treating the theme of the conflict between primitive and civilized values. See *Collected Stories, 1939–1976* (1979). Bowles has also transcribed the legends and tales of Mohammed Mrabet; see *Love with a Few Hairs* (1967).

Camus, Albert, *Exile and the Kingdom* (1957). Four of these six short stories are set in Camus's native North Africa; all explore the theme of spiritual exile.

Canetti, Elias, *The Voices of Marrakesh* (1978). Intelligent, evocative record of the Nobel Prize–winning writer's responses to the mysteries and beauty of the Moroccan city.

Douglas, Norman, *Fountains in the Sand* (1912). Recollections of a visit to Tunisia: "timeless, the quality essential and evocative" (Lawrence Clark Powell). Other English accounts that endure are Hilaire Belloc, *Esto Perpetua: Algerian Studies and Impressions* (1906); Robert B. Cunninghame-Graham, *Mogreb-El-Acka* (1898); Wyndham Lewis, *Filibusters in Barbary* (1932); and George E. Woodberry, *North Africa and the Desert* (1914).

**Gide, André,** *The Immoralist* (1902). Michel gradually rebels against self-sacrifice and other civilized standards of personal conduct. Most of the action of the novel is set in a sensuously detailed Algerian village.

**Julien, Charles A.,** *History of North Africa* (1971). Translation of the 1952 revised edition of the French classic, covering from the Arab Conquest to 1830. The best introduction to the Islamic history of the Mahgreb.

**Macke, August,** *Tunisian Watercolors and Drawings* (1970). Album of enchanting, sun-drenched paintings made by the German artist on his trip to Tunisia with Paul Klee before World War I.

**MacKendrick, Paul,** *The North African Stones Speak* (1980). The classical history of the region, from earliest times to the seventh century. An eloquent chronicle based on study of archaeological ruins.

**Spencer, William,** *Algiers in the Age of the Corsairs* (1976). Fascinating social history of the great Mediterranean city.

## Tropical Africa

**Achebe, Chinua,** *Things Fall Apart* (1958). The Nigerian novelist analyses what white missionaries and governments have done to West African tribal life. See *A Man of the People* (1966).

**Caputo, Philip,** *Horn of Africa* (1980). Exciting novel of contemporary Africa in revolution.

**Cary, Joyce,** *Mister Johnson* (1939). The rise and fall of the inimitable, capering Nigerian clerk who is in love with "civilisation." "A novel which is as breathlessly comic and endlessly ingenious as anything Cary ever wrote ends by making us weep and look at Africa with new eyes" (V. S. Pritchett).

**Conrad, Joseph,** *Heart of Darkness* (1902). Far up the Congo at the turn of the century. One of the finest short novels in English.

**Davidson, Basil,** *The African Genius* (1970). Introduction to the cultural and social history of Africa. See *Africa in History* (1974) and *The Lost Cities of Africa* (rev. 1975). He wrote the text to *Ghana: An African Portrait* (1976), an album of compelling photographs by Paul Strand.

**Dinesen, Isak,** *Out of Africa* (1938). The Danish writer's account of managing a coffee plantation in Kenya, transformed into a vibrant recreation of the beauties of the African landscape and its people. *Shadows on the Grass* (1960) is a collection of short stories set in Africa. See *Letters from Africa, 1914–1931* (1981).

**Emecheta, Buchi,** *The Bride Price* (1976). A Nigerian village in the 1950s is the setting for this novel about a modern girl up against traditional attitudes about women. See *The Slave Girl* (1977), *Destination Biafra* (1982), and *Second Class Citizen* (1974), about African emigrants in London.

**Gide, André,** *Travels in the Congo* (1929). Perceptions of an alert, unromantic mind in contact with new experiences; a fine journal.

**Greene, Graham,** *Journey Without Maps* (1936). A trek through Liberia as a spiritual search for author's own past. An unusual, richly textured book.

**Grzimek, Bernhard and Michael Grzimek,** *Serengeti Shall Not Die* (1961). Passionate account of efforts to save Africa's greatest aggregation of wildlife by director of the Frankfurt Zoo and his son. See *Among Animals of Africa* (1971).

**Hanly, Gerald,** *Warriors and Strangers* (1972). The novelist's early experiences in, and return journey two decades later to, East Africa: autobiography, history, and travelogue. His African novels include *Gilligan's Last Elephant* (1962), *Drinkers of Darkness* (1955), and *Consul at Sunset* (1951).

**Hoagland, Edward,** *African Calliope: A Journey to the Sudan* (1979). His trip to the Sudan — Arab north, black south, equatorial rain forests, encroaching Sahara, 115 different languages, 17 million people.

**Huxley, Elspeth,** *The Flame Trees of Thika* (1959). Poignant childhood memoir. The author's family left Edwardian England for the then-virgin wilds of Kenya. See *The Mottled Lizard* (1982) and *On the Edge of the Rift: Memories of Kenya* (1962).

**Kingsley, Mary H.,** *Travels in West Africa* (1897). This travel classic by the niece of Victorian novelist Charles Kingsley was a sensation in its day. Full of intelligence and humanity.

**Laurence, Margaret,** *The Tomorrow-Tamer* (1964). Collection of short stories about West Africa that portray the impact of technology and civilization on tribal life and individuals. See *This Side Jordan* (1960), a novel, and *New Wind in a Dry Land* (1964), nonfiction about Somaliland.

**Laye, Camara,** *An African Child* (1954). Also called *The Dark Child,* this novel by the popular Guinean writer beautifully describes traditional African life.

**Matthiessen, Peter (t) and Eliot Porter (p),** *The Tree Where Man Was Born* (1972). History, anthropology, and pungent observations of wildlife on a trek through East Africa, splendidly complemented by Porter's beautifully reproduced "living" photographs. See *Sand Rivers* (1981), about the Selous Game Preserve in southern Tanzania, with photographs by Hugo Van Lawick.

**Moorehead, Alan,** *No Room in the Ark* (1960). Affectionate account of an extended journey in East Africa — the plains and mountains, the last great wild-animal herds, the legendary Masai and Karamojong — and a moving plea for the preservation of the continent's creatures.

**Morris, Donald R.,** *The Washing of the Spears: A History of the Rise of the Zulu Nation Under Shaka and Its Fall in the Zulu War of 1879* (1965). Long, prodigiously researched, crisply told story of the Zulus from Shaka's leadership in 1816 to their defeat by the British six decades later.

**Mphahlele, Ezekiel,** *The African Image* (rev. 1974). The "African personality" by one of the continent's foremost literary critics. See *Chirundu* (1981), a novel.

**Musgrove, Virginia,** *Ashanti to Zulu: African Traditions* (1976). This wonderful book for children describes twenty-six African tribes, one for each letter of the alphabet. It is distinguished by the extraordinary Caldecott Medal–winning illustrations by Leo and Diane Dillon. They won the award the prior year for *Why Mosquitos Buzz in People's Ears: A West African Tale* (1975), retold by Verna Aardema. See Gail E. Haley, *A Story, A Story: An African Tale* (1970), also a Caldecott winner.

**Naipaul, Shiva,** *North of South: An African Journey* (1979). Part travelogue of East Africa and part meditation on the contemporary African spirit; a rich montage of portraits and encounters.

**Naipaul, V. S.,** *A Bend in the River* (1979). Political novel about an East African of East Indian descent who goes to live in a newly independent central African nation. A deeply disturbing vision of what happens in a place caught between the dangerous allure of the modern world and its own tenacious past.

**Nesbitt, Lewis Mariano,** *Hell-hole of Creation* (1934). Vivid account of the exploration of the Abyssinian Dankiel, the Great Rift depression where the temperature is frequently over 150 degrees. "The whole is unforgettable and contains many passages of great beauty" (David Garnett). The same country is evoked in Thomas Pakenham, *The Mountains of Rasselas: An Ethiopian Adventure* (1959).

**Ngugi Wa Thiongo,** *Petals of Blue* (1977). Absorbing novel of modern Africa. As James Ngugi, he published several others; see *A Grain of Wheat* (1967).

**Theroux, Paul,** *The Jungle Lovers* (1971). Colorful, full-flavored novel set in a small central African country in the midst of a revolution. *Girls at Play* (1969) also has an African background.

**Tutuola, Amos,** *The Palm-Wine Drinkard* (1952). Classic by a Nigerian novelist — a sort of African *Pilgrim's Progress* — written in pidgin English; mixes myth, legend, and folk tales.

**Van der Post, Laurens,** *Venture to the Interior* (1951). Deeply moving account of journey into an uncharted region of central Africa — and into the human spirit. See *The Hunter and the Whale: A Tale of Africa* (1967), a touching novel set among the whaling fleet based in South Africa during the winter.

**Waugh, Evelyn,** *Black Mischief* (1932). Colonialism on the run: Emperor Seth, who is exploited by a former Oxford classmate, gets carried away attempting to modernize his kingdom. Based on Waugh's trips to Abyssinia, wittily recounted in *They Were Still Dancing* (1931).

**Wykes, Alan,** *Snake Man: The Story of C. J. P. Ionides* (1961). In Tanzania lives the former ivory poacher, white hunter, self-taught herpetologist, animal collector, and full-time, lifelong egoist, who, it has been said, talks like a character from *Stalky and Co.* trying to talk like a character of P. G. Wodehouse and continually swearing at his failure. A little masterpiece about an eminent maverick.

**Wylie, John,** *Skull Still Bone* (1975). The imperturbable and resourceful Dr. Quarshie tracks down a murderer. First of a series of detective novels set in "Arkhana," a young West African republic in which the country doctor plays sleuth.

## Southern Africa

**Abrahams, Peter,** *Mine Boy* (1946). Black South African's sensitive novel about a man's move to the city from the country. His experiences in South Africa before his voluntary exile are recounted in *Tell Freedom* (1954). Other novels include *Wild Conquest* (1950) and *A Wreath for Udomo* (1956).

**Biko, Steve,** *Steve Biko: Black Consciousness in South Africa* (1979). Remarkable record of testimony given by the late black activist at the trial for terrorism of nine black South Africans. See *I Write What I Like: A Selection of His Writings* (1979) and Donald Wood, *Biko* (1980).

**Brink, André P.,** *Rumours of Rain* (1978). Resonant novel about a bigot and apartheid from an Afrikaner's point of view. See *A Dry White Season* (1979). Other Afrikaner novels are Uys Krige, *Orphan of the Desert* (1967) and H. C. Bosman, *Mafeking Road* (1947).

**Fugard, Athol, John Kani, and Winston Ntshona,** *Sizwe Bansi Is Dead* (1973). Award-winning, beautifully written play that offers an insight into black South African life. See Fugard's novel, *Tsotsi* (1980).

**Gordimer, Nadine,** *July's People* (1981). A tragic parable about the travails of a white family in a postrevolutionary South Africa. "For me this is the best novel that [she] has ever written. It is certainly the warmest and the simplest" (Alan Paton). See *Burger's Daughter* (1979) and *Selected Stories* (1976).

**Head, Bessie,** *When Rain Clouds Gather* (1969). Warm, humorous first novel about a woman from South Africa who goes to live in a Botswana village. See *A Question of Power* (1973).

**Hope, Christopher,** *A Separate Development* (1981). Very funny novel narrated by a seventeen-year-old boy of "indeterminate race." Full of telling observations of contemporary South African society.

**Jacobson, Dan,** *The Beginners* (1968). Ambitious, sprawling novel about three generations of a Jewish family. Ranges over South African life. See *The Price of Diamonds* (1957).

**Lessing, Doris,** *The Grass Is Singing* (1958). Powerful first novel by the Rhodesian-born novelist. A disturbing tale of racial struggle in the arid farmlands of South Africa in the early 1950s. See *African Stories* (1965).

**McClure, James,** *The Steam Pig* (1972). The first of a remarkable series of police procedurals that feature Tramp, a Boer cop; his assistant Zondi, a Zulu; and the Trekkersburg police force. A series about a police psychiatrist by Wessel Ebersohn gives a good view of South African political problems; see *Divide the Night* (1981).

**Paton, Alan,** *Too Late the Phalarope* (1953). Haunting novel about a young white South African police lieutenant, idolized in the community, who violates one of the strictest laws of that country governing the relationship between whites and blacks. See *Cry, The Beloved Country* (1948) and *Ah, But Your Land Is Beautiful* (1982).

## Near East

**Bell, Gertrude,** *The Desert and the Sown* (1907). Travels in Syria in 1907 by the English traveler, scholar, archaeologist, mountaineer, explorer, and arabist. Her letters, published in 1927, are fascinating.

**Christie, Agatha,** *Come, Tell Me How You Live* (1946). Light, bouncy memoirs of travels in Iraq and Syria with her archaeologist husband. Christie fans will discover clues to the genesis of some of her mystery novels.

**Dos Passos, John,** *Orient Express* (1927). Observations of people and places while speeding through the Near East on the famous train.

**Kinglake, Alexander William,** *Eothen, or Traces of Travel Brought Home from the East* (1844). Chronicle of an English gentleman's travels and impressions. "Perhaps the best book of travel in the English language" *(Cambridge History of English Literature).*

**Lewis, Bernard,** *Islam in History: Ideas, Men and Events in the Middle East* (1973). Essays by one of the keenest observers of the modern Middle East. He edited and translated *Islam: From the Prophet Muhammed to the Capture of Constantinople* (1976).

**Maxwell, Gavin,** *People of the Reeds* (1958). Vivid, poetic description of the primitive marsh dwellers of remote Southern Iraq. See Wilfrid Thesiger, *The Marsh Arabs* (1964).

**Roditi, Edouard,** *The Delights of Turkey* (1977). Twenty imaginative short stories that capture the essence of Turkey.

**Settle, Mary Lee,** *Blood Tie* (1977). Set in the Turkish Aegean, this National Book Award–winning novel traces the conflicts between old and new and between the price of honor and the cost of corruption.

**Vaczek, Louis and Gail Buckland (eds.),** *Travelers in Ancient Lands: A Portrait of the Middle East 1839–1919* (1981). The "curious" East as viewed through the lenses of early photographers.

## Arabia

**Burton, Sir Richard F.,** *Personal Narrative of a Pilgrimage to Al-Madinah and Meccah* (1855–56). Intrepid traveler and translator of *The Thousand Nights and a Night,* Burton was the first English visitor to Islam's holy cities. "The grim humor, headlong vigor, brilliant descriptions, and insatiable love of adventure make it one of the most exciting and personal volumes in English" (Martin S. Day).

**Doughty, Charles Montagu,** *Travels in Arabia Deserta* (1888). For some, the best travel account in English; for others, its formidable Elizabethan style makes it a ponderous bore. One of the most talked about and least read of books. Edward Garnett edited an abridgement (one-quarter of the original length) in 1931.

**Raban, Jonathan,** *Arabia: A Journey Through the Labyrinth* (1979). Young English journalist's witty and exhilarating account of his journey to the Arab oil states.

**Stark, Freya,** *A Winter in Arabia* (1940). In the tradition of such intrepid English travelers as Lady Anne Blunt (author of *A Pilgrimage to Nejd* [1881]), Stark eloquently details her stay in the southern Arabian town of Hureidha during the winter of 1937–38. See *The Southern Gates of Arabia* (1936). The best of her fine travel writings are collected in *The Journey's Echo* (1964).

**Thesiger, Wilfred,** *Arabian Sands* (1959). The fruit of many journeys through the parched Empty Quarter of Arabia, home of the Beder Tribes. The vivid sketches and anecdotes provide a rare — perhaps a final — glimpse of the ancient Arabian culture. See *The Last Nomads* (1980).

## East Asia

**Black, Gavin,** *The Golden Cockatrice* (1975). One of a series of superb thrillers by a writer whose "irresistible social commentary, inventive characterizations, and knowledge of the Far East make his books pure joy to read, even without their high suspense and mystification" (Dorothy B. Hughes). Under his real name, Oswald Wynd, he has written many fine Asian novels including *The Ginger Tree* (1977) and *Walk Softly, Men Praying* (1967).

**Blunt, Wilfred,** *The Golden Age of Samarkand* (1973). Large, handsome volume with a fund of illustrations about the conquerors and explorers who traveled across the central Asian steppes.

**Cartier-Bresson, Henri,** *The Face of Asia* (1972). Selection of compelling photographs taken over a twenty-year period by the celebrated French photographer.

**Dermout, Maria,** *The Ten Thousand Things* (1958). Strange, fragile, magical first novel by a sixty-seven-year-old woman of Indonesia. Sensually evokes East Indian life; some have called it a minor masterpiece. See *Yesterday* (1959).

**Hedin, Sven,** *Through Asia* (1898). Captivating account of a journey undertaken by a Swedish adventurer in 1893 to "traverse Asia from west to east, from the Caspian Sea to Peking."

**Lewis, Norman,** *Golden Earth: Travels in Burma* (1952). Lively account, full of brilliant descriptive passages, by a tireless, resourceful and perceptive traveler. See *Dragon Apparent: Travels in Indo-China* (1951) and *A Single Pilgrim* (1954), a novel of modern Thailand.

**Matthiessen, Peter,** *The Snow Leopard* (1978). National Book Award winner based on the journal of his trek with field biologist George Schaller in upper Nepal. A wise and beautiful book. An excellent companion volume is Schaller's *Stones of Silence: Journeys in the Himalaya* (1980).

**Maugham, W. Somerset,** *The Gentleman in the Parlour* (1933). A master storyteller's charming account of a journey from Rangoon to Haiphong.

**Naipaul, V. S.,** *Among the Believers: An Islamic Journey* (1981). From his own intensive seven-month journey to Iran, Malaysia, Indonesia, and Pakistan, an unprecedented revelation of the Islamic world today.

**Orwell, George,** *Burmese Days* (1934). Bitter, satirical novel about the British in pre–World War II Burma and the effects of imperialism.

## Oceania

*Art of the Pacific* (1980). Beautiful photographs of art objects from collections of

New Zealand museums and of works by Polynesian and Melanesian artists, plus a lucid text.

**Daws, Gavan,** *A Dream of Islands: Voyages of Self-discovery in the South Seas* (1980). Fascinating stories of Melville, Robert Louis Stevenson, missionary John Williams, political adventurer Walter Murray Gibson, and Gauguin, who sought the line between savagery and civilization.

**Day, A. Grove (ed.),** *Best South Sea Stories* (1964). Fine collection of short stories guaranteed to fuel the reader's tropical isle fantasies. See *Explorers of the Pacific* (1966) and *Rascals in Paradise* (1957), written with James A. Michener.

**Froude, James Anthony,** *Oceana* (1887). Engaging, provocative record of his journey to the South Pacific. The American painter John LaFarge's *Reminiscences of the South Seas* (1912) is an account of his travels with his friend Henry Adams.

**Heyerdahl, Thor,** *Fatu-Hiva: Back to Nature on a Pacific Island* (1975). The famed skipper of *Kon-tiki* lyrically describes the remote island in the Marquesas where he spent his honeymoon in the 1930s.

**Michener, James A.,** *Tales of the South Pacific* (1947). Pulitzer Prize–winning sketches about marines, seabees, and nurses amid the island-hopping warfare of World War II. Basis of Rodgers & Hammerstein musical *South Pacific.* See *Return to Paradise* (1951).

**Moorehead, Alan,** *The Fatal Impact: An Account of the Invasion of the South Pacific, 1767–1840* (1966). The devastating effects of the white man since Captain Cook on Tahiti, the east coast of Australia, and Antarctica.

**Nordhoff, Charles and James Hall,** *The Bounty Trilogy* (1932–34). Fact-based popular novels about the mutiny against Captain Bligh, his journey to safety, and the life of the mutineers on Pitcairn Island.

**Stevenson, Mrs. Robert Louis,** *Our Samoan Adventure* (1955). Diary by the famous writer's wife of three years of their life together in the South Seas before his death in 1894. See Joseph W. Ellison, *Tusitala of the South Seas: The Story of Robert Louis Stevenson's Life in the South Pacific* (1953) and Stevenson's own *Vailima Letters* (1896).

**Vayda, Andrew P. (ed.),** *People and Cultures of the Pacific: An Anthropological Reader* (1968). Nontechnical essays by such noted anthropologists as Mead and Malinowski about their work with Pacific islanders.

# COUNTRIES

## *Canada*

**Berton, Pierre,** *Klondike Fever: The Life and Death of the Last Great Gold Rush* (1958). Tells with drama and humor the story of the Klondike gold rush of 1897–99. See *The Wild Frontier* (1977) and *My Country* (1976).

**Blais, Marie-Clair,** *A Season in the Life of Emmanuel* (1966). Beautifully composed novel about the family of a poor Quebec farmer viewed through the eyes of the youngest of sixteen children. See *St. Lawrence Blues* (1974).

**Callaghan, Morley,** *Now That April's Here* (1936). Collection of realistic stories, distinguished by the author's perception and humanity. See *Stories* (1959) and *Close to the Sun* (1978).

**Creighton, Donald Grant,** *John A. MacDonald* (1953–56). Biography of the chief architect of the Dominion of Canada and its first prime minister. See *The Story of Canada* (1961), a one-volume history.

**Davies, Robertson,** *The Salterton Trilogy* (1952–58). Like Trollope's Barsetshire novels, these take a satirical look at an Ontario community (in fact, Kingston). The first of the novels is *Tempest Tost.*

**Galbraith, John Kenneth,** *The Scotch* (1964). Graceful, anecdotal memoir of the Scotch community in Ontario where he grew up.

**Gallant, Mavis,** *My Heart Is Broken* (1964). Volume of short stories whose locales range from the Canadian north woods to the Italian Riviera, by a writer with the ability to make the ordinary seem eccentric and vice versa. See *From the Fifteenth District* (1979).

**Grant, Rev. George M.,** *Ocean to Ocean: Sandford Fleming's Expedition Through Canada in 1872* (1873). First-person account of Fleming's journey from Halifax to Victoria in search of a transcontinental railway route. The Lewis and Clark expedition of Canada.

**Hoagland, Edward,** *Notes from the Century Before: A Journal from British Columbia* (1969). Encounters with the trappers, traders, prospectors, and explorers who opened the last frontier, by one of America's most gifted writers. "A beautiful book: so sharp and persistent in rendering the visible world, and yet so strangely wild with feeling" (Philip Roth).

**Laurence, Margaret,** *A Jest of God* (1966). About a thirty-four-year-old virgin and her neurotic mother, it is one of the Manawaka Quintet of novels about life in a bleak town on the Manitoba plains, each distinguished by penetrating characterization. See *The Stone Angel* (1964) and *The Diviners* (1974).

**MacLennan, Hugh,** *The Colour of Canada* (1967). Thoughtful book about Canada by one of its most distinguished novel-

ists; beautifully illustrated by leading photographers. See his classic novels, *Two Solitudes* (1946) and *Each Man's Son* (1951).

**Munro, Alice,** *Lives of Girls and Women* (1973). Semiautobiographical novel about growing up in rural Canada, told with unusual skill and sensitivity. See *The Beggar Maid: Stories of Flo and Rose* (1979).

*Reader's Digest Canadian Book of the Road* (1979). An exceptionally handsome, 400-page all-inclusive motoring guide, with detailed color maps. See *Scenic Wonders of Canada* (1979).

**Stegner, Wallace,** *Wolf Willow* (1962). Amalgam of history, reminiscences, and fiction recreates the last Plains frontier — southern Saskatchewan. That province is further portrayed in R. D. Symons, *Silton Seasons* (1975) and Sinclair Ross's novel, *As for Me and My House* (1941).

**Woodstock, George,** *The Canadians* (1980). Lively, candid, well-illustrated interpretative account of Canada by its leading man of letters. Interesting to compare with *O Canada: An American's Notes on Canadian Culture* (1965), by his American counterpart, Edmund Wilson.

## Mexico

**Bedford, Sybille,** *The Sudden View: A Traveller's Tale from Mexico* (rev. 1960). The perceptions and prejudices of the noted English writer are in full evidence in a book which is "remarkably acute, delicate and vivid" (Aldous Huxley). Huxley's own book of Mexican recollections, *Beyond the Mexique Bay* (1934), is also enjoyable.

**Calderón de la Barca, Frances E.,** *Life in Mexico* (1843). This travel classic is the diary of Fanny Inglis, a Scotswoman who married the first Spanish ambassador to Mexico and spent two amazed years there.

**Diaz del Castillo, Bernal,** *Discovery and Conquest of Mexico* (1632). Written by one of Cortes's lieutenants, this frank and captivating chronicle of the conquistadors ranks with the great historical memoirs.

**Dobie, J. Frank,** *Tongues of the Monte* (1935). Beautifully understated tales based on a trip to Mexico by the Texan writer.

**Fuentes, Carlos,** *The Death of Artemio Cruz* (1964). Richly textured novel of power and imagination; a panorama of modern Mexican history in one man's life. See *Terra Nostra* (1976), *The Hydra Head* (1978), and *A Change of Skin* (1968).

**Greene, Graham,** *Another Mexico* (1939). Superbly written narrative of a journey in the wake of the Mexican revolution through Tabasco and Chiapas, from which emerges an impression of a violent and forbidding land. Greene called it a background book for *The Power and the Glory*.

**Krutch, Joseph Wood,** *The Forgotten Peninsula: A Naturalist in Baja California* (1961). Informal, rambling portrait of Baja by a wise observer of the natural world.

**Lawrence, D. H.,** *Mornings in Mexico* (1927). Luminous, brief book about encounters with Mexican Indians.

**Paz, Octavio,** *The Labyrinth of Solitude* (1962). Classic essays about the Mexican character; sensitive, urbane scholarship by a brilliant poet. Paz's own poetry can be sampled in *Early Poems 1935–1955* (rev. 1973), translated by Muriel Rukeyser.

**Prescott, William Hickling,** *Conquest of Mexico* (1843). Classic account of the fall of the Aztec empire before the Spanish legions by an American historian with a feeling for landscape and pageant and a colorful, often purple, prose style.

**Reyes, Alfonso,** *Mexico in a Nutshell and Other Essays* (1964). Wide-ranging essays by a master stylist who was Mexico's ranking man of letters at the time of his death in 1959.

**Rodman, Selden,** *A Short History of Mexico* (1981). From the Aztecs to the current oil boom in a concise, brief, informal volume by the American poet, art critic, and hispanophile.

**Rulfo, Juan,** *The Burning Plain and Other Stories* (1967). Sympathetic pictures of peasants' lives leavened by Catholicism and Aztec paganism. See *Pedro Paramo* (1959).

**Simon, Kate,** *Mexico: Places and Pleasures* (rev. 1979). Since its first appearance in 1963, this charming guide cum book of essays has been the standard companion for travelers to Mexico. The best budget guide is Carl Franz, *The People's Guide to Mexico* (curr. rev.).

**Traven, B.,** *The Night Visitor, and Other Stories* (1966). Set mainly in the back country, this collection of stories is an excellent introduction to one of the leading interpreters of Mexican history and culture.

## Cuba

**Barbour, Thomas,** *A Naturalist in Cuba* (1944). Facts and adventures described by an urbane writer and naturalist.

**Cabrera Infante, Guillermo,** *Three Trapped Tigers* (1971). Set on the eve of Castro's victory in Havana, a remarkable novel with Joycean humor and Cuban vernacular. Another dazzling Cuban novelist is José Lezama Lima; see *Paradiso* (1974).

**Carpentier, Alejo,** *The Lost Steps* (rev. 1967). Originally published in Spanish in 1953, this audacious novel revolves around a quest in the Amazon jungle for the marvelous and magical Latin American reality. See *Explosion in the Cathedral* (1963).

**Dorschner, John,** *The Winds of December* (1980). Lively, smoothly written journalistic account of the Cuban Revolution based on extensive interviews and U.S. State Department documents.

**Thomas, Hugh,** *Cuba: The Pursuit of Freedom* (1971). Long but popular and graceful history.

## Haiti

**Dunham, Katherine,** *Island Possessed* (1969). Personal, honest account of the noted American dancer's love affair with Haiti. Three decades earlier another American black woman, Zora Neale Hurston, published an account of her visit to the island in *Tell My Horse* (1938).

**Greene, Graham,** *The Comedians* (1966). Three men caught up in a revolution against Papa Doc Duvalier in an absorbing and surprisingly optimistic novel.

**Rodman, Selden,** *Haiti, The Black Republic* (rev. 1963). Poetic look at the country by an American poet long resident there. More prosaic is Edmund Wilson's *Red, Black, Blond, and Olive* (1956), the "Black" section of which is about Haiti.

**Roumain, Jacques,** *Masters of the Dew* (tr. by Langston Hughes and Mercer Cook, 1944). Highly colorful novel of black life in a Haitian peasant village in vivid, lyrical, and simple prose.

**Thoby-Marcelin, Philippe and Pierre Marcelin,** *The Beast of the Haitian Hills* (1946). Folk wisdom, fable, and voodoo in a novel in which "the skill, grace and spice of the storytelling are art from a distant and neglected world" (Arna Bontemps). See *All Men are Mad* (1970).

## Brazil

**Amado, Jorge,** *Gabriela, Clove, and Cinnamon* (1962). Sensuous, playful novel about the effect of a lovely woman on the inhabitants of a sleepy seaport. See *Dona Flor and Her Two Husbands* (1969) and *Home is the Sailor* (1964). His earlier novels, such as *The Violent Land* (1945), are broad-scaled studies of social injustice.

**Bishop, Elizabeth and Emanuel Brasil (eds.),** *An Anthology of Twentieth-Century Brazilian Poetry* (1972). Superbly translated selection of a unique and exciting body of verse. For a survey of contemporary fiction, see William L. Grossman (ed.), *Modern Brazilian Short Stories* (1974). A valuable older work is Samuel Putnam's *Marvelous Journey: Four Centuries of Brazilian Literature* (1948).

**Burns, E. Bradford,** *A History of Brazil* (rev. 1980). Best single-volume history, it is a panoramic interpretation of Brazil's past from its discovery to the present.

**Cunha, Euclides da,** *Rebellion in the Backlands* (1902). A singular, amazing, somewhat enigmatic epic which reads like a novel; it has been termed the "Bible of Brazilian nationality." William Gass has declared that it "will be recognized, worldwide, as one of the greatest masterpieces of Western prose."

**Dos Passos, John,** *Brazil on the Move* (1963). The product of the writer's travels during his late years, it has the novelist's feel for the land and its people. Thirty years earlier, Peter Fleming's journey to the interior resulted in the worldwide best seller, *Brazilian Adventure* (1934), which is still delightful reading.

**Freyre, Gilberto,** *Masters and the Slaves* (1964). Brazil's greatest social historian uses buildings as symbols of his country's transition from Portugese colony to modern nationhood. See *The Gilberto Freyre Reader* (1974).

**Guimaraes Rosa, João,** *The Devil to Pay in the Backlands* (1956). Intricate, baroque epic by a writer who has been called "beyond dispute Latin America's greatest novelist" (Emir Rodriguez Monegal).

**Lins de Rego, Jose,** *Plantation Boy* (1966). Part of the Sugar Cane Cycle of novels about life in rural northeast Brazil.

**Machado de Assis, Joachim Maria,** *Epitaph of a Small Winner* (1880). From beyond the grave, a witty and cynical ghost recalls his life — his illicit love affairs, his political ambition, his personal jealousies — and decides that, though dead, he is still ahead of the game; by a brilliant novelist who has been said to combine the psychological probing of Henry James with the whimsy of Laurence Sterne.

**Ramos, Gracilianos,** *Barren Lives* (1938). A poor family in the pitiless regional droughts. An eloquent, spare novel.

**Wagley, Charles,** *An Introduction to Brazil* (rev. 1971). Concise illustrated story of modern Brazil. See *Amazon Town: A Study of Man and the Tropics* (rev. 1976) and *Welcome of Tears: The Tapirape Indians of Central Brazil* (1977).

## Argentina

**Borges, Jorge Luis,** *Borges: A Reader* (1981). Superbly edited and annotated translations by Emir Rodriguez Monegal and Alistair Reid of the essential works of Jorge Luis Borges; brilliant stories that blend elements of essay, science fiction, detective stories, fantasy, literary criticism, and autobiography.

**Guiraldes, Ricardo,** *Don Segundo Sombra* (1926). Classic novel of gauchos.

**Hudson, W. H.,** *Idle Days in Patagonia* (1893). Considered by many to be the Argentine-born naturalist's finest book, it is an account of his journey down the Rio Negro to the Patagonian plains. More recent Patagoniana are Bruce Chatwin's *In Patagonia* (1978); Gerald Durrell's *The Whispering Land* (1962); and George G. Simpson, *Attending Mercies: A Patagonia Journal* (1934).

**Puig, Manuel,** *Betrayed by Rita Hayworth* (1971). Comic novel about small town in bleakest Argentine flatlands where, to combat the boredom and hopelessness of life, people adopt gestures and attitudes from Hollywood films of the thirties and forties. See *Kiss of the Spider Woman* (1979).

**Sabato, Ernesto,** *On Heroes and Tombs* (1961, tr. 1981). Baroque tales about Argentinian life; they mix reality and hallucination.

## England

**Blythe, Ronald (ed.),** *Places: An Anthology of Britain* (1981). Essays and poems by over forty writers on the places that have personal resonance for them. Included are Sir John Betjeman, Jan Morris, Alan Sillitoe, and Barbara Pym.

**Cobbett, William,** *Rural Rides* (1830). Vigorous descriptions of country life. Other nineteenth-century masters of the genre appear in E. D. H. Johnson (ed.), *The Poetry of Earth: A Collection of English Nature Writings* (1966).

**Defoe, Daniel,** *A Tour Through the Whole Island of Great Britain* (1724). Vivid portrait of early eighteenth-century English life. Combines a poetic vision with a gift for observation and the telling anecdote.

**Fisher, Lois H.,** *A Literary Gazetteer of England* (1980). Tour of literary England; strewn throughout with pictures and quotes.

**Hawkes, Jacquetta,** *A Land* (1963). Imaginative study of the relationship of the land and structures of Britain to its people from prehistory onward. A moving book.

**Hawthorne, Nathaniel,** *Our Old Home* (1863). Charming sketches by the New England writer, who was ever alert to the variety of the people he met during his consulship in England. His contemporary, Ralph Waldo Emerson, wrote of his British experiences in *English Traits* (1856). See Henry Steele Commager (ed.), *Britain Through American Eyes* (1974) and Richard Kenin, *Return to Albion: Americans in England, 1760–1940* (1979).

**Hudson, W. H.,** *Afoot in England* (1909). One of many elegantly written books in which he relates his observations of the natural beauty of England. See *Nature in Downland* (1900). Other skillful nature writing of Hudson's time includes Richard Jeffries, *Round About a Great Estate* (1880) and Edward Thomas, *The Countryside: A Selection of His Prose and Verse* (1977).

**James, Henry,** *English Hours* (1905). Collection of fugitive essays that interpret English life and are marked by enthusiasm and curiosity.

**Morton, H. V.,** *In Search of England* (rev. 1960). Impressions of a high-spirited car journey "over the roads and through the lanes of England . . . during that brief, golden age after the War." A decade later, in the heart of the Depression, J. B. Priestley made a similar ramble, recounted in *English Journey* (1934).

**Priestley, J. B.,** *The English* (1973). Social history in impressionistic essays and illustrations on the theme of "Englishness," in which the author concludes that the English are a haunted people.

**Taine, Hippolyte,** *Notes on England* (1874). Intelligent and inquisitive observations of Victorian life. Other noteworthy accounts by nineteenth-century Continental visitors are Louis Simond, *Journal of a Tour and Residence in Great Britain* (1811) and Prince Hermann Pückler-Muskau, *A Tour of England, Ireland and France* (1828).

*Treasures of Britain* (rev. 1976). Published for the Automobile Association of England, this beautifully illustrated handbook guides the visitor to all the great historic and cultural sites of the island. Required reading for all planning a trip to Britain. See the AA's *Book of British Villages* (1981) and *Where to Go in Britain* (1981).

**Trevelyan, G. M.,** *History of England* (rev. 1959). First published in 1926, its command of narrative has made it the finest single-volume history of England. See *English Social History* (rev. 1978). A fine companion is Malcolm Falkus and John Gillingham (eds.), *Historical Atlas of Britain* (1981).

**White, Gilbert,** *The Natural History and Antiquities of Selborne* (1789). This book, by a country parson and naturalist with a reverence for nature and a scientific attention to detail, is remarkable not only for its accurate descriptions of the Hampshire countryside but for its knowledgeable picture of eighteenth-century English rural life.

## Wales

**Borrow, George,** *Wild Wales* (1862). English vagabond's journeys through the Welsh countryside.

**Cordell, Alexander,** *The Rape of the Fair Country* (1959). Wales of the nineteenth century in a novel brimming with the joy of life and the strangeness of the Welsh language.

**Davies, Rhys,** *The Best of Rhys Davies* (1979). His love of his native countryside and for the tenacious stock from which he came permeates his short stories.

**Hanley, James,** *A Kingdom* (1978). Novel set at a mountain farm: two sisters clash when they are reunited before their father's funeral. See *The Welsh Sonata* (1954).

**Llewellyn, Richard,** *How Green Was My Valley* (1940). Nostalgic novel, with a genuine feeling for the Welsh people, about a coal-mining town during the last century.

**Richards, Alun (ed.),** *The Penguin Book of Welsh Short Stories* (1976). Fine selection: for an anthology of poetry, see Gwyn Jones (ed.), *The Oxford Book of Welsh Verse in English* (1977).

**Roberts, Kate,** *The Loving Sleep* (1978). Novel of marital infidelity, by the best novelist writing in Welsh today.

**Thomas, Dylan,** *Under Milk Wood* (1954). A moving, hilarious account of a spring day in a Welsh fishing village. Conceived for the radio. *Portrait of the Artist as a Young Dog* (1940) contains waggish stories of the poet's boyhood in South Wales.

**Thomas, Gwyn,** *The World Cannot Hear You* (1951). The rivalry between two brothers supplies the action in this strangely humorous novel about the grubby, passionate dwellers of a Welsh valley. Thomas's fine autobiography, *A Few Selected Exits* (1969), is about his impoverished boyhood in a coal-mining town.

**Williams, Emlyn,** *George: An Early Biography* (1961). Recollections of the remarkable childhood of the Welsh actor and playwright.

## Ireland

**Behan, Brendan,** *Brendan Behan's Island* (1962). Completed a couple of years before his death, this "Irish sketchbook" is full of delights. Drawings by Paul Hogarth.

**Bernen, Robert,** *Tales from the Blue Stacks* (1978). An American living in the sheep-herding country of Donegal — the Blue Stacks — presents these elegant and economical stories to "preserve a true picture of some aspects of Blue Stack life at the moment of its final disappearance . . . into the modern world around it."

**Carleton, William,** *Stories of Irish Life* (1970). Selections from the classic sketches of peasant life written in the 1830s. Full of colorful speech and vigor.

**Dangerfield, George,** *The Damnable Question: A Study of Anglo-Irish Relations* (1971). Elegant and vivid study of the "damnable question" between 1800 and 1922 with some characterizations of the leading players.

**Debreffny, Brian,** *The Land of Ireland* (1979). Sumptuous picture book with accompanying poetry. See *The Irish World: The Art and Culture of the Irish People* (1977). The best concise history is John Ranelagh, *Ireland: A History* (1981).

**Edgeworth, Maria,** *Castle Rackrent* (1800). Dissipation, depravity, and dissolution — all in one fictional eighteenth century Anglo-Irish family of landlords — as described with wit and candor by the family servant.

**Gill, Bartholomew,** *McGarr and the Politician's Wife* (1977). The first of a fine series of crime novels detailing the exploits of Peter McGarr, Chief Inspector of Detectives of the Irish Police.

**Heaney, Seamus,** *Poems 1965–1975* (1980). Works by the Ulster poet: earthy and wise. See *Field Work* (1979).

**Hinkson, Pamela,** *Irish Gold* (1947). Warm, reflective evocation of the charm of Irish country-house life by the daughter of poet Katharine Tynan. Another picture of country living is David Thomson, *Woodbrook* (1976).

**Kiely, Benedict,** *The State of Ireland* (1980). Novella and seventeen short stories, in richly idiomatic prose by a Northern Irishman.

**Lavin, Mary,** *Collected Stories* (1971). Artful short stories, intensely felt, ranging over many aspects of modern Irish life. See *The Shrine and Other Stories* (1977).

**Marlow, Joyce,** *The Uncrowned Queen of Ireland: The Life of Kitty O'Shea* (1975). Her ten-year affair with and eventual marriage to Parnell. This story of the doomed lovers gives a fine picture of late nineteenth-century Ireland. See Jules Abels, *The Parnell Tragedy* (1966).

**Moore, Brian,** *The Mangan Inheritance* (1980). "Return of the native" novel "evokes the character of an entire people — the inhabitants of western Ireland" (Joyce Carol Oates).

**O'Brien, Edna,** *Mother Ireland* (1976). Intimate narrative, mixing history and myth, which conjures up the spirit of the place and its people. The author's short stories can be sampled in *A Scandalous Woman and Other Stories* (1974).

**O'Connor, Frank,** *Collected Stories* (1981). Robust short stories by the writer Yeats called the Chekhov of Ireland.

**O'Faolain, Sean,** *Selected Stories of Sean O'Faolain* (1978). Superb stories written over five decades by one of Ireland's most distinguished men of letters. *The Irish* (1949) is a nonfiction work about his country.

**Somerville, E. O. and Martin Ross,** *The Real Charlotte* (1894). By two cousins who collaborated on a number of popular novels of Irish life from the Protestant Anglo-Irish point of view. Choice use of Irish dialect and idiom and sly wit. This is their best effort and is "the one great Irish novel of the 19th century" (V. S. Pritchett).

**Synge, J. M.,** *Playboy of the Western World* (1907). Powerful tragicomedy of Irish peasant life set in a little inn on the wild west coast. Its lyrical dialogue, robust and imaginative, makes this one of the great plays of the century.

**Tracy, Honor,** *The Straight and Narrow Path* (1956). Witty, astringent novel by a gifted Anglo-Irish writer. A complementary nonfictional work is *Mind You, I've Said Nothing: Forays in the Irish Republic* (1958).

**Woodham-Smith, Cecil,** *The Great Hunger* (1962). The Irish famine of the 1840s; it is "among the most terrible and moving epics ever written of the near-destruction and tremendous tenacity of a whole people" (Sean O'Faolain).

## Scotland

**Beckwith, Lillian,** *The Hills Is Lonely* (1959). The first in a series: stories full of hilarious incidents and delightful characters about the author's life in the Hebrides.

**Brockie, Keith,** *Keith Brockie's Wildlife Sketchbook* (1981). Sketches and watercolors of nature and animals of Scotland's islands and seashore, forests, lochs and rivers, and mountains and moorland.

**Brown, George Mackey,** *Greenvoe* (1972). A poetic novel, by a native, about the people of a village in the Orkney Islands. See *A Time to Keep and Other Stories* (1969) and *Magnus* (1972), a novel.

**Crichton, Robert,** *The Camerons* (1972). Skillfully written, earnest novel about lives in a mining town and the workers' struggle there for improved conditions.

**Gibbon, Lewis Grassic,** *A Scots Quair Trilogy* (1932–34). Comprising *Sunset Song, Cloud Howe,* and *Grey Granite,* it is the great modern Scottish work of fiction. See *Scottish Scene* (1934) written with Hugh MacDiarmid.

**Hunter, Mollie,** *You Never Knew Her as I Did* (1981). This story of a boy who tries to rescue Mary, Queen of Scots from prison is one of her many fine historical novels for young readers set in her native Scotland. See *The Stronghold* (1975) and *The Ghosts of Glencoe* (1969).

**Jenkins, Robin,** *Fergus Lamont* (1980). Rousing novel about a poet of the Glasgow slums, it tells us something about the soul of modern Scotland. See *The Cone Gatherers* (1981).

**Johnson, Samuel,** *A Journey to the Western Islands of Scotland* (1775). Delightful account of the tour he took at age sixty-four with Boswell to the Highlands and Skye. Boswell's account in *The Journal of a Tour of the Hebrides* (1785) is even more spirited for having Dr. Johnson as its subject. See Israel Shenker, *In the Footsteps of Johnson and Boswell* (1982).

**McKelway, St. Clair,** *The Edinburgh Caper: A One-Man International Plot* (1962). While visiting Scotland the *New Yorker* writer imagined that there was a plot afoot by the Russians to kidnap President Eisenhower, who was planning to attend a summit conference there. "The wacky episode is related in his impeccable prose — nobody tells a story better than he does — and the whole thing is like — and as charming as — *Alice in Wonderland*" (P. G. Wodehouse).

**Mackenzie, Compton,** *Tight Little Island* (1950). Amusing novel about the agony on a Hebridean island when war brought a whisky shortage.

**McPhee, John,** *The Crofter and the Laird* (1970). Gracefully written narrative about the people of the island of Colonsay in the Hebrides.

**Macqueen, John and Tom Scott (eds.),** *The Oxford Book of Scottish Verse* (1967). Best one-volume anthology, a rich collection ranging from poets of the thirteenth century to those born before 1930.

**Moncreiffe of That Ilk, Sir Iain,** *The Highland Clans: The Dynastic Origins, Chiefs and Background of the Clans Connected with Highland History and Some of Their Families* (1968). Handsome volume, vivid and cheerful, with good color photos.

**Muir, Edwin,** *The Story and the Fable* (rev. 1954). Memoir of childhood on a farm in the Orkneys and youth in and around Glasgow. Chiefly a story of the inner man — the world of thought and imagination. See *Scottish Journey* (1935) and *The Scots and Their Country* (1946).

**Ostrow, Johanna, . . .** *In the Highlands Since Time Immemorial* (1970). Lyrical novel about a man returning to the uncomplicated life of a Highland farmer. Expressively evokes the harsh land and a vanishing culture.

**Stevenson, Robert Louis,** *Kidnapped* (1886). Ostensibly about David Balfour's search for his inheritance, it is "essentially . . . a topographical novel about Scotland in 1751" (David Daiches). The unfinished *Weir of Hermiston* (1896), which some consider his masterpiece, also has a Scottish background.

**Tey, Josephine,** *Singing Sands* (1953). Highly atmospheric mystery novel with a vividly rendered Outer Hebrides background. Another Scotland-set murder mystery is Michael Innes's *Lament for a Maker* (1938).

# France

**Balzac, Honoré de,** *La Comedie Humaine* (1830–50). This is the title given by Balzac to the entire body of his prodigious fictional output, a vast realistic panorama of the France of his time — from the fall of Napoleon to 1848. A handy *Michelin* is Felicien Marceau, *Balzac and His World* (1967).

**Bernen, Robert,** *In the Heat of the Sun* (1981). Sketches of Paris and southern France: people, nature, and culture, written with rare immediacy and literary grace.

**Chevallier, Gabriel,** *Scandals of Clochemerle* (1936). Satirical novel about French village life and manners in the 1930s. Full-blooded, Rabelaisian, it is irrepressibly amusing. See *Wicked Village: A Story of Clochemerle* (1956).

**Daudet, Alphonse,** *Adventures of Tartarin of Tarascon* (1872). Good-humored stories of the great boaster painted against a background of the Provencal countryside. More modern portraitists of the Provencal peasant, more mystical than Tartarin, are Henri Bosco, *Farm in Provence* (1947) and Jean Giono, *Joy of Man's Desiring* (1940).

**Fisher, M. F. K.,** *Map of Another Town* (1964). Casual memoir of the American author's stay in Aix-en-Provence. *A Considerable Town* (1978) is a witty and affectionate look at Marseilles.

**Ford, Ford Madox,** *Provence: From Minstrels to the Machine* (1935). "The expansiveness of spirit, the embracing knowledge of the place, that bodies forth in Ford's long love affair with Provence will always give this book a joyous life of its own" (Eudora Welty). Another good English traveler's account is James Pope-Hennessy, *Aspects of Provence* (1967).

**Freeling, Nicolas,** *A Dressing of Diamond* (1974). This novel introduces Henri Castang, a member of the Police Judicaire in a provincial French town, whose further adventures are continued in series. Chief Inspector Damiot is another French cop worth knowing; his premier appearance is in Vincent McConner's *The Provence Puzzle* (1980).

**Guerard, Albert,** *France in the Classical Age: The Life and Death of an Ideal* (1928). Brilliantly written history of France between the sixteenth and eighteenth centuries. Later years are masterfully considered in Theodore Zeldin's *France, 1848–1945* (1973–77).

**James, Henry,** *A Little Tour in France* (1885). These charming impressions of the author's journey through Loire, Provence, and Languedoc find him more companionable than in his novels.

**Pilkington, Roger,** *Small Boat Through France* (1964). Lively description of an amiable Englishman's journey in a forty-five-foot craft through the French waterways. See *Small Boat to Alsace* (1962), *Small Boat in Southern France* (1965), and *Small Boat on the Moselle* (1968).

**Shattuck, Roger,** *The Banquet Years: The Arts in France, 1885–1918* (1958). Four artists — Henri Rousseau, Erik Satie, Alfred Jarry, and Guillaume Apollinaire — contribute to a masterly portrait of an age decisive in the flowering of modern art.

**Stendhal,** *Travels in the South of France* (1970). Notes on a tour made in 1838, illustrated with contemporary drawings. A fascinating book: "Stendhal the tourist is always the servant of Stendhal the novelist. His strength is as a connoisseur of human beauty and foibles" (A. Alvarez). See *Memoirs of a Tourist* (1962), his gossipy recollections of a journey through France, Geneva, and Genoa.

**Stevenson, Robert Louis,** *Travels with a Donkey in the Cévennes* (1879). Cosy account of the Scotsman and his faithful donkey, Modestine, on a journey through the south of France. *An Inland Voyage* (1878) is about a canoe trip through France and Belgium.

**White, Freda,** *Three Rivers of France: The Lot, Dordogne, and Tarn* (1952). Beautiful descriptions of the river country of Rouergue. A classic of its kind. See *West of the Rhone: Languedoc, Roussillon, the Massif Central* (1964) and *Ways of Acquitaine* (1968).

**Zola, Émile,** *The Rougon-Macquart Series* (1871–93). Cycle of twenty novels that minutely and mercilessly describe the world of one family in Zola's naturalistic style and serve as a microcosm for the society of the French Second Empire. Highly documentary but variable; *The Downfall* (1892) and *The Soil* (1888) are among the best.

## Spain

**Alberti, Rafael,** *The Lost Grove* (1976). Lovely autobiography by the Spanish poet: from his youth in Andalusia at the turn of the century to his years as a poet and painter in Madrid before the civil war.

**Borrow, George,** *The Bible in Spain* (1842). The colorful English traveler's adventures, some apocryphal, while peddling Bibles during the Carlist upheavals.

**Brenan, Gerald,** *South from Granada* (1957). The English author was the first of the post–World War I Spanish expatriates and came to know the country as few non-Spaniards have. This is one of his best books, all of which blend "meditation, poetry and disillusion with an unexpected interest in botany, sociology, anthropology and the picaresque" (Cyril Connolly).

**Ford, Richard,** *Handbook for Travellers in Spain* (1845). The Victorian travel writer's discernment and sympathy contributed to making this "probably the best guide-book ever written" (V. S. Pritchett). See *Gatherings from Spain* (1846).

**Jiménez, Juan Ramón,** *Platero and I* (1917). Lyrical prose poem portraying life in and around a remote village in Andalusia as told to his donkey Platero. For the poetry of the Nobel Prize–winning poet, see *Juan Ramón Jiménez: Three Hundred Poems* (1957).

**Lee, Laurie,** *As I Walked out One Midsummer Morning* (1969). Beautiful recollection of the English poet's tramp through Spain in 1934, a time in which signs of impending civil war were clearly visible. *A Rose for Winter* (1956) is a memorable record of a season in Andalusia.

**Marse, Juan,** *The Fallen* (1979). Novel of postwar Barcelona — a Goyesque fresco of corrupted lives seen through the eyes of a gang of street-wise slum kids. See *Golden Girl* (1981).

**Maugham, W. Somerset,** *Don Fernando, or, Variations on Some Spanish Themes* (1935). Collection of informal pieces on a variety of topics, from Spanish food and wines to El Greco.

**Michener, James A.,** *Iberia: Spanish Travels and Reflections* (1968). Spacious, never dull view of a country and culture the author loves. Other American novelists who have written accounts of their Spanish travels include William Dean Howells, *Familiar Spanish Travels* (1913); and John Dos Passos *Rocinante: To the Road Again* (1922).

**Morris, Jan,** *Spain* (1979). Revision of the text from the 1964 coffee-table book, *The Presence of Spain;* a profound and witty book by a travel writer very sensitive to Spanish life and landscape.

**Perez Galdos, Benito,** *Fortunata and Jacinto: Two Stories of Married Women* (1886). This story of love and destructive jealousy of two women is at the foreground of this vast panorama of bourgeois life in Madrid by "the supreme Spanish novelist of the 19th century . . . and takes its place among those Victorian masterpieces that have presented the full-length portrait of a city" (V. S. Pritchett). See *Dona Perfecta* (1876).

**Pritchett, V. S.,** *The Spanish Temper* (1955). Analysis of the Spanish character by the English man of letters who "never for a moment abandons his own point of view, remaining throughout ironic, humane, dispassionate and English to the core. . . . Everyone should read this wise, witty and beautiful book" (Honor Tracy). Many of Pritchett's early short stories are set in Spain; see *Marching Spain* (1928).

**St. Martin, Hardie (ed.),** *Roots and Wings: Poetry from Spain 1900–1975* (1976). Machado, Jiménez, Unamuno, Lorca, and many others are represented in this fine bilingual anthology.

**Tracy, Honor,** *Silk Hats and No Breakfast: Notes on a Spanish Journey* (1956). The first of a trio of affectionate Spanish travel books by the Anglo-Irish novelist who has a knack for conveying a sense of place. See *Spanish Leaves* (1964) and *Winter in Castile* (1974).

**Yglesias, Jose,** *The Goodbye Land* (1967). Masterful account of a trip to author's father's Galician village; it has been acclaimed a "little masterpiece" (Gerald Brenan). See *The Franco Years* (1977).

## Portugal

**Campbell, Roy,** *Portugal* (1957). Amazing — for its vituperation and vivacity — profile by the South African poet and man of action of the country where he made his home.

**Dos Passos, John,** *The Portugal Story: Three Centuries of Exploration and Discovery* (1969). Excellent popular history of the Lusitanian empire. The authoritative history is C. R. Boxer, *The Portugese Seaborne Empire, 1415–1825* (1969).

**Eca de Queiroz,** *The Relic* (1880). The adventures of Raposo, a Portugese playboy make up "one of the truly delightful novels of the world — a classic of that most rarely successful of literary types, the serio-comic. It will live because it is a faithful reflection of life, set in a perfect artistic form" (Francis Steegmuller). Another novel by the great Portugese stylist is *The City and the Mountains* (1885).

**Fielding, Henry,** *Voyage to Lisbon* (1735). Spirited travel book, full of the special charm of the creator of *Tom Jones,* who died and was buried in Lisbon. Another eighteenth-century English novelist's recollection of Iberia is William Beckford's charming *Journal in Portugal and Spain, 1787–1788* (1954).

**Macaulay, Rose,** *Fabled Shore: From the Pyrenees to Portugal* (1949). Fine travel writing about a journey to Portugal by the English novelist. Another peripatetic countryman, Sacheverell Sitwell, published his impressions *In Portugal and Madeira* (1954).

## Italy

**Alvaro, Corrado,** *Revolt in Aspromonte* (1930). Powerful brief novel about justice, set among the poor of Calabria.

**Barzini, Luigi,** *The Italians* (1964). Refreshing look at the author's fellow Italians in a style "as bright and sparkling and clear as a glass of Valpolicella" (Gilbert Highet). See *From Caesar to the Mafia* (1971).

**Berenson, Bernard,** *Passionate Sightseer* (1960). Beautifully made, photo-enhanced, book of selections from the last diaries of the art connoisieur. Written when, as an old man, he revisited much of Italy to reconsider its works of art. Candid, conversational, fresh, witty; in all, delightful reading.

**Brooks, Van Wyck,** *The Dream of Arcadia: American Writers and Artists in Italy, 1760–1915* (1958). Hawthorne, Howells, and James are a few of the men and women discussed in this scholarly, yet charming and even picturesque, work by the distinguished American literary historian.

**Cornilesen, Ann,** *Torregreca* (1969). Exquisitely written account of the founding by an indomitable American woman of a charity-sponsored nursery school in an impoverished Italian hill town. "Heart raising and heart breaking, tenderly ruthless, terrifyingly honest, coldly truthful and warmly human . . . deserves to become recognized as an all-time classic" (Sean O'Faolain). See *Vendetta of Silence* (1972).

**Dogo, Guiliano,** *Treasures of Italy* (1976). Gazetteer, each entry telling about the art works to be found there. This beautifully illustrated survey of Italian art can serve as a valuable and practical companion to those journeying to the country.

**Douglas, Norman,** *Old Calabria* (1919). Classic informal view of the region by the English author of *South Wind* and numerous Mediterranean travel books.

**Fernandez, Dominique,** *The Mother Sea* (1967). Unhurried but lively tour of southern Italy, Sardinia, and Sicily by a sometimes insufferable Frenchman with a contempt for Italians.

**Gissing, George,** *By the Ionian Sea: Notes on a Ramble in Southern Italy* (1901). The English Victorian novelist's travels inspired a "honey-toned thing, this study of Greek Italy, mellow as old marble lying warm in the sun" (Cornelius Weygandt). A more contemporary English wanderer is H. V. Morton, and his book *A Traveller in Southern Italy* (1969).

**Goethe, J. W.,** *Italian Journey, 1786–1788* (1962). Large, handsomely illustrated edition, translated by W. H. Auden and Elizabeth Mayer, about the Italian landscape, art, and people as seen and felt by "a monster of intelligence and of creative force" (Paul Valéry).

**James, Henry,** *Italian Hours* (1909). James loved Italy. Here his fondness for detail is fused with joy in Italy's beauty and antiquity.

**Jovine, Francesco,** *The Estate in Abruzzi* (1952). Regional classic which captures the full flavor of peasant life around Abruzzi. Gabriele D'Annunzio's Nietzschean art-nouveau novel, *Triumph of Death* (1896) is set in his native Abruzzi.

**Kubly, Herbert,** *An American in Italy* (1955). National Book Award–winning collection of pieces, mainly about people, which read like short stories.

**Lawrence, D. H.,** *Sea and Sardinia* (1921). Revealing not only of the stony island of Sardinia, but of Lawrence himself. "No English writer of his time was so 'aware' . . . so unerringly right in picking out just those aspects of a foreign scene which bring it vividly before the reader to whom it is all strange and unknown" (Richard Aldington). See *Twilight in Italy* (1916), *Etruscan Places* (1932), and Leo Hamalian, *D. H. Lawrence in Italy* (1981).

**Menen, Aubrey,** *Speaking the Language like a Native: Aubrey Menen on Italy* (1962). Collection of pieces by English novelist long resident in Italy. Many of his comic novels, such as *The Duke of Gallodoro* (1952) and *The Fig Tree* (1959) have Italian backgrounds. See *Rome for Ourselves* (1961) and *Venice* (1976).

**Moravia, Alberto,** *Time of Desecration* (1980). Written in the form of a conversation, a powerful indictment of contemporary Italian society. *The Conformist* (1951) and *The Time of Indifference* (1929) are psychological studies of a passive personality caught up in the fascism of his times.

**Newby, Eric,** *When the Snow Comes They Will Take You Away* (1971). An English writer tells of his escape from POW camp during World War II and of the Italian people who aided and sheltered him.

**O'Faolain, Sean,** *A Summer in Italy* (1950). Account of a season in Italy in which he tells of his brief lapse from Roman Catholicism; it has been called

"one of the best evocations of place in modern travel literature" (Martin S. Day).

**Pavese, Cesare,** *The Moon and the Bonfire* (1950). This lyrical, realistic, and compassionate novel attempts nothing less than an analysis of the whole of Italian life. See *The Selected Works of Cesare Pavese* (1968).

**Vailand, Roger,** *The Law* (1957). Greed, misery, and lust for power in a small southern seaport town. "Every paragraph and every sentence of this novel has been carefully cast and seems to be locked into position, creating a structure which is solid and formal, and yet always lively" (V. S. Naipaul).

## Sicily

**Brancati, Vitaliano,** *Bell'Antonio* (1949). Taking on *gallismo* — Don Juanism Italian style — this seriocomic tale superimposes love, sex, and politics.

**Durrell, Lawrence,** *Sicilian Carousel* (1977). One of the novelist's "island" travel books. Another impression by an English visitor is Vincent Cronin, *The Golden Honeycomb* (1954).

**Lampedusa, Giuseppe di,** *The Leopard* (1960). This novel of exquisite refinement by the prince of Lampedusa portrays the impact on a Sicilian prince and his family of Garibaldi's invasion of Sicily and unification of Italy.

**Levi, Carlo,** *Words are Stones: Impressions of Sicily* (1959). Three different journeys to Sicily by the northern Italian writer; vivid journalism with outrage at the deplorable conditions of the people.

**Lewis, Norman,** *The Honored Society: A Searching Look at the Mafia* (1964). A chilling report on the Sicilian Mafia by an outstanding English writer. Another outsider's look at the dark side of Sicily is Gavin Maxwell, *The Ten Pains of Death* (1959).

Mangione, Jerre, *A Passion for Sicilians: The World of Danilo Dolci* (1968). Absorbing, eloquently written account of the northern Italian–born social reformer's nonviolent crusade against misery and violence in western Sicily. See Dolci's own *The Man Who Played Alone* (1969) and *Sicilian Lives* (1981).

Pirandello, Luigi, *Short Stories* (tr. 1965). Naturalistic stories by Sicily's most celebrated writer, the Nobel Prize winner best known for his plays.

Sciascia, Leonardo, *Candido, or, A Dream Dreamed in Sicily* (1979). Slim novel about a man with an irresistible propensity for telling the truth and the disastrous consequences that ensue. By a "writer of great importance, one of a holy trinity whose other incarnations are Italo Calvino and Alberto Moravia" (Anthony Burgess). See *The Council of Egypt* (1963).

Verga, Giovanni, *The House by the Medlar Tree* (1881). Story of the fall, through three generations, of a peasant family of fishermen. "One of the great novels and the product of a rich poetic imagination" (Anthony West). See *Little Novels of Sicily* (1925), translated by D. H. Lawrence.

Vittorini, Elio, *In Sicily* (1949). Novel about a city man's rediscovery of himself and the basic values of life when he returns for a visit to the primitive Sicilian village where he was born.

## Germany

Agee, Joel, *Twelve Years: An American Boyhood in East Germany* (1981). Written from the unusual perspective of a member of a family that chose to live in Communist Europe, this beautifully written book about coming of age by the son of James Agee is "one of those rare personal memoirs that bring to life a whole country and an epoch" (Christopher Isherwood).

Becker, Jurek, *Sleepless Days* (1979). Short novel by East German living in the

West that "with its claustrophobic atmosphere of almost unconscious conformism has the power to disturb us all" (D. M. Thomas). Other notable fiction by East German writers includes Reiner Kunze, *The Wonderful Years* (1977) and Christa Wolf, *No Place on Earth* (1982).

Bedford, Sybille, *A Legacy* (1956). Profound novel about the pre–World War I Hohenzollern Reich.

Böll, Heinrich, *Billiards at Half-past Nine* (1962). The entire German experience, from the days before World War I to the 1960s, in the lives of one family. Powerful and humane. Other novels by the Nobel Prize–winning writer include *The Clown* (1965), *Group Portrait with Lady* (1971), and *The Safety Net* (1982).

Grass, Günter, *The Tin Drum* (1963). Madly inventive picaresque tale of twentieth-century Germany as seen through the eyes of Oskar, a dwarf who deliberately stopped growing when he was three years old. The other novels of the Danzig Trilogy are *Cat and Mouse* (1963) and *Dog Years* (1965).

Hamburger, Michael (ed.), *German Poetry, 1910–1975: An Anthology* (1976). Collection of not only the well-known poets, but many not previously translated into English. See *East German Poetry* (1972).

Laqueur, Walter, *Weimar: A Cultural History 1918–1933* (1975). Stimulating, balanced survey of the Weimar renascence. See Peter Gay, *Weimar Culture* (1968).

Lenz, Siegfried, *The Heritage: The History of a Detestable Word* (1981). The word is "homeland," and this tale, set in an East Prussian town in the early part of the century, attempts to reclaim it from the Nazis. See *The German Lesson* (1971).

Pachter, Henry M., *Modern Germany: A Social, Cultural, and Political History* (1978). Overview of the volatile nation that initiated two world wars. See Gordon

Craig's fine *Germany: 1866–1945* (1978) and Andreas Hillgruber's brilliant *Germany and the Two World Wars* (1981).

**Read, Piers Paul, *The Junkers*** (1969). First-person novel about young British diplomat who falls in love with a German woman and discovers that her family is connected with a certain notorious war criminal.

**Sander, August, *Photographs of an Epoch, 1909–1959*** (1980). The pictures of life between the wars by the German photographer are remarkable. Another album by a native German photographer is *Eisenstadt: Germany* (1981).

**Shirer, William L., *The Rise and Fall of the Third Reich*** (1960). Monumental history by American journalist who was eyewitness to Hitler's ascent to power. For an inside view see *Inside the Third Reich* (1970) by Albert Speer, Hitler's architect and minister of armaments and war production.

**Spender, Stephen (ed.), *Great German Short Stories*** (1960). Includes such modern masters as Kafka, Mann, and Rilke.

## Greece

**Durrell, Lawrence, *Prospero's Cell*** (1945). The first of his superb Aegean travel books, this is about Corfu; *Reflections on a Marine Venus* (1953) is about Rhodes, and *The Greek Islands* (1978) is comprehensive. They are classics of the leisurely-meditative-evocation-of-cherished-place school of travel writing. The novel *The Dark Labyrinth* (1962) is set in Crete.

**Fermor, Patrick L., *Mani: Travels in the Southern Peloponnese*** (1958). An "incomparable nature study of the place" (Lawrence Durrell). See *Roumeli: Travels in Northern Greece* (1966).

**Haviaris, Stratis, *When the Tree Sings*** (1979). A boy comes of age in a mountain village during the German occupation.

This epic narrative is about heroism, resistance, and survival. Theodore Vrettos's *Birds of Winter* (1980), set in a similar place and time, is rich in Greek traditions and history.

**Kazantsakis, Nikos, *Zorba the Greek*** (1953). The memorable Zorba dominates this picaresque tale, full of life and the color of Crete. See *The Greek Passion* (1953) and *Journey to the Morea* (1966), an evocative account of the novelist's 1937 trip to the Peloponnesus.

**Levi, Peter, *The Hill of Kronos*** (1981). Glowing, deeply personal memoir of his love affair with Greece. See his fine introduction to the ruins of ancient Greece, *Atlas of the Greek World* (1981).

**Longford, Elizabeth, *Byron's Greece*** (1976). The poet's two journeys to Greece, in a beautiful mix of travelogue and biography.

**Merrill, James, *The (Diblos) Notebook*** (1965). This ingenious novel-about-a-novel, ostensibly about a Greek-American who goes back to Greece to find his roots, is "a disciplined, adventurous performance in the best tradition of fictional experiment" (Wilfrid Sheed).

**Miller, Henry, *The Colossus of Maroussi*** (1941). Shimmering evocation of Greece and of the brilliant raconteur Katsimbalis, the Colossus of Maroussi. Miller's most genial book, "it gives you a feeling of the country and the people that I have never gotten from any modern book" (Edmund Wilson).

**Myrivilis, Stratis, *The Mermaid Madonna*** (1949). Filled with sunlight and sparkling color, the novel chronicles daily life in a small fishing port on the Aegean Sea.

**Seferis, George, *Delphi*** (1963). Brief, evocative book by the Nobel Prize–winning poet, with astounding photographs; it conveys awe for and mystery of the home of the ancient oracle.

## Poland

**Andrzejewski, Jerzy,** *Ashes and Diamonds* (1948). Memorable novel about the political chaos in a small Polish town trapped between two tyrannies at the end of World War II.

**Hlasko, Marek,** *Eighth Day of the Week* (1958). Stark, moving novel of people longing to free themselves from the nightmare of their everyday lives; "the sort of book you read at one sitting and remember the rest of your life" (Paul Engle). See *Next Stop — Paradise* (1960).

**Kuniczak, W. S.,** *Thousand Hour Day* (1971). Richly textured novel about the first thousand hours of World War II, in which Poland was conquered by blitzkrieg. *The March* (1979) is a sequel.

**Milosz, Czeslaw,** *The Captive Mind* (1953). The Nobel Prize–winning émigré poet's trenchant testimony to the plight of Polish artists after the Second World War. See *The History of Polish Literature* (1969), *Postwar Polish Poetry* (1965), and *The Seizure of Power* (tr. 1982), his first novel.

**Watt, Richard M.,** *Poland and Its Fate: 1918 to 1939* (1978). Lucid political history of the first Polish republic, which was dominated by Marshal Pilsudski. See M. K. Dziewanowski, *Poland in the Twentieth Century* (1977).

## Czechoslovakia

**Hermann, H. H.,** *A History of the Czechs* (1976). From Bohemia's pre-Slav times in 400 B.C. to the Russian invasion of 1968, by a Yugoslavian-born English journalist.

**Kahout, Pavel,** *The Hangwoman* (1981). Unusual fairy tale about a fifteen-year-old girl enrolled in the new school of executionary sciences.

**Kundera, Milan,** *The Joke* (1969). Satire by Czechoslovakia's leading novelist of a university student whose practical joke has tragic repercussions. *Laughable Loves* (1974) and *The Book of Laughter and Forgetting* (1981) are collections of short stories.

**Skvorecky, Josef,** *Miss Silver's Past* (1975). Witty satire on the Czech publishing world and the frustrating atmosphere of controlled intellectual life. See *The Cowards* (1970).

**Vaculík, Ludvik,** *The Guinea Pigs* (1973). Disturbing, often humorous, antitotalitarian fable. See *The Axe* (1973).

## Yugoslavia

**Andric, Ivo,** *The Bridge on the Drina* (1959). The Nobel Prize–winning Serbian author's epic novel artfully weaves stories and fables to tell the 350-year history of the bridge between Bosnia and Serbia. See *Bosnian Story* (1958) and *The Woman from Sarajevo* (1966).

**Cosic, Dobrica,** *A Time of Death* (1977). Finely crafted novel about the Serbian army during World War I. See *Reach to Eternity* (1979) and *South to Destiny* (1981).

**Djilas, Milovan,** *The Stone and the Violets* (1972). Powerful stories set in Montenegro, the native region of this man of politics and letters. See *Under the Colors* (1971).

**Durrell, Lawrence,** *White Eagles over Serbia* (1955). Espionage thriller marked by its evocative descriptions of the wild Serbian mountains.

**West, Rebecca,** *Black Lamb and Grey Falcon* (1941). Travels throughout Yugoslavia by the writer and her husband. Fascinating information and reflections and fine prose. Dusko Doder, *The Yugoslavs* (1978) is a congenial contemporary view of the country.

# Russia

**Billington, James H.,** *The Icon and the Axe: An Interpretation of Russian Culture* (1966). A thousand years of Russian cultural history in imaginative prose. "Probably the single finest American book on Russia and one of the most impressive achievements of American scholarship since the end of World War II" (Marshall Berman).

**Conquest, Robert,** *The Great Terror: Stalin's Purge of the Thirties* (rev. 1973). Crisp, restrained account of one of this century's greatest horrors, one that sent millions to death or to gulags. By an English scholar, poet, and novelist. See his edition of Tibor Szamuely's *The Russian Tradition* (1974).

**Crankshaw, Edward,** *The Shadow of the Winter Palace: Russia's Drift to Revolution, 1825–1917* (1976). The seeds of revolution, from the Decembrist uprising through entry into World War I, by "a superbly literate historian who can squeeze out of the driest documents an understanding of the human dimension that lesser practitioners of the art invariably miss" (Richard Pipes).

**Cummings, E. E.,** *Eimi* (1933). Remarkable travel diary, highly personal and ultramannered, of a thirty-six day stay in that "uncircus of noncreatures calling itself 'Russia.'" A "marvelous cinema of Cummings, provincial, Cambridge-bred American poet, attempting to high hat an entire social system" (Horace Gregory).

**Farson, Negley,** *The Lost World of the Caucasus* (1958). Foreign correspondent's evocative recollection of a journey through the remote southern Soviet Union in 1929.

**Hare, Richard,** *The Art and Artists of Russia* (1966). Fine survey of art from the earliest Byzantine period to early twentieth century, especially good on unfamiliar folk art and icons. Another good survey is *The Horizon Book of the Arts of Russia* (1970).

*The Horizon History of Russia* (1970). Splendid illustrated introduction to the rich history of Russia, the best for the general reader. Another excellent general history is Michael Florinsky, *Russia: A Short History* (1964).

**Kaiser, Robert G.,** *Russia from the Inside* (1980). Unique collection of photographs by former citizens now living in the West. See Vladimir Sichov and Eugene Sihanoff, *The Russians* (1981), a book of stunning but bleak photographs smuggled out of the country.

**Kennan, George,** *Tent Life in Siberia* (1867). Minor travel classic by an American who spent two years installing a telegraph line across Siberia. The best modern report on the land and people is Farley Mowat, *The Siberians* (1971).

**Maclean, Fitzroy,** *To the Back and Beyond* (1975). Journey in the Central Asian Republics and Mongolia. The first part of *Eastern Approaches* (1950) describes Maclean's exploratory expeditions deep into the heart of Russia in the 30s.

**Pasternak, Boris,** *Dr. Zhivago* (1958). The struggle of Yuri Zhivago, physician and poet, to maintain his humanity, in a complex novel "of truth and courage and beauty, a work of art toward which one's final response is nothing less than a feeling of reverence" (Irving Howe).

**Pipes, Richard,** *Russia Under the Old Regime* (1974). Provocative, insightful study which draws parallels between the repressive policies of the old regime and the Soviet state.

**Rosmer, Alfred,** *Moscow Under Lenin* (1953). French revolutionary's vivid picture of the early enthusiasm and confusion in the city from 1920 to Lenin's death in 1924.

**Seton-Watson, Hugh,** *The Russian Empire 1801–1917* (1967). Upon its publication, the *New York Times* hailed it as "the most complete, up-to-date, and authoritative history presently available in any language, Russian included." The heart of the imperial period is treated in Isabel de Madariaga's *Russia in the Age of Catherine the Great* (1981). A graphic companion volume is Chloe Obolensky's fascinating collection, *The Russian Empire: A Portrait in Photographs* (1979).

**Shalamov, Varlam,** *Kolyma Tales* (1980). Collection of short stories of life inside the prison camps in Kolyma in Siberia. More stories appear in *Graphite* (1981). See Robert Conquest, *Kolyma: The Arctic Death Camps* (1978).

**Smith, Hedrick,** *The Russians* (1976). First-hand profile of the Soviet people by former chief of the *New York Times* bureau in Moscow. Another excellent report by an American correspondent is Elizabeth Pond, *From the Yaroslavsky Station* (1981).

**Solzhenitsyn, Aleksandr I.,** *The Gulag Archipelago 1918–1956* (1974–78). About the prisons scattered across the Soviet Union. This three-volume epic text defies classification; its moral outrage makes it "the greatest and most powerful single indictment of a political regime ever to be leveled in modern times" (George F. Kennan).

**Tertz, Abram,** *The Makepeace Experiment* (1965). About an eccentric dictator with the power of psychological magnetism who has a provincial town declare its independence. An imaginative satire, full of intricate Joycean associations and published pseudonymously. Under his real name, Andrei Sinyavsky, he has written *A Voice from the Chorus* (1976).

**Voinovich, Vladimir,** *The Life and Extraordinary Adventures of Private Ivan Chonkin* (1977). The hilarious adventures of the country bumpkin Chonkin satirize Soviet life. "Call it a masterpiece of a new form — Socialist surrealism. Call it the Soviet *Catch 22* as written by a latter-day Gogol" (Theodore Solotaroff). See *Pretender to the Throne: The Further Adventures of Private Ivan Chonkin* (1981), and *In Plain Russian* (1979).

## Egypt

**Critchfield, Richard,** *Shahhat: An Egyptian* (1978). Living and working with the peasant Shahhat's family for more than two years, he captures the essence of traditional peasant life, a timeless, hidden world on the brink of modernity.

**Durrell, Lawrence,** *The Alexandria Quartet* (1957–60). The Mediterranean city and its people rendered with dazzling lucidity and suave finesse in four parts. "One of the strangest and most poetic works of fiction in modern English" (Gilbert Highet). A quarter-century earlier E. M. Forster described the fascination of Alexandria in *Pharos and Pharillon* (1923).

**Flaubert, Gustave,** *Flaubert in Egypt* (1978). An artfully edited volume by Francis Steegmuller of Flaubert's letters and notes about his journey through Egypt.

**Gornick, Vivian,** *In Search of Ali Mahmoud: An American Woman in Egypt* (1973). Engrossing, brilliantly alive account by a Jewish writer from New York of her personal odyssey to Cairo. Another, quite different, book of impressions is Hans Koning, *A New Yorker in Egypt* (1976).

**Newby, P. H.,** *The Picnic at Sakkara* (1955). High comedy of the English in Egypt in fine prose. Among his other novels set in Egypt are *Kith* (1977), *Something to Answer For* (1968), and *Revolution and Roses* (1957).

## Israel

**Amichai, Yehuda,** *Songs of Jerusalem and Myself* (1973). Compressed, honest verses that evoke the landscape and history of Israel.

**Anati, Emmanuel,** *Palestine Before the Hebrews* (1963). Superb history and a literary achievement as well.

**Bauer, Yehuda,** *Flight and Rescue: Brichah* (1970). Riveting history of the organized escape by the Jewish survivors of the Holocaust from eastern Europe to Israel in the years following the war. A real exodus that reads like a modern detective story. See *A History of the Holocaust* (1982).

**Bellow, Saul,** *To Jerusalem and Back* (1976). Personal account by the American Nobel laureate of his journey to Israel. Another travel recollection by a novelist is Jakov Lind, *A Trip to Jerusalem* (1978).

**Davidson, Lionel,** *The Menorah Men* (1966). Thriller by English writer living in Israel. See *Smith's Gazelle* (1971) and *The Sun Chemist* (1976).

**Eban, Abba,** *Abba Eban: An Autobiography* (1977). Stylish memoir by the former ambassador and Foreign Minister. Other good political autobiographies are Golda Meir, *My Life* (1975); Moshe Dayan, *Story of My Life* (1976); and Yitzhak Rabin, *The Rabin Memoirs* (1979).

**Frankel, William,** *Israel Observed* (1981). Probably the best introduction to the government and society.

**Gruber, Ruth,** *Raquela, A Woman of Israel* (1978). The times of a ninth-generation Jerusalemite whose life mirrors the history of Israel.

**Koestler, Arthur,** *Thieves in the Night* (1946). This documentary novel of Palestine of 1937–38, "in its study of social groups and political manifestations, is full of the psychological insights which are the only things that make history intelligible and the writing of it a humanistic art" (Edmund Wilson).

**Levin, Meyer,** *The Settlers* (1972). A massive, highly colored, family-history novel set in Palestine from the turn of the century to the Balfour Declaration. The saga is continued in *The Harvest* (1978).

**Magnusson, Magnus,** *Archaeology of the Bible* (1978). Clear, scholarly guide to the discrepancies and concordances between the archeological and biblical records. See

Avraham Negev, *Archaeology in the Land of the Bible* (1978).

**Megged, Aharon,** *Living on the Dead* (1970). Subtle, intense novel about the conflict between generations. See *King of Flesh and Blood* (1958), *The Short Life* (1980), and *Asahel* (1982).

**Michener, James,** *The Source* (1965). Twelve thousand years of history in a popular epic built around a fictional archaeological site, "makor."

**Netanyahu, Jonathan,** *Self-Portrait of a Hero* (1981). Letters (1963–1976) of a man killed leading the Entebbe raid; touching, elegant, and witty.

**Rennert, Maggie,** *Shelanu: An Israel Journal* (1979). Intelligent, witty record by an American who emigrated to Israel in 1973 and finally became *shelanu* — "one of ours."

**Sachar, Howard M.,** *A History of Israel* (1976). Spacious history from the rise of Zionism to our time. See *The Mamma Camel* (1980), a novel.

## *Iran*

**Browne, Edward Granville,** *A Year Amongst the Persians* (1927). Classic of travel literature; he describes in lively style impressions of the character and thought of the Persians in 1887.

**English, Barbara,** *The War for a Persian Lady* (1971). With a pungent writing style and witty portraits, she describes the political and diplomatic background to the Persian war with Great Britain of 1856–57. A fascinating study of Victorian pigheadedness.

**Esfadiary, F. M.,** *Identity Card* (1966). Most celebrated novel of modern Iran paints a grim portrait of the country under the rule of the Shah. It was smuggled out and printed in the U.S.

**Morier, James,** *The Adventures of Hajji Baba of Ispahan* (1824). Written by an

English ambassador to Persia, this picaresque romance about the roguish Hajji
Baba afoot in nineteenth-century Persia
remains a delight to read.

**O'Donnell, Terence,** *Garden of the Brave
in War* (1980). This American lived for
fifteen years in Iran and gained a keen
insight into the Iranian character. A superb storyteller. Other companionable
travel books by Americans include Curtis
Harnack, *Persian Lions, Persian Lambs*
(1965) and Anne Mehdavi, *Persian Adventure* (1953).

**Payne, Robert,** *Journey to Persia* (1952).
His travels to such sites of ancient Persian
glory as Persepolis and Isfahan and his
romantic reflections on the masterpieces
of art he found there.

**Sackville-West, V.,** *Twelve Days: An Account of a Journey Across the Bakhtieri
Mountains in Southern Persia* (1928). One
of the fruits of her residence in Iran as the
wife of diplomat Harold Nicolson. See
*Passenger to Teheran* (1927).

**Sa'edi, Gholam-Hossein,** *Dandil: Stories
from Iranian Life* (1968, tr. 1981). Moving
stories by one of Iran's leading writers
explore the country's alienation from the
West.

**Smith, Anthony,** *Blind White Fish in
Persia* (1953). This strangely titled book is
the lighthearted account of a summer in
Persia by four Oxford undergraduates on
a scientific expedition.

**Stark, Freya,** *The Valleys of the Assassins*
(1934). Chronicle of journeys in the less
accessible regions of Iran — including
one to remote valleys where an ancient
sect called the "Assassins" once practiced
its sinister rites. Distinguished by a sensitive understanding of primitive people.

## Afghanistan

**Byron, Robert,** *The Road to Oxiana*
(1937). Paul Fussell calls this "artfully
constructed great myth in the form of an

apparently spontaneous travel diary" of
Byron's trip to the Near East "the *Ulysses*
or *The Waste Land* of modern travel
books."

**Kessel, Joseph,** *The Horseman* (1968). Adventure story of peasant life in modern
Afghanistan with haunting descriptions
of the countryside.

**Levi, Peter,** *The Light Garden of the
Angel King: Journeys in Afghanistan*
(1973). A Jesuit priest-archaeologist in
search of the farthest eastern reaches of
the Greek empire shares his rich, many-
layered perceptions in exceptionally fine
writing. Other modern travelers are Freya
Stark, *The Minaret of Djam* (1971) and
David Chaffetz, *A Journey Through Afghanistan* (1981).

**Michaud, Roland and Sabrina Michaud,**
*Caravans to Tartary* (1978). Extraordinary
color photographs decorate the authors'
account of their trek by camel with Tartar
caravans in remote east Afghanistan.

**Newby, Eric,** *A Short Walk: A Preposterous Adventure* (1958). Beautifully funny
book about two Englishmen who combine
the most blatant physical and mental un-
preparedness with outrageous nerve while
wandering in the Hindu Kush mountains
of eastern Afghanistan.

**Wood, John,** *Journey to the Source of the
Oxus* (1841). An intrepid English explorer's expedition into the interior. Another Victorian Afghan classic is George
Robertson, *The Káfirs of the Hindu-Kush*
(1896).

## India

**Ackerley, J. R.,** *Hindoo Holiday* (1932).
Journal of an Englishman who went to
India as a maharajah's private secretary.
A "work of high literary skill and very
delicate aesthetic perception and it deals
with a character and a milieu which are
novel and radiantly delightful" (Evelyn
Waugh).

**Banerji, Bibhutibhushan,** *Pather Panchali* (1928–29). Autobiographical novel of childhood in Bengal village that is "the only modern Indian novel (written in an Indian language) of true artistry . . . a world classic as well as a Bengali masterpiece" (Martin Seymour-Smith).

**Basham, A. L.,** *The Wonder that Was India: A Survey of the Culture of the Indian Sub-continent Before the Coming of the Muslims* (rev. 1968). Sympathetic, scholarly history, copiously illustrated, of India from 3000 B.C. to the mid-sixteenth century.

**Belfrage, Sally,** *Flowers of Emptiness: Travels to an Indian Guru* (1981). Diary of an American woman's experiences at the Poona ashram of Bhagwan Shree Rajneesh. For a picture of blissed-out Westerners in India see Gita Mehta, *Karma Cola* (1979).

**Blaise, Clark and Bharati Mukherjee,** *Days and Nights in Calcutta* (1977). Candid impressions by an American writer and his Indian-born wife of a journey through her country.

**Collins, Larry and Dominique Lapierre,** *Freedom at Midnight* (1975). Enthralling journalistic account of the eclipse of the British Raj and the birth of modern India and Pakistan.

**Desai, Anita,** *Clear Light of Day* (1980). Richly atmospheric novel set in modern Delhi about two sisters of a decaying family, by a part-Indian writer who blends toughness with poetic imagination. See *Fire on the Mountain* (1978) and *Games at Twilight* (1978).

**Forster, E. M.,** *A Passage to India* (1924). The confrontation of Indian and Western cultures is at the heart of this masterpiece. "Great as the problem of India is, Forster's book is not about India alone; it is about all of human life" (Lionel Trilling). An interesting background to this novel is found in Forster's letters from India during the 1920s in *The Hills of Devi* (1953).

**Godden, Jon,** *The Seven Islands* (1956). Novel about a holy man living alone on a small island in the Ganges, told with the simplicity of a fable. See *The City and the Wave* (1954). She and her sister have collaborated on *Two Under the Indian Sun* (1966), an engaging memoir of their childhood in India during the second decade of the century, and *Shiva's Pigeons: An Experience in India* (1972).

**Godden, Rumer,** *The River* (1946). Sensitive, fragile novel about two adolescent girls, the daughters of an Anglo-Indian family living in Bengal. Her other novels set in India include *Kingfishers Catch Fire* (1953) and *Dark Horse* (1982). See *Gulbadan: Portrait of a Rose Princess at the Moghul Court* (1980) and *Mooltiki: Stories and Poems from India* (1957).

**Jhabvala, Ruth Prawer,** *Travelers* (1973). The author, a European who has lived in India for twenty years, is "one of the few quietly subtle writers working in this loud, brash age. The central character in *Travelers,* as in her other books, is India, which for her is not so much a country as an experience, after which no one is ever the same" (Ved Mehta). See *Heat and Dust* (1975) and *How I Became a Holy Mother* (1976).

**Keating, H. R. F.,** *Perfect Murder* (1964). Debut of Inspector Ganesh Ghote of the Bombay Criminal Investigation Department. The loveable, downtrodden detective is called upon to solve unusual murders in a long series of expert novels.

**Kipling, Rudyard,** *Plain Tales from the Hills* (1887). His first published fiction, a collection of well-plotted Anglo-Indian short stories of picturesque adventure. He glorified imperialism in this and other works about India, but there is no doubt that he was a born storyteller.

**Markandaya, Kamala,** *Nectar in a Sieve* (1955). Lyrical, haunting story of human suffering and the hard peasant life of south India. See *Two Virgins* (1973) and *The Golden Honeycomb* (1977).

**Masters, John,** *Nightrunners of Bengal* (1951). First of a sequence of action-packed popular novels tracing an Anglo-Indian family from the seventeenth century to the present. Others include *Bhowani Junction* (1954) and *Far, Far the Mountain Peak* (1957). *The Road Past Mandalay* (1961) is an account of Masters's participation in Wingate's "Chindit" campaign in World War II.

**Mehta, Ved,** *Portrait of India* (1970). Modern India by one of its most gifted writers. See *Walking the Indian Streets* (1961).

**Moorhouse, Geoffrey,** *Calcutta* (1972). Compassionately written, nightmarishly vivid portrait of a problem city.

**Naipaul, V. S.,** *India: A Wounded Civilization* (1977). The brilliant Trinidad-born novelist's intelligent, angry, humane, and passionate portrait of the land of his forebears and his perceptive conclusions on why India cannot fully be modernized. See *An Area of Darkness* (1964).

**Narayan, R. K.,** *The Man-Eater of Malgudi* (1963). One of the enchanting novels, full of dry, ironic humor, set in a fictional town in south India. Narayan, who writes in English, has been called the "Gogol of India." "Without him I could never have known what it was like to be an Indian" (Graham Greene). See *The English Teacher* (1945) and *Malgudi Days* (1982).

**Painter-Downes, Mollie,** *Ooty Preserved: A Victorian Hill Station in India* (1967). A *New Yorker* profile of Ootacamund, an old English mountain resort; "the effect is ghastly, but sociologically interesting, and with a particular poignancy of its own" (Malcolm Muggeridge).

**Rao, Raja,** *The Serpent and the Rope* (1960). Demanding, metaphysical novel grounded on the vedantic notion of reality and illusion, that paints a discerning "psychographic" portrait of India. See *Kanthapura* (1938).

**Rushdie, Salman,** *Midnight's Children* (1981). Novel about a man born at midnight on the day of Indian liberation in 1948, his history being entwined with that of his country, by a writer "with startling imaginative and intellectual resources, a master of perpetual storytelling. Like Garcia Marquez . . . he weaves a whole people's capacity for carrying its inherited myths . . . into a kind of magic carpet" (V. S. Pritchett). See *Grimus* (1982).

**Scott, Paul,** *The Jewel in the Crown* (1966). The first novel of the Raj Quartet: masterful setting of the entire psychic tapestry of India at the time of the British collapse. The others are *The Day of the Scorpion* (1968), *The Towers of Silence* (1972), and *A Division of Spoils* (1975).

**Sivasankara, Pillai Thakazhi,** *Chemmeen* (1962). Simple, haunting novel of love and hate in a fishing village of south India.

**Wolpert, Stanley,** *A New History of India* (rev. 1982). The best introductory survey for the general reader.

**Worswick, Clark and Ainslie Embree,** *The Last Empire: Photography in British India, 1885–1911* (1976). Fascinating portrait of the British Raj and of India itself.

## China

**Arnold, Eve,** *In China* (1980). Beautiful volume of haunting photographs of the country and its people by an American photographer. Another camera artist is Marc Riboud; see *Visions of China: Photographs of Marc Riboud, 1957–1980* (1981).

**Bloodworth, Dennis,** *The Chinese Looking Glass* (rev. 1980). Entertaining, provocative study that ranges with confidence and authority across 7,000 years of history, philosophy, literature, and day-to-day living, tracing the invisible strands that form the character of present-day China.

**Chen, Jo-hsi,** *The Execution of Mayor Yin and Other Stories from the Great Proletarian Cultural Revolution* (1978). Collection of artful short stories by a disillusioned writer now living in the West.

**Chen, Yuan-Tsung,** *The Dragon's Village* (1980). Autobiographical novel, based on the author's experiences during the Cultural Revolution, that Harrison Salisbury called the Chinese equivalent of Sholokhov's *And Quiet Flows the Don.*

**Fairbank, John King,** *The United States and China* (rev. 1979). Classic text by the dean of American China scholars; reputedly the best introduction to China. *Chinabound* (1982) is a memoir.

**Fleming, Peter,** *One's Company* (1934). Civilized, wry narrative of a journey ("a superficial account of an unsensational journey," are the author's words) to "Manchukuo and Red China." Several years later two other English writers recorded their impressions of a trip to China; see W. H. Auden and Christopher Isherwood *Journey to a War* (1939).

**Garside, Roger,** *Coming Alive: China After Mao* (1981). Superb, expert look at contemporary China by a British diplomat.

**Goodrich, L. Carrington and Nigel Cameron,** *The Face of China: As Seen by Photographers & Travelers, 1860–1912* (1978). Fascinating pictures with quotations from early travelers.

**Hibbert, Christopher,** *The Dragon Wakes: China and the West, 1793–1911* (1971). Vivid history of Anglo-Chinese relations — the Opium Wars, the Boxer Rebellion, etc. "Like our greatest historians, he has a novelist's sensibilities, a care for the past intensified by a concern for the future. His book is remarkably and disturbingly alive — one to trust and study" (Paul Theroux).

**Hinton, William,** *Fanshen: A Documentary of Revolution in a Chinese Village* (1966). Long, ardently sympathetic narrative of six months in a northern village when the new Communist power was establishing itself.

**Lattimore, Owen,** *High Tartary* (1930). Erudite, lively account of Chinese Turkes-

tan by an early American sinologist who writes in a style reminiscent of Doughty. See *Mongol Journey* (1941) and *Desert Road to Turkestan* (1929).

**Leys, Simon,** *Chinese Shadows* (1977). Belgian art historian's provocative, superbly written criticism of contemporary Chinese cultural values.

**Liu, Wu-chi and Irving Yucheng Lo** **(eds.),** *Sunflower Splendor: Three Thousand Years of Chinese Poetry* (1976). Largest and best collection of translated Chinese poems to have appeared in English.

**Lord, Bette Bao,** *Spring Moon* (1981). Saga of a Chinese "courtyard" family chronicles the House of Chang from the last days of imperial rule through Nationalist government and the Communist revolution. An absorbing first novel.

**Lu Hsun,** *Selected Stories* (1972). Much revered since his death in 1936 for his reformist stance, he was the first short-story writer to break away from the strictures of the classical form. "No writer of modern Chinese prose can match either his economy or the degree of human feeling that gets into his stories" (Martin Seymour-Smith).

*Nagel Travel Guide to China* (curr. rev.). Comprehensive; the best guide.

**Polo, Marco,** *Travels* (1300–24). Observations and stories by the Venetian merchant about his travels to Cathay and his seventeen years in the court of Kublai Khan. See Henry H. Hart, *Marco Polo, Venetian Adventurer* (rev. 1967).

**Prishvin, Mikhail,** *The Root of Life* (1980). A Russian hunter and an old Chinese ginseng gatherer are the protagonists of this poetic, austere novel set in the wilderness of northern Manchuria.

**Smedley, Agnes,** *Chinese Destinies: Sketches of Present Day China* (1933). China of a half-century ago was in revolutionary turmoil and the American author was there recording it in sharp, evocative, outspoken, partisan observations. See *China's Red Army Marches* (1934) and *Battle Hymn of China* (1943). Selections from these and others are in *Portraits of Chinese Women in Revolution* (1976).

**Snow, Edgar,** *Red Star over China* (rev. 1968). One of the first books by an American journalist to report on the growing strength of the Chinese Communists. See *The Other Side of the River* (1962) and his autobiography *Journey to the Beginning* (1958).

**Spence, Jonathan,** *The Death of Woman Wang* (1978). Eminent American China scholar's reconstruction of seventeenth-century life; "cutting swatches of trials, episodes, case histories from his materials, Spence bodies forth better than anybody else I have ever read, the brutality, cruelty and horror that underlies modern Chinese history" (Theodore H. White). See *Ts'ao Yin and K'ang-hsi Emperor: Bondservant and Master* (1967).

**Sullivan, Michael,** *Symbols of Eternity: The Art of Landscape Painting in China* (1979). "For anyone who loves art but knows little about Chinese painting, and would like to approach a little closer to one of the greatest artistic traditions of the world." See *The Arts of China* (rev. 1977) and *The Meeting of Eastern and Western Art* (1973).

**Suyin, Han,** *The Crippled Tree* (1965). The first installment of her autobiography, which tells the story of China too. A tendentious but enthralling work; followed by *The Mortal Flower* (1965) and *My House Has Two Doors* (1980).

**Terril, Ross,** *Flowers on an Iron Tree: Five Cities of China* (1975). A China scholar's graphic, informal picture of ordinary life in Shanghai, Dairen, Hangchow, Wuhan, and Peking. See *800,000,000: The Red China* (1972) and *Mao: A Biography* (1980).

**Tuchman, Barbara,** *Stilwell and the American Experience in China, 1911–1945* (1971). Really two books in one: the biography of "Vinegar Joe" Stilwell, the controversial American general, and the history of the Chinese-American relationship. It is a "fantastic and complex story, finely told" (Jonathan Spence). See Theodore H. White (ed.), *The Stilwell Papers* (1948).

**Van Gulik, Robert,** *The Chinese Gold Murders* (1959). One of a radiant series of detective novels about the seventh-century Judge Dee by a Dutch diplomat and sinologist. "Those who weary of routine crime may, like me, find the Chinese detective story . . . one of the most habit-forming drugs exported by the Orient" (Anthony Boucher).

## Tibet

**David-Neel, Alexandra,** *My Journey to Lhasa* (1927). The French explorer, Buddhist lama, and fluent speaker of the Tibetan language spent fourteen fascinating years in that country. Continued in *Magic and Mystery in Tibet* (1932). Other engaging accounts by Europeans include Sven Hedin, *A Conquest of Tibet* (1934) and Marco Pallis, *Peaks and Lamas* (rev. 1974).

**Fleming, Peter,** *Bayonets to Lhasa* (1961). Enthralling account of the Young-Husband mission — the British invasion of Tibet in 1904.

**Harrar, Heinrich,** *Seven Years in Tibet* (1953). Memoir by an Austrian mountaineer who served as tutor to the young Dalai Lama at Lhasa after escaping from a British internment camp in India during World War II.

**Suyin, Han,** *Lhasa, The Open City: A Journey to Tibet* (1977). A nonromantic account of the transformation of Tibet since its takeover by the Chinese in 1959. For an incisive scrutiny of the country today see the splendidly designed, large-format *Tibet* (1981) by a team of Tibetan scholars and Chinese photographers.

**Thubten, Jigme Norbu,** *Tibet Is My Country* (1960). Intimate life story of the Dalai

Lama's eldest brother. See Chogyam Trungpa, *Born in Tibet* (1966). Perhaps the most unusual spiritual autobiography is that of the German monk Lama Anagarika Govinda, *The Way of the White Clouds: Buddhist Pilgrim in Tibet* (1965).

## Hong Kong

**Clavell, James,** *Tai-Pan* (1966). Adventure story about the beginning of Hong Kong, from 1841 with the British acquisition after the first Opium War to the destruction of Queen's Town during a typhoon. *Noble House* (1981) is also a historical epic about the colony. John Gordon Davis, *Years of the Hungry Tigers* (1974) is a saga of modern Hong Kong.

**Elegant, Robert S.** *Dynasty* (1977) Popular "generations" novel by an old Hong Kong hand. See *Hong Kong* (1977), one of the Time-Life Great Cities series.

**Hughes, Richard,** *Hong Kong: Borrowed Place, Borrowed Time* (1968). Excellent illustrated overview by a long-time foreign correspondent. James Pope-Hennesey, *Half-Crown Colony: A Historical Profile of Hong Kong* (1970) is a chatty mix of travel and history.

**Marshall, William,** *Sci-Fi* (1981). One of the Yellowthread Street series of madcap thrillers featuring Inspector Harry Feiffer and his disorganized but earnest crew of Hong Kong cops.

**Suyin, Han,** *A Many-Splendored Thing* (1952). Poignant memoir of her love affair with an English newspaperman in 1949 and his tragic death in Korea just before their wedding. Another love story, fictional and of an entirely different sort, is Richard Mason's *The World of Suzie Wong* (1957).

## Japan

**Adachi, Barbara,** *The Living Treasures of Japan* (1973). Interviews with great contemporary artisans, called "living treasures," with photographs of their works, which derive from natural materials. Conveys a deep love of craft and tradition.

**Bashō, Matsua,** *The Narrow Road to the Deep North and Other Travel Sketches* (c. 1680). Masterpiece of poems and narrative about journeys to remote parts of Japan by the Zen-inspired founder of the modern school of haiku. See *Back Roads to Far Towns* (c. 1680).

**Benedict, Ruth,** *The Chrysanthemum and the Sword: Patterns of Japanese Culture* (1946). This classic anthropological study is today of historical interest, as the Japan it describes exists more in tradition than in reality. *Japanese Society* (1970) by Chie Nakane, known as the Margaret Mead of Japan, explores the individual's commitment to the group.

**Chand, Meira,** *Last Quadrant* (1982). A typhoon bears down on an orphanage in Kobe, where a storm is brewing inside too. A fine, evocative novel. See *The Gossamer Fly* (1980).

**Clavell, James,** *Shogun* (1975). Fast-paced, popular, half-million-word novel about a shipwrecked English sea pilot in feudal seventeenth-century Japan.

**Dazai, Osamu,** *The Setting Sun* (1951). Powerful novel about the reaction of an upper-class family to the Second World War. See *No Longer Human* (1958).

**Hearn, Lafcadio,** *Glimpses of Unfamiliar Japan* (1874). The American writer visited Japan at age forty in search of the exotic and stayed there the rest of his life, becoming a Japanese citizen. Of his many books about his adopted country, this is the best.

**Hokusai, Katsushika,** *Thirty-Six Views of Fuji* (1832). Famous series of woodblock prints produced when the great artist was past seventy and at last satisfied with his achievement. Its genre pictures of men and women in their ordinary activities are a summation of the daily life of nine-teenth-century Japan.

**Ibuse, Masuji,** *Black Rain* (1969). Unforgettable fictional reconstruction of the tragedy of Hiroshima. See John Hersey's extraordinary reportage in *Hiroshima* (1946).

**Kawabata, Yasunari,** *The Master of Go* (1972). Elegiac, poignant, and symbolic novel about the defeat of a traditional grand master of Japanese chess by a younger, more modern-minded man.

**Keene, Donald (ed.),** *Modern Japanese Literature* (1967). Anthology which introduced many Japanese writers to the West. Howard Hibbett (ed.), *Contemporary Japanese Literature* (1977), an anthology of postwar writing, is a good companion volume.

**Mishima, Yukio,** *The Sea of Fertility Tetralogy* (1972–74). Comprising *Spring Snow, Running Horses, The Temple of Dawn,* and *The Decay of the Angel,* it is a work of cosmic scope and human drama that charts, with satirical verve and resonant feeling, the progress of a soul through several incarnations.

**Murasaki Shikibu,** *The Tale of Genji* (c. 1000). Considered the first novel ever written, it chronicles the aristocratic society at Heian, the capital at the time. The newest and most readable translation, beautifully illustrated, is by Edward Seidensticker, published in 1976. Ivan Morris, *The World of the Shining Prince* (1964) provides a luminous background history of the times.

**Natsume, Soseki,** *Grass on the Wayside* (1919). Somber autobiographical novel by the greatest novelist of the Meiji period about the futility of human relationships. See *The Wayfarer* (1916) and *I Am a Cat* (1905), his comic masterpiece.

**Niwa, Fumio,** *The Waiting Years* (1956). A discursive novel, quintessentially Japanese in its lack of concern with plot, that probes a man's spiritual crisis and gives the reader an unvarnished look at contemporary temple life.

**Paterson, Katherine,** *The Master Puppeteer* (1975). Superb novel for young readers, handsomely illustrated and set in a beautifully evoked feudal Japan. Winner of National Book Award. The same period is background for *The Sign of the Chrysanthemum* (1973); *Of Nightingales that Weep* (1974); and *The Crane Wife* (1981), her translation of Sumiko Yagawa's retelling of an old folktale.

**Reischauer, Edwin O.,** *Japan: The Story of a Nation* (rev. 1981). Concise interpretative history by distinguished Harvard professor and former U.S. ambassador to Japan. See *The Japanese* (1977).

**Rexroth, Kenneth,** *One Hundred Poems from the Japanese* (1955). Fine translations by a distinguished American poet. He has created, with remarkable success, English versions which stand as poems in their own right. See *One Hundred More Poems from the Japanese* (1976).

**Richie, Donald,** *The Inland Sea* (1972). Informative, charming journal of a voyage through the Inland Sea by a former curator of New York's Museum of Modern Art who has lived half his life in Japan. See *Introducing Japan* (1972) and *The Japanese Movie* (rev. 1982).

**Shiga, Naoya,** *A Dark Night's Passing* (1921–37). Compelling, intensely personal novel about a young writer in search of himself.

**Shonagon, Sei,** *The Pillow Book* (c. 967). Witty, polished diary by a lady-in-waiting in the Heian court that brilliantly reflects traditional upper-class life of the period. Excellent translations by Arthur Waley (1928) and by Ivan Morris (1967). Another interesting portrait of feudal Japan can be found in the thirteenth-century diary, *The Confessions of Lady Nijo* (tr. 1973).

**Statler, Oliver,** *Japanese Inn* (1961). Original and fascinating book that details four turbulent centuries of Imperial Japanese history: the emperors and bandits, the warlords and merchants, the actors and artists, and the famous inn that stood at its crossroads.

**Suzuki, Daisetz T.,** *Zen and Japanese Culture* (1959). The foremost authority of his time on Zen shows how it influenced the cult of swordsmanship, the tea ceremony, the haiku form of poetry, and the Japanese love of nature. See Thomas Hoover, *Zen Culture* (1977).

**Tanizaki, Junichiro,** *Seven Japanese Tales* (1963). Collection of stories on theme of obsession by one of Japan's greatest modern novelists.

**Wichmann, Siegfried,** *Japonisme* (1981). Lavish reproductions and photographs make this comprehensive chronicle of the Japanese influence on Western art in the nineteenth and twentieth centuries a feast for the eye.

**Worswick, Clark (ed.)** *Japan: Photographs, 1854–1905* (1979). One hundred twenty photographs that offer a fascinating glimpse of an unfamiliar Japan.

## Malaysia

**Burgess, Anthony,** *The Long Day Wanes* (1964). American edition of the Malayan Trilogy, which was published in England in the late fifties.

**Farrell, J. G.,** *The Singapore Grip* (1979). Ironic novel about the doomed city from the thirties to its fall to the Japanese in 1942.

**Maugham, W. Somerset,** *The Casuarina Tree* (1926). Early collection of stories about the English of the Malay Peninsula and Borneo (all republished in the *Complete Short Stories*). Maugham at his storytelling best.

**Theroux, Paul,** *The Consul's File* (1977). Dry, comic stories, about dispirited expatriates, that center on a U.S. consulate in a remote Malaysian village. *Saint Jack*

(1973) has a colorful Singapore background.

**Wallace, Alfred Russel,** *The Malay Archipelago* (1869). An English scientist and thinker's decade in Malaya. It has been called the best piece of first-hand narrative exploration in the English language.

## New Guinea

**Harrar, Heinrich,** *I Came from the Stone Age* (1965). Exciting account of an Austrian mountaineer's encounters with nature and curious Stone Age tribes on his trek across the western part of New Guinea. Another tale of true adventure is Forbes Wilson, *The Conquest of Copper Mountain* (1981).

**Kirk, Malcolm,** *Man as Art: New Guinea* (1981). Large-format photographs of New Guineans in full tribal dress by a man who over thirteen years spent months at a time living with various tribes.

**Matthiessen, Peter,** *Under the Mountain Wall: A Chronicle of Two Seasons in the Stone Age* (1962). The naturalist and novelist portrays the life of the primitive Kurelu tribe. "What he has described in beautiful and poignant writing is the way of savages. . . . They are ourselves in miniature" (Loren Eiseley).

**Read, Kenneth E.,** *The High Valley* (1965). Well-written, introspective report of two years in the village of Susuroka in the Central Highlands.

**Williams, Maslyn,** *The Stone Age Island: New Guinea Today* (1964). Written by an Australian film maker, "this splendid book is a disclosure of pure fact that reads with the elixir and rush of a fine novel" (Russell Peterson).

## Australia

*A Day in the Life of Australia* (1981). On March 6, 1981, one hundred top photographers set out to capture the life of Australia over the course of one day. Result:

A photojournalistic milestone, as the Aussie stereotypes are blown away. An incisive portrait of a land and its people.

**Davidson, Robyn,** *Tracks* (1980). A twenty-seven-year-old woman's 1700-mile, six-month trek across the rugged bush with four camels and a dog.

**Grzimek, Bernhard,** *Four-Legged Australia: Adventures with Animals and Man in Australia* (1967). Chatty account by a German zoologist of his meetings with the kangaroo, koala, platypus, and other endangered wildlife of Australia.

**James, Clive,** *Unreliable Memoirs* (1981). Boyhood and coming of age to his arrival in England at twenty-two recollected in a book which is savagely funny, facetious, scatological, puerile, and moving.

**Keneally, Thomas,** *The Chant of Jimmy Blacksmith* (1972). Tragic, chilling novel, based on a true murder story, about a Christian-reared aborigine torn between two worlds.

**Marshall, James Vance,** *Walkabout* (1959). Sympathetic, haunting tale of two American children who find themselves the sole survivors of a plane crash on the virtually uninhabitated outback and of their encounter with an aborigine boy. See *A Walk to the Hills of the Dreamtime* (1970).

**Moorehead, Alan,** *Cooper's Creek* (1964). The nineteenth-century Burke and White expedition across Australia, which ended in terror and disaster. *Rum Jungle* (1953) is a return-of-the-native memoir by the gifted Australian-born journalist.

**Richardson, Henry Handel,** *Fortunes of Richard Mahony* (1930). The title of a classic trilogy begun in 1917 with *Australia Felix* and set in the mid-nineteenth century. It tells the tragic story of a man's fight to overcome impending insanity. Another classic historical novel is Eleanor Dark, *Timeless Land* (1941).

**Upfield, Arthur W.,** *Lure of the Bush* (1928). Premier volume of the long-lived series of detective novels about Inspector Napoleon "Bony" Bonaparte, the part-aborigine sleuth with the ability to read "the Book of the Bush" and reason superbly.

**Ward, Russel,** *A Different Frontier: The Australian Legend* (rev. 1979). Classic study blending history, sociology, and folklore into a lively text. With illustrations. See *The History of Australia: The Twentieth Century* (1978). Another good introduction to Australia is David Horne's *The Lucky Country* (1974).

**White, Patrick,** *Voss* (1957). Novel by the Nobel laureate about a German explorer's trek across the desert that ended in mutiny and death. See *The Edge of the Storm* (1974) and his self-portrait *Flaws in the Glass* (1982).

## New Zealand

**Ashton-Warner, Sylvia,** *Spinster* (1959). Novel about a brilliant, compassionate, impulsive woman teaching in a remote Maori schoolhouse. "Alive with passion and beauty; it has a poetic quality that reminds me of Emily Dickinson, so precisely does it register a special kind of experience" (Herbert Read). See *Greenstone* (1966), *Bell Call* (1964), and *Incense to Idols* (1960).

**Bone, Robert W.,** *The Maverick Guide to New Zealand* (1981). Excellent travel companion.

**Lockley, Ronald,** *Man Against Nature* (1971). Dramatic story, attractively illustrated, of the changes in the New Zealand ecology caused by man and the animals he has introduced to the island.

**Sargeson, Frank,** *Collected Stories* (1974). New Zealand's greatest short-story writer, especially noted for his studies of women and childhood. The best of the new generation of short-story writers is Margaret Sutherland; see her *Dark Places, Deep Regions and Other Stories* (1980).

Shadbolt, Maurice, *The Lovelock Version* (1981). Large, sweeping novel of modern New Zealand by one of that country's most graceful writers. See *Strangers and Journeys* (1972) and *Among the Cinders* (1965).

# UNITED STATES

Adams, Ansel and Nancy Newhall, *This Is the American Earth* (1960). Already a classic, the splendid photos — half by Adams, the others selected by him — and Newhall's simple text, a prose poem really, are an ecological alert which must be heeded.

*American Heritage Guide, Great Historic Places* (rev. 1980). Guidebook to over a thousand historic sites, arranged alphabetically by state and by town.

Dickens, Charles, *American Notes* (1842). Volume of travel sketches that offended the sensibilities of Americans for its position on abolition and international copyright. Other amusing nineteenth-century American travel books by English novelists include Frances Trollope, *Domestic Manners of the Americans* (1832), Frederick Maryatt, *A Diary in America* (1839), and Rudyard Kipling, *American Notes* (1899).

*Federal Writers Project, American Guide Series* (1935–41). Books written during the Depression as a WPA project for unemployed writers: one for each state, plus some regions and cities. Many have been revised, but the originals are still invaluable for history, geology, and geography.

Frank, Robert, *The Americans* (1958). Classic gallery of candid and sardonic photos taken by the Swiss photographer during a two-year journey across America on a Guggenheim grant.

James, Henry, *The American Scene* (1907). In his full late Jacobean style, he describes his native land after an absence of twenty years.

Jensen, Oliver, and Joan Kerr, *American Album* (1968). Sumptuous photographs documenting the country's history.

Linklater, Eric, *Juan in America* (1931). Robust lampoon of a grotesque America, both joyous and cruel. The best work of the Scottish novelist, it is a modern picaresque classic.

Matthiessen, Peter, *Wildlife in America* (1959). A "decline and fall" of American wildlife, its account of the obliteration of the wilderness is "a dramatic, unsettling story, skillfully told in a clean, strong prose not often found in the literature of conservation" (Archie Carr). See Hal Borland, *The History of Wildlife in America* (1975).

*Mobil Travel Guides* (curr. rev.). Published by Rand McNally, these regional handbooks are the best accommodation guides on the market. See the *Rand McNally Road Atlas* (curr. rev.), a must for any cross-country driving.

Nash, Roderick, *Wilderness and the American Mind* (rev. 1973). An historian traces the evolution of the American attitude toward the wilderness. See Arthur A. Ekirich, *Man and Nature in America* (1963), a historical study of the conflict between harmonious living with, and exploitation of, nature in America.

Pachter, Marc (ed.), *Abroad in America: Visitors to the New Nation 1776–1914* (1976). Published in association with the National Portrait Gallery, this beautifully executed volume matches travelers' accounts with hundreds of superb illustrations. See Peter Conrad's *Imagining*

*America* (1980), a witty treatment of nineteenth- and twentieth-century literary British travelers.

**Steinbeck, John,** *Travels with Charley* (1962). Ten thousand miles through thirty-four states in the good truck *Rocinante* with his faithful poodle, Charley.

Another on-the-road report by an American novelist is Henry Miller, *The Air-Conditioned Nightmare* (1945).

**Stewart, George R.,** *American Place-names* (1970). Selective dictionary for continental U.S. Great fun to browse through the 12,000 entries.

# NEW ENGLAND

**Hale, Nancy (ed.),** *New England Discovery* (1963). The Boston-born novelist's anthology of regional writing. George F. Whicher (ed.), *Poetry of the New England Renaissance, 1790–1890* (1950) is the best collection for the period.

**Mitchell, Edwin Valentine,** *It's an Old New England Custom* (1946). Good, old-fashioned tidbits of historical crotchets, from bundling to epitaphs. His other delightful books include *The Horse and Buggy Age in New England* (1937) and *Yankee Folk* (1948).

**Snow, Edward,** *Mysterious Tales of the New England Coast* (1961). Score of the most fascinating puzzles that have emerged along these shores, many of which may never be solved, by a master teller of sailing stories. See *Fantastic Folklore and Fact: New England Tales of Land and Sea* (1968).

**Strand, Paul (p) and Nancy Newhall (ed.),** *Time in New England* (rev. 1980). Strand's classic photographs are matched with selections of memoirs, poems, letters, and tall tales from writers about New England's past in a book that is "a model of its kind that has never been eclipsed" (Hilton Kramer). Of the making of picture books of New England there is no end; some of the best are Hal Borland (t) and B. A. King (p), *A Place to Begin: The New England Experience* (1976); Samuel Chamberlain (p) and Stewart Beach (t), *New England in Color* (1969); Robb Sagendorph (t) and Anthony Griffin (p), *New England* (1963); and Martin W. Sandler, *This Was New England: Images of a Vanished Past* (1977).

**Tanner, Ogden,** *New England Wilds* (1974). Handsomely produced volume about the region's wilderness areas, part of the Time-Life American Wilderness series. Superb companion volumes are Alfred J. Godin, *Wild Mammals of New England* (1978) and its field guide edition (1981).

## *Connecticut*

**Borland, Hal,** *This Hill, This Valley* (1957). Reflections and descriptions by the naturalist and writer of life on his farm near Salisbury in northern Connecticut. See *Hill County Harvest* (1967).

**DeForest, John W.,** *History of the Indians of Connecticut* (1853). Indian life from the earliest known period to 1850 by a novelist who lived in New Haven.

**Gannett, Lewis,** *Cream Hall* (1949). Account of life on a northwest Connecticut hilltop farm by a former New York reporter and book reviewer. He was a family man and, in his own words, no Thoreau, but he went back to the country.

**Morath, Inge (p) and Arthur Miller (t),** *In the Country* (1977). Coffee-table book of beautiful photographs with personal, impressionistic, and nostalgic sketches by the playwright, long a resident of Connecticut.

**Rolleston, Sara Emerson,** *Heritage Houses: The American Tradition in Connecticut, 1660–1910* (1979). Forty houses, inns, and taverns that display a 250-year-old regional architectural tradition.

**Sandler, Martin W.,** *This Was Connecticut: Images of a Vanished World* (1977). Two hundred photographs by T. S. Bronson of Connecticut life from 1855 to 1914, with a perceptive narrative. A superbly designed volume.

**Taber, Gladys,** *The Best of Stillmeadow* (1976). A dozen books have issued from the seventeenth-century Connecticut farmhouse, each filled with the author's warmth of feeling and enjoyment of the landscape and its seasons. This is a selection from those writings.

**Taylor, Robert J.,** *Colonial Connecticut: A History* (1979). Good comprehensive history from the days of original settlement to the Declaration of Independence. See Charles McLean Andrews's *Connecticut's Place in Colonial History* (1924); Jane DeForest Shelton's rich detailing of day-to-day colonial life in *Salt Box House: 18th Century Life in a New England Hill Town* (1900); and Christopher Collier's *Roger Sherman's Connecticut: Yankee Politics and the American Revolution* (1971). The early years of statehood are covered in Richard J. Purcell, *Connecticut in Transition, 1775–1818* (1919).

**Teale, Edwin Way,** *A Walk Through the Year* (1978). Inspired by Thoreau's proposal: "it would be pleasant to write the history of one hillside for one year," Teale culled his journal of over twenty years to fashion a year of days at Trail Wood. A companion volume is *A Naturalist Buys an Old Farm* (1974).

**Van Dusen, Albert E.,** *Connecticut* (1961). This fully illustrated large-format book is the best single-volume history of the state. *Connecticut: Past and Present* (1939) is an affectionate, personal blend of history, geography, topography, and sentiment by Odell Shepard, a Pulitzer Prize–winning writer who based his book on twenty years of rambling throughout the state.

## Maine

**Beston, Henry,** *Northern Farm: A Chronicle of Maine* (1948). Meditative account, suffused with his warmth and pleasure in little things, by a naturalist of a year on a Kennebec farm. The best of his writings have been collected in *Especially Maine: The Natural World of Henry Beston* (1970).

**Brace, Gerald Warner,** *Between Wind and Water* (1966). Maine's summer coast by a novelist, many of whose works have a Maine setting; see *The World of Carrick's Cove* (1957).

**Chase, Mary Ellen,** *Windswept* (1941). One of the best novels set on the coast of Maine by this writer, a descendant of sailors and farmers of the state. Other regional novels are Ruth Moore, *Sarah Walked Over the Mountain* (1979); Elizabeth Ogilvie, *An Answer in the Tide* (1978); and Elizabeth Savage, *Toward the End* (1980).

**Coffin, Robert P. Tristram,** *Lost Paradise: A Boyhood on a Maine Coast Farm* (1934). The Pulitzer Prize–winning poet's charming evocation of his down-east childhood. His verse includes *Maine Ballads* (1938), and of his informal prose works about Maine, outstanding are *Yankee Coast* (1947), *Maine Doings* (1950), and *Kennebec* (1937), one of the Rivers of America series.

**Gould, John,** *And One to Grow On: Recollections of a Maine Boyhood* (1949). Growing up in the twenties in Freeport. A reader would be "hard put to it to find an account of a small town boyhood more amusingly, humanely, and satisfyingly described" (Henry Beston). A distaff memoir of yankee youth is Helen V. Taylor, *A Time to Recall: The Delights of a Maine Childhood* (1963).

**Jewett, Sarah Orne,** *The Country of the Pointed Firs* (1896). Set in a small town not unlike the author's native Berwick, these old-fashioned stories, "or sketches, rather, light as smoke, or wisps of sea-fog, (are) charged with the odors of mint, wild roses and balsam. . . . No one since Hawthorne had pictured this New England world with such exquisite freshness of feeling" (Van Wyck Brooks).

**Rich, Louise Dickinson,** *The Peninsula* (1958). This illustrated description of the Gouldsboro Peninsula is "a beautiful and moving book . . . full of the sights and the sounds and the feeling of that remote Maine coast and its people" (Rachel Carson). See her unabashedly partisan informal histories and guides, *State O'Maine* (1964) and *The Coast of Maine* (rev. 1975). *My Neck of the Woods* (1950) is about the primitive fifteen years she and her husband spent in the high wilderness of northwestern Maine.

**Roberts, Kenneth,** *Trending into Maine* (rev. 1944). One of this historical novelist's paeans to his state. See *We Took to the Woods* (1942), *Don't Say That About Maine* (1950), and *Good Maine Food* (1939).

**Thoreau, Henry David,** *The Maine Woods* (1864). Sights, sounds, and scents of the poet-naturalist's trips to Mount Katahden, Moosehead Lake, the West Branch of the Penobscot, Lake Chesunesok, the famous Allegash River, and the East Branch. More recent accounts of the Maine woods are Lew Dietz, *The Allegash* (1968) and Helen Hamlin, *Nine Mile Bridge: Three Years in the Maine Woods* (1945).

**White, E. B.,** *One Man's Meat* (1942). In his late thirties, White and his wife and young son went to live on a salt-water farm in Maine and stayed for five years. Contemplating through long winters, writing of small events in the course of his farming, he composed a series of monthly columns for *Harper's* called "One Man's Meat." They are gathered here.

## Massachusetts

**Cummings, Abbot Lowell,** *The Framed Houses of Massachusetts Bay, 1625–1725*

(1979). Two hundred eighty splendid photographs and drawings of classic colonial homes.

**Dubus, Andre,** *Finding a Girl in America* (1980). Many of the stories in this and earlier collections of short stories take place among the lower-middle-class and blue-collar families near Newburyport, in the northeast corner of the state. See *Adultery and Other Stories* (1977) and *Seperate Flights* (1975).

**Freeman, Mary Wilkins,** *A New England Nun; and Other Stories* (1891). "Local color" classic, short stories about the frustrated, repressed men and women in eastern Massachusetts who stayed when people were moving west.

**Hough, Henry Beetle,** *Mostly on Martha's Vineyard: A Personal Record* (1975). For over forty years Hough published and edited the *Vineyard Gazette* and wrote many books about the island. This one, about his early days, is one of the best. He collaborated with photographer Alfred Eisenstadt on a beautiful picture book, *Martha's Vineyard* (1970).

**Marquand, John P.,** *Timothy Dexter Revisited* (1960). In 1925 Marquand published *Lord Timothy Dexter,* a biography of the amazing eighteenth-century eccentric; thirty-five years later he reminisced about Newburyport, his and Dexter's home town. It provided the inspiration for his novel *Wickford Point* (1939).

**Morison, Samuel Eliot,** *The Maritime History of Massachusetts* (rev. 1941). Classic account of the rise and development of Massachusetts as a sea power from 1783 to 1860.

**Taylor, Robert J.,** *Western Massachusetts in the Revolution* (1954). Frontier politics, Shay's Rebellion, the Great Awakening, and other events around the time of the War for Independence.

**Wharton, Edith,** *Ethan Frome* (1911). Brief, stark, tragic novel of love among poor high-villagers in the Berkshires.

**Whitehill, Walter Muir and Norman Kotker,** *Massachusetts: A Pictorial History* (1976). Copiously illustrated, large-format, well-written survey to delight all lovers of the Commonwealth.

**Wood, James Playsted,** *The People of Concord* (1970). Vibrant sociocultural history of the extraordinary town of Emerson, Thoreau, Alcott, and others.

## Cape Cod

**Beston, Henry,** *The Outermost House: A Year of Life on the Great Beach of Cape Cod* (1928). The Quincy-born, Harvard-educated naturalist spent a year in a two-room cabin on the outer dunes of Cape Cod. This record of that time is about the vividness of small events and also about man's relationship to the cosmos. A classic in American nature writing.

**Hay, John,** *The Great Beach* (1963). Lyrical evocation of nature's beauty on the Cape. See *The Run* (rev. 1965) and *Nature's Year: The Seasons of Cape Cod* (1961).

**Leighton, Clare,** *Where Land Meets Sea: The Tide Line of Cape Cod* (1954). A resident's hymn of praise, full of sharp observation and fine woodcuts. Other writers in the contemplative tradition of Beston include Wyman Richardson, *The House on Nauset Marsh* (1955) and Robert Finch, *Common Ground: A Naturalist's Cape Cod* (1981).

**Thoreau, Henry David,** *Cape Cod* (1865). Posthumously published account of three walking trips made over a six-year period that describes the environment and people of "the bared and bended arm of Massachusetts" with relish and good humor.

**Vorse, Mary M.,** *Time and the Town: A Provincetown Chronicle* (1942). Beautiful book that combines autobiography with local history. Plenty of amusing and revealing anecdotes.

## New Hampshire

**Atkinson, Brooks and W. Kent Olson,** *New England's White Mountains: At Home in the Wild* (1978). Celebration of the rugged wilderness in a splendid selection of photographs and prose by people drawn to its beauty. One man so drawn was Cornelius Weygandt who annually summered near the Sandwich country and wrote *White Hills: Mountain New Hampshire, Winnepesaukee to Washington* (1934) and *New Hampshire Neighbors: Country Folks and Things in the White Hills* (1937).

**Blos, Joan W.,** *A Gathering of Days: A New England Girl's Journal 1830–32* (1979). Newberry Award–winning novel that captures the hardship and tranquility of early American farm life and the sturdiness and tenderness of the people whose way of life it was. A pendant volume is Donald Hall's *Ox-cart Man* (1979), winner of the Caldecott Medal for Barbara Cooney's superb illustrations that suggest early American paintings on wood.

**Cannon, LeGrand, Jr.,** *Look to the Mountain* (1942). Pioneer life in the shadow of Mt. Chocorua. A moving love story. See *A Mighty Fortress* (1937). Ann Miller Downes, *The Pilgrim Soul* (1952) is also a popular novel of pioneering days.

**Frost, Robert,** *New Hampshire* (1923). Pulitzer Prize–winning collection of New England stories told in blank verse, the title poem describing New Hampshire as "one of the two best states in the Union, Vermont's the other." See *North of Boston* (1914).

**Hawthorne, Nathaniel,** *The Great Stone Face, and Other Tales of the White Mountains* (1889). Tales and short stories set in New Hampshire by the great New England writer.

**Hebert, Ernest,** *The Dogs of March* (1979). The slide downhill of a middle-aged, barely literate man by a novelist with an ear for the vernacular. Other novels of contemporary New Hampshire are Ruth Doan MacDougall, *Aunt Pleasantine* (1978) and Russel Banks, *Hamilton Stark* (1978).

**Milne, Lorus J. and Margery Milne,** *The Valley: Meadow, Grove and Stream* (1963). Husband and wife chronicled the environmental happenings around their house in the Oyster River Valley and the tidewater estuary at Durham. See *Gift from the Sky* (1967), about a female mute swan that settled down on a mill pond in Durham, and see John R. Quinn's *The Winter Woods* (1977) and *The Summer Woodlands* (1980).

**Sarton, May,** *Kinds of Love* (1970). Sensitive novel of life in a small hill town. In her collection of poems, *As Does New Hampshire* (1967), she celebrates the life of the village and countryside where she has put down roots.

**Tolman, Newton F.,** *North of Monadnock* (1961). Shrewdly observant view of country living in the uplands by a man whose family roots in Nelson go back several generations. Other observers of country and village live are Philbrook Paine, whose gusty anecdotes are in *Squarely Behind the Beaver* (1963), and Haydn S. Pearson, whose books include *New England Flavor* (1961).

**Williams, Thomas,** *Town Burning* (1959). National Book Award–winning novelist's incisive study of small, static town, distinguished by rich characterization. See *Whipple's Castle* (1968) and *The Followed Man* (1978).

## Rhode Island

**Bridenbaugh, Carl,** *Fat Mutton and Liberty of Conscience: Society in Rhode Island 1636–1690* (1974). Fine study of the economic life of the seventeenth-century settlers. Other good books on this period are Sydney V. James, *Colonial Rhode Island* (1975) and S. H. Brockunier, *The Irrepressible Democrat, Roger Williams* (1940).

**Downing, A. F. and Vincent J. Scully, Jr.,** *The Architectural Heritage of Newport, Rhode Island, 1640–1915* (rev. 1967). Hundreds of beautiful reproductions. Newport of the 1870s and 1880s is delightfully recollected in *This Was My Newport* (1944), by Maud Howe Elliott.

**Lippincott, Bertram,** *Indians, Privateers and High Society: A Rhode Island Sampler* (1961). Informal historical sketches of the smallest state. Humorous and dramatic.

**Plante, David,** *The Family* (1978). Fine novel about growing up in a French-Canadian working-class family in Providence. See *The Country* (1981).

**Winterich, John T.,** *Another Day, Another Dollar* (1947). Delightful reminiscences of the author's youth in Providence during the first decades of the century.

## Vermont

**Davis, Deane C.,** *Justice in the Mountains* (1980). The former governor recounts tales and stories of his days as a country lawyer in the twenties and thirties in an easy feet-on-the-fender style.

**Delbanco, Nicholas,** *Sherbrookes Trilogy* (1977–80). Commencing with *Possession,* the novels trace the claims of history, love, and blood ties on an eccentric rich family in rural Vermont, in a prose "offered with the precision of heavy, precious coins being counted in the palm" (Frederick Busch).

**Duffus, R. L.,** *Williamstown Branch* (1958). These "impersonal memories of a Vermont boyhood" by a former *New York Times* editorial writer are an enchanting exercise in nostalgia in their evocation of turn-of-the-century small-town life. See *Waterbury Record* (1959) and *West Hill* (1942), a novel.

**Fisher, Dorothy Canfield,** *Vermont Tradition: The Biography of an Outlook on Life*

(1953). Spiritual biography of an adopted state. Filled with the familiar warmth of understanding and the admiration of the simple basic virtues that marked her work. See *Memories of Arlington* (1957).

**Hill, Ralph Nading,** *Contrary Country* (rev. 1960). Engaging look at Vermont's distinctly private flavor by one of its most ardent celebrants. See *Yankee Kingdom: Vermont and New Hampshire* (1961). He was a coeditor of the beautiful photographic album *Vermont: A Special World* (1969) and its sequel *Vermont for Every Season* (1980) and editor of *Vermont Album: A Collection of Early Vermont Photographs* (1974).

**Jellison, Charles A.,** *Ethan Allen: Frontier Rebel* (1969). Lively biography of the leader of the Green Mountain Boys and Revolutionary War hero that serves as a good introduction to the times. The ensuing years of statehood are graphically related in *Social Ferment in Vermont, 1791–1850* (1939).

**Johnson, Charles W.,** *The Nature of Vermont* (1980). First-rate introduction and guide to the environment.

**Merrick, Elliot,** *Green Mountain Farm* (1948). Warm, thoughtful, larded with fine anecdotes, this account of rural life by a man who moved to Vermont with his wife and child during the Depression is more than a "joys of country living" book. See his novel, *From This Hill Looks* (1934). Other moving and amusing books by ex-urbanites are Kathleen B. Granger's *The Hills of Home: A Vermont Idyll* (1966) and Marguerite Hurrey Wolf's *I'll Take the Back Road* (1975).

**Mosher, Howard Frank,** *Where the Rivers Flow North* (1978). The austere, beautiful Jay Peak country by the Canadian border is Mosher's special province. These finely crafted stories capture the rugged land and the people it shapes. See *Disappearances* (1977).

**Swift, Esther Munroe,** *Vermont Placenames: Footprints of History* (1977). Seven hundred-page, twenty-years-in-the-making volume with in-depth accounts of the places named. A must for self-respecting lovers of the Green Mountains.

**Van de Water, Frederic F.,** *A Home in the Country* (1937). Candid and witty account of how he and his wife, New Yorkers, found a home in Vermont. He wrote many books about his adopted state, including a four-novel cycle about "early Vermont's desperate struggle for self-ownership" that begins with *Reluctant Rebel* (1948).

# MIDDLE ATLANTIC STATES

## *Delaware*

**Canby, Henry Seidel,** *The Age of Confidence: Life in the Nineties* (1934). A bittersweet interpretation of life in Wilmington and America. *American Memoir* (1947) and *Family History* (1945) are also autobiographical. *The Brandywine* (1941) is his fine contribution to the Rivers of America series and is illustrated by Andrew Wyeth.

**Lunt, Dudley Cammett,** *Taylors Gut in the Delaware State* (1967). Wildlife experiences of the author, a wildfowl hunting enthusiast, around Taylors Gut, a tidal inlet on the Atlantic coast. See *Thousand Acre March* (1959) and *The Woods and the Sea* (1965).

**Mosley, Leonard,** *Blood Relations: The Rise and Fall of the Duponts of Delaware* (1980). Popular history of the 150-year American dynasty that has had great influence on the state.

**Ward, Christopher,** *The Dutch and Swedes on the Delaware, 1609–64* (1930).

Enthusiastic, entertaining popular history of the region before the English gained control of it. For a revisionist view see C. A. Weslager, *The English on the Delaware: 1610–1682* (1968).

**Weslager, C. A.,** *Delaware's Buried Past: A Story of Archeological Adventure* (1968). Chronological record of Delaware's beginnings by a noted local historian.

## Maryland

**Barth, John,** *The Sot-weed Factor* (1960). Rollicking satire of historical novels set among the tobacco planters of seventeenth-century Maryland.

**Klingel, Gilbert C.,** *The Bay: A Naturalist Discovers a Universe of Life Above and Below the Chesapeake* (1951). Enthusiastic, delighted observer "with the endless patience of a true naturalist has recorded the details of the pageant of life enacted by jelly-fish and fiddler crabs, barnacles and all the rest of the bay's creatures" (Rachel Carson).

**Michener, James A.,** *Chesapeake* (1978). Four-century panorama of the Eastern Shore through the fictional interweaving of three families and the Indians, blacks, and Irish immigrants who settled there.

**Tyler, Anne,** *Celestial Navigation* (1974). Extraordinarily moving and beautiful portrait of a Baltimore artist by a novelist who has been praised "for her ability to infuse the homeliest details from daily lives and environment with a kind of luminous intensity — a process in which extreme accuracy of vision is combined with a poetic instinct for startling possibilities" (Robert Towers). See *Searching for Caleb* (1976), *Morgan's Passing* (1979), and *Dinner at the Homesick Restaurant* (1982).

**Warner, William W.,** *Beautiful Swimmers: Watermen, Crabs and the Chesapeake Bay* (1976). Awarded the Pulitzer Prize, it is not only a complete natural history of the pugnacious, succulent Atlantic blue crab, it is also a colorful report on the Bay and on the frank-talking watermen who make their living in the crab's pursuit. For more about these interesting watermen see George Carey, *A Faraway Time and Place* (1971).

## New Jersey

**Beck, Henry Charlton,** *Fare to Midlands: Forgotten Towns of Central New Jersey* (1939). One of several flavorful books by a newspaperman that mix fact and folklore about the forgotten and abandoned towns in the state: the fruit of years of sympathetic exploration and listening. See *Forgotten Towns of Southern New Jersey* (1936), *Forgotten Towns of Central New Jersey* (1939), and *The Roads of Home: Lanes and Legends of New Jersey* (1956).

**Lundin, Leonard,** *Cockpit of the Revolution: The War for Independence in New Jersey* (1940). Thorough, lively narrative survey of New Jersey in the Revolution. For a fictional treatment of the war there, see Thomas Fleming, *Liberty Tavern* (1976).

**McPhee, John,** *The Pine Barrens* (1968). Beautifully written, compassionate portrait of the land and people of the wilderness in south central New Jersey; a unique blend of folklore and the natural processes the author found there. An edition with photographs by Bill Curtsinger was published in 1981.

**Peterson, Russell,** *Another View of the City* (1967). A naturalist's fresh, genial account of a cycle of seasons in the natural environment of the northeastern tip of New Jersey, within sight of New York's Empire State Building! Other suburban nature observations are Eve Rodimer, *The Year Outdoors* (1966) and William Jon Watkins, *Suburban Wilderness* (1981).

**Tice, George A.,** *Urban Landscapes: A New Jersey Portrait* (1976). Large-format collection of black-and-white photographs, beautifully reproduced, of buildings in various towns and cities. With a nuance of tonal shading that haunts the viewer.

## New York

**Carmer, Carl,** *My Kind of Country* (1966). "Undefined gleanings" from thirty years' writings by an author who has come to be identified with upstate New York. See *The Tavern Lamps Are Burning: Literary Journeys Through Six Regions and Four Centuries of New York State* (1964), a personal collection of prose and poetry; *The Hudson* (rev. 1968); and *Genesee Fever* (1941), a novel.

**Dangerfield, George,** *Chancellor Robert R. Livingstone of New York, 1746–1813* (1960). This elegant biography of the eighteenth-century statesman, a member of one the great landowning families of New York, is a "unique study of the times and an unforgettable portrait of a Colonial aristocrat caught up in the turbulence of a revolutionary age, during which most of what he stood for was bound to disappear sooner or later" (Carl Bridenbaugh).

**Edmonds, Walter,** *Rome Haul* (1929). The famous historical novelist drew on his lifelong environment of the Mohawk Valley/Cherry Valley/Erie Canal region for the background of most of his novels. This one, as well as *Erie Water* (1933) and *The Wedding Journey* (1947) are set in the great days of the Erie Canal before the advent of railroads. Samuel Hopkins Adams, *Canal Town* (1944) also takes place at that time.

**Howat, John K.,** *The Hudson River and Its Painters* (1972). Large-format volume of paintings by Hudson River School painters accompanied by a pro-conservation text. See Raymond J. O'Brien, *American Sublime: Landscape and Scenery of the Lower Hudson Valley* (1981).

**Irving, Washington,** *Knickerbocker's History of New York* (1809). In droll fashion, this mock-heroic epic of Dutch New York brings to life old New Amsterdam and the gallant Peter Stuyvesant. See *The Sketch Book* (1819), containing his most popular stories, "Rip van Winkle" and "The Legend of Sleepy Hollow." A more serious history of the state can be found in Marshall B. Davidson, *New York: A Pictorial History* (1977).

**Kammen, Michael G.,** *Colonial New York: A History* (1975). Judicious, elegant, monumental study, by Pulitzer Prize–winning historian.

**Keller, Jane Eblen,** *Adirondack Wilderness: A Story of Man and Wilderness* (1980). Engaging story of the Adirondack Mountain Wilderness, the largest public park in the U.S. Other Adirondackiana include the photojournalistic volumes by Lincoln Barnett, *The Ancient Adirondacks* (1974); William C. White, *Adirondack Country* (1967); and Hugh Fosburgh's *One Man's Pleasure* (1960), a journal of a year spent at his house in the forest.

**Rattray, Everett T.,** *The South Fork: The Land and the People of Eastern Long Island* (1979). Publisher of the East Hampton *Star* eloquently relates the natural history of the South Fork, not the *haute monde* of the Hamptons, with marvelous descriptive skill. Other interesting Long Island books include Robert Arbib, *The Lord's Wood* (1971) and Jeanette Rattray, *Ship Ashore* (1955).

**Wallace, Anthony F. C.,** *The Death and the Rebirth of the Seneca: The History and Culture of the Great Iroquois Nation, Their Destruction and Demoralization, and Their Cultural Revival at the Hands of the Indian Visionary Handsome Lake* (1970). The epic story of the collapse and renascence of the greatest of the northeast Indian tribes. A masterpiece of anthropological and historical investigation.

**Wilson, Edmund,** *Upstate: Records and Recollections of Northern New York* (1971). His memories of twenty years in the Old Stone House in Talcottville is also an account of a region and its people, "a haunting book that will be read hundreds of years from now to learn what the twentieth century was about" (Christopher Lehmann-Haupt).

## Pennsylvania

**Allen, Hervey,** *The City in the Dawn* (1950). Abridgement of the trilogy of documentary local-color novels that begin in the 1760s in the mountains east of today's Pittsburgh. Other good novels of the eighteenth century include Elsie Singmaster, *A High Wind Rising* (1942) and Herbert H. Stover, *Song of the Susquehanna* (1949).

**Bartlett, Virginia K.,** *Pickles and Pretzels: The World of Food in Pennsylvania* (1979). Lively look at the historical and ethnic foods of the Commonwealth.

**Brand, Millen (t) and George A. Tice (p),** *Fields of Peace: A Pennsylvania German Album* (1970). Happy combination of photographs and prose make this a haunting picture of the German (not Dutch) Americans of Lancaster County. Brand, who lived for many years on Crow Hill, near Bally, is the author of a fine book of poems about them, *Local Lives* (1975).

**Constantine, K. C.,** *The Rocksburg Railroad Murders* (1972). First of a series of intelligent and moving detective novels about Mario Balzic, the "half hunkie, half dago" police chief of a small western Pennsylvania town.

**Dolson, Hildegarde,** *The Great Oildorado: The Gaudy and Turbulent Years of the First Oil Rush* (1959). Bouncy, anecdotal account of the Pennsylvania oil fields, 1859–80.

**O'Hara, John,** *49 Stories* (1962). Fine collection of short stories that take place in Gibbsville, the eastern Pennsylvania town of much of the author's fiction. It is also the setting for his National Book Award–winning novel, *Ten North Frederick* (1955).

**Richter, Conrad,** *The Light in the Forest* (1953). White child taken prisoner by Delaware Indians and adopted into a family tries to return to the forest. Compelling in its observation of the white man from the viewpoint of the Indian and in giving an authentic sensation of life in mid-eighteenth-century America. See the companion novel, *A Country of Strangers* (1966).

**Swetnam, George and Helene Smith,** *A Guidebook to Historic Western Pennsylvania* (1976). Well-organized, richly informative Baedeker to the myriad points of historical interest in the area.

**Updike, John,** *The Olinger Stories* (1964). These early stories set in Olinger, Pennsylvania, the mythical town not unlike the author's native Shillington, are not really regional stories, for his territory is the conflict of daily life and the sense of something more, and the urgencies of sex and death.

**Wildes, H. E.,** *William Penn* (1974). Fresh look at the man who was the "true and absolute proprietor" of the 45,000 square miles of virgin territory later known as Pennsylvania.

## Washington, D.C.

**Adams, Henry,** *Democracy* (1880). The Washington of Grant's second administration, the mid-1870s, the Washington of vote-buying and fixed elections, slanderous competition, preposterous graft. The true authorship of this incisive and entertaining work was not revealed until after Adams's death in 1918. Another interesting novel of the Grant years is John William DeForest's *Honest John Vane* (1875).

**Cameron, Robert,** *Above Washington* (1979). Large, handsome book of spectacular color photographs taken from the air. For a less elevated view, the best informal guide to the capital is E. J. Applewhite, *Washington Itself* (1981).

**Dos Passos, John,** *District of Columbia* (1952). Omnibus edition of trilogy published over the interval 1939–49 made up of *Adventures of a Young Man, Number*

*One,* and *The Grand Design,* a gloomy but extremely interesting work about Washington of the thirties and forties.

**Green, Constance Winsor,** *Washington: Village and Capital, 1800–1878* (1962). Pulitzer Prize–winning history, written with spirit and sympathy, that is "lucid, authoritative . . . enthralling" (Arthur R. Schlesinger, Jr.). The second volume is *Washington: Capital City, 1879–1950* (1964).

**Halle, Louis J.,** *Spring in Washington* (1947). Man and nature in the capital, especially around Rich Creek Park, as viewed by a professor and scholar of diplomacy; "In this fresh and lovely writing [he] tells the story of the way spring comes to Washington, from the first chill, spare beginnings until the full oppressive splendor of summer sweeps in" (Donald Culross Peattie).

**Just, Ward,** *The Congressman Who Loved Flaubert, and Other Washington Stories* (1973). Subtle, sophisticated tales of the world of Washington. See *Nicholson at Large* (1975).

**Leech, Margaret,** *Reveille in Washington* (1941). The capital during the Civil War. "It is the mingling of the deep current of history with all the bubbles of rumor and despair and hope that floated on its surface, of the great event with the small detail, that makes [this] so fascinating, so alive, and so contemporaneous" (Stephen Vincent Benet). Awarded the Pulitzer Prize for history.

**Slaydon, Ellen Maury,** *Washington Wife: Journal of Ellen Maury Slaydon from 1897–1919* (1963). Honest, ebullient diary of social, political, and historical events by a Congressman's wife.

**Teague, Michael (ed.),** *Mrs. L: Conversations with Alice Roosevelt Longworth* (1981). Theodore Roosevelt's daughter had been a living monument of Washington social life for a half-century when she died in 1980 at age ninety-six. These skillfully edited taped conversations reveal her sparkling personality and are practically a course in unofficial capital history.

**Vidal, Gore,** *Washington, D.C.* (1967). Entertaining page-turner about presidential aspirants in the Washington of 1937–52, with some walk-ons by real politicians. Other modern Washington-based popular novels include Allen Drury, *Advise and Consent* (1959); Barbara Howar, *Making Ends Meet* (1967); and William Safire, *Full Disclosure* (1977).

# GREAT LAKES

## Illinois

**Bradbury, Ray,** *Dandelion Wine* (1957). Warm, poetic novel about a twelve-year-old boy's summer of 1928 in Green Town by the science fiction writer from Waukegan.

**Eberle, Nancy,** *Return to Main Street* (1982). In 1978 the author and her husband sold their Evanston house and moved with their three children to a 200-acre farm at the edge of a small Illinois town. This is the thoughtful chronicle of their experience.

**Grierson, Francis** *The Valley of Shadows: Recollections of the Lincoln Country 1858–63* (1909). Sensitive memoir of boyhood in antebellum Illinois blends poetry and realism into a unique evocation of pioneer America that "deserves to become a classic" (Edmund Wilson).

**Masters, Edgar Lee,** *The Sangamon* (1942). The Spoon River poet's contribution to the Rivers of America series describes the history of, and life on, the prairie through which the Sangamon flows and is handsomely decorated with illustrations by Lynd Ward. See *Illinois*

*Poems* (1941) and *The Tale of Chicago* (1933).

**Maxwell, William,** *Time Will Darken It* (1948). The scene is a small town in 1912, the protagonist is a man of impossibly high ideals. A novel of great character.

**Sandburg, Carl,** *Always the Young Strangers* (1953). Boyhood memoirs of the poet, born of Swedish parents in Galesburg in 1878, that carefully portrays the life of a prairie town during the gaslit era. A piece of authentic Americana, remarkable for its utter honesty.

## Indiana

**Hubbard, Kin,** *Abe Martin of Brown County, Indiana* (1906). One of a long series of books collecting the sayings, mostly in dialect, of the fictitious Abe Martin, created by Hubbard in his syndicated column. Clifton Fadiman dubbed the great cracker-barrel philosopher "a Hoosier Rochefoucauld."

**Lewin, Michael Z.,** *Ask the Right Question* (1971). The first adventure of Indianapolis private eye Albert Sampson, broke, fast-talking, and hard-boiled. One of the best contemporary detective series.

**Lockridge, Ross,** *Raintree County* (1948). A day — July 4, 1892 — in the life of a man in a mythical Indiana county. A novel large in intention, fine, and flawed but ripe with acute observation and feel for the region and its way of life.

**Tarkington, Booth,** *The Gentleman from Indianapolis: A Treasury of Booth Tarkington* (1970). A taste of Tarkington, a sampler that includes all of *Alice Adams, The Magnificent Ambersons,* and *Penrod,* and the finest short stories that sparkle with warm humor and deep understanding.

**West, Jessamyn,** *The Witch Diggers* (1951). Described as "Indiana, 1899, Brueghel," it is a macabre, rowdy, symbolic story set on a poor farm; a "good, long, warm, generous and curious novel" (Eudora Welty). See *The Massacre at Fall Creek* (1975).

## Michigan

**Harrison, Jim,** *Farmer* (1976). The love affairs of a Swedish-American schoolteacher-farmer in Upper Michigan, middle-aged and handicapped. A serene, satisfying novel richly evocative of small-town and farm life. See *Wolf* (1970) and *Warlock* (1981).

**Hemingway, Ernest,** *The Nick Adams Stories* (1972). Collects all the stories about the Hemingway alter ego; told in a characteristic controlled, informed, but always impersonal tone.

**Lutes, Della,** *Gabriel's Search* (1940). As in her earlier *Country Kitchen* (1939), this story of frontier life in the 1830s serves as a peg for the author to display her exhaustive knowledge of early Michigan customs. Other nineteenth-century historical novels include Vivian Parsons, *Not Without Honor* (1941); George White, *Free as the Wind* (1942); and Cecile Matschat, *Preacher on Horseback* (1940).

**Stadtfield, Curtis K.,** *From the Land and Back* (1972). Luminous story of "my farming forefathers, of how they picked a somewhat inhospitable portion of central Michigan, put their roots down, made farms and homes and futures, and how all that they had for generations was swept away almost overnight by technological change."

**Traver, Robert,** *Anatomy of a Murder* (1958). Bestselling novel written pseudonymously by Michigan Supreme Court justice John Voelker about a murder trial in northern Michigan, where he was a district attorney for fourteen years. His other novels evocative of the north country are *Danny and the Boys* (1951), *Laughing Whitefish* (1965), and *People Versus Kirk* (1981).

## Ohio

**Baskin, John,** *New Burlington: The Life and Death of an American Village* (1976). A memoir of the town through first-person recollections, artfully organized and edited, serves as a paean to the rural culture that flourished in America between the Civil War and World War II. Another Ohio town is portrayed in Peter Davis, *Hometown* (1982).

**Gold, Herbert,** *Therefore Be Bold* (1960). Amusing story of adolescents in a Cleveland suburb in the late thirties by a distinctive stylist. Another Depression-era Cleveland coming-of-age novel is James T. Maher, *The Distant Music of Summer* (1979). Don Robertson's *The Greatest Thing Since Sliced Bread* (1965) is also set in Cleveland, on the day in 1944 when nine-year-old Morris Bird III searches for his friend Starky.

**Howells, William Dean,** *Years of My Youth* (1916). When he was almost eighty, Howells looked back at the ambitions and dreams of his boyhood in Ohio. His other autobiographical works about his life in frontier Ohio include *A Boy's Town* (1890), *My Year in a Log Cabin* (1893), *Impressions and Experiences* (1896), and *New Leaf Mills* (1913).

**Richter, Conrad,** *The Ohio Trilogy* (1940–50). Comprising *The Trees, The Fields,* and *The Town,* the Pulitzer Prize–winning series that depicts the settling of Ohio between 1790 and 1860 through the life of Sayward Wheeler and his family "pulses from beginning to end with the passion of the land, the flesh, and the spirit. It has America's heartbeat in it. Cut it and it bleeds American" (Edward Wagenknecht). It was published in a one-volume edition in 1966 as *The Awakening Land.*

**Robertson, Don,** *Paradise Falls Saga* (1967–78). *Miss Margaret Ridpath and the Dismantling of the Universe, Paradise Falls,* and *Mystical Union* are a trilogy of novels by a writer who has been called the "Trollope of small-town middle America."

## Wisconsin

**Derleth, August,** *Walden West* (1961). Comprises, like *Return to Walden West* (1970), entries from his extensive journals: sharp observations of town life and the natural life around it. It is "probable that they are classics of their kind" (Mark Schorer). *Wisconsin Earth: A Sac Prairie Sampler* (1948) contains pieces from his spacious historical novels about the Black Hawk country.

**Eifert, Virginia S.,** *Journeys in Green Places: The Shores and Woods of Wisconsin's Door Peninsula* (1963). The beauty of woods, bogs, birds, and plants of a remote environment.

**Havighurst, Walter,** *The Winds of Spring* (1940). Novel of pioneering, 1840–70, with a different slant: the hero is a scholarly ornithologist in a paradise of new subjects. Other novels of early Wisconsin are Jessica Nelson North, *Morning in the Land* (1941); Leslie Schlytter, *Tall Brothers* (1941); and Laban C. Smith, *No Better Land* (1946).

**Leopold, Aldo,** *A Sand County Almanac* (1949). One of the great classics of nature and ecology writing. Sketches, arranged seasonally, about what the author and his family see and do at their weekend "shack." "On this sand farm in Wisconsin, first worn out and then abandoned by our bigger-and-better society, we try to rebuild, with shovel and axe, what we are losing elsewhere. It is here that we seek — and still find — our meat from God."

**Wescott, Glenway,** *Grandmothers* (1927). As a young man flips through an old album of photographs, he reconstructs the lives of his pioneer ancestors he sees there. The unhappy, frustrated lives of the members of two Wisconsin families thus unfold in a superb, moving novel. See *Goodbye, Wisconsin* (1928), a collection of short stories.

# THE BORDER STATES

## Appalachia

**Arnow, Harriet,** *Seedtime on the Cumberland* (1960). Frontier life in Cumberland valley, 1780–1803, as lived by the pioneers. Written in an easy narrative style, it was followed by *Flowering of the Cumberland* (1963).

**Bake, William A.,** *The Blue Ridge* (1977). Magnificent photographic album of the great mountain range by "the Ansel Adams of the Blue Ridge." See Alberta Pierson Hannum, *Look Back with Love* (1967), a recollection of the Blue Ridge, and Stephen Goodwin, *Blood of Paradise* (1979), a novel of contemporary life there.

**Caudill, Harry M.,** *Night Comes to the Cumberlands* (1963). Classic account by Appalachia's best known advocate of how the region became depressed. In *The Watches of the Night* (1976) he returned to find that federal programs had turned the mountain people into welfare clients and failed to halt the ruin of the land. See *The Mountain, The Miner, and the Lord* (1980), a collection of tales told him by his mountain neighbors.

**Caudill, Rebecca,** *My Appalachia* (1966). Reminiscences by a teacher and writer who grew up there and witnessed the tragic erosion of the land and its people. She wrote several novels and children's books set in the region. See *Tree of Freedom* (1949).

**Dykeman, Wilma,** *The Tall Woman* (1962). Novel about a North Carolina mountain woman in the years following the Civil War. See *The French Broad* (1955), her classic account of the east Tennessee-North Carolina river.

**Ogburn, Charlton,** *The Southern Appalachians: A Wilderness Quest* (1975). Invaluable account of the area that "seems to touch on everything of significance in Appalachia, from the flame azalea to the black bear, from the Cherokee Indians to the Winnebago tourists, from Daniel Boone to the Appalachian Trail, from geology to morphology" (Edward Abbey). See Jerome Dolittle, *The Southern Appalachians* (1975) and Maurice Brooks, *The Appalachians* (1965).

**Porter, Eliot (p) and Edward Abbey (t),** *Appalachian Wilderness: The Great Smoky Mountains* (1970). Majestic color photographs and forthright prose make a splendid tribute to the grandeur of the mountains.

**Shackleford, Laurel and Bill Weinberg,** *Our Appalachia* (1977). Expressive and fascinating oral history.

**Slone, Verna Mae,** *What My Heart Wants to Tell* (1979). Plain, direct account of Appalachian life by a member of the tenth generation of Slones to live in Pippa Passes, Kentucky. A lyrical, illustrated companion volume is Craig E. Royce, *Country Miles Are Longer than City Miles* (1976).

**Wigginton, Eliot (ed.),** *The Foxfire Book* (1972). The first of a series put together from magazine articles written by Georgia high school students. Interviews and photographs of the hill people. A marvelous preservation of the traditional ways of Appalachia.

## Kentucky

**Arnow, Harriet Simpson,** *Hunter's Horn* (1949). Lyrical novel about a poor white farmer's obsession with killing a fox. Great feeling for the Kentucky countryside and its people.

**Bakeless, John E.,** *Master of the Wilderness: Daniel Boone* (1939). Dramatic, broad-canvas biography of the famous frontiersman in which "some of the characters are as thrilling as a Beadle Dime Novel, some of the anecdotes as improbable as Mike Fink stories" (Henry Steele Commager).

**Berry, Wendell,** *The Memory of Old Jack* (1974). Deeply moving novel about a man who has spent a lifetime close to the land, living out his final years in a small Kentucky River town.

**Clark, Thomas D.,** *Kentucky: Land of Contrast* (1968). The best concise history by the most eminent historian of Kentucky.

**Gordon, Caroline,** *None Should Look Back* (1937). Distinguished Civil War novel about a wealthy family; it focuses on the exploits of General Nathan Bedford Forrest. Other Kentucky historical novels are *Penhally* (1931) and *Green Centuries* (1941). Her skillfully written short stories are gathered in *The Collected Stories of Caroline Gordon* (1981).

**Mason, Kathryn Harrod,** *James Harrod of Kentucky* (1951). Biography of the founder of the first settlement in the state by his descendant. Evokes the spirit of the frontier with considerable charm.

**Roberts, Elizabeth Madox,** *The Time of Man* (1926). Powerful, bleak novel about poor, illiterate folks of the hill country in central Kentucky. See *The Great Meadow* (1930), an outstanding novel of Kentucky pioneer life.

**Still, James,** *River of Earth* (1940). Affectionate novel about three years in the life of a small boy and his family in the coal-mining country of Appalachia. Spare, colorful, sure in its command of the mountain idiom, and poetic in its evocation of the mountain setting. See *Hounds on the Mountain,* a collection of poems, and *The Run for Elbertas* (1981), a volume of short stories.

**Stuart, Jesse,** *A Jesse Stuart Harvest* (1965). Novelist, short-story writer, poet

identified for decades with the mountain region of the state and its people; this sampler is a door through which to enter the richness and variety of his work.

**Warren, Robert Penn,** *Night Rider* (1939). Novel about the Tobacco War between growers and manufacturers in the early 1900s; imbued with moral themes that haunt all his work. Other Kentucky settings can be found in *Band of Angels* (1955), a novel, and *Brother to Dragons: A Tale in Verse and Voices* (1953).

## North Carolina

**Betts, Doris,** *The River to Pickle Beach* (1971). Her first novel, it richly evokes the state. Her fine short stories are collected in *Beasts of the Southern Wilds* (1973) and *The Astronomer* (1966). See *Heading West* (1981), a novel.

**Davis, Burke,** *The Summer Land* (1965). Nostalgic fictional reminiscences by an accomplished novelist historian about life on a poor tobacco farm; reads like a folk tale.

**Ehle, John,** *The Landbreakers* (1964). Novel about the early pioneers in the Carolina mountain country "recreates the time, the place, and the settler's relationship to the wilderness with notable vigor and reality" (Hal Borland). The first of five novels chronicling the Wright and King families over several generations. See *The Winter People* (1982).

**Fletcher, Inglis,** *Raleigh's End* (1940). The first of the Carolina Series of historical novels, full of pageantry and high romance and set in the Albemarle district.

**Harris, Bernice K.,** *Sweet Beulah Land* (1943). Rich, panoramic novel about everyday life of poor white sharecroppers, "an intimate landscape with its times of planting and harvest, characters filling it by the score with precisely expressive faces, spontaneous pantomines, colored costumes and possessions and toys in hand, all somewhat like a painting of Peter Breughel's" (Eudora Welty).

**Mebane, Mary E.,** *Mary* (1981). To be black in the South: her life near Durham, North Carolina.

**Pierce, Ovid Williams,** *On a Lonesome Porch* (1968). Sensitive, quiet novel about the lives of two women living on a plantation right after the Civil War; a moving, poetic novel.

**Stick, David,** *Graveyard of the Atlantic: Shipwrecks of the North Carolina Coast* (1952). Dramatic stories told informally. See *The Outer Banks of North Carolina, 1584–1958* (1959).

**Terres, John K.,** *From Laurel Hill to Siler's Bay: The Walking Adventures of a Naturalist* (1970). Years of close observation of a tract of wild land near Chapel Hill by the former editor of *Audubon Magazine* resulted in this entrancing book. "Because this book is a work of art we are held in its spell in a timeless world" (May Sarton).

**Wolcott, Reed,** *Rose Hill* (1976). Oral history of one small North Carolina town — the words of its inhabitants without comment or analysis: an American *Akenfield.* Tarheel town life is the subject of Ernest Seeman's intriguing novel *American Gold* (1978) and Sylvia Wilkinson, *Bones of My Bones* (1982).

## Tennessee

**Ford, Jesse Hill,** *The Liberation of Lord Byron Jones* (1965). Divorce suit by a respected black man against his wife for having an affair with a white cop sets off a chain reaction that ends in violence. This powerful, moving novel of racial strife was followed by *Fishes, Birds and Sons of Men* (1967), a collection of short stories set in the same town. See *The Raider* (1975), a novel of the Tennessee frontier and the Civil War.

**Green, Ely,** *Ely: An Autobiography* (1966). Memoir of boyhood in rural Tennessee by a man born half-black, half-white, and illegitimate. "A most extraordinary document" (Lillian Smith).

**Haun, Mildred,** *The Hawk's Done Gone* (1940). Collection of superb human-filled short stories of life in remote Smokies country.

**Jones, Madison,** *Passage Through Gehenna* (1978). Meticulously made novel of rural life by the writer whom Allen Tate called the "Thomas Hardy of the South." See *A Buried Land* (1963), *A Cry of Absence* (1971), and *Season of the Strangler* (1981).

**Lytle, Andrew,** *The Velvet Horn* (1959). Novel of two families who soon after the Civil War lived in the forest of the Cumberlands. Realistic and allegorical, it is a neglected "landmark in American fiction" (Caroline Gordon).

**McCarthy, Cormac,** *Child of God* (1973). Concise, chilling horror story that explores the limits of degradation. Set against the pastoral backdrop of the eastern Tennessee hill country. See *The Orchard Keeper* (1965), *Outer Dark* (1968), and *Suttree* (1979).

**Maddux, Rachel,** *The Orchard Children* (1977). Account of her flight with her husband from city living to a farm and their experience in a foster-child custody fight that ensued. Her novel, *Abel's Daughter* (1960) has a Tennessee setting.

**Rourke, Constance,** *Davy Crockett* (1934). "Born on a mountain top in Tennessee," he of the coonskin cap and the tall tale memorialized in a swift-paced, old-fashioned biography.

**Taylor, Peter,** *Collected Stories of Peter Taylor* (1969). Stories of middle Tennessee told simply and without pretension by a writer "unsurpassed in portraying the critical moment when an ordinary person has an inner revelation of the fallibility of social order" *(Harvard Guide to Contemporary Writing).*

**Warren, Robert Penn,** *Flood* (1964). Novel about people of a small western Tennessee town coming to terms with themselves when the town is ruined by the building of a dam. Other Tennessee fiction by the distinguished poet, critic, and nov-elist includes *The Cave* (1959), *At Heaven's Gate* (1943), and *Circus in the Attic and Other Stories* (1948).

.

# THE DEEP SOUTH

**Agee, James (t) and Walker Evans (p),** *Let Us Now Praise Famous Men* (1941). On journalistic assignment in the Depression-gaunt South, Agee shared the lives of three sharecropper families and produced a reportorial masterpiece that with Evans's haunting photographs depicts a bygone era and vividly records the human condition.

**Bartram, William,** *The Travels of William Bartram* (1791). Classic account by the Philadelphia Quaker, one of America's early naturalists, of his journey through North and South Carolina, Georgia, and Florida.

**Caldwell, Erskine (t) and Margaret Bourke-White (p),** *You Have Seen Their Faces* (1937). Powerful picture text of Southern sharecroppers by the Georgian novelist and the photojournalist, husband and wife at the time.

**Campbell, Will D.,** *Brother to a Dragon-fly* (1977). Two interwoven stories: a recollection of his older brother whose drug addiction killed him and his involvement in the civil rights movement. Together they make an emotional, "scrupulous honest statement of what it has been to be a Southerner, of what it is to be a human being" (Walker Percy). See Thomas Connelly, *Will Campbell and the Soul of the South* (1982).

**Cash, W. J.,** *The Mind of the South* (1941). Illuminating, finely written cultural and psychological analysis of Southern ways.

**Frady, Marshall,** *Southerners* (1980). Collection of expanded magazine articles by a perceptive journalist — a Southern *Odyssey*. Other journalistic excursions include Roy Blount, Jr., *Crackers* (1980)

and Paul Hemphill, *The Good Old Boys* (1974).

**Meine, Franklin J. (ed.),** *Tall Tales of the Southwest* (1930). Flavorful, graphic collection of nineteenth-century Southern humor. "It is the best anthology of any kind I know of" (J. Frank Dobie).

**Shuptrine, Hubert (ill.) and James Dickey (t),** *Jericho: The South Beheld* (1974). Large, beautifully produced album of superb watercolors and drawings coupled with the distinguished poet's narrative captures the rural South.

**Terrill, Tom E. and Jeradd Hirsch (eds.),** *Such as Us: Southern Voices of the Thirties* (1978). Entrancing gleanings from the Southern Life History Project of the Federal Writers' Program of the Depression in which anonymous Southerners talked about their lives. A rich portrait of the variety of the region.

**Woodward, C. Vann,** *Origins of the New South* (rev. 1972). Study of the new South, 1877–1914; a "thoroughgoing and well-written volume that is a work of real distinction and great importance" (Dumas Malone). See *The Strange Career of Jim Crow* (rev. 1974).

## *Alabama*

**Carmer, Carl,** *Stars Fell on Alabama* (1934). The life of the times in a rich blend of folklore and history. A more contemporary, but equally flavorful, mixture of stories, folklore, and humor is Kathryn Tucker Windham, *Alabama: One Big Front Porch* (1975).

**Hannah, Barry,** *Ray* (1980). Ray is a physician in Tuscaloosa. A verbally exuberant, lusty novel. See *Airships* (1978), a short-story collection.

**Lee, Harper,** *To Kill a Mockingbird* (1960). Pulitzer Prize–winning novel in which a six-year-old girl, "Scout" Finch, tells what happened in her town in the 1930s when her father, a lawyer, was appointed to defend a black man charged with raping a white woman. A memorable, much-loved, popular novel.

**Murray, Albert,** *Train Whistle Guitar* (1974). Growing up black in Gasoline Point, Alabama, in the 1920s: an autobiographical novel that moves with the rhythm of the blues. See *South to a Very Old Place* (1972).

**Rosengarten, Theodore,** *All God's Dangers: The Life of Nate Shaw* (1974). Skillfully edited transcription of tapes made when he was 90, of an illiterate black tenant farmer — a man of great dignity and humor. Paints an absorbing portrait of the rural South during much of this century.

## Arkansas

**Jones, Douglas C.,** *Weedy Rough* (1981). Wonderful novel about a boy's growing up in the hamlet of Weedy Rough in the twenties and early thirties.

**Harrington, Donald,** *The Architecture of the Arkansas Ozarks* (1975). Rollicking good story made up of tall tales and myths about a family in Stay More, in the Ozarks. The mountains are at the center of Otis Welton Coan, *Rocktown, Arkansas: An Ozark Novel* (1953) and Bob Minick (p) and Roger Minick (t), *Hills at Home: The Rural Ozarks of Arkansas* (1975), a collection of fine photographs accompanied by stories by the photographer's father, a "native Ozarker."

**Pharr, Robert Deane,** *The Book of Numbers* (1969). Supple novel, vital and powerful, about a couple of numbers racket men in the black ghetto.

**Randolph, Vance,** *We Always Lie to Strangers: Tall Tales from the Ozarks* (1951). One of many delightful volumes assembled by the folklorist on his trips in the mountains. See *Pissing in the Snow, and Other Ozark Folktales* (1976).

**Simon, Charlie May,** *Straw in the Sun* (1945). One woman's experiences homesteading in the hills in the early thirties. Her husband, John Gould Fletcher, wrote an impressionistic, anecdotal description of the state in *Arkansas* (1947).

## Florida

**Douglas, Marjorie Stoneman,** *The Everglades: River of Grass* (rev. 1977). Classic of the Rivers of America series, rich in history and the environment of the unique river of water and grass. See *Florida: The Long Frontier* (1967) and *Road to the Sun* (1952), a novel. See also Archie Carr, *The Everglades* (1973), a lushly illustrated volume in the Time-Life Wilderness of America set.

**Hurston, Zora Neale,** *Their Eyes Were Watching God* (1937). This novel about one woman's three marriages is a beautiful book, earthy, shining with humor, and written in a fascinating rich folk speech. See *Seraph on the Sewanee* (1948), about a Florida cracker woman, and *I Love Myself when I Am Laughing . . . : A Zora Neale Hurston Reader* (1979), edited by Alice Walker.

**Jahoda, Gloria,** *The Other Florida* (1967). A transplanted Northerner's loving description of the Florida panhandle beyond Pensacola and the wet and dry savannas, pine barrens, and jungle hammocks extending from the elbow of St. John River to the Gulf at Cedar Keys.

**MacDonald, John D.,** *The Deep Blue Goodbye* (1964). The first of more than twenty colorful mysteries featuring Travis McGee, the cynical salvage expert and philosopher who lives aboard his boat, the *Busted Flush*. They portray the water life in Florida as a background to McGee's sleuthing, loving, and commentary on the state of the world.

**McGuane, Tom,** *Ninety-two in the Shade* (1973). Postcounterculture novel about conviction, courage, manliness, and, finally, death as played out by two fishing guides near Key West, by a writer who "shares with Celine a genius for seeing the profuse, disparate materials of everyday life as a highly organized nightmare" (L. E. Sissman). See *Panama* (1978).

**Pratt, Theodore,** *The Barefoot Mailman* (1943). Light, entertaining novel about the man who carried the mail, on foot, between Palm Beach and Miami during the 1890s. Vivid descriptions of the coast. See *Florida Roundabout* (1959).

**Rawlings, Marjorie Kinnan,** *The Yearling* (1939). Pulitzer Prize–winning novel about a boy and deer growing up in the hammock region of central Florida about 1870. *Cross Creek* (1942) describes the life and the people of the remote village where the author lived, raised oranges, and wrote stories.

**Rudloe, Jack,** *The Living Dock at Panacea* (1977). A marine specimen collector's lively and charming description of the sealife of Florida's Gulf Coast. See *The Sea Brings Forth* (1968) and *The Erotic Ocean* (1971).

**Wilder, Robert,** *Bright Feather* (1948). Rousing popular novel set in the 1830s about the great Seminole hero Asseola. The author "has not only dealt justly with one of the greatest Indian heroes but he has brought to turbulent and boiling life one of the least known periods in Southern, as well as American life" (Marjorie Stoneman Douglas). Edith Everett Pope, *River in the Wind* (1954) also deals with the Seminole Wars.

**Yglesias, Jose,** *The Truth About Them* (1972). Affectionate autobiographical novel about a Cuban-American working-class family that emigrated to Tampa in the 1890s. Touches on many concerns of the Latino community. See *A Wake in Ybor City* (1963).

## Georgia

**Caldwell, Erskine,** *God's Little Acre* (1933). A fine novel full of great characterization — particularly Ty Ty Walden, homespun philosopher — delightful folk humor, and Rabelaisian gusto. See *Tobacco Road* (1932) and *Georgia Boy* (1943).

**Cheney, Brainard,** *River Rogue* (1942). Vigorous, detailed popular novel about the raftsmen along the Oconee and Altamaka rivers of the 1880s. Another Georgian historical novelist is Caroline Miller, author of *Lebanon* (1944) and the Pulitzer Prize–winning *Lamb in His Bosom* (1933), both about life on the frontier.

**Crews, Harry,** *Childhood: The Biography of a Place* (1978). The place is rural Bacon County in the southeast part of the state; the time is the years prior to World War II. Growing up on a hardscrabble farm, with its attendant poverty and cruelty, recalled in a memoir that reads like a novel. The place has been superbly evoked in Crews's fiction as well; see *Gospel Singer* (1968), *This Thing Don't Lead to Heaven* (1970), and *Feast of Snakes* (1976).

**Dickey, James,** *Deliverance* (1970). Novel about four Atlanta businessmen on a weekend canoe and hunting trip that turns into a nightmare. Dickey's award-winning poetry often deals with Southern themes; see *Buckdancer's Choice* (1965) and *Exchanges* (1971).

**Fancher, Betsy,** *The Lost Legacy of Georgia's Golden Isles* (1971). Beautiful evocation of the haunting spirit and historical richness of these Atlantic islands.

**Kemble, Fanny,** *Journal of a Residence on a Georgian Plantation* (1863). The English actress toured America in the 1830s and married Pierce Butler, owner of a plantation with 700 slaves. She wrote the journal in 1839, but published it in 1863 to influence English opinion against the South, whose "peculiar institution" she despised. It is probably the most penetrating account of American slavery ever written. Her remarkable life is told in J. C. Furnas, *Fanny Kemble* (1981).

**Kluger, Richard,** *Members of the Tribe* (1977). Novel about the Jewish experience in the South; the first half is luminous depiction of Savannah from 1870 to the First World War. The other half is a provocative fictionalization of the famous Frank murder trial and lynching.

**Mitchell, Margaret,** *Gone With the Wind* (1936). The great bestseller that portrays the lives of Rhett and Scarlett against the background of antebellum and Civil War Georgia. Despite its melodramatic conventions it has kept its hold over readers. For a different view of the period read Margaret Walker's *Jubilee* (1966), a fictional story of the author's great-grandmother, born a slave.

**O'Connor, Flannery,** *The Complete Stories* (1971). National Book Award–winning collection of stories set in her native Georgia, by a writer who "expresses something secret about America, called 'the South,' with that transcendent gift for expressing the real spirit of a culture that is conveyed by those writers . . . who become nothing but what they see" (Alfred Kazin). See *Flannery O'Connor's Georgia* (1980), with photos and text by Barbara McKenzie.

**Williams, Vinnie,** *Walk Egypt* (1960). The not-so-happy life of a young girl in the hills of north Georgia. A novel distinguished by its richness of regional speech and folk wisdom. See *Greenbones* (1968).

## Louisiana

**Corrington, John William,** *The Southern Reporter* (1981). Fine collection of stories, mostly set in Louisiana. See *And Wait for the Night* (1964), a beautifully written novel of the last days of the Civil War and the occupation of Shreveport during 1865, and *The Upper Hand* (1967).

**Gaines, Ernest J.,** *Catherine Carmer* (1964). The first of several novels about black life in rural Louisiana by a writer with a masterful command of the Louisiana black and Cajun dialects. See *Of Love and Lust* (1968), *Autobiography of Miss Jane Pittman* (1971), and *In My Father's House* (1978).

**Grau, Shirley Ann,** *The Hard Blue Sky* (1958). Novel presenting in rich detail the lives of the people of a remote island and a "sense of the community, as it carries on its usual tasks, as it faces the various crises that are the book's themes" (Granville Hicks). See *The Black Prince* (1955), a collection of short stories.

**Hallowell, Christopher,** *People of the Bayou: Cajun Life in Lost America* (1979). Anecdotal social history of the distinctive people who survive by dredging oysters or fur trapping at the edge of the marshland on the Gulf of Mexico. See William F. Rushton's vivid portrait *The Cajuns: From Acadia to Louisiana* (1979).

**Liebling, A. J.,** *The Earl of Louisiana* (1961). Masterful record of the volcanic and shrewdly entertaining Earl Long's 1960 gubernatorial campaign, with its stump-speaking tours through swampwater hamlets. A closeup portrait of a master politician in action by a journalist who "writes like an angel, with a pen dipped in brandy and acid" (Stephen Longstreet).

## Mississippi

**Carter, Hodding,** *Where Main Street Meets the River* (1953). Autobiography of the liberal newspaperman from 1932 when he started his first paper through his years of opposition to the likes of Senator Bilbo and Huey Long.

**Douglas, Ellen,** *The Rock Cried Out* (1979). Young man who has spent several years in the North returns to his native Mississippi seeking country peace and is caught up again in a traumatic event that happened years before. Like her other novels, this is set in the mythical river towns of Homochitto and Philippi, just west of, and more accessible than, Yoknapatawpha County. See *A Family's Affairs* (1962) and *Apostles of Light* (1973).

**Faulkner, William,** *Sartoris* (1929). The world that takes shape in this and the succeeding seven novels that constitute the first cycle of the Yoknapatawpha saga is "a Balzacian representation of Southern history. But it is more profoundly the embodiment of Faulkner's imagination of history and myth as modes of human existence. Nothing else like it appears in American literature, or for that matter, world literature" *(Harvard Guide to American Writing).*

**Lowry, Beverly,** *Come Back, Lolly Ray* (1977). Smoothly written satirical portrait of a river-rich delta town and Lolly Ray Lasswell, star baton twirler, who comes to bear the burden of its dreams. See *Emma Blue* (1978).

**Moody, Anne,** *Coming of Age in Mississippi* (1968). Stirring memoir of the life of the daughter of a black sharecropper in Wilkinson County. A history of our time seen from the bottom up.

**Morgan, Berry,** *The Mystic Adventures of Roxie Stoner* (1974). Short stories told from the point of view of an illiterate black woman living in King County that speak of the decay of family and community in the South and say it with humor, poignancy, and the ring of authenticity. See *Pursuit* (1966).

**Morris, Willie,** *North Toward Home* (1967). A young literary man, a success in New York, looks back on his boyhood in small-town Mississippi, eloquently capturing the essence of that experience. See *Yazoo* (1971), an account of a return to his old hometown during its segregation upheavals.

**Percy, William Alexander,** *Lanterns on the Levee* (1941). Fine, lyrical autobiography of a poet, planter's son, and uncle of novelist Walker Percy. It depicts life on the Mississippi Delta during the early years of the century from the patrician point of view.

**Spencer, Elizabeth,** *The Voice at the Back Door* (1956). Set against the changing pattern of race relations in the world of the Mississippi Delta, the question of just how much a decent man must sacrifice in order to gain political advantage is probed in this candid, understated, "practically perfect novel" (Brendan Gill). See *The Stories of Elizabeth Spencer* (1981).

**Welty, Eudora,** *Collected Stories* (1980). Skillful, caring stories about small-town Delta life that display her sensitivity, her keen ear for local idiom, her humor, and her sense of the mythic and mysterious in everyday life. See *The Robber Bridegroom* (1942), a folk tale of bandits in Mississippi's territorial era; *One Time, One Place* (1971) is a collection of poignant snapshots made by the author during the Depression.

## South Carolina

**Carawan, Guy and Candie Carawan** **(eds.),** *Ain't You Got a Right to the Tree of Life?: The People of Johns Island, South Carolina — Their Faces, Their Words, Their Songs* (1966). Husband-and-wife team of folklorists with photographer Robert Yellin put together a fascinating oral history of these unique island people. Thirty years earlier South Carolina novelist Julia Peterkin published a book about another unusual people, the Gullah blacks living along the coast: *Roll, Jordan, Roll* (1934), with photographs by Doris Ulmann.

**Childress, Alice,** *A Short Walk* (1979). A good portion of this novel about the life of a black woman born in 1900 in the Carolina lowlands is set in that region and beautifully captures the rich language of the low country.

**Fox, William Price,** *Moonshine Light, Moonshine Bright* (1967). Two adolescent boys get involved with a bootlegger during a summer in the late 1940s in Columbia, South Carolina in this fresh, humorous novel of a latter-day Huck and Tom. See *Ruby Red* (1971) and *Southern Fried Plus Six* (1968), a collection of short stories.

**Rubin, Louis B., Jr.,** *The Golden Weather* (1961). Account of a thirteen-year-old Jewish boy's summer in Charleston in 1936 captures the special charm of the city. See Robert Molloy, *Charleston: A Gracious Heritage* (1947).

**Wright, Louis B.,** *Barefoot in Arcadia: Memories of a More Innocent Era* (1974). Recollections of boyhood during the first two decades of the century in the God-fearing, Protestant-ethic-subscribing Carolina Piedmont. Another account of upper South Carolina childhood is Ben Robertson, *Red Hills and Cotton: An Upcountry Memory* (1942).

## Virginia

**Dabney, Virginius,** *Virginia: The New Dominion* (1971). Long, elegantly written, popular history from Captain John Smith's landing at Jamestown in 1607 through the demise of the Byrd dynasty in 1970.

**Dillard, Annie,** *Pilgrim at Tinker Creek* (1974). "I am no scientist," says the author, "but a poet and a walker with a background in theology and a penchant for quirky facts." Here is a meditation on mystery, death, beauty, and violence, a mystical excursion into the natural world of a creek in the Roanoke Valley.

**Glasgow, Ellen,** *Barren Ground* (1925). Quiet, stark story about the rural poor by the Pulitzer Prize–winning Richmond novelist. *Vein of Iron* (1935) has a similar setting, while *The Romantic Comedians* (1926) is a satirical novel of manners. See *Collected Stories* (1963).

**Rouse, Parke, Jr.,** *Planters and Pioneers: Life in Colonial Virginia* (1968). The sub-title describes it: "The story in pictures and text of the people who settled England's first successful colony from its planting in 1607 to the birth of the United States in 1789." Its companion volume is *Virginia: The English Heritage in America* (1966).

**Styron, William,** *Lie Down in Darkness* (1951). His first novel, which traces the tragic life of Peyton Loftis, whose wealthy Virginia family could not give her the understanding she desperately needed.

## West Virginia

**Bishop, John Peale,** *Act of Darkness* (1935). The West Virginia–born writer's only novel: set in a small town in 1905 amid Faulkneresque decay, it is "a profound and moving piece of symbolism, a study of the desperation and spiritual chaos that can sometimes overtake a whole generation of men" (Caroline Gordon).

**Grubb, Davis,** *Night of the Hunter* (1953). Tense and moving novel, set in the Ohio Valley during the last century, about two children fleeing a killer. See *Fool's Paradise* (1969).

**Kaser, Paul,** *How Jerem Came Home* (1980). Jerem came home to the Great Smokies from Korea in a wooden box: how his death affected his grandmother and younger brother is the subject of this lyrical first novel.

**Settle, Mary Lee,** *The Beulah Quintet* (1956–80). Fine families-on-the-land saga that begins with *O Beulah Land,* set in the eighteenth century, and spans two centuries of West Virginia life; told in the idiom of the day and place.

**Wilson, Meredith Sue,** *A Space Apart* (1979). A vigorous, sustained first novel about small-town West Virginia life. The same town is the setting for *Higher Ground* (1981).

# THE GREAT PLAINS

**Dick, Everett,** *The Sod House Frontier* (1937). Compiled entirely from letters, documents, old newspaper files, and personal recollections, a racy social history of the plains from 1854 to 1890. See David Dary (ed.), *True Tales of the Old-Time Plains* (1979).

**Manfred, Frederick,** *Conquering Horse* (1959). A young Sioux chieftain's perilous mission to save his life and attain manhood, written with fervor for the Plains region that Manfred refers to as Siouxland. See *Scarlet Plume* (1964) and *Riders of Judgment* (1957).

**Sandoz, Mari,** *Old Jules Country* (1965). Selection from fiction and nonfiction about her region — the High Plains of the Dakotas, Nebraska, Wyoming and eastern Montana, the Black Hills, the Badlands, the sandhills of Nebraska, the North Platte, the Little Missouri, and the Yellowstone. See *Love Song to the Plains* (1961).

**Webb, Walter Prescott,** *The Great Plains* (1931). Many studies during the five decades since this classic history was published have added to our knowledge of the region; Webb's account of how the character of the Plains shaped its history is still superb.

**Wilder, Laura Ingalls,** *The Little House in the Big Woods* (1953). The first of the "Little House" books, based on the experiences of the author, who was born in 1867 in a log cabin on the edge of the big woods of Wisconsin. She traveled with her family by covered wagon through Kansas, Minnesota, and the Dakota Territory.

## Iowa

**Bissell, Richard,** *7-1/2¢* (1953). Probably the only funny novel written about labor union struggle — in this case a pajama factory in the author's native Dubuque. With its natural talk and ways of midwestern life it is pure Americana. A former river pilot, he has written two novels about the Mississippi: *A Stretch on the River* (1950) and *High Water* (1954).

**Garland, Hamlin,** *Boy Life on the Prairie* (1899). A graceful description of what it was like to grow up in northeast Iowa in the years following the Civil War. For a fictional account of those times see Herbert Quick's trilogy, which starts with *Vandemark's Folly* (1922).

**Harnack, Curtis,** *We Have All Gone Away* (1973). Evocative memoirs of growing up on an Iowa farm during the Depression. His Iowa novels include *Love and Be Silent* (1963) and *Limits of the Land* (1979).

**Kantor, Mackinlay,** *Spirit Lake* (1961). Vivid novel about settlement of frontier Iowa that culminates in a bloody massacre by the Indians.

**Stegner, Wallace,** *Remembering Laughter* (1937). First book by the Pulitzer Prize–winning Iowa-born novelist. A tragic story of love on a farm, an Iowa *Ethan Frome.*

## Kansas

**Howe, E. W.,** *The Story of a Country Town* (1883). A melodramatic novel about the narrow life of a Kansas community, this was one of the first important works of naturalistic fiction, and it is still strong. Subsequent country-town novels include Langston Hughes, *Not Without Laughter* (1930) and Joseph Stanley Pennell, *The History of Nora Beckham* (1948).

**Inge, William,** *Picnic* (1953). Pulitzer Prize–winning play by the Kansas-born dramatist about romance, illusions, and frustration under the hot Kansas sun.

**Stratton, Joanna L.,** *Pioneer Women: Voices from the Kansas Frontier* (1981). Clear voices, retrieved and edited: this was what it was like to be a woman on the frontier.

**Vestal, Stanley,** *Queen of the Cowtowns* (1952). Fascinating anecdotal history of Dodge City, in its heyday the cowboy capital of the world.

**Wellmann, Paul,** *The Walls of Jericho* (1948). Popular historical novel set in a fictional Kansas town. Another is *The Bowl of Brass* (1944). See *The Trampling Herd* (1939), the story of the cattle range, and *Death on Horseback* (1947), the history of the Indian wars on the Great Plains.

## Minnesota

**Bly, Carol,** *Letters from the Country* (1981). Essays from a culturally isolated community in western Minnesota that are brimming with good humor and tell about modern life in rural America.

**Havill, Edward,** *Big Ember* (1947). Simple, graphic novel about Norwegian settlers' daily life on the frontier in southern Minnesota. Other historical novels are Dana Faralla, *Circle of Trees* (1955); Walter O'Meara, *Trees Went Forth* (1947); and Evelyn Wise, *The Long Tomorrow* (1938). The feel of the period is conveyed in the letters collected in Theodore Bost and Sophie Bost, *A Frontier Family in Minnesota* (1981).

**Hoover, Helen,** *The Long-Shadowed Forest* (1964). Account of the author's year in a wilderness cabin, written with a poet's sensitivity and a naturalist's eye. See *The Gift of the Deer* (1966), *A Place in the Woods* (1969), and *The Years of the Forest* (1973).

**Lewis, Sinclair,** *Main Street* (1920). The Nobel Prize–winning Minnesota novelist's classic satire about Gopher Prairie, its small-town smugness and apathy, and the few sensitive citizens caught by the "village virus."

**Olson, Sigurd F.,** *Singing Wilderness* (1956). Lyrical description of the wildlife of the "canoe country" of the Quetico-Superior region. Other books about the north country by this eloquent conservationist and naturalist are *Runes of the North* (1964), *Open Horizons* (1969), and *Reflections from the North Country* (1976). Another singer of the wilderness is Paul Lehmberg in *In the Strong Woods* (1979).

## Missouri

**Croy, Homer,** *County Cured* (1943). A popular biographer and novelist writes about growing up on a Missouri farm in the 1880s. See *West of the Water Tower* (1923), a novel.

**Kantor, Mackinlay,** *Missouri Bittersweet* (1969). Sort of a local *Travels with Charley:* journeys around the state and comparisons with the past, all spiked with history and the author's crotchets. His novel *The Romance of Rosy Ridge* (1923) takes place in Missouri.

**Meyerowitz, Joel,** *St. Louis and the Arch* (1980). Magnificent photographs illuminating the cityscape set off against the arch.

**Mott, Frank Luther (ed.),** *The Missouri Reader* (1964). Fine anthology of Missouriana. The best one-volume history is Duane Meyer, *The Heritage of Missouri: A History* (1973).

**Wecter, Dixon,** *Sam Clemens of Hannibal* (1952). Fine biography of Mark Twain through 1853, his eighteenth year, when he left his hometown.

## Nebraska

**Cather, Willa,** *O Pioneers!* (1913). Novel about a heroic woman and the struggles of pioneer farm life in Nebraska. The poignant *A Lost Lady* (1923) also takes place on the Plains.

**Faulkner, Virginia,** *Roundup: A Nebraska Reader* (1957). Dandy sampler of the best writing about the state. The best history is James C. Olson, *History of Nebraska* (1955).

**Janovy, John, Jr.,** *Keith County Journal* (1978). Absorbing account of the land and small animals in the sandhills country of north central Nebraska. See *Yellowlegs* (1980) and *Back in Keith County* (1981).

**Morris, Wright,** *Ceremony in Lone Tree* (1960). One of several sensitive fictional portraits of family relations set in his native state. His early days are the subject of *Will's Boy: A Memoir* (1981). *The Home Place* (1948) and *God's Country and My People* (1968) mix his photographs and prose to evoke a notion of small-town Nebraska.

**Sandoz, Mari,** *Old Jules* (1935). Her masterpiece: the portrait of her larger-than-life father, a Swiss emigrant in western Nebraska in 1884, written "as if she had cut it, like a sod, from the live ground" (Stephen Vincent Benet). See *Slogum House* (1937), a novel about late nineteenth-century Nebraska, and *Son of the Gamblin' Man* (1960), a fictional biography of the painter Robert Henri as a young man in frontier Nebraska.

**Welsch, Roger L. (ed.),** *Treasury of Nebraska Pioneer Folklore* (1967). Marvelous cornucopia of cornhusker lore. See *Sod Walls: The Story of the Nebraska Sod House* (1968).

## North Dakota

**Hudson, Lois Phillips,** *The Bones of Plenty* (1962). Powerful novel portraying the plight of a tenant farm family during the Depression. See *Reapers of the Dust: A Prairie Chronicle* (1964).

**Kelsey, Vera,** *Red River Runs North* (1951). Racy, popular history of the Red River Valley, which marks the border between North Dakota and Minnesota.

**Robinson, Elwyn B.,** *History of North Dakota* (1966). Excellent single-volume text. See Bruce Nelson, *Land of the Dakotahs* (1946).

**Sypher, Lucy J.,** *The Edge of Nowhere* (1972). Novel, as wholesome as buttermilk fresh from the churn, portraying the vanished way of life in a small village in 1916. Continued in *Cousins and Circuses* (1974), *The Spell of Northern Lights* (1975), and *Turnabout Years* (1976).

**Woiwode, Larry,** *Beyond the Bedroom Wall: A Family Album* (1975). Forty-four separate stories that chronicle a family from the 1930s to date, in which the "dramatization of the problem of getting a hold on reality — the problem of fully realizing what lies out at the edge of dream and memories 'beyond the bedroom wall' — is simply brilliant" (John Gardner).

## South Dakota

**Blasingame, Ike,** *Dakota Cowboy: My Life in the Old Days* (1958). Zesty recollections of an old cowboy who spent seven years working for the Matador Land and Cattle Company during the first decade of the century. See Walker D. Wyman, *Nothing But House and Sky* (1954), another cowhand's memoirs of life on the Dakota range.

**Hall, Oakley,** *The Bad Lands* (1978). Thoughtful, well-written story about the impact on the ecology of the Badlands by the settlers. See E. R. Zeitlow, *These Same Hills* (1960), about the passing of an old trapper and his way of life in the Badlands, and Watson Parker, *Gold in the Black Hills* (1966), about mining days.

**Kohl, Edith Eudora,** *Land of the Burnt Thigh* (1938). Simply told account of the struggles of the author and her sister to homestead about thirty miles from Pierre in 1907. A stirring tale of quietly heroic lives. Two novels about the hardships of pioneer farm life are Hamlin Garland, *A Little Norsk* (1892) and Rose Wilder Lane, *Free Land* (1938).

**Milton, John R. (ed.),** *The Literature of South Dakota* (1976). A cornucopia of prose and poetry about the state, from Lewis and Clark to Manfred and Deloria.

See *South Dakota: A Bicentennial History* (1977).

**Rölvaag, Ole,** *Giants in the Earth* (1927). Dramatic novel about a family of Scandinavian settlers in South Dakota in the 1870s; originally written in Norwegian by an immigrant who became an American college professor. An American classic.

# THE MOUNTAIN STATES

**Adams, Ansel (p) and Nancy Newhall (t),** *The Tetons and the Yellowstone* (1970). Classic volume of majestic mountain landscapes by the nature photographer.

**Berry, Don,** *A Majority of Scoundrels: An Informal History of the Rocky Mountain Fur Company* (1961). Fresh, carefully researched account, written with the skill of a novelist. The colorful fur trappers are also the subject of Bernard DeVoto, *Across the Wide Missouri* (1947); David Lavender, *Bent's Fort* (1954); and Stanley Vestal, *Mountain Men* (1937).

**Bishop, Isabelle Bird,** *A Lady's Life in the Rocky Mountains* (1879). English author's letters to her sister about her four-month, 800-mile tour of the Rockies in 1873. A fascinating picture of frontier life.

**Davidson, Levette J. and Forrester Blake (eds.),** *Rocky Mountain Tales* (1947). Yarns and fables of early western trails, the pony express, stage drivers, prairie fires, shootings, and hangings. Full of the swagger of the frontier. See Blake's fine novels, *Joe Christmas* (1948) and *Wilderness Passage* (1953).

**Lavender, David,** *The Rocky Mountains* (1980). Fine narrative history of the region by an outstanding and prolific regional historian. See *One Man's West* (1943), an account of his ranching and mining experiences; *Land of Giants* (1958); *The Big Divide* (1948); and *David Lavender's Colorado* (1976).

## *Colorado*

**Borland, Hal,** *High, Wide, and Lonesome* (1956). This and *Country Editor's Boy* (1970) describe the naturalist-author's childhood in the dry-land town of Flagler. Other remembrances of childhood are Sonora Babb, *An Owl on Every Post: A Recollection of Life on the Colorado Plain* (1970), and Ralph Moody, *Little Britches: Father and I Were Ranchers* (1950).

**Michener, James A.** *Centennial* (1974). Based on extensive research and set in the fictional town of Centennial (perhaps Keota), this sweeping popular story tells of the Indians, explorers, fur trappers, cattlemen, and others who left their mark on Colorado.

**Sprague, Marshall,** *Money Mountain: The Story of Cripple Creek Gold* (1953). Absorbing story of one of the world's greatest gold camps of the 1890s. See *Massacre: The Tragedy at White River* (1957), a reconstruction of the massacre of whites by the Utes in 1879; *The Great Divide* (1964), a history of the Rocky Mountain passes; and *Colorado: A Bicentennial History* (1976).

**Waters, Frank,** *Pike's Peak: A Family Saga* (1977). Based on a trilogy the author published in the thirties, this semiautobiographical novel traces a family from the Golconda days when Leadville boomed, Denver became a big town, and Cripple Creek led the world in gold production through world war and depression. See

*Midas of the Rockies: The Story of Stratton and Cripple Creek* (1937) and *The Colorado* (1946), one of the finest of the Rivers of America series.

**Wolle, Muriel Sibell,** *Stampede to Timberline* (rev. 1974). Written and illustrated by a long-time University of Colorado art professor, it is the best of the many ghost-town books: a much-loved classic.

## Idaho

**Brink, Carol,** *Strangers in the Forest* (1959). The white-pine country of the Panhandle is the setting for this novel of protest against exploitation of the area. See *Buffalo Coat* (1944) and *Snow in the River* (1964).

**Davis, Nelle,** *Stump Ranch Pioneer* (1943). An authentic pioneer story by an observant woman who left her dust bowl ranch for a stump farm in the Panhandle. Another spirited narrative conveying something of the life of a farm woman is Annie Greenwood, *We Sagebrush Folks* (1934). George R. Stewart, *Reluctant Soil* (1936) is a novel of one woman's struggle to eke out an existence from the desert soil of an Idaho farm.

**Fisher, Vardis,** *In Tragic Life* (1932). First installment of a tetralogy; the frank story of boyhood and adolescence of Vridar Hunter, who lives on a farm in the wilderness. See *Dark Bridwell* (1921) and *Toilers of the Hills* (1928), both novels.

**Peterson, Harold,** *The Last of the Mountain Men: A True Story of a Living American Legend* (1969). The story of Sylvan Hart, who deliberately recreated the style and substance of an earlier way of life in the Salmon River wilderness. "A singularly vivid apostrophe to the rocks and water and wildlife of a magnificent slice of this country" (Geoffrey Wolff).

**Stoll, William,** *Silver Strike: The True Story of Silver Mining in the Coeur d'Alenes* (1932). One of the last personal narratives of the frontier; full of color and drama. His life as a young lawyer in the boom-town days during the silver rush of 1883.

## Montana

**Alderson, Nannie,** *The Bride Goes West* (1942). Memoir as told to Helena Huntington Smith by a genteel young Southern woman who married and moved to the Montana frontier in the 1880s. Rich in anecdotes, wisdom, and courage.

**Call, Hughie,** *Golden Fleece* (1942). Reminiscences of a western Montana sheep rancher's wife tell "of an American way of life with a gusto, a sense of humor and a richness of human understanding" (Hal Borland).

**Cushman, Dan,** *The Silver Mountain* (1957). One man's rise to wealth during the 1880s and 1890s. Turn-of-the-century politics is the background for *The Old Copper Collar* (1957). See *The Great North Trail: America's Route of the Ages* (1966).

**Doig, Ivan,** *This House of Sky: Landscapes of a Western Mind* (1978). Superb memoirs of thirty years in Montana. Other good recollections of growing up are Milton Shatraw, *Thrashin' Time: Memories of a Montana Boyhood* (1970) and Chet Huntley, *The Generous Years: Remembrances of a Frontier Boyhood* (1968).

**Glasscock, Carl B.,** *War of the Copper Kings: Builders of Butte and Wolves of Wall Street* (1935). Lively history of the colorful mining days. See the Federal Writers Project, *Copper Camp: Stories of the World's Greatest Mining Town, Butte, Montana* (1943) and Clyde F. Murphy, *The Glittering Hill* (1944), a novel.

**Guthrie, A. B., Jr.,** *The Big Sky* (1947). First of series of historically and geographically faithful novels that make "out of the events of a real world, something like a spiritual epic of the Northwest" (Walter Van Tilburg Clark). Continued in

*The Way West* (1949), *These Thousand Hills* (1956), *Arfive* (1971), and *The Last Valley* (1976).

**Josephy, Alvin M.,** *The Nez Perce Indians and the Opening of the Northwest* (rev. 1971). The heroic flight in 1877 of the Nez Perce through Idaho and Montana, Chief Joseph's leadership, and their final capture in northern Montana. See Merril D. Beal, *"I Will Fight No More Forever"*: *Chief Joseph and the Nez Perce War* (1964).

**Toole, K. Ross,** *Montana: An Uncommon Land* (1959). Dramatic, interpretative history of the fourth-largest state. See *Twentieth Century Montana: A State of Extremes* (1970).

**Van Sickle, Dirck,** *Montana Gothic* (1979). Novel in which the protagonist is the bleak, vengeful land, portrayed from 1913 to the present. Other modern novels of Montana include Donald McCaig, *The Butte Polka* (1980); Robert Lewis Taylor, *A Roaring in the Wind* (1978); Mildred Walker, *Winter Wheat* (1944); and Thomas McGuane, *Nobody's Angel* (1982).

**Welch, James,** *The Death of Jim Loney* (1979). Gripping novel about an alienated half-Indian, half-white man who ends up being hunted in Montana's Little Rockies.

## Nevada

**Clark, Walter Van Tilburg,** *The Track of the Cat* (1949). An attempt by a family of brothers to track down a black panther during a mountain blizzard, it is "one of the great American novels of 'place' — may well be the achievement that twentieth century American regionalism has needed to justify itself" (Mark Schorer). Other good Nevada historical novels include Edwin Corle, *Coarse Gold* (1942); Vardis Fisher, *City of Illusion* (1941); and John Haase, *Big Red* (1980).

**Dunne, John Gregory,** *Vegas: A Memoir of a Dark Season* (1974). Absorbing personal account of a season in Las Vegas. Other offbeat impressions of the city are Hunter S. Thompson, *Fear and Loathing in Las Vegas* (1971) and Mario Puzo, *Inside Las Vegas* (1979).

**Lewis, Oscar,** *Silver Kings* (1947). Colorful account of the four leading men in the early history of the silver mines. See Dan DeQuille's classic *History of the Big Bonanza* (1876).

**Murbarger, Nell,** *Ghosts of the Glory Trail* (1956). Engaging history of the excitement and color of the roaring mining camp era, with a ghost town directory. See Don Ashbaugh, *Nevada's Turbulent Yesterday . . . A Study in Ghost Towns* (1963).

**Twain, Mark,** *Roughing It* (1872). Roisterous, hilarious account of the twenty-five-year-old Sam Clemens's journey west, where he worked for a spell for the *Virginia City Territorial Enterprise*. He vividly portrays the life of the Nevada frontier. A classic.

## Utah

**Abbey, Edward,** *Desert Solitaire: A Season in the Wilderness* (1968). Tough-minded memoir of a season spent living alone as a park ranger at Arches National Monument. "The author is a rebel and an eloquent loner. His is a passionately felt, deeply poetic book. It has philosophy. It has humor. It has its share of nerve-tingling adventures . . . set down in a lean, racing prose, in a close-knit style of power and beauty" (Edwin Way Teale). See *Slickrock: The Canyon Country of Southeast Utah* (1971).

**Anderson, Nels,** *Desert Saints: The Mormon Frontier in Utah* (1942). Mine of information about the fascinating society and history of Utah's Mormon settlers. Vardis Fisher, *Children of God* (1939) is a massive historical novel of the Mormons.

**Burton, Richard F.,** *The City of the Saints and Across the Rocky Mountains to California* (1861). Cheerful, sympathetic account by the English explorer of his visit to Salt Lake City, his comments on polygamy, and his interview with Brigham Young.

**Stegner, Wallace,** *Mormon Country* (1942). The Pulitzer Prize–winning novelist's description of the land and folkways of Utah's Mormons. His novel *Recapitulation* (1979) takes place in Salt Lake City.

**Wise, William,** *Massacre at Mountain Meadow* (1976). Powerful account of an American legend and a monumental crime: the slaughter of the Fancher party in 1857 by Indians and members of the Mormon church.

## Wyoming

**Larson, T. A.,** *History of Wyoming* (1965). Exciting narrative of Wyoming's colorful history.

**Olson, Ted,** *Ranch on the Laramie* (1972). Warm, human memoirs of a boyhood on a ranch during the years before World War I.

**Schaefer, Jack,** *Shane* (1949). Cowboy classic about a hero, a boy, and courage. See *The Collected Short Novels of Jack Schaefer* (1967) and *The Collected Short Stories of Jack Schaefer* (1966). Other good Wyoming westerns include Louis L'Amour, *Bendigo Shafter* (1979); Ernest Haycox, *Deep West* (1937); and James Boyd, *Bitter River* (1939).

**Smith, Helena Huntington,** *The War on Powder River* (1966). Exciting account of the infamous Johnson County cattle war. For a contemporaneous account see Asa Shinn Mercer, *Banditti on the Plains* (1894).

**Stewart, Elinore Pruitt,** *Letters of a Western Homesteader* (1913). Memoir by a woman who, as a widow with a small child, migrated to Burnt Cork, Wyoming, and worked her way up from housekeeper to rancher. A tale with the wholesome tang of the prairie. Homesteading in the 1920s is recollected in the delightful *Seventy Miles from a Lemon* (1947), by Emma Yates.

# THE SOUTHWEST

**Adams, Ansel,** *Photographs of the Southwest* (1976). The Southwestern landscape photographed with the eloquent Adams austerity, plus an essay on the land by Lawrence Clark Powell.

**Austin, Mary,** *The Land of Journey's Ending* (1924). Lyrical tribute to the Arizona/New Mexico area captures its spirit delightfully. See *Lost Borders* (1909) and *One-Smoke Stories* (1934).

**Dobie, J. Frank,** *Coronado's Children* (1930). Almost magical tales of buried Spanish treasures and lost mines in the Southwest by a man considered to be the laureate of that region's writers. The sequel is *Apache Gold and Yaqui Silver* (1939).

**Dutton, Bertha P.,** *Indians of the American Southwest* (1978). The traditions, culture, history, geography of each tribe, by the director of the Museum of Navaho Ceremonial Art. See Edward P. Dozier, *The Pueblo Indians of North America* (1970) and Norman T. Oppelt, *Guide to Prehistoric Ruins of the Southwest* (1981).

**Horgan, Paul,** *Conquistadors in North American History* (1963). Simply told, elegant account of the men who opened up the new world for Spain.

**Kupper, Winifred,** *Golden Hoof: The Story of the Sheep of the Southwest* (1945). Engaging history and description of the sheepherding days of yore.

**Meinig, D. W.,** *Southwest: Three People in Geographic Change* (1971). Outstanding geographical overview of the region and its people. The influence of climate on the lives and culture of the population is eloquently described in the classic *Sky Determines* (1934), by Ross Calvin.

**Powell, Lawrence Clark,** *Southwest Classics* (1974). Wonderful essays on the great books about the arid lands of the Southwest. An absolute must for any lover of the area. Equally indispensable is J. Frank Dobie's *Guide to Life and Literature of the Southwest* (rev. 1952). See Cecil Robinson, *Mexico and the Hispanic Southwest in American Literature* (1977).

**Richter, Conrad,** *The Sea of Grass* (1937). First of three superbly crafted novels of the Southwest: "a kind of prose poem, beautiful and tragic. Lutie, wife of the owner of the grass is perhaps the most successful creation of a ranch woman that fiction has so far achieved" (J. Frank Dobie). See *Tracey Cromwell* (1942) and *The Lady* (1957).

**Tanner, Clara Lee,** *Southwest Indian Painting* (rev. 1973). Collection of contemporary works that blend tribal tradition with outside influences. See *Southwest Indian Craft Arts* (1968) and Polly Schaafma, *Indian Rock Art of the Southwest* (1980).

## Arizona

**Abbey, Edward,** *Cactus Country* (1973). Beautiful photographs accompany the naturalist-novelist's song of the Sonora Desert. See *The Hidden Canyon: A River Journey* (1977).

**Bean, Amelia,** *The Feud* (1960). Swiftly paced novel based on the bloody Graham-Tewksbury feud of the 1880s. A good modern western, about rustlers and full of loving descriptions of Arizona, is William Decker, *The Holdouts* (1979).

**Hall, Oakley,** *Warlock* (1958). A sense of unavoidable tragedy haunts this novel of Tombstone and the Wyatt Earp legend that is "an important addition to the short list of serious novels about the Western frontier" (Granville Hicks). Another novel of Tombstone is John Myers, *The Last Chance* (1950). See Frank Waters, *The Earp Brothers of Tombstone* (1960).

**Krutch, Joseph Wood,** *The Voice of the Desert* (1955). A report on the pattern of the desert world and an adventure into the inner world of a wise and quizzical man. A wise and graceful book. See *Grand Canyon* (1958).

**Lockwood, Francis Cummins,** *Pioneer Days in Arizona* (1932). Topical history from the Spanish occupation to statehood. See Marshall Trimble, *Arizona: A Panoramic History of a Frontier State* (1977) and Lawrence Clark Powell, *Arizona: A Bicentennial History* (1976).

**Rak, Mary Kidder,** *A Cowman's Wife* (1934). With its sequel *Mountain Cattle* (1936) it offers a vibrant first-hand account of the world of the cattle ranchers in Cochise County, still wild and remote.

**Santee, Ross,** *Lost Pony Tracks* (1953). Reflective recollection of ranch life during the early part of the century by a master yarn-spinner. See *Cowboy* (1928) and *Apache Land* (1947).

**Summerhayes, Martha,** *Vanished Arizona* (1908). Recollections of an Army wife on the Arizona frontier in the 1870s, "a story that is peerless in the literature of that time and place. Not only is (it) a primary source for that period when the Apaches had been only temporarily contained, it is also a love story unique in the literature of the Southwest . . . romantic in its evocation of the life led by a frontier officer's young bride" (Lawrence Clark Powell).

**White, Helen C.** *Dust on the King's Highway* (1947). Richly textured novel based on the struggles of the eighteenth-century Spanish missionaries, particularly of Francisco Garces who wandered throughout Arizona ministering to the Indians.

**White, Stewart Edward,** *Arizona Nights* (1907). A blend of fact, fiction, and folklore that vigorously portrays the real Southwest or, as White declared, "the average life in the cattle country before the advent of the movies." A regional classic.

## New Mexico

**Broder, Patricia Janis,** *Taos: A Painter's Dream* (1980). Lavishly illustrated history of the pioneer generation of Taos artists (1915–27) who discovered the spectacular land of the remote village. See Mabel Dodge Luhan, *Taos and Its Artists* (1947).

**Church, Peggy Pond,** *The House at Otowi Bridge: The Story of Edith Warner and Los Alamos* (1970). Story of a remarkable woman who came to the plateau country in 1922 and remained there until her death thirty years later; a story of the people, the land, and the impact of the atomic bomb project there in the 1940s.

**Cleaveland, Agnes Morley,** *No Life for a Lady* (1941). Intimate look at ranch life from an Anglo point of view; for a Hispanic perspective, see Fabiola Cabeza de Vaca, *We Fed Them Cactus* (1954).

**Courlander, Harold,** *The Fourth World of the Hopis* (1971). Collection of traditional accounts of epic events and adventures in the life of the Hopi clans and villages, from legendary to historical times.

**Eastlake, William,** *The Bronc People* (1958). Lyrical tale of life in present-day New Mexico written with the characteristic combination of broad humor, fantasy, and compassion of a novelist whose "prairie-hard prose is as pure and clean as the wind-sanded land that fosters it" (Ken Kesey). See *Go in Beauty* (1956) and *Portrait of an Artist with 26 Horses* (1963).

**Fergusson, Erna,** *New Mexico: A Pageant of Three Peoples* (rev. 1964). Probably the best book ever written about the state. *Dancing Gods: Indian Ceremonials of New Mexico and Arizona* (1931) is a classic of Southwestern literature.

**Fergusson, Harvey,** *Wolf Song* (1927). Historical novel about the mountain men in the Sangre de Cristo, that is "among the best half-dozen novels of the West" (J. Frank Dobie). Republished with two other early novels in *Followers of the Sun: A Trilogy of the Santa Fe Trail* (1936). See *Grant of Kingdom* (1950), a novel based on the huge Maxwell land grant, and *The Conquest of Don Pedro* (1954), a novel about a frontier town shortly after the Civil War.

**Hillerman, Tony,** *Dance Hall of the Dead* (1973). One of an intriguing series of detective novels featuring Joe Leaphorn, a Navaho reservation policeman. Taut and rich in description of Indian tribal ways.

**Horgan, Paul,** *Far from Cibola* (1938). A novel of Depression-torn New Mexico. *A Distant Trumpet* (1960) is a novel of the 1880s; his nonfiction includes *The Habit of Empire* (1939), about New Mexico of the sixteenth century, and *The Centuries of Santa Fe* (1956), brief historical stories of that city.

**La Farge, Oliver,** *Behind the Mountains* (1956). Consuelo Otille Baca was the second wife of the author of *Laughing Boy.* This is the story, told through her husband, of her wonderful girlhood on her family's domain at Rociada, a high valley in the Sangre de Cristos between Santa Fe and Taos. "Here in a few simple artless, artful exercises in the transmutation of one person's memories into another person's prose is the quintessence of northern New Mexico" (Lawrence Clark Powell).

**Luhan, Mabel Dodge,** *Winter in Taos* (1935). She left a great aesthetic salon in New York to visit New Mexico during the First World War and stayed on for forty-six years, establishing herself as the cultural arbiter of Taos. This lovely book is about the region, its seasonal rhythms, and its daily life.

**Marriott, Alice,** *The Valley Below* (1949). Warm, discerning memoir about the life of the anthropologist-author in an adobe house in the Round Valley, near Santa Fe, and the native people of the area.

**Nichols, John,** *The Milagro Beanfield War* (1974). The first novel of a trilogy set in mythical Chamiso County in northern New Mexico, a crucible of Anglo, Chicano, and Pueblo cultures. Nichols wrote the text (and William Davis did the photographs) for *If Mountains Die* (1979), a handsome book about the Taos valley.

**O'Keefe, Georgia,** *Georgia O'Keefe* (1976). Splendid album of the paintings of the artist, long resident in New Mexico, that evoke the spirit and sense of place of her adopted region.

**Waters, Frank,** *People of the Valley* (1941). Provocative novel about the coming of technological change to the Spanish-speaking people living in the town of Mora in the Sangre de Cristos, by an author who is "not only a good writer but what is rarer, a good storyteller, and who possesses perhaps the finest sense of the West's special tatterdalionry" (William Brandon). See *Pumpkin Seed Point* (1969), an autobiographical account of his life among the Hopis, and *Book of the Hopi* (1963).

## Oklahoma

**Giles, Janice Holt,** *The Kinta Years* (1973). Memoirs of childhood in the prairie town of Kinta in the early 1900s.

**Gipson, Fred,** *Fabulous Empire* (1946). Richly anecdotal, fast-paced story of the rise and fall of the 101 Ranch and of the family of George Washington Miller and his sons, who built it up and finally lost it. See Ellsworth Collings, *The 101 Ranch* (1937).

**James, Marquis,** *Cherokee Strip: A Tale of an Oklahoma Boyhood* (1945). Memoir by

the Pulitzer Prize–winning biographer and journalist: an epic of the cattle kingdom.

**Mathews, John Joseph,** *Talking to the Moon* (1945). The story of a nature lover living alone for ten years in the blackjack country of eastern Oklahoma. See *Wah-Kon-Tah: The Osage and the White Man's Road* (1932) and *Sundown* (1934), a novel.

**Williams, Cecil B.,** *Paradise Prairie* (1953). Tender novel about the early days on a farm in central Oklahoma. Another novel of pioneer days is Alberta Winston Constant, *Oklahoma Run* (1954). Contemporary Oklahoma provides the background to Darcy O'Brien, *The Silver Spooner* (1981).

## Texas

**Bedichek, Roy,** *Adventures with a Texas Naturalist* (1947). These descriptions and anecdotes of the great Texas outdoors amount to a hymn to nature. See *Karánkawy Country* (1950).

**Dobie, J. Frank,** *Cow People* (1964). Picturesque stories of old-time Texas ranchers; perhaps the best of his many books. *I'll Tell You a Tale* (1961), a selection of his tales, is a fine doorway into Dobie's Texas.

**Graves, John,** *Hard Scrabble: Observations on a Patch of Land* (1974). A naturalist's sometimes argumentative, always honest, ruminations about his 440-acre place in north central Texas. See *From a Limestone Ridge* (1981).

**Greene, A. C.,** *A Personal Country* (1970). Recollections of his youth in the teens and thirties. Masterly evocations of west Texas.

**James, Marquis,** *The Raven: A Biography of Sam Houston* (1929). Pulitzer Prize–winning biography of the legendary president of the Lone Star Republic and hero of the Texas Revolution. Another good presidential portrait is Herbert Gambrell and L. W. Newton, *Anson Jones: The Last President of Texas* (1948).

**Lea, Tom,** *The Wonderful Country* (1952). Superb historical novel of the frontier by the Texas author-illustrator. *The King Ranch* (1957) is an excellent history of the largest ranch in Texas.

**Loughmiller, Campbell and Lynn Lough-miller (eds.),** *Big Thicket Legacy* (1977). The editors spent nine years interviewing the people of this unique area of south-eastern Texas to produce this fascinating oral history. Brings Big Thicket to life.

**McMurtry, Larry,** *Horseman Pass By* (1961). Novel which, in portraying contemporary rural Texas life in the face of changing times, shatters the glamor of ranching and cowboys. The film *Hud* was based on this book. See *The Last Picture Show* (1966) and *Leaving Cheyenne* (1963).

**Matthews, Sallie Reynolds,** *Interwoven: A Pioneer Chronicle* (1936). Personal narrative of ranch life on the frontier during the second half of the nineteenth century by an intelligent, refined woman.

**Nordyke, Lewis,** *Nubbin Ridge* (1960). These reminiscences of boyhood on a small Panhandle farm in the second decade of the century form "a splendid book, warm with memory, enriched with humor, colloquial to the core, and full of both truth and drama" (Hal Borland). See

*The Great Roundup: The Story of Texas and Southwestern Cowmen* (1955) and *The Truth About Texas* (1957).

**Owens, William A.,** *This Stubborn Soil* (1966). Autobiography: life on a farm in the Red River Valley and his widowed mother's struggle to feed and clothe her family. *A Season of Weathering* (1973) is a sequel.

**Perry, George Sessions,** *Hold Autumn in Your Hand* (1941). Award-winning novel about a courageous sharecropper in the Brazos River bottom; told with wit and humor. See *Texas: A World in Itself* (1942).

**Smith, Erwin E. (p) & J. Evetts Haley (t),** *Life on the Texas Range* (1952). A cowboy took these beautiful photographs of life on a big ranch in west Texas in the early 1900s.

**Webb, Walter Prescott,** *The Texas Rangers* (1935). The basic book on this famous Texas organization. See his study of the frontier, *The Great Plains* (1931). Other good Texas Ranger books are John C. Duval, *Adventures of Bigfoot Wallace* (1870) and James B. Gillett, *Six Years with the Texas Rangers* (1921).

**Wier, Allen,** *Blanco* (1978). Empty lives in a small town: a novel rich in characterization and evocation of modern south central Texas life. See *Things About to Disappear* (1978), a collection of short stories.

# THE PACIFIC STATES

## *Alaska*

**Heller, Herbert L.,** *Sourdough Sagas* (1967). The journals, memoirs, tales, and recollections of the earliest Alaska gold miners, 1883–1923; the first-hand account of struggle, fun, and savage splendor by the conquerors of the last frontier. See Murray Morgan, *One Man's Gold Rush* (1967), an album of pictures taken by an

itinerant photographer during the golden Klondike days.

**McPhee, John,** *Coming into the Country* (1977). Graceful, hard-edged portrait of the Alaskan frontier. A masterpiece of reporting. *Alaska: Images of the County* (1981) is a portfolio of color photographs by Galen Rowell set against a text excerpted from McPhee's book.

**Muir, John,** *Travels in Alaska* (1915). Richly descriptive, charming account of his three visits to Alaska in 1879, 1880, and 1890. Later wilderness reports by naturalists include Sally Carrighar, *Moonlight at Midday* (1958) and Adolph Murie, *A Naturalist in Alaska* (1960).

**Murie, Margaret,** *Two in the Far North* (1962). Camp life in the wilderness shared by author and her husband, Olaus J. Murie. His recollections are collected in *Journey to the Far North* (1973).

**Wright, Billie,** *Four Seasons North: A Journal of Life in the Alaskan Wilderness* (1973). Account of the first year that the author and her husband spent north of the Arctic Circle in a small cabin they built themselves. Sara Machetanz's *The Howl of the Malemute: The Story of an Alaska Winter* (1961) is another woman's wilderness memoir.

## California

**Chase, J. Smeaton,** *California Coast Trails* (1913). Classic account of the author's horseback journey from Mexico to Oregon.

**Clappe, Louisa Smith,** *The Shirley Letters from the California Mines, 1851–1852* (1854). Vividly descriptive letters from a mining camp on a fork of the Feather River, deep in the Sierra Nevada mountains. An outstanding historical work on the times is J. S. Holliday, *The World Rushed In: The California Gold Rush Experience* (1981). For a fictional portrait, see Bret Harte's local color stories. *The Luck of Roaring Camp and Other Sketches* (1870).

**Clelland, Robert Glass,** *The Cattle on a Thousand Hills: Southern California, 1850–1870* (1941). One of many attractive books by a fine regional historian. See *The Place Called Sespe: The History of a California Ranch* (1940).

**McWilliams, Carey,** *Southern California Country: An Island on the Land* (1946). Astounding, revisionist history of California south of the Tehachapi Range. See *California: The Great Exception* (1949) and *Factories in the Field: The Story of Migratory Farm Labor in California* (1939).

**Pitt, Leonard,** *The Decline of the California: A Social History of the Spanish-speaking Californians, 1846–1890* (1966). Colorful, anecdotal picture of a lost world.

**Sanborn, Margaret,** *Yosemite: Its Discovery, Its Wonders and Its People* (1981). Marvelous piece of work, well-researched, gracefully written, about the meeting of nature and humanity in one of the most beautiful valleys on earth.

**Starr, Kevin,** *America and the California Dream, 1856–1915* (1973). Exuberant, brilliant cultural history that probes the inner experience of California's formative years through a series of well-wrought cultural studies.

**Steinbeck, John,** *The Grapes of Wrath* (1939). Modern classic about the Joad family, refugees from the Dust Bowl, and their hard times as migrant laborers in California. His other California fiction includes *The Long Valley* (1938); *Tortilla Flat* (1935) and *Cannery Row* (1945), both set around Monterey; and *To A God Unknown* (1933).

**Stewart, George R.,** *Ordeal by Hunger* (rev. 1960). Riveting story of the tragic Donner Party of 1846. See *Committee of Vigilance* (1964), about early San Francisco, and *East of the Giants* (1938), a novel set in the days before the Gold Rush.

## Hawaii

**Bishop, Isabelle Bird,** *Six Months on the Sandwich Islands* (1875). Classic collection of the English author's cheerful, vividly descriptive letters to her sister. Other noted travelers' accounts of the period are Robert Louis Stevenson, *Travels in Hawaii* (1889) and Mark Twain, *Letters from the Sandwich Islands* (1966).

Bushnell, O. A., *Ka'a'awa: A Novel About Hawaii in the 1850's* (1972). Colorful story of adventure during the reign of Kamehameha III. Other good historical novels are Albertine Loomis, *Grapes of Canaan* (1966) and Marjorie Sinclair, *Kona* (1947).

Cameron, Robert, *Above Hawaii* (1977). Fresh aerial photoperspectives of the islands. Closer to the ground is *The Hawaiians* (1970), an album of a decade's worth of imaginative photographs by former *National Geographic* photographer Robert Johnson.

Daws, Gavan, *Shoal of Time: A History of the Hawaiian Islands* (1969). Concise, fascinating history from the time of Cook's discovery in 1778 to statehood in 1959.

Day, A. Grove and Carl Stroven (eds.), *A Hawaiian Reader* (1959). Gathering of selections, from Robert Louis Stevenson and Jack London to Somerset Maugham and James Jones. *The Spell of Hawaii* (1968) is a companion volume.

Gray, Francine Du Plessix, *Hawaii: The Sugar Coated Fortress* (1972). Compelling, sharply observed report on the problems facing Hawaii by a first-rate writer who has since been characterized by defenders of the islands as opinionated and ultra-liberal.

London, Jack, *Stories of Hawaii* (1965). Collection of his Hawaiian tales that are uneven but interesting for their island background. See his wife Charmian London's *Our Hawaii* (1917), which makes up in exuberance what it lacks in polished literary skill.

Michener, James A., *Hawaii* (1959). The first of Michener's great panoramic pop-historical epics and one of the most interesting.

Smith, Bradford, *Yankee in Paradise: The New England Impact on Hawaii* (1956). Entrancing history of the missionaries during the mid-nineteenth century who came to rid the natives of their heathen ways.

Tempski, Armine Von, *Born in Paradise* (1940). Unpretentious, fresh memoir by an English-Polish woman born on a large cattle ranch in Hawaii at the beginning of the century.

# THE PACIFIC NORTHWEST

Douglas, William O., *My Wilderness: The Pacific West* (1960). The U.S. Supreme Court Justice's first-hand observations of his beloved country, written in a vigorous, spare style. See *Of Men and Mountains* (1950).

Holbrook, Stewart, *The Columbia* (1955). Zesty, informal portrait and history of the great river by a journalist and popular historian who lived on its shores for thirty years. See *Far Corner: A Personal View of the Pacific Northwest* (1952).

Johansen, Dorothy O. and Charles M. Gates, *Empire of the Columbia* (1967). Lively history of the Pacific Northwest. See David Lavender, *Land of Giants: The Drive to the Pacific Northwest, 1750–1950* (1958).

Judson, Katherine B., *Myths and Legends of the Pacific Northwest* (1910). Collection of regional folklore and Indian legends. See Robert H. Ruby and John A. Brown, *Indians of the Pacific Northwest: A History* (1981).

Lucia, Ellis (ed.), *This Land Around Us: A Treasury of Pacific Northwest Writing* (1969). Excellent, wide-ranging anthology of the region's rich literary heritage.

## Oregon

**Ashworth, William,** *The Wallowas: Coming of Age in the Wilderness* (1978). While a college student in the sixties, he began taking excursions to the Wallowas mountains in the Eagle Cap wilderness; here he matures from adventure seeker to nature lover. Living in the wilderness is the subject of Dayton O. Hyde, *Yamsi* (1971) and Irving Petite, *The Elderberry Tree* (1964).

**Balch, Frederick Homer,** *Bridge of the Gods: A Romance of Indian Oregon* (1890). Much-loved retelling of the legend about the origin of the great rock bridge over the Columbia River and the Indians whose existence was dependent on it.

**Berry, Don,** *Trask* (1960). Incredibly exciting novel about fur trappers in the 1840s, full of suspense and authoritative detail. See *Moontrap* (1962) and *To Build a Ship* (1963), both superb historical novels of adventure.

**Churchill, Sam,** *Big Sam* (1965). Powerful first-hand chronicle of a real-life Paul Bunyan and the raw exciting life of the turn-of-the-century lumber camps. Against the story of the rise and fall of the logging industry is set the warm and beautiful story of a son's admiration for his father. See *Don't Call Me Ma* (1977).

**Clark, Malcolm, Jr.,** *The Eden Seekers: The Settlement of Oregon, 1818–1862* (1981). The adventures of several groups of pioneers in a lively history.

**Davis, H. L.,** *Honey in the Horn* (1935). Robust Pulitzer Prize–winning novel about one of America's last frontiers — homesteading in Oregon, 1906. Other Oregon novels are *The Winds of Morning* (1952) and *Distant Music* (1957). *Team Bells Woke Me* (1953) is a short-story collection, and *Kettle of Fire* (1959) contains essays.

**Dye, Eva Emery,** *McLoughlin and Old Oregon* (1936). A favorite historical novel among old Oregonians, about the governor of the Hudson's Bay Company during the wilderness days. He is also the focus of Richard G. Montgomery's *White-Headed Eagle* (1935).

**Gulick, Bill,** *Treasure in Hell's Canyon* (1979). Novel about a lawyer's search for a lost gold mine is far above the level of the ordinary western. See *Bend of the Snake* (1950).

**Kesey, Ken,** *Sometimes a Great Notion* (1964). Ambitious, flawed novel about the struggle between two brothers, distinguished by its rapid shiftings of point of view and its evocation of the dark, alluvial beauty of the logging country.

**Ross, Alexander,** *Adventures of the First Settlers on the Oregon* (1849). Recollections of a man who "went through founding of Astoria, traveled inland among the tribes, and left a remarkable picture behind him. Not only is it an honest book. It is a dramatic and colorful book and ranks with the finest of the first-hand historical chronicles in America" (Ernest Haycox).

## Washington

**Binns, Archie,** *Mighty Mountain* (1940). One of the native Washington writer's many historical novels about the state, this one is about Puget Sound in the mid-nineteenth century. Others include *You Rolling River* (1947), about life in the Columbia River country in the 1890s, and *Timber Beast* (1944), about the conflict between the Wobblies and the lumber barons. See *The Roaring Land* (1942), reminiscences of his youth in the Puget Sound country, and *Gateway: The Story of the Port of Seattle* (1941).

**Clark, Norman,** *Mill Town* (1970). Superb social history of Everett, Washington, from its founding in the 1840s to the infamous "Everett Massacre" of 1916. Other cities are remembered in Lucile F. Fargo, *Spokane Story* (1950) and Thomas Ripley, *Green Timber* (1968), an engaging reminiscence of Tacoma's boom-and-bust days of the early 1890s.

McKay, Allis, *They Came to a River* (1941). Fine novel set during the first two decades of this century in the apple-growing country. See *Two Women at Pine Creek* (1966). Other popular historical novels are Patricia Campbell, *Royal Anne Tree* (1956) and Anita Pettibone, *Light Down, Stranger* (1942).

Morgan, Murray, *Skid Road: An Informal Portrait of Seattle* (rev. 1981). Intimate, picturesque history of the city by a colorful writer whose other Washingtoniana includes *The Viewless Wind* (1949) and *The Dam* (1954). Roger Sale's elegant history *Seattle: Past and Present* (1977) is a model of its kind. That city is also where private eye John Denson operates in a series of crisp detective novels by Richard Hoyt, starting with *Decoys* (1981).

Swan, James G., *The Northwest Coast* (1857). Classic account, told in simple, eloquent prose, of frontier life and the Indians in Washington Territory. See Ivan Doig's *Winter Brothers: A Season at the Edge of America* (1980), in which he interweaves his thoughts with Swan's journal.

# CITIES

## New York City

Abbott, Berenice, *Changing New York* (1939). A great photographer's lyrical portrait of New York in the thirties. Other noteworthy photographic tributes include Andreas Feininger, *New York* (1964); Philip Trager, *Philip Trager: New York* (1980); Helen Devitt, *A Way of Seeing* (rev. 1981); and Reinhart Wolf, *New York* (1981).

Berger, Meyer, *Meyer Berger's New York* (1960). Collection of columns he wrote for the *New York Times* in the late fifties, sketches of the curious that not only provide a fascinating panorama of city life but, as journalism, are a model of their kind. See *The Eight Million: Journal of a New York Correspondent* (1942).

Caro, Robert A., *The Power Broker: Robert Moses and the Fall of New York* (1974). To this 1200-page, superbly researched biography of the man who in four decades as a public official built most of the bridges, parks, and highways around the city, the author brings the highest level of dramatic writing. Awarded a Pulitzer Prize.

Clarke, Donald Henderson, *In the Reign of Rothstein* (1929). In a crudely vigorous style a newspaperman portrays a man who would do anything for a buck and the colorful Broadway characters who flared across the tabloids of the twenties. Highest quality gossip. See Leo Katcher, *Big Bankroll: The Life and Times of Arnold Rothstein* (1959).

Finney, Jack, *Time and Again* (1970). Time-travel story of love and mystery in New York of 1882 as seen through the eyes of a man of our time. A Currier and Ives novel that will charm any New Yorker.

Gordon, John and L. Rust Hills (eds.), *New York, New York: The City as Seen by Masters of Art and Literature* (1965). Big, thick selection of short stories chosen by Hills and 100 paintings and drawings chosen by Gordon, former curator of the Whitney Museum.

Kasson, John F., *Amusing the Million: Coney Island at the Turn of the Century* (1978). Exciting look at Steeplechase, Luna, Dreamland, etc. and what they meant. A pop culture classic.

Kieran, John, *Natural History of New York City: A Personal Report After 50 Years of Study and Enjoyment of Wildlife Within the Boundaries of Greater New York* (1959). Comparable to Izaak Walton and Gilbert White in its universal appeal, this book by the New York City–born journalist-naturalist is "one long delightful trip in the company of a charming and erudite companion" (Edwin Way Teale). An excellent companion volume is Elizabeth Barlow's *The Forests and Wetlands of New York City* (1972).

**Lewis, David,** *When Harlem Was in Vogue* (1981). Wonderful evocation of the spirit of black life as played out in Harlem during the twenties. See Jervis Anderson, *This Was Harlem: A Cultural Portrait 1900–1950* (1982); Nathan Huggins, *Harlem Renaissance* (1971); and Gilbert Orofsky, *Harlem: The Making of a Ghetto* (1966).

**Liebling, A. J.,** *Back Where I Come From* (1938). A native New Yorker's funny, warm-hearted, sometimes frenzied, essays about his "old home town." Liebling's masterful slices of Manhattan life, especially his hilarious profiles of the raffish Broadway characters he encountered, appear in *The Telephone Booth Indian* (1942) and *The Jollity Building* (1962).

**McKelway, St. Clair,** *True Tales from the Annals of Crime and Rascality* (1954). Selections from the gifted *New Yorker* writer's "Annals of Crime" columns about unusual criminals and rogues of the city. More of these delightful tales appear in *The Big Little Man from Brooklyn* (1968).

**Michelin Guide to New York City** (curr. rev.). "The best tourist guide to New York City" (Local History Division, The N.Y. Public Library). Top guides of another sort are *AIA Guide to New York City* (rev. 1978), a comprehensive illustrated look at the buildings and neighborhoods of all five boroughs, and Harmon H. Goldstone, *History Preserved: A Guide to New York City Landmarks and Historic Districts* (1974).

**Mitchell, Joseph,** *The Bottom of the Harbor* (1960). Collection of New York pieces: journalism transmuted into literature. His earlier works, mainly profiles of Dickensian characters, are classics: *McSorley's Wonderful Saloon* (1943) and *Old Mr. Flood* (1948).

**Morris, James,** *The Great Port: A Passage Through New York* (1969). Refreshing look at the city through the perceptive eyes of the English travel writer. Other British observers include Anthony Burgess, *New York* (1976) and V. S. Pritchett, *New York Proclaimed* (1965).

**Moss, Howard (ed.),** *New York: Poems* (1980). Poems about the city selected by the poet and poetry editor of the *New Yorker*.

*The New York Kid's Book: 170 Children's Writers and Artists Celebrate New York City* (1979). Ebullient cornucopia of stories, games, cartoons, things to do. For kids eight and up it is both guidebook and entertainment. Two favorite children's storybooks of the city are George Selden, *The Cricket in Times Square* (1960) and Jean Merrill, *The Pushcart War* (1964).

**Patterson, Jerry E.,** *The City of New York: A History Illustrated from the Collections of the Museum of the City of New York* (1978). Dandy album of prints, photographs, maps, paintings, handbills, theater programs, etc. See Roger Whitehouse, *New York: Sunshine and Shadow: A Photographic Record of the City and Its People from 1850 to 1915* (1974) and Nathan Silver, *Lost New York* (1971).

**Strong, George Templeton,** *Diary* (1952). Selections by Allan Nevins from the forty-year (1835–75) diary of a prominent man of his time. Fluid and acid, it reflects the upper class New York City life of the period; "wherever you glance in the diary so many things touching or funny, so much delight! . . . It will last you a lifetime" (Brendan Gill).

**Wharton, Edith,** *The Age of Innocence* (1920). Pulitzer Prize–winning novel about an affable conformist whose marriage of convenience cannot extinguish his passion for another woman. Set against the constricting New York society of the

1870s, it is "the finest of her novels . . . painted with a richness of color and detail that delights the imagination." (Louis Auchincloss).

**White, E. B.,** *Here Is New York* (1949). There was New York. A personal, thoughtful 8,000-word love letter to his city.

## Chicago

**Ade, George,** *Chicago Stories* (1963). Selection of pieces written for the *Chicago Record* that vividly portray the city during the 1890s.

**Algren, Nelson,** *Chicago: City on the Make* (1951). A Goyaesque picture of the city by a socially conscious novelist who grew up in its slums. "The best evocation of a city's feeling, around and about" (Studs Terkel). For a New Yorker's sharply observant view of the same time see A. J. Liebling, *Chicago: The Second City* (1952).

**Bellow, Saul,** *The Adventures of Augie March* (1953). The picaresque adventures of a young Jewish man of the Chicago streets as he tries to shape his own destiny. A rich, vital, memorable novel by the Chicago-based Nobel Prize–winning novelist.

**Bradley, Mary,** *Old Chicago* (1933). Four short novels about nineteenth-century Chicago, carefully researched and charming. For a not-so-charming picture of the city a century later see Bette Howland's compelling *Blue in Chicago* (1978).

**Burnett, W. R.,** *Little Caesar* (1929). The popular hard-boiled novelist's tale of Prohibition-era Chicago gang leader Rico, made famous by Edward G. Robinson in the screen role. See *The Asphalt Jungle* (1949) and *Good-bye, Chicago* (1981).

**Dreiser, Theodore,** *The Color of a Great City* (1923). Comparing these vignettes to Hopper's paintings or Steiglitz's early photographs, Van Wyck Brooks found them "full of the zest with which Dreiser observed the secret and thrilling in a thousand corners of the city."

**Dubkin, Leonard,** *Enchanted Streets* (1947). These "unlikely adventures of an urban nature lover" offer a refreshing glimpse of the city's birds and insects by a writer who retains his sense of wonder.

**Paretsky, Sara,** *Indemnity Only* (1982). Introducing V. I. Warshawsky, private detective, in a new series of fast-paced thrillers that take our heroine around the city.

**Pierce, Bessie Louis,** *History of Chicago* (1937–57). Comprehensive, clear, a lifetime's work, and a model urban history. A beautiful and affectionate architectural history is David Lowe, *Lost Chicago* (1975).

**Wendt, Lloyd and Herman Kogen,** *Bosses in Lusty Chicago* (1967). Wonderful, anecdotal social history of the old days. Other such informal histories include Emmet Dedmon, *Fabulous Chicago* (rev. 1981); Lloyd Lewis and Henry Justin Smith, *Chicago: The History of Its Reputation* (1929); and Ernest Poole, *Giants Gone: Men Who Made Chicago* (1943).

## Boston

**Amory, Cleveland,** *The Proper Bostonians* (rev. 1972). Anecdotal, impudent study of Boston society and its first families from colonial times. Other informal portraits include Lucius Beebe, *Boston and the Boston Legend* (1935); George F. Weston, *Boston Ways: High, By, and Folk* (1957); and David McCord, *About Boston* (1948).

**Garland, Joseph E.,** *Boston's North Shore* (1978). Between Beverly Cove and eastern point are the resort towns of Boston's "Riviera." This is how they looked at their peak, in summers between 1823 and 1890. See *Boston's Gold Coast: The North Shore, 1890–1929* (1981), a sequel.

**Hale, Edward Everett,** *A New England Boyhood* (1893). The Boston clergyman and man of letters recalls his years growing up in the 1820s and 1830s. His granddaughter, Nancy Hale, evokes Boston of the 1910s and 1920s in her beautiful fictionalized memoir, *A New England Girlhood* (1958).

**Higgins, George V.,** *The Friends of Eddie Coyle* (1972). Fast-paced, hard-boiled excursion into the underbelly of Boston in a novel of small-time hoods by a former prosecuting attorney with a remarkable ear for the colloquial. See *The Digger's Game* (1973) and *The Rat on Fire* (1981).

**Howe, M. A. DeWolfe,** *A Venture in Remembrance* (1941). Memoir by the distinguished biographer of many of his generation's men of letters; it paints a very human picture of proper Boston. See Helen Howe, *The Gentle Americans, 1864–1960: The Biography of a Breed* (1965).

**Howells, William Dean,** *The Rise of Silas Lapham* (1885). Perhaps Howells's greatest novel. A newcomer climbs the ladder of Boston society. See *A Modern Instance* (1882).

**Jones, Howard Mumford and Bessie Zaban Jones (eds.),** *The Many Voices of Boston: A Historical Anthology, 1630–1975* (1975). Carefully selected excerpts from Puritan days to the present provide an outstanding and entertaining social history.

**Kay, Jane Holtz,** *Lost Boston* (1980). Through hundreds of old photographs, the architecture critic of the *Nation* traces the evolution of the city in a well-researched, lucid study.

**McCloskey, Robert,** *Make Way for Ducklings* (1941). For more than four decades this Caldecott Medal–winning picture book about a family of ducks looking for a home in downtown Boston has been enchanting young children.

**Marquand, John P.,** *The Late George Apley* (1937). Pulitzer Prize–winning novel in the form of a fictional biography of a proper Brahmin; a sharply observed satire of upper-crust Boston. More recent Boston novels include Jean Stafford, *Boston Adventure* (1944), Julian Moynahan, *Pairing Off* (1969), and James Carroll, *Mortal Friends* (1978).

**Museum of Fine Arts, Boston,** *Paul Revere's Boston, 1735–1818* (1975). Varied look at the eighty-three years of change that occurred during Paul Revere's lifetime, richly and handsomely illustrated with paintings, silver, furniture, etc. An even earlier period is documented in Darret B. Rutman, *Winthrop's Boston* (1965).

**Morison, Samuel Eliot,** *One Boy's Boston, 1887–1901* (1962). The historian reminisces about his youth in the 1890s. This period is delightfully recalled in Marion L. Peabody, *To Be Young Was Very Heaven* (1967); John Jay Chapman, *In Memories and Milestones* (1915); and Robert Grant, *Fourscore* (1934).

**Parker, Robert B.,** *The Godwulf Manuscript* (1973). Spenser, a tough, wisecracking private eye, is introduced in this novel. Parker "has mastered the idiom of the classic hard-boiled detective story, his people are not given to long periods of soporific introspection, and a lot happens. This is one delightful book" (George V. Higgins).

**Tucci, Douglas Shand,** *Built in Boston: City and Suburb, 1800–1950* (1978). Elegant, scholarly history of the architecture of the city, from Bulfinch to Gropius. The Boston Society of Architects, *Architectural Boston* (1976), with its emphasis on contemporary Boston (Pei, Rudolph, etc.) and restored nineteenth-century buildings, is more than a guidebook, for it illustrates the impact of modern design upon a city already rich in traditional architecture.

**Whitehill, Walter Muir,** *Boston: A Topographical History* (1963). One of several books by Boston's eminent student of its architecture. See *Boston: Portrait of a City*

(1964) and *Boston in the Age of John Fitz-gerald Kennedy* (1966).

## Philadelphia

**Baltzell, E. Digby,** *Philadelphia Gentlemen: The Making of a National Upper Class* (rev. 1979). Classic study of wealth and power in "Penn's Greene Countrie Towne." More informal is Nathaniel Burt, *The Perennial Philadelphians: The Anatomy of an American Aristocracy* (1963), witty sketches of their foibles, attitudes, and rituals.

**Boyer, David,** *The Sidelong Glances of a Pigeon Watcher* (1968). This funny novel about an eccentric Philly cab driver is a favorite modern Philadelphia story. Others are George R. Clay, *Family Occasions* (1978); Tom McHale, *Principato* (1970); and Evelyn Wilde Mayerson, *If Birds Are Free* (1980).

**Bridenbaugh, Carl and Jessica Bridenbaugh,** *Rebels and Gentlemen: Philadelphia in the Age of Franklin* (1942). The life and culture of the city prior to the Revolution, with special focus on Benjamin Franklin.

**Hendriks, Gordon** *The Life and Work of Thomas Eakins* (1974). Insight into the personality of the painter and into the character of turn-of-the-century Philadelphia.

**Lukacs, John,** *Philadelphia: Patricians & Philistines, 1900–1950* (1981). In looking for the unique quality of Philadelphia, the author has written engaging sketches of seven eminent citizens.

**Mitchell, S. Weir,** *Hugh Wynne, Free Quaker* (1897). Highly colored romance of a "fighting Quaker" in vividly rendered Revolutionary Philadelphia, by a prolific historical novelist who was an eminent Philadelphia physician. See *The Red City* (1907).

**Morley, Christopher,** *Travels in Philadelphia* (1920). Delightful, crotchety essays about the author's native city. His novel *Kitty Foyle* (1939) offers a sentimental but often vivid and accurate portrait of Philadelphia life.

**Oberholtzer, Ellis P.,** *The Literary History of Philadelphia* (1906). Presents Philadelphia when it was the most enjoyable, most cultured, and most gracious city in America.

**Pennell, Elizabeth Robins,** *Our Philadelphia* (1914). Charming guide copiously illustrated by the author's husband, Joseph Pennell, both with roots in Philadelphia.

**Repplier, Agnes,** *Philadelphia: The Place and the People* (1925). Delightful description and history by a woman who was one of the foremost essayists of her day. Another nostalgic and genial narrative of that day is Cornelius Weygandt, *Philadelphia Folks: Ways and Institutions in and About the Quaker City* (1938).

## Detroit

**Arnow, Harriet,** *The Dollmaker* (1954). Powerful, compassionate novel about the impact of city life on Gertie Nevels and her family, who had come to Detroit from the Kentucky hills. See *The Weedkiller's Daughter* (1970).

**Conot, Robert,** *American Odyssey* (1974). History of Detroit from 1701 with fictional biographies of ordinary citizens woven into the narrative.

**Leonard, Elmore,** *City Primeval: High Noon in Detroit* (1980). One of his first-rate thrillers set in the city. Other Detroit crime tales include William J. Coughlin, *Day of Wrath* (1980); Loren D. Estleman, *Motor City Blue* (1980); and John A. Jackson, *The Diehard* (1977).

**Litwak, Leo E.,** *Waiting for the News* (1969). To enjoy this novel about Jake Gottlieb's struggle to unionize his fellow laundryworkers in the late thirties you need hold no particular opinion, "but you do need to be responsive to human effort, you must be able to see the grandeur and the misery of the Thirties. . . . [This work is] a fable of moral scope" (Irving Howe).

**Oates, Joyce Carol,** *Them* (1969). Violence in one blue-collar white family is traced from the Depression to the riots of 1967 in a National Book Award–winning novel that has been characterized as urban gothic.

## New Orleans

**Brooks, Charles B.,** *The Siege of New Orleans* (1961). Vivid account of the famous Battle of New Orleans.

**Cable, George Washington,** *Old Creole Days* (1879). Despite the awkward plots and surfeit of dialect in this collection of short stories, its "picture of New Orleans — the place and the people — is still the best that has ever been done" (Shirley Ann Grau). A selection of writings by a later local colorist are gathered in *Grace King of New Orleans* (1973), edited by Robert Bush.

**Cable, Mary,** *Lost New Orleans* (1980). The buildings that no longer exist in a city famed for the buildings that do.

**Chopin, Kate,** *The Awakening* (1899). Beautifully composed, graceful novel of a young woman's awakening from the dull dream of her existence and the tragic consequences that ensue. Mostly set on Grand Isle, the fashionable New Orleans summer resort where the rich merchants deposited their wives and children. See *Bayou Folk* (1894).

**Dufour, Charles (t) and Bernard M. Hermann (p),** *New Orleans* (1980). A knowledgeable, lively text and vibrant color photographs make a fascinating paean to the city. For a succinct historical survey through old photographs, see Leonard V. Huber, *New Orleans: A Pictorial History* (1971).

**Percy, Walker,** *The Moviegoer* (1961). Carnival week in New Orleans — and a

critical week in the life and loves of a young man for whom the insubstantial world of Hollywood myth is more real than his own life — by a novelist who "with compassion and without sentimentality or the mannerisms of the clinic, examines the delusions and hallucinations and the daydreams that afflict those who abstain from the customary ways of making do" (National Book Award citation).

**Saxon, Lyle,** *Fabulous New Orleans* (1928). Early description of New Orleans that is still one of the best for its historical material and its early twentieth-century view of New Orleans life.

**Stanforth, Deirdre,** *The New Orleans Restaurant Cookbook* (1976). Great dishes from the great preparers of the city's distinctive, flavorful cuisine. See *Romantic New Orleans* (1977).

**Stone, Robert,** *A Hall of Mirrors* (1967). Passionate novel about three young people in a hallucinatory New Orleans of race riots, fanaticism, poverty, and Mardi Gras.

**Toole, John Kennedy,** *A Confederacy of Dunces* (1980). Pulitzer Prize–winning novel about the memorable Ignatius J. Reilly and his hilarious, ribald, mock-heroic adventures in a flavorfully rendered New Orleans. Other noteworthy modern novels of the city include Shirley Ann Grau, *The House on Coliseum Street* (1961); Elizabeth Spencer, *The Snare* (1972); and Nelson Algren, *A Walk on the Wild Side* (1955).

## Houston

**Byrd, Sigman,** *Sig Byrd's Houston* (1955). Local columnist of a quarter-century ago — the O. Henry of Houston — writes with sympathy and freshness about the seamier side of the city's life.

**Donahue, Jack,** *The Lady Loved Too Well* (1978). The suspense novel that introduced attorney Harlan Cole, Houston's own Perry Mason, hero of a series of courtroom mysteries.

**Dresel, Gustav,** *Gustav Dresel's Houston Journal: Adventures in North America and Texas 1837–1841* (1955). Travel diary of a young German businessman who spent a couple of years carefully observing life in and around Houston — its street fights, drinking binges, tent shows.

**Haynes, Robert V.,** *A Night of Violence: The Houston Riot of 1917* (1976). Admirable study of a horrendous race riot incited by a mob of black soldiers — the first in which more whites than blacks were killed — that resulted in the largest court-martial in American history and the hanging of more than a score of men.

**Thompson, Thomas,** *Blood and Money* (1976). A mysterious death and its strange consequences are the subject of this riveting journalistic narrative set against a backdrop of moneyed Houston.

## Los Angeles

**Banham, Reyner,** *Los Angeles: The Architecture of Four Ecologies* (1969). An English architectural historian's thoughtful, stimulating celebration of the architecture to be found in the mountains, plains, beaches, and freeways of the city.

*The Best of Los Angeles: A Discriminating Guide* (curr. rev.). Indispensable guide to dining, music, shopping, art, and other amenities by seasoned LA observers.

**Bukowski, Charles,** *Post Office* (1971). The high-energy poet's autobiographical novel about a man tediously working at the Post Office who yearns to be out on the streets meeting women or playing the horses.

**Cain, James,** *Mildred Pierce* (1941). Glendale of the thirties is the setting for this absorbing, hard-edged novel of one woman's tragic life. See *Double Indemnity* (1943).

**Cameron, Robert,** *Above Los Angeles* (1976). Collection of contemporary and nostalgic aerial photographs of greater LA. Remarkable perspectives of one of the country's most ill-defined and beautiful regions.

**Didion, Joan,** *Play It as It Lays* (1970). Sparse novel of a sterile Los Angeles and one woman's attempt to endure, by one of southern California's most reflective and able writers. Other novels of LA-as-moral-wasteland include Alison Lurie, *The Nowhere City* (1966); Paula Fox, *The Western Coast* (1972); Cynthia Buchanan, *Maiden* (1970); and Carolyn See, *Mother Daughter* (1977).

**Fante, John,** *Ask the Dust* (1939). Autobiographical novel about Arturo Bandini's struggle to become a writer. See *Dreams from Bunker Hill* (1982).

**Henstell, Bruce,** *Los Angeles* (1980). Entertaining, illustrated history of the city's first 200 years. See Norman Dash, *Yesterday's Los Angeles* (1976) and John D. Weaver, *Los Angeles: The Enormous Village* (1981).

**Sinclair, Upton,** *Oil!* (1927). One of the best novels that Sinclair ever wrote, it starts with an oil strike in Long Beach and flowers into a captivating, muckraking indictment of the oil scandals of the period, especially the Teapot Dome affair.

**Waugh, Evelyn,** *The Loved One* (1948). Set against a background of embalming rooms, crematoria, and the unforgettable Whispering Glades Memorial Park, this riotous caper in the graveyards of Southern California is — underneath the laughs — as moving as death itself. Another acerbic view of the area provides the background for Aldous Huxley's *After Many a Summer Dies the Swan* (1939).

## San Francisco

**Adams, Alice,** *Beautiful Girl* (1979). Many of these moving, artfully simple short stories are set in modern San Francisco, as are her novels *Listening to Billie* (1978) and *Rich Rewards* (1980). Ella Leffland's *Love Out of Season* (1974) is a beautifully crafted love story set in the city during the sixties.

**Bean, Walton,** *Boss Ruef's San Francisco: The Story of the Union Labor Party, Big Business, and the Graft Prosecution* (1952). The bizarre career of the fabulous political kingpin of turn-of-the-century San Francisco. Freemont Older's *My Own Story* (1926) is a first-hand account of the era by a newspaper publisher who gave Ruef twenty-four hours to get out of town.

**Cameron, Robert,** *Above San Francisco* (1975). Magnificent aerial photographs interspersed with some historical photographs of the same scene.

**Dobie, Charles Caldwell,** *San Francisco: A Pageant* (1933). Informal portrait by one of the city's most fervent celebrants. His local color–ful fiction includes *Portrait of a Courtezan* (1934), *San Francisco Tales* (1935), and *San Francisco Adventures* (1937).

**Gilliam, Harold,** *The Natural World of San Francisco* (1967). Lyrical, yet scientifically precise, descriptions of the majestic play of sea, wind, rock, and sky. See *Between the Devil and the Deep Blue Sea* (1969) and *For Better or For Worse: The Ecology of an Urban Area* (1972).

**Hammett, Dashiell,** *The Maltese Falcon* (1930). Sam Spade on the streets of San Francisco, by the founder of the hard-boiled school of detective fiction. Joe Gores's marvelous tour de force, *Hammett* (1975), a novel about Hammett's Pinkerton days in San Francisco, is great reading.

**Hart, Jerome,** *In Our Second Century* (1931). Fond recollections of turn-of-the-century bohemian days by a long-time editor of the *Argonaut.*

**Lewis, Oscar,** *The Big Four* (1938). Colorful story of the millionaires Huntington, Stanford, Hopkins, and Crocker. See *Bay Window Bohemia: An Account of the Ar-*

*tistic World of Gaslit San Francisco* (1956) and *I Remember Christine* (1942), a novel of the city.

**Norris, Frank,** *McTeague* (1899). The great San Francisco novel; a sensitive story of a disappointed man, full of the color of the city. Basis for Von Stroheim's silent screen classic *Greed.*

**Walker, Franklin,** *San Francisco's Literary Frontier* (1939). Charming, anecdotal story of the days of Twain, Harte, and Bierce (1849–69), when for a moment San Francisco was the literary capital of the nation.

## Toronto

**Atwood, Margaret,** *Life Before Man* (1980). A triangle — two women and a man — in a discerning novel about the changing roles of the sexes. See *Surfacing* (1972) and her much acclaimed study of Canadian literature, *Survival: A Thematic Guide to Canadian Literature* (1972).

**Clarke, Austin,** *The Meeting Point* (1972). First of three novels portraying the fortunes of a group of West Indian domestics, their friends, lovers, spouses, and employers, in Toronto. See *Storm of Fortune* (1973) and *The Bigger Light* (1975).

**Engel, Marian,** *The Year of the Child* (1981). Poignant, funny novel about the wildly varied brood of the vital Harriet Ross that flourish on a small, eccentric Toronto street. Another good Toronto novel is Shirley Faessler, *Everything in the Window* (1980). See Morris Wolfe and Douglas Daymond (eds.), *Toronto Short Stories* (1977).

**Kilbourn, William and Rudi Christi,** *Toronto: In Words and Pictures* (1978). Affectionate view of just about every facet of the city in photographs and witty commentary. See William Dendy, *Lost Toronto* (1979).

**Wright, Richard B.,** *The Weekend Man* (1971). Fresh sad and comic first novel about a young textbook salesman estranged from his wife. "Like *Lucky Jim,* it is singularly unpretentious, funny and almost surreptitiously gifted" (Mordecai Richler). See *Farthing's Fortunes* (1976).

## Montreal

**MacLennan, Hugh,** *The Watch that Ends the Night* (1959). A vivid rendering of Montreal during the Depression, when people caught politics the way they catch religion.

**Newman, Joel,** *Dead Man's Tears* (1981). In a hard-boiled detective novel, private eye Philip Kaufman searches for clues down the mean streets of Montreal.

**Richler, Mordecai,** *The Apprenticeship of Duddy Kravitz* (1959). Jewish-American classic about the adventures of a young man on the make. *Son of a Smaller Hero* (1955) is also set in Montreal.

**Roy, Gabrielle,** *Tin Flute* (1947). Affectionate look at the life of a large French-Canadian family living in the slums of the Saint-Hewn quarter. See *the Cashier* (1955), also set in Montreal.

**Moore, Brian,** *The Luck of Ginger Coffey* (1960). Seriocomic novel of a middle-aged, blundering, mediocre Irishman in Canada. A memorable character portrait.

## London

**Betjeman, John,** *Victorian and Edwardian London from Old Photographs* (1969). The English poet laureate is an authority on Victorian architecture, a knowledge that felicitously informs this collection of rich images from London's past.

**Bowen, Elizabeth,** *The Heat of the Day* (1949). "It is the 'atmosphere' of war-time London, encapsulated so miraculously in [the novel] that survives the strange story of Stella Rodney and her lover" (Anthony Burgess). The period is rendered in

nonfiction by Mollie Panter-Downes, *London War Notes, 1939–1945* (1969).

**Burke, Thomas,** *The Streets of London Through the Centuries* (1941). Lively miscellany of London life through the centuries, embellished by a fine selection of prints, paintings, and photographs. See *Living in Bloomsbury* (1941) and *Limehouse Nights* (1917).

**Cameron, Robert (p) and Alistair Cooke (t),** *Above London* (1980). Large-format album of splendid aerial photographs that offer a unique perspective of the city.

**Conrad, Joseph,** *The Secret Agent* (1907). Suggested by the attempt of anarchists to blow up the Greenwich Observatory, this psychological thriller, set in a grimy, inhuman Edwardian London, traces the pathetic conspiracy of the agent-provocateur Verloc. Other London "terrorist" novels are Henry James, *The Princess Casamassima* (1886) and Paul Theroux, *The Family Arsenal* (1976).

**Dickens, Charles,** *Sketches by Boz* (1833–35). Satires on the daily life of the capital skillfully done by the twenty-one-year-old Dickens. See Alexander Welsh, *The City of Dickens* (1973).

**Gay, John,** *Trivia, or the Art of Walking the Streets of London* (1716). Eighteenth-century London comes to life as the poet and playwright guides the reader through its streets, introducing the strange characters that throng them. Ned Ward, *The London Spy* (1698–1709) is an equally curious guide round the town.

**Graves, Charles,** *Leather Armchairs: The Book of London Clubs* (1964). Anecdotal look at these unique institutions, starting with White's, founded in 1693, and continuing to the present day. One closes the book with the feeling that the author's "heart is sad. He has been inditing of a good matter, like the Psalmist, but he knows that the future lies with Dunkin' Donuts" (Alan Pryce-Jones).

**Hanff, Helene,** *The Duchess of Bloomsbury Street* (1973). Literary New Yorker and incorrigible Anglophile's witty and romantic impressions of her first visit to London.

**Harnett, Cynthia,** *The Drawbridge Gate* (1954). Meticulously researched adventure story for young readers about the real Dick Whittington that is full of the bustle of fifteenth-century London. Complete with illustrations and maps. The same period, the London of publisher William Caxton, is brought to life in *Caxton's Challenge* (1960).

**Hibbert, Christopher,** *London: The Biography of a City* (1970). Exuberant social history by a gifted popular historian, an "illuminating and singularly diverting book" (Jean Stafford). A graphic survey of London's history can be found in J. L. Howgego, *The City of London Through Artist's Eyes* (1969).

**James, Henry,** *The Awkward Age* (1899). Novel set in the social life of London, said to be modeled on the Asquith circle; "a cheese souffle of the leperous crust of society done to a turn and a niceness but where he puts on the *dolcissimo vox humana* stop" (Ezra Pound). Jamesian London is described in Stanley Weintraub's *The London Yankees: Portraits of American Writers and Artists in England, 1894–1914* (1979).

**Lessing, Doris,** *In Pursuit of the English* (1961). "Documentary" of the Southern Rhodesian novelist's first year in England, 1949. The London in which she found herself, "alone with a young child and little money, was a strange, still-postwar land of rations, the black-market and spivs, a vanished era which her book documents with humor and insight" (Gillian Tindall).

**MacInnes, Colin,** *The London Novels* (1969). Three works — *City of Spades* (1957), *Absolute Beginners* (1959), and *Mr. Love and Justice* (1960) — gathered in one volume that focuses on the social problems of the black, adolescent, and criminal subcultures.

**Morrison, Arthur,** *The Hole in the Wall* (1902). Novel by the author of *Tales of Mean Streets;* written from within the East End, the sinister Dockland of the 1880s. V. S. Pritchett called it "a minor masterpiece."

**Piper, David,** *Companion Guide to London* (curr. rev.). The best of the many guidebooks to the city, written with charm and authority by a distinguished art historian. See *London* (1971), an illustrated account of London's artistic and architectural development.

**Pritchett, V. S.,** *London Perceived* (1963). Originally published with photographs by Evelyn Hofer, this witty and knowing distillation of London — a panorama of its history, art, literature, and life — by one of England's leading novelists and literary critics is "one of the great essays in the language" (A. J. Liebling).

**Smith, John Thomas,** *A Book for a Rainy Day, or Recollections of the Events of the Years 1766–1833* (1845). Written by an intimate of the literary and artistic life of London, it is "one of the most entertaining and trustworthy memorials of his time" *(Cambridge History of English Literature).* Much of the same period, but of the sporting, rather than cultural, life is captured in engaging slang in Pierce Egan, *Life in London* (1821).

**Summerson, John,** *Georgian London* (rev. 1979). Learned and lively study of the architecture, and the socioeconomic conditions, during the most glorious century of the city's architecture by the foremost authority on London buildings. See George Rudé, *Hanoverian London* (1971), which does for London's character what Summerson does for its architecture.

**Woolf, Virginia,** *Mrs. Dalloway* (1925). This very readable stream-of-consciousness novel takes place one June day while Mrs. Dalloway wanders through the streets of London. Other good London novels include Margaret Drabble, *The Needle's Eye* (1972) and Iris Murdoch, *Under the Net* (1954).

## Dublin

**Beckett, Samuel,** *More Pricks than Kicks* (1934). Short stories that trace the career of Belacqua Shah — the first of Beckett's antiheroes — and reveal Beckett's underlying theme of bewilderment and suffering that informs his later works in French. Shot through with humor and a strong sense of Dublin.

**Behan, Dominic,** *Tell Dublin I Love Her* (1962). Colorful, raffish celebration of the Behan family and their neighbors of the slums around the block from where Sean O'Casey used to live.

**Donleavy, J. P.,** *The Ginger Man* (1955). Hilarious novel chronicling the roguish adventures of Sebastian Balfy Dangerfield, an American student studying law at Dublin's Trinity College.

**Gogarty, Oliver St. John,** *Mourning Became Mrs. Spendlove and Other Portraits, Grave and Gay* (1948). Miscellany of short stories, portraits, and reminiscences of Joyce, Yeats, and other Irish luminaries and of Dublin itself by the Irish physician and writer who was the model for "stately, plump Buck Mulligan." *As I Was Going Down Sackville Street* (1937) is the first of his lively memoirs. See Ulick O'Connor, *The Times I've Seen: Oliver St. John Gogarty* (1964), a biography.

**Joyce, James,** *Dubliners* (1914). Perhaps the most influential collection of stories written in English in this century: described by the author as a series of chapters in the moral history of his community. While the geographic boundary of the stories may be middle-class, Catholic Dublin, the artistic boundary is set only by Joyce's far-reaching genius. See Frank Delany, *James Joyce's Odyssey: A Guide to the Dublin of "Ulysses"* (1982).

**McGahern, John,** *The Pornographer* (1980). The pornographer is a Dublin writer, the creator of strange adventures of naughty Mavis and her irrepressible colonel. "I know no one who has caught so well the peculiar *hopelessness* of contemporary Ireland" (Anthony Burgess). See *The Leavetaking* (1975), and *The Dark* (1966), set in the rural Ireland of author's childhood.

**O'Brien, Flann,** *At Swim-Two-Birds* (1951). Neo-Joycean pastiche by a writer with a fine ear for Dublin talk, a "comic masterpiece of modern Irish literature that is as dazzling as the aurora borealis and twice as difficult to describe" (Richard Harrity). See *A Flann O'Brien Reader* (1978).

**Plunkett, James,** *Strumpet City* (1969). Novel set against the labor movement struggle in Edwardian Dublin. The city is really the protagonist. *Farewell Companions* (1978) is a companion piece. *The Gems She Wore: A Book of Irish Places* (1972) is nonfiction.

**Pritchett, V. S. (t) Evelyn Hofer (p),** *Dublin: A Portrait* (1967). Delightful book written by a wise and urbane guide with poetic photographs of the city and its people. For a good narrative history see Peter Somerville-Large, *Dublin* (1979).

**Stephens, James,** *The Charwoman's Daughter* (1912). Humorous idyll of the slums of Dublin by a poet and fictionist associated with the Irish literary renaissance. His novel *Crock of Gold* (1912) is a classic of whimsy.

## Paris

**Allen, Tony,** *Americans in Paris: An Illustrated Account of the Twenties and Thirties* (1978). Rich blend of narrative and photographs detailing the colony in Paris in the years after the First World War. See Hugh Ford, *Published in Paris: American and British Writers, Painters and Publishers in Paris, 1920–1939* (1975).

**Atget, Eugene (p) and Marcel Proust (t),** *A Vision of Paris* (1963). Photographs of Atget splendidly matched with Proust's words to evoke a Paris that has since disappeared entirely. Another superb collaboration is *Paris* (1980) by Brassai (p) and John Russell (t).

**Audemars, Pierre,** *The Turns of Time* (1961). Maigret is not alone in keeping the streets of Paris safe. This book introduces the charming M. Pinaud of the Paris Surete whose adventures are continued in subsequent novels. Fin-de-siecle Paris is the setting for Richard Grayson's *The Murders at Impasse Louvain* (1979), the premier case in a series featuring Inspector Jean-Paul Gautier.

**Bemelmans, Ludwig,** *Madeleine* (1939). The first of a classic series of children's picture-story books about the perky Madeleine and her adventures in Paris.

**Callaghan, Morley,** *That Summer in Paris: Memories of Tangled Friendships with Hemingway, Fitzgerald, and Some Others* (1963). Light, anecdotal account of a long-vanished younger generation. "The gift of moral objectivity . . . has enabled him to include in his portraits their unpleasant and outrageous traits and yet never indulge himself in malice" (Edmund Wilson). Another amusing recollection of the period by a Canadian is John Glassco, *Memoirs of Montparnasse* (1970).

**Cobb, Richard (t) and Nicholas Breach (p),** *The Streets of Paris* (1980). With charming erudition, Cobb guides a tour, not of the usual grand vistas but of the unfashionable, out-of-the-way places, in search of the unchanged Paris. Cobb has written absorbing histories of Revolutionary Paris; see *Paris and its Provinces 1792–1802* (1975) and *Death in Paris 1795–1801* (1978).

**Colette,** *The Vagabond* (1910, tr. 1955). Charming novel about a French music hall artist who hated men but could not resist them. Evokes the tangy atmosphere of the Parisian boulevard days. Paris is also richly evoked in *Chéri* and *The Last of Chéri* (tr. 1955).

**Collins, Larry and Dominique Lapierre,** *Is Paris Burning?* (1965). Popular history of the liberation of Paris from the Germans in 1944 and how Nazi General Choltitz helped save the city from the destruction ordered by Hitler. The occupation is recalled in remarkable photographs in David Pryce-Jones, *Paris in the Third Reich* (1981).

**Courthion, Pierre,** *Paris in the Past: From Fouquet to Daumier* (1957). With its companion volume, *Paris in Our Time: From Impressionism to the Present Day* (1957), the history of the city from the fourteenth to the twentieth century, presented in the pictures of the great French painters.

**Flanner, Janet,** *Paris Was Yesterday, 1925–1939* (1972). Selections from the "Letters from Paris" column of the *New Yorker* by a woman who illuminated French life and defined manners and morals. See volumes for 1944–65 and for 1965–71.

**Handke, Peter,** *A Moment of True Feeling* (1977). An Austrian beset with Sartrean nausea wanders through Paris; at every step his feelings are interwoven with acute observation of its streets, buildings, cafes; an evocative journey in a city that is at once supportive and familiar, strange and provocative.

**Hemingway, Ernest.** *A Moveable Feast* (1964). Recollections of Paris during the early twenties, an attempt to clear the record: nostalgic, gossipy, sometimes acerbic and embarrassing, always interesting. A nice complement is Robert E. Gajdusek's *Hemingway's Paris* (1978) with its almost 200 stunning photographs of Paris.

**James, Henry,** *The Ambassadors* (1903). "His supreme offering to Paris," as Cyril Connolly said about this novel. James said, "Nothing is more easy than to state the subject. 'Love all you can; it's a mistake not to.' " See *Parisian Sketches* (1957), a collection of passages from letters James sent to the *New York Tribune* in the 1870s, edited by Leon Edel and Ilsa Dusoir Lind.

Kertesz, Andre, *J'aime Paris: Photographs Since the Twenties* (1974). Beautifully reproduced black-and-white photographs of haunting beauty. Other good albums are Paris/Magnum: *Photographs 1937–1980* (1981) and Alecio de Andrade (p) and Julio Cortagar (t), *Paris, The Essence of an Image* (1981).

Lopez, Claude Anne, *Mon Cher Papa: Franklin and the Ladies of Paris* (1966). Not just another American-in-Paris story — an entertaining account of Benjamin Franklin's friendship with the ladies of the eighteenth-century city and their assistance in his political mission. See Susan Mary Alsop, *The First Americans in Paris* (1982).

Miller, Henry, *Tropic of Cancer* (1934). Thinly fictionalized early experiences of Miller in Paris are the subject of this "gay, fierce, shocking, profound, sometimes brilliant, sometimes madly irritating first novel" (Cyril Connolly).

Queneau, Raymond, *Zazie* (1960). Zazie, a pink-cheeked, decadent, Gaelic Lolita, whose weekend visit to Paris turns into a roller-coaster escapade through burlesqued perversion, civilized absurdities and cultural booby traps. A virtuoso display of verbal pyrotechnics, philosophical gags, social and literary satire, and sheer tease — all woven into a ribald fantasy.

Richardson, Joanne, *La Vie Parisienne, 1852–1870* (1971). Portrait of the age of Flaubert, the Goncourts, Offenbach, and Baudelaire admirably painted. Succeeding decades are handsomely portrayed in Raymond Rudorff, *The Belle Epoque: Paris in the Nineties* (1973) and Nigel Gosling, *The Adventurous World of Paris, 1900–1914* (1978).

Simenon, Georges (t) and Frederick Franck (i), *Simenon's Paris* (1970). Beautifully made book of extracts from Simenon's Paris stories with Franck's sensitive drawings. Another novelist-illustrator collaboration is Irwin Shaw and Ronald Searle, *Paris! Paris!* (1977).

Stein, Gertrude, *The Autobiography of Alice B. Toklas* (1933). Charming, anecdotal, wise record of nearly thirty years of life in an exciting Paris. Nominally the recollections of the author's companion, it is, of course, the biography of Gertrude Stein and of the modern art movement. See James Mellow, *Charmed Circle: Gertrude Stein and Company* (1974).

Wiser, William, *Disappearances* (1980). Complex, richly worded novel of young American in Paris in 1919 on the periphery of Gertrude Stein's charmed circle; his "portrait of Paris may be the best in English since Henry Miller's *Tropic of Cancer*" (Anatole Broyard).

## Rome

Bowen, Elizabeth, *A Time in Rome* (1960). Personal impressions and reflections of Rome rendered in exquisite prose.

Clark, Eleanor, *Rome and a Villa* (1952). Impressions by a National Book Award–winning writer with a "genius for attention, observation and recording [who] sees with beautiful accuracy the differences between things. With a true sense and love of the grand, the tragic, the beautiful, she has that necessary sense of their opposites." (Katherine Anne Porter).

Clough, Arthur Hugh, *Amours de Voyage* (1858). Seriocomic epistolary novel in hexameters by "one of the few Victorians who seem to belong to our age rather than their own. . . . The account of Rome is a wonderful evocation of the Rome that is in our minds, mixed up with our private life and business, our incapacity to answer the numberless questions that come from the city that has more of human fate in each of its stones than any city on earth" (V. S. Pritchett).

Hayes, Alfred, *The Girl on the Via Flaminia* (1949). Slim, spare novel about a love affair between an American GI and a young Roman woman during the last year of World War II. See *All the Conquests* (1946).

**Krautheimer, Richard,** *Rome: Profile of a City 312–1308* (1980). Exemplary profile of medieval Rome, from the time of Constantine to the removal of the papacy to Avignon.

**Hare, Augustus C.,** *Walks in Rome* (1871). First edition of famous early guide book by the English writer and artist that accompanied countless Victorian travelers. It remains informative and amusing. A sparkling view of the city today can be had in Paul Hofmann, *Rome: The Sweet, Tempestuous Life* (1982).

**Morante, Elsa,** *History: A Novel* (1977). Long, rich novel about the brief life of a bastard child from 1941 to 1947, but also a fine portrait of Rome during the war.

**Moravia, Alberto,** *Roman Tales* (1957). Vignettes of life among the city's poor by one of Italy's ranking novelists. See *More Roman Tales* (1963).

**Piranesi, Giovanni Battista,** *Views of Rome* (1748–78). Famous series of etchings of monuments of ancient and Renaissance Rome. *Views of Rome Then and Now* (1976) matches forty-one of the etchings with corresponding photographs.

**Stendhal,** *A Roman Journal* (1829). Grand tour of Rome described with wit and sensitivity. Much of it is pure invention, but it is nevertheless fascinating as a tour of Stendhal.

## Florence

**Cochrane, Eric,** *Florence in the Forgotten Centuries 1527–1800: A History of the Florentines in the Age of the Grand Duke* (1973). A magisterial work, brilliantly conceived and executed, that reads like a novel.

**McCarthy, Mary,** *The Stones of Florence* (1963). Full-bodied living portrait of the glories of Florence in sharply-defined photographs and a brilliant text. Andre Barrett's *Florence Observed* (1974) is also an excellent text-and-photo volume.

**Malaparte, Curzio,** *Those Cursed Tuscans* (1964). Strange and lively extended essay on the author's native region of Tuscany, of which Florence is the principal city. It is inventive, capricious, often affected, exasperating, amazing, and essential for an understanding of the region.

**Pratolini, Vasco,** *The Naked Streets* (1945). One of the Florentine author's novels about the working class, told with verve and clarity. See *A Tale of Poor Lovers* (1946). *Metello* (1955) is the first of an affectionate, realistic trilogy of nineteenth-century Florence.

**Spencer, Elizabeth,** *The Light in the Piazza* (1960). Short novel of subtle and delicate irony about a mother and daughter; "the peculiar quality of Florence permeates the book and the spirit of the City is a force in the story" (Granville Hicks).

## Naples

**Belmonte, Thomas,** *The Broken Fountain* (1979). Eloquent social study by an American anthropologist who lived for a year in a poor Neapolitan neighborhood.

**Burns, John Horne,** *The Gallery* (1947). Naples in ruin near the end of World War II is the setting of this powerful novel which evokes the *Galleria Umberto Primo* where pimps, whores, black-market operators, and thieves as well as the poor, starving, honest people gathered. Gore Vidal called it the best book of World War II.

**Douglas, Norman,** *Siren Land* (1911). Erudite and humanity-filled blend of personal, scenic, historical, and legendary features of the "siren land" — Capri and the Peninsula of Sorrento.

**Hazzard, Shirley,** *The Bay of Noon* (1970). Intelligent, elegant novel about an English girl's loss of innocence in a perfectly drawn Naples. Anna Marie Ortese's *The Bay Is Not Naples* (1955) and Gwyn

Griffin's *A Last Lamp Burning* (1965) also evoke the city wonderfully.

**Lewis, Norman,** *Naples '44* (1979). Unforgettable episodes and memorable bizarre characters in an extraordinary diary of a year in Naples at the time of its occupation by the Allies. Aubrey Menen's *Four Days in Naples* (1979) recounts the bloody street fighting involving Neapolitan street urchins and German soldiers.

## Venice

**Canaletto, Antonio,** *Views of Venice by Canaletto* (1975). Gathering of the eighteenth-century Venetian painter's broad, detailed "views" of the city.

**Howells, William Dean,** *Venetian Life* (rev. 1907). The one-time "dean of American letters" spent the Civil War years in Venice as consul. On his return to America in 1866, he published these letters and impressions, which charmingly evoke nineteenth-century Venice.

**James, Henry,** *The Aspern Papers* (1888). A long story — "the beautiful and blest *nouvelle,*" as James called the form — about a man obsessed by an unnatural passion for the papers of a dead poet and his "battles and strategems" to obtain them during a moodily rendered Venetian summer. *The Portrait of a Lady* and *The Wings of the Dove* have some Venetian backdrops.

**Lauritzen, Peter (t) and Alexander Zielcke (p),** *Palaces of Venice* (1978). Lavish coffee-table volume focusing on forty-five of the most famous palaces, magnificently photographed and expressively described. See *Islands and Lagoons of Venice* (1980) and *Venice: A Thousand Years of Culture and Civilization* (1978).

**McAndrew, John,** *Venetian Architecture of the Early Renaissance* (1980). Offers a knowledge not only of the great churches and palaces but of Venice itself.

**McCarthy, Mary,** *Venice Observed* (1956). Searching observations and splendid

photographs combine to make this personal interpretation of Venice a classic.

**Mann, Thomas,** *Death in Venice* (1913). Masterful short novel about the German writer Aschenbach's infatuation with the Polish boy Tadzio, which serves as a symbol for several of Mann's favorite themes, including the "dizziness on the edge of the abyss of art."

**Morris, James,** *The World of Venice* (rev. 1974). "Highly intelligent portrait of an eccentric city, written in powerful prose and enlivened by many curious mosaics of information. . . . It is a beautiful book to be read and to possess" (Harold Nicolson). See *The Venetian Empire: A Sea Voyage* (1980).

**Pasinette, P. M.,** *Venetian Red* (1960). The vicissitudes of two families of Venice in the years before the Second World War in a warm novel by a Venetian novelist. See *The Smile on the Face of the Lion* (1965). Other modern novels of Venice include Muriel Spark, *Territorial Rights* (1979) and Hans Habe, *Palazzo* (1977).

**Ruskin, John,** *John Ruskin's Venice* (1976). Fine distillation of *The Stones of Venice* (1851–53) and *St. Mark's Rest: The History of Venice* (1877–84). The former was published in a handsome abridged version, edited and introduced by Jan Morris, in 1981.

## Vienna

**Barea, Ilsa,** *Vienna* (1966). Felicitous blend of history and personal memoir that scoops away the whipped cream and reveals the real Vienna.

**Doderer, Heimito Von,** *The Demons* (1961). Huge novel, a large-scale canvas of Vienna in the 1920s. "An intricate, passionately conservative, magnificent book" (Frederic Morton).

**Gainham, Sarah,** *Night Falls on the City* (1967). The first of a trilogy of Strauss-and-Sachertorte novels set in the days of

Franz Joseph by an accomplished and romantic storyteller. Edith de Born's *Fielding Castle* (1959) is another superior romance of the same period.

**Lauterstein, Ingeborg,** *The Water Castle* (1981). Two worlds collide in this novel: the refined world of Austrian aristocracy and the brutal world of Nazi occupation. It is narrated by a Viennese girl who grows from childhood into young womanhood as the Third Reich rises and falls.

**Musil, Robert,** *Man Without Qualities* (1953–60). Unfinished, 1,600 pages long, and set in pre–World War I Vienna, it is Musil's *magnum opus* and has been ranked by some with the works of Mann, Proust, and Joyce. Frank Kermode said, "He was a great man, and everybody should find out why."

**Pick, Robert,** *The Last Days of Imperial Vienna* (1976). Impressionistic view of the end of the Habsburg Empire, 1916–19, as seen from the capital. Other evocations of the Imperial period include Sarah Gainham, *The Habsburg Twilight: Tales from Vienna* (1979); William M. Johnston, *Vienna, Vienna: The Golden Age 1815–1914* (1981); Arthur J. May, *Vienna in the Age of Franz Joseph* (1975); and Frederic Morton, *A Nervous Splendor: Vienna 1888–1889* (1979).

**Pryce-Jones, David,** *Vienna* (1978). English writer presents a bouquet to Vienna, part of the superb Time-Life Great Cities series.

**Schnitzler, Arthur,** *Viennese Novelettes* (1931). Five tales published in the 1920s about prewar Vienna by a dramatist who was also a master of the psychological short story. See *The Little Comedy and Other Stories* (1978) and *My Youth in Vienna* (1971).

**Schorske, Carl E.,** *Fin-de-Siecle Vienna* (1979). Rewarding collection of essays written over a twenty-five-year period that provide a luminous intellectual history of the era of Freud, Wagner, Klimt, and Herzl. The world of painting of the

period is portrayed in Peter Verga, *Art in Vienna, 1898–1918* (1981).

**Wechsberg, Joseph,** *Vienna, My Vienna* (1969). Affectionate illustrated look at the city's history, architecture, music, coffeehouse life, etc. by the Vienna-raised author. See *The Vienna I Knew: Memories of a European Childhood* (1979).

## Berlin

**Berger, Thomas,** *Crazy in Berlin* (1958). The American Carlo Reinhart loose in the bizarre ruins of Berlin at the close of World War II. First of the celebrated Reinhart series of novels.

**Deighton, Len,** *Funeral in Berlin* (1965). Berlin was a popular milieu for cold war thrillers in the sixties. This story about a British agent's attempt to smuggle a Russian scientist out of East Berlin is one of the best. Other Berlin thrillers are Adam Hall, *Quiller Memorandum* (1965); W. T. Tyler, *The Man Who Lost the War* (1979); and David Brierly, *Big Bear, Little Bear* (1981).

**Friedrich, Otto,** *Before the Deluge: A Portrait of Berlin in the 1920's* (1972). Vivid, haunting account of a unique moment in time, a world to itself, a prelude to the deluge that engulfed Europe. See Wolf Von Eckhardt and Sandor L. Gilman, *Bertolt Brecht's Berlin: A Scrapbook of the Twenties* (1975).

**Grosz, George,** *Ecce Homo* (1966). Collection of acidulous drawings by the satiric illustrator whose work defined the Berlin of the twenties. His autobiography, *A Little Yes, A Big No* (1946) is very illuminating of the period. The memoirs of Rheinish playwright Carl Zuckmayer, *A Part of Myself* (1970), bring the times alive.

**Grunfeld, Frederic V.,** *Berlin* (rev. 1967). Part of the Time-Life Great Cities series, it is a beautifully illustrated social and cultural history of the city. See *Prophets Without Honor: A Background to Freud, Kafka, Einstein and Their World* (1979), about the most exciting epoch of modern German intellectual history.

**Isherwood, Christopher,** *The Berlin Stories* (1945). First published in 1935 and 1939, the two related novels, *The Last of Mr. Norris* and *Goodbye to Berlin,* portray a charming city of avenues and cafes, a grotesque city of night people and fantasts — both were Berlin in 1931, the period when Hitler was beginning to make his move to power. The musical *Cabaret* was adapted from this book.

**Johnson, Uwe,** *Two Views* (1965). Story of two lovers who suddenly find themselves separated by the Berlin Wall, by a novelist who has made the two Germanys his literary province. See *The Third Book About Achim* (1967) and *Speculations About Jacob* (1963).

**Kästner, Erich,** *Emil and the Detectives* (1930). Life in Berlin is viewed through the eyes of a small boy who leads a band of his friends in catching a bank robber. A classic for children ten and up.

**Nabokov, Vladimir,** *Laughter in the Dark* (1938). "Once upon a time there lived in Berlin, Germany, a man called Albinus. He was, rich, respectable, happy; one day he abandoned his wife for the sake of a youthful mistress; he loved, was not loved; and his life ended in disaster." So reads the outline on the first page of this strange, skillful novel. Nabokov's other Berlin novels are *King, Queen, Knave* (tr. 1968) and *Mary* (tr. 1970).

**Ryan, Cornelius,** *The Last Battle* (1966). Solidly researched journalistic account of the fall of Berlin to the Soviets in 1945. For a Russian view, see Theodore Plievier, *Berlin* (1956).

## Prague

**Hampl, Patricia,** *A Romantic Education* (1981). A poet who grew up in Minnesota with roots in Czechoslovakia goes to Prague to reflect on and interpret contemporary life in the capital. Her collection of poems, *Women Before an Aquarium* (1978), includes many pieces about her Czech background.

**Hrabel, Bohumel,** *The Death of Mrs. Bottisberger* (1975). Novel about the slightly zany world of some unforgettable, not quite believable, ordinary people of Prague. See *Closely Watched Trains* (1968).

**Kahout, Pavel,** *From the Diary of a Counterrevolutionary* (1972). Juxtaposed diaries, factual and fictional, by the Czech journalist-playwright who was involved in the Prague Spring of 1968; "it is the complicated biography of a generation that grew up questioning its allegiance to a Soviet satellite state" (Sanche de Granmont).

**Korecky, Miroslav,** *Prague in Color* (1977). Handsome large-format book of photographs by a Czech art historian.

**Wechsberg, Joseph,** *Prague: The Mystical City* (1971). Understated, informed journey through Prague by the Austrian-born writer who grew up in the city. In *Homecoming* (1946) he tells of his return as an American soldier to his old home.

## Moscow

**Lee, Andrea,** *Russian Journal* (1981). A young Russian-speaking American spent ten months in the Soviet Union with her husband, a graduate student studying in Moscow. In elegant prose she describes the segment of Russian society that she came to know. George Feifer, *Moscow Farewell* (1976) is an artful "fictional nonfiction" account of an American graduate student.

**Leonov, Leonid,** *The Thief* (1931). Set in vividly evoked "Lower Depths" of Moscow, this long, brawling novel portrays a former cavalry officer who, disaffected with the dull life of serving the Soviet state, becomes a thief.

**Martin, Jay,** *Winter Dreams: An American in Moscow* (1979). For five months

Martin was a visiting professor in the capital, during which time he had many dramatic adventures.

**Muggeridge, Malcolm,** *Winter in Moscow* (1934). Amusingly malicious book by the English journalist who was for eight months Moscow correspondent for the *Manchester Guardian.* Fiercely anti-Soviet, he wittily lampoons such Russia-lovers of the time as Duranty and Nevinson.

**Smith, Martin Cruz,** *Gorky Park* (1981). Gripping detective novel about a triple murder and its solution by Moscow cop Arkady Renko. Another first-rate Moscow thriller is Anthony Olcott, *Murder at the Red October* (1981).

## Jerusalem

**Collins, Larry and Dominique Lapierre,** *O Jerusalem* (1971). Dramatic, swiftly told account of the events in the struggle of 1948 in which the Arabs and Jews fought each other for the city. The battle is the background for Yoram Kaniuk's novel, *Himmo, King of Jerusalem* (1969).

**Oz, Amos,** *The Hill of Evil Counsel* (1978). Three related stories that look at Israel from the perspective of a boy growing up in Jerusalem during the waning days of the British mandate. *My Michael* (1972) is also set in the city.

**Shahar, David,** *News from Jerusalem* (1974). Collection of short stories set in the rich atmosphere of Jerusalem's mingled traditions. See *The Palace of Shattered Vessels* (1975) and *His Majesty's Agent* (1980). Shulamith Hareven's *City of Many Days* (1977) is a sensitively rendered novel about growing up in Jerusalem during the first half of this century.

**Uris, Jill and Leon Uris,** *Jerusalem, Song of Songs* (1981). The enchanting beauty of Jerusalem is revealed in this wedding of photographs with text by the author of the popular *Exodus.* For viewing it in the flesh, the outstanding guide is Sarah Fox Kaminker, *Footloose in Jerusalem: 8 Guided Walking Tours* (rev. 1981).

**Wiesel, Elie,** *A Beggar in Jerusalem* (1970). These stories of people who have gathered at the famous Wailing Wall are imbued with the spiritual and philosophical concerns that distinguish Wiesel's writings. See *Dawn* (1961) and *The Traitor* (1981).

## Other Cities

**McGreevy, John (ed.),** *Cities* (1981). Baker's dozen of personalities write paeans to their favorite cities — Anthony Burgess on Rome, Germaine Greer on Sydney, Studs Terkel on Chicago, etc.

**Menen, Aubrey,** *Cities in the Sand* (1973). Leptis Magna, Timgad, Palmyra, and Petra — once mighty, now reduced to ruins — described in writing rich and sure.

**Morris, James,** *Cities* (1963). Over seventy cities vividly described by the finest contemporary travel writer (now known as Jan Morris). See *Places* (1972), *Travels* (1976), and *Destinations* (1980).

**Time-Life Editors,** *The Great Cities* (1976–81). Twenty-five-volume series of the highest quality photojournalism with well-produced color plates, each volume by a distinguished writer.

**Toynbee, Arnold (ed.),** *Cities of Destiny* (1967). Immense book with magnificent color reproductions about eighteen major cities of different eras, each given a chapter written by a prominent author (e.g., Maurice Bowra on Periclean Athens, Sir Steven Runciman on Christian Constantinople) and a portfolio sampling its artistic life.

# STREETS

**Hiroshige, Ando,** *The Fifty-three Stages of the Tokaido* (1832). Series of marvelous woodblock prints portraying the national highway connecting Tokyo with the capital at Kyoto and the western provinces. Along the way were fifty-three stations in small villages where lodgings and refreshments were available.

**Naipaul, V. S.,** *Miguel Street* (1960). Miguel Street is a sort of Cannery Row of Port of Spain, Trinidad. The eccentric lives of its inhabitants are fictionally portrayed in finely wrought sketches.

**Petry, Ann,** *The Street* (1946). On a street in Harlem, in a tiny dark apartment lives a young black woman and her small son. This powerful novel describes her struggles to earn security for herself against the pressures of social circumstances and the violence of overcrowded streets.

**Richler, Mordecai,** *The Street* (1975). Light, affectionate "semifictional" memoir of growing up Jewish on Montreal's St. Urbain Street in the 1940s. See *St. Urbain's Horseman* (1971) and *Joshua Then and Now* (1980).

**Seuss, Dr.,** *And to Think That I Saw It on Mulberry Street* (1937). One little boy saw the most remarkable things on Mulberry Street in this charming early Dr. Seuss picture book.

# HABITATION

## *House*

**Bowen, Elizabeth,** *The House in Paris* (1935). Through a chance meeting of two children in a house in Paris, the tale of a tragic love affair is revealed. A novel with a supreme subtlety of feeling and atmosphere.

**Fairbrother, Nan,** *The House in the Country* (1965). The author's account of building a family house in England is "a hymn to the spirit of place, sung round a house in the country, the choice, its building, its inhabitants. . . . She has cunningly transformed her house into a work of literature." (Alan Pryce-Jones).

**Girouard, Mark,** *Life in the English Country House* (1978). A classic social and architectural history. Another superb book by this exceptional writer is *The Victorian Country House* (rev. 1979). See Jill Franklin, *The Gentleman's Country House and Its Plan, 1835–1914* (1981).

**Hawthorne, Nathaniel,** *The House of Seven Gables* (1851). The great seven-gabled house of the Pyncheons in Salem, Massachusetts, is the setting for this romance about how the sins of the fathers affect their children.

**Johnson, Josephine W.,** *Seven Houses: A Memoir of Time and Places* (1973). A Pulitzer Prize–winning novelist remembers her childhood homes in the Midwest, not as architecture but as experiences, in a quiet, evocative memoir.

**Lockley, Ronald,** *Orielton: The Human and Natural History of a Welsh Manor* (1978). A naturalist describes his ten years as owner of an 800-year-old manor house and its surrounding acres.

**Lubbock, Percy,** *Earlham* (1922). Earlham Manor was the house of his mother's family in Norfolk, England, where he spent his summers as a boy. A masterpiece of evocation of the best Victorian Quaker traditions.

**Mora, E. S.,** *Japanese Homes and Their Surroundings* (1961). The best introduction to the architectural and domestic aspects of the Japanese home by an unusually sensitive writer. See Bernard Rudofsky, *The Kimono Mind* (1965).

**Sarton, May,** *Plant Dreaming Deep* (1968). A poet and novelist tells of buying an eighteenth-century home in a New Hampshire town and what she learned from the house. A tender, luminous book.

**Walker, Lester,** *American Shelter: An Illustrated Encyclopedia of the American House* (1981). More than 100 different styles of houses are illustrated in chronological order from the Indian earth lodge to projections of space dwellings. Informative and charming.

## Apartment and Boarding House

**Disch, Thomas,** *334* (1974). The lives of the tenants at 334 East Eleventh Street, New York City, a government housing project in the future, are described in this powerful, pessimistic science-fiction novel.

**Taylor, Elizabeth,** *Mrs. Palfrey at the Claremont* (1971). Superb novel about a group of people facing old age in a sad residential hotel in London.

**Trevor, William,** *Mrs. Eckdorf in O'-Neill's Hotel* (1970). Comedy and pathos mix in this story of a group of misfits fighting each other over who will run the place. A beautifully controlled novel. See *The Boarding House* (1965).

**Voinovich, Valdimir,** *The Ivankiad, or the Tale of the Writer Voinovich's Installation in His New Apartment* (1977). This satirical account of how the author wrangled with his neighbor for a two-room apartment in the Moscow Writers' Cooperative is not only very funny but is a window into the workings of the Soviet system.

**Wallant, Edward Lewis,** *The Tenants of Moonbloom* (1963). The rootlessness of urban life is at the heart of this novel about the tenants of a rundown apartment house in New York City.

PART II

# NATURE

# NATURE

**Bateson, Gregory,** *Mind and Nature* (1979). The English anthropologist seeks to find the patterns that connect living things. A demanding work that uses the most recent findings of genetics and evolutionary theory. See *Steps to an Ecology of Mind* (1972).

**Cole, William (ed.),** *A Book of Nature Poems* (1969). Tasteful anthology, ranging from Coleridge to Plath, Emerson to Updike. An excellent prose anthology is Hal Borland (ed.), *Our Natural World* (1969).

**Cottrell, Alan,** *Portrait of Nature: The World as Seen by Modern Science* (1975). "A book that in directness, breadth of learning, and elegant prose style will rank with the very best of the classic science books for the layman" *(Times Literary Supplement).*

**Eiseley, Loren,** *The Immense Journey* (1957). In an unusual blend of scientific knowledge and imaginative vision, the author, an anthropologist and naturalist, meditates on life's endless mysteries. See *The Firmament of Time* (1960) and *The Unexpected Universe* (1969).

**Frisch, Karl Von,** *Man and the Living World* (rev. 1963). Engaging, brilliant study of man and his environment by the Nobel Prize–winning Austrian zoologist and ethologist.

*The Golden Nature Series.* Little paperbacks, informative, beautiful, and inexpensive, on virtually every aspect of nature from fossils to stars, from insects to seashells. Golden Books also publishes a series of very useful field guides.

**Krutch, Joseph Wood,** *The Great Chain of Life* (1956). Fine introduction to natural history by literary critic turned naturalist. See *The Best Nature Writings of Joseph Wood Krutch* (1970).

**Ley, Willy,** *Dragons in Amber* (1951). Good-natured, rambling look at life before man. Pop paleontology at its best.

**Porter, Eliot,** *Intimate Landscapes* (1979). Beautifully composed photographs by a camera artist with an "inward response to nature that imparts a lyric grace to the whole enterprise. What mastery!" (Hilton Kramer). See *In Wilderness Is the Preservation of the World* (1962).

**Rensberger, Boyce,** *The Cult of the Wild* (1977). Thoughtful, well-written nature essays by a *New York Times* science writer.

# PRESERVATION

**Abbey, Edward,** *The Monkey Wrench Gang* (1976). A sort of comic extravaganza about a band of Southwesterners who try to defend the land against "alien" invaders, by a writer who loves unfenced country. See *Good News* (1981), a novel, and his collected nonfiction pieces in *The Journey Home: Some Words in Defense of the American West* (1977), *Abbey's Road* (1979), and *Down the River* (1982).

**Bates, Marston,** *The Forest and the Sea: A Look at the Economy of Nature and the Ecology of Man* (1960). A distinguished zoologist's nontechnical textbook of ecology. See *The Nature of Natural History* (1950).

**Benford, Gregory,** *Timescape* (1981). Award-winning science-fiction novel about a physicist in 1962 who receives a message from a group of scientists in 1998 faced with ecological disaster who want to tell their ancestors what to do to save themselves from a future that has already occurred.

**Berry, Wendell,** *The Unsettling of America: Culture and Agriculture* (1977). Eloquent polemic by a poet who is close to the heart of things and who expresses what America would like to believe it is and may yet be. See *Recollected Essays, 1965–1980* (1981) and *The Gift of Good Land* (1981).

**Bodsworth, Fred,** *Last of the Curlews* (1955). Immense flocks of Eskimo curlews were slaughtered by sportsmen and meat-hunters in the space of a few decades. This is the moving story of the last of these beautiful birds that conservation laws came too late to protect.

**Callenbach, Ernest,** *Ecotopia* (1975). Provocative utopia novel in which northern California, Oregon, and Washington form a nation in which a sane ecology policy dominates. An intriguing and instructive fantasy. See *Ecotopia Emerging* (1981), a "prequel."

**Carson, Rachel,** *Silent Spring* (1962). Landmark book on the environment; a devastating indictment of our use of chemical insecticides. See Frank Graham, *Since Silent Spring* (1970).

**Colinvaux, Paul,** *Why Big Fierce Animals Are Rare* (1978). Complex concepts are gracefully explained in this short, enchanting book by a zoologist-ecologist who has a knack for asking all the right questions. See *Introduction to Ecology* (1973) and *The Fates of Nations: A Biological Theory of History* (1980).

**Commoner, Barry,** *The Closing Circle: Nature, Man and Technology* (1971). Ecological classic in lucid prose about technological pollution of the environment. See *Science and Survival* (1966) and *The Politics of Energy* (1979).

**Dasmann, Raymond,** *Last Horizon* (1963). An ecologist, eloquent and passionate in his beliefs, poses some hard questions and finds there are no easy answers. See *Planet in Peril: Man and the Biosphere Today* (1972) and *The Conservation Alternative* (1975).

**Dorst, Jean,** *Before Nature Dies* (1970). Brilliant survey by leading French zoologist of man's impact on the whole biosphere.

**Ehrenfeld, David,** *Conserving Life on Earth* (1972). Plea for global conservation, with case studies of ecosystems. A level-headed, thought-provoking book.

**Ehrlich, Paul,** *The Population Bomb* (rev. 1971). Modern classic that argues for population control. See *How to Be a Survivor* (1971) and *Extinction: The Causes and Consequences of the Disappearance of Species* (1981).

**Eiseley, Loren,** *The Invisible Pyramid* (1970). Man's landing on the moon is the takeoff point for these eloquent meditations on the environmental crisis.

**Gary, Romain,** *The Roots of Heaven* (1956). An idealist's efforts to save the elephants of equatorial Africa from being hunted to extinction furnishes the action in this dramatic novel of ideas.

**Hardin, Garrett,** *Exploring New Ethics for Survival: The Voyage of the Spaceship Beagle* (1973). Leading ecologist illustrates the competing interests on earth in this fictional log of a spaceship. Includes essays on the environmental situation. See *The Limits of Altruism: An Ecological View of Survival* (1977).

**Hayes, Harold T. P.,** *Three Levels of Time* (1981). In a world of limited resources and increasing demand, can human life survive? He traveled the world to ask Richard Leakey, Archie Carr, E. F. Schumacher, and many other experts. He adds two additional "levels": a cosmic perspective on the origins of life, and a dramatic personal perspective on one man's evasion of almost certain death.

**McHugh, Tom,** *The Time of the Buffalo* (1972). Evolution of the bison and its relationship with three cultures of man; a finely illustrated study.

**McPhee, John,** *Encounters with the Archdruid* (1971). These encounters between a crusading conservationist and three other men "who got their success from a different kind of religion with respect to nature — one that sees man first — take place in continental settings of great splendor . . . [and are written] with conscious balance and sophistication"

(John Hay). A marvelous piece of work by a master prose stylist.

**Orwell, George,** *Coming up for Air* (1939). Engaging novel about a middle-aged man who returns to the village where he was born and surveys the damage done by industrialization. "One of the most powerful novels ever written about the threat to what we now call the environment" (Margaret Drabble).

**Passmore, John,** *Man's Responsibility for Nature* (1974). Subtitled *Ecological Problems and Western Traditions,* it is a thoughtful challenge to the sentimental view of man in nature.

**Sears, Paul B.,** *The Living Landscape* (1967). One of the best writers on conservation describes the planet as a living entity. An eloquent plea for conservation. See *Where There Is Life* (1962).

**Smith, W. Eugene and Aileen M. Smith,** *Minimata* (1975). Minimata is the prefecture in Japan poisoned by methyl mercury. Unforgettable account in photographs and words of the effects of the pollution.

**Snyder, Gary,** *Turtle Island* (1974). The Pulitzer Prize–winning poet's collection of poetry and prose that share a vision: the rediscovery of this land and the ways by which we might become natives of the place instead of invaders. See *Earth House Hold* (1969).

**Swan, Christopher and Chet Roaman,** *YU83: An Eco-fiction of Tomorrow* (1977). Imaginative collection of detailed plans, news items, and other documents about the development of Yosemite Valley into a wilderness area.

# PRINCIPLES: THEORY

## Physical

**Davies, Paul,** *Other Worlds: A Portrait of Nature and Rebellion, Space, Superspace, and the Quantum Universe* (1981). Lucid explanation of the frontiers of quantum physics by English theoretical physicist. See *The Runaway Universe* (1978) and *The Edge of Infinity* (1982).

**Feinberg, Gerald,** *What Is the World Made Of?* (1977). Atoms, leptons, quarks, and other tantalizing particles, of course — all of which you will know and love after reading this concise guide to subatomic phenomena. Two other entertaining introductions to physics for nonscientists are B. K. Ridley, *Time, Space and Things* (1976) and Fred Wolf, *Taking the Quantum Leap* (1981). For a touch of "meta-physics" see Fritjof Capra, *The Tao of Physics* (1975) and Gary Zukov, *The Dancing Wu Li Masters* (1979).

**Gamow, George,** *Thirty Years that Shook Physics: The Story of the Quantum Theory* (1966). Quantum theory lucidly explained with illustrations and anecdotes by a distinguished Russian-American nuclear physicist and master popularizer. See *Gravity* (1962), *Mr. Tompkins in Paperback* (1966), and *The Biography of Physics* (1961).

**Gardner, Martin,** *The Ambidextrous Universe: Mirror Asymmetry and Time-Reversal Worlds* (1979). Mirrors, parity, the fourth dimension, and more felicitously explained in this modern classic by the author of the mathematical games column of *Scientific American.* See *Fads and Fallacies in the Name of Science* (rev. 1957), *Science: Good, Bad and Bogus* (1981), and *Relativity for the Million* (1962).

**McPhee, John,** *The Curve of Binding Energy* (1974). Eloquent portrait of Theodore Taylor, a theoretical physicist bent on creating systems that prevent nuclear materials from falling into the hands of do-it-yourselfers.

**Walker, Jearl,** *The Flying Circus of Physics* (1975). An imaginative, enjoyable introduction to physics made up of 600 questioning paragraphs.

## Chemical

**Asimov, Isaac,** *A Short History of Chemistry* (1965). Excellent popular scientific history. A little more sophisticated is Aaron J. Ihde, *The Development of Modern Chemistry* (1964).

**Curie, Eve,** *Madame Curie* (1937). Classic biography of her mother, the Polish scientist who won Nobel Prizes in chemistry and physics.

**Friend, J. Newton,** *Man and the Chemical Elements* (rev. 1961). Anecdotal history of each of the elements.

**Read, John,** *Prelude to Chemistry* (1966). Alchemy, felicitously explained.

**Smith, Richard F.,** *Chemistry for the Million* (1972). Easy-to-read primer that anchors the science firmly in history and the arts.

## Mathematical

**Bell, Eric Temple,** *The Magic of Numbers* (1946). One of several stimulating math books that can be enjoyed by non-MENSA members. See *Mathematics, Queen and Servant of Science* (1951) and *Men of Mathematics* (1937).

**Courant, Richard and Herbert Robbins,** *What Is Mathematics?* (1941). Provides an elementary approach to ideas and methods: a classic of its kind. Other good introductions are Norman Gowar, *An Invitation to Mathematics,* (1980) and Harold R. Jacobs, *Mathematics: A Human Endeavor* (1970).

**Ellis, Keith,** *Number Power in Nature, Art, and Everday Life* (1978). How the power of number has manifested itself in history, myth, philosophy, and our daily lives.

**Fadiman, Clifton,** *Fantasia Mathematica* (1958). Anthology of stories, cartoons, essays, rhymes, music, anecdotes, epigrams, and other oddments and amusements that will delight mathematicians and amateurs as well. See *Mathematical Magpie* (rev. 1981).

**Gardner, Martin,** *The Incredible Dr. Matrix* (1976). One of many collections of Gardner's celebrated "Mathematical Games" columns in *Scientific American;* must reading for lovers of mathematical puzzles. Another good collection is Paul Berloguen, *100 Numerical Games* (1976).

**Huff, Daniel,** *How to Lie with Statistics* (1954). This genially subversive little book is a classic. See *How to Take a Chance* (1968). Hans Zeisel, *Say It with Figures* (rev. 1968) is a more scholarly introduction to using statistics.

**Kasner, Edward and James R. Newman,** *Mathematics and the Imagination* (1940). Witty, joyful guide to the principles of math. More technical is Newman and Ernest Nagel, *Godel's Proof* (1938). Newman edited *The World of Mathematics* (1956), an anthology of mathematical literature.

**Kline, Morris,** *Mathematics in Western Culture* (1953). Brisk, lucid look at the role of mathematics in our culture. See *Mathematics: The Loss of Certainty* (1980), presenting his controversial view of the decline of self evidence as a criterion for truth, and *Mathematical Thought from Ancient to Modern Times* (1973).

**Ulam, Stanislaw M.,** *Adventures of a Mathematician* (1976). Fascinating autobiography of the brilliant Polish-born prodigy who worked on the Manhattan Project and seems to have known all the great men of nuclear science.

**Wiener, Norbert,** *Ex-prodigy: My Childhood and Youth* (1953). Sometimes crotchety and egotistical, always lively recollections of the author of *Cybernetics,* who lectured at Harvard at age eighteen. See *I Am a Mathematician: The Later Life of a Prodigy* (1956). See also Steve J. Heims, *John Von Neumann and Norbert Wiener: From Mathematics to the Technologies of Life and Death* (1981).

# PRINCIPLES: APPLICATION

## *Technology*

**Burke, James,** *Connections* (1979). Exciting history of technology describes it as a continuing process. With loads of illustrations; based on the absorbing PBS television series.

**DeCamp, L. Sprague,** *The Ancient Engineers* (1963). Engineering in early times colorfully recounted by a master storyteller. See Henry Hodges, *Technology in the Ancient World* (1970).

**Florman, Samuel C.,** *The Existential Pleasures of Engineering* (1976). Brief, engaging, beautifully written corrective to the antitechnologists. See *Blaming Technology: The Irrational Search for Scapegoats* (1981).

**Ordway, Frederick I., III, and Mitchell B. Sharpe,** *The Rocket Team* (1978). Fascinating, authoritative look at Wernher von Braun and the other German scientists who developed the V-2 rocket during World War II before coming to the U.S.

*The Smithsonian Institution Book of Inventions* (1978). Splendid introduction to history of technology: a handsome volume, hundreds of photographs and graphics, and a concise, interesting text. See Ronald W. Clark, *The Scientific Breakthrough: The Impact of Modern Invention* (1976).

## Computers

**Bernstein, Jeremy,** *The Analytical Engine: Computers — Past, Present and Future* (rev. 1981). Superb nontechnical introduction to the world of computers; concise and lucid.

**Convey, H. Dominic and Neal Harding McAlister,** *Computer Consciousness: Surviving the Automated 80's* (1980). Projections of things to come. See Christopher Evans, *The Micro Millennium* (1980) and

Katharine Davis Fishman, *The Computer Establishment* (1981). Do-it-yourselfers, see Robert L. Perry, *Owning Your Own Home Computer* (1980).

**Kidder, Tracy,** *The Soul of a New Machine* (1981). An absorbing tale of how a group of whiz-kid engineers at Data General Corporation built a super-mini computer.

**Roszak, Theodore,** *Bugs* (1981). Intelligent, disturbing horror novel set in the near future that projects where computer technology might lead. Two good computer thrillers are Frederic Vincent Huber, *Apple Crunch* (1981) and Malcolm MacPherson, *The Lucifer Key* (1981).

**Sobel, Robert,** *IBM: Colossus in Transition* (1981). A Wall Street writer's engrossing account of the growth of IBM and its strategy in the computer wars.

# THE LAND

**Calder, Nigel,** *The Restless Earth: A Report on the New Geology* (1972). Superb popular exposition of "plate tectonics" — the theory that the earth's crust is a collection of rocky plates which move on a slippery base.

**McPhee, John,** *Basin and Range* (1981). McPhee ranges across the continent in the company of leading field geologists and conveys the excitement of "reading" the earth.

**Moore, Ruth,** *The Earth We Live On: The Story of Geological Discovery* (1971). Lively illustrated introduction, from old myths to new geophysical theories.

**Rawson, Marion,** *Of the Earth Earthy: How Our Fathers Dwelt upon and Wooed the Earth* (1937). The functions of those mysterious entities so frequently encountered in early literature: such things as the lime kiln, saltpeter bed, charcoal pit, peat bog, and malthouse.

**Redfern, Ron,** *Corridors of Time: 1,700,-000,000 Years of Earth at Grand Canyon* (1980). This big book with its magnificent gatefold photos of Grand Canyon panoramas and lively text serves as a luminous introduction to geological theory.

**Watts, May Theilgaard,** *Reading the Landscape of America* (rev. 1975). Guided ecological field trip designed to relate the flora to their environment and to the history of the continent. See *Reading the Landscape of Europe* (1971).

## Mountains

**Benuzzi, Felice,** *No Picnic on Mount Kenya* (1952). Fascinating story of how the author, an Italian POW in an East African prison camp in 1942, escaped to climb Mt. Kenya.

**Clark, Simon,** *Puma's Claw* (1959). Few had ever seen, and no one had ever climbed, Pumasillo. This account of the 1957 Cambridge Andean Expedition's successful ascent is full of rough camaraderie and humor.

**Conway, W. Martin,** *Mountain Memories* (1920). Classic memoir of his experiences in Tierra del Fuego, Kashmir, Spitzbergen, Karakoram, and elsewhere.

**Jerome, John,** *On Mountains* (1978). Everything you want to know about mountains — geology, weather, glaciation, etc. Clear, relaxed writing.

**King, Clarence,** *Mountaineering in the Sierra Nevada* (1872). Characters, adventures, and mountains in splendid word pictures. A classic.

**Muir, John,** *The Mountains of California* (1894). The Sierra Nevada range and his adventures there: a pinnacle of mountain literature.

**Newby, Eric,** *Great Ascents: A Narrative History of Mountaineering* (1977). A score of the world's toughest mountains, their ascents, photographs, and maps in a handsome volume. See R. I. G. Irving, *The Romance of Mountaineering* (1935).

**Peters, Ed,** *Mountaineering: The Freedom of the Hills* (rev. 1982). Superb instruction guide, from the basics to state-of-the-art techniques.

**Read, Piers Paul,** *Alive: The Story of the Andes Survivors* (1974). Compassionate tale of plane crash victims who survived freezing mountain weather without food after deciding to eat their dead.

**Roberts, David,** *The Mountain of My Fear* (1968). Students scale Alaska's Mount Huntington. *Deborah: A Wilderness Narrative* (1970) describes the ascent of the eastern side of Mt. Deborah, Alaska.

**Roper, Steve and Allen Steck,** *Fifty Classic Climbs of North America* (1979). A must for any serious mountaineer; diagrams of best routes, degree of difficulty, and other essential information.

**Rowell, Galen,** *A Mountaineer's World* (1979). Rowell's superb photographs, with absorbing stories of the climbs that enabled him to take them. See *In the Throne Room of the Mountain Kings* (1978) and *High and Wild* (1980).

**Shipton, Eric,** *Upon that Mountain* (1943). Memoirs of the Alps, East Africa, and the first entry into the apparently inaccessible basin of Nanda Devi.

**Taylor, Rob,** *The Breach: Kilimanjaro and the Conquest of Self* (1981). Ascent of the breach wall of the famous mountain. A remarkable tale of adversity and courage.

**Tilman, H. W.,** *Snow in the Equator* (1937). This book about the author's climbs in Africa is one of several distinguished by literary grace, acuity, and genial humor. See *Mount Everest: 1938* (1948), *Nepal Himalaya* (1952), *Two Mountains and a River* (1949), and J. R. L. Anderson's biography, *High Mountains, Cold Seas* (1981).

**Zwinger, Ann H. and Beatrice E. Willard,** *Land Above the Trees* (1972). An ecologist and artist team up on this superb study of the Alpine Tundra. See Dwight Smith, *Above Timberline: A Wildlife Biologist's Rocky Mountain Journal* (1981).

## The Alps

**Clark, Ronald W.,** *The Alps* (1973). Beautifully written and illustrated "biography" of the great European range conveys the compulsion that has driven mountaineers to pit themselves against it. See *The Day the Rope Broke: The Story of the First Ascent of the Matterhorn* (1965).

**De Beer, Gavin,** *Alps and Elephants: Hannibal's March* (1956). Brief book which attempts to solve the historical puzzle of the route Hannibal took from Carthage to Rome. See *Alps and Men* (1932) and *Early Travellers of the Alps* (1930).

**Harrar, Heinrich,** *The White Spider: The History of the Eiger's North Face* (1959). An enthralling step-by-step description of its scaling by a member of the first party to climb its face.

**Ramuz, Charles-Ferdinand,** *When the Mountain Fell* (1935). Evocative novel in which, weeks after an avalanche in the center of Vaud, a young man emerges to tell his story of survival. Anna Rutgers Van Derloeff-Basinero, *Avalanche* (1958); is an outstanding book for young readers about a similar catastrophe.

**Ratti, Achille,** *Climbs on Alpine Peaks* (1923). Its author became Pope Pius XI; his accounts of climbing the Matterhorn and other mountains assure it a place among the Alpine standards.

**Rebuffat, Gaston,** *Starlight and Storm: The Ascent of Six Great Faces of the Alps* (1968). This account by the French guide who climbed all of the six great northern faces is a paean to his profession. *On Ice and Snow and Rock* (1972) is a classic. See *Men and the Matterhorn* (1973).

**Shirahata, Shiro,** *The Alps* (1980). Album of magnificent photographs.

**Ullman, James Ramsey,** *The White Tower* (1945). Dramatic novel about an ascent on the Alps by a knowledgeable mountaineer. See *And Not to Yield* (1970), *The Age of Mountaineering* (rev. 1964), *High Conquest* (1941). *Straight Up: The Life and Death of John Hardin* (1968), and *Americans on Everest* (1964).

**Wechsberg, Joseph,** *Avalanche!* (1958). Absorbing, richly detailed chronicle of the disastrous slide that destroyed the Austrian village of Blans in 1954.

**Whymper, Edward,** *Scrambles Among the Alps* (1870). The most famous and still the greatest mountaineering account ever written. Other Victorian Alpine classics are A. F. Mummery, *My Climbs in the Alps and Caucasus* (1895); Leslie Stephens, *The Playground of Europe* (1870); and John Tyndall, *The Glaciers of the Alps* (1860).

## The Himalayas

**Bonington, Chris,** *Everest, The Hard Way* (1977). The 1975 British expedition's successful scaling of the South West Face, by an excellent mountaineer-writer. See *Annapurna: South Face* (1971), *Ultimate Challenge* (1974), and his autobiographical volumes *I Chose to Climb* (1966) and *The Next Horizon* (1973).

**Habeler, Peter,** *The Lonely Victory: Mount Everest '78* (1979). Reconstruction of the Everest ascent he made with Reinhold Messner.

**Herzog, Maurice,** *Annapurna* (1952). The scaling of the mighty mountain — the highest ever climbed by man at that time — thrillingly told by a member of the French expedition of 1950.

**Hillary, Edmund,** *High in the Cold Air* (1961). A return to the Himalayas by the tough New Zealander whose name is practically synonymous with Everest. See *Schoolhouse in the Clouds* (1964) and his memoirs, *Nothing Venture, Nothing Win* (1975).

**Hornbein, Thomas F.,** *Everest: The West Ridge* (1965). Astounding, beautifully reproduced photographs taken during the American Mt. Everest expedition; "the most glorious book of color photographs one can ever hope to see" (Robert Payne).

**Hunt, John,** *The Conquest of Everest* (1954). The official report; the chapter on the final ascent was written by Hillary. For other perspectives see Wilfrid Noyce, *South Col: A Personal Story of the Ascent of Everest* (1955) and James Morris, *Coronation Everest* (1958).

**Messner, Reinhold,** *Everest: Expedition to the Ultimate* (1979). Climbing Everest without using bottled oxygen, by an independent-minded, fatalistic individualist. See *Seventh Grade: Most Extreme Climbing* (1975) and *The Big Walls* (1979). See Ronald Faux, *High Ambition* (1982), a biography of Messner.

Shirakawa, Yoshikazu, *Himalayas* (1973). Coffee-table book bursting with hundreds of dramatic photographs. "Each picture is a trophy" (Edward Hoagland).

Smythe, F. S., *Camp Six* (1937). One of the foremost English mountaineers of the twenties and thirties recounts the 1933 Everest expedition. See *Kamet Conquered* (1932) and *The Kanchenpengo Adventure* (1930).

Tenzing, Norgay Sherpa, *Tiger of the Snows* (1955). One of the conquerors of Everest tells of the forty years in which he dreamed of climbing the great mountain. His next quarter-century is recounted in *After Everest: An Autobiography* (1978).

## Forests

Averill, Gerald, *Ridge Runner* (1948). Reminiscences of the forest and its dwellers beautifully told by a Maine woodsman.

Caras, Roger, *The Forest* (1979). A coniferous forest in Washington is described in this moving, novelistic portrait of the complete web of life.

Davis, Millard C., *The Near Woods* (1974). An experienced ecologist's genial and literate tour of the woods and forests he has known all over the U.S., scattered throughout with interesting chips of forest lore.

Ets, Marie Hall, *In the Forest* (1944). Little book for five- and six-year-old children, with fine black-and-white illustrations, about the animals of the forest. Another good story book is May Sarton's *A Walk Through the Woods* (1976), illustrated by Kazue Mizumura, in which the poet and her dog and cat take a leisurely walk.

Le Guin, Ursula K., *The Word for World is Forest* (1972). Award-winning short novel about the earth's colonization of a distant planet, which threatens the forest world of its tranquil inhabitants.

Nance, John, *The Gentle Tasaday: A Stone Age People in the Philippine Rain Forest* (1975). Journalist's informal account of a beguiling people and their idyllic forest environment.

Olson, Sigurd F. (t) and Les Blacklock (p), *The Hidden Forest* (1969). The changing seasons in the forest described with freshness and enthusiasm by an eloquent naturalist and stunningly captured in color photographs.

*Robin Hood and Guy of Gisborne* (1765). One of the most popular ballads of the legendary outlaw and his merry band, who dwell deep in Sherwood Forest. A long-time favorite version for young readers is Howard Pyle's illustrated *The Merry Adventures of Robin Hood* (1883).

Rowlands, John, *Cache Lake Country: Life in the North Woods* (rev. 1978). The best book on the joys and methods of survival in the northern forests, full of woods lore and philosophy.

Rustrun, Calvin, *Once upon a Wilderness* (1973). One of several books by an experienced woodsman on the basics of wilderness living. See *The Wilderness Route Finder* (1967), *The Wilderness Cabin* (rev. 1972), *The New Way of the Wilderness* (1958), and *Chips from a Wilderness Log* (1982).

Sandved, Kjell B. (p) and Michael Emsley (t), *Rain Forests and Cloud Forests* (1979). Large-format collection of dazzling photographs.

Shakespeare, William, *As You Like It* (c. 1600). Pastoral comedy of multiple wooing in the Forest of Arden. One of Shakespeare's most delightful plays.

Stevens, James, *Paul Bunyan* (1925). Collection of tales about the great figure in American folklore and his blue ox, Babe, whose horns were forty-two ax handles and a plug of chewing tobacco apart.

Sutton, Ann and Myron Sutton, *Wildlife of the Forests* (1979). Splendid text-and-photo volume about the forest ecosystem by a knowledgeable husband-and-wife team. See Wallace B. Grange, *Those of the Forest* (1954), a compelling narrative about forest animals, and Rien Poortvliet, *The Living Forest: A World of Animals* (1979), an album of charming pictures of the Dutch woods by the gnomic artist.

**Turnbull, Colin,** *The Forest People* (1961). An anthropologist writes with beauty and great charm of his experiences with the Pygmies of the Ituri Forest of the Congo. See *Wayward Servants* (1965).

## Jungles

**Ayensu, Edward S. (ed.),** *Jungles* (1980). Lavish, folio-sized volume by the director of the Endangered Species Program at the Smithsonian Institution describes the major jungles of the world and how they can be conserved.

**Beebe, William,** *High Jungle* (1949). The biologist and nature writer's expeditions in South America, with philosophical excursions and sympathy for all forms of life. It "stands very high, indeed, on the ridge where literature and natural history meet" (Edwin Way Teale). See *Jungle Days* (1925).

**Burroughs, Edgar Rice,** *Tarzan of the Apes* (1912). The first of a long-lived series about the jungle's most famous denizen. See Philip Jose Farmer's admiring *Tarzan Alive: A Definitive Biography of Lord Greystoke* (1972).

**Chapman, F. S.,** *The Jungle Is Neutral* (1949). True adventure story of a man's endurance for three years in the Malay jungle. Leon Statham, *Welcome, Darkness* (1950) is another suspenseful, true, World War II jungle-survival narrative.

**Fawcett, P. H.,** *Lost Trails, Lost Cities* (1953). Account of eleven years' wandering up and down the jungles of the Amazon Basin, written by an English explorer before he disappeared in 1925. "The style is rich, romantic, loose, but somehow

through the verbiage and the extravagant anecdotes emerges an impression — a sense of wild nature, mystery, fortitude and doom" (Graham Greene).

**Hudson, W. H.,** *Green Mansions* (1904). The famous "romance of the tropical forest" of South America, a tragic love story of Rima, the bird girl, and Mr. Abel.

**Kipling, Rudyard,** *The Jungle Books* (1894–5). Highly imaginative tales of jungle animals who act like people and of Mowgli, the boy leader of the jungle kingdom in which he has been raised.

**Malraux, Andre,** *The Royal Way* (1913). Set in the Cambodian jungle and described as a Conrad novel written by Dostoeveski, it is a novel obsessed with death "by a literary anarchist, likely to evoke as much wonderment as admiration" (Sean O'Faolain).

**Sanderson, Ivan,** *Ivan Sanderson's Book of Great Jungles* (1965). Intriguing, handsomely illustrated, large-format volume by the English-born zoology popularizer with a gift for a good anecdote. See *Green Silence: Travels Through the Jungles of the Orient* (1974).

**Tomlinson, H. M.,** *The Sea and the Jungle* (1913). Classic sketches of travel in the Brazilian jungle and aboard a British tramp steamer.

## Deserts

**Austin, Mary,** *The Land of Little Rain* (1903). In the unchanging border regions of southern California and Arizona the author made her home. This is her portrait of a colorful land, of yucca and creosote, bobcat and coyote. Two other Mojave Desert classics of the period are John C. Van Dyke, *The Desert* (1901) and Ida Strobridge, *In Miner's Mirage Land* (1904).

**Baylor, Byrd,** *The Desert Is Theirs* (1976). A lovely book for six-to-ten-year-olds of

Baylor's free verse accompanied by the beautiful illustrations of Peter Parnell.

**Bodley, Ronald V. C.,** *Wind in the Sahara* (1944). An Englishman's seven years with North African desert nomads.

**Cowles, Raymond B.,** *Desert Journal: Reflections of a Naturalist* (1977). The California desert, in a blend of autobiography and popular science.

**George, Uwe,** *In the Deserts of This Earth* (1978). The genesis, ecology, and our current knowledge of deserts by the German desertologist, with many lively digressions about the sad state of the planet.

**Herbert, Frank,** *Dune* (1965). Science-fiction classic about feudal intrigue on the desert planet of Anakis. See sequels: *Dune Messiah* (1969), *Children of Dune* (1976), and *God Emperor of Dune* (1981).

**Moorhouse, Geoffrey,** *The Fearful Void* (1974). Trek over 2,000 of the hardest miles in the world, across the Sahara by camel, confronting thirst, dysentery, hunger, treachery, and himself.

**Muench, David (p) and Edward Abbey (t),** *Desert Images* (1979). Striking color photographs of the American desert; prose by novelist-naturalist Abbey, author of *Desert Solitaire.*

**Wagner, Frederic H.** *Wildlife of the Desert* (1980). Excellent color photographs and an informed text in a handsomely produced worldwide survey of desert animals.

**Woodin, Ann,** *Home Is the Desert* (1964). Rich and human portrait by a woman who "has made the desert country and its natives, both plant and animal, vividly alive" (Hal Borland).

## Islands

**Bazin, Herve,** *Tristan* (1971). Original, powerful novel about the people of Tristan da Cunha — the Isle of Loneliness

— in the middle of the South Atlantic, whose simple existence was shattered by a volcano in 1969.

**Blond, Georges,** *The Plunderers* (1951). Strange and moving tale of the sea and the fur seals of Goddess Island near the Aleutians.

**Carlisle, Olga,** *Island in Time* (1980). The Russian-born translator and author was a child in 1939 vacationing on the island of Oléron off the west coast of France, when World War II broke out and she had to remain there until 1945. A Microcosm of wartime Europe.

**Chekhov, Anton,** *The Island: A Journey to Sakharin* (1893). Observations on a trip to the Far Eastern prison island "from which there is a great deal to learn about the chaos that reigns on the periphery of huge, centrally administered empires" (Heinrich Böll).

**Conrad, Joseph,** *Victory* (1915). The loner Axel Heyst and the outcast woman Lena on a lonely island of the East Indies in one of Conrad's later novels. His other lost-Europeans-on-tropical-islands novels are *Almayer's Folly* (1896) and *An Outcast of the Islands* (1896).

**Defoe, Daniel,** *Robinson Crusoe* (1719). Based on the true story of one Alexander Selkirk, the "life and strange surprizing adventures" of Robinson Crusoe, shipwrecked on a small island near the Orinoco River, is a perennial favorite.

**Dennis, Nigel,** *Malta* (1973). Witty, delightful illustrated history of the Mediterranean island by the English novelist.

**Douglas, Norman,** *South Wind* (1917). Witty novel à la Peacock, full of allusive conversation and odd English and American characters swayed by the disturbing, warm south wind of the Capriesque island of Nepenthe in the Mediterranean.

**Durrell, Gerald,** *My Family and Other Animals* (1957). Warm and funny recollections of boyhood before World War II with his family (and assorted fauna) on Corfu. A companion volume is *Birds, Beasts and Relatives* (1969).

**Durrell, Lawrence,** *Bitter Lemons* (1957). Affectionate, sympathetic evocation of the once pacific island of Cyprus.

**Edwards, G. B.,** *The Book of Ebenezer LePage* (1981). Ebenezer, a crusty, funny, contrary old man, a man of Guernsey, tells of his life bounded by the sea, the rocks, and the distant coast of France. A brilliant novel by an author who died in 1976.

**Fowles, John (t) and Fay Godwin (p),** *Islands* (1978). Rambling essay (with stark photographs) in which the English novelist uses the Scilly Islands off the Cornwall coast as a springboard for discussion of the island metaphor in literature.

**Gibbons, Boyd,** *Wye Island* (1979). The struggle in the early seventies between land developers and conservationists over the future of an island off the Maryland shore.

**Golding, William,** *Lord of the Flies* (1955). Ralph, Piggy, Jack, and the other school boys wrecked on an uninhabited island attempt to forge a society: a luminous parable about how the restraints of civilization break down under extreme conditions.

**Heckman, Hazel,** *Island in the Sound* (1967). Lyrical descriptions of nature on a remote island in Washington's Puget Sound. See *Island Year* (1972).

**Heyerdahl, Thor,** *Aku-Aku: The Secret of Easter Island* (1958). Adventures in unearthing a piece of Polynesia's past and explanation of how the great monolithic statues that dot the shores were carved and transported.

**Homer,** *The Odyssey* (c. 800 B.C.). "The first novel in world literature is woven of islands and the sea and of solitude and sexuality, which is why it has had a greater influence on subsequent story-tell-

ing, both thematically and technically, than any other single book in human history" (John Fowles). Two noteworthy modern versions are Eyvind Johnson, *Return to Ithaca* (1952) and Nikos Kazantzakis, *The Odyssey: A Modern Sequel* (1938).

**Huxley, Aldous,** *Island* (1962). Pala, an island in Southeast Asia, is the setting for this pedagogic novel of utopia, a far cry from the satiric *Brave New World.*

**Klingel, Gilbert C.,** *Inagua* (1941). The title refers to a lonely and nearly forgotten island on the outer fringes of the Bahamas, where the author was shipwrecked. He writes beautifully of its natural history and natives and his own hardships.

**Laxness, Halldór,** *Independent People* (1934, tr. 1946). Epic social novel set in a bleak fishing village of Iceland. Other novels by the Nobel Prize winner are *The Light of the World* (1937–40) and *Paradise Reclaimed* (1962).

**Lockley, Ronald,** *I Know an Island* (1939). The English ornithologist and his wife and infant daughter lived for several years on the remote island of Skokholm off the coast of Wales. Continued in *Shearwaters* (1943). See *The Sea's a Thief* (1936), a novel, and *In Praise of Islands* (1957), an anthology.

**MacLean, Charles,** *Island on the Edge of the World: The Story of St. Kilda* (1980). Life on an island in the North Atlantic, fifty miles west of the Outer Hebrides, its vanished Gaelic culture and environmentally integrated society.

**MacNeil, Ben** *The Hatterasman* (1959). Eloquent, elegantly produced account of the people living on the islands of Ocracoke and Hatteras on North Carolina's Outer Banks.

**Matthiessen, Peter,** *Oomingmak: The Expedition to the Musk Ox Island in the Bering Sea* (1967). He joined an expedition to Nunivak Island to capture musk ox calves for the Fairbanks, Alaska, zoo and here eloquently describes the tundra and Eskimo life.

**Moore, Tui De Roy,** *Galapagos: Islands Lost in Time* (1980). The unique beauty of the islands radiantly caught by a native. See Kenneth Brower (ed.) and Eliot Porter (p), *Galapagos* (1970), a collection of pieces by Darwin, Melville, and others illustrated with Porter's superb color photographs.

**Morison, Samuel Eliot,** *The Story of Mount Desert Island, Maine* (1960). Brief, amiable reminiscences of life on the rocky island at the mouth of the Penobscot River. See Eliot Porter's photograph album. *Summer Island: Penobscot Country* (1966).

**O'Dell, Scott,** *Island of the Blue Dolphins* (1960). An older children's classic, based on fact, about an Indian girl's eighteen years alone on a northern California island.

**O'Sullivan, Maurice,** *Twenty Years A-growing* (1933). Life on Great Blasket, an island off the Kerry coast of Ireland, written in Irish by a peasant and beautifully translated. Neolithic civilization from the inside. Another Blasket Islander, Tomas O Crohan, is the author of *The Islandman* (1937).

**Steig, William,** *The Bad Island* (1969). A bizarre children's story about an island where everything that lives on it is bad; with Steig's beautiful watercolor illustrations.

**Stevenson, Robert Louis,** *Treasure Island* (1883). Classic adventure romance about buried treasure, Long John Silver, and more: a favorite of younger readers.

**Synge, J. M.,** *The Aran Islands* (1907). The Irish dramatist spent most of six years on the treeless Aran Islands in Galway Bay before writing this portrait of the primitive life of the peasants. His famous one-act tragedy, *Riders to the Sea* (1904), takes place there.

**Thomas, Bill,** *The Island* (1980). The islands along the U.S. coast, from Alaska to Maine, in a sumptuously illustrated volume.

**Wells, H. G.,** *Mr. Blettsworthy on Rampole Island* (1928). Written in the carefree manner of his early novels, it tells the story of a shipwrecked man's attempt to convert the superstitious natives to the way of common sense. A surprise ending adds to the fun.

**Wortman, Elmo,** *Almost Too Late* (1981). Incredible true saga of how the author and his three teenage children, shipwrecked by a gale on a deserted island off British Columbia, survived for two months.

**Wright, Austin,** *Islandia* (1942). Written by a distinguished American law professor, this 1,000-page novel about an imaginary continent in the South Pacific is "one of the most remarkable examples of ingenuity in the history of literary invention" (Clifton Fadiman). See Mark Saxton, *The Islar: A Narrative of Land 3* (1969) and *Havoc in Islandia* (1982), novels of Islandia today.

## The Poles

**Amundsen, Roald,** *South Pole* (1912). His discovery of the South Pole in 1911. In 1928 he disappeared while on a rescue mission at the North Pole. See Roland Huntford, *Scott and Amundsen* (1980) and Kare Holt, *The Race: A Novel of Polar Exploration* (1976).

**Byrd, Richard E.,** *Alone* (1938). The American pilot and polar explorer describes his long isolation for scientific study in Antarctica. See *Little America* (1930).

**Cherry-Garrard, Apsley,** *The Worst Journey in the World: Antarctica, 1910–1913* (1922). Incredible story of a nightmarish five-week journey through the Antarctic darkness to obtain embryos of the emperor penguin. "One of the most interesting books I ever have read or expect to read" (Mark Van Doren).

**Freuchen, Peter,** *Peter Freuchen's Adventures in the Arctic* (1960). Selections by the Danish polar explorer: thrilling combat with ice, bears, hunger, and danger.

**Fuchs, Vivian and Edmund Hillary,** *The Crossing of Antarctica* (1959). Official account of the first crossing of the continent by tractor, led by Fuchs with a supporting force commanded by Hillary. The latter's unofficial account of the expedition is *No Latitude for Error* (1961). The official photographer, George Lowe, is the author of *From Everest to the South Pole* (1961).

**Keneally, Thomas,** *The Survivor* (1969). Subtle novel about the survivor of a disastrous Antarctic expedition who is haunted by the thought that he was responsible for the death of its leader. *Victim of the Aurora* (1978) is also an Antarctic novel.

**Mountfield, David,** *A History of Polar Exploration* (1974). Excellent history, vividly illustrated.

**Nansen, Fridtjof,** *In Night and Ice* (1897). The search for the North Pole by the Norwegian explorer and statesman. See *Farthest North* (1897).

**Peary, Robert E.,** *The North Pole: Its Discovery in 1909* (1910). Classic account of the discovery of the North Pole after eight attempts; includes sidelights on Eskimo life.

**Priestly, Raymond E.,** *Antarctic Adventure: Scott's Northern Party* (1915). Surviving the Antarctic winter, by a scientific member of the expedition from which Scott set out on a mission, never to return.

**Ronne, Finn,** *Antarctica, My Destiny* (1979). The experiences of his nine polar expeditions — with Byrd and on his own.

**Scott, Robert Falcon,** *Scott's Last Expedition: Journals and Reports* (1913). The English explorer reached the South Pole five

weeks after its discovery by Amundsen and died of exposure and hunger on the return trip to base. The journals are very moving: the last entry was made by his dying hand. See *Voyage of Discovery* (1905) and Peter Brent, *Captain Scott and the Antarctic Tragedy* (1977).

**Shackleton, Ernest H.,** *The Heart of the Antarctic* (1909). The experiences of Scott's companion on his 1901 expedition and leader of his own later expeditions. See *South* (1919) and Alfred Lansing, *Endurance: Shackleton's Incredible Voyage* (1959).

**Stefansson, Vilhjalmur,** *Discovery* (1964). Candid autobiography of the Canadian-born explorer and anthropologist whose many books include *My Life with the Eskimo* (1913) and *The Friendly Arctic* (rev. 1943).

**Worsley, Frank,** *Endurance: An Epic of Polar Adventure* (1931). The incredible story of the 1914–17 Antarctic expedition led by Shackleton.

## Rivers

**Cary, Bob,** *The Big Wilderness Canoe Manual* (1978). Concise, detailed guide for planning a trip downriver, with a conservation ethic message. See Verne Huston, *River Camping: Touring by Canoe, Kayak and Dory* (1981) and Calvin Rustrun, *North American Canoe Country* (1964).

**Farmer, Philip Jose,** *To Your Scattered Bodies Go* (1971). Riverworld is a large planet around which winds a 10-million-mile river. On its banks everyone who ever died, from Karl Marx to Tom Mix to Joan of Arc, wakes up the day after death. To find out how and why, read the fascinating science-fiction Riverworld cycle, of which this is the first volume.

**Forbath, Peter,** *The River Congo* (1977). The discovery, exploration and exploitation of what has been called the world's most dramatic river.

Granmont, Sanche De, *The Strong Brown God: The Story of the Niger River* (1976). An expert storyteller describes European exploration of the great African river since its discovery in 1796 by Mungo Park.

Graves, John, *Goodbye to a River* (1961). Lone canoe journey down a 200-mile stretch of Texas's Brazos River, which is doomed by the demands of a modern society. A beautiful lament.

Horgan, Paul, *Great River: The Rio Grande in North American History* (1970). Pulitzer Prize–winning study of the river and the whole Texas-New Mexico area by an accomplished novelist and regional historian. See *The Heroic Triad: Essays in the Social Energies of Three Southwestern Cultures* (1971).

Jerome, Jerome K., *Three Men in a Boat (To Say Nothing of a Dog)* (1889). Hilarious Victorian classic about the adventures of three friends and a fox terrier on holiday on the Thames.

McPhee, John, *The Survival of the Bark Canoe* (1975). Marvelous account of a man who has devoted his life to preserving the Indian craft of birchbark canoe making and of a canoe trip in the Maine woods.

Moorehead, Alan, *The White Nile* (1960). The search for the sources of the Nile during the latter half of the nineteenth century: an extraordinary reading adventure. See *The Blue Nile* (1962).

Neihardt, John, *The River and I* (1910). A trip down the Missouri River from Montana to Iowa taken by the author, the future "Poet Laureate of Nebraska," and two companions.

Newby, Eric, *Slowly down the Ganges* (1967). Wide-eyed record of a 1,200-mile journey down India's holy river. See Edward Rice, *The Ganges: A Personal Encounter* (1974).

Powell, John Wesley, *Exploration of the Colorado River of the West and Its Tributaries* (1875). Scientific report of author's trips down a thousand miles of wild river, from Green River Crossway, Wyoming, to just above the present location of Boulder Dam. Wallace Stegner, whose *Beyond the Hundredth Meridian* (1954) is about Powell's explorations, called it "one of the best adventure stories in American literature." See *Down the Colorado* (1970), an abridgement of Powell's report with stunning photographs by Eliot Porter.

Raban, Jonathan, *Old Glory: An American Voyage* (1981). Inspired by *Huckleberry Finn,* the English writer took a voyage on a sixteen-foot raft down the Mississippi River in 1979. This account of that trip is filled with brilliantly observed portraits of people, places, and events and a sense of history. See Marquis Childs, *Mighty Mississippi* (1982).

Seton, Ernest Thompson, *Arctic Prairies* (1911). The naturalist-author-illustrator canoed 2,000 miles in search of caribou.

Zwinger, Ann, *Run, River, Run: A Naturalist's Journey down One of the Great Rivers of the West* (1975). Down the Green River, through the Southwest canyon country. Vividly recorded with a careful eye for detail and larded with observations on botany, zoology, geology, and earlier explorations. See Robert F. Leslie, *Read the Wild Water: 780 Miles by Canoe Down the Green River* (1966).

## Lakes

Burton, Richard F., *The Lake Region of Central Africa* (1860). This account of the Victorian scholar-gypsy's journey to Lake Tanganyika "remains not only his best book but also, in a field of writing that was remarkably good, one of the best explorer's journals ever written" (Alan Moorehead).

Havighurst, Walter, *Long Ships Passing* (rev. 1975). The story of the Great Lakes since the days of the Indians, explorers, and trappers. See *Three Flags at the Straits* (1966).

**Hill, Ralph Nading,** *Lake Champlain* (1977). The big lake, its natural and social history, described by an old New England hand. See Frederick Van de Water, *Lake Champlain and Lake George* (1946).

**Morgan, Dale L.,** *The Great Salt Lake* (1947). A fact-packed history from earliest geological time through the dramatic Mormon settlement by its banks.

**Wordsworth, William,** *Guide Through the District of the Lakes in the North of England* (1812). The Lake poet's charming tour of Lakes Windermere, Derwentwater, and others.

## Ponds

**Amos, William H.,** *The Life of the Pond* (1967). A marine biologist's guided tour of the myriad life forms coexisting in a pond.

**Reynolds, Christopher,** *The Pond on My Windowsill* (1970). How to build your own "pond" of water insects, snails, worms, and other organisms without a trip to the pet shop, by collecting specimens at your local pond. Great project for kids.

**Russell, Franklin,** *Watchers at the Pond* (1961). The teeming universe of a pond in the Canadian wilderness over the course of a year. A fresh, skillful story by a naturalist.

**Thoreau, Henry David,** *Walden* (1854). "When I wrote [*Walden*] I lived alone, in the woods, a mile from any neighbor, in a house which I had built myself, on the shore of Walden Pond, in Concord, Massachusetts, and earned my living by the labor of my hands only. I lived there two years and two months. At present I am a sojourner in civilized life again." So begins one of the most remarkable books ever written about nature and the meaning of life.

**Tresselt, Alvin,** *The Beaver Pond* (1976). The beautiful illustrations by Roger Duvoisin make this little book for youngsters very special.

# THE SEA

**Beebe, William,** *The Arcturus Adventure* (1926). Classic account of the 1925 voyage of the research vessel *Arcturus* to the Sargasso Sea and the Galapagos islands. See *Beneath Tropic Seas* (1928) and *Half Mile Down* (1934).

**Borgese, Elizabeth Mann,** *The Drama of the Oceans* (1976). Lucid overview of the oceans set off an album of striking illustrations. *See Seafarm: The Story of Aquaculture* (1980).

**Brower, David (ed.),** *Not Man Apart* (1965). Magisterial photographs of the Big Sur coastline of California by Ansel Adams, Eliot Porter, and others; with poetry by Robinson Jeffers.

**Carson, Rachel L.,** *The Sea Around Us* (rev. 1961). An award-winning classic and an enthralling account of the ocean, its geography and its inhabitants. See *The Edge of the Sea* (1955), the story of the tidal world of the Atlantic Coast.

**Cousteau, Jacques-Yves,** *Jacques Cousteau: The Ocean World* (1979). Magnificent color photographs with text adapted from the aquanaut's twenty-volume *The Ocean World of Jacques Cousteau.* See his classic memoir *The Silent World* (1953).

**Culliney, John L.,** *The Forests of the Sea: Life and Death on the Continental Shelf* (1977). A tour of the continental shelf that warns of environmental disaster if human greed is not checked. He wrote (with Edward S. Crockett) *Exploring Underwater: The Sierra Club Guide to Scuba and Snorkeling* (1980).

**Diolé, Philippe,** *4,000 Years Under the Sea* (1954). Account of man's explorations undersea during the past forty centuries. See Frederic Dumas, *30 Centuries Under the Sea* (1976) and Sylvia Earle's lavishly illustrated *Exploring the Deep Frontier: The Adventures of Man in the Sea* (1980).

**Faulkner, Douglas,** *Living Corals* (1979). Amazing pictures taken over a sixteen-year period by perhaps the greatest underwater photographer. Another beautiful album of submarine flora is Leni Riefenstahl, *Coral Gardens* (1978).

**Hardy, Alister,** *The Open Sea* (rev. 1971). A marine biology classic; fine writing and illustrations describe the world of plankton, fish, and fisheries. See *Great Waters* (1968), an account of the *Discovery* expedition to Antarctic waters.

**Steinbeck, John,** *The Log from the Sea of Cortez* (1951). Reissue of the narrative of *The Sea of Cortez,* written with marine biologist Edward F. Ricketts a decade earlier. A journal of travels and undersea research in the Gulf of California, with Steinbeck's metaphysical meditations.

## Sea Creatures

**Abbott, R. Tucker,** *The Kingdom of the Seashell* (1972). Sweeping survey of world of mollusks. *American Seashells* (1974) is the standard reference work.

**Carr, Archie,** *So Excellent a Fishe: A Natural History of Sea Turtles* (1967). Beautifully written account of turtles and terrapins by a leading authority. See Jack Rudloe, *Time of the Turtle* (1978).

**Carson, Rachel L.,** *Under the Sea Wind* (1941). Story of life among birds and fish on the shore, open sea, and sea bottom, by the prize-winning author of *The Sea Around Us.*

**Clark, Eleanor,** *The Oysters of Locmariaquer* (1966). The title gives no inkling of the fascination of this witty, informative, exquisitely written book about the succulent oyster and the men of Brittany who harvest it. National Book Award winner.

**Clarkson, Ewan,** *Halic: The Story of a Gray Seal* (1970). Unsentimental, well-researched story of one North Atlantic seal, rendered in a terse, poetic style. See Ronald Lockley, *The Saga of the Gray Seal* (1955) and Frank Stuart, *A Seal's World* (1959).

**Faulkner, Douglas (p) and Barry Fell (t),** *Dwellers of the Sea* (1976). Astounding pictures, coupled with a lucid text.

**Line, Les and George Reiger,** *The Audubon Society Book of Marine Wildlife* (1980). Exquisite color photographs by some of the most famous wildlife photographers. Everything from barnacles and sea urchins to manta rays and sandpipers.

**Matthiessen, Peter,** *Blue Meridian: The Search for the Great White Shark* (1971). A search over thousands of miles of ocean for the great white shark — a search organized by a millionaire sportsman obsessed with testing the outer limits of human endeavor. See Jacques Cousteau and Philippe Cousteau, *The Shark: Splendid Savage of the Seas* (1970) and Paul Budker, *The Life of the Sharks* (1971).

**Maxwell, Gavin,** *Harpoon Venture* (1952). After the war, Maxwell bought an island in the Outer Hebrides as a shark fishery. This is the wonderfully told story of his adventures with his sharks.

**Migdalski, Edward C. and George S. Fichter,** *The Fresh and Salt Water Fishes of the World* (1976). Popularly written guide with over 500 fine paintings of different fishes.

## Whales and Dolphins

**Brower, Kenneth,** *Wake of the Whale* (1979). The beautiful photographs of William R. Curtsinger make special this appreciation of the Leviathan. Richard Ellis, a marine artist, has embellished *The Book of Whales* (1980) with his superb paintings.

**Lilly, John C.,** *Lilly on Dolphins: Humans of the Sea* (1975). Revised edition of *Man and Dolphin* and *The Mind of the Dolphin* that describe his groundbreaking attempts to communicate with members of a different species. See *Communication Between Man and Dolphin* (1978).

**McIntyre, Joan (ed.),** *Mind in the Water: A Book to Celebrate the Consciousness of Whales and Dolphins* (1974). Moving, richly varied collection of pieces from literature, mythology, science, and firsthand accounts: an eloquent plea for their survival. See Ronald Lockley, *Whales, Dolphins and Porpoises* (1979).

**Merle, Robert,** *The Day of the Dolphin* (1969). Thrilling novel set at a Florida laboratory where dolphin communication has succeeded. Intellectually provocative, serious in its implications, moving, and dramatic. Other dolphin novels include Ted Mooney's speculative *Easy Travel to Other Planets* (1981) and Tristan Jones, *Aka* (1981).

**Mowat, Farley,** *A Whale for the Killing* (1973). The Canadian naturalist tries to save a whale trapped in a tidal pool from being killed by local townspeople. A moving, sad tale.

**Scheffer, Victor B.,** *The Year of the Whale* (1969). Sensitive, poetic "biography" of twelve months in the life of a young sperm whale; "a volume to be treasured" (Loren Eiseley). A similar treatment is given in Jeremy Lucas, *Whale* (1981) and Sally Carrighar, *The Twilight Seas: A Blue Whale's Journey* (1975).

**Slipjer, E. J.,** *Whales* (rev. 1979). Classic work that blends history, anecdote, illustrations, and science. Another accessible cetacean study is Robert Barton, *The Life and Death of Whales* (rev. 1980).

**Small, George L.,** *The Blue Whale* (1971). Poignant account of the slaughter of the largest animal that ever lived. A compassionate signal of distress.

## Man on the Sea

**Adkins, Jan,** *The Craft of Sail: A Primer of Sail* (1973). Guide to handling small boats, great for the beginner. Adkins's superb illustrations can also be seen in *Wooden Ship* (1978).

**Allcard, Edward,** *Single-Handed Passage* (1950). A very literate book by one of the great English lone sailors. See *Temptress Returns* (1953) and *Voyage Alone* (1964).

**Barton, Humphrey,** *The Sea and Me* (1952). Famous British yachtsman's irrepressible and popular ramblings. See *Vertue XXXV* (1951) and *Atlantic Adventurers: Voyages in Small Craft* (1953).

**Belloc, Hilaire,** *The Cruise of the Nona* (1925). Charming work by the eminent English writer with no little knowledge of small boats. A similarly enjoyable work of the period is Sir Arthur Ransome's *Racundra's First Cruise* (1923).

**Bradford, Ernle,** *The Mediterranean: Portrait of a Sea* (1971). Its colorful history by a prolific British sailor-historian. See *Ulysses Found* (1964), an account of his voyage in search of Ulysses's route, *The Wind Commands Me: A Life of Sir Francis Drake* (1965) and *The Sultan's Admiral: The Life of Barbarossa* (1968).

**Caldwell, John,** *Desperate Voyage* (1949). His harrowing adventures crossing the Pacific in a twenty-nine-foot cutter in order to be with the woman he loved.

**Chichester, Sir Francis,** *Gipsy Moth Circles the World* (1967). Account of the fastest solo circumnavigation by the intrepid English sailor. His other works include *Alone Across the Atlantic* (1961), *Atlantic Adventure* (1963), and *The Lonely Sea and the Sky* (1964).

Childers, Erskine, *The Riddle of the Sands* (1900). This classic espionage thriller about a German plot to invade Britain is also one of the all-time great yachting novels.

Conrad, Joseph, *The Nigger of the Narcissus* (1897). Brief, powerful novel on the Conradian theme of men under stress that involves a dying black sailor whose presence influences the linked lives of each member of the crew. *Mirror of the Sea* (1906) is an exciting personal record of Conrad's days at sea.

Dampier, William, *A New Voyage Round the World* (1697). The remarkable experiences of the navigator and privateer generally considered to be the first Englishman to see Australia. He marooned Alexander Selkirk, the prototype of Robinson Crusoe, on Juan Fernandez Island.

Dana, Richard Henry, Jr., *Two Years Before the Mast* (1840). Account of a merchant brig's voyage around Cape Horn to California by a Boston student who signed aboard as a common sailor in order to improve his health. A great sea classic.

Forester, C. S., *The Hornblower Saga* (1937–62). Eleven-novel series in which Horatio Hornblower rises from midshipman to admiral. Set in Lord Nelson's navy during the Napoleonic wars. Forester collaborated with Samuel H. Bryant on *The Hornblower Companion* (1964), must reading for Hornblower lovers.

Gerbault, Alain, *The Flight of the Firecrest* (1926). Around-the-world cruise by the most famous modern French sailor, an iconoclastic, unique man. See *In Quest of the Sun* (1955).

Griffith, Bob and Nancy Griffith, *Blue Water: A Guide to Self-Reliant Sailboat Cruising* (1979). Sea chest of information for old salts.

Guzzwell, John, *Trekka Around the World* (1963). Young Englishman's single-handed sail around the world.

Hanley, James, *The Ocean* (1941). Gripping novel of survival in an open boat during World War II by an English novelist, a former merchant seaman. "Far and away the best writer of the sea and seafaring men since Conrad" (Henry Green).

Hayden, Sterling, *Voyage: A Novel of 1896* (1976). A novel about the around-the-Horn voyage of a huge iron-hulled, four-masted square rigger; big, ambitious, overdrawn, and gripping. In *Wanderer* (rev. 1977), the actor-author describes the trip he took to the South Seas with his four children on a 100-ton schooner.

Herreshoff, L. Francis, *The Complete Cruiser: The Art, Practice and Enjoyment of Boating* (rev. 1980). Breezy classic on how to get the maximum enjoyment out of your boat.

Heyerdahl, Thor, *Kon-Tiki: Across the Pacific by Raft* (1950). To prove his theory that some south Pacific islands could have been settled by people from Peru, the Norwegian anthropologist and crew of five sailed a log raft from Peru. An incredible voyage. See *The Tigris Expedition* (1981), about a similar voyage by a ship made of reed bundles down the Persian Gulf to retrace the routes of Sumerian sailors, and *The Ra Expeditions* (1971).

Hiscock, Eric, *Sou'West in Wanderer IV* (1973). One of the best books of his cruises on the oceans of the world with his wife as first mate. See *Around the World in Wanderer III* (1956), *Beyond the Western Horizon* (1963), and *Cruising Under Sail* (rev. 1982).

Holdridge, Desmond, *Northern Lights* (1939). A professional explorer's joyous voyage with two companions at age eighteen from Nova Scotia northwards along the coast of Labrador to the Button Islands.

Holm, Donald, *The Circumnavigators: Small Boat Voyagers of Modern Times* (1974). Engrossing, delightful stories of outstanding sailors plus a chapter on "the anatomy of a dreamboat."

**James, Naomi,** *Alone Around the World* (1979). Very personal, human story of the author's 272-day circumnavigation.

**Johnson, Irving and Electa Johnson,** *Yankee's Wandering-World* (1949). One of several narratives about their share-the-expense circumnavigation aboard the schooner *Yankee.*

**Jones, Stephen,** *Drifting* (1971). Delightful, tangy anecdotes about dooryards, alleys, lagoons, swamps, and creeks around New Orleans, Cape May, Rhode Island, and other places. See *Backwater* (1979), about the out-of-the-way spots on Long Island Sound, and *Harbor of Refuge* (1981).

**Jones, Tristan,** *Ice!* (1978). The first of several accounts of the voyaging life that read like adventure novels. See *Incredible Voyage* (1977), *Saga of a Wayward Sailor* (1979), and *Adrift* (1980).

**Knapp, Arthur,** *Race Your Boat Right* (rev. 1973). Informal, comprehensive manual on techniques for racing. See Manfred Curry, *Racing Tactics* (rev. 1973).

**Marin-Marie,** *Wind Aloft, Wind Alow* (1947). Two hair-raising singlehanded Atlantic crossings under sail and under power.

**Maury, Richard,** *The Saga of Cimba* (1939). Two-year voyage from Nova Scotia to the South Seas in a thirty-five-foot schooner described in sparkling narrative.

**Melville, Herman,** *Moby-Dick* (1851). Beneath the narrative of maritime adventure on a whaler, this masterpiece "is a parable on human life and cosmic existence, with special reference to all that baffles and cripples the spirit of man" (Lewis Mumford).

**Moitessier, Bernard,** *The First Voyage of the Joshua* (1973). Voyage around Cape Horn by one of the best small-boat bluewater sailors in the world.

**Monsarrat, Nicholas,** *The Cruel Sea* (1951). Novel about the rigors of life on two British ships during World War II. Middling characterization, but it superbly evokes the atmosphere of a small ship at war.

**Mowat, Farley,** *The Boat Who Wouldn't Float* (1970). Hilarious adventures of the Canadian naturalist aboard his pocket schooner. One mishap after another.

**Newby, Eric,** *The Last Grain Race* (1956). At age eighteen he was the only Englishman on a four-masted Finnish barque, lived in the fo'c'sle, worked the ship, and rounded both capes on the historic passage from Australia to England.

**Pardey, Lin and Larry Pardey,** *Seraffin's European Adventure* (1979). Cruising experiences of a couple on a small boat. Entertaining and full of practical advice.

**Parry, J. H.,** *Romance of the Sea* (1981). Elegantly illustrated anecdotal history of the romantic days of sailing ships. See *The Discovery of the Sea* (1974).

**Pidgeon, Harry,** *Around the World Single-Handed* (1932). After Joshua Slocum, Pidgeon is the most famous singlehander. He continued circumnavigating until well into his seventies.

**Poe, Edgar Allan,** *The Narrative of Arthur Gordon Pym* (1838). Fantastic, horrific tale of shipwreck, mutiny, cannibalism, and attack by savages and monsters, in Poe's only novel.

**Robertson, Dougal,** *Sea Survival: A Manual* (1975). Sound, practical advice from one who survived on a raft after a shipwreck, as related in *Survive the Savage Sea* (1973). Other recent true survival sagas include Maurice Bailey and Maralyn Bailey, *Staying Alive* (1974) and Nicholas Angel, *Capsize!: A Story of Survival in the North Atlantic* (1981).

**Robinson, William A.,** *10,000 Leagues over the Sea* (1932). One of the first books by the legendary American sailor about his adventures aboard his Alden ketch, at the time the smallest boat to sail around the world. *To the Great Southern Oceans* (1956) and *Return to the Sea* (1972) are fine books about his *Varua* cruises in the Pacific. See *The World of Yachting* (1966).

**Roth, Hal,** *Two Against Cape Horn* (1978). Well-told tale of his and his wife's voyage round the Horn, during which they were shipwrecked for several days. See *After 50,000 Miles* (1977).

**Sheean, Neil,** *The Arnheiter Affair* (1972). Why Lieutenant Commander Arnheiter was relieved from duty ninety-nine days after assuming command of his ship. A bizarre story of a pathetic man whose heroic fantasies led to the breakdown of morale among his men. An equally odd tale of a crackup at sea is Nicholas Tomalin and Ron Hale, *The Strange Last Voyage of Donald Crowhurst* (1970).

**Slocum, Joshua,** *Sailing Alone Around the World* (1900). The voyage of the *Spray*, the thirty-seven-foot, home-built sloop in which Slocum became the first man singlehandedly to circle the world; "a nauti-cal equivalent of *Walden* . . . one of the American classics" (Van Wyck Brooks).

**Tabarly, Eric,** *Lonely Victory: Atlantic Race, 1964* (1966). From Plymouth to Newport singlehanded in twenty-seven days aboard *Pen Duick II,* the first of a series of innovative trimarans. See *Ocean Racing* (1972).

**Tambs, Erling,** *Cruise of the Teddy* (1934). The Norwegian novelist and his wife journeyed four years all over the world, during which time two children were born. A carefree, high-spirited journey. The adventures of another couple who took to the sea in the thirties are Bill & Phyllis Crowe, *Heaven, Hell & Salt Water* (1957).

**Tilman, H. W.,** *Mischief in Patagonia* (1957). A famous mountaineer took up sailing and wrote a series of exciting books about it. See *Mischief in Greenland* (1964) and *Triumph and Tribulation* (1979).

**Villiers, Alan,** *By Way of Cape Horn* (1930). The hazardous voyage round the Horn in the author's windjammer. His many other books of the sea include *Sons of Sindbad* (1969) and *Monsoon Seas: The Story of the Indian Ocean* (1952).

# THE AIR

## Birds

**Audubon, John James,** *The Birds of America* (1827–38). *The* ornithological classic. The magnificent hand-colored engravings from the renowned Double Elephant Folio have been beautifully reproduced in the Audubon Society's Baby Elephant Folio, arranged by Roger Tory Peterson and Virginia Moore Peterson, and published as *Audubon's Birds of America* (1979). See Roland C. Clement, *The Living World of Audubon* (1974).

**Broun, Maurice,** *Hawks Aloft: The Story of Hawk Mountain* (1949). How he established a mountain sanctuary for migrating hawks, thousands of which had been slaughtered each fall. He "tells one of the most inspiring stories of conservation since the struggle to halt the plume trade a generation and more ago" (Edwin Way Teale). For an update, see Michael Harwood, *The View from Hawk Mountain* (1973).

**Dennis, John V.,** *A Complete Guide to Birdfeeding* (1975). For those who do their bird watching at home. See *Beyond the Bird Feeder* (1981).

**Durden, Kent,** *Gifts of an Eagle* (1972). Amazing story of Lady, a golden eagle who for sixteen years remained in captivity. *Flight to Freedom* (1974) chronicles Lady's life in the wilderness after being set free.

**Eckert, Allan W.,** *The Great Auk* (1963). Absorbing, curiously moving fictionalized account of the life cycle of the last Great Auk, a helpless victim of extinction at the hands of nature and man. See *The Silent Sky: The Incredible Extinction of the Passenger Pigeon* (1965) and *The Water Birds of North America* (1981), with paintings by Karl E. Karelus.

**Feduccia, Alan,** *The Age of Birds* (1980). Large, beautifully illustrated volume tracing the evolution of birds from reptiles.

**Fuertes, Louis Agassiz,** *Pictures of New England Birds* (1932). Sumptuous plates by the greatest bird illustrator of the first half of this century. See *The Birds of Minnesota* (1932) and *Artist and Naturalist in Ethiopia* (1936).

**Gaddis, Thomas E.,** *Birdman of Alcatraz: The Story of Robert Stroud* (1955). He spent thirty-nine years in solitary confinement and became a self-educated authority on diseases of birds.

**Gould, John,** *John Gould's Birds* (1980). Gould was a lithographer and the foremost publisher of ornithological illustration in Victorian England. These plates from his famous *Birds of Great Britain* (1862–73) show his formal, delicate style to perfection.

**Halliday, Tim,** *Vanishing Birds: Their Natural History and Conservation* (1978). Superb consideration of extinct and endangered birds; profusely illustrated.

**Hosking, Eric,** *A Passion for Birds: Fifty Years of Photographing Wildlife* (1979). Over 240 plates from an outstanding bird photographer. See *An Eye for a Bird* (1970).

**Hudson, W. H.,** *Birds of La Plata* (1921). The Argentine-born English author of *Green Mansions,* was a lifelong and acutely perceptive bird fancier. See *Birds and Man* (1901) and *Birds of Town and Village* (1920).

**Hyman, Susan,** *Edward Lear's Birds* (1980). Collection of the Victorian nonsense poet's superb paintings.

**Karmali, John,** *Birds of Africa* (1980). Marvelous photographs covering virtually all the East African families of birds.

**Krutch, Joseph Wood and Paul S. Erekksson,** *A Treasury of Birdlore* (1962). Anthology of the world of birds and bird-writing, ranging from Audubon, Wilson, Muir, and Bartram to Carrighar, Peattie, and Carson.

**Lansdowne, J. F.,** *Birds of the West Coast* (1976). Magnificent paintings by perhaps the greatest of contemporary bird painters. See *Birds of the Eastern Forest* (1968).

**Lawrence, Louise De Kiriline,** *The Lovely and the Wild* (1968). Thirty years of bird watching in Ontario's Pimisi Bay region. She knows individual birds and "writes with the strength and simplicity of Isak Dinesen" (Brooks Atkinson).

**Loates, Glen,** *The Art of Glen Loates* (1979). The Canadian artist's beautiful, precise bird paintings are accurate to the last pinfeather. See *Birds of North America* (1979).

**Lorenz, Konrad,** *The Year of the Greylag Goose* (1979). The renowned ethologist's informal description of the social behavior of a species with which he has had a lifelong fascination, in a volume of sumptuous photographs.

**MacDonald, Malcolm,** *Birds in My India Garden* (1962). With remarkable photographs by Christina Lake. "Although there is a lot of good ornithological observation packed into the pages of this large attractive book, it is written with such a gracious touch that it makes the best sort of armchair or bedside reading" (Roger Tory Peterson).

**Murphy, Robert,** *The Peregrine Falcon* (1963). Novel about the first year of life of one of these superb hunters; full of interesting details about falconry.

**Pasquier, Roger,** *Watching Birds: An Introduction to Ornithology* (1977). Gives the amateur birder the basics in all areas of ornithology. Excellent companion to the field guides.

**Peterson, Roger Tory,** *A Field Guide to the Birds* (rev. 1980). Practical, easy-to-use, copiously illustrated handbook by the dean of American ornithology writers and author of numerous other field guides. See his classic *Birds over America* (rev. 1964) and *The Bird Watcher's Anthology* (1957). See also *The World of Roger Tory Peterson* (1977) by John C. Devlin and Grace Naismith.

**Scott, Peter and The Wildfowl Trust,** *The Swan* (1972). Authoritative work on every aspect of the swan — history, behavior, myth, — with many striking illustrations. Good personal books about these beautiful birds include Marcus MacSwiny of Mashanaglass, *Six Came Flying* (1972) and Budd Schulberg, *Swan Watch* (1975).

**Shortt, Terence Michael,** *Wild Birds of the Americas* (1978). Attractive volume of stunning bird portraits by the former chief artist of the Royal Ontario Museum, plus a brief text about each family of New World birds.

**Strange, Ian,** *The Bird Man: An Autobiography* (1976). Genial book by a man who has dedicated his life to the conservation of birds of the Falkland Islands.

**Sutton, George Mikisch,** *At a Bend in a Mexican River* (1972). Just one of many fine books by an eminent ornithology writer and artist. See *High Arctic* (1971).

**Terres, John K.,** *The Audobon Society Encyclopedia of North American Birds* (1980). Monumental, twenty-years-in-the-making achievement, with over 6,000 entries and superb illustrations by the author of *Songbirds in Your Garden* (rev. 1968) and *Flashing Wings: The Drama of Bird Flight* (1968). See *The Audubon Society Handbook for Birders* (1981) by Stephen W. Kress.

**Wharton, William,** *Birdy* (1978). Sensitive, award-winning first novel about friendship, the nature of reality, and canaries. The hero eventually believes he is one himself.

**White, T. H.,** *The Goshawk* (1951). The author of *The Once and Future King* describes how he tried to train a hawk according to the ancient rules of falconry.

## Man Aloft

**Bach, Richard,** *Stranger to the Ground* (1963). By the creator of Jonathan Livingston Seagull, an eloquent, almost spiritual, record of a pilot's singlehanded transoceanic flight. See *Bi-plane* (1966), a novel.

**Cooper, Henry S. F.,** *A House in Space* (1976). What it is like to live in space — the inside story of the famous Skylab experiments.

**Fallaci, Oriana,** *If the Sun Dies* (1965). In-depth investigation of NASA, with interviews with scientists. Stewart Brand called this by "far the best book on space exploration."

**Foster, Timothy R. V.,** *The Aviator's Catalog: A Source Book of Aeronautics* (1981). Where to get the latest aviation hardware: a book any pilot would enjoy browsing through. See *The Aircraft Owner's Handbook* (1978).

**Gann, Ernest K.,** *Fate Is the Hunter* (1961). Recollection of author's aerial adventures in which fate played a leading role. Gann's many aviation novels include *In the Company of Eagles* (1966). See *Ernest K. Gann's Flying Circus* (1974).

**Knauth, Percy,** *Wind on My Wings* (1961). Joyful account of how the author learned to fly.

**Langewiesche, Wolfgang,** *Stick and Rudder: An Explanation of the Art of Flying* (1944). Classic that clearly explains such basics as how a plane stays up in the air.

**Lindbergh, Anne Morrow,** *North to the Orient* (1935). Her flight with her husband, Charles Lindbergh, to Japan and China in 1931. A beautifully written chapter in aviation history. See *Listen!! The Wind* (1938).

**Lindbergh, Charles A.,** *The Spirit of St. Louis* (1953). "Lucky Lindy's" own hour-by-hour account of his famous flight. See Brendan Gill, *Lindbergh Alone* (1977), in a fiftieth anniversary tribute.

**McPhee, John,** *The Deltoid Pumpkin Seed* (1973). The fantastic true story of the Aereon 7, the embodiment of the dreams, hopes, work, money, and fanatical true grit of perhaps the most bizarre band of men ever to try to revolutionize the concept of manned flight. Exciting, funny, and, finally, moving.

**Maher, Gay Dalby,** *The Joy of Learning to Fly* (1978). Excellent companion for the tyro pilot.

**Murchie, Guy,** *Song of the Sky* (1955). Dramatic, mind-expanding metaphor of the sky being like an ocean, and flying like sailing.

**Park, Edward,** *Nanette* (1977). Vivid memoir of author's fighter squadron in the South Pacific during World War II

that in one pilot's words is "full of the exhilaration of those aerial moments that pilots yearn for and remember fondly."

**Pene Dubois, William,** *The Twenty-One Balloons* (1947). Children's classic about Professor William Waterman Sherman's fabulous voyage around the world in a flying balloon, with a stop on the amazing island of Krakatoa, that mixes scientific fact with absolute nonsense.

**Saint-Exupéry, Antoine de,** *Night Flight* (1931). The perilous world of pioneer aviation set out in a novel of rare beauty and power by an aviator who, "in all he tells us, speaks as one who 'has been through it.' His personal contact with ever-recurrent danger seasons in his book with an authentic and inimitable tang" (Andre Gide). See *Southern Mail* (1933), *Wind, Sand and Stars* (1939), *Flight to Arras* (1942), and Curtis Cates's biography *Antoine de Saint-Exupéry* (1970). Pierre Clostermann's World War II novel *Flames in the Sky* (1948) is in the Saint-Exupéry tradition.

**Steinman, Hy,** *Triumph: The Incredible Saga of the First Transatlantic Flight* (1961). Dramatic resurrection of a forgotten saga — the first transatlantic flight, in 1917 — that reads like an adventure novel.

**Wolfe, Tom,** *The Right Stuff* (1979). Brilliant rendering of the great astronaut saga of the sixties by "a cunning interpreter of American social reality, never unsympathetic even when hilariously critical" (Paul Fussell).

# WEATHER

**Ballard, J. G.,** *The Wind from Nowhere* (1962). Fine English science-fiction writer's first novel about a 550 mph wind that destroys civilization. His other apocalyptic novels are *The Burning World* (1964), *The Drowned World* (1962), and *The Crystal World* (1966).

**Butler, Hal,** *Nature at War* (1977). Disasters — earthquakes, hurricanes, floods, tornadoes, and so forth — engagingly explained.

**Calder, Nigel,** *The Weather Machine* (1975). How the weather works, with striking photographs. Probably the best popular introduction to meteorology.

**Conrad, Joseph,** *Typhoon* (1903). Classic tale about the skipper of the *Nan-Shan,* a solid, unimaginative man who rises to great heights in response to overwhelming challenge. Contains the best description in literature of a sea storm.

**Gaskell, T. F. and Marlin Morris,** *World Climate: The Weather, The Environment and Man* (1980). Concise, clear survey of science's current understanding of climate. See D. S. Halacy, Jr., *Ice or Fire: Surviving Climatic Change* (1978), which sets forth the theory of an upcoming ice age.

**Hughes, Richard,** *In Hazard* (1938). Spare novel whose most outrageous quality is "its daring — to take the same subject as Conrad in *Typhoon,* the simple story of a hurricane and human endurance, to include even a shipload of Chinese; it would be foolhardy if it were not triumphantly justified" (Graham Greene).

**Kals, W. S.,** *The Riddle of the Winds* (1977). The anecdotes and illustrations make this fascinating subject as easy as a breeze.

**Kirk, Ruth,** *Snow* (1978). Nontechnical, well-written; everything you would ever want to know about snow.

**Kyle, Duncan,** *Whiteout* (1976). Adventure novel about the effects of a sudden ice storm on a group of men in the Arctic.

**McCullough, David,** *The Johnstown Flood* (1968). An award-winning historian with a careful eye for detail deftly reconstructs the famous nineteenth-century tragedy. The destruction of Galveston by hurricane is vividly reconstructed in Herbert M. Mason, *Death from the Sea* (1972).

**Mowat, Farley,** *The Serpent's Coil* (1961). The title is a symbol for "cyclone" and this is the true story of a freighter's 100-day ordeal in the midst of one.

**Reifsnyder, William E.,** *Weathering the Wilderness: The Sierra Club Guide to Practical Meteorology* (1980). Manual for understanding and predicting the weather, with detailed climatologies of different regions.

**Sloane, Eric,** *Folklore of American Weather* (1963). Delightful little book on weather sayings and belief. See *Eric Sloane's Weather Book* (1952) and *Eric Sloane's Almanac and Weather Forecaster* (1955).

**Stewart, George R.,** *Storm* (1941). This novel about the life of a wind they called Maria started the tradition of giving storms proper names.

**Watts, Alan,** *Instant Weather Forecasting* (1968). Nicely organized sixty-four page illustrated guide to weather forecasting from the clouds; for use by anyone to whom the weather in the near future is of vital importance.

# THE SEASONS

**Clifton, Lucille,** *Everett Anderson's Year* (1974). A children's book of pensive, honest poems for each month in the year of Everett Anderson, a child of the ghetto. For more seasonal urban verse, see Lee Bennett Hopkins, *I Think I Saw a Snail: Young Poems for City Seasons* (1969).

**Collins, Henry Hill, Jr. (ed.),** *The American Year* (1960). Nature across the land as observed by writers and naturalists, past and present, from Thoreau to Teale. See Hal Borland (t) and Les Line (p), *The Seasons* (1973); Joseph Wood Krutch, *The Twelve Seasons* (1949); and John Burroughs, *Signs and Seasons* (1886).

**Henderson, Harold G.,** *An Introduction to Haiku: An Anthology of Poems and Poets from Basho to Shiki* (1958). The apparently simple seventeen-syllable haiku are traditionally keyed to *ki,* or "season." See *Haiku in English* (1967) and R. H. Blyth's monumental *History of Haiku* (1964).

**Hughes, Ted,** *Season Songs* (1975). The English poet takes us through the year as played out in the Devon countryside. Illustrations by Leonard Baskin. Designed for young readers but good for all.

**Smith, Anthony,** *The Seasons: Life and Its Rhythms* (1979). Reveals the influence of the seasonal cycle on every living thing. Handsome illustrations.

## Winter

**Jaques, Florence and Francis Lee Jaques,** *Snowshoe Country* (1945). Zesty, unpretentious, often profound, description of the authors' winter stay in northern Minnesota. Wisconsin is the scene for Edward Lueders, *The Clam Lake Papers: A Winter in the North Woods* (1979).

**Keats, Ezra Jack,** *The Snowy Day* (1962). The author's luminous collages decorate this story book about a young boy's joy in the first snow of winter.

**Ogburn, Charlton Jr.,** *The Winter Beach* (1966). Eloquent, thoughtful portrait of the Atlantic seashore that is as bracing as a brisk walk on a cold, sunny morning.

**Rustrun, Calvin,** *Paradise Below Zero* (1968). A cold-weather lover describes the rewards of winter living and provides a lot of technical know-how on survival.

**Stokes, Donald W.,** *A Guide to Winter: Northeast and North Central North America* (1977). Handy, illustrated field guide on what to look for in the winter landscape. The really serious winter person should see Edward R. Chapell, *Field Guide to Snow Crystals* (1969).

## Spring

**Clifton, Lucille,** *The Boy Who Didn't Believe in Spring* (1973). Fine illustrations by Brinton Turkle. A book for young children about two city kids — one black, one Italian — who set off in quest of spring.

**Helm, Mackinlay,** *Spring in Spain* (1952). An art historian shares in flowing narrative his impressions of the Spanish primavera.

**Quennell, Peter,** *Spring in Sicily* (1952). A delightful travel chronicle, by the urbane English biographer and memoirist, of a season on the Mediterranean island.

**Scherman, Katharine,** *Spring on an Arctic Island* (1956). Perceptive account of the blossoming of spring on an island in the eastern Canadian Arctic; splashed with vivid descriptive passages.

**Teale, Edwin Way,** *Springtime in Britain* (1970). An American naturalist with a poet's feeling for the landscape describes his 11,000-mile journey through the natural history of Britain from Land's End to John O'Groats.

## Summer

**Barrett, Richmond,** *Good Old Summer Days* (1952). Pleasant, nostalgic look at the social life of the wealthy before the First World War at such watering spots as Newport, Saratoga, Long Branch, Bar Harbor, and Narragansett Pier. See Brendan Gill (t) and Dudley Witney (p), *Summer Place* (1978).

**Dostoevski, Feodor,** *Winter Notes on Summer Impressions* (1955). His visit to Europe in the summer of 1862, and his scathing contempt for bourgeois values of the West.

**Kurelek, William,** *A Prairie Boy's Summer* (1975). A fine book for young readers about the joys and rigors of a prairie summertime. See *A Prairie Boy's Winter* (1973).

**Roy, Gabrielle,** *Enchanted Summer* (1976). Reminiscences of summer in rural Quebec in which the season itself is the major character.

**Wharton, Edith,** *Summer* (1917). Brief, lyrical novel of summer romance between a simple young woman of a New England mountain village and a young man from the outside. "It is a classical story, like that of *Tess of the D'Urbervilles.* The young man will go away, tenderly remembering the summer, leaving the girl devastated by confusion and grief — and pregnancy" (Elizabeth Hardwick).

## Autumn

**Medsgar, Oliver P.,** *Nature Rambles, Autumn* (1930). Simple, conversational portrait of the plants and animals as they appear in the fall months. Part of a series on the seasons, published later as a set.

**O'Faolain, Sean,** *Autumn in Italy* (1953). Shrewd observations, often moving, always interesting, of his journey to the Italian boot and Sicily.

**Teale, Edwin Way,** *Autumn Across America* (1956). Keenly observant tour of autumn across the U.S. This and his volumes on the other seasons have been collected in *The American Seasons* (1976).

**Thomson, James,** *Autumn* (1730). One of four poems which make up *The Seasons* (rev. 1746), by the English poet remembered today as author of "Rule Brittannia." These sublime poems were at the forefront of the back-to-nature movement.

**Tresalt, Alvin,** *Autumn Harvest* (1964). Autumn activities and occurrences: children's book, exquisitely illustrated by Roger Duvoisin. They collaborated on other seasonal books, including *Hide and Seek Fog* (1965), *"Hi, Mister Robin!"* (1950), *White Snow, Bright Snow* (1947), and *It's Time Now!* (1969).

# LIFE

## Molecular Basis

**Crick, Francis,** *Of Molecules and Men* (1966). The English Nobel laureate's dramatic role in the development of molecular biology. See *Life Itself: Its Origin and Nature* (1981).

**Judson, Horace Freeland,** *Eighth Day of Creation: Makers of the Revolution in Biology* (1978). Lucid history of molecular biology that gives a human dimension to the revolutionary events of the new science.

**Monod, Jacques,** *Chance and Necessity: An Essay on the Natural Philosophy of Modern Biology* (1971). Brilliant, provocative meditations; accessible to the serious reader.

**Thomas, Lewis,** *The Lives of a Cell: Notes of a Biology Watcher* (1974). Luminous essays that easily transmit his philosophical view of biology. See *The Medusa and the Snail* (1980).

**Watson, James D.,** *The Double Helix* (1967). Candid, thrilling, personal account of the discovery of the structure of DNA by the corecipient of the Nobel Prize. See *The DNA Story: A Documentary History of Gene Cloning* (1982).

## Evolution

**Attenborough, David,** *Life on Earth* (1981). Triumphant retelling of the 3.5-billion-year story of evolution, charged with uncommon freshness, clarity, and verve and illustrated with astounding photographs; "quite simply the best introduction to natural history ever written" (Desmond Morris).

**Darwin, Charles,** *The Origin of Species* (1859). One of the most influential books ever written; it puts forth his original theory of natural selection. Richard E. Leakey published an abridged and illustrated version in 1979.

**Eiseley, Loren,** *Darwin's Century: Evolution and the Men Who Discovered It* (1961). The great idea and the men who shaped it described deftly. See *Darwin and the Mysterious Mr. X: A New Light on the Evolutionists* (1979) and William Irvine, *Apes, Angels and Victorians: The Story of Darwin, Huxley, and Evolution* (1955).

**Gould, Stephen Jay,** *Ontogeny and Phylogeny* (1978). Lucid account of the development of evolutionary theory and the effect of recent genetic discoveries on its soundness. See *Ever Since Darwin: Reflections in Natural History* (1977) and *The Panda's Thumb: More Reflections in Natural History* (1980).

**Greene, John Colton,** *Death of Adam: Evolution and the Impact on Western Thought* (1959). Chronicle of the rise of the idea of evolution and the decline of the idea of creation in the century and a half from Newton to Darwin.

## Animals

**Adams, Richard,** *Watership Down* (1972). Wonderful fantasy about the quest of renegade rabbits for a new warren. Adams picked up his knowledge of rabbits from Ronald Lockley's *The Private Life of The Rabbit* (1974), the result of a five-year observation of rabbits living in a huge glass-walled warren.

**Beard, Peter H.,** *The End of the Game* (rev. 1977). Documentary of over 700 photographs and drawings of vanishing wildlife; a modern classic on East Africa.

**Carroll, Lewis,** *The Hunting of the Snark* (1876). Nonsensical mock-heroic poem about the elusive, chimerical Snark — which turns out to be a Boojum, you see.

**Colby, C. B.,** *Fur and Fury* (1963). Informal, fascinating account of weasels which, like Gavin Maxwell's otters, are delightful to read about.

**Colette,** *Creatures Great and Small* (1957). Collection of the French stylist's superb writings about animals.

**Cuppy, Will,** *How to Attract the Wombat* (1949). Delightful nonsense in "serious" pieces about animals that have been described as "more or less natural history." See *How to Become Extinct* (1942).

**Day, David,** *The Doomsday Book of Animals* (1981). Beautifully illustrated "natural history of vanished species" — nearly 300 of them that have become extinct since 1680.

**Desmond, Adrian J.,** *The Hot-blooded Dinosaurs* (1976). Iconoclastic study that challenges much of what paleontologists believe about the great beasts of the Mesozoic era. See William Stout's wonderful illustrations in *The Dinosaur* (1981).

**Douglas-Hamilton, Iain and Aria Douglas-Hamilton,** *Among the Elephants* (1975). This account of the lives of elephants (and the authors) over several years in Tanzania has extraordinary photographs of elephant behavior. For an excellent book on elephants generally, see Dan Freeman, *Elephants: The Vanishing Giants* (1981).

**Durrell, Gerald,** *Golden Bats and Pink Pigeons* (1978). His expedition to Mauritius to catch animals he could breed in his Channel Island wildlife preserve and so extend the species. See *Catch Me a Colobus* (1973).

**Fraser Darling, Frank,** *Wild Life in an African Territory* (1960). This English animal watcher and conservationist is always a joy to read. See *A Naturalist on Rona: Essays of a Biologist in Isolation* (1969) and *Pelican in the Wilderness: A Naturalist's Odyssey in North America* (1956).

**Frisch, Karl Von,** *Animal Architecture* (1974). Fascinating, popularly written description of the building activities of animals, from protozoa to mammals.

**Guillot, Rene,** *Sama* (1952). This story of an African elephant is typical of the French author's excellent children's books that stress kindness to animals. See *Oworo* (1955).

**Kinlock, Bruce,** *Sauce for the Mongoose: The Story of a Real-life Rikki-tikki-tavi* (1965). Charmingly told story of Pipa the mongoose, by a chief game warden in Tanganyika.

**Kipling, Rudyard,** *Just So Stories* (1902). Charming collection of whimsical animal fantasy tales that tell readers how the leopard got his spots, how the whale got his throat, and so on.

**Kotzwinkle, William,** *Doctor Rat* (1976). Very contemporary fantasy novel — social science fiction — that is in fact an antivivisection tract.

**Lorenz, Konrad Z.,** *King Solomon's Ring* (1952). The Nobel Prize–winning ethologist's engaging guide to animal behavior.

**McNulty, Faith,** *The Wildlife Stories of Faith McNulty* (1980). Animals in a number of different settings in a dozen stories of quiet wit and singular beauty. See *The Whooping Crane* (1966), *The Great Whale* (1974), and *Must They Die: The Strange Case of the Prairie Dog and the Black-footed Ferret* (1971).

**Maxwell, Gavin,** *Ring of Bright Water* (1961). The life of the author and his two pet otters in the Scottish highlands. "An enchanting, beautifully written, and, above all, a very funny book and everyone should read it as a tonic" (Gerald Durrell). Henry Williamson's *Tarka the Otter* (1927) is an otter classic.

**Milne, Lorus et al.,** *The Secret Life of Animals* (1975). Handsome picture book about the behavior of animals of all kinds. See *The Invertebrates of North America* (1972).

**Murie, Olaus J.,** *A Field Guide to Animal Tracks* (rev. 1975). Classic guide with loads of illustrations. See Ernest Thompson Seton, *Animal Tracks and Hunter Signs* (1958).

**North, Sterling,** *Rascal: A Memoir of a Better Era* (1963). Warmhearted, simply written recollection of the author at twelve and his pet raccoon in Wisconsin, 1918. See *The Wolfling* (1969) and *Raccoons Are the Brightest People* (1966).

**Reader's Digest Association,** *Our Magnificent Wildlife: How to Enjoy and Preserve It* (1975). Handsome illustrations and sound advice distinguish this fine volume. Other good nature books by Reader's Digest are *The Joy of Nature: How to Observe and Appreciate the Great Outdoors* (1977) and *Natural Wonders of the World* (1980).

**Rue, Leonard Lee, III,** *The World of the Beaver* (1964). Definitive, popular study; the fruit of years of personal observation. See *The World of the White Tail Deer* (1962) and *Furbearing Animals of North America* (1981).

**Ryden, Hope,** *God's Dog* (1974). Moving narrative of the coyote of the Southwest, vividly written and illustrated. See *Bobcat Year* (1981).

**Salt, Henry,** *Animal Rights Considered in Relation to Social Progress* (1892). This book "was a masterpiece of its kind; and it remains one of the most lucid and persuasive of all books written in defense of animals" (Keith Thomas). See Salt's autobiography *Seventy Years Among Savages* (1921). For a contemporary argument in favor of animal rights, see Peter Singer, *Animal Liberation* (1975).

**Sanderson, Ivan T.,** *Animal Treasure* (1937). Narrative of expedition into West Africa on behalf of the British Museum; written with charm and lively style.

**Schaller, George B.,** *Golden Shadows, Flying Hooves* (1973). His three years in Serengeti National Park in Tanzania. See *Serengeti: A Kingdom of Predators* (1973) and Hugo van Lawick's extraordinary photographs in *Savage Paradise: The Predators of Serengeti* (1978).

**Stadtfield, Curtis K.,** *Whitetail Deer* (1975). Eloquent summary of a year in the lives of deer in their northern Michigan environment.

**Walker, Ernest P. et al.,** *Mammals of the World* (rev. 1978). Superbly produced two-volume illustrated reference set that describes every genus of mammal, from the egg-laying platypus to modern man.

## Big Cats

**Adamson, Joy,** *Born Free: A Lioness of Two Worlds* (1960). Elsa was raised as a pet and patiently taught to hunt for herself before being set free in the African wilderness. See *Living Free* (1961) and *Forever Free* (1963).

**Bertram, Brian,** *Pride of Lions* (1978). The author studied the same group of lions as did George Schaller, who reported his findings in *The Serengeti Lion* (1972), a scholarly work. This is more accessible to general readers.

**Kessel, Joseph,** *The Lion* (1959). Brilliant adventure story of a girl and the wild denizens of an African game preserve.

**Mountfort, Guy,** *Saving the Tiger* (1981). The head of the World Wildlife Fund tells of the effort to rescue the Asian tiger from extinction. Incredible photographs.

**Murphy, Robert,** *The Mountain Lion* (1969). Novel about the life of a mountain lion in Arizona.

## Apes

**Brewer, Stella,** *The Chimps of Mount Asserik* (1978). She taught zoo chimps how to live in the jungle, that is, how to be "wild."

**Goodall, Jane,** *In the Shadow of Man* (1972). Vivid introduction to the wild chimpanzees at Combe National Park by Lake Tanganyika. Packed full of superb photographs. See *My Friends the Chimpanzees* (1968).

**Patterson, Francine and Eugene Linden,** *The Education of Koko* (1981). Koko, a young lowland gorilla, was taught American Sign Language and to respond to some spoken English. See John MacKinnon, *The Ape Within Us* (1978) and H. S. Terrace, *Nim* (1979).

**Rey, H. A.,** *Curious George* (1941). The first of a popular series of picture story books about the hilarious adventures of the hypercurious little monkey.

**Schaller, George B.,** *The Year of the Gorilla* (1964). Classic study: well-written, incisive, illustrated.

## Bears

**Bond, Michael,** *A Bear Called Paddington* (1958). The first of a series of children's books about a bumbling little bear from "darkest Peru" who is adopted by a London family.

**Engel, Marian,** *Bear* (1976). Strange, compelling story of the relationship of a woman and a big bear in the wilderness.

**Ford, Barbara,** *Black Bear: The Spirit of the Wilderness* (1981). Everything a sixth-to-eighth-grader could possibly want to know about black bears, vividly told by a woman who views them as an important part of wilderness ecology. Grownups will like this book too.

**Milne, A. A.,** *Winnie the Pooh* (1926). The merry adventures of the honey-loving bear, his animal friends, and Christopher Robin. An ursus minor classic. See *The House at Pooh Corner* (1928).

**Russell, Andy,** *Grizzly Country* (1967). He spent five years studying grizzlies in remote Alaska and Canada. This is what he saw. See *Trails of a Wilderness Wanderer* (1971) and *Andy Russell's Adventures with Wild Animals* (1978).

## Wolves

**Aiken, Joan,** *The Wolves of Willoughby Chase* (1964). Wicked wolves without and a grim governess within the great English country house. A brilliant mixture of suspenseful Victorian melodrama and humor. An enchantment from start to finish. See *Black Hearts in Battersea,* (1964), a sequel.

**Caras, Roger A.,** *The Custer Wolf: Biography of an American Renegade* (1966). Exciting, realistic fictional biography of a wolf that ravaged South Dakota between 1910 and 1920.

**DeRegniers, Beatrice Schenk,** *Red Riding Hood* (1972). Retelling in verse of the Brothers Grimm version for boys and girls to read themselves, with illustrations by Edward Gorey. Other modern illustrated retellings of classic wolf tales include Robin and Jocelyn Wild, *Little Big Pig and the Big Bad Wolf* (1972) and Erik Blegvad, *The Three Little Pigs* (1980).

**Fox, Michael W.,** *The Soul of the Wolf* (1980). Provocative look at the similarities between human and wolf societies. See *Behavior of Wolves, Dogs, and Related Canids* (1972).

**George, Jean Craighead,** *Julie of the Wolves* (1972). Beautiful story for young readers of an Eskimo girl alone on the Alaskan tundra who, in order to survive, learns to communicate with the wolves. Winner of the Newberry Award. See *The Moon of the Gray Wolves* (1969), nonfiction.

**Lawrence, R. D.,** *Secret Go the Wolves* (1980). How he hand-reared two wolf pups. Another true story of friendship between man and wolf is Robert F. Leslie, *In the Shadow of a Rainbow* (1974).

**Lopez, Barry,** *Of Wolves and Men* (1978). The role of the wolf in myth.

**Mech, L. David,** *Wolf: The Ecology and Behavior of an Endangered Species* (1970). Mech describes in nontechnical language the wolf's behavior, its relations with other animals, and its environment on Isle Royale. Durward L. Allen, *Wolves of Minong: Their Vital Role in a Wild Community* (1979) is also a study of the Isle Royale timber wolf. Ewan Clarkson, *Wolf Country: A Wilderness Pilgrimage* (1975) is a more literary, popular book about the island.

**Mowat, Farley,** *Never Cry Wolf* (1963). The summer he spent in the arctic with a pack of wolves.

**Zimen, Eric,** *The Wolf: A Species in Danger* (1979). Provocative study based on his first-hand experiences with Bavarian wolves.

## Horses

**Chipperfield, Joseph E.,** *Banner, the Pacing White Stallion* (1972). Set in the Rockies of the vanishing frontier, this story for older children is about some men's obsession with capturing the legendary last of the wild white stallions. Another fine story about horses is his *Ghost Horse: Stallion of the Oregon Trail* (1962).

**Cunninghame Graham, R. B.,** *The Horses of the Conquest* (1930). The story of the horses of the Spanish conquest of the New World rendered with great charm by the half-Scottish, half-Spanish writer. Tom Lea's superb novel, *The Hands of Cantú* (1964), is about the horses of the Conquistadors.

**Dobie, J. Frank,** *The Mustangs* (1952). History of the wild horses of the American West by the Texan master of the good yarn.

**Goble, Paul,** *The Girl Who Loved Wild Horses* (1978). Paintings sweep and stampede across the pages of this story for young readers about a Native American girl's love of horses. Awarded the Caldecott Medal.

**Goodall, Daphne Machin,** *Horses of the World* (rev. 1974). An illustrated survey, with over 320 photographs of breeds of horses and ponies. See *Flight of the East Prussian Horses* (1973).

**Green, Ben K.,** *Horse Tradin'* (1967). The author's many trading experiences, starting back in the twenties, in the tangy language of the Texas storyteller.

**Griffiths, Helen,** *The Wild Heart* (1963). Beautifully told story for younger readers about a mare in the Argentine pampas. See *Horses in the Clouds* (1957) and *The Wild Horses of Santander* (1966).

**Henry, Marguerite,** *King of the Wind* (1948). Newberry Award–winning story of a real horse written for fourth-to-sixth-graders by a popular writer of many horse stories. See *Misty of Chincoteague* (1947) and *Stormy, Misty's Foal* (1963).

**Hope, Charles E. G.,** *The Horseman's Manual* (1972). Contains practically everything a horse owner could want to know; probably the finest general manual. Also of interest to an owner is Steven D. Price et al. (eds.), *The Whole Horse Catalog* (1978).

**Podhajsky, Alois,** *My Dancing White Horse* (1965). Autobiography of the director of the Spanish Riding School of Vienna, famous for its white Lipizzaners. See *The Riding Teacher: A Basic Guide to Correct Methods of Classical Instruction* (1973) and Milan Volenc, *Lipizzaner: The Story of the Horses of Lipica* (1981).

**Seth-Thomas, Michael (ed.),** *The Horse* (1980). The horse in history — war, art, work, sport — lavishly illustrated in color. See Fred Urquhart (ed.), *The Book of Horses: The Horse Through the Ages in Art and Literature* (1981).

**Ryden, Hope,** *America's Last Wild Horses* (1971). Photographic account of the battle

to protect the last herds from commercial exploitation. See *Mustangs: A Return to the Wilds* (1972).

**Sewell, Anna,** *Black Beauty* (1877). This classic fictional autobiography has been enjoyed by children for over a century. Other horses that have long been popular are Walter Farley, *The Black Stallion* (1941) and Mary O'Hara, *My Friend Flicka* (1941).

**Silvester, Hans,** *Horses of the Camargue* (1976). Astounding photographs taken by a man who lived among these wild horses in southern France.

**Vavra, Robert,** *Equus: The Creation of a Horse* (1977). Poetic photographs of wild horses accompanied by literary quotations that will thrill any horse lover. See *Such Is the Real Nature of Horses* (1979) and *All Those Girls in Love with Horses* (1981).

## Dogs

**Ackerley, J. R.,** *My Dog Tulip* (1956). He describes, with great affection and skill, the ties that often bind man to dog. See *We Think the World of You* (1961).

**Chekhov, Anton,** *Kashtanka* (1961). Story of a mongrel who becomes a circus performer: humor and pathos, honest realism, and engaging fantasy.

**Dodson, Kenneth,** *Hector the Stowaway Dog* (1958). True nautical story of a dog's odyssey from Vancouver to Japan in search of his master.

**Glover, Harry (ed.),** *A Standard Guide to Pure-Bred Dogs* (1978). Fine illustrations and writing. An authoritative, useful, and pleasurable work. The American Kennel Club's *The Complete Dog Book* (rev. 1979) is also very good.

**Griffiths, Helen,** *León* (1968). A mongrel sheepdog in a Spanish village left with indifferent people while his master went off to war.

Kantor, Mackinlay, *The Voice of Bugle Ann* (1935). Eloquent story of a foxhound in rural Missouri that is "a short epic of this truly American sport. . . . It holds the interest, but one reads the book for the races, the sessions around the camp fire, the glimpses of Bugle Ann" (Caroline Gordon). See *The Daughter of Bugle Ann* (1953).

Lawick, Hugo Van, *Solo: The Story of an African Wild Dog* (1974). Vivid, expert description. With his wife, Jane Goodall, he has written *Innocent Killers* (1971) about the Cape hunting dog, the spotted hyena, and the golden jackal.

London, Jack, *White Fang* (1906). A cross-breed dog sacrifices his life to save that of the man who had saved him from a cruel owner. The dramatic quality of London's dog stories is revived in Joseph E. Chipperfield, *Storm of Dancerwood* (rev. 1967), Nicholas Kalashnikoff, *Toyon* (1950), and R. D. Lawrence, *The North Runner* (1979).

Lorenz, Konrad Z., *Man Meets Dog* (1955). The famous zoologist focuses with great wit on the relationship between people and their dogs.

Mowat, Farley, *The Dog Who Wouldn't Be* (1957). A boy and his dog, this time on the Canadian plains; told with rare humor and style.

Muir, John, *Stickeen* (1909). A short novel about a man, a dog, a storm, and a glacier, set in Alaska.

Sendak, Maurice and Matthew Margolis, *Some Swell Pup: or Are You Sure You Want a Dog?* (1976). Marvelous Sendak illustrations in a realistic book about the responsibilities involved in raising a dog.

Smith, Dodie, *Hundred and One Dalmatians* (1957). Warm, humorous fantasy for dog lovers of all ages about a London couple with two beloved dalmatians who end up with 101 beloved dalmatians.

Vladimov, George, *Faithful Ruslan* (1979). A dog's view of the gulag in a novel about a guard dog at a Siberian prison camp.

## Cats

Blackbeard, Bill and Malcolm Whyte, *Great Comic Cats* (1981). Comprehensive history of the cat in caricature and comic narrative from the Cowardly Lion and the Cheshire Cat to Felix, Krazy Cat, Poosy, Gato, Fritz, Fat Freddy's Cat, and Garfield.

Bond, Simon, *101 Uses for a Dead Cat* (1981). Tenth through one-hundred-tenth lives for your cat: ingenious and hilarious. Cat-haters will also enjoy Skip Morrow, *I Hate Cats Book* (1980).

Briggs, Katherine, *Nine Lives: The Folklore of Cats* (1980). Famed folklorist's farrago of fascinating, often funny, feline folklore.

Eliot, T. S., *Old Possum's Book of Practical Cats* (1939). Something of a literary curiosity, a book of Learesque light poems about cats. There is a 1982 edition illustrated by Edward Gorey.

Gág, Wanda, *Millions of Cats* (1938). Classic picture storybook, charmingly illustrated, about an old man who cannot decide which cat to adopt, so he takes them all — "millions and billions and trillions of cats."

Gallico, Paul, *The Abandoned* (1950). A sentimental fantasy about a boy turned into a cat; full of interesting cat lore. See *The Silent Miaow* (1964).

Lessing, Doris, *Particularly Cats* (1967). Absorbing, simply-told account of experiences with cats she has known.

Macbeth, George and Martin Booth (eds.), *The Book of Cats* (1977). Hefty volume containing literary selections, both poetry and prose, and illustrations that will tickle the whiskers of any ailurophile. See Jean Burden (ed.), *A Celebration of Cats: An Anthology of Poems* (1974).

Pond, Grace, *The Complete Cat Encyclopedia* (1973). All that a cat fancier or breeder would want to know in one volume. See *A Standard Guide to Cat Breeds* (1979).

Sarton, May, *Fur Person* (1957). The saga of Tom Jones, whose decision to find just the right home proved successful; told with great charm.

Tangye, Derek, *Somewhere a Cat Is Waiting* (1976). Nice, sometimes moving and funny, story of the winning of the author from the ranks of cat haters.

Van Vechten, Carl, *The Tiger in the House* (1920). As the author says, this is a book about "the manners and customs of the cat, his graces and calineries [sic], the history of his subjugation of humankind."

## Insects and Spiders

Dethier, Vincent G., *To Know a Fly* (1963). Clear and witty explanation of the purpose and methods of studying the behavior of the black blowfly.

Duren, Bernard et al., *Insects Etc.: An Anthology of Arthropods, Featuring a Bounty of Beetles* (1982). Exquisite paintings of bugs, grasshoppers, beetles, and the like by Duren, with lively text and quotes.

Evans, Howard E., *Life on a Little-known Planet* (1968). Entertaining, authoritative introduction to the world of insects. See *Wasp Farm* (1963).

Fabre, J. Henri, *The Insect World of J. Henri Fabre* (1942). Selections, edited by Edwin Way Teale, from the writings of the pioneer French entomologist. Teale's own *The Strange Lives of Familiar Insects* (1962) and *Near Horizons: The Story of an Insect Garden* (1942) are delightful.

Frisch, Karl Von, *The Dancing Bees: An Account of Life and Senses of the Honey Bee* (rev. 1965). A summation of a lifelong study of the bee's behavior by the Nobel Prize–winning Austrian zoologist. See *Bees: Their Vision, Chemical Senses, and Language* (rev. 1971). The most curious book about bees is Maurice Maeterlinck's sentimental and mystical *The Life of the Bee* (1903), while the most remarkable is Bernd Heinrich's *Bumblebee Economics* (1979).

Howe, William H. (ed.), *The Butterflies of North America* (1975). Outstanding introduction to lepidopterology. Kjell Sandved (p) and Jo Brewer (t), *Butterflies* (1976) is a large-format volume with magnificent photographs.

Lehane, Brendan, *The Compleat Flea* (1969). Light-hearted compendium of lore, odd facts, literary allusions, and social comments on one of man's oldest enemies.

Linsenmaier, Walter, *Insects of the World* (1972). A sparkling scientific text and magnificent illustrations and photographs join in a vivid exploration of the complex "other world." More local in interest is Alexander Klots and Elsie Klots, *Insects of North America* (1971). The best field guides are Donald J. Borror and Richard E. White, *A Field Guide to the Insects of America North of Mexico* (1970) and Herbert Levi and Lorna Levi, *Spiders and Their Kin* (1968).

Tweedie, Michael, *Insect Life* (1977). With considerable charm, the author introduces the reader to insect life all over the world.

White, E. B., *Charlotte's Web* (1952). Children's classic, illustrated by Garth Williams, about the heroic, intelligent spider named Charlotte and her efforts to save the life of Wilbur the pig.

## Plants

Anderson, Edgar, *Plants, Man and Life* (1952). In a rambling, felicitous style, a "plant anthropologist" explores the relationship between common plants and man.

**Andrews, Henry N.,** *The Fossil Hunters: In Search of Ancient Plants* (1980). Lucid, anecdotal sketches of scientists who devoted themselves to the study of fossil plants. Here is the human side of science. See Barry Thomas, *The Evolution of Plants and Flowers* (1981).

**Bailey, Liberty Hyde,** *How Plants Got Their Names* (1933). A knowledgeable book that with charm and eloquence traces the genesis of the scientific names of plants.

**Christopher, John,** *No Blade of Grass* (1957). Imaginative scenario of a disastrous world famine resulting from a blight on grass crops. Christopher's other catastrophe novels include *The Long Winter* (1962) (brief ice age) and *The Ragged Edge* (1966) (earthquakes).

**Colette,** *For a Flower Album* (1960). Translation of a slender 1949 work in which flowers and plants provide the themes for Colette's sensual, exquisitely phrased pieces; with watercolors by Manet.

**Conti, Alice,** *The Book of Flowers* (1973). Beautiful large-format book about flower illustration. See *The Treasury of Flowers* (1975) and Martyn Rix, *The Art of the Plant World: Great Botanical Illustrators and Their Work* (1981).

**Dowden, Anne Ophelia,** *Wild Green Things in the City: A Book of Weeds* (1972). Take this with you to identify that plant tenaciously growing in a crack at the curb; look at the drawings of the plants in their "natural habitat" — amid old cigarette packs and bottle caps. Great for city kids.

**Galston, Arthur W.,** *Green Wisdom* (1981). Brief pieces from the author's columns in *Natural History* magazine about plants and their relationship to the world. Fine writing and illustrations.

**Gordon, Lesley,** *Green Magic: Flowers, Plants and Herbs in Lore and Legend* (1977). Sumptuously illustrated collection of myths, stories, and quotes about the significance of plants.

**Kramer, Jack,** *Cacti and Other Succulents* (1978). Lavish volume laden with beautiful photographs that is also a first-rate guide to cacti. See *Orchids: Flowers of Romance and Mystery* (1975), *Gardening in Small Spaces* (1979), and *An Illustrated Guide to Flowering Houseplants* (1981).

**Leonni, Leo,** *Parallel Botany* (1977). Precision, authority, wit, and scholarship in the first full-scale guide to the world of parallel plants — a vast, ramified, extremely peculiar, and wholly imaginary plant kingdom. Unique, definitive, hilarious.

**Marsh, Jean (t) and Kate Greenaway (i),** *The Illuminated Language of Flowers* (1978). Rearrangement of the 1884 classic, beautifully done and full of Victorian charm and exquisite Greenaway drawings.

**Masefield, G. B. et al.,** *The Oxford Book of Food Plants* (1969). Wonderful book for anyone interested in planting and cooking. Origins, life cycles, geographical distribution, etc.; with color illustrations.

**Meeuse, B. J. D.,** *The Story of Pollination* (1961). All about pollination, with superb drawings.

**Milne, Lorus and Margery Milne,** *Living Plants of the World* (1967). Fine nontechnical introduction to the world of plants; a mine of fascinating information. Other good primers are E. J. H. Corner, *The Life of Plants* (1964) and Fritz W. Went, *The Plants* (1963).

**Moore, Ward,** *Greener than You Think* (1947). Science fiction satire about a new chemical that enables plants to transform and use any material for growth, which leads to the obliteration of everything on earth. Other good botany-fiction novels are John Boyd, *The Pollinators of Eden* (1969); Thomas Disch, *The Genocides*

(1965); and John Wyndham, *The Day of the Triffids* (1951).

**Niering, William,** *The Audubon Society Field Guide to North American Wildflowers* (1979). The Eastern edition of the first-rate handbook. The Western edition is by Richard Spellenberg and Nancy Olmstead. *The Audubon Society Book of Wildflowers* (1978) is a lovely picture album by Les Line (p) and Walter H. Hodge (t).

**Parker, Loni and David T. Jenkins,** *Mushrooms: A Separate Kingdom* (1979). Handsome book about facts and folklore surrounding mushrooms, embellished with calligraphy and color illustrations. For mushroom hunters the best guide is Orsan K. Miller, Jr., *Mushrooms in North America* (1979).

**Penn, Irving,** *Flowers* (1980). Album of gorgeous, sensual color photographs of flowers.

**Richie, Donald (ed.),** *The Masters' Book of Ikebana: Backgrounds and Principles of Japanese Flower Arrangement* (1966). Large, splendidly made book, full of luminous photographs and authoritative information about this ancient Japanese art.

## Trees

**Collis, John Stewart,** *The Triumph of the Tree* (1954). Almost poetic amalgam of botany, conservation, and philosophy about our relation to trees and a plea for reforestation of our vanishing woodlands.

**Fowles, John (t) and Frank Horvat (p),** *The Tree* (1979). Haunting photographs by the French photographer with the lyrical prose of the English novelist.

**Jackson, James P.,** *The Biography of a Tree* (1979). The 250-year life of a white oak, from acorn to natural death, in a sensitive, illustrated book. A valuable lesson in forest ecology.

**Johnson, Hugh,** *The International Book of Trees* (1974). Big, beautiful book, brimming with color photographs, that serves as a complete guide to the major forest and garden trees of the temperate world. A similar visual treat is Les Line (p) and Ann and Myron Sutton (t), *The Audubon Society Book of Trees* (1981).

**Kieran, John,** *Introduction to Trees* (1954). Absorbing elementary guide to common trees of America. See Frank C. Brockman, *Trees of North America: A Field Guide to the Major Native and Introduced Species North of Mexico* (1968).

**Peattie, Donald Culross,** *A Natural History of Western Trees* (1953). The author had not only an extensive scientific knowledge as a naturalist, but a lyric gift for words. "One of the most eloquent and authoritative studies ever written of America's woodlands" (Hal Borland). See *A Natural History of Trees of Eastern and Central North America* (1950).

**McPhee, John,** *Oranges* (1967). A minor classic of reportage and perhaps the last word on the subject: sketches of orange growers, discussions of the orange-juice industry, a history of oranges, botanical descriptions, and the like.

**Silverstein, Shel,** *The Giving Tree* (1964). "Once there was a tree . . . and she loved a little boy." So begins a parable of rare perception, beautifully written and illustrated, about the gift of giving.

**Symonds, George W.,** *The Tree Identification Book* (1973). Easy-to-use manual that enables you to identify a tree by looking up any one part — bark, seeds, leaves, twigs, flowers. See *The Shrub Identification Book* (1963).

**Treuer, Robert,** *The Tree Farm* (1977). How the author gave up his job and moved to the wilds of Minnesota to start a tree farm.

# PART III

# PEOPLE

# HUMANKIND

**Berne, Eric,** *Games People Play: The Psychology of Human Relationships* (1964). A psychiatrist looks at the "games" we play in order to get "strokes" from other people. A book that is enlightening and disturbing.

**Bronowski, J.,** *The Ascent of Man* (1973). Bronowski's wide learning and enthusiasm make this history of human scientific ingenuity exciting reading.

**Dickson, Paul,** *The Official Rules* (1978). Offbeat compendium of laws, principles, and instructions for coping in a world increasingly dominated by impersonal institutions, uncontrolable objects, and unpredictable human behavior. See *The Official Explanations* (1980).

**Dixon, Dougal,** *After Man* (1981). He describes the forms of life on earth 50 million years from now. Brilliantly imaginative, yet firmly based on zoological, botanical, and geological fact. Gene Bylinsky, *Life in Darwin's Universe: Evolution and the Cosmos* (1981) makes a provocative companion.

**Dixon, W. Macneile,** *The Human Situation* (1938). An extraordinarily fertile mind eloquently and wittily ranges over basic problems of living. See Weston La-

Barre, *The Human Animal* (1954), in which a social anthropologist speculates on humankind.

**Dubos, René J.,** *So Human an Animal* (1968). Environmental and genetic influences on man's development are examined in this Pulitzer Prize–winning work. See *Beast or Angel: Choices that Make Us Human* (1974) and *Celebration of Life* (1981).

**Farb, Peter,** *Humankind* (1978). An absorbing account of the rise and development of humankind that continually probes in search of the causes of things.

**Gould, Stephen Jay,** *The Mismeasure of Man* (1981). Incisive, far-ranging historical study of scientific racism as it influenced the observations of IQ theorists. Winner of National Book Critics Circle Award.

**Huxley, Thomas H.,** *Man's Place in Nature* (1863). Victorian classic of biology about the meaning of evolution. Its ethical significance is taken up in George Gaylord Simpson, *The Meaning of Evolution* (rev. 1967).

**Johanson, Donald and Maitland Edey,** *Lucy: The Beginnings of Mankind* (1981). Johanson, an American paleoanthropologist, explains the significance of his discovery of the bones of "Lucy" — the oldest erect-walking human ancestor ever found — and disputes the Leakeys' claim about when man first appeared.

**Leakey, Richard E. and Roger Lewin,** *Origins* (1977). What the new paleontological discoveries reveal about the emergence of our species and its possible future. See *People of the Lake: Mankind and Its Beginnings* (1978). See also John Reader, *Missing Links: The Hunt for Earliest Man* (1981), a stunningly illustrated survey of the quest for our roots, from Darwin to the Leakeys.

**Montagu, Ashley,** *On Being Human* (rev. 1966). Eloquent refutation of the status of competition and rugged individualism as laws of life; he finds cooperation dominant. Further elucidated in *Man and Aggression* (1973), in which he takes on Lorenz and Ardrey. See *Man's Most Dangerous Myth: The Fallacy of Race* (1974), *The Human Connection* (1979), and *Growing Young* (1981).

**Sheehy, Gail,** *Passages: Predictable Crises of Adult Life* (1976). Based on the latest scientific research, she uses lively case histories to help us prepare for the watersheds of life. See *Pathfinders: Overcoming the Crises of Adult Life and Finding Your Own Path to Well-Being* (1981).

**Stapledon, Olaf,** *Odd John* (1936). Fictional biography of a strange young Englishman who is in fact the next evolutionary step beyond man. One of the great works of science fiction. Other novels on this theme are Theodore Sturgeon, *More than Human* (1953) and A. E. Van Vogt, *Slan* (1946).

**Teilhard De Chardin, Pierre,** *The Phenomenon of Man* (1959). The French Jesuit and paleontologist tells of man's role in the evolutionary process: his continuing part in organizing the "Noosphere" and guiding it toward the "Omega Point." See *The Future of Man* (1964).

**Wilson, Edward O.,** *On Human Nature* (1978). The sociobiologist argues that so-cial behavior is primarily the result of genetic predetermination. As a corrective, see Ashley Montagu (ed.), *Sociobiology Examined* (1980).

## Jews

**Agnon, S. Y.,** *The Bridal Canopy* (1937). The Nobel Prize–winning writer's novel about Reb Yudel — a Jewish Don Quixote — on the road in search of husbands for his three daughters. A wise and comic work, rich in Jewish folklore. See *Guest for the Night* (1968) and *Twenty-one Stories* (1970).

**Aleichem, Sholom,** *The Best of Sholom Aleichem* (1979). Selection of short stories of Russian-Jewish village life by the writer on whose tales *Fiddler on the Roof* is based.

**Dann, Jack,** *Wandering Stars: An Anthology of Jewish Science Fiction* (1974). Delightful offbeat collection of shlemiels in orbit, space rabbis, and so forth. See *More Wandering Stars* (1981).

**Grayzel, Solomon,** *History of the Jews* (1968). Succinct, comprehensive account of the long history of the Jewish people. A good popular survey is Chaim Potok, *Wanderings: Chaim Potok's History of the Jews* (1978).

**Kahler, Erich,** *The Jews Among the Nations* (1967). A masterpiece of condensation by a distinguished scholar.

**Laqueur, Walter,** *A History of Zionism* (1972). Sympathetic, balanced, and thoughtful study. See *The Terrible Secret: Suppression of the Truth About the "Final Solution"* (1981) and *The Missing Years* (1980), a novel.

**Malamud, Bernard,** *The Fixer* (1966). Pulitzer Prize–winning novel set in Czarist Russia, about an ordinary man accused of ritual murder and his heroic victory over brutality and degradation. For an account of the real fixer, see Maurice Samuel, *Blood Accusation: The Strange History of the Beiliss Case* (1966).

Neugroschel, Joachim (ed.), *The Shtetl: A Creative Anthology of Jewish Life in Eastern Europe* (1979). Rich and varied collection of writings about village life form the eighteenth-century tales of the Baal Shem Tov to twentieth-century fiction. Other basic anthologies are Leo Schwartz (ed.), *The Jewish Caravan: Great Stories of 25 Centuries* (1976), Howard Schwartz and Anthony Rudolf (eds.), *Voices Within the Ark: The Modern Jewish Poets* (1981), and William Novak and Moshe Waldoks (eds), *The Big Book of Jewish Humor* (1981).

Patai, Raphael, *The Jewish Mind* (1977). Analysis of the characteristics associated with the "Jewish personality." See *The Vanished World of the Jews* (1981) and *The Myth of the Jewish Race* (1975).

Rosten, Leo, *Leo Rosten's Treasury of Jewish Quotations* (1972). A dazzlement of 4,352 proverbs, folk sayings, witticisms, and the like collected and freshly translated or rewritten. See *The Joys of Yiddish* (1968).

Roth, Cecil, *Doña Gracia of the House of Nasi* (1941). Engaging portrait of a fascinating woman and the struggle by the secret Jews (Marranos) of the sixteenth century for freedom of conscience. See *The House of Nasi: The Duke of Naxos* (1948). Other works by the Anglo-Jewish historian include *The Jewish Contribution to Civilization* (1938), *History of the Jews* (rev. 1970), and *Jewish Art* (rev. 1971).

Schwarz-Bart, Andre, *The Last of the Just* (1961). Novel depicting the drama of Jewish suffering, martyrdom, and transfiguration begins with a pogrom in the twelfth century and ends in a gas chamber.

Singer, I. J., *Of a World that Is No More* (1971). The elder brother of Isaac Bashevis Singer beautifully evokes his childhood in a small Polish town at the turn of the century. For a stunning look at that world, see Lucjan Dobroszycki and Barbara Kirshenblatt-Gimblett, *Image Before My Eyes: A Photographic History of Jewish Life in Poland, 1864–1939* (1978).

Singer, Isaac Bashevis, *The Collected Stories of Isaac Bashevis Singer* (1981). Rich, hypnotic tales that enfold the reader into the author's world of imps, demons, lovers, and other mischievous creatures in prewar Poland and in the America of Yiddish-speaking immigrants from Poland.

Wiesel, Elie, *The Jews of Silence: A Personal Report on Soviet Jewry* (1966). Eloquent account of the plight of the Jews in the Soviet Union by a reflective, morally concerned writer, himself a survivor of Auschwitz. See *A Jew Today* (1979) and his powerful novels of the Holocaust, *The Oath* (1973), *The Town Beyond the Wall* (1964), and *Splinters* (1982).

## The Holocaust

Améry, Jean, *At the Mind's Limit: Contemplations by a Survivor on Auschwitz and Its Realities* (1980). A Belgian journalist offers bleak testimony about life and death in the concentration camps.

Appelfeld, Aharon, *Badenheim 1939* (1980). Novel about Jews at an Austrian spa in the summer of 1939 who are bent on their little pleasures and fail to see what is happening around them. Called "a small masterpiece" (Irving Howe) it takes its power from the disparity between its graceful writing style and the horror that the reader knows will ensue. See *The Age of Wonders* (1982).

Bettelheim, Bruno, *Surviving* (1979). The Vienna-born psychiatrist, himself a survivor of the concentration camps, here collects some writings over the last forty years, mainly on the Holocaust.

Dawidowicz, Lucy S., *The War Against the Jews 1933–1945* (1975). Step-by-step account that is "as lucid and complete a rendering of these ghastly events in all their political and bureaucratic concatenations as we are likely to get in a single volume" (Robert Alter). See *A Holocaust Reader* (1976), *The Jewish Presence* (1977), and *The Holocaust and the Historian* (1981).

**Des Pres, Terrence,** *The Survivor: An Anatomy of Life in the Death Camps* (1976). Based on his reading of "original testimony" of survivors, he argues that there is a connection between staying alive in one of Hitler's or Stalin's death camps and staying human. A powerful, elegant, and provocative book.

**Epstein, Leslie,** *King of the Jews* (1979). The hero of this novel heads the Judenrat and reigns as virtual dictator in the ghetto of an unnamed Polish city. Based on fact, it is a fine literary attempt to come to terms with the Holocaust.

**Hersey, John,** *The Wall* (1950). Long novel in the form of a diary of the courageous resistance by the Jews of the Warsaw ghetto from 1939 to 1943, when the Germans finally destroyed it. For a nonfictional account see Ber Mark, *Uprising in the Warsaw Ghetto* (1975).

**Klüger, Ruth and Peggy Mann,** *The Last Escape* (1973). Compelling account of the attempted rescue of Europe's Jews by members of the Massad, the secret organization of the Jewish settlement in Palestine.

**Morganstern, Soma,** *The Third Pillar* (1955). Symbolic novel of Nazi destruction of the Polish Jews rendered in Old Testament cadences "enables us to grasp in a vision the meaning of a dread episode in human history which a hundred straightforward reports have failed to convey" (Maurice Samuel).

**Rothchild, Sylvia (ed.),** *Voices from the Holocaust* (1981). Dramatic oral history by survivors. "The voices in this book must be listened to. They are the embodiment of a powerful and anguished call to life, to

faith, to salvation" (Elie Wiesel). See Azriel Eisenberg (ed.), *Witness to the Holocaust* (1981).

## Gypsies

**Borrow, George,** *Lavengro* (1851). Fictionalized memoirs of the author's life among the gypsies of England, full of roving adventure and eccentric characters. *The Romany Rye* (1857) is a sequel.

**Koudelka, Josef,** *Gypsies: Photographs* (1975). An eye-riveting album of photographs taken mainly in East Slovakia during the sixties.

**Leland, Charles Godfrey,** *The Gypsies* (1882). An American Borrow, this "most engaging of minor men of letters . . . [was] famous for two generations as a lover of the marvellous, the forbidden, the droll and the wild" (Van Wyck Brooks). His *Memoirs* (1893) are full of picturesque charm.

**Starkie, Walter,** *Raggle-Taggle: Adventures with a Fiddle in Hungary and Roumania* (1933). A latter-day scholar-gypsy, a British professor, fiddled his way among the gypsies and writes of his adventures with grace and enthusiasm.

**Yoors, Jan,** *The Gypsies* (1967). At age twelve, the author ran away from home to join a gypsy caravan and lived among them for ten years. He wrote this fascinating inside view "as a protest against oblivion, as a cry of love for this race of strangers who have lived among us for centuries and remained apart." See *Crossing: A Journal of Resistance and Survival in World War II* (1971).

# HUMANITY

## The Body

**Clark, Kenneth,** *The Nude* (1956). This "study in ideal form" is a classic, a bril-

liant account of the human body in art. A good companion is Constance Sullivan's fine study of the body in photography, *The Nude* (1980).

Lowen, Alexander, *Depression and the Body: The Biological Basis of Faith and Reality* (1972). The creator of Bioenergetics advocates reestablishment of communication with our one instrument of self-expression via a series of simple exercises. See *The Betrayal of the Body* (1967) and *The Language of the Body* (1969).

Nilsson, Lennart and Jan Lindberg, *Behold Man: A Photographic Journey of Discovery Inside the Body* (1974). Striking photographs, many enlarged tens of thousands of times, depicting the abstract magnificence of the internal body.

*Rand McNally Atlas of the Body and Mind* (1976). Exciting, illustrated look at ourselves. See *The Johns Hopkins Atlas of Human Functional Anatomy* (1978) and C. Yokochi, *Photographic Anatomy of the Human Body* (1971).

Ratcliff, J. D., *Your Body and How It Works* (1975). Based on the popular "I Am Joe's Body" and "I Am Jane's Body" series in *Readers Digest,* it is a good popular survey of the basics, clearly presented with useful illustrations. See John S. Collis, *Living with a Stranger: A Discussion of the Human Body* (1979) and Bernard Knight, *Discovering the Human Body* (1981).

## Men

Arpino, Giovanni, *A Crime of Honor* (1962). Novel about the notion of southern Italian males that a crime committed to revenge sexual betrayal is honorable.

Brickner, Richard P., *My Second Twenty Years: An Unexpected Life* (1976). With unsparing honesty he tells how an automobile accident left him with the challenge of building a life from a wheelchair. It was a struggle to grow into manhood, not once but twice.

Dubbert, Joe L., *A Man's Place: Masculinity in Transition* (1979). Traces the evolution of man's identity since the mid-nineteenth century.

Fasteau, Marc, *The Male Machine* (1976). Liberating look at the role of contemporary man.

Goldberg, Herb, *The Hazards of Being Male: Surviving the Myth of Masculine Privilege* (1976). How American men are conditioned by society to play a role whose impossible demands psychically cripple and eventually kill them. See *The New Male: From Self-destruction to Self-care* (1979).

Hemingway, Ernest, *Men Without Women* (1927). Hard-edged, realistic short stories about hard-edged, realistic Hemingway men.

Julty, Sam, *Men's Bodies, Men's Selves* (1979). This "complete guide to the health and well-being of men's bodies, minds, and spirits" was inspired by the women's *Our Bodies, Ourselves.* See *Male Sexual Performance* (1975).

Kriegel, Leonard, *On Men and Manhood* (1979). Highly personal look at the concept of manhood and the changing role of men in American life today. He edited *The Myth of American Manhood* (1978), an anthology that traces the evolution of the masculine identity in America from colonial times to the present.

Levinson, Daniel J., *The Seasons of a Man's Life* (1978). The fruits of a ten-year study on the life cycle of males, which served as the basis for Gail Sheehy's best-selling *Passages.*

McGrady, Mike, *The Kitchen Sink Papers: My Life as a Househusband* (1975). After sixteen years of marriage he switched roles with his wife to become housekeeper to his family of five. Amusing and insightful. Another househusband heard from is Mike Clary, *Daddy's Home* (1982).

Mailer, Norman, *An American Dream* (1964). Outrageous, pop-art novel principally about the masculine experience as personified in the supermacho sexual athlete Stephen Rojack.

**Malone, Michael,** *Heroes of Eros: Male Sexuality in the Movies* (1979). Provocative analysis of how film makers have portrayed men. Lots of big glossies.

**Michaels, Leonard,** *The Men's Club* (1981). Seven men, friends and strangers, gather to form a men's group. Over the course of the evening their violence, lusts, miseries, and loves tumble out. A novel that explores the role of men in the age of liberated women.

**Perlman, Jim (ed.),** *Brother Songs: A Male Anthology of Poetry* (1979). Collection of poetry by contemporary American male poets that confronts traditional notions of "maleness" and how males relate to each other.

**Roth, Philip,** *My Life as a Man* (1974). Absorbing, humorous, incisive novel about a contemporary American novelist as contemporary American man.

**Silber, Sherman J.,** *The Male: From Infancy to Old Age* (1981). Clearly written, informative description of male sexuality, impotence, the prostate, puberty, and all other aspects of being a man.

**Wagenvoord, James and Peyton Bailey (eds.),** *Men: A Book for Women* (1978). Also *Women: A Book for Men* (1979). One of them will help you understand the members of the opposite sex. Delightful graphics.

## Women

**Boston Women's Health Book Collective,** *Our Bodies, Ourselves* (rev. 1976). Large-format feminist handbook of female physiology and self-care for women by women.

**Coles, Robert and Jane Hallowell Coles,** *Women of Crisis: Lives of Struggle and Hope* (1978). Compelling oral histories that unveil the innermost concerns and emotions of a migrant worker, a Chicano, an Eskimo, an "Appalachian," and an urban white housekeeper. See *Women of Crisis II: Lives of Work and Dreams* (1980).

**de Beauvoir, Simone,** *The Second Sex* (1952). Learned, enlightening feminist classic about woman and her "historical and contemporary situation in Western culture."

**Flexner, Elizabeth,** *Century of Struggle: The Women's Rights Movement in the United States* (rev. 1979). Sympathetic and distinguished work of scholarship that surveys the entire struggle.

**French, Marilyn,** *The Women's Room* (1977). Feminist novel that traces the lives of a group of women across several decades as they cope with their hard-won independence. Other good women's novels of the seventies include Gail Godwin, *The Odd Women* (1976) and Judith Rossner, *Any Minute I Can Split* (1973).

**Friedan, Betty,** *The Feminine Mystique* (1963). One of the key books that started the feminist renaissance in the sixties, it is a luminous sociocultural study of the way American women had come to view themselves. See *The Second Stage* (1981).

**Gilman, Charlotte Perkins,** *Herland* (1915). A witty, instructive, lost feminist Utopian novel by a socialist feminist. See *The Charlotte Perkins Gilman Reader* (1980).

**Gray, Francine Du Plessix,** *Lovers and Tyrants* (1976). Elegantly written first-person narrative that chronicles the life of a young woman and her relationships and concludes that lovers *are* tyrants.

**Greer, Germaine,** *The Female Eunuch* (1971). Passionate, lively examination of the ways in which the myths of society have conditioned women and forced them into impotent roles. See *The Obstacle Race: The Fortunes of Women Painters and Their Work* (1979).

**Moffat, Mary Jane and Charlotte Painter,** *Revelations: Diaries of Women* (1974). Collection of nineteenth- and twentieth-century women's diary entries on the themes of love, power, and work; includes the unknown and forgotten with such professional writers as Sand, Nin, George Eliot, and Gertrude Stein.

**Oates, Joyce Carol,** *The Goddess and Other Women* (1974). Searing short stories about the crises of ordinary women. See *Marriage and Infidelities: Short Stories* (1972).

**Rosen, Marjorie,** *Popcorn Venus: Women, Movies and the American Dream* (1973). Lively look at the continually evolving role of women in the movies. See Molly Haskell, *From Reverence to Rape: The Treatment of Women in the Movies* (1974).

**Russ, Joanna,** *The Female Man* (1975). A feminist science-fiction novel that uses various literary devices to explore women's condition. See *The Two of Them* (1978).

**Shulman, Alix Kates,** *Memoirs of an Ex-Prom Queen* (1972). Coming of age in America for one eloquent white, upper-middle-class woman: her typical and often painful experience of sexual initiation, marriage, divorce, abortion, and child rearing.

**Woolf, Virginia,** *A Room of One's Own* (1929). Exquisitely written book ostensibly on the theme of women and fiction, it is actually a devastating and inspiring exposition of feminism. See *Three Guineas* (1938).

## Sex and Sexuality

**Barbach, Lonnie Garfield,** *For Yourself: The Fulfillment of Female Sexuality.* (1976). A guide to orgasmic experience that endeavors to educate a woman to the wisdom of her own body via a unique step-by-step program. See *Shared Intimacies: Women's Sexual Experiences* (1980).

**Bengis, Ingrid,** *Combat in the Erogenous Zone* (1972). Intensely personal account of a woman's experiences in relations between and among the sexes.

**Calderone, Mary S. and Eric W. Johnson,** *The Family Book About Sexuality* (1981). Creative interpretation of all aspects of human sexuality in a family setting.

**Carrera, Michael,** *Sex: The Facts, The Acts & Your Feelings* (1981). Very useful book, with question-and-answer sequences, candid line drawings. Comprehensive, direct, sensitive.

**Comfort, Alex,** *The Joy of Sex* (1972). The sensitive, liberated approach and graphic illustrations have made this "Gourmet Guide to Lovemaking" and its successor, *More Joy of Sex* (1975), phenomenal best-sellers. For men and women who are familiar with the basics and want to go on from there.

**Gordon, Sol,** *Girls Are Girls and Boys Are Boys — So What's the Difference?* (1979). A leading sex educator's fine book for children explaining the facts of life. *Did the Sun Shine Before I Was Born?* (1975) is a book for youngsters to read with their parents. For teenagers he has written *Facts About Sex for Today's Youth* (1979).

**Hite, Shere,** *The Hite Report* (1976). With its companion report on male sexuality (published in 1981), a provocative study based on thousands of questionnaires. Revealing and stimulating.

**Jong, Erica,** *Fear of Flying* (1973). Popular novel about the liberated Isadora Wing in a quest for the "zipless fuck." See *How to Save Your Own Life* (1977).

**Le Guin, Ursula K.,** *The Left Hand of Darkness* (1969). Science-fiction masterpiece about a planet inhabited by androgynous human beings who are capable of becoming male or female as the occasion demands. Boldly challenges conceptions about sexuality.

**Marcus, Stephen,** *The Other Victorians* (1966). Superb cultural history of sexual repression in mid-nineteenth-century England. For the ultimate in Victorian libido see "Walter," *My Secret Life* (1966).

**Mayle, Peter,** *Where Did I Come From?* (1973). Superb, no-nonsense illustrated sex primer for children.

**Mead, Margaret,** *Sex and Temperament in Three Primitive Societies* (1936). Close study of three New Guinea tribes that advances her theory that "masculine" and "feminine" characteristics are based on cultural traits. "Combines the charm of *Gulliver's Travels* and *Erewhon* with that of *Alice in Wonderland*" (Joseph Wood Krutch).

**Morris, Jan,** *Conundrum* (1974). "I was three or perhaps four years old when I realized that I had been born into the wrong body, and should really be a girl." So opens this astonishing account of James Morris's sex-change operation, a view that reveals the full scope of human sexuality.

**Nin, Anaïs,** *Delta of Venus* (1977). Written in the 1940s for a dollar a page when the author was hard up for cash, the stories are elegant and sensuous. See *Little Birds* (1979).

**Offit, Avodah K.,** *Night Thoughts: Reflections of a Sex Therapist* (1981). Wide variety of sexual topics touched upon with clarity and wit by a psychiatrist called "the Montaigne of human sexuality." See *The Sexual Self* (1977).

**Reage, Pauline,** *The Story of O* (1966). Pornographic classic about the sexual enslavement of a woman by a man, written with Gallic matter-of-factness.

**Rossner, Judith,** *Looking for Mr. Goodbar* (1975). Loosely based on an actual case, an absorbing novel about a nice, quiet Catholic schoolteacher whose search for sexual adventures in New York's singles bars resulted in her murder.

**Tannahill, Reay,** *Sex in History* (1980). Lively, absolutely riveting look at the role of sex down through the ages.

**Thurber, James and E. B. White,** *Is Sex Necessary? or, Why You Feel the Way You Do* (1929). Sendup of the pseudoscientific books on sexuality. A classic spoof.

**Zilbergeld, Bernie,** *Male Sexuality: A Guide to Sexual Fulfillment* (1978). Physical and emotional aspects of sex for men explained in honest, nonjudgmental, everyday terms.

## Homosexuality

**Adair, Nancy and Casey Adair (eds.),** *Word Is Out: Stories of Some of Our Lives* (1978). Byproduct of the popular documentary film; twenty men and women of various ages, races, and lifestyles tell all.

**Brown, Rita Mae,** *Rubyfruit Jungle* (1973). Wonderfully funny autobiographical novel of coming of age as a lesbian. See *Six of One* (1978). Other contemporary lesbian novels include Isabel Miller, *Patience and Sarah* (1970), Jane Delynn, *In Thrall* (1982), and Valerie Taylor, *Prism* (1981).

**Crisp, Quentin,** *The Naked Civil Servant* (1977). Memoir by an outrageous queen of England; "a classic of autobiography" (Michael Holroyd). See *How to Become a Virgin* (1982).

**Fairchild, Betty and Nancy Hayward,** *Now That You Know: What Every Parent Should Know About Homosexuality* (1979). Excellent supportive guide. See Charles Silverstein, *A Family Matter: A Parent's Guide to Homosexuality* (1977).

**Friedel, Richard,** *The Movie Lover* (1981). Felicitous gay novel about one man's obsession with the elegance depicted in thirties movies. Other good modern gay novels include Andrew Holleran, *The Dancer from the Dance* (1979); Daniel Curzon, *Something to Do in the Dark* (1971); Patricia Nell Warren, *The Front Runner* (1974); David Watmough, *No More into the Garden* (1978); and Charles Nelson, *The Boy Who Picked up Bullets* (1981).

Hansen, Joseph, *Gravedigger* (1982). One of a well-written series of detective novels set in Los Angeles about the adventures of Dave Brandstetter, insurance investigator and self-styled "aging homosexual." See *Skinflick* (1979).

Heger, Heinz, *The Men with the Pink Triangles* (1980). Homosexuals had to wear pink triangles under the Nazi regime. This is the story of their fate in the Holocaust.

Leduc, Violette, *La Bâtarde* (1965). The hard life and loves of the lesbian writer, honestly and graphically recounted in a sensuous prose style. Continued in *Mad in Pursuit* (1971). See *Therese and Isabelle* (1967), a novel.

Millett, Kate, *Sita* (1977). A lesbian feminist's candid, agonizing account of a painful love affair.

Rechy, John, *Rushes* (1980). Set in a leather-and-western bar, like his other novels it depicts with raw energy the frenetic search for sexual satisfaction. See *This Day's Death* (1970) and *The Sexual Outlaw: A Non-fiction Account of 3 Days & Nights in the Sexual Underground* (1977).

Reid, John, *The Best Little Boy in the World* (1973). Insightful, upbeat out-of-the-closet confessional.

Russo, Vito, *The Celluloid Closet: Homosexuality in the Movies* (1981). Informative, witty look at Hollywood's portrayal of homosexuals.

Secrest, Meryle, *Between Me and Life: A Biography of Romaine Brooks* (1974). Admirable life of a remarkable American painter in the Parisian lesbian world during the twenties. The biography of her companion is also excellent on this circle of women: George Wickes, *The Amazon of Letters: The Life and Loves of Natalie Barney* (1976).

Silverstein, Charles and Edmund White, *The Joy of Gay Sex* (1977). Lightly written, encyclopedic manual of gay male sex. Its female counterpart is Emily L. Sisley and Bertha Harris, *The Joy of Lesbian Sex* (1977).

Vida, Ginny (ed.), *Our Right to Love: A Lesbian Resource Book* (1978). Fine collection of essays about the values and needs of gay women. Two other valuable books are Sidney Abbott and Barbara Love, *Sappho Was a Right-on Woman: A Liberated View of Lesbianism* (1972) and Del Martin and Phyllis Lyon, *Lesbian/Woman* (1972).

White, Edmund, *States of Desire: Travels in Gay America* (1980). A novelist's report on the state of the gay nation. See *Nocturnes for the King of Naples* (1979), a novel.

## Pregnancy and Childbirth

Arms, Suzanne, *Immaculate Deception: A New Look at Women and Childbirth in America* (1975). Challenging look at how women have given up their responsibility for conscious, affirmative childbirth to the medical profession. See *A Season to Be Born* (1973), an album of childbirth photographs.

Bradley, Robert, *Husband-Coached Childbirth* (rev. 1974). The Bradley method of natural childbirth explained in a humane, informal way.

Chesler, Phyllis, *With Child: A Diary of Motherhood* (1979). An ardent feminist and scholar speaks engrossingly of her pregnancy, childbirth, and first year of motherhood.

Drabble, Margaret, *The Millstone* (1966). A novel of compassion and humor about an emancipated woman who unintentionally gets pregnant. Probes the way that pregnancy and motherhood changes a woman's life. A similar situation is at the center of Lynne Reid Banks, *The L-Shaped Room* (1960).

Fallaci, Oriana, *Letters to a Child Never Born* (1977). The Italian journalist recounts her unwanted pregnancy and reveals the profundity of her symbiotic relationship with the child in a book which is ultimately life-affirming.

**Keneally, Thomas,** *Passenger* (1979). A fine novelist brings off an interesting experiment: the narrator is a fetus, a "passenger."

**Kitzinger, Sheila,** *The Complete Book of Pregnancy and Childbirth* (1980). A perceptive, compassionate childbirth educator and mother of five explains everything in words and pictures. Her other books include *Birth at Home* (1979) and *The Experience of Childbirth* (1972).

**Kotzwinkle, William,** *Swimmer in the Secret Sea* (1975). Strange novel — lovely and terse — narrated by the father of a stillborn child that begins in the last stages of labor and ends after the burial of the child.

**Lamaze, Fernand,** *Painless Childbirth: The Lamaze Method* (1956). Classic guidebook to a once revolutionary and now accepted childbirth idea. See Marjorie Karmel, *Thank You, Dr. Lamaze: A Mother's Experiences in Painless Childbirth* (1959). An excellent modern guide is Elizabeth Bing, *Six Practical Lessons for an Easier Childbirth* (rev. 1977).

**Millinaire, Catherine,** *Birth* (1974). Affirmative, joyful book of interviews with mothers about the childbirth experience; with photos.

**Nilsson, Lennart,** *A Child Is Born: The Drama of Life Before Birth* (rev. 1977). Incredible color photographs of the growth stages of the fetus. An awesome book.

**Queenan, John T., M.D. (ed.),** *A New Life: Pregnancy, Birth, and Your Child's First Year* (1979). Superb guide to pregnancy and early parenthood that is comprehensive, easy to understand, and beautifully illustrated.

**Sanger, Margaret,** *Margaret Sanger: An Autobiography* (1938). Moving and witty story of a remarkable woman and of her pioneering efforts to promote birth control in this country.

**Santamaria, Frances Karlen,** *Joshua, Firstborn* (1970). Charming, witty account by an American woman of her journey to Greece to give birth in an Athenian natural childbirth clinic.

**Whelan, Elizabeth M.,** *A Baby? . . . Maybe: A Guide to Making the Most Fateful Decision of Your Life* (1975). Expert aid, written with sensitivity, humor, intelligence, and compassion. See Merle Bombardieri, *The Baby Decision* (1981).

## Adoption

**Braithwaite, E. R.,** *Paid Servant* (1962). Touching story of a London welfare worker's frustrating search for parents to adopt a four-year-old racially mixed boy.

**Hartog, Jan De,** *The Children: A Personal Record for the Use of Adoptive Parents* (1968). The experiences of adopting two Korean children. Other narratives by people who adopted Asian children are Frank W. Chinnock, *Kim: A Gift from Vietnam* (1969) and Marjorie Margoles and Ruth Gruber, *They Came to Stay* (1975).

**Lifton, Betty Jane,** *Twice Born: Memoirs of an Adopted Daughter* (1975). Account by an adopted child, now an adult, of her search for her natural origins and roots. See *Lost and Found: The Adoption Experience* (1979). Nina Bawden's novel *Familiar Passions* (1979) is about an adoptee's search for her parents.

**Stein, Sara B.,** *The Adopted One: An Open Family Book for Parents and Children Together* (1979). Fine little picture book for an adopted child to read with adoptive parents.

**Wishard, Laurie and William Wishard,** *Adoption: The Grafted Tree* (1979). A lawyer and his adopted daughter, a social worker, explain the legal and psychological process of adoption for natural parents, present and prospective adoptive parents, adopted children, and their families.

## Childhood

**Aksakov, Sergei,** *Years of Childhood* (1858). Beautiful memories of author's early boyhood in the Russian steppes to 1799, when he went to school in Kazan. Continued in *The Family Chronicle* (1856) and *A Russian Schoolboy* (1856).

**Angelou, Maya,** *I Know Why the Caged Bird Sings* (1970). In this first volume of an extraordinary life story she recounts her early years growing up black, poor, and frightened in Stamps, Arkansas. See *Gather Together in My Name* (1974), *Singin' and Swingin' and Gettin' Merry Like Christmas* (1976), and *The Heart of a Woman* (1981).

**Aries, Philippe,** *Centuries of Childhood* (1963). Lively social history of family life between the Middle Ages and the early nineteenth century, with a wealth of anecdotes and illustrations.

**Bawden, Nina,** *Tortoise by Candlelight* (1963). Fourteen-year-old Emmie acts as mother of her small family, which inhabits a world of fright and fun — a weird yet wonderful domain adults cannot understand and in which they cannot be understood. This English writer with a special knowledge of children also wrote *A Little Love, A Little Learning* (1966).

**Burnett, Francis Hodgson,** *The Secret Garden* (1910). A richly textured book for children about the restorative effect of a neglected garden on the heroine and her friends. See *A Little Princess* (1905).

**Byars, Betsy,** *The Summer of the Swans* (1971). Written for fourth-to-ninth graders, this unforgettable story of fourteen-year-old Sara and her mentally retarded little brother is full of sensitivity and humor. Winner of the Newberry Award. See *The Pinballs* (1977).

**Canetti, Elias,** *The Tongue Set Free: Remembrance of a European Childhood* (1980). Born in Bulgaria and writing in German, he remembers his early life and the events, personalities, and intellectual forces that shaped him; intellectually engaging, moving, and witty. See *The Torch in the Ear* (1982), about his youth in Vienna.

**Carossa, Hans,** *A Childhood* (1922). A German writer's exquisite remembrances of his youth. See *Boyhood and Youth* (1932).

**Cary, Joyce,** *A House for Children* (1941). Autobiographical novel about an idyllic Irish childhood of the 1890s.

**Church, Richard,** *Over the Bridge* (1956). An English minor poet's moving narrative of lower-middle-class boyhood in South London between the Boer War and World War I. "No one comes to mind, except Proust, who has probed with such devotion, honesty and exquisite tact into a boy's love for his mother" (May Sarton). Continued in *The Golden Sovereign* (1957) and *The Voyage Home* (1966).

**Cleary, Beverley,** *Ramona the Brave* (1975). Ramona is a spunky little girl created by the popular children's writer and is featured in a series illustrated by Alan Tiegreen that kids adore. See *Ramona Quimby, Age 8* (1981).

**Del Castillo, Michel,** *A Child of Our Time* (1958). Heartbreaking autobiographical novel of the effects of World War II on a child. Other works about children caught in the Holocaust include Saul Friedlander, *When Memory Comes* (1979), Jerzy Kosinski, *The Painted Bird* (1965), Elie Wiesel, *Night* (1960), and Uri Orlev, *The Lead Soldiers* (1980).

**Dickens, Charles,** *David Copperfield* (1849–50). Dickens put much of his own early life into this magnificent classic, which is peopled with some of his most famous characters — Micawber, Uriah Heep, Steerforth.

**Erikson, Erik H.,** *Childhood and Society* (rev. 1963). Classic study that emphasizes the importance of early frustration in the development of the adult.

**Finney, Charles,** *Past the End of the Pavement* (1939). This touching and hilarious account of the adventures of two boys in a small midwestern town has been called one of "the few classics about boy-life that have been written in America" (Edward Wagenknecht).

**Fitzhugh, Louise,** *Harriet the Spy* (1964). Refreshing, sparkling book for young readers about a nasty little girl who keeps a secret notebook filled with honest comments on her family and friends. *The Long Secret* (1965) is a sequel. See *Nobody's Family Is Going to Change* (1974).

**France, Anatole,** *Little Pierre* (1921). With its sequel, *Bloom of Life* (1923), a charming and beautiful autobiography of youth by the Nobel Prize–winning French novelist. See *The Book of My Friend* (1885).

**Gascar, Pierre,** *The Seed* (1959). This stark, tender portrait of a melancholy childhood, told through the eyes of a ten-year-old boy, is "beyond question one of those imaginative truthful novels that are destined to survive and to be recognized as literature of value for a long time to come" (Anthony West).

**Godden, Rumer,** *An Episode of Sparrows* (1955). Novel about the change in the lives of two London street urchins when they drop a packet of seeds on the street. Godden is good at showing how children perceive the behavior of adults. Children are also at the center of *The Greengage Summer* (1958) and *The Battle of Villa Fiorita* (1963).

**Gorey, Edward,** *The Hapless Child* (1961). One of a series of delightfully catastrophic little books illustrated by the author in which the most macabre things happen to children. See *The Gashlycrumb Tinies* (1963), *The Insect God* (1963), and *The Beastly Baby* (1962).

**Greene, Graham,** *A Sort of Life* (1971). A poignant and personal account of his childhood and youth, a masterpiece of controlled self-examination. Continued in *Ways of Escape* (1981).

**Hughes, Richard,** *A High Wind in Jamaica* (1929). Splendid novel about young children aboard a pirate ship; one of the best books about children.

**Humphrey, William,** *Farther Off from Heaven* (1977). Memoir of a happy childhood in Red River County, Texas, that ends in disaster when the author's father is killed in a bloody auto accident.

**James, Henry,** *What Maisie Knew* (1897). The world and its immorality as seen through the eyes of a precocious child who is undergoing the complications of her parents' divorce.

**Johnson, Crockett,** *Harold and the Purple Crayon* (1955). A whimsical paper odyssey of a little boy who creates his own adventures with his purple crayon. An ingenious illustrated treat for children. Another delightful classic of the fifties is Ruth Krause, *A Hole Is to Dig: A First Book of First Definitions* (1952), illustrated by Maurice Sendak.

**Kismaric, Susan,** *American Children: Photographs from the Collection of the Museum of Modern Art* (1980). Exhibition catalogue of poignant black-and-white photographs of children.

**Koch, Kenneth,** *Wishes, Lies, and Dreams: Teaching Children to Write Poetry* (1971). An avant-garde poet at P.S. 91 in New York City tells of his success in getting children to express themselves in verse. See *Rose, Where Did You Get That Red?: Teaching Great Poetry to Children* (1973).

**Lee, Laurie,** *The Edge of Day: A Boyhood in the West of England* (1959). Wonderful childhood reminiscences of village life in the Cotswolds by "a man who is glad to be alive and can praise life in terms that ring as true as bird song; as we read we share his gladness and echo his praise" (T.

S. Matthews). Other fine books about English country childhood include Richard Jeffries, *The Story of My Heart* (1883); A. L. Rowse, *A Cornish Childhood* (1942); and Alison Uttley, *The Country Child* (1931).

**Lewis, C. S.,** *Surprised by Joy: The Shape of My Early Life* (1955). Mainly his spiritual ups and downs, from his initial atheism to Christian conversion; contains penetrating childhood recollections of boarding school.

**Lopate, Philip,** *Being with Children* (1975). Wise and tender account of a poet's experiences teaching imaginative writing at a school on New York's Upper West Side.

**McCarthy, Mary,** *Memories of a Catholic Girlhood* (1957). Collection of autobiographical pieces: indignant, observant, always interesting.

**McEwan, Ian,** *The Cement Garden* (1978). Four sly, unpleasant kids, newly orphaned, conceal their mother's death so as not to be taken into care. Narrated by one of the children, a bizarre novel with dark hints of aberration. A very similar plot is in Julian Gloag, *Our Mother's House* (1963).

**Milne, Christopher,** *The Enchanted Places* (1975). The son of A. A. Milne — the Christopher Robin of his father's Pooh stories — recalls his childhood among the Milne creatures. It is a lost domain somewhere between the storybook world and the real world.

**Moberg, Vilhelm,** *When I Was a Child* (1956). Autobiographical novel of a boy's life in rural Sweden at the turn of the century: brooding and moving.

**Morante, Elsa,** *Arturo's Island* (1959). Poetic, delicately constructed novel about the boyhood and early adolescence of a strange boy on a primitive island in the Bay of Naples.

**Nabokov, Vladimir,** *Speak, Memory* (rev. 1966). A great writer's autobiography of his childhood in old Russia, "a delightful idyll of youth, and a powerful image of the growth of the soul under stress . . . one of the most charming autobiographies written in our time" (Gilbert Highet).

**Nesbit, E.,** *The Story of the Treasure Seekers* (1899). The first of her novels for children about the attempts of the six Bastable children to raise badly needed money and end the family's financial troubles. Followed by *The Wouldbegoods* (1901) and *New Treasure Seekers* (1904).

**O'Connor, Frank,** *An Only Child* (1961). In this recollection of his life as a child in a Cork slum and his youth as a revolutionary, "he brings his great gifts to the writing of autobiography, and the result is a beautiful book" (Granville Hicks).

**Opie, Iona and Peter Opie,** *The Lore and Language of School Children* (1959). Contributions from thousands of British children compose an utterly charming gathering of jeers and torments, pranks, half-beliefs, parody, repartee, and other oral traditions.

**Pritchett, V. S.,** *A Cab at the Door* (1968). Luminous memoir of his Edwardian childhood. Continued in *Midnight Oil* (1971).

**Read, Herbert,** *The Innocent Eye* (1933). The English poet and art critic recounts with sensuous detail his childhood on a Yorkshire farm. "Perhaps the best autobiography in our language" (Graham Greene).

**Reid, Forrest,** *Young Tom* (1944). Award-winning novel by the Irish writer known for his particular sensitivity to the spirit of childhood.

**Renan, Ernest,** *Recollections of My Youth* (1883). The French historian and critic traces in limpid prose his early years in Brittany and his loss of faith while a student in Paris.

**Roth, Henry,** *Call It Sleep* (1934). Set among immigrant Jews of New York's Lower East Side before the First World

War, this finely wrought novel about little David Schearle is a work of great poignancy and intelligence.

**Sartre, Jean-Paul,** *The Words* (1964). Penetrating, inward-turning childhood recollections of unexpected charm by the brilliant French writer. The youthful remembrances of his companion, Simone de Beauvoir, are in the splendid *Memoirs of a Dutiful Daughter* (1958).

**Schulz, Bruno,** *The Street of Crocodiles* (1962). First published in the author's native Poland in 1934, these highly original stories of his boyhood blend the humorous and the brutal in a work of fantastic realism.

**Singer, Isaac Bashevis,** *In My Father's Court* (1966). The Nobel Prize–winning writer describes his childhood in Warsaw as the son of a poor rabbi. Continued in *A Little Boy in Search of God* (1976), *A Young Man in Search of Love* (1978), and *Lost in America* (1981).

**Steig, William,** *Small Fry* (1944). A hundred observant, funny drawings of kids doing the things that kids do. See *Dreams of Glory* (1953).

**Thompson, Thea,** *Edwardian Childhoods* (1980). Nine little lives are contrasted in "an exceptional book . . . a model of how to present oral autobiography and social history" (Ronald Blythe).

**Warner, Sylvia Townsend,** *Scenes of Childhood* (1981). A series of luminous glimpses into the English novelist's Edwardian childhood.

**Wright, Richard,** *Black Boy* (1945). Eloquent, poignant autobiography of the novelist's boyhood and youth in the South. Continued in *American Hunger* (1977).

## Adolescence

**Alain-Fournier,** *Big Meaulnes* (1913). Also translated as *The Lost Domain* and *The Wanderer,* it is a magical novel in which the adolescent hero's romantic adventure at a seemingly enchanted house mingles reality and dream. "It is a book one never quite forgets, a book like a secret garden" (John Fowles).

**Armour, Richard,** *Through Darkest Adolescence* (1964). A tongue-in-cheek satire of that difficult stage with heart-rending illustrations by Susan Perl. More laughter at adolescence is in Delia Ephron's *Teenage Romance or How to Die of Embarrassment* (1981), wiggily illustrated by Edward Koren.

**Blume, Judy,** *Tiger Eyes* (1981). Fifteen-year-old Davey sees her father murdered. How she deals with death and violence is at the heart of this novel by a writer with a remarkable sensitivity to teenagers. Her other popular books avidly read by adolescents include *Are You There, God? Its Me, Margaret* (1970), *Deenie* (1973), *Starring Sally J. Freedman as Herself* (1977).

**Bowers, John,** *No More Reunions* (1973). Nostalgic novel of a boy's sometimes painful growing up in Tennessee during the forties. Other good coming-of-age novels include Julian Moynahan, *Where the Land and Water Meet* (1979); Michael Blankfort, *Take the "A" Train* (1976); Ella Leffland, *Rumors of Peace* (1979); and Theodore Weesner, *The Car Thief* (1972).

**Capote, Truman,** *Other Voices, Other Rooms* (1948). Lush, haunting, precocious novel (Capote's first, written at age twenty-three) about a thirteen-year-old boy who goes to live with his father in a run-down Louisiana mansion peopled with eccentric characters and comes to an awareness of the light and shadows of the adult world and his own homosexuality.

**Conroy, Frank,** *Stop-time* (1967). An extraordinary, exciting recollection of the teenage years, one of the finest books about growing up. "On its own level and scale, there are reminders of Wordsworth's *Prelude* in the book: discovery of

the self en route to art" (Stanley Kauffmann).

**Frank, Anne,** *The Diary of a Young Girl*
(1952). The extraordinary diary of an intelligent and sensitive Jewish girl in hiding
from the Nazis in Amsterdam.

**Goodman, Paul,** *Growing Up Absurd:*
*Problems of Youth in the Organized Sys-*
*tem* (1960). Two decades later, this impassioned assault on American "phony" culture by a literary iconoclast is still on
target.

**Joyce, James,** *A Portrait of the Artist as*
*a Young Man* (1916). This autobiographical and imaginative record of Stephen
Dedalus's Irish Catholic upbringing is "so
mesmeric, so hypnotic a book that I can
never speak of it to young readers without
murmuring, *Enter these enchanted woods*
*ye who dare*" (Sean O'Faolain).

**Lee, Tanith,** *Don't Bite the Sun* (1975).
The coming of age of a most unusual girl
(sometimes boy). Set in a far future city,
this funny science-fiction novel depicts its
heroine in a society where adolescents
amuse themselves changing sex, shoplift-
ing, committing suicide, and rejuvenating
themselves. *Drinking Sapphire Wine*
(1976) is a sequel.

**Mayle, Peter,** *What's Happening to Me?*
(1975). Fine blend of text and pictures explains the changes of puberty to teenagers.
Another excellent book for adolescents on
sex and relationships is *Changing Bodies,*
*Changing Selves* (1981), by Ruth Bell in
the *Our Bodies, Ourselves* format.

**Panshin, Alexei,** *Rite of Passage* (1968). In
a spaceship fleeing from postapocalypse
earth, a fourteen-year-old girl must go
through a coming-of-age ritual.

**Salinger, J. D.,** *The Catcher in the Rye*
(1951). The celebrated novel about Holden
Caulfield's hectic underground weekend
in New York.

**Stafford, Jean,** *Mountain Lion* (1947).
Subtle, understanding novel about a

brother and sister emerging from childhood into adolescence and knowledge of
the way of the world.

**Zindel, Paul,** *The Pigman* (1968). Classic
realistic young-adult novel. About two
teenagers' involvement with an elderly
man, it is filled with contemporary lingo,
odd characters, and strange situations.
See *The Pig Legacy* (1980).

## Middle Age

**Bellow, Saul,** *Herzog* (1964). Moses Herzog, sufferer, joker, cuckold, charmer,
and survivor of disasters both public and
private. Winner of National Book Award
for fiction.

**Drabble, Margaret,** *The Middle Ground*
(1980). A woman in her forties tries to sort
out her life: a wryly observant novel by an
English writer who exerts a pure, old-
fashioned narrative skill.

**Fried, Barbara,** *The Middle Age Crisis*
(rev. 1976). Lucid, witty study of the problems that plague men and women entering
the middle years. See Luree Miller, *Late*
*Bloom: New Lives for Women* (1980) and
Henry Sill, *Surviving the Male Mid-life*
*Crisis* (1977).

**Lessing, Doris,** *Summer Before the Dark*
(1973). A charming, intelligent, attractive
forty-five-year-old woman, her husband
away for the summer, is beckoned by a
young lover to an exciting future that
turns into a confrontation with her past.

**Lindbergh, Anne Morrow,** *Gift from the*
*Sea* (1955). Calm, slender book in which
the author eloquently ponders the per-
plexities of middle age. Her graceful letters and diaries also reflect her thoughtfulness; the first of the five collections is
*Bring Me a Unicorn* (1972).

**Simmons, Charles,** *Wrinkles* (1978). In-
triguingly constructed out of forty small
descriptions of aspects of his life, this
novel paints a simple and powerful portrait of a middle-aged man.

**Tanizaki, Junichiro,** *The Key* (1961). Story of the pathological effect of the fear of impotence and its tragic impact on a middle-aged man married to a younger woman.

**Walser, Martin,** *Runaway Horse* (1980). Elegant psychological study of two men who confront middle age.

**Wax, Judith,** *Starting in the Middle* (1979). A perceptive, funny woman in her forties writes of her own and others' experiences of finding themselves "in the middle."

**Wilson, Angus,** *The Middle Age of Mrs. Eliot* (1948). Admirable novel of an intelligent woman trying to make something of her life in widowhood and reduced circumstances.

**Wright, Richard B.,** *In the Middle of a Life* (1973). Three days in the life of a middle-aged salesman who lives in a small apartment in one of the seedier parts of Toronto.

## Aging

**Bellow, Saul,** *Mr. Sammler's Planet* (1970). Compassionate National Book Award–winning novel about a Polish Jewish refugee in his seventies who accurately, reluctantly, and frequently divines the sickness of the present and recalls the madness of the past.

**Blythe, Ronald,** *The View in Winter: Reflections of Old Age* (1979). Unflinching oral history done in England and Wales which provides an inside view of aging. Another English study comprising mostly interviews is sociologist Peter Townsend's sympathetic *Family Life of Old People: An Inquiry in East London* (1958).

**Colette,** *Break of Day* (1961). Semiautobiographical novel about the renunciation of love after the breakup of a woman's second marriage and about the difficulties of aging and death.

**Comfort, Alex,** *A Good Age* (1976). In encyclopedia format, this solid compendium of useful information is at once poetic, practical, and tough-minded.

**Cowley, Malcolm,** *The View from 80* (1980). Written when the literary critic was eighty-two, this brief book is "eloquent on the felt disparity between an unchanged self and the costume of altered flesh" (Donald Hall). Other personal essays on aging include Henry Beetle Hough, *To the Harbor Light* (1976); Elizabeth Vining, *Being Seventy: The Measure of a Year* (1978); and May Sarton, *Journal of a Solitude* (1973).

**Cunningham, Imogen,** *After Ninety* (1977). Album of portraits of men and women over ninety taken by the renowned photographer when she was ninety-two. A moving celebration of age.

**Curtin, Sharon R.,** *Nobody Ever Died of Old Age: In Praise of Old People, In Outrage at Their Loneliness* (1972). Polemical, personal, and often moving survey of the variety of life styles adopted by old people in America.

**de Beauvoir, Simone,** *Coming of Age* (1971). Massive philosophical, historical, and psychological study of what it means and how it feels to become old.

**Knopf, Olga, M.D.,** *Successful Aging: The Facts and Fallacies of Growing Old* (1975). The psychological and medical aspects of aging discussed in a clear and authoritative book. She wrote it at age eighty-five!

**Koch, Kenneth,** *I Never Told Anybody: Teaching Poetry Writing in a Nursing Home* (1977). A poet documents the use of poetry for exploration and healing in a book which has been described as a "humane document of the spirit."

**Meyerhoff, Barbara,** *Number Our Days* (1979). Written by an anthropologist with a novelist's sensibilities, this fine book about a group of first-generation elderly

Jews living in Venice, California, may teach us more about the proper way to live than all the self-help books combined.

**Montherlant, Henri De,** *The Bachelors* (1934). The French novelist uses his austere and ironic style in a moving story of the old age of two decadent aristocrats "perishing in their pride."

**Olsen, Tillie,** *Tell Me a Riddle* (1961). Superb story revolving around the crises of old age and terminal illness that reveals much about working class life, the Depression, the family, cowardice, and courage.

**Rabinowitz, Dorothy and Yedida Nielsen,** *Home Life* (1971). Dramatization of nursing home life; illuminating to those on the outside.

**Sarton, May,** *As We Are Now* (1973). Novel in the form of a diary of a retired schoolteacher who was put in nursing home by her relatives. A powerful portrayal of a desolating experience.

**Scott, Paul,** *Staying On* (1977). The Smalleys, an old English couple, have stayed on in their seedy annex of Smith's Hotel in an Indian hill section after the British left. This deep attachment and Col. Smalley's death are movingly portrayed "by one of the best novelists to emerge from Britain's silver age" (Robert Towers).

**Silverstone, Barbara and Helene Hyman** *(rev. 1982). You and Your Aging Parent: The Modern Family's Guide to Emotional, Physical, and Financial Problems.* Resource guide filled with essential and expert information.

**Spark, Muriel,** *Memento Mori* (1959). The characters of this audaciously witty "geriatric frolic" of a novel "preserve in the face of death a quality of faith, and even of humor, that encourages us" (Alfred Kazin).

**Stegner, Wallace,** *The Spectator Bird* (1976). National Book Award–winning novel that quietly and absorbingly tours through the landscape of a man's life as he approaches seventy.

**Uris, Auren,** *Over 50: The Definitive Guide to Retirement* (1979). A 600-page comprehensive guide in which the author not only presents the facts but weaves in first-person stories.

# FAMILY LIFE

## Wedding

**Kramer, Jane,** *Honor to the Birds Like the Pigeon that Guards Its Grain Under the Olive Tree* (1971). In describing the events leading up to the wedding of a thirteen-year-old Moroccan girl, this nonfiction novel offers an engaging glimpse into the Moroccan culture and mind.

**McCullers, Carson,** *The Member of the Wedding* (1946). Charming fantasy about twelve-year-old Frankie, in frightening transition between childhood and adolescence, who yearns in vain to accompany her brother and his bride on their honeymoon and is protected psychologically by the friendship of the devoted housekeeper.

**Norfleet, Barbara,** *Wedding* (1979). One hundred fifty black-and-white American wedding pictures taken by studio photographers over the last 100 years.

**Strachey, Julia,** *Cheerful Weather for the Wedding* (1932). Brief satirical novel about the absurdities of the wedding day. "This is a very small book but a very perfect one revealing a rich sense of humor and very great literary and dramatic skill" (David Garnett).

**Welty, Eudora,** *Delta Wedding* (1946). Quiet story of the relationships in a "county family" of the Mississippi Delta that is gathered for a wedding. Great atmosphere.

## Married Couples

**Albee, Edward,** *Who's Afraid of Virginia Woolf?* (1963). A riveting drama about a travesty of a modern marriage that is played out by George and Martha on one long evening.

**Arlen, Michael,** *Exiles* (1970). A son's haunting, bittersweet memoir of his father, a best-selling novelist, and his mother, a Greek noblewoman, who moved in the international literary circles of the 1920s.

**Bergman, Ingmar,** *Scenes from a Marriage* (1974). Television screenplay chronicling the simultaneous decline of a marriage and increasing self-knowledge of its partners.

**Browning, Robert and Elizabeth Barrett Browning,** *Love Letters* (1899). The poets' correspondence portrays a passion sublimated in idealistic love. See Francis Winwar, *Immortal Lovers* (1950).

**Carver, Raymond,** *What We Talk About When We Talk About Love* (1981). Slim collection of stories of exhausted men and women within or just after marriage that is written with an eerie intensity of focus and in "so spare a manner that it takes a time before one realizes how completely a whole culture and a whole moral condition is represented by even the most seemingly slight sketch" (Frank Kermode). See *Will You Please Be Quiet, Please?* (1976).

**Connell, Evan S.,** *Mrs. Bridge* (1957). In a sequence of episodes, this and its companion novel, *Mr. Bridge* (1969), capture the manners of the provincial white U.S. middle class and constitute a "saga of sweet joylessness and blunted sensibility of marriage, family, and middle age on the Plains of Protestantism" (Webster Schott).

**Cronin, Vincent,** *Louis and Antoinette* (1975). Sparkling biography of Louis XVI and his queen by a stylistically graceful English writer. Other good biographies of French royal couples include Frances Mossiker, *Napoleon and Josephine: The Biography of a Marriage* (1965) and Jasper Ridley, *Napoleon III and Eugénie* (1980).

**Enchi, Fumiko,** *The Waiting Years* (1971). A wealthy man in the Meiji period sends his wife to Tokyo to bring him back a mistress. A battle of wills ensues, and disaster.

**Fitzgerald, F. Scott,** *Tender Is the Night* (1934). The tragic and haunting story of Dick Diver, a young psychiatrist whose career is thwarted and his genius numbed through marriage to the exquisite and wealthy Nicole Warren. A revision by Malcolm Cowley was published in 1951.

**Fontane, Theodor,** *Effi Briest* (1895). The story of a marriage — prearranged, unromantic — a misstep, and the inexorable consequences, in a novel comparable in its probing of feminine psychology and in its perfection of style to *Madame Bovary.*

**Fox, Paula,** *Desperate Characters* (1970). Beautifully wrought novel about a loveless, middle-aged marriage between two upper-middle-class New Yorkers. Reveals the delicate balance of human love enduring severe stress from the sickness of society.

**Gelb, Barbara,** *So Short a Time: A Biography of John Reed and Louise Bryant* (1973). "A sensitive and compassionately written account of the short, frenetic careers of two courageous and mildly talented persons caught up in a vast historical transformation which they romanticized without understanding its costs and fateful consequences" (Sidney Hook).

**Handke, Peter,** *The Left Handed Woman* (1978). Brief, memorable novel tracing the breakdown of the marriage of a young couple in their thirties; austere, hard-edged prose.

**Hardy, Thomas,** *The Return of the Native* (1878). Affecting study of a stormy and unsuitable marriage — that of the idealistic Clym Yeobright and passionate Eustacia Vye — doomed to tragedy from its inception.

**Lash, Joseph,** *Eleanor and Franklin* (1971). Superb Pulitzer Prize–winning biography of the Roosevelts; its sequel is *Eleanor: The Years Alone* (1972). Prior presidential couples are portrayed in Alfred Leland Crabb, *Home to the Hermitage: A Novel of Andrew and Rachel Jackson* (1948); Virginia Moore, *The Madisons* (1979); and Lynne Withey, *Dearest Friend: A Life of Abigail Adams* (1981).

**Lurie, Alison,** *The War Between the Tates* (1974). Finely crafted novel of manners about a college professor's affair with a student and its effect on his seventeen-year-old marriage.

**Marlow, Joyce,** *The Oak and the Ivy: An Intimate Biography of William and Catherine Gladstone* (1977). Gracefully written peek into the private lives of the Victorian prime minister and his wife. Mary Soames, *Clementine Churchill: The Biography of a Marriage* (1979) is an engrossing story of the fifty-seven years of marriage to Winston Churchill, as told by his youngest daughter.

**Massie, Robert K.,** *Nicholas and Alexandra* (1967). Fine popular biography of the last of the Romanovs. Some other noteworthy regal biographies are Robert Browning, *Justinian and Theodora* (1970); Joanne Richardson, *Victoria and Albert* (1977); and J. Bryan III and Charles J. V. Murphy, *The Windsor Story* (1981), about Edward VIII and Wally Simpson.

**Mortimer, Penelope,** *The Pumpkin Eater* (1962). A crisis in the heroine's fourth marriage is the focus of a novel "so touching, so moving, so funny; so desperate, so alive" (Elizabeth Janeway).

**Nicolson, Nigel,** *Portrait of a Marriage* (1973). A son's account of the remarkable marriage between Vita Sackville-West, a writer, and Harold Nicolson, an English diplomat and writer — whose love deepened with time although each was constantly and by mutual consent unfaithful to the other.

**Robertson, Don,** *Abelard and Heloise* (1972). Historically accurate retelling of the fascinating story of the tragic love and secret marriage between the eleventh-century theologian Pierre Abélard and Héloïse. See Helen Waddell, *Peter Abelard* (1933), a novel.

**Rogin, Gilbert,** *Preparation for the Descent* (1981). A subtle, intelligent novel, gracefully written, about the effects of a failing marriage on one feckless man.

**Schwartz, Lynne Sharon,** *Rough Strife* (1980). Fine first novel about marriage told with compassion and wit. Other contemporary novels about trapped wives include Sheila Ballantyne, *Norma Jean the Termite Queen* (1977); Sue Kaufman, *Diary of a Mad Housewife* (1967); Anne Roiphe, *Up the Sandbox* (1970); Alan Saperstein, *Mom Kills Kids and Self* (1979); and Hilma Wolitzer, *In the Flesh* (1977).

**Shakespeare, William,** *The Taming of the Shrew* (c. 1594). The swift courtship and marriage of Petruchio and Katherina forms the central plot of one of Shakespeare's funniest comedies.

**Spater, George and Ian Parsons,** *A Marriage of True Minds* (1979). Handsomely illustrated story of Leonard and Virginia Woolf's life together.

**Stegner, Wallace,** *Angle of Repose* (1971). Pulitzer Prize–winning novel that switches between the present and the turn-of-the-century West about a gifted woman in conflict with the burdens of marriage. "For all the breadth and sweep [it] achieves an effect of intimacy . . . and experience newly minted rather than a pageantable re-creation" (William Abrahams).

**Thomas, Helen,** *As It Was* (1926). The widow of Edward Thomas, the English Georgian poet killed in World War I, movingly relates their meeting, their love, and their life together. See *World Without End* (1931).

**Tomkins, Calvin,** *Living Well Is the Best Revenge* (1971). Affectionate story of Gerald and Sara Murphy, an elegant and striking American couple, friends of the Fitzgeralds, Stein, Picasso, and Hemingway. Beautifully evokes the romantic tempo of the 1920s. Must reading for lovers of *Tender Is the Night.*

**Updike, John,** *Too Far to Go* (1979). Collects the stories about the Maples, about the decline and fall of a marriage, of a million mundane moments shared. According to Updike, "the point of these stories is that all blessings are mixed."

**Yates, Richard,** *Revolutionary Road* (1961). "An extraordinarily precise, vivid and wholly credible account of the swift and miraculous burst of spirit that revives and then, quite literally, kills off a particular suburban marriage" (Alice Adams).

## *Adultery*

**Eca de Queiroz,** *Cousin Bazilio* (1878). A superb stylist's realistic and "sensual novel about Luiza, the Portugese Emma Bovary, so charming in her own right, so like and yet so unlike her French counterpart" (Francis Steegmuller). This tale of illicit love was translated by Roy Campbell in 1953.

**Flaubert, Gustave,** *Madame Bovary* (1857). Set amid the stifling atmosphere of nineteenth-century bourgeois France, it is at once an unsparing depiction of a woman's gradual corruption, a savagely ironic study of human shallowness and stupidity, and "possibly the most beautifully written book ever composed; undoubtedly the most beautifully written novel" (Frank O'Connor).

**Greene, Graham,** *The End of the Affair* (1951). Sarah Miles, a married woman, ends her affair with the novelist Bendrix because of a prayer being answered; a novel that probes good and evil, the damned and the saved.

**Hawthorne, Nathaniel,** *The Scarlet Letter* (1850). One of the great American novels, about Hester Prynne and the Rev. Arthur Dimmesdale, adultery, and illegitimacy in a vividly rendered seventeenth-century Puritan Boston.

**James, Henry,** *The Golden Bowl* (1904). Elaborate novel in the late Jamesian style about a young American woman, married to an Italian prince in London, who discovers him to be carrying on an affair with her friend.

**Shaplen, Robert,** *Free Love and Heavenly Sinners* (1957). With consummate narrative skill, the story of the famous trial of Henry Ward Beecher for adultery — the great "passion drama" of the period — is unfolded.

**Tolstoy, Leo,** *Anna Karenina* (1874–76). The story of Anna and her lover Count Vronsky is the central panel of a magnificent work of art, certainly one of the greatest novels ever written.

## *Divorce*

**Abeel, Erica,** *Only When I Laugh* (1978). Moving and humorous chronicle of the devastating year after her divorce and her resultant loss of self-confidence; it teaches something about love and living with grace. Other good personal narratives include Eve Baguedor, *Separation* (1972); Susan Braudy, *Between Marriage and Divorce* (1975); and Marilyn Murray Willison, *Diary of a Divorced Mother* (1980).

**Alvarez, A.,** *Life After Marriage: An Autobiography of a Divorce* (1982). His honest exercise in taking stock and surviving. See Jonathan Gathorne-Hardy, *Marriage, Love, Sex and Divorce* (1982).

**Epstein, Joseph,** *Divorced in America: Marriage in an Age of Possibility* (1974).

In fluent style the author mixes confession, reporting, and analysis with a defense of traditional marriage.

**Gardner, Richard A.,** *Boys' and Girls' Book About Divorce* (1971). Written for children nine and up it is a practical guide to coping with divorce and all its ramifications. Norma Klein has written a couple of novels for teenagers about divorce and single parents, *It's Not what You Expect* (1973) and *Mom, The Wolfman and Me* (1972).

**Schickel, Richard,** *Singled Out: A Civilized Guide to Sex and Sensibility for the Suddenly Single Man — or Woman* (1981). Based on his own experiences, a writer describes the social and sexual etiquette for the recently divorced. Novels about suddenly single men include Schickel's own *Another I, Another You* (1978); Don Carpenter, *Getting Off* (1971); Bruce Jay Friedman, *About Harry Towns* (1974); and Dan Wakefield, *Starting Over* (1973).

## Generations

**Arlen, Michael J.** *Passage to Ararat* (1975). Compelling book in which the author endeavors to find the Armenian heritage that his father, the English novelist Michael Arlen, had put behind him.

**Bergamini, John D.,** *The Spanish Bourbons: The History of a Tenacious Dynasty* (1974). Gossipy, entertaining sketches of the Bourbons from 1700, when Philip V ascended the throne, down to the present day. Other lively histories of European dynasties include Joseph Calmette, *The Golden Age of Burgundy* (1963); Virginia Cowles, *The Romanovs* (1971); and Walter Henry Nelson, *The Soldier Kings: The House of Hohenzollern* (1970).

**Bowen, Elizabeth,** *Bowen's Court* (1942). Three centuries of her family in "a sympathetic picture of a class often denigrated beyond its entire deserts, and the results,

in human character, of their really tragic isolation" (Louise Bogan).

**Butler, Samuel,** *The Way of All Flesh* (1903). Several generations of the Pontifex family are studied in this ironic, bitter novel about the struggle between father and son and the hypocrisy of the Victorian religious and education system.

**Clark, Ronald W.,** *The Huxleys* (1968). Fine portrait of a brilliant family, with principal focus on Thomas, Sir Julian, and Aldous. Other good English family histories include Lord David Cecil, *The Cecils of Hatfield House* (1973) and A. L. Rowse, *The Churchills* (1966).

**Clifton, Lucille,** *Generations* (1976). Unassuming poetic portrait of the author's family back to her great-great-grandmother, who was born in Africa and brought to America in chains.

**Greenslet, Ferris,** *The Lowells and Their Seven Worlds* (1946). A remarkable American literary family pictured through seven generations. See C. David Heyman, *American Aristocracy: The Lives and Time of James Russell, Amy and Robert Lowell* (1980).

**Kupferberg, Herbert,** *The Mendelssohns* (1972). Chronicle of a brilliant and fascinating German Jewish family, including Mose Mendelssohn, the philosopher; Dorothea Veit, the wife of Friedrich Schlegel; and Felix Mendelssohn, the composer.

**Maxwell, William,** *Ancestors* (1971). In tracing the genealogy of his family he provides a miniature history of the U.S.

**Shepherd, Jack,** *The Adams Chronicles: Four Generations of Greatness* (1975). Handsomely illustrated volume depicting four generations of overachievers, as Daniel Boorstin calls them in his admirable introduction. The classic history is James Truslow Adams, *The Adams Family* (1930).

# FAMILY

**Cheever, John,** *The Wapshot Chronicle* (1957). Rich, sweeping Rabelaisian chronicle of a New England family named Wapshot that stubbornly refused to let the sap of life run dry. Winner of National Book Award. See *The Wapshot Scandal* (1963).

**Galsworthy, John,** *The Forsyte Saga* (1906–21). Popular three-generation family saga chronicling, from late Victorian times to just after World War I, the evils of acquisitiveness.

**Guest, Judith,** *Ordinary People* (1976). Conrad, the teenage son, narrates this novel about his family, the Jarretts, just ordinary people — and they are coming apart.

**Hayward, Brooke,** *Haywire* (1977). Memoir of Hollywood childhood and family disintegration by the daughter of Leland Hayward and Margaret Sullivan.

**Irving, John,** *The Hotel New Hampshire* (1981). The wild and weird saga of the Berry family, which includes a midget, a deaf child, a homosexual, a bear, a lesbian who thinks she's a bear, a stuffed dog, a neurotic rape victim, an incestuous brother and sister, and a blind Jew named Freud. A bizarre neo-Dickensian tale. See *The World According to Garp* (1978).

**Larsson, Carl,** *A Home* (1974). Lovely, luminous watercolors of painter Larsson's family at their rural Swedish home at the turn of the century. See *A Farm* (1976) and *A Family* (1980).

**Matthiessen, F. O.,** *The James Family* (1947). Chiefly comprising selections from the writings of Henry James Sr., William, Henry, and Alice James, with comments by the author. An interesting perspective on the family can be drawn from Jean Strouse's biography, *Alice James* (1980).

**Mitford, Nancy,** *The Pursuit of Love* (1946). Delightful novel about a rebellious young family — surely the Mitfords — whose domineering and eccentric father forces everyone around him to extreme and unconventional behavior. Many of its characters reappear in *Love in a Cold Climate* (1949). The remarkable Mitfords are wonderfully described in Jessica Mitford's *Daughters and Rebels* (1960).

**O'Neill, Eugene,** *Long Day's Journey into Night* (1956). Riveting four-act play, based on O'Neill's own family history, about the Tyrones, their illusions and delusions, their drinking, and their verbal attacks on each other.

**Robison, Mary,** *Oh!* (1981). Hilarious and serious first novel about the madcap Cleveland family.

**Rugoff, Milton,** *The Beechers* (1981). Story of preacher Lyman Beecher and his remarkable children, of whom Henry Ward and Harriet Beecher Stowe are the most famous. Another American family of the nineteenth century is portrayed in Madelon Bedell, *The Alcotts* (1980).

**Salinger, J. D.,** *Franny and Zooey* (1961). Part of the Glass family stories. Like *Raise High the Roof Beam, Carpenters* and *Seymour: an Introduction* (1963), it is narrated by Buddy Glass, the second oldest; it tells of the youngest members, Franny and Zooey, and the latter's help in his sister's recovery from a nervous breakdown. Seymour, who committed suicide in "A Perfect Day for Bananafish," one of the *Nine Stories* (1953), is at the center of the last two novellas.

**Saltykov-Schedrin, M. E.,** *The Golovlyov Family* (1872–76). Portrait of an unforgettably horrible family in a novel that is "the most somber and pitiless instance of black comedy in Russian literature of the 19th century" (V. S. Pritchett).

**Simpson, Jeffrey,** *The American Family: A History in Photographs* (1977). Celebration of family life in a rich and varied collection of images. An earlier photographic tribute was *Family* (1965), done in collaboration by Margaret Mead and Ken Heyman.

**Stead, Christina,** *The Man Who Loved Children* (1940). This American novel by an Australian writer about the Pollit family has the quality that only a "great book has: it makes you a part of one family's immediate existence as no other book quite does" (Randall Jarrell).

**Taylor, Mildred D.,** *Song of the Trees* (1975). Set in Mississippi at the height of the Depression, it tells in powerful language and rich characterization the story of the Logan family's struggle to maintain integrity and pride. Its sequel, *Roll of Thunder, Hear Me Cry* (1977) won the Newberry Medal as the most distinguished children's book of the year. Followed by *Let the Circle be Unbroken* (1981).

**Waugh, Evelyn,** *Brideshead Revisited: Sacred and Profane Memories of Charles Ryder* (1945). Novel about the Marchmains, a titled Roman Catholic family of wealth, between the world wars. Sentimental, snobbish, and full of Catholic apologetics, but completely absorbing.

**West, Rebecca,** *The Fountain Overflows* (1956). Sparkling novel about the eccentric and gifted Aubrey family of Victorian England.

**Wolfe, Thomas,** *Look Homeward, Angel* (1929). Sprawling, lyrical, humorous, richly evocative novel about the Gants of Catawba, based on Wolfe's own early experiences in Asheville, North Carolina. "The best of his prose combines splendor and eloquence with an all-embracing humanity and conquering, affirmative vision of man's earthly struggles" (Andrew Turnbull).

## Child Care

**Caplan, Frank (ed.),** *The First Twelve Months of Life* (1973). Month-by-month guide put together by the Princeton Center for Infancy and Early Childhood. Indispensable. See *The Second Twelve Months of Life* (1978) and *The Parenting Advisor* (1977).

**Cottin-Pogrebin Letty,** *Growing up Free: Raising Your Child in the 80's* (1981). Thoughtful guide to role-free family life by a concerned feminist bent on ridding the sexes of cumbersome stereotypes.

**Dodson, Fitzhugh,** *How to Parent* (1970). Practical guide written by a psychologist and father of three who recommends a commonsense combination of love and discipline. See *How to Father* (1974), *How to Discipline with Love* (1977), and *How to Grandparent* (1981).

**Dreikurs, Rudolf with Vicki Soltz,** *Children: The Challenge* (1964). Classic on parenting: how to become a match for children by applying tested solutions and a consistent philosophical approach to discipline that neither lets children run wild nor stifles them. See Rebecca Costa et al., *A Parents' Guide to Children: The Challenge* (1978), a programmed guide to Dreikurs's book.

**Faber, Adele and Elaine Mazlish,** *Liberated Parents, Liberated Children* (1974). Zesty, honest account of how a group of parents guided by Dr. Haim Ginott discovered that his methods of communicating offer them options. See *How to Talk So Kids Will Listen and Listen So Kids Will Talk* (1980).

**Fraiberg, Selma H.,** *The Magic Years: Understanding and Handling the Problems of Early Childhood* (1959). Shows how the child confronts the world and learns to cope with it; with great warmth and perception, discusses problems at each stage of development, revealing the qualities that can provide the right answer at critical moments.

**Gordon, Tom,** *P.E.T.* (1975). The basic text of Parent Effectiveness Training — the "no-lose program for raising responsible children." See *P.E.T. in Action* (1976).

**Gross, Leonard H.** (ed.), *The Parents' Guide to Teenagers* (1981). Hundreds of questions that parents ask, answered knowledgeably and clearly. See John Schowalter and Walter Anyon, *The Family Book of Adolescence* (1979).

**Jones, Sandy,** *Good Things for Babies* (rev. 1980). Useful guide to infant products; sort of a *Whole Earth Catalog* for baby goods. See *Learning for Little Kids: A Parents' Source Book for the Years 3 to 8* (1979).

**Leach, Penelope,** *Your Baby & Child: From Birth to Age Five* (1978). Comprehensive, authoritative, sensitive guide to child care and development; elegantly designed and illustrated.

**Salk, Lee and Rita Kramer,** *How to Raise a Human Being* (1969). Parents' guide to emotional health from infancy through adolescence according to Dr. Salk. See *Preparing for Parenthood* (1974) and *What Every Child Would Like His Parents to Know* (1972).

**Scharlatt, Elisabeth L.** (ed.), *Kids: Day In and Day Out* (1979). Compendium of ideas, recommendations, insights, inspirations, facts and suggestions, problems, and solutions for living with kids every day. Combines the best qualities of Dr. Spock and *The Whole Earth Catalog.*

**Spock, Benjamin,** *Baby and Child Care* (rev. 1976). The bestseller of the century; this classic, which has raised two generations "according to Spock," is the greatest handbook for parents on the everyday problems of child raising.

## Fathers

**Corman, Avery,** *Kramer Versus Kramer* (1977). Engaging novel about a father who discovers the joys and miseries of being a single parent when his wife leaves him.

**Daley, E. A.,** *Father Feelings* (1978). Brief, informal observations on the joys and minor trials of suburban, middle-class fatherhood by a minister, former teacher, and writer for "Mr. Rogers' Neighborhood."

**Kundera, Milan,** *The Farewell Party* (1976). A brilliant Czech writer's novel on the theme of fatherhood — biological, adoptive, spiritual, moral, and legal.

**Parke, Ross D.,** *Fathers* (1981). Frank, well-written, up-to-date study on the role of the father. See Maureen Green, *Fathering* (**1976**).

**Sullivan, S. Adams,** *The Father's Almanac* (1980). Lots of practical ideas and advice for men who take pleasure in the challenge and enjoyment of raising young children. Another good adviser is Sara Gilbert, *What's a Father For?* (1975).

## Fathers and Sons

**Ackerley, J. R.,** *My Father and Myself* (1969). Lucid memoir of author's emotional relationship with his father, shadowed by his own homosexuality; often humorous and courageously candid. See *The Ackerley Letters* (1975).

**Day, Clarence,** *Life with Father* (1935). Sentimental classic about his upper-middle-class father. Delightful illumination of the gaslight era of New York City.

**Gold, Herbert,** *Fathers* (1966). A father seen through the eyes of a son in a memoir-novel that points to the dislocation between generations. See *Family* (1981).

**Gosse, Edmund,** *Father and Son* (1907). Classic autobiography. The story of his Calvinistic father's treatment of him offers an inside view of a family of Plymouth Brethren in Victorian England and of the development of an inquiring mind.

**Henderson, Bill,** *His Son: A Child of the Fifties* (1981). Fine memoir about the author's relationship with his father and his endeavor to discover principles by which to live.

**Mauriac, Francois,** *The Desert of Love* (1925). A tale, set in Bordeaux, about a father and son who, unbeknownst to each other, strive for the love of the same woman.

**Mehta, Ved,** *Daddyji* (1972). This absorbing recollection of his remarkable father is also an account of the disintegration of the colonial world.

**Shakespeare, William,** *Henry IV, Part I* (1598). The greatest of historical dramas, about King Henry IV and his son Prince Hal, rebellion in the kingdom, the Battle of Shrewsbury, and the figure of Falstaff.

**Sitwell, Osbert,** *Tales My Father Taught Me* (1962). A pendant to his five-volume autobiography, *Left Hand, Right Hand,* he elaborates on its greatest character, the wildly improbable comic figure of his father. Sitwell-lovers will adore it; others will find his prose style overwrought.

**Wolff, Geoffrey,** *The Duke of Deception* (1979). A writer's harsh but wonderfully affectionate memories of his father. Not only an account of one son's attempt to find his father, but a stripping of the veneer that hides all fathers.

## Fathers and Daughters

**Balzac, Honoré De,** *Pere Goriot* (1834). One of his Scenes of Parisian Life, the tragic story of a saintly but weak father of two ungrateful daughters, who humiliate and finally abandon him. A Gallic Lear.

**Gordon, Mary,** *Final Payments* (1978). A disillusioned Irish Catholic woman has spent the last decade caring for her invalid father. Now at thirty she must begin a life. A rich novel about friendship, grief, love.

**James, Henry,** *Washington Square* (1881). Small, quiet masterpiece about Catherine Sloper at home in Washington Square under the emotional dominance of her father.

**Shakespeare, William,** *King Lear* (c. 1605). Powerful tragedy of Lear and his daughters Regan, Goneril, and Cordelia that ends in their slaying and the king's total mental disintegration and death from grief.

**Swanberg, W. A.,** *Whitney Father, Whitney Heiress: Two Generations of America's Richest Families* (1980). Fascinating lives of millionaire William C. Whitney, his wife Flora Payne Whitney, and their daughter, Dorothy Payne Whitney.

## Mothers

**Barber, Virginia and Merrill Skaggs,** *The Mother Person* (1975). Cuts through the romantic assumptions and myths about motherhood that do not prepare women for what it is.

**Emecheta, Buchi,** *The Joys of Motherhood* (1979). Powerful novel set in modern Nigeria about the rigors of motherhood and the demands of society that make women prisoners of their sex.

**Friedland, Ronnie and Carol Kort (eds.),** *The Mothers' Book: Shared Experiences* (1981). Superb collection of essays by mothers about myriad aspects of motherhood. Realistic and moving.

**Kelly, Margaret and Ella Parsons,** *The Mother's Almanac* (1975). With wit and affection they cover just about everything a parent of an infant to a six-year-old would want to know. Filled with advice, projects, recipes, and much more, it is both useful and fun.

**Kitzinger, Sheila,** *Women as Mothers* (1978). A childbirth educator, social anthropologist, and mother, she writes sensitively of what being a mother means to a woman as a person.

**Lazarre, Jane,** *The Mother Knot* (1976). Painfully honest reflections by a sensitive writer on her experiences of childbirth and motherhood.

**Rich, Adrienne,** *Of Woman Born: Motherhood as Experience and Institution* (1976). By a poet and feminist, a brilliant and passionate exploration of the joy and pain, the myth and the reality, of motherhood.

## Mothers and Sons

**Bazin, Hervé,** *Viper in the Fist* (1947). A French novelist's depiction of a psychological battle between a spiteful mother and her young son.

**Dahlberg, Edward,** *Because I Was Flesh* (1963). This autobiography is as much the "tough, but, in its own way, epic story of his mother, the immigrant itinerant lady barber who found her son entering the literary world as a revolutionary leftist" (Harvey Swados). His famous proletarian novel *Bottom Dogs* (1929) tells much the same story in fictional form.

**Lawrence, D. H.,** *Sons and Lovers* (1913). Autobiographical in origin, this is the magnificent story of an English coal-mining family at the turn of the century, particularly of one son, Paul, and his unsatisfied, unfulfilled mother.

**Olsen, Paul,** *Sons and Mothers: Why Men Behave as They Do* (1981). Informal, anecdotal study by a psychotherapist on the mother-son relationship; written with insight and thoughtfulness.

**Roth, Philip,** *Portnoy's Complaint* (1969). "Portnoy's Complaint" is a disorder in which strongly felt ethical and altruistic impulses war perpetually with extreme, often perverse, sexual language. Many of its symptoms can be traced to the mother-child relationship. A wildly comic novel with an unforgettable Jewish mother. An equally outrageous caricature of the Jewish mother-son relationship is drawn in Bruce Jay Friedman, *A Mother's Kisses* (1964).

**Seabrook, Jeremy,** *Mother and Son* (1980). This mother ran a butcher shop in Northampton, England, during and after World War II. He writes of "complicated emotions and states of mind with rare verbal clarity and chilling honesty, and every line gives good value" (Alan Sillitoe).

## Mothers and Daughters

**Brown, Rosellen,** *The Autobiography of My Mother* (1976). A novel that dramatizes "in meticulous detail, through the very nuances of speech, the tragic differences between an indefatigable civil rights attorney and her 29-year-old 'withered flower-child' daughter" (Joyce Carol Oates). Other contemporary novels to explore the mother-daughter relationship include E. M. Broner, *Her Mothers* (1975); Gail Godwin, *A Mother and Two Daughters* (1982); Susan Richards Shreve, *A Woman Like That* (1977); and Anne Roiphe, *Long Division* (1972).

**Colette,** *My Mother's House/Sido* (1929). A set of lyrical reminiscences of her early years and her beloved mother, Sido. Simone de Beauvoir wrote about her mother in *A Very Easy Death* (1965).

**Moravia, Alberto,** *Two Women* (1958). An elemental tale, moving and compassionate, about a peasant mother and her daughter victimized in wartime Italy.

**Murphy, Dervla,** *Wheels Within Wheels* (1980). An extraordinary woman's honest, bitter memories of her first thirty years in a small Irish village, the only child of an intellectual, strong, house-proud, crippled mother.

## Brothers

**Dostoevski, Fedor,** *The Brothers Karamazov* (1880). Four brothers driven by intense passion become involved in the brutal murder of their own father. A compelling, profound, complex novel.

**Dunne, John Gregory,** *True Confessions* (1977). A grimy, corrupt Los Angeles in the forties is the setting for this novel about a gruesome slaying as it affects the lives of two Irish-Catholic brothers, a cop and a priest.

**Joyce, Stanislaus,** *My Brother's Keeper* (1958). Memoir of James Joyce by his younger brother illuminates his Dublin youth and early works. See *Dublin Diary* (1952).

**Machado de Assis, Joaquin Maria,** *Esau and Jacob* (1904). The rivalry between two brothers serves as the vehicle for a novel of society in the last days of the old Brazilian empire.

**Singer, I. J.,** *The Brothers Ashkenazai* (1936). Story of a set of very different twin brothers that chronicles the rise and decline of the Russian city of Lodz from the 1870s to the Revolution. "One of the greatest 20th century social novels . . . an extraordinary, searing work of art" (Alfred Kazin).

## Sisters

**Austen, Jane,** *Sense and Sensibility* (1811). Superb novel of manners that revolves around sisters Elinor, the one with sense, and Marianne, the one with sensibility, and their unfortunate romances.

**Baker, Dorothy,** *Cassandra at the Wedding* (1962). Highly polished writing distinguishes this novel, on the relationship between two sisters, that "presents what is probably as incisive a portrait of any in literature of a girl who is hopelessly in love with another girl" (Robert Phelps).

**Bennett, Arnold,** *The Old Wives' Tale* (1908). Long novel that traces the lives of two sisters from the pottery district of the Five Towns, who are "unforgettable, both as individual characters and as preoccupied with industry, patriotism and thrift" (V. S. Pritchett).

**Green, Martin,** *The Von Richthofen Sisters* (1974). Story of Else and Frieda von Richthofen and their husbands, Max Weber and D. H. Lawrence; a work that combines biography, history of ideas, literary criticism, and study of culture.

**Hazzard, Shirley,** *The Transit of Venus* (1980). Award-winning novel that traces the arcs of two sisters' lives through love at mid-twentieth century. Other contemporary novels chronicling the lives of sisters include Rachel MacKenzie, *The Wine of Astonishment* (1974) and Richard Yates, *The Easter Parade* (1976).

**Lawrence, D. H.,** *Women in Love* (1920). Two sisters, Gudrun and Ursula, living in a Midlands colliery town are at the center of this powerful novel which examines their relationship and that of their lovers as they clash in thought, belief, and passion. Their earlier lives are chronicled in *The Rainbow* (1915).

**Lehmann, Rosamond,** *The Echoing Grove* (1953). Elegant psychological novel about a triangle involving two sisters: the man's wife and his mistress. "This is her very best. It is, I think, a masterpiece" (Elizabeth Janeway).

**Sendak, Maurice,** *Outside Over There* (1981). A little girl rescues her infant sister from the clutches of goblins in a superb children's book, dreamy and symbolic with haunting watercolors.

**Tanizaki, Junichiro,** *The Makioka Sisters* (1948). Japan in the 1930s is the setting for this masterly novel that chronicles the fortunes of four sisters. It has been called a modern-day *Tale of Genji* and "the seamy side of Jane Austen" (Kenneth Rexroth).

**Tharp, Louise,** *The Peabody Sisters of Salem* (1950). One founded the American kindergarten, one married Horace Mann, and one married Nathaniel Hawthorne.

## Brother and Sister

**Cocteau, Jean,** *The Holy Terrors* (1929). Haunting novel of the beauty and cruelty of adolescence and the claustrophobic dreamworld inhabited by a brother and sister.

**Eliot, George,** *The Mill on the Floss* (1860). Dorclote Mill on the river Floss is the scene for this novel about Tom and Maggie Tolliver, a brother and sister who begin life with affection, fall out, and reunite in death.

**Hartley, L. P.,** *Eustace and Hilda Trilogy* (1944–47). Traces the lives of Eustace and his sister Hilda from childhood through the drama of their grownup lives. It was described by Lord David Cecil as "in any age and by any standard . . . a masterpiece."

**James, Henry,** *The Turn of the Screw* (1898). Classic horror novel about an evil curse surrounding the beautiful children Miles and Flora and their governess's desperate attempts to ward off the "ghosts" that threaten them.

**Peters, H. F.,** *Zarathustra's Sister: The Case of Elizabeth and Friedrich Nietzche* (1977). Strange and fascinating love/hate story between the German philosopher and his manipulative sister.

## Uncles

**Dickens, Charles,** *The Mystery of Edwin Drood* (1870). Did the sinister John Jasper murder his nephew Edwin Drood? As Dickens left the novel unfinished, we will never know his intentions. But Leon Garfield "concluded" the story in a 1981 edition.

**Le Fanu, Joseph Sheridan,** *Uncle Silas, A Tale of Bartram-Haugh* (1864). This Victorian classic of terror about an evil uncle's machinations to murder his niece and ward, Maud Ruthyn "is not the last, belated Gothic romance but the first (or among the first) of the psychological thrillers" (Elizabeth Bowen).

**Markus, Julia,** *Uncle* (1978). Beautiful little novel about Uncle Irv, a man willing to make any sacrifice for others; Suzanne, his niece; and a season at summer camp.

**Morris, Wright,** *My Uncle Dudley* (1942). A wild car journey from Los Angeles to Chicago, the young nephew at the wheel, Uncle Dudley directing the action, in a broadly picaresque novel.

**Welty, Eudora,** *The Ponder Heart* (1954). Short tragicomic novel about the strange, overgenerous Uncle Daniel; Welty at her frolicsome best.

## Aunts

**Capote, Truman,** *The Grass Harp* (1951). Sensitive, unwanted boy goes to live with his remarkable old aunt and her menage in a tree house.

**Dennis, Patrick,** *Auntie Mame* (1955). The inspiration for the popular play and musical, it tells of the narrator's upbringing by an eccentric aunt in New York City and the comic escapades that she gets involved in.

**Forster, E. M.,** *Marianne Thornton, A Domestic Biography, 1797–1887* (1956). The English novelist constructed this biography of his great aunt from her letters. He appears in the final section as a very small boy experiencing the impact of a very old woman. A witty, elegant nineteenth-century social history.

**Greene, Graham,** *Travels with my Aunt* (1969). Richly comic novel about a bachelor nephew and his ever-amazing Aunt Augusta, who in their adventures teaches him how to live.

**Purdy, James,** *The Nephew* (1960). The nephew is missing in action in Korea. His spinster aunt, who brought him up, searches for his personality.

## Grandparents

**Hall, Donald,** *String Too Short to Be Saved* (1960). The poet reminisces about the summer spent on the family farm in New Hampshire while a boy and his special relationship with his grandfather.

**Holman-Hunt, Diana,** *My Grandmothers and I* (1961). The granddaughter of pre-Raphaelite British painter William Holman-Hunt unsentimentally chronicles her girlhood spent shuttling between two strongly contrasting grandmothers. A "triumphant recreation of a child's memories" (Evelyn Waugh). See *My Grandfather, His Wives and Loves* (1970).

**Jury, Mark and Dan Jury,** *Gramp* (1976). In unsentimental text and photos the account of a family's decision to care for the senile grandfather at home, its effect on them, and his death three years later.

**Ruark, Robert,** *The Old Man and the Boy* (1957). A newspaperman-novelist remembers his North Carolina boyhood and his outdoorsman grandfather. A similar relationship is given fictional gloss in Janet Majerus, *Grandpa and Frank* (1976).

# HEALTH AND MEDICINE

**Boyd, Doug,** *Rolling Thunder: A Personal Exploration into the Secret Healing Powers of an American Indian Medicine Man* (1974). Magical story of a year spent touring with a Cherokee medicine man who possessed the ability to bring about "miraculous" cures.

**Correy, Lee,** *Space Doctor* (1981). Science-fiction novel notable for its imaginative projections of the state of medicine in the future. See Groff Conklin and Noah D. Fabricant (eds.), *Great Science Fiction About Doctors* (1963).

**Crichton, Michael,** *The Andromeda Strain* (1969). Thriller about world's first biological crisis, ignited when an unmanned NASA satellite is recalled. *The Terminal Man* (1972) also has a medical background. See *Five Patients: The Hospital Explained* (1970), nonfiction, and Jeffrey Hudson, *A Case of Need* (1968), pseudonymous Edgar-winner.

**Dubos, René,** *Mirage of Health: Utopias, Progress, and Biological Change* (1959). The distinguished microbiologist shows that a utopia in which disease is conquered and the only thing left to die of is old age is neither possible nor desirable.

**Duffy, John,** *The Healers: The Rise of the Medical Establishment* (1976). Carefully researched, fluidly written history of American medicine. For a large-format pictorial survey see Albert S. Lyons and Joseph Petrucelli, *Medicine: An Illustrated History* (1979).

**Fisher, M. F. K.,** *A Cordiall Water: A Garland of Odd and Old Recipes to Assuage the Ills of Man & Beast* (1961). The author's sensitivity to nature and taste for strangeness and anecdote make this collection of folk remedies delightful.

**Flexner, James Thomas,** *Doctors on Horseback: Pioneers of American Medicine* (1937). Portraits of seven extraordinary pioneer physicians drawn with the vigor of fiction.

**Glasser, Ronald,** *The Body Is the Hero* (1976). The body's immune system is the focus of this clear, exciting book. See *Ward 402* (1973).

**Goodfield, June,** *An Imagined World: A Story of Scientific Discovery* (1981). The product of five years with an immunologist involved in cancer research: a lucid and intelligent account of the hard work and drama that constitute scientific creativity. See *The Siege of Cancer* (1975) and *Playing God: Genetic Engineering and the Manipulation of Life* (1977).

**Le Baron, Charles,** *Gentle Vengeance* (1981). Inside look at the rigors of the first year at Harvard Medical School.

**Miller, Jonathan,** *The Body in Question* (1979). Topical history of medicine, shot off from the BBC TV series, by the erudite and witty physician.

**Molière,** *The Imaginary Invalid* (1673). Entertaining and scathing attack on the pretensions of doctors. One of the great French comic dramatist's masterpieces. His other sendups of the medical profession are *The Physician in Spite of Himself* (1666) and *The Doctor in Love* (1665).

**Nolen, William A.,** *The Making of a Surgeon* (1971). Anecdotal, rambling account of a young surgeon's training, "remarkable for its wit and honesty. As a description of how men work against impossible odds, it is both human and heroic in a fascinating way" (Michael Crichton). See *A Surgeon's World* (1972). For a fictional gloss see John Hejinian, *Extreme Remedies* (1974).

**Nourse, Alan,** *The Bladerunner* (1974). One of several sci-fi novels for teenagers about medicine by an experienced science writer who was once a physician. His books for adults include *Inside the Mayo Clinic* (1979) and *The Practice* (1978), a novel.

**Roueché, Berton,** *Eleven Blue Men and Other Narratives of Medical Detection* (1954). Collection of fascinating pieces originally published in the *New Yorker* about pathology investigation. See *The Incurable Wound and Further Narratives of Medical Detection* (1958), *The Medical Detectives* (1980), and *Curiosities of Medicine, 1552–1962* (1963).

**Selzer, Richard,** *Mortal Lessons: Notes on the Art of Surgery* (1976). Collection of essays on medicine and mortality, written with urgency and poetic feeling. See *Confessions of a Knife* (1979) and *Letters to a Young Surgeon* (1982).

**Shainberg, Lawrence,** *Brain Surgeon: An Intimate View of His World* (1979). Compelling portrait by a writer who spent a year with a renowned chief of neurosurgery. Good companion volumes are I. S.

Cooper, *The Vital Probe: My Life as a Brain Surgeon* (1981) and Edward M. Restak, *The Brain: The Last Frontier* (1979).

**Time-Life Editors,** *Life Library of Health* (1980–). Series of judicious, clear, beautifully illustrated volumes on every aspect of health.

**Toynbee, Polly,** *Patients* (1977). An English "new journalist" spent five months at London Hospital observing the intimate moments of other people's lives. A nonsentimental, involving book.

**Young, James H.,** *The Medical Messiahs* (1967). Social history of health quackery in twentieth-century America. See *The Toadstool Millionaires* (1962).

## Infectious Diseases and Epidemics

**Camus, Albert,** *The Plague* (1948). The scene of this modern masterpiece is laid in the Algerian port of Oran, where a ravaging epidemic of bubonic plague — symbolic of other spiritual and political plagues — has thrown the city into a harrowing agony.

**De Kruif, Paul,** *Microbe Hunters* (1926). Man's fight against disease chronicled in vivid biographies of pioneering bacteriologists. A classic of its kind. See *Men against Death* (1934); Greer Williams, *Virus Hunters* (1959); and Sinclair Lewis, *Arrowsmith* (1925), a novel about a microbe hunter.

**Giono, Jean,** *Horseman on the Roof* (1954). The French lyrical novelist's story of the devastating cholera epidemic of 1838 in Provence "is a remarkably beautiful piece of writing about a remarkably ugly subject" (Anthony West).

**McNeill, William H.,** *Plagues and People* (1976). A historian proposes that the course of human events has been decisively shaped by the arbitrary forces of epidemic disease. A speculative, provocative book.

**Powell, John H.,** *Bring out Your Dead: The Great Plague of Yellow Fever in Philadelphia in 1793* (1950). Dramatic story of an epidemic that killed 4,000 of a city's 55,000 inhabitants. Mildred A. Jones, *Echo of the Flute* (1958) is a novel about the plague.

**Shurkin, Joel N.,** *The Invisible Fire* (1979). Story of mankind's triumph over smallpox.

**Stewart, George R.,** *Earth Abides* (1949). Science-fiction classic about a plague that covers the earth and the survivors' vain efforts to restore civilization.

**Swift, Jonathan,** *A Journal of the Plague Year* (1722). This account of the London plague of 1665 was published as an authentic journal — a literary hoax, as the events described occurred before he was born. Fascinating reading, anyhow.

**Vallery-Radot, Pasteur,** *Louis Pasteur: A Great Life in Brief* (1958). Intimate, admiring biography by the grandson of the French scientist who proved that microbes cause sickness.

**Zinsser, Hans,** *Rats, Lice and History* (1935). Classic biography of infectious diseases and the various roles they have played in history.

## Encounters with Illness

**Cousins, Norman,** *Anatomy of an Illness as Perceived by the Patient: Reflections on Healing and Regeneration* (1979). Using his own remarkable self-cure from a crippling disease and the case histories of others, the author discusses the importance of the patient's attitude and natural healing.

**Ellis, A. E.,** *The Rack* (1959). A novel — long, grim, completely absorbing — about life in a tuberculosis sanitorium; speaks of the ordeal of the human spirit and the will to live.

**Massie Robert and Suzanne Massie,** *Journey* (1975). Poignant account of their years caring for a son stricken with genetic hemophilia and of his survival.

**Mee, Charles L., Jr.,** *Seizure* (1979). Case history of a young music student afflicted by a brain tumor: as gripping as a suspense thriller.

**White, Robin,** *Be Not Afraid* (1972). A parent's honest account of his child's long ordeal with epilepsy and the strain it placed on the rest of the family.

## Cancer

**Alsop, Stewart,** *Stay of Execution: A Sort of Memoir* (1974). The well-known columnist developed leukemia and recorded his emotional response to being told that he could be expected to live no more than one year. He recovered.

**Cook, Stephani,** *Second Life* (1981). More than a story of a painful illness, its disastrous consequences, and recuperation — a remarkable odyssey of a woman's discovery of her own inner resources.

**Israel, Lucien,** *Conquering Cancer* (1978). Lucid, argumentative discussion of available treatments for cancer and outline of current medical theories and practices.

**Lee, Laurel,** *Walking Through Fire* (1977). Courageous account of her battle with Hodgkin's Disease, told with wit and beauty. *Signs of Spring* (1980) is an epilogue detailing her post-remission experiences. Elaine Ipswitch, *Scott Was Here* (1979) is about an unsuccessful struggle with this form of cancer.

**Lund, Doris,** *Eric* (1974). Mother's story of her son's ordeal with leukemia. Beautifully written, it is a story not of dying, but of living intensely.

**Rollin, Betty,** *First You Cry* (1976). Unsparing and inspiring account of her mastectomy and her coming to grips with its physical and psychological consequences. See Dorothy Abbott, *Nothing's Changed: Diary of a Mastectomy* (1981); Rose

Kushner, *Breast Cancer: A Personal History and an Investigative Report* (1975); and Penelope Mortimer, *My Friend Says It's Bulletproof* (1968), a novel. For an alternative to mastectomy, see Oliver Cope, *The Breast: Its Problems — Benign and Malignant — and How to Deal with Them* (1977).

**Ryan, Cornelius,** *A Private Battle* (1978). Day-by-day log of coping with cancer achieves a humble power through the frank expression of his awareness of his fate. Another moving narrative is Bernard Sloan, *The Best Friend You'll Ever Have* (1980).

**Solzhenitsyn, Aleksandr,** *The Cancer Ward* (1968). Based on his own treatment for cancer, this novel about the cancer ward of a hospital in the 1950s (and the political cancer corrupting Soviet life) is "for all its external atmosphere of the clinic basically a celebration of human life" (Clifton Fadiman).

**Sontag, Susan,** *Illness as Metaphor* (1979). Inspired by her own response to cancer and threat of death, Sontag attacks the metaphoric thinking about disease that makes it more traumatic than it would be in itself. An intellectually stimulating work.

**Wolitzer, Hilma,** *Ending* (1974). A realistic novel about a young couple with two small children all going through the agony of the husband's death from bone cancer. Told with feeling and even humor.

## Cardiovascular Problems

**The American Heart Association,** *Heartbook: A Guide to Prevention and Treatment of Cardiovascular Disease* (1980). Thirty-one leading heart specialists have contributed to this comprehensive overview; graphically illustrated and lucidly written.

**Halberstam, Michael and Stephan Lesher,** *A Coronary Event* (1976). Alter-

nating narratives of the physician and his heart patient: witty, intelligent, and informative.

**Hodgins, Eric,** *Episode: Report on an Accident Inside My Skull* (1969). At sixty, the journalist-author underwent a "cardiovascular accident" — a stroke. This stirring account of his eighteen months of recovery is written with "intense feeling, acute perception, flashing humor — and entertaining rascality" (Frank G. Slaughter).

**Lear, Martha Weinman,** *Heartsounds* (1980). Eloquent, stirring book about her husband and his five years of medical crises, including neglect and mistreatment. About loving as much as about dying, and reads like a novel.

**MacKenzie, Rachel,** *Risk* (1971). A writer's deeply personal, affecting account of her ordeal of open-heart surgery.

## Exceptional Children

**Axline, Virginia,** *Dibs: In Search of Self* (1964). The deeply moving account of the emergence by means of "play therapy" of intelligence and emotion in a five-year-old boy so withdrawn that his own parents judged him mentally defective. A psychoanalyst tells of his patient struggle with a similar child in Richard D'Ambrosio, *No Language but a Cry* (1970).

**Featherstone, Helen,** *A Difference in the Family: Life with a Disabled Child* (1980). During the first year of Jody's life, his parents learned that he was severely disabled; they responded not with bitter unhappiness, but a "calm, wise, unflinching and heart-mending book" (John Leonard).

**Greenfeld, Josh,** *A Child Called Noah* (1972). Fascinating, terrible story of the Greenfelds' gradual awareness that their son was developmentally disabled. Continued in *A Place for Noah* (1978). Two inspiring accounts of parents battling to get through to their children diagnosed as autistic are Barry Neil Kaufman, *Son Rise* (1976) and Clara Claiborne Park, *The Siege* (rev. 1982).

**Hill, Archie,** *Closed World of Love* (1977). Stepfather's gentle tribute to his wife's unselfish love for her severely handicapped son. He learned to share in the boy's care until the latter's death thirteen years later.

**Killilea, Marie,** *Karen* (1952). Courage, patience, and finally triumph in the author's struggle to help her daughter, a victim of cerebral palsy. A touching, gallant book. See Helene Brown, *Yesterday's Child* (1976).

## Blindness

**Bjarnhof, Karl,** *The Stars Grow Pale* (1958). Sensitive, life-affirming novel by a blind Danish writer about a child doomed to blindness. See *The Good Light* (1960), a sequel.

**Butler, Beverly,** *Light a Single Candle* (1962). Based on the author's own experiences, a moving novel of a girl blinded at fourteen and her struggle to take her place again in her school crowd. See *Gift of Gold* (1972), a continuation.

**Chevigny, Hector,** *My Eyes Have a Cold Nose* (1946). Nonsentimental, swiftly paced account of the author's experiences, since being struck blind at middle age, with his seeing-eye dog. Sheila Hocken, *Emma and I* (1978) is about a woman's relationship with her guide dog.

**Green, Henry,** *Blindness* (1926). This first novel about a seventeen-year-old boy who is struck blind was written when Green was an undergraduate at Oxford.

**Keller, Helen,** *The Story of My Life* (1903). The story of a remarkable woman, blind and deaf since birth, who became a world figure. The relationship between her and her "miracle worker," Anne Sullivan

Macy, is beautifully described in Joseph Lash, *Helen and Teacher* (1980).

**Kendrick, Baynard H.,** *Odor of Violets* (1941). Private investigator Captain Duncan Maclain is introduced in this detective novel in which, aided by his seeing eye dog and partner "Spud" Savage, he uses his remaining senses to track down a killer. The first of all blind detective series is that about Max Carrados, created by Ernest Bramah; see *The Eyes of Max Carrados* (1923).

**Mehta, Ved,** *Face to Face* (1957). The Indian-born writer tells about "facial vision" — the ability to see without eyes — and his experiences at a wonderful school for the blind in the U.S.

**Potok, Andrew,** *Ordinary Daylight: Portrait of an Artist Going Blind* (1980). In an absorbing, controlled work, a forty-year-old artist tells about his loss of sight from an inherited disease.

**Russell, Robert,** *To Catch an Angel: Adventures in a World I Cannot See* (1962). Warm, inspiring story of a man blinded in childhood who went through Yale and Oxford to become an English professor. *The Island* (1973) is a sequel.

**Yates, Elizabeth,** *The Lighted Heart* (1960). A novelist and children's writer touchingly describes her husband's adjustment to blindness at middle age. See Eleanor Clark, *Eyes, Etc.* (1978).

## Alcoholism

**Fitzgibbon, Constantine,** *Drink* (1979). With considerable charm, the author details his personal struggle with alcoholism. An absorbing, informative story. Another good confessional is Paul Molloy, *Where Did Everybody Go?* (1981).

**Goodwin, Donald W.,** *Alcoholism: The Facts* (1981). A psychiatry professor's down-to-earth look at the problem clears up much misinformation about alcoholism.

**Jackson, Charles,** *The Lost Weekend* (1944). Novel depicting the psychological hell of a five-day drunken fling.

**Lowry, Malcolm,** *Under the Volcano* (1947). A novel of great power, set in Mexico, about the British consul and his horrific alcoholic last days. Beautifully written, touching on themes of love, guilt, and salvation. Lowry's life ended in alcoholic suicide.

**O'Hara, John,** *Appointment in Samarra* (1934). Haunting story of an aristocratic drunkard, Julian English, over a three-day bender in which his life spirals downward with dizzying speed to an untimely appointment with destiny. A hard-boiled classic.

**Rebeta-Burditt, Joyce,** *The Cracker Factory* (1977). The pressures and responsibilities of her life turn the heroine to the bottle. After an attempted suicide she finds herself institutionalized. Despite its serious theme, it is a novel full of humor.

**Straus, Robert,** *Escape from Custody* (1974). Social study of skid-row drinking that moves like a novel.

**Weiner, Jack B.,** *Drinking* (1976). A recovered alcoholic and journalist looks at the world of alcoholics and some of the programs that offer help.

**Yates, Richard,** *Disturbing the Peace* (1975). A finely crafted, grim novel of a man's descent into alcoholic oblivion. Other novels on this theme include Hans Fallada, *The Drinker* (1952) and Donald Newlove, *Sweet Adversity* (1978).

**Zola, Émile,** *The Dram-Shop* (1877). Translation of *L'Assommoir,* a compassionate novel written in the language of the Paris slums and intended to dramatize the disastrous effects of drinking on the working class.

## Drug Use

**Abel, Ernest L.,** *Marihuana: The First Twelve Thousand Years* (1981). The rise

and fall of cannabis chronicled by a psychopharmacist who has done his research. For a swift-paced look at its use today see Albert Goldman, *Grass Roots: Marijuana in America Today* (1979).

**Burroughs, William,** *Junkie* (1953). Harrowing, brutal document of the world of hard-drug users, pushers, and narcs. His experimental novel *The Naked Lunch* (1959) is distinguished by its drug-crazed flights of poetic imagination. With Allen Ginsberg he wrote *The Yage Letters* (1963) about their South American drug experiences.

**De Quincey, Thomas,** *Confessions of an English Opium-Eater* (1822). This classic by a superb writer addicted for fifty years is a series of digressive pieces beaded upon the chain of a "confession." See Grevel Lindop, *The Opium Eater: A Life of Thomas De Quincey* (1981). Two other English opium eaters of letters are Coleridge — see Molly Lefebvre, *Samuel Taylor Coleridge: A Bondage of Opium* (1974) — and Francis Thompson — see John Walsh, *Strange Harp, Strange Symphony; The Life of Francis Thompson* (1967).

**Harris, David,** *The Last Scam* (1981). Absorbing novel about life and death in the marijuana-smuggling run between Mexico and America. A nonfiction account of smuggling that reads like fiction is Robert Sabbag's engrossing *Snowblind: A Brief Career in the Cocaine Trade* (1976).

**Huxley, Aldous,** *The Doors of Perception* (1954). A brilliant mind observes itself under the influence of hallucinogens. See *Moksha: Writings on Psychedelics and the Visionary Experience* (1977). Other literary "travel" journals are Henri Michaux, *Light Through Darkness* (1963) and Alan Watts, *The Joyous Cosmology* (1963).

**Lamb, F. Bruce,** *Wizard of the Amazon: The Story of Manuel Cordova-Rios* (1974). Cordova's amazing experiences as a captive of an Amazonian Indian tribe at the beginning of the century and his use of the powerful hallucinogen native to those parts.

## Mental Disintegration

**Atwood, Margaret,** *Surfacing* (1972). In a novel hailed for its spare tension, a journey into the wilderness occasions the heroine's vision into those primordial aspects of life from which we have become almost fatally severed.

**Beers, Clifford,** *A Mind that Found Itself* (1908). Classic autobiographical account of mental illness and mistreatment in mental hospitals and a history of the mental hygiene movement founded by the author.

**Dostoevski, Fedor,** *The Double* (1846). An early, short novel of the Russian master, it depicts with remarkable realism the mental disintegration of a petty civil servant, ending with his being carried away to the madhouse. *The Idiot* (1868), more a novel of ideas, has as its protagonist a man who relapses into idiocy at the end of the story.

**Gibson, Margaret,** *The Butterfly Ward* (1980). Sensitive short stories set in and out of institutions that explore the fragile border between sanity and insanity. See *Considering Her Condition* (1981).

**Gilman, Charlotte Perkins,** *The Yellow Wallpaper* (1892). Bitter story of a young woman driven to insanity by a loving husband-doctor who, with the purest intentions, imposes a severe rest cure.

**Gogol, Nikolai,** *Diary of a Madman* (1835). Astounding fictional view of the mind of a St. Petersburg civil servant who believes himself to be the king of Spain.

**Green, Hannah,** *I Never Promised You a Rose Garden* (1972). An accurate, unflinching account of the world of the mentally ill: an emotionally gripping novel. That world is expertly presented in nonfiction in Susan Sheehan, *Is There No Place on Earth for Me?* (1982).

**Howland, Bette,** *W-3* (1974). After attempting suicide, the author landed in a psychiatric ward. This is her powerful story of life in that ward.

**Jackson, Shirley,** *The Bird's Nest* (1954). Frightening, sometimes funny, novel of a young woman with multiple personalities. Many of her other novels deal with disturbed young people; see *We Have Always Lived in the Castle* (1962) and *The Haunting of Hill House* (1959).

**Kafka, Franz,** *The Metamorphosis* (1915). One fine morning Gregor Samsa awakes to find himself transformed into a giant insect. A brilliant, nightmarish fantasy.

**Kesey, Ken,** *One Flew over the Cuckoo's Nest* (1962). Set in a mental hospital, this funny and poignant novel of one vital man's effect on his fellow inmates and the institution is a cry of the spirit, a roar of protest.

**Keyes, Daniel,** *The Minds of Billy Milligan* (1981). Compelling story of a young man, the first person in U.S. history to be found not guilty of a major crime because he had multiple personalities. See *The Fifth Sally* (1980), a novel about such a person. Earlier accounts of such a phenomenon include Corbett Thigpen and Hervey M. Cleckley, *Three Faces of Eve* (1957) and Flora Schreiber, *Sybil* (1973).

**Lessing, Doris,** *Briefing for a Descent into Hell* (1971). An "inner-space fiction" by a novelist who believes that society's treatment of the mentally ill is a great and dangerous blind spot, that through the minds of the "broken-down" appear truths that we choose to shut out.

**Neufeld, John,** *Lisa, Bright and Dark* (1969). Written for teenagers, this novel portrays the plight of a mentally ill adolescent girl whose parents refuse to recognize that there is anything wrong with her.

**Plath, Sylvia,** *The Bell Jar* (1971). Esther Greenwood's painful month in New York is the start of a crackup that eventually leads to madness and attempted suicide.

A riveting novel by a poet who took her own life.

**Poe, Edgar Allan,** *The Tell-Tale Heart* (1843). A killer tormented by what he believes to be the heartbeat of his victim blurts out his guilt to the police. Poe is the master of this sort of macabre tale.

**Sigal, Clancy,** *Zone of the Interior* (1976). Set in London at a sanctuary for schizophrenics who live in equality with the staff, a devastating satire on Laingian therapy.

**Stevenson, Robert Louis,** *The Strange Case of Dr. Jekyll and Mr. Hyde* (1886). The classic tale of the dual personality — benign Dr. Jekyll and demonic Mr. Hyde — that serves as a psychological allegory of the good and evil in all of us.

**Ward, Mary Jane,** *The Snake Pit* (1946). The horrors of life in an insane asylum skillfully told from point of view of an inmate. Another inside-an-institution novel is Janet Frame, *Faces in the Water* (1961).

**Wechsler, James et al.,** *In a Darkness* (1972). The ten-year effort to relieve his son's schizophrenia, ending with his son's suicide at age twenty-six. An angry, unnerving, heart-rending book.

## Psychoanalysis

**Balchin, Nigel,** *Mine Own Executioner* (1945). Intriguing English novel about a lay psychiatrist and his handling of a young psychopathic murderer.

**Clark, Ronald W.,** *Freud: The Man and the Cause* (1980). Judicious, absorbing biography of the father of psychoanalysis. A more flattering portrait is the three-volume *The Life and Work of Sigmund Freud* (1953–57) by the Welsh analyst Ernest Jones.

**Flügel, John,** *The Psychology of Clothes* (1930). Psychoanalytic approach to the wearing of clothing in a book that is learned, instructive, and often entertaining.

**Freud, Anna,** *Psychoanalysis for Parents and Teachers* (1935). Freud's daughter, a leading psychoanalytic theorist, explains the Oedipus complex, the latency period, and other watersheds of childhood development.

**Freud, Sigmund,** *Psychopathology of Everyday Life* (1914). The great man's most accessible work.

**Fuller, Peter,** *Art and Psychoanalysis* (1981). Survey of the work of Marion Milner, Melanie Klein, Charles Rycroft, Freud, Jung, and others. See Marion Milner, *On Not Being Able to Paint* (rev. 1967).

**H.D.,** *Tribute to Freud: With Unpublished Letters by Freud to the Author* (1951). An American poet's subtle, poignant recollections of being psychoanalyzed by Freud in London.

**Jung, C. G.,** *Memories, Dreams, Reflections* (1963). "With its copious disclosures of his inner life, it is perhaps as near as one can get to literary confession. . . . It was the hidden domain of his life that he valued, and this is what, in his final backward glance, he chose mainly to expose" (Lewis Mumford).

**Kaplan, Louise,** *Oneness and Separateness: From Infant to Individual* (1978). Traces evolution of a baby's experience of oneness with his mother into that of separation from her.

**Le Guin, Ursula K.,** *The Lathe of Heaven* (1971). About a man who has dreams that alter reality, and his analyst, who attempts to exploit that power over the world. Absorbing, mind-expanding science fiction.

**Malcolm, Janet,** *Psychoanalysis: The Impossible Profession* (1981). Artfully rendered portrait of a psychoanalyst and a well-researched critique of the profession.

**Rycroft, Charles,** *The Innocence of Dreams* (1979). Elegantly written volume in which the author goes beyond Freud and Jung in expounding his theory on the "innocence" of dreams. Other books on the subject include Freud's classic *The Interpretation of Dreams* (1900); Norman MacKenzie, *Dreams and Dreaming* (1966); and Sandra Shulman's intriguing *Nightmare* (1979).

**Sechehaye, Marguerite,** *Autobiography of a Schizophrenic Girl* (1970). Remarkable book by a Swiss psychoanalyst about a new method of therapy, "symbolic realization," as applied to a case of schizophrenia.

**Svevo, Italo,** *The Confessiosn of Zeno* (1923). Modernist classic novel in the form of a self-analysis written by Zeno for his psychoanalyst that brilliantly underlines the contradictions between his expressed and his internal desires.

**Thomas, D. M.,** *The White Hotel* (1981). Beautifully written, intelligent novel that begins with a tormented opera singer undergoing psychoanalysis with Freud and climaxes with the massacre of Russian Jews at Babi-Yar.

## Death

**Agee, James,** *A Death in the Family* (1957). Set in rural Tennessee, this Pulitzer Prize–winning novel poignantly focuses on the effect of a man's death on his young son and the religious zeal it inspires in his wife.

**Becker, Ernest,** *The Denial of Death* (1973). Brilliant synthesis of Freud, Rank, Jung, Fromm, and others on man's failure to acknowledge death. Awarded the Pulitzer Prize.

**Buck, Pearl,** *A Bridge for Passing* (1962). An interweaving of the passing of her husband and her ensuing grief with an account of a journey to Japan. Other writers who have written of their deceased spouses are C. S. Lewis, *A Grief Observed*

(1961) and Alan Paton, *For You Departed* (1974).

**Caine, Lynn,** *Widow* (1974). The realities of a husband's death and her grief. A graceful book. See *Lifelines* (1978).

**Cook, Bruce and Diane Christian,** *Death Row* (1980). Interviews with inmates on death row in a Texas prison. See Doug Magee, *Slow Coming Dark: Interviews on Death Row* (1980).

**Craven, Margaret,** *I Heard the Owl Call My Name* (1973). A young Anglican vicar is sent to minister to British Columbian Indians and must learn to come to terms with his terminal illness.

**Cristofer, Michael,** *The Shadow Box* (1978). Powerful drama that takes a hard look at the way people face death. Awarded the Pulitzer Prize.

**Gunther, John,** *Death Be Not Proud* (1949). Moving memorial to his son's courageous fifteen-month battle against a brain tumor, which finally killed him at age seventeen. See Christopher Leach, *Letter to a Younger Son* (1982), a touching book about a father's grief occasioned by the death of his son.

**Kapleau, Philip (ed.),** *The Wheel of Death: A Collection of Writing from Zen Buddhism and Other Sources on Death, Rebirth, Dying* (1971). Shards of wisdom from the East.

**Kluge, Eike-Henner W.,** *The Ethics of Death* (1975). Accessible critical exposition of the philosophical arguments surrounding suicide, abortion, infanticide, euthanasia, and senicide.

**Krementz, Jill,** *How It Feels When a Parent Dies* (1981). Eighteen children tell of their feelings when their mother or father died. With Krementz's photographs. This is a deeply moving book which can provide solace for a grieving youngster.

**Kübler-Ross, Elisabeth,** *On Death and Dying* (1969). A physician who has pioneered understanding of the terminally ill tells what the dying have to teach doctors, nurses, clergy, and their own families. See *Living with Death and Dying* (1981).

**Leca, Ange-Pierre,** *The Egyptian Way of Death: Mummies and the Cult of the Immortal* (1981). Fascinating look at a culture that mummified 500 million bodies.

**Lerner, Gerda,** *A Death of One's Own: Fragments from My Life* (1978). With sensitivity and spirit, the author chronicles her husband's slow death from a brain tumor. A similar ordeal is recounted in Hila Colman, *Hanging On* (1977).

**Moody, Raymond A., Jr.,** *Life After Life: The Investigation of a Phenomenon — Survival of Bodily Death* (1976). Speculations on what it is like to die, based on interviews with people who had clinically died but lived to relate their comforting near-death experiences.

**Panger, Danier.,** *The Dance of the Wild Mouse* (1979). Novel about the experience of dying in the alienated environment of a modern hospital.

**Smith, Alexander,** *Dreamthorp* (1863). This book of gentle meditations on death in a remote English village is "the quietest book of essays I know. To read it is like sinking under the leaves and grass of a gentle and caring cemetery and being profoundly glad to be there" (James Dickey).

**Tolstoy, Leo,** *The Death of Ivan Ilyich* (1886). A man's discovery that he has terminal cancer is the starting point for a lonely journey of contemplative discovery of the meaning of life and the acceptance of death.

**White, Helen Dean,** *With Wings as Eagles* (1953). A mother finds that her grief over the death of her son in World War II was an enriching spiritual experience. See

Lewis Mumford, *Green Memories* (1947), about his son killed in that war.

**Zorza, Victor and Rosemary Zorza,** *A Way to Die* (1981). This wrenching account of their twenty-five-year-old daughter's two-year battle with cancer is notable for its picture of the family-centered care she received at a hospice in England during her final days.

## Suicide

**Alvarez, A.,** *The Savage God: A Study of Suicide* (1972). Personal, literary, and existential exploration, with account of Sylvia Plath's suicide and of the author's attempt on his own life.

**Barth, John,** *The Floating Opera* (rev. 1967). His first novel; a man inquires into the reasons for not having committed suicide thirteen years before.

**Handke, Peter,** *A Sorrow Beyond Dreams: A Life Story* (1975). Understated narrative of his mother's dead-end life (she committed suicide at age fifty-one). Reads like one of his novels.

**Mannes, Marya,** *Last Rights* (1974). Succinct, passionate argument that the right to choose death when life no longer holds meaning is the last human right. See Christian Barnard, *Good Life/Good Death: A Doctor's Case for Euthanasia and Suicide* (1980).

**Sexton, Anne,** *Live or Die* (1966). Pulitzer Prize–winning collection of poems painfully reflects her inner torments about death and suicide.

**Sulzberger, C. L.,** *How I Committed Suicide* (1982). He thinks about suicide through the ages, tours through Europe, and then "kills" himself and his beloved dog. A reverie.

# HUMAN QUALITIES

## Courage and Cowardice

**Bukovsky, Vladimir,** *To Build a Castle: My Life as a Dissenter* (1978). A Russian exile who has spent most of his adult life in prison for his beliefs describes with perception and wit his painful experiences.

**Conrad, Joseph,** *Lord Jim* (1900). Tormented by his cowardice in abandoning 800 pilgrims on a sinking ship in order to save himself, Lord Jim becomes a wanderer, finally finding atonement for his moral lapse in the sacrifice of himself. A masterpiece.

**Crane, Stephen,** *The Red Badge of Courage* (1895). Classic novel, set at a brilliantly depicted Civil War battle, of an ordinary, inexperienced soldier who deserts the field in cowardice to return the next day with courage. A penetrating psychological study of men at war.

**Fitzgibbon, Constantine,** *20 July* (1955). Skillfully told account of the band of German officers who conspired to overthrow Hitler in 1944.

**Flowers, Desmond, and James Reeves (eds.),** *The Taste of Courage* (1960). Over a thousand pages of eyewitness battle accounts of World War II strung together in continuous narrative. "There is more of the scent and sound of battle, the sacrifice and bewilderment of the home front than you will find in a dozen novels" (Drew Middleton).

**Hemingway, Ernest,** *The Old Man and the Sea* (1952). Brief, carefully told novel about an old Gulf fisherman who proves his courage when he hooks a giant marlin.

**Kennedy, John Fitzgerald,** *Profiles in Courage* (1956). Written while he was a senator and awarded a Pulitzer Prize, it is comprised of pieces about politicians who had the courage to stand up for what they believed in.

**Mackenzie, Compton,** *Certain Aspects of Moral Courage* (1962). Gallery of Englishmen who displayed moral or political integrity, ranging from D. H. Lawrence to those who stood by Oscar Wilde during his infamous trial.

**Moore, William,** *The Thin Yellow Line* (1975). A strangely moving account of the courts-martial and subsequent executions of British soldiers accused of cowardice in World War I.

**Sperry, Armstrong,** *Call It Courage* (1940). This "Story of Mafatu, the Boy Who Was Not Afraid" is about a young Polynesian who overcomes his fear of the sea to become a hero. A lovely Newberry Award–winning tale for children.

## Ambition

**Dreiser, Theodore,** *Sister Carrie* (1900). Dreiser's first and greatest novel traces the fortunes of a poor country girl as she works her way up the ladder of success, first in Chicago and later in New York, only to find loneliness at the top. The original version was published in 1981. In *The Financier* (1912), the first of the Cowperwood trilogy, he charts the ruthless climb to power of a typical nineteenth-century robber baron.

**Epstein, Joseph,** *Ambition: The Secret Passion* (1981). The editor of *The American Scholar* probes the role of ambition in

American society, finding it to have positive value, to be "the fuel of achievement."

**Fitzgerald, F. Scott,** *The Great Gatsby* (1925). This now classic portrait of the twenties is a novel of romantic love, infidelity, and inevitable violence and the ambition of Jay Gatsby, who "believed in the green light, the orgiastic future that year by year recedes before us." One of the great American novels of our century.

**Hardy, Thomas,** *The Mayor of Casterbridge* (1886). Set in Wessex, England, shortly before 1830, it tells the story of Michael Henchard, an itinerant laborer who, in a moment of drunken despair, sold his wife at auction. This act came to haunt him, and finally to destroy him.

**Heller, Joseph,** *Something Happened* (1974). Written in a deliberately flat prose that accentuates the despair of the main character, it is about ambition, greed, love, lust, hate and fear, marriage and adultery.

**Maupassant, Guy De,** *Bel-Ami* (1885). The hero is an unprincipled social climber of limitless ambition; all the other characters are equally nasty, but very much alive; and the background of Parisian boulevard life is masterfully portrayed.

**Schulberg, Budd,** *What Makes Sammy Run?* (1941). Energetic first novel tracing the attempt of the grasping Sammy Glick to scale the top of the Hollywood heap. The heap of the "rag trade" is climbed by the equally obnoxious Harry Bogen in the remorseless and vivid *I Can Get It for You Wholesale* (1937) by Jerome Weidman.

**Shakespeare, William,** *Macbeth* (c. 1606). Spurred on by his ambitious wife, Macbeth's ambition to become king of Scotland is fulfilled at the cost of murder. Some of Shakespeare's most memorable scenes occur in this play.

**Stendhal,** *The Red and the Black* (1830). Julien Sorel's drive for power, masterfully depicted in one of the great psychological novels.

**Wharton, Edith,** *The Custom of the Country* (1913). Powerful and brilliant novel of manners about Undine Spragg clawing her way to the top of New York society.

## *Failure*

**Bellow, Saul,** *Seize the Day* (1956). Brief, intense novel in the chronicle of a miserable single day in the life of Tommy Wilhelm, broke, unemployed, middle-aged, separated from his family.

**Burgess, Anthony,** *Enderby* (1968). Hilarious and touching novel about Enderby, a fat, flatulent, middle-aged poet, who is whisked from obscurity to the pinnacle of pop fame but cannot cohabit with the bitch goddess, Success. A splendid comic portrait of the artist.

**Exley, Frederick,** *A Fan's Notes* (1968). Fictional memoir of a young man's searing descent into alcoholism, impotence, and insanity. A melancholy, funny, savage, and penetrating book about the American dream of fame and success. A brilliant attempt to tell the truth. See *Pages from a Cold Island* (1975).

**Goncharov, Ivan,** *Oblomov* (1859). The eponymous hero, a landowner living in St. Petersburg, spends almost all his time in robe and slippers lounging on his couch while his business affairs are going to ruin. His name has entered the Russian language as a synonym for sloth and ineffectiveness. A masterpiece of high comedy.

**Miller, Arthur,** *The Death of a Salesman* (1949). The tragedy of Willy Loman and of his sons, Biff and Happy. A moving, thoughtful drama about success and failure, self-deception, and responsibility.

## Friendship

**Bell, Millicent,** *Edith Wharton and Henry James* (1965). "I would include her book in my special series for the insomniac's bedside — books which transport us to a more enchanting world than the present and induce a state of grace" (Cyril Connolly).

**Greene, Bette,** *The Summer of My German Soldier* (1973). A lonely Jewish girl in Jenkinsville, Arkansas, forms a tragic friendship with a runaway German POW. A fresh, moving novel for teenage readers.

**Lobel, Arnold,** *Frog and Toad Are Friends* (1970). First of a series of irresistible children's tales about two special amphibious friends, illustrated by the author.

**McCarthy, Mary,** *The Group* (1962). Novel chronicling the lives of eight friends from the Vassar class of '33 as they cope with the realities of everyday life. A social history of one preliberation generation of women.

**Marquis, Don,** *archy and mehitabel* (1927). Collects the delightful stories of archy, the literary cockroach, and his companion mehitabel, a cat whose motto is "toujours gai." Written in a wacky free verse, a mordant satire on the state of the world.

**Maxwell, William,** *The Folded Leaf* (1945). Sensitive, disciplined portrait of the relationship between two adolescent boys in Chicago.

**Meynell, Viola,** *Francis Thompson and Wilfrid Meynell: A Memoir* (1953). Intimate details of the famous friendship between Thompson, a poet with a taste for opium, who lived in squalor in turn-of-the-century London until saved, physically and spiritually, by the Meynells.

**Morrison, Toni,** *Sula* (1973). The bond between two women over forty years, and the world in which it is destroyed, is brilliantly evoked in a clear, dark, resonant novel.

**Paterson, Katherine,** *Bridge to Terabitiha* (1977). A boy and a girl, fifth graders at a rural school, become close friends until death. A book for pre-teens; rich character development; awarded the Newberry Medal.

**Sachs, Marilyn,** *Class Pictures* (1981). Sensitive book for young teenage readers about the friendship between Pat and Lolly. Full of freshness, humor, and insight. See *Amy and Laura* (1966) and *Peter and Veronica* (1969).

**Scholem, Gershon,** *Walter Benjamin: The Story of a Friendship* (1981). A scholar recalls his intense intellectual camaraderie with the brilliant German-Jewish critic, who committed suicide in 1940. Other literary reminiscences include Mary Colum and Padraic Colum, *Our Friend James Joyce* (1958); William Dean Howells, *My Mark Twain* (1910); and Willie Morris, *James Jones: A Friendship* (1978).

**Steinbeck, John,** *Of Mice and Men* (1937). Set against ranch life in California's central valley, this brief novel tells the tragic tale of the bond between the slow-witted giant, Lennie, and the sensible George.

**Uhlman, Fred,** *Reunion* (1977). Provocative and touching short novel in which the Jewish narrator, thirty years later, recalls his doomed friendship with the son of a nobleman in Nazi Germany.

**Wakefield, Dan,** *Going All the Way* (1970). Indianapolis, 1954, is the scene of this funny and poignant story of two friends trying to reckon with the middle-class values of their community.

**Weldon, Fay,** *Female Friends* (1974). Three women now in their forties, who became friends as children during the evacuation of wartime London, are at the center of this novel about the predicament of civilized females in our times. By an English writer with a gift for crisp, witty dialogue.

## Loneliness

**Cassola, Carlo,** *An Arid Heart* (1964). After experiencing two unhappy love affairs, a young woman retreats into a life of isolation. A fine Italian novel.

**Fox, Paula,** *The Stone-Faced Boy* (1968). Beautifully crafted young-adult novel about a boy who displays neither happiness nor displeasure. See *Blowfish Live in the Sea* (1970) and *Portrait of Ivan* (1969).

**McCullers, Carson,** *The Heart Is a Lonely Hunter* (1940). The influence of a deaf-mute on the lonely lives of a small Georgia town; poignant and restrained.

**Moore, Brian,** *The Lonely Passion of Judith Hearne* (1955). Moving and compassionate story of a lonely, middle-aged spinster living in a Belfast boardinghouse, who finds herself caught between two profound passions and in the end sees her last hope for love and domesticity destroyed. A small masterpiece.

**Pym, Barbara,** *Quartet in Autumn* (1978). Fine English novel describing, with wit and compassion, the coming together of four lonely old folks. See *The Sweet Dove Died* (1979).

**Rubens, Bernice,** *I Sent a Letter to My Love* (1978). Three old people in a small Welsh town have the routine of their lives changed when one of the women advertises for a "gentleman companion."

**Seabrook, Jeremy,** *Loneliness* (1975). The voices of these few hundred English men and women tell us more about loneliness than a dozen statistical studies.

**Trevor, William,** *Elizabeth Alone* (1974). A lonely, divorced woman who enters a

London hospital for a hysterectomy is warded with three other women and comes out braver and more content with her life. A sensitive, tragicomic novel.

**West, Nathanael,** *Miss Lonelyhearts* (1933). Frenetic, garish, compelling novel about an advice-to-the-lovelorn columnist who is told by his feature editor that he is one of America's twentieth-century priests. "One of the . . . finest American novels of our century" (Stanley Edgar Hyman).

**Yates, Richard,** *Eleven Kinds of Loneliness* (1962). Compassionate collection of short stories offering poignant, revealing glimpses into the lives of lonely New Yorkers.

## Good and Evil

**Doctorow, E. L.,** *Welcome to Hard Times* (1961). Story of a man who rides into the small western town of Hard Times at the end of the last century and casually levels it to the ground; and of another man who devotes his life to reconstructing it. An exceptional novel of good intentions and the fascination of evil.

**Greene, Graham,** *The Heart of the Matter* (1948). What is good and what is evil, who are the damned and who are the saved, explored in this novel, set in West Africa, about a basically honest British civil officer driven to suicide by the torment of his sins. Another African novel, *A Burnt-Out Case* (1961), is also on this theme.

**Macdonald, George,** *The Princess and the Goblin* (1872). Splendid Victorian fairy story, and allegory, about a young and beautiful princess, her mysterious grandmother, and their exciting adventures in warding off a tribe of evil goblins.

**Wilder, Thornton,** *Heaven's My Destination* (1934). George Brush, a holy innocent on the road, determined to convert a materialistic America.

Williams, Charles, *All Hallows' Eve* (1945). Like his other "metaphysical" thrillers, this is an exciting novel in which good and evil do battle. See *The Greater Trumps* (1932).

## Loss of Innocence

Bowen, Elizabeth, *The Death of the Heart* (1938). Subtle atmospheric novel about a sixteen-year-old girl who falls in love with an insensitive young man.

Dickens, Charles, *Great Expectations* (1860–61). Perhaps his finest novel, it chronicles the coming into manhood of Pip, a young man who means well and often does wrong, but who through disillusionment and sadness becomes a man of character.

Hartley, L. P., *The Go-Between* (1953). A tragic love affair is seen but not understood by the boy who serves as messenger for the adults involved. A novel of innocence massacred by experience and evil.

James, Henry, *The Portrait of a Lady* (1881). Sought after by rich and handsome suitors, Isabel is at once too proud, too intelligent, and too naive. She rejects them all, only to succumb to the deceptive charms of a fortune hunter. The first of James's novels on the theme of American innocence confronted by European guile, it has been described as "a great leisurely built cathedral" (Graham Greene).

Laclos, Pierre Choderlos de, *Les Liaisons Dangereuses* (1782). A classic of demonic cynicism, the story in the form of letters of the systematic corruption of the innocent by two partners for their own amusement.

## Revenge

Doyle, Arthur Conan, *A Study in Scarlet* (1887). Sherlock Holmes's first case involves murders of revenge, which the incomparable sleuth traces back to Utah and the Mormons.

Leffland, Ella, *Mrs. Munck* (1970). Author's suspenseful first novel, set in a backwater California town, about an act of vengeance that took twenty-five years to complete.

Manfred, Frederick, *Lord Grizzly* (1954). The agony, courage, and strange revenge of a nineteenth-century mountain man deserted and left to die by his companions. A robust, authentic legend of the West.

Portis, Charles, *True Grit* (1968). Warm and funny novel set in the 1870s about a spunky fourteen-year-old girl, out to avenge her father's death, and a mean and tough U.S. marshal who befriends her.

Shakespeare, William, *Hamlet* (1603). An endlessly fascinating play of revenge about the melancholy Dane and his plot to kill those responsible for his father's death.

## Alienation and Despair

Beckett, Samuel, *Molloy* (1950). A novel with two narratives: old Molloy passes time telling himself stories and remembering his past journeys; and a private detective is sent to find him. Part of a trilogy that includes *Malone Dies* (1951) and *The Unnameable* (1952), it is a disturbing, memorable work of genius.

Del Castillo, Michel, *The Guitar* (1959). A Spanish dwarf seeks to move his fellow men by the magic of his guitar playing, but they regard it as witchcraft and stone him. A work of utter despair.

Ellison, Ralph, *Invisible Man* (1952). Driving, honest, searing, allusive, and existential novel about an American antihero's journey in search of himself.

Kavan, Anna, *Julia and the Bazooka* (1975). Powerful, anguished stories of despair and loneliness reflecting the author's drug addiction and hallucinatory terror. See *Asylum Piece* (1980).

**Sartre, Jean-Paul,** *Nausea* (1938). A novel in the form of the impressionistic diary of a French writer who ruthlessly catalogues his every feeling and sensation about the world and people around him. His thoughts culminate in a pervasive, overpowering feeling of nausea, which gives Sartre the opportunity to dramatize the tenets of his existentialist creed.

## Decadence

**Green, Martin,** *Children of the Sun: A Narrative of "Decadence" in England After 1918* (1976). All you will ever want to know about the bright young literary dandies who came to prominence at the end of World War I.

**Huysmans, J. K.,** *Against the Grain* (1884). The granddaddy of decadent literature, it is the story of Des Esseintes, the supremely effete aesthete who has organized his life "against the grain," seeking sensation in the rare and aberrant. A perversely absorbing novel. See James Laser, *The First Decadent: Being the Strange Life of J. K. Huysmans* (1955).

**Julian, Philipe,** *Dreamers of Decadence: Symbolist Painters of the 1890's* (1971). Richly detailed and illustrated account of a minor but fascinating group of artists that included Beardsley and Mucha.

**Wilde, Oscar,** *The Picture of Dorian Gray* (1891). Famous fantasy of a beautiful young man on the degenerate path and his supernatural portrait, which mirrors his inner being. Full of sparkling prose and aphorisms.

**Wolff, Geoffrey,** *Black Sun: The Brief Transit and Violent Eclipse of Harry Crosby* (1976). The tragic, bizarre tale of a decadent poet manqué who committed suicide in 1920 at the age of thirty-one.

## Love

**Austen, Jane,** *Pride and Prejudice* (1813). Pride must be humbled and prejudice extinguished before the delightful Elizabeth Bennet and Darcy are engaged in this superb novel of Regency manners.

**Brontë, Charlotte,** *Jane Eyre* (1847). The romance of Jane Eyre, a shy, plain girl of quiet determination, who matures into a women of strength and intelligence, and Mr. Rochester, the handsome, sardonically proud aristocrat, is at the center of this moving story of tender love and violent passions.

**Brontë, Emily,** *Wuthering Heights* (1847). Set against the dark and rugged Yorkshire moors, it introduces two of the most startling characters in all literature: Heathcliff, an unfathomable mixture of savagery and gentleness, and Catherine, the woman he loved but drove to madness. One of the strangest love stories ever.

**Colette,** *The Pure and the Impure* (tr. 1967). This "odd masterpiece [is] about men and women, a lot of them real people, who love for the passions" (Elizabeth Hardwick).

**Colwin, Laurie,** *Happy All the Time* (1980). A modern comedy of manners of contemporary Manhattan, this love story about two couples is unusual in that it is not sad: everyone lives happily ever after. A breezy, endearing, unabashedly modern romance. Her short stories in *The Lone Pilgrim* (1981) are also about men and women in love.

**Congreve, William,** *The Way of the World* (1700). Sparkling Restoration comedy of plots and machinations to be overcome before the witty lady of fashion, Millamant, and the young, equally witty gentleman about town, Mirabell, can be engaged.

**Daudet, Alphonse,** *Sappho* (1884). Touching love story set in Paris of a young man and a worldly woman by "one of the magicians of the surface of life, one of the masters of the moments of the heart" (V. S. Pritchett).

**Ede, H. S.,** *Savage Messiah* (1931). Story of the passionate love affair between an eighteen-year-old French sculptor, Henri Gaudier, and a thirty-eight-year-old Pole, Sophie Brzeska, told through their letters and diaries.

**Goethe, Johann Wolfgang Von,** *The Elective Affinities* (1809). This psychological study of a husband and wife, each of whom is in love with another person, is "one of the most extraordinary novels ever written" (W. H. Auden). The best translation is by Elizabeth Mayer and Louise Bogan.

**Hardy, Thomas,** *Jude the Obscure* (1894). The powerful passion of Jude Fawley for his cousin, Sue Bridehead, continues through the marriage of each to another and ultimately brings dark tragedy to all four. One of the most perceptive works in English on the complex theme of sex and human instincts.

**Hemingway, Ernest,** *A Farewell to Arms* (1929). Played out against a war-torn Italy and an idyllic Switzerland, this story of the romance between Frederic Henry and Catherine Barkley is one of the greatest American novels of the century, written in "musical crystal-clear style; blown like glass from the white-heat of violence" (Cyril Connolly).

**Kawabata Yasunari,** *Snow Country* (1956). Moving tale of a doomed love affair between a Tokyo dilettante and a young geisha. Other novels by the Japanese Nobel Prize–winning writer about love and sex are *Thousand Cranes* (1959) and *The Sound of the Mountain* (1970).

**La Farge, Oliver,** *Laughing Boy* (1929). Pulitzer Prize–winning novel about the tragic love of Laughing Boy, a Navajo silversmith and horse trader, for Slim Girl. Blends realism with romanticism.

**Lawrence, D. H.,** *Lady Chatterley's Lover* (1928). Lawrence said that the real point of this once-banned novel about sensual love shared by Lady Chatterley and her gamekeeper is that "men and women be able to think sex, fully, completely, honestly, and cleanly." Although it is not his best novel, those who read it "with a sympathetic eye and an open mind will find it full of meat and wine" (Lawrence Durrell).

**Mitford, Nancy,** *Voltaire in Love* (1958). The long and successful liaison between the great eighteenth-century French writer and philosopher and Marquise Emile du Châtelet. Told with polish and wit.

**Nabokov, Vladimir,** *Lolita* (1955). Dark comic novel about middle-aged Humbert Humbert's passion for the twelve-year-old "nymphet" Lolita. Full of sharp observations about American life.

**Origo, Iris,** *The Measure of Love* (1957). Five biographical essays about various nineteenth-century figures for whom love was at the heart of their lives. See *Last Attachment* (1949), a fascinating account of Lord Byron and Teresa Guccioli.

**Percy, Walker,** *Second Coming* (1980). A novel of ideas with an enchanting love story at its center between two improbable people — a retired Wall St. lawyer and a schizophrenic young woman.

**Price, Reynolds,** *A Long and Happy Life* (1962). A small North Carolina town is the bower for the romance between Rosacoke Mustian and Wesley Beaver. "It is a love story, and one of the simplest and most poignant I have ever read" (Granville Hicks).

**Radiguet, Raymond,** *The Devil in the Flesh* (1923). Written by a seventeen-year-old boy, this famous French novel reveals, with extraordinary frankness and understanding, the heart-rending romance of a young student and a married woman. "It exposes naturally, graciously, cruelly, modestly, and immodestly the lowest depths to which none of us can any longer descend" (Jean Cocteau).

**Robinson, Jill,** *Bed/Time/Story* (1974). Candid, potent account of the author's profound love affair. A love story of our hectic times.

**Shakespeare, William,** *Antony and Cleopatra* (c. 1607). The tragic drama of two of history's most famous lovers. See *Romeo and Juliet* (c. 1595). Love's lighter side is portrayed in *Much Ado About Nothing* (c. 1598) and *Love's Labour's Lost* (c. 1594).

**Singer, Isaac Bashevis,** *The Slave* (1962). Set in seventeenth-century Poland, it is the simple and moving love story of two persecuted lovers — a Jew and a Polish peasant — united only in death. See *Shosha* (1978) and *Enemies: A Love Story* (1972).

**Spencer, Scott,** *Endless Love* (1979). Gripping, lyrical novel of sex, obsession, and endless love. See *Preservation Hall* (1977).

**Steegmuller, Francis (ed.),** *"Your Isadora": The Love Story of Isadora Duncan and Gordon Craig* (1974). In letters and diaries the touching story of the love between two talented, egotistical figures.

**Tanizaki, Junichiro,** *Some Prefer Nettles* (1955). Autobiographical novel about a loveless marriage and a husband's search for peace through the rediscovery of Japanese traditions.

**Taylor, Elizabeth,** *A Game of Hide-and-Seek* (1951). Childhood lovers meet again at middle age in a London tea-shop. A love story by a novelist whose "prose is one of the most beautiful and exact instruments of precision in use today. In a phrase . . . she can lay bare a heart and indicate a life" (Elizabeth Janeway).

**Turgenev, Ivan,** *Torrents of Spring* (1871). Graceful and penetrating short novel about a man who forsakes the love of a young, innocent girl for an older, "ex-perienced" woman and regrets it for the remainder of his life. *First Love* (1870) and *Smoke* (1867) are also love stories.

## Jealousy

**Balzac, Honoré De,** *Cousin Bette* (1846). The eponymous character, a cold harridan who hides her bitterness behind a mask of benevolence, destroys her niece's romance out of jealousy. One of the best of the Human Comedy series of novels.

**Colette,** *Duo* (1934). Superb novel about the destruction of a man and his marriage by jealousy.

**Paterson, Katherine,** *Jacob Have I Loved* (1980). Newberry Award–winning novel for teenagers set on a little known island off the Maryland coast in the 1940s. A fresh telling of the ancient story of an older twin's lost birthright.

**Shaffer, Peter,** *Amadeus* (1981). Fascinating play about the nature of the creative personality, focusing on the composer Salieri's great jealousy of Mozart. See Alexander Pushkin's one-act tragedy *Mozart and Salieri* (1830).

**Shakespeare, William,** *Othello* (c. 1604). The tragedy of the Moor of Venice who "lov'd not wisely but too well." Enraged by the "green-eyed monster" of jealousy he strangles his bride and kills himself.

## Avarice

**Balzac, Honore De,** *Eugenie Grandet* (1833). One of Balzac's Scenes of Provincial Life, a greedy old miser destroys his daughter's romance because of her suitor's lack of wealth and so condemns her to unhappiness.

**Dickens, Charles,** *Our Mutual Friend* (1865). Rich, spacious novel, full of remarkable characters, in which Dickens inveighs against avarice and the evils of wealth. His *A Christmas Carol* (1843) is about one of the greatest misers in all English literature: Ebenezer Scrooge.

**Eliot, George,** *Silas Marner* (1861). Classic novel of how a man living in miserly isolation is redeemed through the love of a little girl.

**Jonson, Ben,** *Volpone* (1606). Drama about the wealthy miser Volpone, who pretends that he is dying so that his rich and greedy friends will give him valuable gifts in order to be named his heir. A wildly funny, harsh satire on human avarice.

**Traven, B.,** *The Treasure of Sierra Madre* (1935). Three American derelicts search for a lost gold mine in the Mexican wilderness. A masterful social and psychological novel.

# PART IV

# SOCIETY

# COMMUNITIES

## Tribe

**Alland, Alexander, Jr.,** *When the Spider Danced* (1975). An anthropologist's eloquent, compassionate account of the ways of the Abron people of the Ivory Coast.

**Bellow, Saul,** *Henderson the Rain King* (1959). Sparkling novel that recounts the picaresque adventures of Eugene Henderson, a prodigious American millionaire, in a mythic Africa among the Arnewi and Wariri tribes.

**Benedict, Ruth,** *Patterns of Culture* (rev. 1959). Anthropological classic which describes three tribal cultures — the Zuni Indians of New Mexico, the Dobu of Melanesia, and the Kwakiutl of Vancouver Island — and shows how varied customs produce varied behavior.

**Dickinson, Peter,** *The Glass-Sided Ants' Nest* (1968). Scotland Yard's Inspector Pibble must solve the murder of the headman of the remnants of a New Guinea tribe living in the heart of London. Full of native customs and lore, it is an offbeat and beautifully done detective novel.

**Levi-Strauss, Claude,** *Tristes Tropiques* (1955). Observations and reflections stemming from the French anthropologist's work with Amazonian Indians. "Rigorous, subtle, and bold in thought . . . beautifully written and, like all great books, bears an absolutely personal stamp and speaks with a human voice" (Susan Sontag).

**Melville, Herman,** *Typee* (1846). Semiautobiographical adventure story about an American sailor who deserts ship and finds refuge with a tribe of savages on one of the Marquesas Islands of the South Pacific. Keen observations of native moral, religious, and social standards.

**Riefenstahl, Leni,** *The Last of the Nuba* (1974). Timeless photographs, taken during visits over ten years "give us fresh comprehension of man in, as might be, his original majesty and acceptance of life, in his vanity and courage, his beauty, vulnerability, pride" (Eudora Welty). See *The People of Kau* (1976).

**Sokolov, Raymond,** *Native Intelligence* (1975). Cerebral, clever, buoyant novel about a linguistic genius fresh from Harvard who joins the Peace Corps and is dispatched to remote Qatab in South America and sent up the Mishmash River to lead a sanitation project for the Xixi tribe.

**Thomas, Elizabeth Marshall,** *The Warrior Herdsmen* (1965). Affectionate, impressionistic account of the Dodoth tribe caught up in the tribulations of an emerging Africa. See *The Harmless People* (1959), an absorbing, sympathetic study of the Bushmen.

**Turnbull, Colin M.,** *The Mountain People* (1972). Overwhelming, sad story of the Ik, an African tribe that, having lost its ancestral hunting ground, lives on the edge of starvation. Appalling implications for modern man. See *The Lonely African* (1962).

**Van Der Post, Laurens,** *The Lost World of the Kalahari* (1958). Compelling picture of the Bushmen of South West Africa seasoned with a little Jungian mysticism. "I cannot recall a story more touched with fascination or more curious — in fact magical" (Rumer Godden). See *The Heart Is the Hunter* (1962) and *A Mantis Carol* (1976). The Bushmen appear in the novel *A Story Like the Wind* (1972) and its sequel, *A Far-off Place* (1974). See Marjorie Shostak's fascinating *Nisa: The Life and Words of a !Kung Woman* (1981).

## Village

**Critchfield, Richard,** *Villages* (1981). Remarkable account of the lives of people whom the peripatetic author has met since 1959, when he began studying peasant life in the Third World: from Tibetan refugees in the Himalayas and Moroccan criminals in the underworld of Casablanca to Bedouin herdsmen along the Iran-Iraq border. See *The Golden Bowl Be Broken: Peasant Life in Four Cultures* (1973).

**Deane, Shirley,** *In a Corsican Village* (1967). Affectionate, understanding chronicle of a year's cycle in a tradition-shackled, self-sufficient, remote community.

**Dore, Ronald P.,** *Shinohata: A Portrait of a Japanese Village* (1979). An English sociologist's intimate, sensitive, even humorous account of changes in a Japanese hamlet over several decades.

**Fejes, Claire,** *Villagers* (1981). With words and drawings she sensitively paints a picture of Athabaskan village life in remote Alaska.

**Fraser, Ronald,** *Tajos: The Story of a Village in the Costa del Sol* (1973). Woven together from the voices of sixty men and women of the village, it shows how rural Andalusia has changed over the decades since the area became a popular resort area.

**Hélias, Pierre-Jakez,** *The Horse of Pride: Life in a Breton Village* (1978). Childhood recollections of the early part of the century provide an enthralling picture of the last generation of Breton peasant culture before its recent extinction.

**Levi, Carlo,** *Christ Stopped at Eboli* (1945). In 1935, Levi was exiled by the Fascists to live in a village in southern Italy so remote that even Christianity had never come to it. His vivid, touching story of a year's stay there, of the suffering and social oppression, is a monument to the human spirit.

**Mohanti, Prafulla,** *My Village, My Life* (1974). Moving portrayal of Nanpur, the English-educated author's native village south of Calcutta, rendered in the individual voices of the inhabitants.

**Myrdal, Jan,** *Report from a Chinese Village* (1965). Account by the Swedish anthropologist and his artist-photographer wife which vividly describes a month in the lives of villages in northern Shensi province. "A book rich in accounts of human conditions, that made change inevitable and also made Communist social leadership and organization acceptable to the village poor" (Edgar Snow). See Jack Chen, *A Year in Upper Felicity: Life in a Chinese Village During the Cultural Revolution* (1973).

**Peattie, Donald Culross,** *Immortal Village* (1945). This warm, rich history of the beautiful Provencal town of Vence, where the author briefly lived in the 1920s, is intended as a microcosm for the Europe that will not die. Laurence Wylie's *Village in the Vaucluse* (1957) is a beautiful study of daily life in a French village.

**Tolstoy, Leo,** *The Cossacks* (1852–53). Fine novel about life in a Cossack village in the Caucasus. Mikhail A. Sholokhov's *The Silent Don* (1934–40) is a vivid panorama of life in the Cossack village of Tatarsk during the turbulent years of the revolution.

## English Village and Town

**Blythe, Ronald,** *Akenfield: Portrait of an English Village* (1969). Uncompromising portrait of the nature and quality of life in a rural Suffolk village, whose inhabitants speak for themselves. An oral history that dissolves the myth of the peace and wisdom of the pastoral scene.

**Crabbe, George,** *The Village* (1783). Somber-colored poem in heroic couplets describing in unidealized fashion the hard life of the village poor.

**Eliot, George,** *Middlemarch: A Study of Provincial Life* (1871). Set in a Warwickshire town of the Reform period and principally concerned with the intellectual life — Virginia Woolf termed it "one of the few English novels written for grown-up people" — its broad canvas, character, and humor have made it in the opinion of many the greatest novel of the Victorian age. *Adam Bede* (1859) portrays village life before the Industrial Revolution.

**Gaskell, Elizabeth,** *Cranford* (1853). "This intimate record of a few ordinary lives in a Cheshire village combines humour and pathos with an irresistible touch of delicate understanding and it has taken unquestioned rank as one of our minor prose classics" *(Cambridge History of English Literature).* See *Wives and Daughters* (1866).

**Klivert, Francis,** *Klivert's Diary, 1870–1879* (1938–40). Journal of an English cu-

rate in a small Welsh town in the 1860s and 1870s; full of his love of life, his delight in natural beauty, and sharp observations of village life.

**Mitford, Mary Russell,** *Our Village* (1824–32). Delightful "sketches of rural life, character, and scenery" of Three Mile Cross, near Reading.

**Muir, Richard,** *The English Village* (1980). Charmingly written, beautifully illustrated trove of information about the English village from Anglo-Saxon times to the present. See Alan C. Jenkins, *A Village Year* (1981).

**Read, Miss,** *Chronicles of Fairacre* (1977). Omnibus volume of three nominally autobiographical books of the late 1950s, which felicitously and unsentimentally relate the goings-on in a remote South Downs hamlet. She has also written a charming series of novels about Thrush Green, a sleepy postcard Cotswold village, the first of which is *Thrush Green* (1960).

**Thompson, Flora,** *Lark Rise to Candleford* (1945). Collection of books that evocatively and quietly recount her growing up in a small village in the 1890s. See *Still Glides the Stream* (1948).

**Williamson, Henry,** *The Village Book* (1930). Sketches of a Devonshire village that capture "the over-soul of English rural life, that permeating quality that one can appreciate only after living through several years at least in one place" (Richard Church).

## Small-Town America

**Anderson, Sherwood,** *Winesburg, Ohio* (1919). Collection of stories, told intensely and with a poet's feeling, about the sensitive and imaginative souls of Winesburg, the "grotesques," as viewed by a young journalist. Windy McPherson's *Son* (1916) and *Poor White* (1920) also deal with life in small towns.

**Bailey, Anthony,** *In the Village* (1971). A leisurely view of Stonington, Connecticut, and an engaging brief for small-town living by an English Americanophile who adopted the town.

**Lesy, Michael,** *Wisconsin Death Trip* (1973). Through period photographs taken in one midwestern town in the nineteenth century, the author, a historian — an "archaeologist of the commonplace" — has related the bleakness of provincial life in this "dark and somber excavation of lost time and buried horror" (Wright Morris).

**Lewis, Sinclair,** *Babbitt* (1922). Zenith, the Zip City, satirically dissected in a portrait of its eminent booster, George Folonsbee Babbitt.

**Lingeman, Richard,** *Small Town America* (1980). Comprehensive narrative history of the small-town world from 1620 to the present.

**Masters, Edgar Lee,** *Spoon River Anthology* (1915). Collection of free verse epitaphs from a cemetery of a small midwestern town, in which the buried candidly reveal their secret lives, most often at odds with the pious epitaphs chiseled on their gravestones.

**Robinson, Edwin Arlington,** *Tilbury Town* (1953). Gathering by Lawrence Thompson of all of Robinson's poems set in the imaginary New England town in which dwell Miniver Cheevy, Richard Cory, Eben Flood, and others in conflict with the town's standards of morality.

**Spyker, John Howland,** *Little Lives* (1979). Written pseudonymously by novelist Richard Elman, these folksy vignettes about life in a small township in rural upstate New York — "the human condition north of Albany" — are in the *Spoon River/Our Town* tradition. Another town in the same region is the focus of Frieda Arkin's novel, *The Dorp* (1969).

**Twain, Mark,** *The Adventures of Tom Sawyer* (1876). Wonderful tale of the adventures of Tom and his friend, Huck Finn, in the sleepy Mississippi River town of St. Petersburg, Missouri — a nostalgic evocation of the author's boyhood in Hannibal.

**Wilder, Thornton,** *Our Town* (1938). Grover's Corners, New Hampshire, "a typical American town," is the setting of this much-loved, life-affirming play which, according to Wilder, attempts to vivify "something way down deep that's eternal about every human being."

## City

**Barth, Gunther,** *City People: The Rise of Modern City Culture in Nineteenth Century America* (1981). Fascinating study by a professor of history which is "like an old Cecil B. DeMille 'Spectacular,' only much better. [He] has an immense fund of knowledge, which he uses with wit and a fine sense of proportion" (Anatole Broyard).

**Calvino, Italo,** *Invisible Cities* (1974). Prophetic work, blending philosophy and fantasy, about an empire in which cities grow from heroic dreams to mammoth nightmares.

**Clarke, Arthur C.,** *The City and the Stars* (1956). Classic science-fiction novel set in the far distant future about Diaspar, the last city of earth and an imaginatively conceived (and resplendently described) technological Shangri-La. For other projections of urban futures see Ralph Clem et al., *The City 2000 A.D.: Urban Life Through Science Fiction* (1976) and Damon Knight (ed.), *Future City* (1973).

**Geddes, Patrick,** *Cities in Evolution: An Introduction to the Town Planning Movement and to the Study of Civics* (1915). Summary of the thoughts of the English planner who was the first to lay emphasis on the needs of people in building cities.

**Goodman, Paul and Percival Goodman,** *Communitas* (rev. 1960). Analysis in words and pictures of the plans of the past and what alternatives are available for the future. "A witty, penetrating, provocative and, above all, on many essential matters, a wise book; for it deals with the underlying values and purposes, political and moral, on which planning of any sort must be based" (Lewis Mumford).

**Jacobs, Jane,** *The Death and Life of American Cities* (1961). That the prime concern of city planning and urban renewal should be people, argued with wit and passion.

**Liebow, Elliot,** *Tally's Corner: A Study of Negro Streetcorner Men* (1967). Absorbing and entertaining urban study. An anthropologist makes us understand the life of a small streetcorner society in a Washington, D.C. ghetto.

**Mumford, Lewis,** *The City in History: Its Origins, Its Transformations, and Its Prospects* (1961). Lengthy, broad-scaled, enthralling history narrated with desperate urgency by the leading authority on urban culture. He views the city as the chief container of human culture. A book of far-reaching insights and challenge. For an excellent concise, illustrated history see Leonardo Benevolo, *The History of the City* (1980).

**Raban, Jonathan,** *Soft City* (1974). "Soft" because "we mould them in our images; they, in their turn, shape us by the resistance they offer when we try to impose our own personal form on them." Fine personal account of the struggle to live humanely in a large city; London, in the author's case.

**Terkel, Studs,** *Division Street: America* (1967). "A city speaks uninhibitedly through this book. Reading it, one learns the night-thoughts of urban man. . . . Studs Terkel is a wonderfully skilled interviewer, with an instinctive ability to put the question that unlocks defenses and coaxes self-revelation" (Nadine Gordimer).

## *Suburbia*

**Beattie, Ann,** *Falling in Place* (1979). Low-key novel about young disaffected people of the seventies inhabiting a spiritually dingy suburbia. See her short-story collection *Secrets and Surprises* (1978).

**Cheever, John,** *The Stories of John Cheever* (1978). Collects the subtle, satiric *New Yorker* stories of Shady Hill and other suburban landscapes by a keen and close observer of "the way some people live." Winner of Pulitzer Prize.

**De Vries, Peter,** *Reuben, Reuben* (1964). Satirical novel of an exurbanite Connecticut community from the perspectives of three different outsiders by a literary craftsman who is "surely one of the great prose virtuosos in modern America" (Anthony Burgess). *The Tunnel of Love* (1954) and *Comfort Me with Apples* (1956) are also set in suburbia.

**Friedman, Bruce Jay,** *Stern* (1962). Friedman's first novel, about a Jewish schlemiel in a WASP suburbia, is "a delight, at once uproarious and heartbreaking" (Stanley Edgar Hyman).

**Johnson, Diane,** *Burning* (1971). A raging brushfire serves as the backdrop for this witty novel about a microcosmic southern California suburb.

**Oates, Joyce Carol,** *Expensive People* (1968). A fat teenage genius narrates his "confession" of how he killed his mother in a novel about narcissistic suburban life.

**Owens, Bill,** *Suburbia* (1973). Collection of wry photographs of some residents of one San Francisco suburb "at home." Captures an entire life style.

**Updike, John,** *Couples* (1968). The lives of ten middle-class couples of the imaginary Boston suburb of Tarbox portrayed in a stylish novel of sexual obsession and infidelity.

**Wilson, Edmund,** *Memoirs of Hecate County* (1946). Banned as obscene when published (but revised and republished in 1959), this satire of the vacuous lives of denizens of mythical Hecate County, near

New York City, serves as a peg on which to hang some of his social and esthetic ideas.

**Zelver, Patricia,** *A Man of Middle Age and Twelve Stories* (1980). Upper-middle-class suburban California malaise.

## Commune

**Caute, David,** *Comrade Jacob* (1962). Intelligent novel about the Diggers, a communal sect that briefly thrived in Cromwellian England.

**Diamond, Stephen,** *What the Trees Said: Life on a New Age Farm* (1971). Firsthand, deeply felt account of a city-bred radical journalist's experiences on a New England communal farm. Raymond Mungo, *Total Loss Farm* (1971); Edward Connolly, *Deer Run* (1971); Richard Wizansky (ed.), *Home Comforts: Stories and Scenes of Life on Total Loss Farm* (1973); and Robert Mouriet, *Getting Back Together* (1971) also deal with sixties commune experiments.

**Hawthorne, Nathaniel,** *The Blithedale Romance* (1852). The Fourier-inspired community of transcendentalists at Brook Farm of the 1840s was the inspiration for this absorbing novel of love and ideas.

**Nordhoff, Charles,** *The Communistic Societies of the United States* (1875). Classic report by New York journalist of his personal visits to such communal experiments as the Shakers, Amana, and Oneida. A good modern survey is Kenneth Rexroth's *Communalism: From Its Origins to the Twentieth Century* (1974). For a look at contemporary American communes, see Benjamin Zablocki, *Alienation and Charisma* (1980).

**Young, Marguerite,** *Angel in the Forest: A Fairy Tale of Two Utopias* (1945). Poetic portrait of Harmony and New Harmony, Indiana, which is "a true book, conceived as great poems are conceived, and composed with the same exciting, inexhaustible energy. New Harmony was . . . a mad

thing. Miss Young, though with method, is appropriately and beautifully mad" (Mark Van Doren).

## Teen-age Gang

**Hinton, S. E.,** *The Outsider* (1967). Remarkable juvenile classic written by a seventeen-year-old girl about a young member of the "Greasers." Gang ritual, class warfare, and coming of age are treated with honesty and immediacy. *That Was Then, This Is Now* (1971) is a sequel.

**Hoenig, Gary,** *Reaper: The Inside Story of a Gang Leader* (1975). Case study, which reads like a novel, about a leader of a tough Bronx gang.

**Miller, Warren,** *The Cool World* (1960). Duke Custis, leader of the "Royal Crocadiles" of Harlem, is the focus of this novel written in the argot of the streets. "Because they are seen so clearly and made so real, the drama they act out contains implications which go far beyond the squalid, claustrophobic world they inhabit" (James Baldwin).

**Price, Richard,** *The Wanderers* (1974). The coming of age of an Italian gang in the North Bronx in a potent blend of sex, violence, and humor by a novelist with an extraordinary ear for the street talk of the early sixties.

**Yurick, Sol,** *The Warriors* (1965). Compelling, grim, angry novel about a New York gang trying to get home to its "turf." Full of interesting details about gang protocol. Another good New York gang novel is Alice Hoffman, *Property Of* (1977).

## Military Base

**Cozzens, James Gould,** *Guard of Honor* (1948). Pulitzer Prize–winning novel, set at a Florida air force base during World War II, about the human condition and human illusions.

**Jones, James,** *From Here to Eternity* (1951). Long, powerful, and convincing story of life in a garrison in Hawaii during the months preceding the bombing of Pearl Harbor. Winner of National Book Award.

**McCullers, Carson,** *Reflections in a Golden Eye* (1941). Brief, macabre tale of misplaced loves and the resultant violence of a group of men and women in an army camp in the South before the Second World War.

**Regan, Helen,** *Mixed Company* (1981). A fine book about the trials and triumphs of women in the modern American army.

**Smith, William Jay,** *Army Brat* (1981). A poet's felicitous memoirs of growing up on a peacetime army base; small, unpretentious, "it is a book full of humanity and comedy" (Paul Fussell). An officer's wife's experiences of base life are hilariously recounted by Ann Combs in *Smith College Never Taught Me to Salute* (1981).

**Styron, William,** *The Long March* (1952). Powerful, brief novel about forced training march of marines at Parris Island, South Carolina, in which eight men died. Edwin McDowell's *To Keep Our Honor Clean* (1980), set at the same base at about the same time, is a more affectionate look at the Marine Corps.

## Utopia

**Butler, Samuel,** *Erewhon* (1872). Satirical fantasy about the land of Erewhon (an anagram of nowhere), which attacks nearly every phase of Victorian life. Its sequel, *Erewhon Revisited* (1901) is "one of the world's most merciless assaults upon human credulity" (Martin S. Day).

**Karp, David,** *One* (1953). Chilling novel about a benign totalitarian state and the struggle of the protagonist to stave off obliteration of his identity.

**Manuel, Frank E. and Fritzie P. Manuel,** *Utopian Thought in the Western World* (1979). Covering the last 2,500 years, this brilliant, gracefully written book is "the finest single historical study of Western utopias to be found anywhere" (Robert Nisbet). Lewis Mumford's *The Story of Utopias* (rev. 1959) is another lucid long-range history.

**Skinner, B. F.,** *Walden II* (1948). Inventive and fascinating behaviorist community fictionally created by the celebrated Harvard psychologist. For a description of a commune inspired by the novel, see Kathleen Kinkade, *A Walden Two Experiment* (1973).

**Wells, H. G.,** *A Modern Utopia* (1905). Portrait of a technologically developed society ably ruled by a benevolent elite; although occasionally marred by Wells's socialist preaching, it remains one of his most interesting novels of the future. For a more recent sci-fi view, see Thomas M. Disch (ed.), *The New Improved Sun: An Anthology of Utopian Science Fiction* (1976).

## Exile

**Brodsky, Joseph,** *A Part of Speech* (1980). Translations of the brilliant Russian emigre's poems about the experience of exile.

**Carr, E. H.,** *The Romantic Exiles: A 19th Century Portrait Gallery* (1933). Fascinating account of Alexander Herzen and friends, Russian revolutionists living in London, that is "a masterpiece of biography, spirited, enthralling, and profound" (Francis Steegmuller).

**Chapman, Hester,** *The Tragedy of Charles II* (1964). The king's exile from England from 1630 to 1660, when he took the throne after Cromwell's death.

**de la Mare, Walter,** *The Three Mulla Mulgars* (1910). Delightful children's classic by the English poet about a trio of royal monkeys driven into exile.

**Lang, David Marshall,** *The Armenians: A People in Exile* (1981). Absorbing history of the Armenian dispersal over the centuries. See the classic *Armenia: Cradle of Civilization* (rev. 1980).

**Martineau, Gilbert,** *Napoleon's St. Helena* (1964). The daily life of the emperor during his six years' island exile in a carefully researched book. See *Napoleon Surrenders* (1971), about the period between his defeat at Waterloo and his departure for St. Helena.

**Mphahlele, Ezekiel,** *The Wanderers* (1971). Novel by a distinguished African writer about life for black South African political exiles on the run in Nigeria and Kenya.

**Nabokov, Vladimir,** *Pnin* (1957). Memorable, amusing portrait of an exiled Russian entomology professor caught up in the mystifying and perilous intrigues of a small upstate New York college. One of his most accessible novels.

**Shakespeare, William,** *The Tempest* (1611). Poetic drama laid on an enchanted isle of exile on which live Prospero, the ousted Duke of Milan, his daughter Miranda, the spirit Ariel, and the monster Caliban. A drama of shipwreck, sorcery, retribution, and forgiveness.

**Staël, Madame de,** *Ten Years in Exile* (1821). Engaging, vivid memoirs of a remarkable woman of great intelligence exiled from Paris by Napoleon for her outspoken criticism of his reign.

**Wolfe, Bernard,** *Trotsky Dead* (1975). Gripping novelized history of the Russian revolutionary's Mexican exile, which is "important as the only accessible popular account of the strange and terrible tale of the murder of Leon Trotsky" (Bertram D. Wolfe). See Jean Van Heijenhoort, *With Trotsky in Exile: From Prinkipo to Corpoacán* (1978).

## Monastery

**Byron, Robert,** *The Station: Athos, Treasures and Men* (1928). Highly colorful depiction of the art and architecture of the Greek monastery at Mt. Athos in an altogether "remarkable book to have been written by a young man of 22. It is a book lyrical, learned, spirited, fiercely curious and intellectually reckless" (V. S. Pritchett).

**Curzon, Robert,** *Visits to the Monasteries of the Levant* (1845). Victorian travel classic in which an English peer recollects his journeys to monasteries in Egypt, Palestine, and Greece in quest of ancient manuscripts.

**Merton, Thomas,** *The Seven Storey Mountain* (1948). Simple and luminous odyssey of a soul; a poet's conversion to Catholicism and ordination as a Trappist monk. *The Waters of Siloe* (1949) is the story of the Trappist order.

**Miller, Walter M., Jr.,** *A Canticle for Liebowitz* (1959). Science-fiction classic about the struggle to survive and rebuild civilization after a nuclear holocaust, as reflected in the trials of a monastic order over an 1800-year period.

**Pennington, Basil M.,** *O Holy Mountain!; Journal of a Retreat on Mount Athos* (1978). Account by American Trappist monk, the first Catholic in 800 years to be permitted an extended visit to the famous Greek Orthodox monastery.

**Peters, Ellis,** *Monk's Hood* (1981). One of a series of witty detective novels featuring Brother Cadfael, a twelfth-century Benedictine monk, which have the feel of medieval England.

**Sitwell, Sacheverell,** *Monks, Nuns, and Monasteries* (1965). Elegant depiction of monastic architecture and its role in the cenobitic life.

**Wetering, Janwillem van de,** *The Empty Mirror: Experiences in a Japanese Zen Monastery* (1974). Dutch student's wry and objective account of his one and a half years in a Zen priory. See *A Glimpse of Nothingness: Experiences in an American Zen Community* (1975). Giei Sato's *A*

*Diary of a Zen Monastic Life* (1971) offers another perspective.

## Convent

**Bernstein, Marcelle,** *The Nuns* (1976). Why do some women choose to become nuns? One journalist's answer based on interviews of over 500 sisters in Europe and America.

**Diderot, Denis,** *The Nun* (1760). Novel about a nun who takes the vows under duress, her sufferings in the cloister, and her escape, in which the brilliant French writer takes issue with misconceived Christianity.

**Godden, Rumer,** *In This House of Brede* (1969). An insightful novel which traces the journey of a career woman in her forties from novice toward final vows as a Benedictine nun at Brede Abbey in England. See *Five for Summer, Ten for Joy* (1979).

**Holmes, H. H.,** *Nine Times Nine* (1940). First of three novels by a mystery writer best known as Anthony Boucher about Sister Mary Ursula, O.M.B., a Los Angeles nun with a keen mind for solving crimes. A modern series features the curmudgeonly old Sister Mary Teresa; see Monica Quill, *Not a Blessed Thing* (1981).

**Hulme, Kathryn,** *The Nun's Story* (1956). Novelization of true account of Belgian sister who gave up the veil after seventeen years "bursts all doctrinal bonds and transcends mere theology in its fair, objective, and merciful portrayal of the human conscience, of the never-ending struggle of the awakened human spirit, intent on redeeming, in whatever surroundings, its loaned three score and ten" (Mary Ellen Chase).

**Huré, Anne,** *The Two Nuns* (1964). Conflict in a French Benedictine abbey between the letter and spirit of church law is the theme of this thoughtful novel written with dignity and simplicity.

**O'Faolain, Julia,** *Women in the Wall* (1975). Based on the life of Queen Radegunde, the patron saint of prisoners and captives, who spent most of her life as an ordinary nun in sixth-century Gaul, this poignant and powerful novel employs her as symbol of the buried individuality of womanhood.

**Warner, Sylvia Townsend,** *The Corner that Held Them* (1948). Thirty-five years of life in a fourteenth-century English convent in a novel which "is mosaic, is tapestry, is the most colorful weaving. And the details are exquisite as capitals in illuminated manuscripts, the curl of a B's loops or the filigree of an M: sardonic humor peppering the whole" (Anne Freemantle).

**Webster, Elizabeth C.,** *Ceremony of Innocence* (1949). Audacious morality tale about the Second Coming and its effect on a South African Anglican convent.

## Prison

**Abbott, Jack Henry,** *In the Belly of the Beast: Letters from Prison* (1981). These celebrated letters to Norman Mailer by a brutalized man who lived in the violence of prisons for most of his life, a man with a mind that acquired, said Mailer, "the meat and bones of culture without the soup," present a raw vision of the realities of prison life, mixed with political rhetoric.

**Behan, Brendan,** *Borstal Boy* (1959). Sprawling chronicle of author's three years in English reform school is "dramatic, high-spirited, funny, tender, compassionate, and intelligent. . . . [He] is no gifted leprauchan. He is a highly conscious, craftsmanlike, accomplished writer" (John Wain). Subsequent prison experiences serve as the basis of his two plays, *The Quare Fellow* (1956) and *The Hostage* (1958).

**Bowen, Robert O.,** *Weight of the Cross* (1952). Harrowing, powerful novel about the spiritual regeneration of a man interned as a Japanese POW.

**Braly, Malcolm,** *On the Yard* (1967). Hard-hitting novel by an ex-convict who got out of the revolving prison door and became a fine writer. "Surely the greatest American prison novel" (Kurt Vonnegut). *False Starts* (1976) is a memoir of San Quentin and other prisons.

**Charriere, Henri,** *Papillon* (1970). Enthralling bestseller memorializing the author's life in prison and fantastic escapes. His later exploits are detailed in *Banco* (1973).

**Cheever, John,** *Falconer* (1977). The tribulations of a middle-aged college professor in prison, a heroin addict convicted of murdering his brother, is the focus of this "extraordinary novel . . . a Dark Night of the Soul, a purification, a period of suffering in order to re-enter the ceremonies of innocence" (Joan Didion).

**Clavell, James,** *King Rat* (1962). Taut popular fiction, set in a Japanese prison camp, that examines the moral dilemmas facing the prisoners.

**Cummings, E. E.,** *The Enormous Room* (1922). More an imaginative memoir than a true novel, it is based on the poet's experience of being imprisoned in France on suspicion of correspondence with the enemy during World War I. A vivid, sometimes lyrical, impassioned work.

**Dostoevski, Fedor,** *The House of the Dead* (1861). Based on the Russian novelist's own experiences in the Omsk prison, it is a powerful portrayal of Siberian prison life.

**Fallada, Hans,** *The World Outside* (1934). German novel about a man who prefers the security of prison life to the precarious existence outside its walls; "a painful, brutal but uncommonly moving and absorbing book" (Peter Quennell).

**Foucault, Michel,** *Discipline and Punish: The Birth of the Prison* (1978). His most accessible book, on the genesis of modern notions of punishment.

**Ginzburg, Eugenia,** *Journey into the Whirlwind* (1967). Extraordinary, deeply moving memoir of author's experiences in a Soviet concentration camp. A spellbinding survival saga. The story of her eighteen years in Siberia is continued in *Within the Whirlwind* (1981).

**Himes, Chester,** *Cast the First Stone* (1952). Intense, not very pretty story, by a novelist who spent seven years in prison for armed robbery, succeeds "in recreating the inferno of a penitentiary and in recording the ordeal of a convict's emotional growth" (Frederic Morton).

**Kantor, Mackinlay,** *Andersonville* (1955). Searing novel about the notorious Confederate prison. "On to the warp of history [he] has woven with the stuff of imagination an immense and terrible pattern, a pattern which finally emerges as a gigantic panorama of the war itself, of the nation that tore itself to pieces in war. Out of fragmentary and incoherent records, [he] has wrought the greatest of our Civil War novels" (Henry Steele Commager).

**Pellico, Silvio,** *My Prisons* (1832). The poet-patriot's hymn to the imprisoned human spirit recounts his eight years in a Venetian prison. It is permeated with patient suffering and a Christian tone of forgiveness and was one of the most influential works of the Italian romantic movement.

**Reid, P. R.,** *The Colditz Story* (1953). Pace, suspense, and even humor in a classic tale of escape from the supposedly escape-proof castle, high on a pinnacle of rock, in which the Germans of World War II incarcerated the toughest and most ingenious of Allied prisoners of war. See *Men of Colditz* (1954).

**Salas, Floyd,** *Tattoo the Wicked Cross* (1967). Eloquent, powerful first novel about Aaron D'Aragon, sent at age fifteen to a California juvenile prison farm.

**Serge, Victor,** *Men in Prison* (1924). Grim, honest autobiographical novel of a man who found victory in what was one of the most brutal penal systems in Europe. It is the first of a trilogy about revolutionaries that includes *Birth of Our Power* (1931) and *Conquered City* (1932).

**Solzhenitsyn, Aleksandr,** *The First Circle* (1968). Semiautobiographical novel, set in a Russian scientific research center staffed by political prisoners, is laced with theoretical digressions, documentary chap-

ters, and the introduction of historical figures.

**Wicker, Tom,** *A Time to Die* (1975). A journalist who was there mixes documentary reporting and personal feelings in this saga of the 1971 insurrection at New York's Attica prison.

**Zeno,** *Life* (1968). Blunt, sparely poetic account of prison experience of a convicted murderer who spent nine years of a life sentence in London's Wormwood Scrubs before being paroled.

# MANNERS AND BEHAVIOR

**Aresty, Esther B.,** *The Best Behavior* (1970). Fascinating and witty history of etiquette books.

**Castiglione, Baldassare,** *The Book of the Courtier* (1528). Renaissance manual of gracious living in the form of dialogues at the palace of the Duke of Urbino.

**Cooper, Jilly,** *Class* (1981). English media personality wittily dissects British snobbery.

*Debrett's Etiquette and Modern Manners* (1981). By the *Debrett's Peerage* people, it is veddy, veddy British. An anglophile's treat.

**Goffman, Erving,** *Relations in Public: Microstudies of the Public Order* (1971). About the habits and rituals that guide our public interactions. Enthralling and somewhat disturbing. See *Interaction Ritual: Essays on Face-to-Face Behavior* (1967), *Presentation of Self in Everyday Life* (1959), and *Forms of Talk* (1981).

**Joslin, Seslye,** *What Do You Say, Dear?* (1958). The delightful illustrations by Maurice Sendak enhance this wacky etiquette primer for children. See *What Do You Do, Dear?* (1961).

**Mitford, Nancy (ed.),** *Noblesse Oblige: An Enquiry into the Identifiable Characteris-*

*tics of the English Aristocracy* (1956). In identifying some words as "U" (upperclass) and others as "non-U," terms coined by linguist Alan Ross, it set off a fireworks display of comments when published a quarter-century ago. It has been felicitously updated in Richard Buckle (ed.), *U and non-U Revisited* (1979).

**Nicolson, Harold,** *Good Behaviour: Being a Study of Certain Types of Civility* (1956). Refreshing, curious essays about how the best people behave in Ancient China and Greece and modern France, England, and Germany; a model of urbanity and ease by "the best-mannered writer of prose among our contemporary essayists" (V. S. Pritchett).

**Sutherland, Douglas,** *The English Gentleman* (1978). A self-parody by an English gentleman in which he wittily guides the reader to what is considered gentlemanly behavior. See *The English Gentleman's Wife* (1979) and *The English Gentleman's Child* (1980).

**Vanderbilt, Amy,** *The Amy Vanderbilt Complete Book of Etiquette* (rev. 1979). Classic "guide to contemporary living," revised and expanded by Letitia Baldridge. The "other" etiquette book is, of course, *The New Emily Post's Etiquette* (rev. 1975). *Charlotte Ford's Book of Modern Manners* (1980), an informal, often humorous guide, is the newest contender for social arbiter.

# EDUCATION

**Barzun, Jacques,** *Teacher in America* (1945). On the failure of the American teaching profession to produce truly educated students, by a famous scholar who taught for many years at Columbia University.

**Coles, William E.,** *The Plural I: The Teaching of Writing* (1978). Fictionalized treatment of how the author taught a group of students to become serious writers capable of choosing a self or a plural for viewing subjects or confronting experiences.

**Conroy, Pat,** *The Water Is Wide* (1971). Account of the author's experiences teaching eighteen black children in a two-room schoolhouse on Yamacraw Island, South Carolina. Reads like a novel.

**Cremin, Lawrence A.,** *The Transformation of the School* (1961). This story of the progressive education movement by a noted educational historian is "one of the freshest, most beautifully focused books on the history of American education that has ever been published" (Kenneth Lynn).

**Dennison, George,** *The Lives of Children* (1969). Author's experiences teaching in an "alternative" school, the First Street School in New York; "one of the handful of books in which the best qualities of the 1960's remain alive and humanly available" (Thomas R. Edwards).

**Dewey, John,** *Experience & Education* (1938). His most concise and most readable statement on education. By the man acknowledged to be the preeminent educational theorist of the twentieth century.

**Hayden, Torey L.,** *Somebody Else's Kids* (1981). Emotion-filled log of a school year in author's "Resource" room to which the educational misfits from other schools have been sent. See *One Child* (1980).

**Highet, Gilbert,** *The Art of Teaching* (1950). A humanist-scholar relates his general principles of teaching with wit, elegance, and understanding. See *The Immortal Profession: The Joys of Teaching and Learning* (1976).

**Holt, John,** *How Children Fail* (1965, rev. 1982). The first book of several by the perceptive, tradition-shattering spokesman for the school reform movement. Also *How Children Learn* (1968), *The Underachieving School* (1969), *What Do I Do Monday?* (1971), *Freedom and Beyond* (1972), and *Escape from Childhood* (1974). See *Teach Your Own* (1981).

**Kohl, Herbert,** *36 Children* (1968). A touching account of author's tenure as a sixth-grade teacher in Harlem. See *Basic Skills: A Plan for Your Child, a Program for All Children* (1982).

**Kozol, Jonathan,** *Death at an Early Age: The Destruction of the Hearts and Minds of Negro Children in the Boston Public Schools* (1967). Award-winning classic by a fourth-grade teacher in Roxbury, which "I expect will be read in the future, as *Nicholas Nickleby* is now, by those whose habit it is to look back in wonder at the barbarisms of past civilizations" (Nat Hentoff). See *On Being a Teacher* (1981).

**Krishnamurti, J.,** *Education and the Significance of Life* (1953). These calm thoughts of an Eastern teacher "pierce to the roots of our western problem of conformity and loss of personal values" (Rollo May).

**Leonard, George,** *Education and Ecstasy* (1968). Celebrates the joy, the unity, of learning and living. An inspiring book about what education should be.

**MacCracken, Mary,** *Lovey — A Very Special Child* (1976). A heartrending, memorable account of the work of a teacher of emotionally disturbed children with a remarkable child, thought to be autistic. See *A Circle of Children* (1973) and *City Kid* (1981).

**Mein, R. C. (ed.),** *Montessori: Her Method and the Movement: What You Need to Know* (1974). Question-and-answer formatted version of the basic ideas, motives, and goals of the Montessori method.

**Nasaw, David,** *Schooled to Order: A Social History of Public Schooling in America* (1979). The evolution of public education in a well-written history.

**Postman, Neil,** *Teaching as a Conserving Activity* (1979). Well-reasoned argument that teaching must engender respect for the institutions of the school. Interesting to compare with *Teaching as a Subversive Activity* (1969), wherein Postman asserted that traditional methods of education were harmful.

**Russell, Bertrand,** *Education and the Good Life* (1926). Lucid, beguiling ideas on education by one of this century's most courageous thinkers.

**Scott, Rachel,** *A Wedding Man Is Nicer than Cats, Miss: A Teacher at Work with Immigrant Children* (1972). A touching and funny meeting of two cultures, recounted by an English schoolteacher: her experiences teaching the children of Indian and Pakistani immigrants.

**Tolstoy, Leo,** *Tolstoy on Education* (1866). Based on his experiences with the experimental school for peasant children he founded on his estate, Yasnaya Polyana. The great Russian writer's thoughts on such topics as permissiveness seem very modern even today.

## American Teachers

**Barth, John,** *End of the Road* (rev. 1967). Early novel of ideas by the National Book Award–winning novelist that is set at a teachers' college. *Sabbatical* (1982), a rollicking tale of love, also has an academic setting.

**Cross, Amanda,** *Death in a Tenured Position* (1981). English professor-amateur detective Kate Fansler is called on to solve a murder at Harvard. Other Cambridge mysteries include Timothy Fuller, *Harvard Has a Homicide* (1936) and Jane Langton, *The Memorial Hall Murder* (1978).

**Davies, Robertson,** *The Rebel Angels* (1982). Magical novel offering the spectacle of murder, theft, perjury, love, and scholarship at a modern university. A wise and witty book that is at once both comical and deadly serious. Other good contemporary campus novels are James Howard Kunstler, *A Clown in the Moonlight* (1981), Joyce Carol Oates, *Unholy Loves* (1979), and John B. Rosenman, *The Best Laugh Last* (1982).

**Jarrell, Randall,** *Pictures from an Institution* (1954). Clever, satiric novel about a novelist using her year of teaching a creative writing course at a progressive college for women to gather material for a mean-spirited novel. The only novel by the poet and critic, it was written in response to Mary McCarthy's novel of academe.

**McCarthy, Mary,** *The Groves of Academe* (1952). The struggle between the president of a small, liberal college for women and an unpleasant professor provide the plot for this witty, acerbic satire of faculty life.

**Malamud, Bernard,** *A New Life* (1961). At once a devastating satire on academia, a ribald comedy, an ironic commentary on East Coast experience and West Coast innocence, and above all, a profoundly moving fable of redemption and rebirth. Other novels about teaching in the 1950s are Alison Lurie, *Love and Friendship* (1962) and Philip Roth, *Letting Go* (1961).

## British Teachers

**Amis, Kingsley,** *Lucky Jim* (1954). The humorous "angry young man" classic about a young lower-middle-class university instructor.

**Bradbury, Malcolm,** *The History Man* (1976). Depiction of an ambitious radical sociologist at a "new" university. An "extremely witty, readable and alarming book [which] raises questions about the nature of civilization" (Margaret Drabble). His other academic novels are *Eating People Is Wrong* (1960) and *Stepping Westward* (1966).

**Carpenter, Humphrey,** *The Inklings: C. S. Lewis, J. R. R. Tolkein, Charles Williams, and Their Friends* (1979). Skillfully written narrative about a quirky coterie of one-time Oxford English professors best known for their fantasy novels and Christian apologetics. A good picture of the Oxford gentleman-don of the first half of this century is J. C. Masterman's autobiography *On the Chariot Wheel* (1975).

**Lodge, David,** *Changing Places* (1975). Comic novel about two professors, one English, one American, who exchange academic positions and, eventually, wives. Another witty academic novel is D. J. Enright, *Academic Year* (1955).

**Snow, C. P.,** *The Masters* (1951). Novel about the election of a new head of a Cambridge college.

## Oxford and Cambridge

**Beerbohm, Max,** *Zuleika Dobson* (1911). Satiric fantasy about the devastating effect of a lovely adventuress on Oxford's undergraduates.

**Crispin, Edmund,** *The Case of the Gilded Fly* (1944). Also published as *Obsequies at Oxford.* The erudite detective Gervase Fen hunts the murderer of one of the college repertory actresses. Fen figures in other Crispin Oxford mysteries, including *The Moving Toyshop* (1946).

**Forster, E. M.,** *The Longest Journey* (1907). The picture of Cantabrigian intellectual and social life is most memorable in this novel, which "is perhaps the most brilliant, the most dramatic, and the most passionate" of Forster's novels, but an imperfect one which "does not so much fall apart as fly apart" (Lionel Trilling).

**Larkin, Philip,** *Jill* (1946). Oxford during World War II is the setting for this novel by a distinguished English poet. A 1964 reissue contains an autobiographical preface.

**Morris, Jan (ed.),** *The Oxford Book of Oxford* (1978). Witty, informative anecdotal history of the university, occasioned by the 500th anniversary of the Oxford University Press. See *Oxford* (1965). See also A. L. Rowse's very personal chronological history, *Oxford in the History of England* (1975).

**Sayers, Dorothy L.,** *Gaudy Night* (1935). Highly atmospheric, highbrow mystery about a women's college by a writer who knows and loves Oxford. Other donnish mysteries are Tim Heald, *A Small Masterpiece* (1982); J. C. Masterman, *An Oxford Mystery* (1933); and Howard Sharp, *Death of a Don* (1981).

**Sharpe, Tom,** *Porterhouse Blues* (1974). Amusing, nasty novel about a crusty college at Cambridge.

**Sinclair, Andrew,** *My Friend Judas* (1959). Cambridge in the fifties is happily evoked in this novel with a cheerfully iconoclastic hero. Julian Mitchell, *Imaginary Toys* (1961) and Auberon Waugh, *Path of Dalliance* (1963) also imaginatively recreate Oxford during the fifties.

**Stewart, J. I. M.,** *The Gaudy* (1975). The first of the Staircase in Surrey series of novels set at Surrey College, Oxford. Especially revealing on academic politics. Stewart's mystery novels are written under the name of Michael Innes, and some, such as *Seven Suspects* (1937), have academic settings.

**Thwaite, Ann and Ronald Hayman (eds.),** *My Oxford, My Cambridge* (1979). Varied and interesting personal reminiscences of university life by twenty-five distinguished graduates.

## High School

**Kaufman, Bel,** *Up the Down Staircase* (1964). Rollicking novel, witty and wise, about a young woman's first frustrating and furious year as a teacher in a large New York high school.

**Keyes, Ralph,** *Is There Life After High School?* (1976). Nostalgic look at high-school life and its profound effects on later life, written in a humorous, anecdotal style, with perceptive insights.

**Owen, David,** *High School* (1981). The former editor of the *Harvard Lampoon* "infiltrated" the senior class of a New York high school and filed this lively report. Cameron Crowe, *Fast Times at Ridgemont High: A True Story* (1981) is about life in a Southern California high school.

**Powers, John R.,** *Do Black Patent Leather Shoes Really Reflect Up?: A Fictional Memoir* (1975). Comic goings-on at Chicago's St. Patrick Bremmer High will divert any reader, but if you ever attended parochial school you will laugh aloud. Powers's pre–high school days are wittily described in *The Last Catholic in America* (1973).

**Updike, John,** *The Centaur* (1963). Both a realistic narrative about a few days at Olinger High School and the Greek myth about the centaur Chiron. Brilliant shifting of planes. Awarded the National Book Award for fiction.

## Prep School

**Auchincloss, Louis,** *The Rector of Justin* (1964). Fine novel about the founder and headmaster of a New England Episcopal boys' school as told by the people who knew him, loved him, and hated him. Real headmasters are the subjects of John McPhee, *The Headmaster* (1968), about Frank L. Boyden, the "magnanimous despot" of Deerfield Academy; Frank D. Ashburn, *Peabody of Groton* (rev. 1967); Claude M. Fuess, *Independent Schoolmaster* (1952), the memoir of an Andover headmaster; and John D. Verdery, *Partial Recall* (1981), the "afterthoughts" of the master of Wooster School.

**Birnbach, Lisa (ed.),** *The Official Preppy Handbook* (1981). Hilarious sendup of the preppy style which will guide the preppy manqué through the nuances of proper attire, language, and behavior. For those not too old for the real thing, consult *Lovejoy's Prep School Guide* or Joan Barrett and Sally F. Goldfarb, *The Insider's Guide to Prep Schools* (1979).

**Knowles, John,** *A Separate Peace* (1959). Popular classic about the relationship of two seniors at the exclusive Devon School during World War II. *Peace Breaks Out* (1981) is a sequel.

**Prescott, Peter S.,** *A World of Our Own: Notes on Life and Learning in a Boy's Preparatory School* (1970). Using his own alma mater Choate as an example, the author looks at the prep school system and finds it wanting.

**Yates, Richard,** *A Good School* (1978). Graceful, wry portrait of the fictional Dorset Academy, "a funny little school that nobody ever heard of," in what is really a memoir.

## Girls' School

**Apffel, Edmund,** *The Last Days at St. Saturn's* (1981). The belles of St. Saturn's are thoroughly modern in this very funny first novel.

**Brontë, Charlotte,** *Villette* (1853). Partly autobiographical novel about a young English woman teaching in a girls' school in

Brussels and her growing fascination with the professor Paul Emmanuel.

**Colette,** *Claudine at School* (1901). The first of four semiautobiographical novels about a precocious French schoolgirl. *The Complete Claudine* (1976, tr. Antonia White) collects all four.

**Forest, Antonia,** *The Autumn Term* (1948). One of the author's fine stories for girls about traditional upper-middle-class English schools. See *The Attic Term* (1976). See also Mary K. Harris, *The Bus Girls* (1965).

**Kerr, M. E.,** *Is That You, Miss Blue?* (1975). One of the best-loved writers of novels for young teenagers shows her understanding, compassion, and humor in this swift-paced story of the funny and sad adventures of a fourteen-year-old sent to boarding school. See *Little Little* (1981).

**North, Elizabeth,** *Dames* (1981). Dames, an upper-class English boarding school, is at the center of this enjoyable novel about the fortunes of its headmistress and two students over two decades. Janice Elliot's *Secret Places* (1982) is another good novel of boarding-school life.

**Searle, Ronald,** *Hurrah for St. Trinian's* (1948). Searle's superb pen-and-ink drawings of the frolicsome, mischievous girls of this mythical English boarding school are a triumph of hilarity. D. B. Wyndham Lewis did the text for the sequel, *The Terrors of St. Trinian's* (1952).

**Spark, Muriel,** *The Prime of Miss Jean Brodie* (1961). A ruthless comedy, set in an Edinburgh girls' school in the thirties, about a preposterous teacher and her students.

**Tey, Josephine,** *Miss Pym Disposes* (1948). Murder at a physical training college. A leisurely English mystery in most civilized prose. Other school mysteries are Amanda Cross, *Theban Mysteries* (1971); Charlotte McLeod, *Rest You Merry* (1978); and John Wainwright, *Dominoes* (1980).

**White, Antonia,** *Frost in May* (1933). Five years at an English convent public school by the daughter of a Catholic convert, in a novel of power and charm.

## English Public School

**Benedictus, David,** *The Fourth of June* (1962). Bitingly funny first novel set on the playing fields of Eton.

**Dickens, Charles,** *Nicholas Nickleby* (1838–39). The first part of this novel exposes the brutality of the conditions in many English schools, some of which were as woeful as the fictional Dotheboys Hall where young Nicholas served as usher.

**Fuller, Roy,** *The Distant Afternoon* (1959). A small-scale, accomplished novel by a poet about a sensitive boy at a second-rate boarding school.

**Gathorne-Hardy, Jonathan,** *The Old School Tie* (1978). The development of the English public school described in a colorful, anecdotal, and penetrating style.

**Hilton, James,** *Goodbye Mr. Chips* (1934). Short, lachrymose tale of Mr. Chips of Brookfield dreaming away his last days within the sight and sound of the school.

**Hughes, Thomas,** *Tom Brown's School Days* (1857). An "old boys' " popular classic, set at Rugby, that paints a realistic picture of the often cruel world of the Victorian boys' school.

**Johnson, Pamela Hansford,** *The Honours Board* (1970). Civilized novel, written with wit and insight, about a couple teaching during the declining days of the upper-middle-class school of Downs Park.

**Kipling, Rudyard,** *Stalky & Co.* (1899). Nonsentimental autobiographical stories about a trio of boys bent on making life miserable for the school's masters. See G. C. Beresford, *School Days with Kipling: The True Story of Stalky & Co.* (1936).

**Le Carré, John,** *A Murder of Quality* (1962). This novel finds George Smiley outside his accustomed world of espionage, as an amateur investigator of a private murder at one of England's great public schools. Other superior boys' school mysteries are Nicholas Blake, *A Question of Proof* (1935); Leo Bruce, *Case with Ropes and Rings* (1949); L. P. Davies, *The Paper Dolls* (1966); and Michael Gilbert, *The Night of the Twelfth* (1976).

**Mackenzie, Compton,** *Sinister Street* (1914). Novel about Michael Fane, the illegitimate child of wealthy parents, at St. Paul's School in London.

**Mayne, William,** *A Swan in May* (1955). A much-admired English writer of books for young people has based this story, one in a cathedral-school series, on his own experiences at choir school.

**Orwell, George,** *Such, Such Were the Joys* (1953). The title piece of this collection of essays, a reminiscence of preparatory school days, is "his most important autobiographical fragment and perhaps his best essay" (Cyril Connolly). It was originally undertaken as a sort of pendant to Connolly's *Enemies of Promise* (1938), which included a long sketch about the same school, which he attended at the same time as Orwell.

**Powell, Anthony,** *A Question of Upbringing* (1951). The emergence from adolescence, just after World War I, of Nick Jenkins and three other boys. Set at Eton, in France, at Oxford, and in London. The first segment of the series A Dance to the Music of Time, which mixes irony, understatement, and subtle humor to create a world as large and complex as Proust's.

**Waugh, Evelyn,** *Decline and Fall* (1928). Waugh has a delightful time taking the public school and other sacred cows of England for a blithe and madcap ride.

**Wodehouse, P. G.,** *Enter Psmith* (1935). Sprightly tale of the school days of Psmith, later to become a member of Wodehouse's permanent gallery of characters.

## Other Schools

**Kästner, Erich,** *Flying Classroom* (1934). Engaging story for young readers about a boarding school in Bavaria.

**Musil, Robert,** *Young Törless* (1906). The great Austrian writer's remarkable novel of sexual and intellectual awakening, set within the confines of a military boarding school. A work of art and of prophetic psychological insight.

**Peyfritte, Roger,** *Special Friendships* (1950). Finely crafted tragic tale of the furtive friendship of two French boarding-school boys.

**Vargas Llosa, Mario,** *The Time of the Hero* (1966). Harsh look at a military academy in Peru from the viewpoint of the cadets. A powerful novel.

**Willingham, Calder,** *End as a Man* (1947). The unforgettable Jocko de Paris, the despicable upperclassman, is at the center of this brutally honest novel about life inside a Southern military college. Pat Conroy, *Lords of Discipline* (1980) is also set at a Southern military academy, but during the late sixties.

# ECONOMICS

## Capitalism

**Barnet, Richard,** *The Lean Years: Politics in the Age of Scarcity* (1980). In *Global Reach: The Power of the Multinational Corporations* (1974), he and Ronald Muller exposed the unprecedented power of the great corporations; here he analyzes the economic, political, and military crises we face in the immediate future.

**Eichner, Alfred S. (ed.),** *A Guide to Post-Keynesian Economics* (1979). "For anyone who wishes to know what is going on in the world of economic thought, it is, I believe, indispensable" (Robert L. Heilbroner).

**Friedman, Milton,** *Capitalism and Freedom* (1963). The dean of the Chicago school of conservative economics sets forth, in a lively writing style, his views on individual freedom, capitalistic enterprise, and government intervention.

**Galbraith, John Kenneth,** *The Affluent Society* (rev. 1976). Contemporary liberal classic of economics. See *The New Industrial State* (1968) and *Economics and the Public Purpose* (1973).

**Gilder, George,** *Wealth and Poverty* (1981). Argument for supply-side economics — the cornerstone of the Reagan economic plan. Another Reaganomic primer is Lester Thurow's *The Zero Sum Society* (1980).

**Heilbroner, Robert L.,** *The Worldly Philosophers* (rev. 1980). Lives, times, and ideas of the great economic thinkers. See his excellent *The Making of Economic Society* (rev. 1975) and *Five Economic Challenges* (1981), written with Lester Thurow.

**Lekachman, Robert and Baron Van Loon,** *Capitalism for Beginners* (1981). An informal, concise paperback which succinctly tells you everything you always wanted to know about capitalism. Lekachman is the author of *Economist at Bay* (1976) and *Greed Is Not Enough* (1982).

**Moskowitz, Milton et al.,** *Everybody's Business: An Almanac* (1981). This irreverent guide to corporate America tells who runs whom, who makes what, and how the billion-dollar corporations made it to the top. Absolutely fascinating for friends, foes, and neutral observers of American business.

**Rand, Ayn,** *Atlas Shrugged* (1942). In this novel by the libertarian polemicist the world's capitalists go on strike to protest the forces of creeping socialism.

**Schumpeter, Joseph A.,** *Capitalism, Socialism, and Democracy* (rev. 1950). One of the great conservative economists of the century reexamines the ideas of Marxist socialism and finds them to stultify society, compared with those of capitalism.

**Silk, Leonard,** *The Economists* (1976). The views of five contemporary economists — Boulding, Friedman, Galbraith, Leontief, and Samuelson — lucidly presented. See *Economics in Plain English* (1978).

## Socialism

**Heilbroner, Robert L.,** *Marxism: For and Against* (1980). Concise analysis of Marxist economic theories. See *Between Capitalism and Socialism: Essays on Political Economics* (1971).

**Lichtheim, George,** *A Short History of Socialism* (1970). Simple, clear introduction to the subject. Michael Harrington, *Socialism* (1972) is an excellent contemporary restatement.

**MacKenzie, Norman and Jeanne MacKenzie,** *The Fabians* (1977). About the English socialist group, the Fabian Society, founded in 1884 and most often identified with Beatrice and Sidney Webb and George Bernard Shaw.

**Revel, Jean Francois,** *The Totalitarian Temptation* (1977). Highly readable polemic against eurocommunism and for a true global socialism based on the reform of capitalism, by the author of *Without Marx or Jesus* (1971).

**Swanberg, W. A.,** *Norman Thomas: The Last Idealist* (1977). Admiring, often moving, biography of the American socialist leader who ran for president six times.

## Money

**Lathen, Emma,** *Banking on Death* (1961). The novel that launched John Putnam Thatcher, senior vice-president of Sloan Guaranty Trust Company and urbane, charming sleuth, in a series of scrupulously researched Wall Street crime novels. See *Green Grow the Dollars* (1982).

**Mayer, Martin,** *The Fate of the Dollar* (1980). Lucid explanation of the great financial crises of our time, from the gold drain of 1958 to the panics of 1978–79. See *The Bankers* (1974).

**Porter, Sylvia,** *Sylvia Porter's New Money Book for the 80's* (1979). The financial columnist's tips on "how to beat the high cost of living and use your earnings, credit savings and investments to better your life." Other good money books are Jane Bryant Quinn, *Everyone's Money Book* (1978) and Richard E. Blodgett, *The New York Times Book of Money* (1979).

**Shapiro, Max,** *The Penniless Billionaires* (1981). Fascinating exploration of four great inflationary eras of the past — why they arose, who caused them, how family fortunes survived or were destroyed, and what warnings each superinflation shouts out to us today.

**Smith, Adam,** *Paper Money* (1981). Sane, cheerful account of how the age of paper money arrived, what it means, and how it has changed our lives. See *The Money Game* (1968) and *Supermoney* (1972).

## Stock Market

**Brooks, John,** *Once in Golconda: A True Story of Wall Street, 1920–1938* (1969). Absorbing story of Richard Whitney, a president of the New York Stock Exchange who was convicted of embezzlement in 1938. Provides a good social and economic history of the times. See *The Go-Go Years* (1973), an anecdotal account of Wall Street during the sixties, and *The*

*Game Players: Tales of Men and Money* (1980).

**Engel, Louis in collaboration with Peter Wyckoff,** *How to Buy Stocks* (rev. 1977). One of the best of many guides to investment in the stock market.

**Galbraith, John Kenneth,** *The Great Crash* (rev. 1972). Classic account of the stock market crash of 1929.

**Rukeyser, Louis,** *How to Make Money in Wall Street* (rev. 1976). A sound, well-written guide by the genial and informed host of the PBS television series "Wall Street Week."

**Tobias, Andrew,** *The Only Investment Guide You'll Ever Need* (1979). You will need others, but this one is a sensible, clear aid by a contributing editor of *Esquire.* See *Getting By on $100,000 a Year, and Other Sad Tales* (1980).

## Agriculture

**Berry, Wendell,** *Farming: A Hand Book* (1970). Poems, mainly pastoral, that spring from Berry's life in Kentucky, where he farms.

**Bromfield, Louis,** *Malabar Farm* (1947). Fine diary packed full of farm lore by a novelist who went back to his Ohio farm and rebuilt it using organic methods. A homesteading classic. See *Pleasant Valley* (1945).

**Conrat, Maisie and Richard Conrat,** *The American Farm: A Photographic History* (1977). Superb collection of photographs selected from archives around the country show how farming changed from a self-sustaining way of life for most Americans to the agribusiness of today.

**Darley, Gillian,** *The National Trust Book of the Farm* (1981). A beautiful and informative book about an old but thriving British institution.

**Gibbons, Stella,** *Cold Comfort Farm* (1932). Wonderfully comic novel parodying the literature of rustic pessimism of such Hardy followers as Mary Webb.

**Hamsun, Knut,** *The Growth of the Soil* (1920). The rigors of pioneering and of eking out an existence from the land in a novel by the Nobel Prize–winning Norwegian author.

**Kramer, Mark,** *Three Farms: Making Milk, Meat and Money from the American Soil* (1980). Lively journalistic look at the forces shaping modern American agriculture; each of the three farms represents the past, present, and future of farming.

**Perrin, Noel,** *First Person Rural* (1978). Wry, elegant essays about rural Vermont by a transplanted New Yorker, now "sometimes farmer." See *Second Person Rural* (1980). Walter Needham's *A Book of Country Things* (1965) is another fine book about Vermont farming.

**Schreiner, Olive,** *The Story of an African Farm* (1883). Published under the pseudonym Ralph Iron, this novel about three childhood friends offers a realistic glimpse of Boer farm life and its confining conventions, especially on women.

**Thomas, Sherry,** *We Didn't Have Much, but We Sure Had Plenty* (1981). Deeply felt oral histories of American farm women.

**Virgil,** *Georgics* (37–30 B.C.). Ostensibly a didactic poem about farming, animal husbandry, beekeeping, and the like, it is philosophic and national in scope, reflecting the poet's love of nature, his patriotism, and his preoccupation with the mystery of life.

**White, Patrick,** *The Tree of Man* (1956). Long, lyrical novel about a family living on an Australian bush farm at the turn of the century.

## Labor Organizations

**Brill, Steven,** *The Teamsters* (1978). Biographical sketches of nine men in the country's largest trade union.

**Stegner, Wallace,** *Joe Hill* (1950). Also published as *The Preacher and the Slave,* it is a stirring novel about the I.W.W. leader Joseph Hillstrom, who was executed in 1916. Other novels about the old-time labor days are Steve Chapple, *Don't Mind Dying* (1980); Robert Houston, *Bisbee '17* (1979); and Leonard Kriegel, *Quitting Time* (1982).

**Steinbeck, John,** *In Dubious Battle* (1936). Steinbeck's early, hard-hitting novel about a California fruit pickers' strike and radical agitators.

**Yount, John,** *Hardcastle* (1980). Novel about a mining strike in Depression-era Kentucky.

**Zola, Emile,** *Germinal* (1885). Great tragic novel about a miners' strike in northern France. Zola, with consummate artistry, brings a whole community to life.

## Slavery

**Alford, Terry,** *Prince Among Slaves* (1977). Astounding account of an African prince who was captured by slavers and brought to America, where he endured ten years of bondage before being freed and returned to Africa.

**Bontemps, Arna (ed.),** *Great Slave Narratives* (1969). Collection of pieces which gives an eloquent picture of slavery through nonwhite eyes. See Julius Lester, *To Be a Slave* (1968).

**Davis, David Brion,** *The Problem of Slavery in Western Culture* (1966). Pulitzer Prize–winning classic which displays a mastery of the vast source material and the contradictory factors that influenced opinion on slavery.

**Koestler, Arthur,** *The Gladiators* (1930). The revolt of the Roman gladiators under the leadership of Spartacus: a realistic, critical novel by the Hungarian-born writer. Howard Fast's *Spartacus* (1951) is a popular novel about the famous slave rebellion.

**Pope-Hennessy, James** *Sins of the Fathers: A Study of the Atlantic Slave Traders, 1441–1807* (1968). Based on contemporary letters and journals, a vivid account of human misery. The authoritative history is James A. Rawley, *The Transatlantic Slave Trade* (1981).

## Poverty

**Dostoevski, Fedor,** *Poor Folk* (1846). Brief, powerful, epistolary novel about a poor clerk and his hopeless love for an equally poor young woman who lives nearby.

**Jesus, Carolina Maria De,** *Child of the Dark: The Diary of Carolina Maria de Jesus* (1963). This outcry from the slums of São Paulo, Brazil, is a "sad book to read, but it is not easy to forget. Its style is simple, blunt, repetitive, but brisk and tasty. . . . It is a minor classic because it is one of the very few books that have ever been written about the lowest and poorest, *les miserables,* by one of themselves" (Gilbert Highet).

**Lewis, Oscar,** *The Children of Sanchez* (1960). A classic of oral history that reads like a novel; it captures the soul of a Mexican slum family. See *Five Families: Mexican Case Studies in the Culture of Poverty* (1959).

**Mayhew, Henry,** *London Labour and the London Poor* (1861). A journalist records his investigations into the lives of the city's underprivileged. A classic. Peter Quennell distilled the voluminous work in *Mayhew's London* (1949), *Mayhew's Characters* (1951), and *London's Underworld* (1950).

**Orwell, George,** *The Road to Wigan Pier* (1937). Searing yet beautiful account of the poverty Orwell encountered "on the road to Wigan Pier," and a discussion of why socialism had so little appeal. "A masterpiece. It is also a basic document in the intellectual history of this century" (Richard H. Rovere). See *Down and Out in Paris and London* (1933). A fictional companion work is his satire on poverty, *Keep the Aspidistra Flying* (1936).

# POLITICS

## Political Theory

**Aristotle,** *Nicomachean Ethics* (4th cent. B.C.). The famous treatise inquiring into the nature of the Good wherein he develops the Doctrine of the Mean as a guide to human conduct. See *Politics.*

**Machiavelli, Niccolo,** *The Prince* (1517). Classic work on power politics in which Cesare Borgia emerges as the model ruler.

**Marx, Karl,** *The Communist Manifesto* (1848). Perhaps the simplest expression of his beliefs. See Peter Singer, *Marx* (1980), a succinct introduction to Marx's key ideas in fewer than 100 pages.

**Montesquieu, Charles de,** *The Spirit of Laws* (1748). Treatise on "the relationship which law must have to the constitution of each government, to mores, religion, commerce, etc." One of the most influential political volumes ever published and a pleasure to read.

**Plato,** *The Republic* (4th cent. B.C.). One of the great masterpieces of all literature, it is a dialogue in which Socrates, in seeking an answer to the question What is justice? expounds on the nature of the ideal state, the republic.

## Democracy

**Dewey, John,** *Freedom and Culture* (1939). Written when he was eighty years old, a recapitulation of much of his humanistic and liberal thinking and a setting out of the conditions on which true democracy is based.

**Lippmann, Walter,** *The Essential Lippmann: A Political Philosopher for Liberal Democracy* (1963). Selected writings of over fifty years by the eminent political commentator.

**Niebuhr, Reinhold and Paul E. Sigmund,** *The Democratic Experience: Past and Present* (1969). Cross-disciplinary, cross-cultural examination which finds that as a prerequisite for democracy there must be national unity and free participation.

**Tocqueville, Alexis de,** *Democracy in America* (1838). Incisive observations on American institutions and the advantages and disadvantages for them of democracy. A classic, which 150 years later tells much about America. See Richard Reeves, *American Journey* (1982), an account of his findings about the condition of democracy on a retracing of Tocqueville's trail.

**Wills, Garry,** *Confessions of a Conservative* (1979). Brisk intellectual autobiography and political treatise by a leading conservative writer and thinker.

## Totalitarianism and Communism

**Arendt, Hannah,** *The Origins of Totalitarianism* (rev. 1966). A provocative, demanding study which argues that totalitarianism originated in anti-Semitism and nineteenth-century imperialism.

**Crossman, Richard (ed.),** *The God that Failed* (1950). André Gide, Richard Wright, Ignazio Silone, Stephen Spender, Arthur Koestler, and Louis Fischer describe their journeys into communism and their disillusioned return.

**Djilas, Milovan,** *The New Class: An Analysis of the Communist System* (1957). An "Anticommunist manifesto," a tough-minded examination of Communist the-

ory, coolly impersonal and objective, written while the author was in a Yugoslavian prison.

**Koestler, Arthur,** *Darkness at Noon* (1941). An aging revolutionary, in process of being purged and under pressure to confess preposterous crimes, relives a career that embodies the terrible ironies and human betrayals of a totalitarian movement masking itself as an instrument of deliverance.

**Kopelov, Lev,** *To Be Preserved From* (1977). By a Russian veteran of the gulag who "has managed to isolate the universal human process underlying the violence of bureaucratic reaction to dangerous critics, the spiteful origins of so much political accusations, the crabbed enemy behind the idealogue's purity" (Arthur Miller).

**Mandelstam, Nadezhda,** *Hope Against Hope* (1970). Narrative of the terrible story of her husband, poet Osip Mandelstam; his last years as he was hounded and eventually destroyed by the purges. One of the most remarkable books of our times. See *Hope Abandoned* (1971).

**Nabokov, Vladimir,** *The Gift* (1937, tr. 1963). Novel in the form of an autobiography of a Russian expatriate in Berlin after World War I, which examines the native Russian roots of Marxism-Leninism. See *Bend Sinister* (1964).

**Orwell, George,** *Animal Farm* (1945). Wise, illuminating "fairy story" that attacks the pig-headed, gluttonous, and avaricious rulers of an imaginary totalitarian state.

**Wilson, Edmund,** *To the Finland Station* (1940). Brilliant "study in the writing and acting of history" which traces the revolutionary tradition in Europe and the rise of socialism. One of the best guides to the Western sources of Marxism-Leninism.

**Zinoviev, Alexander,** *The Yawning Heights* (1979). Russian emigre's comic epic about an imaginary country with an imaginary ideology. A Swiftian fable about life in a faceless society. See *The Radiant Future* (1981).

## Fascism

**Bassani, Giorgio,** *The Gold-Rimmed Spectacles* (1960). Fascist Italy is the backdrop for this brief, polished novel about a respected physician who becomes involved in a series of increasingly overt homosexual incidents. Shows the Fascist mind victimizing homosexuals and Jews. See *The Garden of the Finzi-Continis* (1965).

**Fallaci, Oriana,** *A Man* (1980). Painful and truthful depiction, cast as a novel, of the torture and murder of her friend and lover, a Greek patriot, at the time of the Fascist regime in Greece.

**Nolte, Ernst,** *Three Faces of Fascism: Action Française, Italian Fascism, National Socialism* (1965). An "attempt on a grand scale, on a massive factual basis and by a scholar of great knowledge and depth, to explain one of the central phenomena of our time" (Walter Laqueur). For a less theoretical, more factual study see F. L. Carsten, *The Rise of Fascism* (1967). The best introduction to the Italian model is Elizabeth Wiskemann, *Fascism in Italy* (1969).

**Silone, Ignazio,** *Bread and Wine* (rev. 1962). Powerful but restrained novel about a revolutionary who returns to his native Italy in the thirties, disguised as a priest, to try to organize the peasants against the Fascist government. See *Fontamara* (1934) and *Mr. Aristotle* (1935).

**Timerman, Jacobo,** *Prisoner Without a Name, Cell Without a Number* (1981). By a former Buenos Aires newspaper publisher who spent two and a half years in an Argentine prison, it contains chilling comments about repression and anti-Semitism under a military dictatorship.

## American Radicalism

**Aaron, Daniel,** *Writers on the Left: Episodes in American Literary Communism* (1961). Combining history, biography, and criticism, an expert chronicle of left-wing writing during the interwar years.

**Doctorow, E. L.,** *The Book of Daniel* (1971). The son of Communist parents, Bronx Jews who were executed in the early fifties for conspiring to steal atomic secrets for Russia, the narrator searches for truth about his parents and about himself in this bitter, deeply felt work that Stanley Kauffmann called "the political novel of our age."

**Chambers, Whittaker,** *Witness* (1952). Memoirs of Communist Party days by one of the notorious Hiss-Chambers case principals. "The name of the author, the theme of his work, the nature of our times all conspire to make this volume one of the most significant autobiographies of the 20th century" (Sidney Hook).

**Gornick, Vivian,** *The Romance of American Communism* (1978). Sympathetic collection of "oral histories" of ex-Communists, "a moving story of the human dimension of the Communist experience in which the Stalinist robots who inhabited those Joe McCarthyite movies and books about the party in the 50's disappear and people emerge" (Michael Harrington).

**Kempton, Murray,** *Part of Our Time: Some Ruins and Monuments of the Thirties* (1955). A look at the failed social myth of the "Red Decade": "a striking piece of work. It is easily the best essay on American Communism and Communists that anyone has done" (Richard H. Rovere).

**Mitford, Jessica,** *A Fine Old Conflict* (1977). Witty, frank "no regrets" memoir of the muckraking Mitford's C.P. days during the thirties and forties.

**Richmond, Al,** *A Long View from the Left* (1973). These "memoirs of an American revolutionary," a long-time journalist for the leftist press, is "a brilliant analytical (and often very amusing) memoir that deserves to be a classic" (Jessica Mitford).

**Sigal, Clancy,** *Going Away* (1962). As the novel's protagonist speeds across country by car, the reader is given a chronicle of the American left from the thirties through the fifties and a sense of the shattering effect that the demise of the Communist dream had on the party's sympathizers.

**Swados, Harvey,** *Standing Fast* (1970). Absorbing, grandly conceived novel tracing a small sect of powerless militants through the years between the outbreak of World War II and the assassination of JFK: "a document of accuracy, integrity and compassion" (John Leonard).

**Trilling, Lionel,** *The Middle of the Journey* (1947). Finely crafted, demanding novel of ideas in which the protagonist questions the basic assumptions of his life as they are reflected in his personal loyalties and political stand.

## American Conservatism

**Buckley, William F., Jr. (ed.),** *Did You Ever See a Dream Walking?: American Conservative Thought in the Twentieth Century* (1970). A valuable anthology of short pieces by leading modern conservatives. *Up from Liberalism* (1968) is good for an understanding of conservatism.

**Burnham, James,** *Suicide of the West* (1964). "Masterful analysis by a masterful strategist of our struggle with Communism" (William F. Buckley, Jr.).

**Hayek, Friedrich,** *The Road to Serfdom* (1944). A distinguished economist argues that tyranny is the end result of government intervention in economic activity. See "anti-Keynesian" Henry Hazlitt's *Economics in One Lesson* (1979), which provides an excellent introduction to libertarian economics.

**Kendall, Willmore and George W. Carey,** *The Basic Symbols of the American Political Tradition* (1970). The conservative interpretation of the American Revolution. The Civil War is analyzed in Henry Jaffa, *The Crisis of the House Divided: An Interpretation of the Issues in the Lincoln-Douglas Debates* (1973).

**Kirk, Russell,** *The Conservative Mind* (1953). Study of English and American conservative thought from Burke to Santayana which "may be credited with inaugurating the modern conservative intellectual movement in America" (William F. Buckley, Jr.). George Nash's *The Conservative Intellectual Movement in America* (1976) is a history of subsequent events. Kirk edited *The Portable Conservative Reader* (1982).

## Anarchism

**Berkman, Alexander,** *Prison Memoirs of an Anarchist* (1912). Chamber of horrors of prison life by labor radical who was incarcerated for fourteen years.

**Carr, E. H.,** *Michael Bakunin* (1937). The nineteenth-century rival of Marx and founder of anarchism, in "one of the best documented, best written, most important biographies of our time" (Isaiah Berlin).

**Drinnon, Richard,** *Rebel in Paradise* (1961). Lively biography of the remarkable Emma Goldman, the anarchist leader who was twice jailed and finally deported from the U.S. in 1919. Her autobiography is *Living My Life* (1931).

**Kropotkin, Peter,** *Memoirs of a Revolutionist* (1899). Account of the social action in Russia during the reign of Alexander II by the anarchist theorist who was exiled in 1876, not to return until 1917, when he was just as hostile to the Bolsheviks as he had been to the Czarist regime.

**Woodcock, George,** *Anarchism: A History of Libertarian Ideas and Movements* (1962). Solid, readable presentation of the principal arguments, as well as the careers, of advocates of anarchism.

## Practical Politics

**Brammer, Billy Lee,** *The Gay Place* (1961). Trio of related novels about politics in a state much like Texas and about a politician much like LBJ, by a knowledgeable writer.

**Conrad, Joseph,** *Nostromo* (1904). Conrad's masterpiece, an impressionistic political novel set in a fictional Latin American republic; a study of capitalist exploitation, revolution, and the corrupting power of obsessive material concerns, which F. R. Leavis called "one of the world's great novels."

**Disraeli, Benjamin,** *Coningsby* (1844). Written before the author became prime minister of England and very much concerned with the political issues of its time; its picture of society, its wit, and its modern sensibility have made it endure. See *Sybil, or The Two Nations* (1845).

**Dominic, R. B.,** *The Attending Physician* (1980). Good example of witty, pertinent suspense novels about Congressman Ben Safford, full of inside Washington detail and written in an easy style by the authors who also write as Emma Lathen.

**Flynn, Edward Joseph,** *You're the Boss* (1947). Apologia for bosses and machines, by a former Democratic Party boss of the Bronx; so frank and revealing that it is "clearly destined to become a small political classic" (Arthur M. Schlesinger, Jr.).

**Sheed, Wilfrid,** *People Will Always Be Kind* (1973). Good inside view of politics in a novel about an Irish-American politician who overcomes polio to run for president.

**Stendhal,** *The Charterhouse of Parma* (1839). The novel opens with a magnificent description of the Battle of Waterloo and traces the career of Fabrizio del Dongo through the intrigues of a small Italian court and finally to the priesthood. "The masterpiece of the Literature of Ideas . . . a book in which sublimity glows from chapter to chapter" (Honoré de Balzac).

**Trollope, Anthony,** *Phineas Finn* (1869). The first of the Palliser novels, about the fortunes of a poor young Irishman who is elected to Parliament and comes to London. Later volumes are more about Plantagenet Palliser and Lady Glencora.

**Voegelen, Eric,** *The New Science of Politics: An Introduction* (1952). Traces history of radical challenges to civilized order from the Greek polis onwards. Considered by conservatives to be a basic text. See Eugene Webb, *Eric Voegelen: Philosopher of History* (1981).

**Wicker, Tom,** *Facing the Lions* (1973). An authentic and sincere novel about the clash between a senator in quest of the presidency and a newspaperman.

# LAW

**Baldwin, Joseph G.,** *The Flush Times of Alabama and Mississippi* (1853). These anecdotes, humorous sketches, and serious biographies of outstanding lawyers and judges give an unusually vivid picture of the bench and bar during the "shinplaster era" of the antebellum South.

**Bedford, Sybille,** *The Faces of Justice: A Traveller's Report* (1961). Instructive and entertaining report on the criminal courts of England, Germany, Switzerland, Austria, and France concocted in pleasing style.

**Cahn, Edmond N.,** *The Moral Decision* (1955). Well-written, impassioned discussion of right and wrong in the light of American law.

**Cardozo, Benjamin N.,** *Selected Writings* (1947). Collection of extrajudicial pieces by the great liberal and literary U.S. Supreme Court justice.

**Cecil, Henry,** *Brief Tales from the Bench* (1968). Short fictional tales about barristers written pseudonymously by an English judge. His other witty legal fictions include *Brothers in Law* (1955) and *Sober as a Judge* (1958).

**Clark, Walter Van Tilburg,** *The Ox-Bow Incident* (1940). Violence and quick justice on the frontier is probed with relentless honesty in a classic western.

**Darrow, Clarence,** *Attorney for the Damned* (1957). The great defense lawyer's most famous pleas as counsel make a remarkable and illuminating work.

**Dickens, Charles,** *Bleak House* (1853). The Jarndyce estate case, dragging its course through the Court of Chancery decade after decade and blighting the hopes and desperate expectations of countless litigants, is at the center of this ambitious, angry, ironic, comic, and unforgettable novel.

**Friedman, Lawrence M.,** *A History of American Law* (1973). Concise social history of the law by a Stanford law professor who believes national legal development to be connected with and molded by social and economic factors.

**Gard, Wayne,** *Frontier Justice* (1949). Informal study of the rise of law and order west of the Mississippi, where order often came before law; maximum of colorful anecdotes, minimum of abstract discussion.

**Hand, Learned,** *The Spirit of Liberty* (1952). Collection of the nonjudicial papers and addresses of one of America's wisest judges. See *The Craft of Judging: The Decisions of Judge Learned Hand* (1969).

**Hare, Cyril,** *Tragedy at Law* (1942). Mystery novel, by an English judge, which renders a realistic picture of a judge on circuit. Other English detective novel classics with a legal setting are Edward Grierson, *Reputation for a Song* (1952); Edgar Lustgarten, *One More Unfortunate* (1947); and Raymond Postgate, *Verdict of Twelve* (1940).

**Harris, Richard,** *Freedom Spent* (1976). Three case studies that demonstrate that individual rights will be protected by the legal system only so long as citizens remain vigilant. See *Honor Bound* (1982), a novel about a lawyer who goes outside the law to avenge the death of a friend.

**Hirsch, H. N.,** *The Enigma of Felix Frankfurter* (1981). Intelligent, provocative psychobiography of the brilliant Supreme Court Justice. See Frankfurter's *Reminiscences* (1960) and *Of Law and Life and Other Things that Matter* (1965).

**Holmes, Oliver Wendell and Sir Frederick Pollock,** *The Holmes-Pollock Letters* (1941). Nearly sixty years' correspondence between the two contains both profundity and charm and confirms "the conviction that Justice Holmes was not only the most distinguished jurist but the most distinguished citizen of his generation" (Henry Steele Commager). See Holmes's classic *The Common Law* (1881), a fine example of his distinct mind and liberal views.

**Kluger, Richard,** *Simple Justice* (1977). Through an analysis of *Brown v. Board of Education,* the seminal school desegregation case of 1954, he shows how the civil rights movement used the law. A moving and fascinating book.

**Lewis, Anthony,** *Gideon's Trumpet* (1963). Gripping story of a fight through the thicket of the judicial system to the U.S. Supreme Court that resulted in its decision giving an indigent defendant the constitutional right to counsel.

**Maitland, Frederic W.,** *The Constitutional History of England* (1908). Read with his classic *History of English Law Before the Time of Edward I* (1895), which was cowritten with Sir Frederick Pollock, these Cambridge lectures provide a comprehensive history through the nineteenth century and are marked by profound erudition and great clarity. See *Selected Essays* (1936).

**Rembar, Charles,** *The Law of the Land: The Evolution of our Legal System* (1980). Good popular anecdotal history from Anglo-Saxon times to the most recent decisions of the Supreme Court. Another good historical survey is Grant Gilmore, *The Ages of American Law* (1977).

**Schwartz, Bernard,** *The American Heritage History of the Law in America* (1974).

Thorough, well-organized presentation, with a selection of vivid photographs and drawings.

**Strick, Anne,** *Injustice for All* (1978). How our adversary system of law victimizes litigants and perverts justice.

**White, G. Edward,** *The American Judicial Tradition: Profiles of Leading American Judges* (1976). Excursion inside judicial minds, from John Marshall to Earl Warren, that clearly shows what the job of judging is all about, in a style which is "brilliantly clear, always interesting and frequently amusing" (Louis Auchincloss).

# CRIME

## *Murder*

**Barden, John Franklin,** *The Deadly Percheron* (1946). Midgets, horses, hibiscus-wearing gentlemen, lovely ladies, and lots of action are featured in this mystery novel of murder, mayhem, and torture in New York by a writer who published three haunting suspense novels in the forties and then dropped from sight. See *Devil Take the Blue-Tail Fly* (1948).

**Bedford, Sybille,** *The Trial of Dr. Adams* (1959). Luminous, suspenseful account of the longest murder trial ever held in the Old Bailey.

**Berger, Thomas,** *Killing Time* (1967). Strange and comic novel about a young, amiable taxidermist who is responsible for a series of bizarre murders.

**Bester, Alfred,** *The Demolished Man* (1953). A flamboyant writer's novel about murder in a future telepathic society. A science-fiction *Crime and Punishment.*

**Cain, James M.,** *The Postman Always Rings Twice* (1934). Tough-guy classic about a sexy woman (a Lana Turner type)

and a drifter (a John Garfield type) who plot to murder her husband.

**Camus, Albert,** *The Stranger* (1942). Short novel about an ordinary little man living quietly in Algiers who commits an ostensibly gratuitous murder. An indelible picture of a human being helpless in life's grip.

**Capote, Truman,** *In Cold Blood* (1966). Cold-blooded study, in the form of a novel, of two multiple murderers; based on interviews by Capote.

**Coates, Robert,** *Wisteria Cottage* (1948). Based on an actual murder case, this is a frightening imaginative trip into the mind of a reluctant multiple murderer with a messiah complex.

**Dostoevski, Fedor,** *Crime and Punishment* (1866). On one level the story of a murder and its consequences, a tale of suspense without equal. On a more profound level, an unsurpassed study of guilt and redemption, pride and rebellion, far-reaching in its implications.

**Dreiser, Theodore,** *An American Tragedy* (1925). Powerful, pessimistic view of the tragedy of life wherein a weak young man trapped by social circumstance ends up being executed for murder.

**Goodman, Jonathan,** *The Killing of Julia Wallace* (1969). Fascinating analysis of the murder in 1931 of a Liverpool housewife, a "classic" which has puzzled authorities ever since.

**Iles, Francis,** *Malice Aforethought* (1931). A murder without mystery, where the reader is told all and yet is kept guessing. Its cynical humor, its picture of English middle-class country life, and its surprise ending have made it a crime novel standard. *Before the Fact* (1932), upon which the movie *Suspicion* was based, is also a thriller of high order.

**Johnson, Pamela Hansford,** *On Iniquity* (1967). An extended essay by an English novelist on the notorious Moors murders.

**Kennedy, Ludovic,** *Ten Rillington Place* (1961). A remarkable 1949 London murder and what the author claims was a miscarriage of justice.

**Kirst, Hans Helmut,** *The Night of the Generals* (1964). Thriller about three similar murders of prostitutes that is "one of the best detective novels I have ever read — indeed a very model of how the formal tale of detection may serve as a vehicle for the literary analysis of character, culture and society" (Anthony Boucher). See *Brothers in Arms* (1967).

**Levin, Meyer,** *Compulsion* (1956). The Leopold-Loeb case was the factual basis for this gripping novel of murder and justice.

**Loomis, Stanley,** *A Crime of Passion* (1967). The Duc de Praslin's murder of his wife shook France in 1847, as related in this "wonderfully rich examination of an epoch and one of its most illustrative events" (Jean Stafford).

**Lustgarten, Edgar,** *The Murder and the Trial* (1958). Seventeen classic murder cases and their courtroom resolutions, expertly recounted.

**Mailer, Norman,** *The Executioner's Song* (1979). Finely crafted, Pulitzer Prize–winning nonfiction novel about convicted murderer Gary Gilmore. Based on extensive interviews, it is more a study of the American West than of crime and punishment.

**Millar, Margaret,** *How Like an Angel* (1962). A bizarre manhunt plunges a young widow into an ordeal of terror in this novel by one of the most skillful writers of the suspense genre. See *Beast in View* (1955).

**Monteilhet, Hubert,** *The Praying Mantises* (1960). Brilliant novel of murder, skillfully and economically documented; all is "suspense, irony and style — a cool, swift, elegant, ruthless tale that will spoil the intelligent man's taste for the lesser product" (Sybille Bedford).

**Porter, Katherine Anne,** *Noon Wine* (1937). Short, intense, novel about a Texas farmer who kills a stranger he believes is attacking his hired man. "A high point of Miss Porter's superb art . . . I believe it to be a masterpiece" (Clifton Fadiman).

**Raymond, Ernest,** *We, the Accused* (1935). Highly dramatic, emotional novel of a little man driven to murder his wife. An English *An American Tragedy*.

**Rendell, Ruth,** *Judgment in Stone* (1978). Compelling murder mystery with masterful characterization and vivid atmosphere. Besides her superb psychological mysteries, Rendell is the author of a series of detective novels featuring the civilized, middle-aged Chief Inspector Wexford; see *Wolf to the Slaughter* (1968).

**Russell, Francis,** *Tragedy in Dedham: The Story of the Sacco-Vanzetti Case* (1962). The plight of Sacco and Vanzetti and their dubious conviction have spawned numerous literary works. This rapid, flowing narrative is an absorbing summary of the case.

Sayers, Dorothy L. and Robert Eustace, *The Documents in the Case* (1930). Chilling tale of death and devotion presented entirely by "documents in the case."

Soderberg, Hjalmar, *Doctor Glas* (1905). The question of ethical murder is examined in this brief fictional journal of a man moved to despair.

Symons, Julian, *The Progress of Crime* (1960). This novel of murder is just one of the many superb crime fictions by a modern master of the genre. See *The Broken Penny* (1963) and *The 31st of February* (1950).

Tey, Josephine, *The Daughter of Time* (1966). A classic detective novel in which bedridden Inspector Alan Grant investigates the alleged murder by Richard III of the princes in the Tower of London. See *Brat Farrar* (1949), and *The Franchise Affair* (1948).

Thomsen, Helen, *Murder at Harvard* (1971). Popular account of the celebrated murder of a prominent Boston physician in 1849, full of the excitement that gripped Boston at the time. A more serious analysis of the case is Robert Sullivan, *The Disappearance of Dr. Parkman* (1971).

Trilling, Diana, *Mrs. Harris and the Death of the Scarsdale Diet Doctor* (1981). Account of the trial of Jean Harris for the murder of her lover, Dr. Herman Tarnower.

Warren, Robert Penn, *World Enough and Time* (1951). Novel based on the "Kentucky Tragedy," a famous nineteenth-century murder case; "whatever its faults, a book written at the full strength of Warren's power by a writer who has great talents, and possibly more" (Elizabeth Janeway).

Zola, Émile, *Thérèse Raquin* (1867). Penetrating psychological novel about a *crime passionelle:* a wife and lover murder her husband and are driven to suicide from guilt over the deed.

## Assassination

Bishop, Jim, *The Day that Lincoln Was Shot* (1955). Exciting journalistic minute-by-minute reconstruction of April 14, 1865, the day President Lincoln was assassinated. See *The Day Kennedy Was Shot* (1968).

Condon, Richard, *The Manchurian Candidate* (1959). Stylish novel about a former Korean POW programmed for assassination by the Chinese. It crackles with excitement. *Winter Kills* (1974) is a novel about a Kennedy-like assassination.

Forsythe, Frederick, *The Day of the Jackal* (1971). His mission: kill President Charles de Gaulle; his code name: Jackal; his price: half a million dollars; his demand: total secrecy, even from his employers. A skillfully contrived, utterly enthralling thriller.

Shakespeare, William, *Julius Caesar* (1599). Brutus, Cassius, et al. conspire to assassinate Caesar in one of the great tragedies. Thornton Wilder used the same event for his novel *The Ides of March* (1948).

Wolpert, Stanley, *Nine Hours to Rama* (1962). Exciting, intricate novel detailing the nine hours preceding the fatal shooting of Mahatma Gandhi and focusing on the assassin.

## Treason

Bakeless, John E., *Turncoats, Traitors and Heroes* (1959). Well-written, exciting record of treasonous espionage in the Continental and British armies. See *Spies of the Confederacy* (1970).

Chapman, Guy, *The Dreyfus Case* (1956). The trial and conviction of an obscure Jewish officer of the French army in 1894 for betraying military secrets became "a struggle of European and later almost of cosmic importance . . . the struggle between right and wrong, justice and injustice, civilization and barbarism" (Leonard Woolf).

**Flexner, James Thomas,** *The Traitor and the Spy: Benedict Arnold and John Andre* (1953). Dual biography of the Revolutionary War general who plotted to deliver the West Point garrison to the British and the agent with whom he was working; carefully researched and dramatically presented.

**Greene, Graham,** *The Human Factor* (1978). Masterful novel about an English double agent, not unlike Kim Philby, leaking secrets to the Russians; raises questions about the nature of good and evil.

**Inglis, David,** *Roger Casement* (1974). Absorbing story of the controversial man hanged by the British in 1914 for trying to secure armed assistance from Germany for the Irish independence movement at the time the First World War broke out.

**Lindsey, Robert,** *The Falcon and the Snowman: A True Story of Friendship and Espionage* (1979). Two affluent young men sell secret documents to the Russians in this riveting real-life spy story.

**Moorehead, Alan,** *The Traitors* (rev 1963). Dramatic tale of three men — Allan Nunn May, Klaus Fuchs, and Bruno Pontecorvo — who, in the author's words "chose, with marvellous arrogance, to betray us for our own good" by passing atomic bomb information to the Russians.

**Nelson, Truman,** *The Old Man: John Brown at Harper's Ferry* (1973). How the famous abolitionist led the raid on a federal arsenal in 1859 and was captured and hung for treason by the state of Virginia; told with the immediacy of a novel.

**Roy, Jules,** *The Trial of Marshal Pétain* (1968). Exciting day-by-day account of the 1945 trial that led to the French Vichy leader's conviction for treason.

**West, Rebecca,** *The New Meaning of Treason* (rev. 1964). Dissects the cases of Lord Haw-Haw and the Soviet espionage agents in the fifties and sixties. A penetrating and provocative analysis of traitorous conduct.

# ETHNIC AMERICANS

## *Afro-Americans*

**Baldwin, James,** *Go Tell It on the Mountain* (1953). Powerfully wrought novel of young John's conversion on his fourteenth birthday and his relationships with various members of his father's Harlem fundamentalist church. *Notes of a Native Son* (1955) and *Nobody Knows My Name* (1961) are collections of intense personal essays.

**Berlin, Ira,** *Slaves Without Masters: The Free Negro in the Antebellum South* (1975). Broad-gauged study of the free black's precarious world in the South. Other important studies of the period are Eugene D. Genovese, *Roll, Jordan, Roll: The World the Slaves Made* (1974) and

Leon Litwack, *Been in the Storms So Long: The Aftermath of Slavery* (1979).

**Brown, Claude,** *Manchild in the Promised Land* (1965). Hard-hitting narrative of growing up in the Harlem streets; written with unvarnished honesty.

**Coombs, Orde and Chester Higgins, Jr.,** *Some Time Ago: A Historical Portrait of Black Americans, 1850–1950* (1981). Powerful photographs which "are not snapshots, but images communicating the essences of people, times and places" (Julius Lester).

**Demby, William,** *Beetlecreek* (1950). Compelling novel about a black boy who arrives in small West Virginia town to live with his aunt and uncle, his involvement with a strange lonely old white man, and the effect of that involvement. See *The Catacombs* (1965).

**Douglass, Frederick,** *My Bondage and My Freedom* (1855). Classic autobiography of the fugitive slave who became the preeminent black man of the nineteenth century. See Nathan Irvin Huggins, *Slave and Citizen: The Life of Frederick Douglass* (1980).

**Du Bois, W. E. B.,** *W. E. B. Du Bois: A Reader* (1970). Anthology of writings by the prolific sociologist and novelist, including selections from his classic *The Souls of Black Folk* (1903). See *Autobiography* (1968).

**Dunham, Katherine,** *Touch of Innocence* (1959). Third-person memoirs of her first twenty years. In searing, graphic prose it is a summary of growing up black in America and "one of the most exhausting life-stories I have ever read, but it is told with such complete understanding that it is clear her words are precise" (Elizabeth Janeway).

**Franklin, John Hope,** *From Slavery to Freedom* (rev. 1974). The definitive history of the black experience in the United States. For a provocative and interpretative survey see Mary F. Berry and John W. Blassingame, *Long Memory: The Black Experience in America* (1982).

**Gutman, Herbert C.,** *The Black Family in Slavery and Freedom, 1750–1925* (1976). An important study which, in contradicting earlier works that argued that slavery destroyed black family life, has brought about a reevaluation of the slave experience.

**Gwaltney, John Langston,** *Drylongso* (1980). Oral history by ordinary black Americans as told to a social scientist; it "entertains even as it instructs and enlightens, and I wouldn't be at all surprised if it should come to be regarded as a classic" (Ralph Ellison).

**Haley, Alex,** *Roots* (1976). The extraordinary book in which Haley traces his family back seven generations to a small West African village and in doing so summarizes the entire Afro-American experience.

**Harding, Vincent,** *There Is a River: The Black Struggle for Freedom in America* (1981). The historical roots of the civil rights movement. "A searing reinterpretation. . . . At once poetic and scholarly, tempered and explosive" (Eugene D. Genovese).

**Hughes, Langston,** *The Langston Hughes Reader* (1958). Poet, dramatist, novelist, and anthologist, Hughes was probably the most influential black writer of his generation. See his comic stories in *The Best of Simple* (1961) and his two-part autobiography, *The Big Sea* (1940) and *I Wonder as I Wander* (1956).

**Jackson, George,** *Soledad Brother* (1970). The letters of George Jackson from Soledad Prison are both poignant and angry. "In one of the finest pieces of black writing ever to be printed, [he] summarizes 300 years of rage for untold millions of blacks, alive and dead" (Julius Lester). See Clark Howard, *American Saturday* (1981), a provocative telling of the Jackson story.

**Morrison, Toni,** *Song of Solomon* (1977). Lyrical novel, blending allegory and fantasy, about the son of a prosperous black midwestern family and his journey through the South where he solves some old mysteries about his origins. Winner of National Book Critics Circle Award. See *Tar Baby* (1981).

**Toomer, Jean,** *Cane* (1923). Piercing, lyrical celebration of black life in stories, verses, and drama, drawing on Toomer's experiences as a teacher in Georgia.

**Walker, Alice,** *Meridian* (1976). Set mostly in the deep South and New York, this moving, affirmative novel tells the story of one woman's pilgrimage to free herself from the guilt of the past and of the development of her commitment to the poor and the black. Other fiction by this gifted poet and lyrical novelist are *In Love and Trouble* (1974), *You Can't Keep a Good Woman Down* (1981), and *The Color Purple* (1982).

**Williams, John A.,** *The Man Who Cried I Am* (1967). Passionately told story of the assassination of a black writer, one of the best American novels of the sixties. See *!Click Song* (1982).

**Wright, Richard,** *Native Son* (1940). The compelling story of Bigger Thomas, a black youth of the Chicago slums, who, victimized by prejudice and his own errors, is brought to trial for murder. *Uncle Tom's Children* (1938) and *Eight Men* (1961) are excellent collections of Wright's short fiction.

**X, Malcolm,** *Autobiography* (1965). A modern classic, written with Alex Haley, by a tough street-wise criminal who evolved into an eloquent spokesman for his people before being shot down in 1965. See Peter Goldman, *The Death and Life of Malcolm X* (1973).

## Asian-Americans

**Chen, Jack,** *The Chinese of America* (1981). The best-written, most comprehensive history of the Chinese experience in the U.S. San Francisco's Chinatown is the setting for C. Y. Lee's novel *The Flower Drum Song* (1957) and Jade Snow Wong's memoirs *Fifth Chinese Daughter* (1950) and *No Chinese Stranger* (1975).

**Houston, Jeanne Wakatsuki and James D. Houston,** *Farewell to Manzanar* (1973). Straightforward, vivid account of one woman's experiences during and after her internment in a camp for Japanese-Americans at the time of World War II. See Monica Sone's memoir, *Wiser Daughter* (1953).

**Kingston, Maxine Hong,** *The Woman Warrior: Memories of a Girlhood Among Ghosts* (1976). A Chinese-American

woman eloquently recounts memories and myths in the form of "talk stories" told her by her mother in an attempt to reconcile past and present cultures. Awarded National Book Critics Circle Award. See *China Men* (1980).

**Santos, Bienvenido N.,** *Scent of Apples* (1980). Collection of quiet stories about displaced Filipinos in the United States by a celebrated Filipino writer.

**Wilson, Robert A. and Bill Hosokawa,** *East to America: A History of the Japanese in the United States* (1980). Good, comprehensive account. See Hosokawa's *Thirty-Five Years in the Frying Pan* (1978), a collection of his columns from the *Pacific Citizen.*

## Mexican-Americans

**Acuño, Rodolfo,** *Occupied America: A History of Chicanos* (rev. 1980). The definitive history of Mexican-Americans.

**Gonzales, Rodolfo,** *I Am Joaquin: Yo Soy Joaquin: An Epic Poem with a Chronology of People and Events in Mexican and Mexican American History* (1972). Stirring poem, presented in both Spanish and English, with illustrations. See Gary Soto, *The Elements of San Joaquin* (1977).

**Rodriguez, Richard,** *Hunger of Memory: The Education of Richard Rodriguez* (1982). Sensitive autobiographical essay by a Mexican-American scholar-writer who did not learn English until he was sixteen.

**Romano V., Octavio I.,** *El Espejo/The Mirror: Selected Chicano Literature* (rev. 1972). Bilingual anthology of representative contemporary Chicano authors; includes excerpts from novels and short stories. *Aztlan: An Anthology of Mexican American Literature* (1972), edited by Luis Valdez and Stan Steiner.

**Villareal, Jose Antonio,** *Pocho* (1959). Perceptive, graceful, and honest novel of the youth and awakening of a Californian

Mexican-American boy. See *The Fifth Horseman* (1974). Other excellent novels of Chicano life are Ron Arias, *The Road to Tamazunchale* (1975) and Rudolfo Anaya, *Bless Me Ultima* (1972).

## Puerto Rican–Americans

**Bethancourt, T. Ernesto,** *Where the Deer and the Cantaloupe Play* (1981). A New York City Puerto Rican boy's fantasy of the wild west starts this "young adult" novel that can be enjoyed by readers of all ages. See *New York Too Far from Tampa Blues* (1975).

**Levine, Barry B.,** *Benjy Lopez: A Picaresque Tale of Emigration and Return* (1980). This could be called "activist nonfiction." It tells the life story of one man as he develops a positive self-image.

**Lewis, Oscar,** *La Vida: A Puerto Rican Family in the Culture of Poverty, San Juan and New York* (1966). A moving study of several branches of a large family, rendered mostly in the words of the individual members. Deep understanding of the lives and problems of the poor. Winner of the National Book Award.

**Mohr, Nicholasa,** *El Bronx Remembered* (1975). Short fictions of the everyday struggles of Puerto Ricans in the South Bronx related with humor and pathos. See *Nilda* (1975) and *In Nueva York* (1977).

**Thomas, Piri,** *Down These Mean Streets* (1967). Powerful autobiography of one man's journey from childhood to maturity in the violent world of Spanish Harlem. See *Seven Long Times* (1974).

## Irish-Americans

**Coleman, Terry,** *Going to America* (1972). Story of the refugees from the Irish potato famine of the mid-nineteenth century; their interesting, often heart-rending individual experiences make compulsive reading.

**Farrell, James T.** *Studs Lonigan* (1932–35). Trilogy of hard-hitting, naturalistic novels about the adolescence and young manhood of Studs Lonigan on Chicago's South Side from 1912 through the early thirties. Written with a feeling for the language of the streets, often in stream-of-consciousness style.

**O'Connor, Edwin,** *The Edge of Sadness* (1961). Set in the Irish-American community of an unnamed city that is obviously Boston, it tells, through the voice of Fr. Hugh Kennedy, the story of Charlie Carmody, a contentious family patriarch. Awarded the Pulitzer Prize.

**Shannon, William V.,** *The American Irish* (rev. 1964). Compassionate, well-written history which in charting the journey from immigration to assimilation, dispels the Pat-and-Mike stereotype. See William D. Griffin, *A Portrait of the Irish in America* (1981).

**Smith, Betty,** *A Tree Grows in Brooklyn* (1943). Nostalgic, warm-hearted, poetic novel about the inimitable Francie Nolan growing up in the Irish slums of Brooklyn during the first years of the century; a classic of its kind.

## Italian-Americans

**DiDonato, Pietro,** *Christ in Concrete* (1939). Written in a lyric, robust prose molded to Italian forms of speech, this first novel about bricklayers, wrote Jerre Mangione at the time of its publication, "more than any other book I have read, . . . conveys a genuine feeling about Italians in this country working and living together." Bricklayers play a part in John Fante's richly written *Wait Until Spring, Bandini* (1938) the story of an Italian mason's family in Colorado. See his *Dago Red* (1940).

**Mangione, Jerre,** *Mount Allegro* (1941). Novel which lovingly recreates a childhood in Sicilian-American neighborhood of Rochester, New York. Another boyhood, one of survival in a tough Brooklyn ghetto, is chronicled in Joseph N. Sorrentino's frank autobiography, *Up from Never* (1971).

**Pellegrini, Angelo M.,** *Americans by Choice* (1952). Gallery of candid and tender sketches of West Coast Italian-Americans of the older generation. Jo Pagano's *The Paisanos* (1940) is a series of fictional sketches of Italian family life in California.

**Puzo, Mario,** *The Fortunate Pilgrim* (1965). The "rise" of an Italian immigrant girl in New York is traced in this novel noteworthy for its feel for American city life. New York's Little Italy is the setting for Vincent Patrick's *The Pope of Greenwich Village,* a fast-paced crime novel full of sparkling street-wise dialogue, and Francine Prose, *Household Saints* (1981).

**Rolle, Andrew F.,** *The Immigrant Upraised: Italian Adventurers and Colonists in an Expanding America* (1970). Landmark study develops the thesis that the Italians' migration to the American West improved their status. The classic work in the field is Robert Foerster, *Italian Emigration of Our Times* (1919). See Rolle's psychohistory, *The Italian Americans: Troubled Roots* (1980), and Alexander De Conde's *Half Bitter, Half Sweet* (1972), a lucidly written "excursion into Italian-American history."

## Jewish Americans

**Aaron, Chester,** *About Us* (1967). Touching, beautifully written novel about the problems of a Jewish family in a Gentile community in the thirties and forties.

**Antin, Mary,** *The Promised Land* (1912). Recollections by the Russian-born writer of her life in the "old country," her emigration at age thirteen, and her new life in Boston.

**Behrman, S. N.,** *The Worcester Account* (1953). Memoirs of growing up in a small devout Jewish community in New England at the turn of the century; "a book

of warmth and nostalgia, and it is sometimes very touching" (Saul Bellow).

**Bellow, Saul,** *The Victim* (1947). Brief, intense novel about the relationship between the persecuted and the persecutor.

**Cahan, Abraham,** *The Rise of David Levinsky* (1917). The great immigrant novel about the rise of one man to the top of the garment trade reflects the great age of New York's Lower East Side between 1885 and 1915. See *Yekl, a Tale of the New York Ghetto* (1896).

**Chotzinoff, Samuel,** *A Lost Paradise* (1955). Early reminiscences of immigrant Jewish family life in the slums: a "wonderfully evocative book, perhaps the richest of its kind in English" (Irving Howe).

**Fuchs, Daniel,** *The Williamsburg Trilogy* (1934–37). Novels about Jewish slum life in New York that probe beneath the surface violence and hardship with irony and an extraordinary sense for detail.

**Hapgood, Hutchins,** *The Spirit of the Ghetto* (1902). Classic collection of sketches of Lower East Side life.

**Howe, Irving,** *World of Our Fathers* (1976). Lucid and sensitive account of the journey of the East European Jews to America and the life they found and made. A companion volume is *How We Lived: A Documentary History of Immigrant Jews in America 1880–1930* (1979).

**Malamud, Bernard,** *The Assistant* (1957). Honest novel on the theme of redemption through suffering, about a Gentile thief who robs a poor Jewish store owner, then helps him, and finally takes his place. See author's short stories collected in *The Magic Barrel* (1958) and *Idiots First* (1963).

**Potok, Chaim,** *The Chosen* (1967). Set in the Williamsburg section of Brooklyn in the 1940s, this novel about the friendship of two boys explores the tension between mysticism and rationalism and between father and son. See *The Promise* (1969),

*My Name is Asher Lev* (1972), and *The Book of Lights* (1981).

**Roiphe, Anne,** *Generation Without Memory: A Jewish Journey in Christian America* (1981). A novelist and assimilated Jew asks intelligent, provocative questions about the modern Jewish-American experience.

**Roth, Philip,** *Goodbye, Columbus* (1959). Roth's first book, a short novel and five short stories, which won the National Book Award, is marvelously observant of Jewish life, as well as energetic and witty.

**Schwartz, Delmore,** *In Dreams Begin Responsibilities and Other Stories* (1978). Eight fine delineations of New York Jews in the 1930s and forties capture the time when "intellectual children of immigrant Jews are finding their way into the larger world while casting uneasy, rueful glances over their backs" (Irving Howe).

**Yezierska, Anzia,** *Red Ribbon on a White Horse* (1950). Poignant memoir of novelist and short-story writer who immigrated to America in 1901 at age sixteen. Her chronicles of life in the ghetto and sweatshops can be sampled in *The Open Cage: An Anzia Yezierska Collection* (1979).

## Native Americans

**Andrist, Ralph K.,** *The Long Death* (1964). Swiftly paced history of the last days of the Plains Indians, who were decimated by the U.S. Army during the last half of the nineteenth century.

**Borland, Hal,** *When the Legends Die* (1963). Novel about a young Ute boy who returns to his ancestral ways, alone, in the wilderness.

**Brandon, William,** *The Last American: The Indian in American Culture* (1974). Probably the finest single-volume history of the American Indian, comprehensive and eloquent. Alvin Josephy, Jr., *The Indian Heritage in America* (1968) is also very good.

**Brown, Dee,** *Bury My Heart at Wounded Knee: An Indian History of the American West* (1971). Angry account of the settlement of the West as the Indians saw it.

**Comfort, Will Levington,** *Apache* (1931). Moving fictional biography of the Apache chieftain, Mangus Colorado (Red Sleeves), in which the author "has created for us the real Indian, his absurdity and his greatness, in a manner that few scientists and no other writers have achieved" (Oliver La Farge). Edwin Corle, *Fig Tree John* (1935) is another classic novel of the Apache.

**Cushman, Dan,** *Stay Away, Joe* (1953). Roisterous novel set in Montana, on the "return of the native" theme. An outrageous story with unbelievable characters, but full of good humor.

**Deloria, Vine, Jr.,** *Custer Died for Your Sins* (1970). Written by a Standing Rock Sioux, a former director of the National Congress of American Indians, this Indian manifesto was much read during the heyday of the Red Power movement. See *Behind the Trail of Broken Treaties: An Indian Declaration of Independence* (1974).

**Highwater, Jamake,** *Song from the Earth: American Indian Painting* (1976). Fine presentation by a Blackfoot-Cherokee writer trained in history and anthropology. His other books include *Ritual of the Wing: North American Indian Ceremonies, Music, and Dances* (1977), *Many Smokes, Many Moons: A Chronology of American Indian History Through Indian Art* (1978), *The Sweet Grass Lives On: Fifty Contemporary North American Indian Artists* (1980), and *The Primal Mind: Visions and Reality in Indian America* (1981).

**Kroeber, Theodora,** *Ishi in Two Worlds: A Biography of the Last Wild Indian in North America* (1962). Beautiful, compelling book about the last survivor of the massacred Yaki Indians of California, who came down from the hills in 1911. See

*The Inland Whale: Nine Stories Retold from California Indian Legends* (1959).

**Long Lance, Chief Buffalo Child,** *Long Lance* (1928). "Vivid, moving account of a Blackfoot Indian in whom the spirit of the tribe and the natural life of the Plains during the buffalo days were incorporated" (J. Frank Dobie).

**McNickle, Darcy,** *The Surrounded* (1936). Beautiful, dramatic novel of a young man on a western Montana reservation torn between loyalty to his tribe and the draw of wider horizons. See *Wind from an Evening Sky* (1978).

**Mails, Thomas E.,** *The Mystic Warriors of the Plains* (1972). Stunning book about the daily life of the Plains Indians with illustrations by the author. See *The People Called Apache* (1974) and *Fools Crow* (1979).

**Momaday, N. Scott, Jr.,** *The Way to Rainy Mountain* (1969). Blending legend, history, and contemporary experience, the author traces back the history of his tribe, the Kiowas, to the world they knew "after they emerged from their hollow log somewhere in the Yellowstone country." Continued in *The Names: A Memoir* (1977). Momaday, a poet of note, also wrote a Pulitzer Prize–winning novel of contemporary Indian life, *House Made of Dawn* (1968).

**Neihardt, John C.,** *Black Elk Speaks* (1932). The life story of an Oglala Sioux, a man of rare wisdom and vision, born in 1863. A memorable book.

**Sandoz, Mari,** *Cheyenne Autumn* (1953). Sympathetic account of the poignant journey of a band of Northern Cheyenne from their incarceration on the Indian Territory of Oklahoma to Yellowstone. "Not only in American history but in all history, it is hard to find stories as moving, noble and dramatic as this one" (Oliver La Farge). See *Crazy Horse* (1942), *Battle of the Little Big Horn* (1966), *The Buffalo Hunters* (1954), and *These Were the Sioux* (1961).

**Silko, Leslie Marmon,** *Ceremony* (1977). Lyrical, singular novel celebrating the author's Pueblo and Mexican heritage. See *Storyteller* (1981).

**Storm, Hyemeyohsts,** *Seven Arrows* (1972). Sort of an allegorical oral history of the author's Northern Cheyenne tribe, this beautifully illustrated volume combines the traditional teaching stories of the Plains Indian with the narrative techniques of a Western novel. See *Song of Heyoehkah* (1981). An elegant companion volume is Peter J. Powell, *People of the Sacred Mountain: A History of the Northern Chiefs and Warrior Societies 1830–1879* (1981).

**Waters, Frank,** *The Man Who Killed the Deer* (1942). Classic novel of a Pueblo Indian caught between the ritual ways of his tribe and the alien twentieth-century ways of the white man; a man who lives as a stranger to both. See *Masked Gods: Navaho and Pueblo Ceremonialism* (1950).

**Welch, James,** *Winter in the Blood* (1974). Fine novel about the identity crisis of a contemporary Indian living in Montana.

**Wilson, Edmund,** *Apologies to the Iroquois* (1960). An introduction to the lively and tragic world of the modern Iroquois of New York in which Wilson came "to understand fully what very few non-Indians seem able to realize, the intense desire of most American Indians to remain Indians, to keep their identity. . . . This is a work to be read for sheer pleasure, for the sake of a fascinating true story delightfully told" (Oliver La Farge).

## Other Americans

**Algren, Nelson,** *Never Come Morning* (1942). Story of Bruno Bicek's brutal life in the Polish section of Chicago's West Side, by "the poet of the Chicago slums."

**Cather, Willa,** *My Ántonia* (1918). Moving novel about the life of Bohemian immigrants on the Nebraska frontier farmland and its effects on the heroine, Ántonia Shimerda. One of the best-loved classics of American fiction. "No *romantic* novel ever written in America . . . is one-half as beautiful" (M. L. Mencken).

**Kuniczak, W. S.,** *My Name is Million* (1978). Illustrated history of the Poles in America.

**Marshall, Paule,** *Brown Girl, Brownstones* (1959). Finely crafted first novel about growing up black and female in a West Indian immigrant community in Brooklyn.

**Moberg, Vilhelm,** *The Emigrants* (1951). The first of a trilogy of novels about Swedish immigrants who settle on the Minnesota frontier. Continued in *Unto a Good Land* (1954) and *The Last Letter Home* (1961).

**O'Connor, Richard,** *The German-Americans* (1968). The best popular history of America's largest minority group.

**Petrakis, Harry Mark,** *A Petrakis Reader* (1978). A sampling of the author's fine short stories about Greeks in America. See his novels *Pericles on 31st Street* (1966) and *A Dream of Kings* (1967).

**Riis, Jacob,** *The Making of an American* (1901). Classic immigrant autobiography of the Danish-born journalist, photographer, and reformer who came to New York in 1870 and remained to battle slum conditions.

**Saroyan, William,** *My Name Is Aram* (1940). Charming, sentimental autobiographical fiction about a boy's days among the Armenians of Fresno, California. Other good novels of the Armenian experience are Richard Hagopian, *Faraway the Spring* (1952) and Marjorie Housepian, *A Houseful of Love* (1953).

**Williams, William Carlos,** *White Mule* (1937). Novel, the first of a trilogy, about an Alsatian husband and Norwegian wife adjusting to life in America, and in which the prose, "the lean, straight, fast-stepping American of Williams is a joy to read for itself alone" (Alfred Kazin).

# TRANSPORTATION

## Aviation

**Bryan, C. D. B.,** *The National Air and Space Museum* (1979). Lavishly illustrated history of aviation and space science based on artifacts from the museum's collection.

**Solberg, Carl,** *Conquest of the Skies: A History of Commercial Aviation in America* (1979). From the barnstormers of the twenties to the corporate giants of the seventies in a concise history.

**Time-Life Editors,** *Epic of Flight* (1980–). Superbly produced illustrated series tracing the history of aviation.

**Vecsey, George and George C. Dade,** *Getting Off the Ground: The Pioneers of Aviation Speak for Themselves* (1979). The fa-

mous and the obscure, each of whom played a part in aeronautical development, talk in "a book of almost haunting enchantment" (Ernest K. Gann).

**Wright, Orville and Wilbur Wright,** *Miracle at Kitty Hawk* (1951). The famous brothers come alive in these intimate, revealing, and absorbing letters. See Harry Combs, *Kill Devil Hill: Discovering the Secret of the Wright Brothers* (1979), a highly readable account of how they made the world's first successful airplane.

## Seafaring

**Baldwin, Leland D.,** *The Keelboat Age in Western Waters* (1941). Entertaining epic of the river migration of flatboats and rafts in early nineteenth-century America.

See Madeline S. Waggoner, *Long Haul West: The Great Canal Era* (1958).

**Clark, Merriam,** *Ford's International Cruise Guide* (annually). The standard of ocean travel. See *Ford's Freighter Travel Guide* (biennially).

**Flexner, James Thomas,** *Steamboats Come True* (rev. 1978). Award-winning historian's account of the competition to develop the first commercially successful steamboat; "more than steamboats coming true. It is the mysterious genius and initiative of humanity being realized" (R. Buckminster Fuller).

**Laing, Alexander,** *The American Heritage History of Seafaring America* (1974). Large-format, sumptuously illustrated production in the best tradition of American Heritage. See Laing's epic about clipper-ship days, *The Sea Witch* (1933), and prose works, *Clippership Men* (1945) and *American Ships* (1972).

**Kemp, Peter (ed.),** *The Oxford Companion to Ships and the Sea* (1976). First-rate, comprehensive reference volume, in dictionary form, with over 3,700 entries. A joy to browse in.

**Kennedy, Ludovic (ed.),** *A Book of Sea Journeys* (1981). Compilation of fact and fiction drawn from a wide range of sources, from Dickens to Sylvia Plath, as well as from many of the great explorers, and illustrated with prints and drawings.

**Maxtone-Graham, John,** *The Only Way to Cross* (1972). Nostalgic look at the heyday of the great luxury liners of the Atlantic.

**Mostert, Noel,** *Supership* (1974). Electrifying description of author's voyage on a super oil tanker; contains an eloquent ecological message.

**Stevenson, Robert Louis,** *The Amateur Emigrant* (1894). Entertaining recollection of the author's voyage as a second-class passenger across the Atlantic, "from the Clyde to Sandy Hook."

**Time-Life Editors,** *The Seafarers* (1978–). A series: vivid writing, colorful treasury of illustrations; from pirates to whalers, from U-boats to clippers.

**Traven, B.,** *The Death Ship* (1926). Eloquent, hard-hitting first-person narrative of an American sailor in the hellish stokehold of a derelict ship which the owners intend to sink for insurance money. A powerful novel of social protest against all government.

**Twain, Mark,** *Life on the Mississippi* (1883). A folk epic, one of the most salty and vigorous American books, about the nineteen-year-old Sam Clemens's fulfillment of his ambition to learn the river and become a Mississippi river pilot.

## Railway

**Beebe, Lucius and Charles Clegg,** *Hear the Train Blow: A Pictorial Epic of America in the Railroad Age* (1952). Elegant blend of text and pictures which felicitously recaptures a bygone era. See *Great Railroad Photographs, U.S.A.* (1964). Oliver Jensen's *The American Heritage History of Railroading in America* (1975) is also a fine pictorial survey.

**Cookridge, E. H.,** *The Orient Express* (1978). Lively life and times of the world's most famous train and its colorful passengers. Thrillers about it include Agatha Christie, *Murder on the Orient Express* (1933) and Graham Greene, *Orient Express* (1932).

**Kennedy, Ludovic (ed.),** *Railway Journeys* (1980). Delightful anthology of rail-inspired literature, from Twain to Theroux, accompanied by charming period illustrations. Another literary anthology is Bill Pronzini (ed.), *Midnight Specials* (1977).

**McCague, James,** *Moguls and Iron Men* (1964). The standard history of the building of the transcontinental railroad, an unusually colorful excursion into a high order of Americana. Other readable accounts are Dee Brown, *Hear that Lonesome Whistle Blow* (1977) and Wesley S. Griswold, *A Work of Giants* (1962).

**Norris, Frank,** *The Octopus* (1901). Powerful naturalistic classic of the battle between California wheat farmers and the railroad — the "octopus" that strangles them. Continued in *The Pit* (1903).

**Piper, Watty,** *The Little Engine that Could* (1920). Children's classic, illustrated by Ruth Sanderson, about the little blue train which tries, tries, and finally succeeds. Other old favorites are Marian Potter's *The Little Red Caboose* (1953) and Virginia Lee Burton's *Choo-Choo* (1957). A beautifully illustrated modern picture book is Donald Crews, *Freight Train* (1978).

**Schivelbusch, Wolfgang,** *The Railway Journey: Trains and Travel in the 19th Century* (1980). Beautifully designed and illustrated volume about the effect of rail travel on the public consciousness and landscape of nineteenth-century France, England, and America.

**Theroux, Paul,** *The Great Railway Bazaar: By Train Through Asia* (1975). "With the eyes and ears of the novelist and the avidity of the responsive traveller, [he] . . . awakens us to the horror, laughter, compassion at the sight of the shameless private will to live" (V. S. Pritchett). Further impressions of this exuberant, curious, and witty traveler are in *The Old Patagonian Express: By Train Through the Americas* (1979).

**Tupper, Harmon,** *To the Great Ocean: Siberia and the Trans-Siberian Railway* (1965). "Utilizes the remarkable history of the railway as a strand upon which to string much of the tale of Siberia from the 16th century empire-building days . . . to the great power politics of the 19th century" (Harrison E. Salisbury). For a delightful account of a trip on the railway see Eric Newby, *The Big Red Train Ride* (1978).

**Whitaker, Roger E. M. and Anthony Hiss,** *All Aboard with E. M. Frimbo,*

*World's Greatest Railroad Buff* (1974). The *New Yorker's* train aficionado recounts some of his most delightful journeys.

## Coach

**Banning, Captain William and George Hugh Banning,** *Six Horses* (1930). Vivid reconstruction of stagecoach days in America.

*Coaching Days of England* (1966). Elegant, huge volume chock-full of period drawings and prints, with an introduction by Anthony Burgess, celebrating the grand and curious English coaches of 1750–1850.

**Loeper, John J.,** *The Flying Machine: A Stagecoach Journey in 1774* (1976). Illustrated with period woodcuts, this charming book for young readers follows the journey from Philadelphia to New York in the stagecoach, *The Flying Machine.*

**Poole, Ernest,** *Nancy Flyer: A Stagecoach Epic* (1949). Ingratiating, colorful yarn by a Pulitzer Prize–winning novelist about stage coaching in New Hampshire before railroads took over.

**Smollett, Tobias,** *The Expedition of Humphrey Clinker* (1771). Amusing adventures of the Bramble family and Humphrey Clinker, a ragged ostler whom they pick up as postilion, as they go coaching through England and Scotland.

## Motorcycle

**Beagle, Peter,** *I See by My Outfit* (1965). Enchanting account of a 3,000-mile odyssey across the face of the nation by two young men on motor scooters.

**Gutkind, Lee,** *Bike Fever* (1973). Journal of a trip around the United States, with informative asides about motorcycle gangs, daredevils, etc.

**Pirsig, Robert,** *Zen and the Art of Motorcycle Maintenance* (1974). This "inquiry into values" is on one level the story of a month's cross-country motorcycle trip taken by the author and his son and on a deeper level, a visit to the author's past and a search for the very meaning of existence. An honest, personal, provocative book.

**Simon, Ted,** *Jupiter's Travels* (1980). Compelling recollection of English journalist's four-year motorcycle trip around the world; candid, sensitive quest for self.

**Thompson, Hunter S.,** *Hell's Angels* (1967). "A strange and terrible saga" of pop sociology and an inside view of the notorious motorcycle gang by the pioneer of gonzo journalism.

## Automobile

**Carson, Richard Burns,** *The Olympian Cars* (1976). Coffee-table book in the grand style showcasing the great American luxury automobiles of the twenties and thirties. Pierre Dumont et al., *Automobiles and Automobiling* (1965) is an album of rare photographs of fine cars.

**Murray, Spence (ed.),** *Basic Auto Repair Manual* (curr. rev.). Excellent, understandable guide to repair and maintenance. *Reader's Digest Complete Car Care Manual* (1981) is also very good.

**Partridge, Bellamy,** *Fill 'Er Up!: The Story of Fifty Years of Motoring* (1952). Delightful first-hand social history, mixing reminiscences and research, of the automobile in American life.

**Pomeroy, Laurence,** *The Grand Prix Car* (rev. 1954). The first of a three-volume English series on the history and development since 1906 of international formula racing cars. "The reigning work in the field of auto racing history" (Eliot Fremont-Smith). See L. K. Setreght, *The Grand Prix Car, 1954–1966* (1968).

**Sears, Stephen W. (ed.),** *The American Heritage History of the Automobile in America* (1977). Large, astonishingly diverse collection of auto-related illustrations.

## The Road

**Duffus, R. L.,** *The Santa Fe Trail* (rev. 1971). About one of the three great trails of the last century (the others being the Oregon Trail and the Chisholm Trail), this is the definitive book on the subject, a "vivacious and accurate chronicle of one of the great highways of commerce" (Henry Steele Commager).

**Hamblin, Dora Jane and May Jane Grunsfeld,** *The Appian Way* (1974). A felicitous recreation of the life and times of the famous Roman road. See N. H. H. Sitwell, *Roman Roads of Europe* (1981), a witty discourse on the subject.

**Holbrook, Stewart H.,** *The Old Post Road: The Story of the Boston Post Road* (1962). Colorful history of the famous post road linking Boston and New York and of the historic taverns and curious places along its course.

**Jordan, Philip D.,** *The National Road* (1948). Spirited story of the great Cumberland Road, the first turnpike constructed by the federal government.

**Moody, Ralph,** *The Old Trails West* (1964). Lively history of the overland routes used during the settlement of the West.

## On the Road

**Bruns, Roger A.,** *Knights of the Road: A Hobo History* (1980). Sophisticated, unromantic study of ramblers, tramps, and vagabonds.

**Cervantes, Miguel De,** *Don Quixote* (1615). The misadventures of the "knight-errant" of La Mancha on the road with his "squire," Sancho Panza, tilting at windmills, "rescuing" damsels in distress, "battling" hostile armies. Its humor, its colorful Spanish background, its profundity, its basic humanity have made it a tragicomic masterpiece.

**Dickens, Charles,** *The Pickwick Papers* (1837). The "perambulations, perils, travels, adventures" of the members of the Pickwick Club in a book "something nobler than a novel," which emits "that sense of everlasting youth — a sense as of the gods gone wandering in England" (G. K. Chesterton).

**Dolan, J. R.,** *The Yankee Peddlers of Early America* (1964). Lively, humorous, and carefully researched narrative of the history of the early American traveling salesman.

**Fielding, Henry,** *Tom Jones* (1749). Long, rollicking history of the lively Tom Jones, plotted like clockwork and replete with humor, adventure, and wonderful characters that he encounters in his wanderings.

**Kerouac, Jack,** *On the Road* (1957). Narrator Sal Paradise and his hero-saint Dean Moriarty roaming America with irrepressible abandon, searching for affirmation in this classic novel of the beat generation.

# CONFLICT

## Wars and Battles

**Andreyev, Leonid,** *The Red Laugh* (1904). Novel, by one of the literary masters of prerevolutionary Russia, set amid the horrors of the Russo-Japanese War.

**Aristophanes,** *Lysistrata* (411 BC). The Greek comic poet's anti–Peloponnesian War drama in which the women of Athens unite in abstaining from sexual relations with their husbands until peace with Sparta is made.

**Brecht, Bertolt,** *Mother Courage and Her Children* (1939 tr. E. Bentley 1963). Epic morality play set in seventeenth-century Europe during the Thirty Years' War traces the wanderings of Mother Courage, whose livelihood is dependent on the war, as each of her three children is corrupted by the seemingly perpetual combat.

**Caesar, Julius,** *The Gallic War* (58–44 B.C.). Straightforward, lucid commentaries on the war in which Caesar annexed Gaul to the Roman Empire. It is considered a classic of military history and concise writing. An illustrated modern translation by Anne and Peter Wiseman was published in 1980.

*The Camera at War: A History of War Photography from 1848 to the Present Day* (1980). More than 300 photographs illustrate this overview of combat photography.

**Capa, Robert,** *Images of War* (1964). Stark, moving photojournalism accompanied by text from the books and letters of the photographer who covered five wars and was killed by a mine in Indochina.

**Čapek, Karel,** *War with the Newts* (1939). Written by a Czech on the eve of the First World War, this superb satirical novel tells of a bizarre new animal that eventually swamps humanity.

**Clausewitz, Carl Von,** *On War* (1833 tr. Howard-Paret 1976). The classic study, and still relevant.

**Dayan, Moshe,** *Diary of the Sinai Campaign* (1966). Account of the 1965 war by the Israeli commander.

**Dupuy, R. Ernest,** *Encyclopedia of Military History* (1977). Everything you wanted to know about war and a few things you did not even know you wanted to know. Other good military reference books are David Eggenburger, *Dictionary of Battles* (1967) and George Bruce, *Harbottle's Dictionary of Battles* (rev. 1981).

**Euripides,** *The Trojan Women* (415 B.C.). Lament over war by those who often suffer most — the women — in a poetic drama which empties war of its glory.

**Gellhorn, Martha,** *The Face of War* (1959). Collection of pieces from four wars — by a superb foreign correspondent. A haunting panorama of tragedy and a luminous antiwar book.

**Goya, Francisco de,** *The Disasters of War* (1863). Series of etchings which scream against the inhumanity and misery of war.

**Grimmelhausen, Hans,** *Simplicissimus* (1668). Picaresque novel of the development of the eponymous hero set against the horrific backdrop of the Thirty Years' War.

**Haldeman, Joe,** *The Forever War* (1974). Award-winning antiwar war novel set in an infernal theater of war in the future. In contrast is Robert Heinlein's classic *Starship Troopers* (1959) a more glorified projection of what the army of the future might be like. For a nonfictional scenario see John W. Macvey, *Space Weapons — Space War* (1982).

**Herodotus,** *The Persian Wars* (c. 450 B.C.). A rich storehouse of interesting digressions, marvelous anecdotes, and superb descriptions of the battles of Salamis, Thermopylae, and Marathon, all rendered in a vivid narrative by "the father of history." An enduring masterpiece. See Aubrey de Selincourt, *The World of Herodotus* (1982).

**Hibbert, Christopher,** *Agincourt* (1964). Luminous reconstruction of the famous battle in which the English forces under Henry V defeated a superior force of French in 1415. Its vivid, unpedantic style and excellent illustrations make it entrancing reading.

**Homer,** *Iliad* (c. 850 B.C.). The wrath of Achilles during the long course of the Trojan War is the focus of the first and greatest epic poem. The blank verse trans-

lation by Robert Fitzgerald published in 1976 is recommended.

**Horne, Alistair,** *The Fall of Paris* (1966). Journalistic account of the siege of Paris by the German army during the Franco-Prussian War and the Commune established thereafter "told with such vivid verisimilitude that the reader feels he is inside the beleaguered city and turns the pages anxiously to learn what will be his fate" (Barbara W. Tuchman). See *Terrible Year: The Paris Commune, 1871* (1971). The standard history of the war is Michael Howard, *The Franco-Prussian War* (1961). Zola realistically depicted it in his novel, *The Downfall* (1892).

**Keegan, John,** *The Face of Battle* (1976). Was it more terrifying to stand under the cloud of arrows at Agincourt, face the leveled muskets of Waterloo, or plod on into the rain of steel at the Somme? This astounding book, which describes what a set battle is like for the man in the thick of it, is "the most brilliant evocation of military experience written in our time" (C. P. Snow). See *The Nature of War* (1981) and *Six Armies in Normandy* (1982).

**Leach, Douglas E.,** *Flintlock and Tomahawk* (1958). Expert history of King Philip's War, which 100 years before the American Revolution gave the colonists their first test of battle against the native population.

**Liddell Hart, B. H.,** *Strategy* (rev. 1967). Theory and history of military strategy illustrated by wars of the last 200 years by distinguished English military historian.

**Millis, Walter,** *Arms and Men: A Study of American Military History* (1956). A military historian's expert, well-written survey. See T. Harry Williams, *The History of American Wars from 1745 to 1968* (1981).

**Montgomery of Alamein,** *A History of Warfare* (1968). Comprehensive survey by the famous English field marshal. Other broad studies include J. F. C. Fuller, *A Military History of the Western World*

(1954–56); Walter Markov, *Battles of World History* (1979); and Theodore Ropp, *War in the Modern World* (1959).

**Pakenham, Thomas,** *The Boer War* (1980). Succinct, beautifully written account of the last great imperial war. See Deneys Reitz, *Commando: A Boer Journal of the Boer War* (1930), a simply told, true adventure classic written by a twenty-one-year-old after the war.

**Rowse, A. L.,** *Bosworth Field and the Wars of the Roses* (1966). Expert history of the long war between the houses of Lancaster and York, which ended at Bosworth in 1485 with the defeat and death of Richard III. See Shakespeare's historical tragedy, *Richard III.*

**Runciman, Sir Steven,** *The Fall of Constantinople, 1453* (1965). Smoothly told story of the siege of the great capital by the Ottomans.

**Seward, Desmond,** *The Hundred Years War: The English in France, 1337–1453* (1978). Expert history of the prolonged war, which ended with the English being expelled from almost all of France.

**Thucydides,** *History of the Peloponnesian War* (c. 410 B.C.). Dramatic recounting of the Athens-Sparta war by a former general with superb literary skill and power. "There is no prose composition in the world that I place so high as the seventh book of Thucydides. It is the *ne plus ultra* of human art" (Thomas Babington Macauley).

**Tinkle, Lon,** *Thirteen Days to Glory* (1958). Carefully planned, smoothly written account of the most celebrated disaster in American history: the siege of the Alamo and the massacre of its defenders.

**Trask, David F.,** *The War with Spain in 1898* (1981). Lively history of the Spanish-American War. See Charles Johnson Post, *The Little War of Private Post* (1960), the memoirs of a foot soldier illustrated with his vivid drawings of battle and camp scenes.

**Tucker, Glenn,** *Poltroons and Patriots: A Popular Account of the War of 1812* (1954). Narrative of the last war between England and the U.S. by a writer who has "the journalistic sense of action and of character, the readiness to find room for an anecdote" (Henry Steele Commager).

**Wedgwood, C. V.,** *The Thirty Years War* (1939). The internecine holy war, which ranged over sixteenth-century Europe, described by one of England's most literary historians in a book which is "so interesting, so easy and rewarding, to read. It is a remarkable achievement" (A. L. Rowse).

**Woodham-Smith, Cecil,** *The Reason Why* (1953). Painstakingly researched and beautifully written account of the advance of the light cavalry brigade in the Crimean War, considered one of the bravest and stupidest charges in military history. A modern classic. See Christopher Hibbert, *The Destruction of Lord Raglan: A Tragedy of the Crimean War, 1854–55* (1962). For a Russian perspective see Leo Tolstoy, *Sketches of Sevastopol* (1855).

**Xenophon,** *Anabasis* (c. 375 B.C.). He led 10,000 Greek mercenaries, hired by Cyrus the Younger to usurp the Persian throne from his brother, on a march through Persian territory to the Black Sea. The *Anabasis* is his account of that expedition and is one of the great tales of adventure in literature.

## Napoleonic Wars

**Chalfont, Lord (ed.),** *Waterloo: Battle of Three Armies* (1980). Collection of outstanding accounts by modern British, French, and German writers of the decisive battle of June 18, 1815. See David Chandler, *Waterloo: The Hundred Days* (1981). The prelude to Waterloo is the subject of Edith Saunders, *The Hundred Days: Napoleon's Final Wager for Victory* (1964).

**Cornwell, Bernard,** *Sharpe's Eagle: Richard Sharpe and the Talavera Campaign,*

*July 1809* (1981). First of a series of action-packed novels about England's Lieutenant Sharpe in a landlubber's Hornblower saga. Another good English adventure novel is Anthony Forrest, *Captain Justice* (1981).

**Delderfield, R. F.,** *The Retreat from Moscow* (1967). Dramatic account of the aftermath of the disastrous Russian campaign of 1812. See *Imperial Sunset: The Fall of Napoleon 1813–14* (1968) and *Napoleon's Marshals* (1966).

**Glover, Michael,** *The Napoleonic Wars: An Illustrated History 1792–1815* (1981). Vivid survey of the colorful era when European affairs were dominated by one man.

**Hardy, Thomas,** *The Dynasts* (1904–08). Epic drama of the Napoleonic wars in unadorned blank verse which "as poetry, drama and history . . . is a great and enriching contribution to literature" *(Cambridge History of English Literature).*

**Herold, J. Christopher,** *Bonaparte in Egypt* (1963). Fascinating, fresh retelling of a story that is both resplendent and sordid. See the elegantly illustrated *The Age of Napoleon* (1963). Herold translated and edited *The Mind of Napoleon: A Selection from His Written and Spoken Words* (1955).

**Hibbert, Christopher,** *Corunna* (1960). Reconstruction of the 1809 battle by a writer who knows how to use historical detail without letting it encumber the flow of the story. A well-written history of the war of which Corunna was a segment is Jan Read, *War in the Peninsula* (1977).

**Manceron, Claude,** *Austerlitz: The Story of a Battle* (1966). The French novelist-historian's detailed, graphic portrayal of Napoleon's most brilliant military success. See *Napoleon Recaptures Paris, March 20, 1815* (1969).

**Ségur, Philippe Paul de,** *Napoleon's Russian Campaign* (1824). Classic first-hand narrative of Bonaparte's march on Moscow and the subsequent disastrous retreat. See *With Napoleon in Russia* (1935) by the emperor's intimate, Armand de Caulaincourt.

**Terraine, John,** *Trafalgar* (1977). Nelson's decisive 1805 naval triumph vividly rendered by eyewitness accounts and superb illustrations. See Gregory Bennett, *The Battle of Trafalgar* (1977).

**Tolstoy, Leo,** *War and Peace* (1864–69). Against the backdrop of Napoleon's invasion, Tolstoy portrays the whole of Russian life. Its history, sociology, psychology, politics, philosophy, the panoramic sweep of its story, and the force and interest of its characters have made this, in the opinion of many, the greatest novel ever.

## World War I

*The American Heritage History of World War I* (1964). With text by S. L. A. Marshall, this is probably the best objective pictorial account of the war. Other good illustrated volumes are Laurence Stallings, *The First World War* (1962) and Susanne Everett, *World War I: An Illustrated History* (1981). Hanson Baldwin's *World War I: An Outline History* (1962) is also authoritative.

**Barbusse, Henri,** *Under Fire* (1917). The French novelist's brutal depiction of the soldier in the trenches. A pacifist classic.

**Blunden, Edmund,** *Undertones of War* (1928). Memoirs based on the poet's experiences with the Royal Sussex during the war.

**Boyd, Thomas,** *Through the Wheat* (1927). Classic American novel written with passionate sobriety about a psychologically deadened Marine hero.

**Brittain, Vera,** *Testament of Youth* (1933). This "autobiographical study of the years 1900–1925" is the intimate, deeply felt record of the writer's life and attempts to show what the war and the years immediately following meant to her generation.

Later years are covered in *Testament of Friendship* (1940) and *Testament of Experience* (1957).

**Chapman, Guy,** *A Passionate Prodigality: Fragments of Autobiography* (1933). Moving recollections of English writer who was in combat in the trenches.

**Cobb, Humphrey,** *Paths of Glory* (1935). Powerful antiwar novel based on a case in which three French soldiers were arrested, tried, and executed for cowardice and mutiny.

**Dos Passos, John,** *Three Soldiers* (1921). Story of three privates of very different backgrounds who go to war; all survive but are broken by Army life. An intense, socially conscious novel with some historical vignettes in which Dos Passos argues that the war was fought to protect American financial interests abroad.

**Findley, Timothy,** *The Wars* (1978). Fine novel of a young Canadian at Ypres and elsewhere and the family tragedy that haunts him.

**Fussell, Paul,** *The Great War and Modern Memory* (1975). Splendid interpretative study of the literature of the war, which attempts to demonstrate that the modern mode of irony sprang from the ashes of the innocence that was consumed in the trenches. Winner of National Book Award.

**Gardner, Brian (ed.),** *Up the Line to Death: The War Poets, 1914–1918* (1967). Owen, Sassoon, Brooke, and seventy other poets. See John Lehmann, *The English Poets of the First World War* (1982).

**Graves, Robert,** *Goodbye to All That* (1929). Autobiography written at the age of thirty-three, most of which deals with the intensity of life in trench warfare and in which Graves says goodbye to England, his own innocence, and that of his world. A classic of its kind.

**Hašek, Jaroslav,** *The Good Soldier Schweik* (1923). Epic satire on the absurdity of war that features the comic misadventures of the kindhearted Schweik, a kind of Czech Don Quixote. "To my mind the greatest comic novel of our century" (Milan Kundera).

**Horne, Alistair,** *The Price of Glory: Verdun, 1916* (1963). Carefully documented account of the long, bloody defense of the French town by the troops of Marshal Pétain.

**Manning, Frederick,** *Her Privates We* (1929). Also published as *The Middle Part of Fortune*. Hemingway said that he read this novel about fighting on the Somme front every year on the anniversary of the month when he was wounded "and it all comes back again as though . . . it were this morning before daylight and you were waiting there dry-mouthed, for it to start."

**March, William,** *Company K* (1933). Novel comprising a series of brief sketches, each of which is a first-person narrative by one of the members of Company K. "It is the only war-book I have read which has found a new form to fit the novelty of the protest. The prose is bare, lucid, without literary echoes, not an imitation but a development of 18th century prose" (Graham Greene).

**Montague, C. E.,** *Disenchantment* (1922). Beautifully written, honest commentaries on the Western Front by the chief editorial writer of the *Manchester Guardian,* who enlisted in 1914 as a private.

**Moorehead, Alan,** *Gallipoli* (1956). "The story is told superbly. Because [he] knows what a battlefield looks, smells and sounds like, the reader gets the 'feel' of the battle. There is the uncertainty, the confusion, the narrow edge between heroism and cowardice. I have read no better piece of descriptive writing about either world war than [his] account of life in the Anzac bridgehead on Gallipoli and the repulse of the first great Turkish assault!" (Drew Middleton). See Roger McDonald, *1915* (1979), a novel.

**Renn, Ludwig,** *War* (1929). Harsh, matter-of-fact novel about trench warfare endures as a devastating comment on man's inhumanity to man.

**Romains, Jules,** *Verdun* (1939). Part of his Men of Good Will cycle, this novel "is a motion picture of a great battle and the events leading up to it, a picture taken with a wide-angle lens. No single novel can give the war complete, but *Verdun* comes close to it" (Clifton Fadiman).

**Sassoon, Siegfried,** *A Long Journey: The World of an English Officer During World War I* (1981). The three semiautobiographical novels by the English poet, earlier published as *Memoirs of George Sherston,* which include the classic *Memoirs of an Infantry Officer* (1930), edited by Paul Fussell and containing contemporary photographs and illustrations.

**Solzhenitsyn, Aleksandr,** *August, 1914* (1972). Vivid portrayal of the Russians' collapse at the Battle of Tannenberg at the onset of the war. One of the exiled writer's most accessible books.

**Terraine, John,** *To Win a War: 1918, The Year of Victory* (1981). Lively account of the period when the war moved into its climax. See *Mons: The Retreat to Victory* (1961).

**Trumbo, Dalton,** *Johnny Got His Gun* (1939). Tough, compelling novel about an anonymous soldier whose body has been destroyed, but whose mind survives as a testament to the horror of war.

**Tuchman, Barbara W.,** *The Guns of August* (1962). In a skillful blend of vivid narrative, anecdotal history, and personal profiles, the story of the battles during the first month of war. The *Zimmermann Telegram* (1958) is an account of how the U.S. got into the war in 1917.

**Wolff, Leon,** *In Flanders Fields: The 1917 Campaign* (1958). The most tragic episode in British military history brought vividly to life in a work which captures the roar of battle. "It is something more than good

military history; it is epic tragedy unrolled by a master storyteller" (S. L. A. Marshall).

## World War II

**Beach, Edward L.,** *Run Silent, Run Deep* (1955). Slightly fictionalized novel by a submarine commander about underwater war patrol in the Pacific. *Submarine!* (1952) is a nonfictional account; see also Clay Blair, Jr., *Silent Victory: The U.S. Submarine War against Japan* (1975). For a vivid rendering of daily life in the undersea war from the German perspective, see Lothar-Günther Buchheim, *U-Boat War* (1978).

**Böll, Heinrich,** *Adam, Where Art Thou?* (1955). Spare, illuminating novel by the Nobel Prize–winning German writer captures the mood at the Eastern front. His first novel, one of his best, *The Train was on Time* (1949), is also about the war.

**Brown, Harry,** *A Walk in the Sun* (1944). Short novel about an American platoon dug in on an Italian beachhead, by a soldier who was also a poet.

**Burgess, Alan,** *Seven Men at Daybreak* (1961). Tensely narrated story of one of the most daring underground missions of the war — a group of Free Czechs parachuted into Czechoslovakia to assassinate S. S. General Heydrich.

**Churchill, Winston,** *The Second World War* (1948–54). Six-volume history by the only statesman to be awarded the Nobel Prize for literature.

**Clark, Ronald W.,** *The Man Who Broke Purple* (1977). The esoteric system of code breaking and other intelligence techniques are touched upon in this admirable account of one of the great cryptographic breakthroughs of the war.

**de Gaulle, Charles,** *The War Memoirs* (1958–60). "The austerity of the prose, the economy of the words, the classic beauty of the images call to mind the finest passages of Caesar's *Commentaries*" (David Schoenbrun).

**Deighton, Len,** *Fighter: The True Story of the Battle of Britain* (1978). Gracefully written account of the air battle of 1940. England at war furnishes the backdrop for two of the author's thrillers, *SS-GB* (1979) and *XPD* (1981).

**Feldt, Eric A.,** *The Coastwatchers* (1946). Classic account of the coastwatchers in the southwest Pacific who reported Japanese movements and rescued Allied airmen from behind enemy lines. See Walter Lord, *Lonely Vigil: Coastwatchers of the Solomons* (1977).

**Guderian, Heinz,** *Panzer Leader* (1952). These memoirs of Hitler's foremost tank expert are the "most vivid of the high-level German military memoirs" (Telford Taylor). See Kenneth Macksey, *Guderian: Creator of the Blitzkrieg* (1976).

**Heggen, Thomas,** *Mister Roberts* (1946). On a cargo ship in the back waters of the Pacific during the waning days of the war, Mister Roberts finds himself playing guardian angel, referee, and diplomat to some 180 men. An authentic, moving, and humorous novel.

**Heller, Joseph,** *Catch-22* (1961). Black-humor classic about a handful of bizarre Air Force officers on a tight little Mediterranean island. An uproarious, apocalyptic masterpiece which just might be "the best American novel to come out of World War II" (Nelson Algren).

**Hersey, John,** *Hiroshima* (1946). The impact of the A-bomb attack on six survivors simply and movingly related. *Men on Bataan* (1942) and *Into the Valley* (1943) are accounts garnered from his experience as a war correspondent for *Time.*

**Hillary, Richard,** *Falling Through Space* (1942). Also known as *The Last Enemy.* Written by a twenty-two-year-old R.A.F. pilot, it "goes a little below the surface, to deal not only with adventure, but with its aftermath, and its effects upon a personal

philosophy" (V. S. Pritchett). Other good personal narratives by airmen are Elmer Bendiner, *The Fall of Fortresses* (1980) and Bert Stiles, *Serenade to the Big Bird* (1952).

**Horne, Alistair,** *To Lose a Battle: France 1940* (1969). Fine reconstruction of the fall of France to the Germans.

**Irving, David,** *The War Between the Generals: Inside the Allied High Command* (1981). Fascinating book which illuminates the infighting, some rather shocking, among the top commanders.

**Jones, James,** *The Thin Red Line* (1962). This, Jones's best novel, centers on an infantry company on Guadalcanal. He wrote the narrative to a superb collection of illustrations and paintings of the war entitled *World War II* (1975). The most revealing nonfiction book about Guadalcanal is Richard Tregaskis, *Guadalcanal Diary* (1943).

**Lewin, Ronald,** *Ultra Goes to War: The Secret Story* (1979). The facts of the secret British intelligence operations, which have only been revealed in recent years. See *The American Magic: Codes, Ciphers and the Defeat of Japan* (1982). Other cryptic works are R. A. Haldane, *The Hidden War* (1978); R. V. Jones, *The Wizard War: British Scientific Intelligence, 1939–1945* (1978); and J. C. Masterman, *The Double-Cross System* (1972).

**Liddell Hart, B. H.,** *History of the Second World War* (1971). Superb recapitulation and interpretation of the events of the war. James L. Stokesbury, *A Short History of World War II* (1980) is a good concise history.

*Life Goes to War: A Pictorial History of World War II* (1977). Hundreds of photographs compiled entirely from wartime issues of the magazine with the best photojournalists.

**Lingeman, Richard, R.,** *Don't You Know There's a War Going On?* (1971). Carefully researched, well-written detailing of just about everything that happened on the American home front during the war years. See Roy Hoopes's oral history, *Americans Remember the Home Front* (1977).

**Lord, Walter,** *Incredible Victory* (1967). Minute-by-minute reconstruction of the war's most stunning naval battle — Midway. See *A Day of Infamy* (1957).

**Marshall, S. L. A.,** *Night Drop: The American Airborne Invasion of Normandy* (1962). The greatest airborne invasion in military history is the subject of this "memorable account, stunning in its force and vast in its humanity . . . you will find no better writing on war than in the last sixty-nine pages of *Night Drop*" (John Toland). See *Bastogne: The First Eight Days* (1946) and *Island Victory* (1944).

**Montagu, Ewan,** *The Man Who Never Was* (1954). Detailed account of British plans to mislead the Germans about the invasion of Sicily. Reads like a thriller.

**Moorehead, Alan,** *The March to Tunis: The North African War, 1940–1943* (1967). Splendid history by an Australian journalist whose coverage of the British campaigns in Africa and the Middle East are considered by many to be the finest military reporting of the war. *Eclipse* (1946) is an account of the final stages of the war in Europe.

**Morison, Samuel Eliot,** *The Two-Ocean War: A Short History of the U.S. Navy in the Second World War* (1963). This one-volume condensation of his fifteen-volume history is "not only a brilliant reconstruction of the greatest naval war in history, but at moments intensely dramatic" (Denis Brogan).

**Mowat, Farley,** *And No Birds Sang* (1979). The Canadian naturalist's combat memoirs are a "grim, moving, eloquent account [which] reads like a novel and fixes images on the mind like a movie — a cross between *The Red Badge of Courage* and *Apocalypse Now*" (Jean Strouse).

**Ooka, Shohei,** *Fires on the Plain* (1952). The best Japanese novel about the war, it is an account of the horrors the hero witnesses as he wanders through the jungles of Leyte; "what makes this a work of memorable strength and artistry is his attempt to discover a meaning in the panorama of agony and destruction before him" (Donald Keene).

**Plievier, Theodor,** *Stalingrad* (1948). A documentary novel, a nightmare in words, about the monumental battle in which some 450,000 people were killed. The defense of Stalingrad is the subject of Konstantin Simonov's novel *Days and Nights* (1945).

**Ryan, Cornelius,** *A Bridge Too Far* (1974). The greatest military gamble of the war, and almost the greatest disaster — Arnhem — is the subject of this solidly researched and swiftly paced journalistic narrative. See *The Last Battle* (1966).

**Sajer, Guy,** *The Forgotten Soldier* (1971). Probably the most horrifying story ever written about a war, any war, these recollections of a former Wehrmacht officer hold the reader's attention in a kind of death grip.

**Scott, Paul,** *Mask of the Warrior* (1958). Exciting psychological novel about the Japanese invasion of British-held Burma. The East Asian front is also the scene for David Piper, *Trial by Battle* (1969), Oswald Wynd, *The Blazing Air* (1981) and H. E. Bates, *The Jacaranda Tree* (1949).

**Settle, Mary Lee,** *All The Brave Promises: Memories of Aircraft Woman 2nd Class 2146391* (1966). American novelist's experiences in England during the war. "Among the few really good books to come out of the Second World War" (Alan Pryce-Jones).

**Time-Life Editors,** *World War II* (1976–). Comprehensive treatment of all aspects of the war in over twenty-five volumes of text and pictures.

**Toland, John,** *The Last 100 Days* (1966). First-rate popular account of the closing months of the war. See *Battle: The Story of the Bulge* (1959).

**Trevor-Roper, H. R.,** *The Last Days of Hitler* (1947). He conducted an official inquiry into the events leading up to Hitler's death. His "ability in combining the scraps of evidence into a continuous account is matched by the skill and lucidity with which he tells his story. And of all the stories ever told this must surely rank as one of the strangest and most fascinating" (Allan Bullock).

**Waugh, Evelyn,** *Sword of Honor* (1965). The trilogy about Guy Crouchback combines elements of farce and nostalgia in an ambitious, difficult work which is "one of the few masterpieces of recent English fiction" (Brigid Brophy). Much of the detail is based on Waugh's wartime service in the Royal Marines and the Commandos.

**Werth, Alexander,** *Russia at War, 1941–1945* (1964). Broad-gauged, profound study of the Soviet role in the war, superbly written by an English correspondent stationed in Russia during most of the war. For a Russian view see Ilya Ehrenburg, *The War: 1941–1945* (1965).

**White, William L.,** *They Were Expendable* (1942). The first book to come from the war in the Pacific, it is the story of Bataan — America's little Dunkirk — by four young officers "as told to" the author. A "tale of gallantry, hardship, action, ingenuity. Simply and forcefully told, it ranks with the great tales of war. These are the men and this is what they did" (Stephen Vincent Benét).

**Wouk, Herman,** *The Winds of War* (1971). Big popular novel with big theme, it chronicles the military and political events which led up to America's decision to enter the war, with plenty of room for family drama and love interests. The story is continued in *War and Remembrance* (1978).

## Korean War

**Deane, Philip,** *I Was a Captive in Korea* (1953). Harrowing adventures of a British war correspondent held captive by the Communists for thirty-three months in which he describes his brainwashing and torture.

**Frankel, Ernest,** *Band of Brothers* (1959). Fast, exciting war novel about the epic retreat of the U.S. Marines from the Yalu River to Hungnan. Another good novel is Jonathan Rubin, *Barking Deer* (1974).

**Goulden, Joseph C.,** *Korea: The Untold Story of the War* (1982). Fresh telling of the causes and course of the "police action" of the 1950s. See E. J. Kahn, Jr., *The Peculiar War: Impressions of a Reporter in Korea* (1952).

**Kim, Richard E.,** *The Martyred* (1964). South Korean intelligence officer assigned to find out why, of the fourteen Christian ministers captured by the Communists, two were spared from the firing squad. Not a war novel, but a Christian novel, written in flat, unemphatic language which artfully counterpoints its mythic significance.

**Marshall, S. L. A.,** *The River and the Gauntlet* (1953). Gripping reconstruction of the defeat of the eighth Army by the Chinese Communists in November, 1950, in the Battle of the Chong Chen River. See *Pork Chop Hill* (1953) and *The Military History of the Korean War* (1963).

## Vietnam War

**Bryan, C. D. B.,** *Friendly Fire* (1976). The elemental tragedy of war is sharply caught in this report of the impact on an Iowa farm family of the death of a son killed by an American artillery shell.

**Caputo, Philip,** *A Rumor of War* (1977). Magnificent memoir of a young Marine officer who found out what it was like to fight in Vietnam.

**Duncan, David Douglas,** *War Without Heroes* (1970). Album of the faces of war.

**Duncan, Donald,** *The New Legions* (1967). Illuminating book, part war stories, part exposé, by a former career Army officer and Green Beret who resigned in opposition to the war.

**Emerson, Gloria,** *Winners and Losers: Battles, Retreats, Gains, Losses and Ruins from a Long War* (1976). Powerful and passionate book about the war by a *New York Times* correspondent.

**FitzGerald, Frances,** *Fire in the Lake: The Vietnamese and the Americans in Vietnam* (1972). Brilliant historical study of the war. Pulitzer Prize, National Book Award, Bancroft Prize.

**Glasser, Ronald J.,** *365 Days* (1971). Moving account of the horrors of the war as seen and heard by an American army doctor in Japan. A portrait of the war by a doctor who spent 365 days in Vietnam and saw misery and highjinks is John A. Parrish, *12, 20 & 5* (1972).

**Greene, Graham,** *The Quiet American* (1956). Exciting thriller set in prewar Saigon about an American operative on a mysterious mission. An indictment of U.S. intervention in Asian affairs, it foresees much.

**Griffith, Philip Jones,** *Vietnam, Inc.* (1971). Photographs by a Welsh journalist who spent five years in Vietnam taking pictures from the viewpoint of that country's beleaguered civilians. Cartier-Bresson called this the greatest description of war since Goya.

**Groom, Winston,** *Better Times than These* (1978). Hard-hitting novel of combat. Other good battle novels include Robert Olen Butler, *The Alleys of Eden* (1982); James Webb, *Fields of Fire* (1978); and Richard E. Ogden, *Green Knight, Red Morning* (1981).

**Herr, Michael,** *Dispatches* (1977). Collection of tough, compassionate articles based on the author's journalistic experiences in Vietnam. Already acclaimed as a classic of its kind. Its evocation of the macabre excitement and fascination of war is masterly.

**Kovic, Ron,** *Born on the Fourth of July* (1976). The anguished testament of an all-American gung-ho marine who became a paraplegic antiwar activist.

**O'Brien, Tim,** *Going After Cacciato* (1978). Realism and fantasy in a National Book Award–winning novel about a squad of soldiers chasing after Cacciato, who has "left" the war to hike to Paris. The author, who was a foot soldier in Vietnam, recorded his impressions in *If I Die in a Combat Zone* (1973).

**Rabe, David,** *Sticks and Bones/The Basic Training of Pavlo Hummel/Streamers* (1969–76). Award-winning trilogy of plays, by a Vietnam veteran, with strong antiwar themes. Interestingly, none of the plays is set in the combat zone.

**Santoli, Al,** *Everything We Had: An Oral History of the Vietnam War by 33 American Soldiers Who Fought It* (1981). Eloquent, moving record of war by the men of battle. See Mark Baker, *Nam: The Vietnam War in the Words of the Men and Women Who Fought There* (1981).

## Revolution and Rebellion

**Arendt, Hannah,** *On Revolution* (1963). Erudite, exhilarating, demanding, this is a study of two classic models of revolution — American and French — and their lessons for the future. Another excellent theoretical study is Crane Brinton, *The Anatomy of Revolution* (rev. 1965).

**Billington, James H.,** *Fires in the Minds of Men: Origins of the Revolutionary Faith* (1980). Revolution as the major secular religion of modern times, from its "incarnation" of 1789 in Paris to the "Second Coming" of 1917 in St. Petersburg.

**Duveau, Georges,** *1848: The Making of a Revolution* (1966). Vivid, detailed account of the second French revolution, which led to the short-lived Second Republic under the rule of Louis Napoleon. Gustave Flaubert's historical novel, *The Sentimental Education* (1869), is set against the backdrop of the Revolution of 1848.

**Fall, Bernard,** *Hell in a Very Small Place* (1967). The noted historian-journalist's account of the fall of Dien Bien Phu during the Indochina War. See Jules Roy, *The Battle of Dienbienphu* (1965).

**Farwell, Bryon,** *Prisoners of the Mahdi* (1968). Highly entertaining history of the Sudan Rebellion, which led to the fall of Khartoum. See *Queen Victoria's Little Wars* (1972) and *Mr. Kipling's Army* (1981).

**Flanagan, Thomas,** *The Year of the French* (1979). The year was 1798, when three tall French ships sailed into a County Mayo harbor to help a band of desperate, romantic Irish men and women rise up against their English oppressors. This novel won the National Book Critics Circle Award.

**Fleming, Peter,** *Siege at Peking* (1959). Graphic reconstruction of the fifty-five-day siege of the diplomatic legations in Peking by the Boxers, a fanatic, antiforeign faction, in 1900.

**Gorky, Maxim,** *The Life of a Useless Man* (1917). The 1905 revolution obliquely viewed through the eyes of a repellent, cowardly, slow-witted police informer. A gripping look at provincial Russia on the brink of epochal change.

**Guevara, Ernesto,** *Episodes of the Revolutionary War* (1968). Personal, simply told recounting of Che Guevara's activity as a guerrilla in the Sierra Maestra mountains during the Cuban struggle.

**Hibbert, Christopher,** *The Great Mutiny* (1980). Absorbing account of the Sepoy Rebellion of 1857, a mutiny by Indian troops of the British Army which quickly spread to other parts of the Raj. James Leasor, *Follow the Drum* (1973) and J. G. Farrell, *The Siege of Krishnapur* (1974) are good adventure novels based on the mutiny.

**Horne, Alistair,** *A Savage War of Peace: Algeria 1954–62* (1978). Dramatic panoramic history of the tragic Algerian war against French colonists.

**James, C. L. R.,** *The Black Jacobins: Toussaint L'Ouverture and the San Diego Revolution* (1938). Dramatic Marxist history of the Haitian revolution.

**Kazantsakis, Nikos,** *Freedom or Death* (1956). Set in 1889, this epic novel of Cretan-Turkish life traces the slow maturing of a revolution in one village.

**Lawrence, T. E.,** *Revolt in the Desert* (1927). A shortened version of *Seven Pillars of Wisdom,* written a year earlier but not published until 1935, about helping the Arab revolt against the Turks during World War I.

**Levy, Alan,** *Rowboat to Prague* (1972). An American journalist's personal recollections of the Prague Spring, the brief revolt against Russian domination that was quashed by Soviet troops. See *Good Men Still Live!* (1974).

**Malraux, Andre,** *Man's Fate* (1934). Shanghai during an abortive Communist insurrection. The novel is unequalled as a study of conspiracy, of men caught in the desperate clash of ideologies, betrayal, expediency, and free will. See *The Conquerors* (1929).

**Michener, James,** *The Bridge at Andau* (1957). Gripping documentary account of the Hungarian uprising of 1956. Tamas Szabo's *Boy on the Rooftop* (1958) is a graphic recollection by a fifteen-year-old boy who was in on the action.

**Pearlman, Moshe,** *The Maccabees* (1973). Beautifully illustrated narrative of the Hanukkah epic, the revolt of the second-century Jewish guerrillas against the Seleucid Empire of Antiochus.

**Pope, Dudley,** *The Black Ship* (1964). The violent mutiny on His Majesty's ship *Hermione* in 1797, by English writer of popular sea novels.

**Prebble, John,** *Culloden* (1962). Colorful, exciting recounting of the 1746 battle in which Prince Charles's Scottish army was defeated by the duke of Cumberland. See *The Highland Clearances* (1963) and *Glencoe* (1966).

**Spence, Jonathan,** *The Gates of Heavenly Peace: The Chinese and Their Revolution 1895–1980* (1981). Masterly study of one of the longest and most important social changes of the century.

**Styron, William,** *The Confessions of Nat Turner* (1967). Controversial novel chronicling the slave rebellion of 1831 from a black point of view. Awarded the Pulitzer Prize. Arna Bontemps, *Black Thunder* (1936), is a fictional recreation of the Gabriel Insurrection of 1800 in which 1,000 slaves planned to capture Richmond, Virginia.

**Tolstoy, Leo,** *Hadzhi Murad* (1911). Superb short novel, one of Tolstoy's last, about a leader of a Cossack uprising in the Caucasus who deserts to the Russians and then attempts to return to his own people.

**Traven, B.,** *The Rebellion of the Hanged* (1936). Set in Mexico, the novel is about the exploitation of Indian lumber-camp workers at the time of the revolt against Diaz in 1910.

**Trevelyan, G. M.,** *The English Revolution, 1688–1689* (1939). The traditional Whig view of Locke, Burke, and Macauley. "In its crisp, brisk narrative which condenses the fall of a dynasty into a hundred and seventy small pages, one acknowledges the hand of a master historian" (Garrett Mattingly). For a lively reinterpretation, see J. R. Jones, *The Revolution of 1688 in England* (1974).

## American Revolution

*The American Heritage Book of the Revolutionary War* (1958). Grand pictorial panorama with a fine introduction by J. H. Plumb.

**Bailyn, Bernard,** *The Ideological Origins of the American Revolution* (1967). Lucid Pulitzer Prize–winning study. It has been said that one cannot claim to understand the revolution without having read this book.

**Bird, Harrison,** *March to Saratoga: General Burgoyne and the American Campaign* (1963). Swiftly paced account of the decisive battle of the war.

**Bradford, Sydney,** *Liberty's Road: A Guide to Revolutionary War Sites* (1976). Detailed guide to battlefields and other points of historical interest for those on pilgrimage or just armchair traveling.

**Commager, Henry Steele and Richard B. Morris (eds.),** *The Spirit of 'Seventy-Six: The Story of the American Revolution as Told by Participants* (rev. 1975). Rich in variety, this is history straight from the source. Another fine blending of contemporary accounts is George F. Scheer and Hugh F. Rankin, *Rebels and Redcoats* (1957).

**Davis, Burke,** *The Ragged Ones* (1951). Exciting novel about Nathanael Greene's southern campaign against Cornwallis. *The Cowpens-Guilford Courthouse Campaign* (1962) is a nonfictional account. Another good pair is the novel *Yorktown* (1952) and its factual counterpart *The Campaign that Won America: The Story of Yorktown* (1970). See *George Washington and the American Revolution* (1975).

**Dupuy, Colonel R. Ernest and Colonel Trevor N. Dupuy,** *The Compact History of the Revolutionary War* (1964). One-volume military history. For social history as well, see John Alden Richard, *A History of the American Revolution* (1969) and Page Smith, *A New Age Begins: A*

*People's History of the American Revolution* (1976).

**Edmonds, Walter D.,** *Drums Along the Mohawk* (1936). Classic popular novel about militia battling the British and the Indians in the Mohawk Valley of central New York.

**Fleming, Thomas,** *Beat the Last Drum: The Siege of Yorktown, 1781* (1963). Dramatic telling of the American victory over Cornwallis. See *Now We Are Enemies: The Story of Bunker Hill* (1960) and *The Forgotten Victory: The Battle for New Jersey, 1780* (1963).

**Forbes, Esther,** *Johnny Tremain* (1943). Revolutionary days in Boston and the Battle of Lexington supply the background to this exciting novel for young readers by a Pulitzer Prize–winning writer. Howard Fast's *April Morning* (1961) is also an imaginative reconstruction of the fighting at Lexington from a young participant's perspective.

**Fowler, William M.,** *Rebels Under Sail: The American Navy During the Revolution* (1976). A little-known part of the war. See *The Baron of Beacon Hill: A Biography of John Hancock* (1980).

**Gross, Robert,** *The Minutemen and Their World* (1976). View of the war through the experiences of the farmers who fought it. Awarded the Bancroft Prize.

**Maier, Pauline,** *The Old Revolutionaries: Political Lives in the Age of Samuel Adams* (1981). Beautifully written minibiographies of the earlier generation of revolutionaries who inspired the activists of 1776. See *From Resistance to Revolution* (1972).

**Nebenzahl, Kenneth and Don Higginbotham,** *The Atlas of the American Revolution* (1974). Wonderful way to follow the military progress of the war: over fifty beautifully reproduced theater-of-war maps actually published during the Revolution.

**Pancake, John S.,** *1777: The Year of the Hangman* (1977). Graceful and witty argument that 1777 could have been the crucial year in the war.

**Roberts, Kenneth,** *Arundel* (1930). Stirring recreation of Benedict Arnold's overland journey across Maine to attack Quebec. "Nobody better than he can bring a battle, a siege, a toilsome march, a wrestle with overmastering moral and material forces, vividly before us" (Allan Nevins). Continued in *Rabble in Arms* (1933). *March to Quebec* (1939) is a selection edited by Roberts from the journals of Arnold's men.

**Snow, Richard F.,** *Freelon Starbird* (1976). Fictional narrative for teenage readers about the extraordinary hardships suffered by an accidental soldier in a beaten army during the winter of 1776.

**Wheeler, Guy,** *Cato's War* (1980). Enjoyable, fast-paced novel about a British officer in the southern campaign.

# French Revolution

**Carlyle, Thomas,** *The French Revolution* (1837). More a collection of vivid portraits than a comprehensive account, it "resembles no other history. It is an epic in prose, flashing with the lightning and reverberating with the thunder of stormy events" *(Cambridge History of English Literature).*

**Dickens, Charles,** *A Tale of Two Cities* (1859). This highly colored novel of Paris and London during the Terror, modeled on Carlyle, is one of "the richest mines of misinformation I know, but grand old melodrama, and still the most popular of all historical romances" (Albert Guerard).

**Herold, J. Christopher,** *Mistress to an Age: A Life of Madame de Staël* (1958). National Book Award–winning biography that, in wittily and brilliantly exposing the dramatic personality of Germaine de Staël and relating it to the revolutions in politics, ethics, and literature she exemplified, "hands the intelligent reader a cornucopia of good reading" (Rebecca West). See *Madame de Staël on Politics, Literature and National Character* (1968), translated and edited by Monroe Berger.

**Hibbert, Christopher,** *Days of the French Revolution* (1980). Enthralling popular chronology of the events of the revolution.

**Karmel, Alex,** *My Revolution* (1970). An entertaining tour de force which uses the diary of Restif de la Bretonne to compose a fictional picture of the revolution as viewed from the underworld of Paris.

**Lefebvre, Georges,** *The French Revolution* (1951, tr. 1962–64). By an authority on the revolution; many historians consider this admirably objective work the best short history of the revolution. For a revisionist interpretation see William Doyle, *Origins of the French Revolution* (1981).

**Loomis, Stanley,** *Paris in the Terror* (1964). Excellent popular history of the horrific days following the revolution. *The Fatal Friendship* (1972) is about Marie Antoinette and Count Fersen and their flight to Verennes.

**Manceron, Claude,** *Twilight of the Old Order* (1977). First of a projected eight-volume leisurely history of the revolution by a French historian, written in the present tense and rich in characterization. Each volume is self-contained, but together they make a full picture.

**Orczy, Baroness,** *The Scarlet Pimpernel* (1905). Costume romance about the adventures of Percy Blakeney, leader of the League of the Scarlet Pimpernel — a band of young Englishmen dedicated to rescuing distressed victims of the Reign of Terror.

**Sabatini, Rafael,** *Scaramouche* (1921). Brilliant example of the Dumas *père* sword-and-cloak school of romantic fiction; its hero, full of revolutionary zeal, uses his powers to further the republican cause.

## Irish Rebellion

**McHugh, Roger (ed.),** *Dublin, 1916* (1966). Eloquent across-the-board collection of contemporary writings about the Sinn Fein Rebellion of Easter week, 1916.

**O'Casey, Sean,** *The Plough and the Stars* (1926). Powerful tragicomedy set in the tenements of Dublin during the Easter Rebellion. Its tumultuous reception made O'Casey leave Ireland for permanent voluntary exile in England.

**O'Connor, Frank,** *The Big Fellow: Michael Collins and the Irish Revolution* (rev. 1965). Lively anecdotal story of the spectacular career of the dynamic hero who died at the hands of his own countrymen in the civil war following the Easter Rebellion. Constantine Fitzgibbon's *High Heroic* (1969) is a novel about Collins.

**O'Faolain, Sean,** *A Nest of Simple Folk* (1933). Novel by the distinguished writer and staunch nationalist about a group of ordinary Irish men and women moving toward a decision to join in the rebellion.

**O'Flaherty, Liam,** *The Informer* (1925). Brutal yet compassionate story of Gypo Nolan, the destitute revolutionary, who informs on a fugitive comrade and then seeks forgiveness. See *The Stories of Liam O'Flaherty* (1956).

## Mexican Revolution

**Azuela, Mariano,** *The Underdogs* (1916). Sharp, spare novel about the leader of a band of impoverished peasants in the revolution. *The Bosses* (1917) and *The Flies* (1918) examine the revolution's political impact.

**Guzman, Martín Luis,** *The Eagle and the Serpent* (1928). Lively autobiographical vignettes about his campaigns with Pancho Villa.

Reed, John, *Insurgent Mexico* (1914). Based on Reed's experiences as a correspondent during the revolution, this "rapid fire of snap-shots" is "the best portrait in all probability that was ever to be written of the 'reckless and romantic' Villa" (Van Wyck Brooks).

Womack, John, *Zapata and the Mexican Revolution* (1969). Classic account of the legendary revolutionary leader, Emiliano Zapata.

Yañez, Agustín, *Edge of the Storm* (1947). A murder and a young woman's running away with a band of rebels are connected in this Faulknerian tale of a backwoods village at the edge of the 1910 revolution. Considered to be the greatest Mexican novel of the century.

## Russian Revolution

Moorehead, Alan, *The Russian Revolution* (1958). The most gracefully written of the many popular accounts of the revolution.

Reed, John, *Ten Days that Shook the World* (1919). Excellent journalistic account of the November coup in which the Bolsheviks seized power. Lenin recommended it as the most vivid and truthful recounting of the events.

Sukhanov, Nicolai N., *The Russian Revolution, 1917: A Personal Record* (1955). Abridgement of seven-volume memoirs by the only theoretician of any importance actually present in St. Petersburg when the revolution broke out; "a highly personal, quarrelsome, colorful record, set down with uncompromising honesty in alternative highhandedness and perceptiveness" (Bertram D. Wolfe). Other personal memoirs include Paul Miliukov, *Political Memories* (1955) and Victor Serge, *Memoirs of a Revolutionary* (1963).

Trotsky, Leon, *The History of the Russian Revolution* (1936). The three-volume English translation is available in single-volume abridgement (1959), edited by F. W. Dupee. "This will probably be Trotsky's masterpiece. A vivid narrative, heightened by excursions into Marxist interpretation, mostly very keen and even sensible. . . . *The Revolution Betrayed* [1937] is a bitter and interesting attack on the then regime in Russia, which he himself christened 'Thermidorean' " (Crane Brinton).

Wolfe, Bertram D., *Three Who Made a Revolution* (rev. 1964). A fair-minded biographical history focusing on the lives of Lenin, Trotsky, and Stalin. On its original publication in 1948, Edmund Wilson called it "the best book in its field in any language."

## Civil War

Babel, Isaac, *Red Cavalry* (1926). Based on his service with the Red Cossacks in the Russian Civil War, the novel is a masterful blend of tradition, sentiment, skepticism, violence, and gentleness by "one of the great writers of our century" (Robert Conquest).

O'Ballance, Edgar, *The Greek Civil War, 1944–1949* (1966). Vivid rendering of the postwar battling for power. See D. G. Konsoulas, *Revolution and Defeat: The Story of the Greek Communist Party* (1966).

Shakespeare, William, *Richard II* (c. 1595). Historical tragedy about the fourteenth-century English king who was overthrown by the army of Henry Bolingbroke (later Henry IV).

Wedgwood, C. V., *The King's War* (1958). With its predecessor, *The King's Peace* (1955), this is a two-paneled portrait in flowing narrative of the reign of Charles I and the English Civil War. See Ivan Roots, *The Great Rebellion, 1642–1660* (1966) and Richard Ollard, *The War Without an Enemy* (1976), a lavishly illustrated history.

Younger, Colton, *Ireland's Civil War* (1969). Lively account, rich in detail and incident, of the war among the southern Irish that followed the signing of the Anglo-Irish treaty in 1921.

## American Civil War

*The American Heritage Pictorial History of the Civil War* (1960). A remarkably handsome book of almost 1,000 illustrations and maps and a lucid, terse narrative by Bruce Catton, "it would be difficult to find a better introduction to the Civil War than this sumptuous book" (Henry Steele Commager). Awarded the rarely bestowed special Pulitzer Prize. See *The American Heritage Century Collection of Civil War Art* (1974).

**Basso, Hamilton,** *Beauregard: The Great Creole* (1933). Sympathetic, always interesting portrait of the Louisiana general who began the War Between the States by firing the first volley at Fort Sumter and was the victor at Manassas.

**Catton, Bruce,** *Centennial History of the Civil War* (1961–65). Eloquent trilogy composed of *The Coming Fury, Terrible Swift Sword,* and *Never Call Retreat.* Among his many other books on the Civil War are the Pulitzer Prize–winning *A Stillness at Appomattox* (1953) and *This Hallowed Ground* (1956).

**Chesnut, Mary Boykin,** *A Diary from Dixie* (1905). Although the diary of the wife of a Confederate cabinet member was actually written many years after the war, it remains "an extraordinary document — in its informal deportment, a masterpiece" (Edmund Wilson). A one-volume selection, edited by C. Vann Woodward, was published in 1981. See Elizabeth Muhlenfeld, *Mary Boykin Chesnut: A Biography* (1981).

**Davis, Burke,** *Sherman's March* (1980). Richly detailed narrative of the devastating trek through Georgia and the Carolinas that serves as a corrective to the romanticizing of *Gone with the Wind.* Other books by this skilled popularizer include *They Called Him Stonewall*

(1954), *Jeb Stuart* (1957), and *To Appomattox* (1959).

**Davis, William C. (ed.),** *Shadows of the Storm* (1981). Admirable first volume of a projected six-part photographic history entitled *The Images of War: 1861–1865.*

**DeForest, John William,** *Miss Ravenel's Conversion from Secession to Loyalty* (1867). Neglected novel by Union army officer, "the finest of our writers of fiction to deal seriously with the events of the Civil War" (Edmund Wilson). See his posthumously published memoirs, *A Volunteer's Adventures* (1946) and *A Union Officer in the Reconstruction* (1948).

**Donald, David,** *Charles Sumner and the Coming of the Civil War* (1960). Brilliant study of the controversial Massachusetts senator who spearheaded the Northern opposition to the South. Winner of the Pulitzer Prize.

**Eggleston, George Cary,** *Rebel's Recollections* (1874). A literate Confederate soldier's anecdotes and vivid vignettes make up "one of the most charming books ever written about the Civil War" (David Donald).

*Fodor's Civil War Sites* (1979). Invaluable *vade mecum* for touring the battlefields.

**Foote, Shelby,** *The Civil War: A Narrative* (1958–74). The opening shot at Fort Sumter through the surrender at Appomattox in a three-volume American *Iliad* by a historian who is also a gifted novelist. See his Civil War novel *Shiloh* (1952).

**Fowler, Robert H.,** *Jim Mundy* (1977). Action-filled novel about a common soldier of the Confederacy that captures the terrible tenor of the times.

**Freeman, Douglas Southall,** *Lee's Lieutenants: A Study in Command* (1942–44). Three-volume study of the remarkable commanders of General Lee's Army of Northern Virginia and the methods by which they waged — and almost won — the war.

**Henry, Robert S.,** *The Story of the Confederacy* (1932, rev. 1957). The classic account, accurate, clear, and inclusive, of the rise and fall of the Confederate states, written with rare charm and style. See *"First with the Most" Forrest* (1944).

**Higginson, Thomas Wentworth,** *Army Life in a Black Regiment* (1870). The New England writer was colonel of the first black regiment, and these memoirs taken from his diary of its southern campaign are, for the period, unusually simple and unpretentious.

**Jones, Douglas C.,** *Elkhorn Tavern* (1980). Novel which unsentimentally focuses on the anonymous homesteaders in the Missouri territories — the victims of the war — rather than the soldiers.

**Kantor, Mackinlay,** *Long Remember* (rev. 1956). About the Battle of Gettysburg, it is "undoubtedly the best historical novel of the old-fashioned, spectacular genre in American literature" (Allen Tate). Michael Shaara's Pulitzer Prize–winning novel, *Killer Angels* (1975) and Don Robertson's *The Three Days* (1959) are also about Gettysburg. See William A. Frassanito's haunting photographic recreation of the famous battleground in *Gettysburg: A Journey in Time* (1975).

**Keneally, Thomas,** *Confederates* (1980). Exciting epic novel about Antietam in the summer of 1862, one of the bloodiest battles of the war. See Don Robertson, *By Antietam Creek* (1961).

**Melville, Herman,** *Battle-Pieces and Aspects of the War* (1866). Volume of poems; "of the great American writers who lived through the war but did not participate in it, perhaps none has left a more touching record" (Alfred Kazin).

**Myrers, Robert Manson (ed.),** *The Children of Pride: A True Story of Georgia and the Civil War* (1972). Massive volume of 1,200 letters written among several brothers of one family between 1854 and 1865; an incomparable record of the rise and fall of nineteenth-century Southern civilization.

**Parish, Peter J.,** *The American Civil War* (1975). Perhaps the best single-volume history of the war. James G. Randall and David Donald, *Civil War and Reconstruction* (1969) is also very good.

**Pennell, Joseph Stanley,** *The History of Rome Hanks and Kindred Matters* (1944). Big, strange first novel, with magnificent battle scenes of Shiloh and Gettysburg, and suffused with the emotional intensity and power of a Thomas Wolfe novel.

**Wheeler, Richard,** *The Siege of Vicksburg* (1978). A you-are-there account of the critical battle, based on quotes from its participants, skillfully woven into a narrative. The author's other eyewitness histories include *Voices of the Civil War* (1976) and *Sherman's March* (1978).

**Whitman, Walt,** *Specimen Days and Collect* (1882). The poet's great diary of his observations and experiences as a volunteer nurse in the hospitals of Washington, D.C.; "there is no better book on the Civil War" (Alfred Kazin).

**Williams, T. Harry,** *Lincoln and His Generals* (1952). Fascinating portrait of Lincoln as commander-in-chief — "A full-bodied, swift-paced narrative. . . . Still, the reader will gain as clear and shrewd an overall comprehension of the Northern effort from this volume as from any other in print" (Allan Nevins). See *Hayes of the Twenty-Third: The Civil War Volunteer Officer* (1965).

**Wilson, Edmund,** *Patriotic Gore: Studies in the Literature of the American Civil War* (1962). Rich and many-sided masterpiece of personalized, interior history which Alfred Kazin called "quite the greatest single work of Wilson's unique career. . . . It makes the passion that went into the war, and the disillusionment that followed it, more effective than has any book in recent memory." See Daniel

Aaron, *The Unwritten War: American Writers and the Civil War* (1973).

## Spanish Civil War

**Barea, Arturo,** *The Forging of a Rebel* (1946). Highly personal autobiography which affords a panorama of Spain from 1890 to 1939 and "has all the impact of a powerful novel, and a range of adventure, historical and personal, such as few novelists would venture to attempt. In it is exhibited with unique completeness and articulateness the soul of a contemporary Spaniard" (Bertram D. Wolfe).

**Koestler, Arthur,** *Spanish Testament* (1938). While covering the war as an English newspaper correspondent, he was captured by the Fascists, imprisoned, and sentenced to death. Although the political analyses have dated, the autobiographical aspects — how it feels to be under sentence of death in solitary confinement — haven't. See *Dialogue with Death* (1942).

**Malraux, André,** *Man's Hope* (1937). Novel based on the distinguished French writer's experiences as a Loyalist fighter and whose "distinction springs not from his knowledge but from the quality of his sympathy; it is not a novel of Loyalist Spain he has written, but a study of contemporary man on one field of battle" (Alfred Kazin).

**Orwell, George,** *Homage to Catalonia* (1938). Orwell fought for the Loyalists and was wounded. On his return to England he wrote these recollections, a book which endures for its idealism and humanity as well as for the superior quality of its reporting.

**Thomas, Hugh,** *The Spanish Civil War* (1961). Brilliant, spacious, authoritative history of the war by a writer with "two great gifts: one for untangling political complications and presenting them clearly and another for describing battles . . . and . . . the historian's most important quality, a tremendous appetite for detail and a grasp for the essential" (Cyril Connolly). To be read with Ronald Fraser's masterly *Blood of Spain: An Oral History of the Spanish Civil War* (1979).

# SPORTS AND RECREATION

## Gardening

**Blaikie, Thomas,** *Diary of a Scotch Gardener at the French Court at the End of the 18th Century* (1932). Blaikie laid out English gardens — then all the rage in France — for the aristocracy. Something more than a mere archaeological curiosity, "it brings back the curious flavour of a period when a modern garden was diversified by grottos, hermitages, 'tombs of Mahomet,' Chinese bridges, pavilions, and little pagodas, against a background of shady boscage and wandering walks" (Peter Quennell).

**Boland, Bridget,** *Old Wive's Lore for Gardeners* (1976). Genial blend of fact and whimsy. See *Gardener's Magic and Other Old Wive's Lore* (1978).

**Crockett, James Underwood,** *Crockett's Victory Garden* (1977). First of the popular television gardener's trio of sensible, informal growing guides. See *Crockett's Indoor Garden* (1978) and *Crockett's Flower Garden* (1981).

**Fairbrother, Nan,** *Men and Gardens* (1956). Spirited look at curiosities of gardening history with delightful literary discursions. See *The Nature of Landscape Design* (1974).

**Faust, Joan Lee,** *The New York Times Book of House Plants* (1973). Excellent care and feeding manual; handsomely illustrated, concisely written. Also good is *Rodale's Encyclopedia of Indoor Gardening* (1980).

**Findhorn Community,** *The Findhorn Garden* (1975). Through contact with various nature spirits this spiritual community in northern Scotland has produced almost miraculous results with fruit, vegetables, and flowers. See *Faces of Findhorn* (1982).

**Fish, Margery,** *Carefree Gardening* (1972). Practical, well-written advice by one of England's foremost gardening writers.

**Gillespie, Janet,** *Peacock Manure and Marigolds: A "No-Poison" Guide to a Beautiful Garden* (1964). Citing her experiences with her New Hampshire garden, the author offers with enthusiasm, humor, and great charm, advice on how to garden "naturally."

**Hebb, Robert S.,** *Low Maintenance Perennials* (1974). Extremely useful how-to; clear and well written.

**Huxley, Anthony,** *Huxley's House of Plants* (1978). One of several fine books on horticulture and flowers by the son of Julian Huxley. See *An Illustrated History of Gardening* (1978), *Plant and Planet* (1975), and *Garden Terms* (1971).

**Jacob, Dorothy,** *Flowers in the Garden: A Personal Reminiscence of 70 Years of Gardening* (1971). This English horticultural autobiography is "so sincere, so personal, and so full of the observations of a practical yet reflective gardener that one feels that gardens and trees and home landscaping go far beyond the plants involved" (Katherine S. White).

**Jekyll, Gertrude,** *On Gardening* (1964). Excerpts from books by one of England's most influential gardeners of the turn of the century — books that not only retain their literary merit but remain practical as well. See *A Gardener's Testament* (1937).

**Johnson, Hugh,** *The Principles of Gardening: The Science, Practice and History of the Gardener's Art* (1979). Informative, beautifully illustrated, and a pleasure to read.

**Keswick, Maggie,** *The Chinese Garden* (1978). Handsomely illustrated volume on the history, art, and architecture of the Chinese formal garden that carefully renders scrutable what is often bewildering to Westerners.

**King, Ronald,** *The Quest for Paradise: A History of the World's Gardens* (1979). Large-format, sumptuously illustrated volume by the former secretary of the Royal Botanical Gardens at Kew.

**Krutch, Joseph Wood (ed.),** *The Gardener's World* (1960). Delightful anthology of the best writing on gardening from Homer to Thoreau, from Boccaccio to Edwin Way Teale. Great flowerbedside reading.

**Lloyd, Christopher,** *The Well-tempered Garden* (1971). Another one of those English gardeners who write so felicitously of their passion, here mixing earthy prose and advice. Still another English gardener-prose stylist is Rosemary Verey, *The Scented Garden* (1982).

**Mandry, Kathy and Joe Toto,** *How to Grow a Jelly Glass Farm* (1974). Absolutely delightful text and illustrations in a book for children about planting seeds in a variety of places — old sneakers, saucers, and jelly glasses. A charming, instructive book. Another great children's gardening book is Alice Skelsey and Gloria Huckaby, *Growing up Green* (1973).

**Mitchell, Henry,** *The Essential Earthman* (1981). The columnist for the *Washington Sunday Post* mixes dry wit with dry mulch in this collection of florid pieces.

**Organic Gardening Magazine Staff,** *The Encyclopedia of Organic Gardening* (rev. 1978). The *sine qua non* reference work for the organic gardener.

**Perényi, Eleanor,** *Green Thoughts: A Writer in the Garden* (1981). Wonderful little essays by a writer who delights in working with the soil.

*Reader's Digest Illustrated Guide to Gardening* (1978). First-rate aid, authoritative and attractive. Other *Reader's Digest* gardening books include *Encyclopedia of Garden Plants and Flowers* (1977) and *Successful House Plants* (1979).

**Sackville-West, V.,** *A Joy of Gardening* (1958). This engaging book of selections from earlier works by the semi-Bloomsbury writer brims over with the expertise, imagination, and love she showered upon her celebrated gardens at Sissinghurst. See *Country Notes* (1940), a collection of splendid essays on country life.

**Scott-James, Anne,** *The Pleasure Garden: An Illustrated History of British Gardening* (1981). Wonderful, rare essays with drawings by her husband, Osbert Lancaster, that will entrance even nongardeners. See *The Cottage Garden* (1981), a brief history of the English cottage garden.

*Sunset Magazine, New Western Garden Book* (rev. 1979). Flagship volume of series of sensible large paperbacks on almost every aspect of home gardening; although written for the western gardener, they can be used by Easterners who keep in mind climatic differences.

**Swain, Roger,** *Earthly Pleasures* (1981). Collection of "Science and the Gardener" columns from *Horticulture* magazine by a man happily adept at writing about science for the lay reader and who can write refreshingly about such familiar things as woodchucks and rotten apples.

**Takakuwa, Gisei,** *Japanese Gardens Revisited* (1974). Superb introduction to the sublime gardening of Japan, adorned with exquisite plates and useful maps. See the beautiful *The Japanese Garden* (1972) by Takeji Iwamiya and Teiji Ito and Mitchell Bring and Josse Wayenbergh, *Japanese Gardens: Design and Meaning* (1981).

**Thomas, Graham Stuart,** *Great Gardens of Britain* (1979). Handsomely illustrated with photographs and watercolors, this is an expert guided tour of the National Trust gardens by one of England's foremost horticultural writers. See Peter Coats, *Great Gardens of Britain* (1977).

**Time-Life Editors,** *Encyclopedia of Gardening* (1971–79). Virtually every aspect of horticulture is covered through easy-to-understand how-to instructions and colorful photographs in thirty volumes.

**White, Katherine S.,** *Onward and Upward in the Garden* (1979). One need not have a green thumb to enjoy this posthumous collection of pieces on the theory and practice of gardening edited and introduced by E. B. White.

**Wyman, Donald,** *Wyman's Gardening Encyclopedia* (rev. 1977). Gardening classic, covering trees, shrubs, vegetables, fruit, flowers, and the rest. Another respected single-volume encyclopedia is James and Louise Bush-Brown, *America's Garden Book* (rev. 1980), a standard work since 1939, revised by the New York Botanical Garden.

# Hunting

**Beckford, Peter,** *Thoughts on Hunting* (1781). English hunting classic, in the form of letters, by a scholar and master of foxhounds.

**Bourjaily, Vance,** *The Unnatural Enemy* (1963). A novelist's thoughts about duck hunting. See *Country Matters: Collected Reports from the Fields and Streams of Iowa and Other Places* (1973).

**Buckingham, Nash,** *The Best of Nash Buckingham* (1973). Selection of writings by one of America's foremost outdoor writers and conservationists that span ninety years of his life. Will charm any duck hunter out of his blind.

**Capstick, Peter,** *Death in the Long Grass* (1978). Exciting tales and thoughts on hunting by former professional big game hunter in Africa. A harsh corrective to the preservationists. See *Death in the Silent Places* (1981) and *Maneaters* (1982).

**Colgate, Isabel,** *The Shooting Party* (1981). Fine multi-charactered novel about three days of shooting and partying on a huge English estate in 1913.

**Dobie, J. Frank,** *The Ben Lilly Legend* (1950). Medley of fact and fable, delivered in a characteristically genial and robust narrative, about the professional bear and lion hunter of the Rockies who was "chief huntsman" to Theodore Roosevelt. Full of great yarns about an extraordinary man.

**Elman, Robert (ed.),** *The Complete Book of Hunting* (1981). International team of writers and photographers weaves technique, strategy, and woodlore in a comprehensive, richly illustrated volume.

**Faulkner, William,** *Big Woods* (1955). Not merely a collection of his hunting stories from Yoknapatawpha County, but "a unified and integrated book that contains some of his best work" (Malcolm Cowley).

**Gordon, Caroline,** *Aleck Maury, Sportsman* (1934). Fictional autobiography of a man whose long life has been dominated by his love of hunting and fishing; considered a minor masterpiece for its "superb craftsmanship, the profound character drawing, the poetry the novel achieves in the meaningful relationship of all its elements" (Peter Taylor).

**Herbert, Henry William,** *On Upland Shooting* (1951). Herbert, under the name Frank Forester, was a celebrated late-nineteenth-century writer on hunting and fishing. This collection of pieces edited by A. R. Beverley-Giddings shows his work to have remained bright and fresh.

**Lytle, John Horace,** *Point!* (1954). Delightful yarn-filled reminiscences by America's foremost pointing-dog authority of his day.

**Mitchell, John G.,** *The Hunt* (1980). Discerning, thoughtful, Hemingwayesque reporting about hunting in America.

**Renard, Jules,** *Hunting with the Fox* (1896). The French writer's poetic sketches of country life, especially animals.

**Surtees, R. S.,** *Jorrocks' Jaunts and Jollities* (1838). The collected adventures of John Jorrocks, the sporting grocer, that with vigorous and broad humor describes the nineteenth-century English sporting life, especially that of the fox hunt. See *Mr. Sponge's Sporting Tour* (1853).

**Whyte-Melville, G. J.,** *Market Harborough* (1861). One of the soldier-writer's many novels about hunting, this one is set in the Pytchley Hunt country of England. He was killed while hunting the year his *Riding Recollections* (1878) was published.

## *Fishing*

**Bergman, Ray,** *Fishing with Ray Bergman* (1970). Fine writing about angling by the author of the classic *Trout* (rev. 1952).

**Berners, Dame Juliana,** *Fishing with an Angle* (1496). Treatise by an English prioress which is, with Walton, *the* angling classic and remains one of the finest essays ever written on the sport. John McDonald's *The Origins of Angling* (1963) contains a new printing of the famous treatise.

**Burns, Eugene,** *An Angler's Anthology* (1952). Tasteful selection of pieces dating back to Berners and going right up to the mid-twentieth century. A fine illustrated anthology is Lee Eisenberg and De Courcy Taylor (eds.), *The Ultimate Fishing Book* (1981).

**Deindorfer, Robert G.,** *The Incompleat Angler: Fishing Izaak Walton's Favorite Rivers* (1977). With descriptive flair and wit, the author chronicles his hegira to the

English rivers fished by the Compleat Angler in the seventeenth century.

**Gordon, Theodore, *The Complete Fly-Fisherman*** (1947). John McDonald has collected and annotated the best writings of Gordon, who died in 1915. He was the leading American angling authority of his time and the man who introduced the dry fly in American streams. See McDonald's *Quill Gordon* (1973).

**Grey, Zane, *Zane Grey's Adventures in Fishing*** (1952). The prolific western novelist was also a deep-sea and fresh-water fisherman of note. This book gathers several of his fishing books.

**Haig-Brown, Roderick, *The River Never Sleeps*** (1971). He is more than just a great authority on angling; his book is full of rich talk and insight. See *The Master and His Fish* (1981).

**Henken, Harmon, *The Complete Fisherman's Catalog: A Source Book of Information About Tackle and Accessories*** (1977). In *Whole Earth Catalog* format; written with wit; a delight to browse.

**Holder, Charles Frederick, *The Log of a Sea Angler: Sport and Adventures in Many Seas with Spear and Rod*** (1906). Angling standard based on author's experiences in Florida, southern California, Cape Cod, and Rio Grande.

**Humphrey, William, *My Moby Dick*** (1978). Attempt to land a thirty-pound trout in a Massachusetts stream is the frame for this interesting, digressive essay on fishing and lesser things by a respected novelist. See *The Spawning Run* (1971).

**McClane, A. J., *McClane's New Standard Fishing Encyclopedia*** (rev. 1974). The sport fishers' bible, packed with colorful illustrations, comprehensive, and written in fine style by the former executive editor of *Field and Stream*. See *McClane's Secrets of Successful Fishing* (1980), *Fishing with McClane* (1975), and *Encyclopedia of Fish Cooking* (1977).

**McGuane, Tom, *An Outside Chance: Essays on Sport*** (1980). Collection of lively sporting pieces by the novelist, most of which deal with fly-fishing. His novel, *The Sporting Club* (1969), contains a good deal of fine writing about fishing and hunting.

**MacLean, Norman, *A River Runs Through It, and Other Stories*** (1976). "In our family there was no clear line between religion and fly fishing." So begins the title short novel about how MacLean learned to fish and how it figured in his relationship with his father and brother. He describes the craft of fly fishing with authority, grace, and gusto.

**Marinoso, Vincent, *The Modern Day Fly Code*** (1950). Indispensable volume for anyone serious about fly fishing. See Helen Shaw's superb *Fly-tying* (1963).

**Miller, Alfred, *Fishless Days, Angling Nights by Sparse Grey Hackle*** (1971). Witty and knowing pieces by a leading expert on trout fishing who wrote under the name of Sparse Grey Hackle.

**Schweibert, Ernest, *Trout*** (1975). The last word on the subject; three volumes, 1,745 pages on everything there is to know about America's favorite game fish in a limpid prose style and graceful illustrations. See *Matching the Hatch* (1955), *Nymphs* (1973), and *Salmon of the World* (1974).

**Scrope, William, *Days and Nights of Salmon Fishing in the Tweed*** (1843). The salmon classic, and still one of the freshest of all angling volumes. Other famous "salmoniana" include George M. L. LaBranche, *Salmon and the Dry Fly* (1951); Jock Scott, *Greased Line Fishing for Salmon* (1935); and Lee Wulfe, *The Atlantic Salmon* (1958).

**Walton, Izaak, *The Compleat Angler, or the Contemplative Man's Recreation*** (1653). An English literary monument and a favorite for over 300 years for what it reveals of the author's amusing and handsome personality rather than for its value as an angling treatise. In the fifth edition, published more than forty years later, Charles Cotton added a section about fly fishing which is still a valuable guide.

**Waterman, Charles F.,** *Fishing in America* (1975). A handsome volume, lavishly designed and containing a thoughtful text. See *Modern Fresh and Salt Water Fly Fishing* (1974) and *The Practical Book of Trout Fishing* (1977).

**Weeks, Edward,** *Fresh Water* (1968). Excellent accounts of fishing days on many waters enriched with a wealth of literary anecdotes.

## Walking

**Aurnosseau, Marcel,** *Highway into Spain* (1930). Leisurely, old-fashioned book, full of interesting literary digressions, recounting the Australian author's walk from Paris to Madrid in 1926. This volume covers France, while *Beyond the Pyrenees* (1932) takes him into Spain.

**Bharata, Swami Agehananda,** *The Ochre Robe* (rev. 1970). Autobiography of a monk, born Leopold Fischer of Vienna, who traveled the length of India on foot as a mendicant. Another peripatetic holy man is the subject of Hallam Tennyson, *India's Walking Saint: The Story of Vinoba Bhave* (1955).

**Davies, W. H.,** *The Autobiography of a Super-Tramp* (1917). Casual account, written with great charm, of an English poet's five years in the U.S., tramping about, picking crops, riding the rods, and existing on handouts.

**Fermor, Patrick Leigh,** *A Time of Gifts: On Foot from the Hook of Holland to Middle Danube* (1977). A fine writer shares his experiences, often humorous, of his solo ramble in the early thirties.

**Fletcher, Colin,** *The Man Who Walked Through Time* (1967). In words and pictures, the author relates his perceptions and awe during the two solitary months he hiked the entire length of the Grand Canyon. His *The New Complete Walker* (1974) is enlightening for anyone planning a backpacking trip.

**Garvey, Edward B.,** *Appalachian Hiker II* (1978). For anyone planning a journey along the Appalachian Trail, a valuable aid by one who walked the length of it. See Steve Sherman and Julia Older, *Appalachian Odyssey: Walking the Trail from Georgia to Maine* (1977) and Cindy Ross, *A Woman's Journey* (1982).

**Hillaby, John D.,** *A Walk Through Britain* (1969). At fifty, the author fulfilled his long-cherished dream of walking the length of England from Land's End to John O'Groats. A keen, close observer of nature, a student of history and literature, his memorial of that journey is refreshingly readable. See Hamish Brown, *Hamish's Groats End Walk: One Man and His Dog on a Hill Route Through Britain and Ireland* (1982).

**Jenkins, Peter,** *A Walk Across America* (1979). Honest, thoughtful, naive narrative about the author's walk from Connecticut to New Orleans. The second half of his trip is recounted in *The Walk West* (1981).

**Lindsay, Vachel,** *A Handy Guide for Beggars* (1916). High-spirited account of the poet's famous walks around the country in which he carried only his pamphlet *Rhymes to Be Traded for Bread*. Sometimes garrulous and mawkish, they are still fraught with bold images and the joy of the open road. See *Adventures While Preaching the Gospel of Beauty* (1914).

**Manning, Harvey,** *Backpacking: One Step at a Time* (rev. 1980). The basics clearly set out; for many, the bible of backpacking. Another favorite is Robert S. Wood, *Pleasure Packing* (rev. 1980).

**Muir, John,** *A Thousand Mile Walk to the Gulf* (1916). Recollections by the mountain man of letters of his saunter from Indiana to Florida in 1867.

**Oakes, George W. and Alexander Chapman,** *Turn Right at the Fountain* (rev.

1981). Handy guide to walking tours of twenty-one major European cities. See Adam Nicholson, *The National Trust Book of Long Walks in England, Scotland, and Wales* (1981).

**Rawicz, Slavomer,** *The Long Walk: A Gamble for Life* (1956). Unbelievable tale of human endurance: a young Pole sentenced to Siberia escaped with six others and walked 3,000 miles back to freedom.

**Ryback, Eric,** *The High Adventure of Eric Ryback: Canada to Mexico on Foot* (1971). Account of author's trek of 2,500 miles in 132 days along the John Muir Trail. See *The Ultimate Journey: Canada to Mexico down the Continental Divide* (1973).

**Zochert, Donald (ed.),** *Walking in America* (1974). Anthology of short pieces about the pleasures and adventures of peripatetic wandering; a perfect armchair walking volume.

## Running

**Bloom, Marc,** *The Marathon: What It Takes to Go the Distance* (1981). Covers everything from the great races and runners to training programs. See Bill Rodgers, *Marathoning* (1980) and Mark Kram, *Miles to Go* (1982), a novel.

**Fixx, James F.,** *The Complete Book of Running* (1977). Every aspect of running succinctly covered. See *Jim Fixx's Second Book of Running* (1980).

**Glanville, Brian,** *The Olympian* (1972). The Great English Track Novel by a knowledgeable sports enthusiast and respected writer.

**Lovesey, Peter,** *Five Kinds of Distance* (1981). A running account of five major long-distance immortals, from Deerfoot in the 1860s to Emil Zapotek in the 1950s, by an English student of sports history and creator of the Sgt. Cribb Victorian detective novels, one of which, *Wobble to Death* (1970), is about a six-day freestyle walking race.

**Sheehan, Dr. George,** *Running & Being* (1978). Enthusiastic joy-of-running book by the guru of runners. See *This Running Life* (1980).

## Bicycling

**Bridge, Raymond,** *Bike Touring: The Sierra Club Guide to Outings on Wheels* (1979). Its simple, clear style makes this the best in the field. See Sue Browder, *The American Biking Atlas & Touring Guide* (1975).

**Murphy, Dervla,** *Full Tilt: Ireland to India with a Bicycle* (1965). Wry, whimsical recollection of her realization of a childhood dream. A Scotswoman's spirited adventures across America on her collapsible bike are recounted in Christian Miller, *Daisy, Daisy* (1981).

**Sloan, Eugene,** *The All New Complete Book of Bicycling* (rev. 1980). The classic *vade mecum* for every serious cyclist. A good companion volume is John Marino et al., *John Marino's Bicycling Book* (1981).

**Smith, Robert A.,** *A Social History of the Bicycle* (1972). Beautifully illustrated volume, especially good on the early bicycling days of the 1890s.

**Sumner, Lloyd,** *The Long Ride* (1978). Account of Sumner's epic bike tour around the world, which took four years and covered almost 30,000 miles. Another fine cycling memoir is Daniel Behrman, *The Man Who Loved Bicycles* (1973).

## Winter Sports

**Caldwell, John H.,** *Cross-Country Skiing Today* (rev. 1981). The latest in equipment for touring and competition. See *Caldwell on Competitive Cross-Country Skiing* (1980).

**Fassi, Carlo,** *Figure Skating with Carlo Fassi* (1980). Written with Gregory Smith.

The noted coach of Peggy Fleming and Dorothy Hamill spells out the basics in this fine introduction to the sport. Jill Krementz, *A Very Young Skater* (1979) is a lovely photo-illustrated book for children which shows not only the glamor, but the hard work it takes to be a figure skater.

**Osgood, William E. and Leslie J. Hurley,** *The Snowshoe Book* (1975). *The* book on snowshoeing, illustrated with photographs and drawings. See *Ski Touring: An Introductory Guide* (1969).

**Ski Magazine Editors,** *Ski Magazine Encyclopedia of Skiing* (rev. 1979). From equipment to locales, from history to principles of skiing. See *Ski Magazine's Complete Book of Ski Technique* (1975).

**Snellman, Walt,** *Mastering the Mountain: The New American Teaching Method to Downhill Skiing* (1981). Clearly sets forth the basics developed over the last decade by professional ski instructors.

## Baseball

**Angell, Roger,** *The Summer Game* (1972). Collection of author's stylish pieces from the *New Yorker*. See *Five Seasons* (1977) and *Late Innings* (1982).

**Asinof, Eliot,** *Eight Men Out* (1963). Good journalistic account of the 1919 Black Sox World Series scandal.

**Bouton, Jim,** *Ball Four Plus Five: An Update 1970–1980* (1981). *Ball Four* (1970) ushered in the candid, irreverent sports memoir. Here is a new edition plus fifty pages extra about what Bouton has been up to since 1970. Other literate inside diaries are Jim Brosnan, *The Long Season* (1960) and Bill Freehan, *Behind the Mask* (1970).

**Boyd, Brendan C. and Fred C. Harris,** *The Great American Baseball Card Flipping, Trading and Bubble Gum Book* (1973). Tip-Topps nostalgia book.

**Cobb, Ty,** *My Life in Baseball: The True Record* (1961). Written with Al Stump. The great hall-of-famer tells all.

**Coover, Robert,** *The Universal Baseball Association, J. Henry Waugh, Prop.* (1968). Not really a baseball novel, it is about an accountant who has devised a baseball game played with dice. Mixing baseball with theology, it will especially delight followers of the former.

**Creamer, Robert W.,** *Babe* (1974). Lucid, intelligent biography of Babe Ruth, the best of many books about the colorful Yankee. His teammate Lou Gehrig is sensitively portrayed in Frank L. Graham's *Lou Gehrig: A Quiet Hero* (1942).

**Durant, John,** *The Story of Baseball in Words and Pictures* (rev. 1973). The standard illustrated history. See Lawrence Ritter and Donald Honig, *The Image of Their Greatness: An Illustrated History of Baseball from 1900 to the Present* (1979).

**Dykes, Jimmy,** *You Can't Steal First Base* (1967). The feisty manager's very entertaining memoirs. Other manager books include Leo Durocher, *Nice Guys Finish Last* (1975) and Norman MacLean, *Casey Stengel* (1976).

**Einstein, Charles,** *The Baseball Reader* (1980). Collection of the best pieces — essays, fiction, cartoons, photos — from *The Fireside Books of Baseball,* one of the literature's great anthologies. Other good anthologies are Jerome Holtzman (ed.), *Fielder's Choice* (1979) and Daniel Okrent and Harris Lewine (eds.), *The Ultimate Baseball Book* (1979).

**Fleming, G. H.,** *The Unforgettable Season* (1981). A day-by-day reconstruction of the 1908 season of the New York Giants in the words of the sports writers of the era may sound dull, but it is not. It was "the most exciting and calamitous race of all time," according to the author, who has lovingly and felicitously revived a vanished time.

**Gifford, Barry,** *The Neighborhood of Baseball: A Personal History of the Chicago Cubs* (1981). Gifford grew up near Wrigley Field in the fifties and delightfully mixes club history with personal anecdotes about being a diehard fan of the hapless Cubs.

**Golenblock, Peter,** *Dynasty: The New York Yankees, 1949–1964* (1975). Affectionate account of the glory years. Other Yankee-ana of note: John Mosedale, *The Greatest of All: The 1927 New York Yankees* (1975); Whitey Ford, Mickey Mantle, and Joseph Durso, *Whitey & Mickey: A Joint Autobiography of the Yankee Years* (1977); Sparky Lyle, *The Bronx Zoo* (1979); Bob Marshal, *Diary of a Yankee Hater* (1981); and Donald Honig, *The New York Yankees: An Illustrated History* (1981).

**Harris, Mark,** *The Southpaw* (1953). The first, and the best, of the Henry W. Wiggen books, the set of novels by a writer with an unfailing ear for the sound of the dugout. See *Bang the Drum Slowly* (1956).

**Hemphill, Paul,** *Long Gone* (1979). Far from the glory of the big leagues, the characters in this funny and poignant novel toil on a Class D team in Florida in the 1950s. Another novel set in the minors is Eliot Asinof, *Man on Spikes* (1955).

**Honig, Donald,** *Baseball When the Grass Was Real: Baseball from the Twenties to the Forties, Told by the Men Who Played It* (1975). Oral history brimming with wonderful anecdotes and old photographs of Depression-era players. See *Baseball Between the Lines: Baseball after World War II* (1976), *The Man in the Dugout* (1977), and *The Last Great Season* (1979), a novel.

**Kahn, Roger,** *The Boys of Summer* (1972). Loving recollection of the Dodgers of the fifties by a fine writer. See *Season in the Sun* (1977) and *The Seventh Game* (1982), a novel. More about da Bums can be found in Donald Honig, *The Brooklyn Dodgers: An Illustrated History* (1981). See David Ritz's witty novel, *The Man Who Brought the Dodgers Back to Brooklyn* (1981).

**Lardner, Ring,** *You Know Me Al* (1916). Collection of stories in the form of "a busher's letters" that details the career of a baseball tyro in the "racy" vernacular of the day.

**Lieb, Fred,** *Baseball As I Have Known It* (1977). Vivid first-hand memories of great moments and players over seven decades by the dean of baseball writers.

**Malamud, Bernard,** *The Natural* (1952). The award-winning writer's first novel was one of the first to deal with baseball in a serious manner; it remains interesting, although marred by allegory. If you like allegory mixed with baseball, try Barry Beckham, *Runner Mack* (1972); Jerome Charyn, *The Seventh Babe* (1979); and W. P. Kinsella, *Shoeless Joe* (1982).

**O'Connor, Philip,** *Stealing Home* (1979). Poignant novel about a father coaching his son's Peewee League team in suburban Ohio breathes freshness into the baseball-as-life metaphor.

**Reichler, Joseph L. (ed.),** *The Baseball Encyclopedia: The Complete and Official Record of Major League Baseball* (curr. rev.). Statistics on every one of the more than 13,000 professional players and managers. And much, much more. A fan's delight. See *The Great All-Time Baseball Record Book* (1981).

**Ritter, Lawrence S.,** *The Glory of Their Times* (1966). Interviews with old-time ball players.

**Roth, Philip,** *The Great American Novel* (1973). Wild, side-splitting, myth-drenched fantasy about the outrageous Patriot League in a wonderfully failed, baseball-loving novel.

**Tunis, John R.,** *The Kid from Tomkinsville* (1940). The kid is Roy Tucker, ace hurler, and the hero of a series of wonderful boys' baseball books by the master of the genre.

## Basketball

**Axthelm, Pete,** *The City Game* (1970). Basketball in New York City, from the Knicks to the playgrounds, graphically laid out by an accomplished sportswriter. Other books that successfully evoke inner city playground basketball are Rick Telander, *Heaven Is a Playground* (1976) and David Wolf, *Foul!: The Connie Hawkins Story* (1972).

**Halberstam, David,** *The Breaks of the Game* (1981). Passionate account of the 1979–80 season of the Portland Trail Blazers that takes a hard look at the wedding of professional sports and big business.

**Hollander, Zander,** *The Modern Encyclopedia of Basketball* (rev. 1979). Thorough one-volume reference tool handy for browsing and settling arguments. Hollander edited the *NBA's Official Encyclopedia of Pro Basketball* (rev. 1981).

**Holzman, Red,** *Defense! Defense!* (1974). A book of winning strategy and tactics by the respected pro coach. See *A View from the Bench* (1980). Not to be missed by Knicks' fans is Lewis Cole, *Dream Team* (1981), about the championship team of 1969–70.

**Isaacs, Neil D.,** *All the Moves: A History of College Basketball* (1975). Hundreds of photographs make this concise survey entertaining and informative.

**Jordan, Pat,** *Chase the Game* (1979). An unusual sport book: about failures, rather than winners. Follows three young players from Bridgeport, Connecticut, as they unsuccessfully bid for careers in the NBA.

**McPhee, John,** *A Sense of Place* (1965). Lyrical portrait of Bill Bradley at Princeton by a superb literary stylist. See Bradley's own *Life on the Run* (1976). Other "star" autobiographies of literary merit are Wilt Chamberlain, *Wilt* (1973) and Bill Russell, *Second Wind* (1979).

**Rosen, Charles,** *God, Man and Basketball Jones* (1979). A former semipro player and

prolific writer explains why pro basketball is a "perfect game." See *Have Jump Shot, Will Travel* (1975) and *A Mile Above the Rim* (1976), both novels about the pros; also *Scandals of '51* (1978) and *Players and Pretenders* (1981).

**Walton, Todd,** *Inside Moves* (1978). Exceptional Cinderella novel narrated by a disabled Vietnam vet about his friend with bad legs who, after a successful operation, becomes a pro superstar. Deeply felt, fully realized characterization and setting. Other good novels are Jay Neugeborn, *Big Man* (1966); Bob Levin, *The Best Ride to New York* (1978); Barry Beckham, *Double Dunk* (1981); and Leo Rutman, *5 Good Boys* (1982).

**Wielgus, Chuck, Jr., and Alexander Wolff,** *The In-Your-Face Basketball Book* (1980). A sly appreciation of the world of pickup basketball, from the hotshots and hot spots around the country, to its folkways and the forbidden fundamentals no coach dared to teach you.

## Boxing

**Gardner, Leonard,** *Fat City* (1969). Tightly written novel about the squalid world of third-rate boxers in a California valley town. Among the few good boxing novels are W. R. Burnett, *Iron Man* (1930); Edward Hoagland, *The Circle Home* (1960); and Budd Schulberg, *The Harder They Fall* (1947).

**Graziano, Rocky,** *Somebody Up There Likes Me* (1955). Better than average rags-to-riches autobiography of ghetto boy who fights his way to the top of big time boxing. Other superior examples of the genre are Jake La Motta, *Raging Bull* (1970) and Sugar Ray Robinson, *Sugar Ray* (1970).

**Liebling, A. J.,** *The Sweet Science* (1956). Collection of articles which originally appeared in the *New Yorker* by a superb sportswriter, masterful at describing fights.

**Shaw, George Bernard,** *Cashel Byron's Profession* (1886). After poleaxing his teacher, our hero runs away to Australia, returns to England, and becomes the most famous fighter of his age. Shaw's only novel; it was the basis of the blank verse play, *The Admirable Bashville.*

**Tunney, Gene,** *Arms for Living* (1941). Memoirs of the former heavyweight champion who retired undefeated. Other heavyweight tomes include Nat Fleischer, *John L. Sullivan, Champion of Champions* (1955); Muhammed Ali, *The Greatest* (1975); Finis Farr, *Black Champion: The Life and Times of Jack Johnson* (1964); Everett Skebran, *Rocky Marciano* (1977); and Joe Louis, *My Life History* (1978).

## Bullfighting

**Conrad, Barnaby,** *Gates of Fear* (1957). Collection of pieces about the *corrida* by an American aficionado with some experience in the bullring. See *La Fiesta Brava: The Art of Bullfighting* (1953) and *The Death of Manolete* (1957).

**Daley, Robert,** *The Swords of Spain* (1966). Not the usual bullfighting book, but a beautiful and informative blend of text and photographs that gives "the best idea of what a bullfighter's life is really like that I have read anywhere" (Barnaby Conrad).

**Hemingway, Ernest,** *Death in the Afternoon* (1932). This famous chronicle of the novelist's passion for bullfighting is really a "book about sport in general and, since this particular sport is really an art, a book about artistic appreciation and literary criticism, yes, and the art of living, of drinking, of dying, of loving the Spanish land" (Malcolm Cowley).

**Picasso, Pablo,** *Toros y Toreros* (1962). Album of sketches of bulls and bullfighters that the great Spanish painter did in the late fifties, with text by the famous matador Dominguin.

**Tynan, Kenneth,** *Bull Fever* (1955). An English litterateur's account of a dozen bullfights, the bulls and the fighters, the styles and the rivalries, as they were in the summer of 1952 in Spain.

## Football

**Blount, Roy, Jr.,** *About Three Bricks Shy of a Load* (1974). Subtitled "a highly irregular lowdown on the year the Pittsburgh Steelers were super but missed the Bowl," it is a journalistic masterpiece that brings alive the fascinating and repelling world of pro football.

**Cope, Myron,** *The Game that Was: The Early Days of Pro Football* (1970). The days before big television contracts and big salaries, the hardscrabble days of the thirties and forties.

**DeLillo, Don,** *End Zone* (1972). Visionary novel about football as ritual, set at a Texas college, and full of laughs and insights.

**DeLuca, Sam,** *The Football Handbook* (1978). A manual for the TV fan, it is the best guide, straightforward, informative, by a former AFC player and broadcaster. See Frank Barrett and Lynn Barrett, *How to Watch a Football Game* (1980).

**Kramer, Jerry,** *Instant Replay* (1968). Very literate diary of the triumphant 1967 season, kept by the Green Bay guard in order "to show what it's like to push yourself beyond endurance for [Vince Lombardi] who considers pain only something that you must shrug off."

**Lombardi, Vince,** *Run to Daylight!* (1963). One week in Green Bay's 1962 season inimitably chronicled by the Packers' legendary coach. See *Vince Lombardi on Football* (1973), edited by George L. Flynn.

**Merchant, Larry,** *And Every Day You Take Another Bite* (1971). Pomposity-deflating analysis of pro football by the popular New York sports columnist. See *The NFL Lottery* (1973).

*The NFL's Official Encyclopedia & History of Pro Football* (rev. 1977). It's all here; a cornucopia of information about the pros.

**Plimpton, George,** *Paper Lion* (1966). What it is like to play quarterback for the Detroit Lions smoothly related by jock manque Plimpton. See *Mad Dogs and Bears* (1974) and *One More July: A Football Dialogue with Bill Curry* (1977).

**Whitehead, James,** *Joiner* (1971). The father of the "good ol' boys" pigskin novels, this one about Sonny Joiner and football, booze, and wild, wild women. Others in this subgenre are Pete Gent, *North Dallas Forty* (1973) and Dan Jenkins, *Semi-Tough* (1972).

## Golf

**Alpert, Hollis et al.,** *How to Play Double Bogey Golf* (1975). Hilarious sendup of the bewildering instructional manual guaranteed to happily resign the reader to his present game.

**Bartlett, Michael,** *The Golf Book* (1980). Anthology of great golf writing that will delight any armchair duffer.

**Darwin, Bernard,** *Mostly Golf: A Bernard Darwin Anthology* (1976). Darwin was the golf correspondent for the *London Times* from 1907 to 1953 and a distinguished writer. Other collections by English literary golf writers are Henry Longhurst, *The Best of Henry Longhurst* (1978) and Peter Dolreiner, *The World of Golf: The Best of Peter Dolreiner* (1981).

**Jenkins, Dan,** *The Dogged Victims of Inexorable Fate* (1970). Collects the funny, perceptive golf pieces that this talented writer did for *Sports Illustrated* in the 1960s.

**Jones, Robert T., Jr.,** *Golf Is My Game* (1960). Unpretentious, charming memoir by the Grand Slam immortal. See *Down the Fairway* (1927).

**McCarthy, Colman,** *The Pleasures of the Game: The Theory Free Guide to Golf* (1977). Nontechnical volume by a fine writer, brimming with ideas on every aspect of the game.

**Plimpton, George,** *The Bogey Man* (1968). What happened to him during a month on the professional circuit.

**Wind, Herbert Warren,** *Herbert Warren Wind's Golf Book* (1971). The best of the *New Yorker* writer's fine pieces on the game over the decades. See *On Tour with Harry Sprague* (1958).

**Wodehouse, P. G.,** *Wodehouse on Golf* (1940). Gathers the early golf stories by the sparkling English humorist.

*The World Atlas of Golf* (1976). Guide to 170 golf courses around the world, with superb photographs and text by leading writers and players. A treat to be treasured by any golfer. See Geoffrey S. Cornish and Ronald E. Whitten, *The Golf Course* (1981).

## Horse Racing

**Ainslie, Tom,** *Ainslie's Complete Guide to Thoroughbred Racing* (rev. 1979). Wealth of information: systems, handicapping, how to read a tip sheet, and more. See *Ainslie's Encyclopedia of Thoroughbred Handicapping* (1978) and *Ainslie's New Complete Guide to Harness Racing* (1981).

**Barich, Bill,** *Laughing in the Hills* (1980). Very personal look around a northern California racetrack interspersed with luminous digressions on philosophy, the Renaissance, the state of the Union, and other things. Well-written, informative, captivating.

**Beyer, Andrew,** *My $50,000 Year at the Races* (1978). Entertaining account of how one player made out, and a great picture of back-racetrack life. See *Picking Winners: A Horse Player's Guide* (1975).

**Francis, Dick,** *The Whip Hand* (1980). The best of an award-winning series of English detective novels revolving around horses, trainers, bookies, and the turf. Francis is an ex-jockey and has written a fine autobiography, *The Sport of Queens* (1969).

**Toperoff, Sam,** *Crazy over Horses* (1969). One man's lifelong attraction to racing recollected in a funny and moving book. Paints a lively picture of the horse-racing world, especially the unusual people he has met at the racetrack.

## Tennis

**Braden, Vic,** *Vic Braden's Tennis for the Future* (1977). Helpful illustrations make this instruction manual by the PBS pro particularly valuable.

**Fadiman, Edwin, Jr.,** *The Professionals* (1973). Engaging novel about life on the pro circuit. Other entertaining tennis novels are William Brinkley, *Breakpoint* (1978); Peter Brennan, *Sudden Death* (1978); and Jane Boyer and Burt Boyer, *World Class* (1975).

**McPhee, John,** *Levels of the Game* (1969). Unsurpassed narrative of the Forest Hills match between Arthur Ashe and Clark Graebner. One of the masterpieces of sports journalism.

**Tilden, William C.,** *My Story* (1948). Memoirs of the tennis great of the twenties. See Frank Deford, *Big Bill Tilden: The Triumphs and the Tragedy* (1976). Other noteworthy court biographies are Don Budge, *A Tennis Memoir* (1967); Jack Kramer, *The Game: My 40 Years in Tennis* (1979); and Peter Rowley, *Ken Rosewall: 20 Years at the Top* (1976).

**U.S. Tennis Association,** *Official Encyclopedia of Tennis* (rev. 1979). Only major reference source for the game, it is stocked full of statistics, interesting text, and photographs.

## Other Sports

**Barnaby, Jack,** *Winning Squash Racquets* (1979). One of the best manuals for an increasingly popular racket game. Also recommended are Al Molloy, Jr., *Winning Squash* (1978) and John Truby, *The Science and Strategy of Squash* (1975).

**Byrne, Robert,** *Byrne's Standard Book of Pool and Billiards* (1978). Lively illustrated volume by a top player and professional writer.

**Chapin, Kim,** *Fast as White Lightning* (1981). Rollicking good report on stock car racing on the "good ol' boys" circuit. Informative and fun.

**Ding Shu-De et al.,** *The Chinese Book of Table Tennis* (1981). Fascinating, easy-to-follow manual that will reward beginners as well as seasoned competitors. The information on the game as played in the People's Republic of China is fascinating.

**Fischler, Stan (ed.),** *These Were the Days: The Lore of Hockey, by the Legends of the Game* (1976). A prolific hockey writer has gathered reminiscences of the good old days by the great players of the past. Among his many other books are *This Is Hockey* (1975) and *Fischler's Hockey Encyclopedia* (1975).

**Glanville, Brian,** *A Book of Soccer* (1979). Good, thorough guide to the sport by the soccer correspondent of the *Sunday Times* of London. His novel, *The Rise of Jerry Logan* (1965), and many of his short stories deal with soccer.

**Herrigel, Eugen,** *Zen in the Art of Archery* (1953). "In this wonderful little book a German philosopher who came to Japan and took up the practice of archery toward an understanding of Zen gives an illuminating account of his own experience" (D. T. Suzuki).

**Hoban, Russell,** *How Tom Beat Captain Najork and His Hired Sportsmen* (1974). Wonderfully ridiculous children's story of how young Tom defeats his Aunt Fidget Wonkham-Strong at the games of womble, muck, and sneedball. Illustrations by Quentin Blake.

**Powell, John T.,** *Inside Rugby: The Team Game* (1976). All the basics, well illustrated, make this lucid book an ideal introduction to rugby.

**Smither, Graham Buxton,** *Behind the Scenes of Gymnasts* (1981). Great action shots highlight this book about the world of gymnastics training, especially in the Eastern bloc countries.

**Wendel, Tim,** *Going for the Gold: How the United States Won at Lake Placid* (1981). Enthusiastic, behind-the-scenes chronicle of the U.S. hockey team's amazing victory at the 1980 Winter Olympics.

## Bridge

**Daniels, David,** *The Golden Age of Bridge* (1980). Popular, fascinating glimpse of the men and women who have shaped the game.

**Goren, Charles H.,** *Goren's Bridge Complete* (rev. 1973). One of many books by the man whose name is practically synonymous with contract bridge.

**Kaplan, Edgar,** *Duplicate Bridge* (1968). Considered the finest introduction to tournament bridge for the experienced rubber bridge player.

**Reese, Terence,** *Begin Bridge with Reese* (1979). Good book on basics by top British player and prolific bridge writer. See *The Most Puzzling Situations in Bridge Play* (1978) and *The Bridge Player's Alphabetical Handbook* (1981). *The Story of an Accusation* (1967) is a lively account of his role in the cheating scandal in the sixties that rocked the bridge world.

**Sontag, Alan,** *The Bridge Bum: My Life and Play* (1977). Interesting inside look into the world of tournament bridge by top player.

## Chess

**Byfield, Brian and Alan Orpin,** *Every Great Chess Player Was Once a Beginner* (1974). Superb introduction to the game for young people. Big and expensive, but its fine graphics and witty text make it a standout. For adults T. D. Harding, *Better Chess for Average Players* (1977) is excellent.

**Chernev, Irving (ed.),** *The Chess Companion* (1968). Subtitled "a merry collection of tales of chess and its players, together with a cornucopia of games, problems, epigrams and advice, topped off with the greatest games of chess ever played," it is the jolliest of a score of books by the experienced chess writer. See *The Most Instructive Games of Chess Ever Played* (1965) and *The Golden Dozen: The Twelve Greatest Chess Players of All Times* (1976).

**Cockburn, Alexander,** *Idle Passion: Chess and the Dance of Death* (1975). Through a strange and fascinating history of chess, Cockburn explores the realities of play, the drives that it serves, and the fantasies that surround it.

**Darrach, Brad,** *Bobby Fischer v. The Rest of the World* (1974). The best journalistic piece about the enigmatic chess genius. See George Steiner, *Fields of Force: Fischer and Spassky at Reykjavik* (1974) and Robert G. Wade and Kevin J. O'Connell (eds.), *Bobby Fischer's Chess Games* (1972).

**Gavin, Thomas,** *King-kill* (1977). Unusual, rich novel based on the life of the nineteenth-century chess champion, the hunchbacked William Schlumberger, who nightly manipulated the "Celebrated Automated Chess Player" in a tawdry medicine show. Other modern chess novels include John Brunner, *The Squares of the City* (1965) and James Whitfield Ellison, *Master Prim* (1968).

**Horowitz, I. A.,** *All About Chess* (1971). This "potpourri of problems and fantasies," drawn from the author's chess columns in the *Saturday Review,* is one of over forty chess books by the former U.S. titleholder and genial writer. See *How to Win at Chess* (1968), *Chess Openings* (1964), and *How to Think Ahead in Chess* (1964).

**Lawson, David,** *Paul Morphy* (1977). Biography of the nineteenth-century American chess prodigy whose games are "to the world of chess what Mozart's string quartets are to chamber music literature" (Harold C. Schoenberg). He is the subject of Frances Parkinson Keyes's romantic novel, *The Chess Players* (1960).

**Nabokov, Vladimir,** *The Defense* (1964). Dazzling, cerebral novel about a chess prodigy, first published in Russian in 1930. Another European chess novel of distinction is Stefan Zweig's *The Royal Game* (1941).

**Reti, Richard,** *Modern Ideas of Chess* (1923). Classic work by the Czech player-theoretician which changed the thinking about the game. Written in a clear and forceful style, it abounds in brilliant descriptive passages. See *Mastering the Chessboard* (1933).

**Schoenberg, Harold C.,** *Grandmasters of Chess* (1973). The distinguished music critic's fine history of modern chess in the lives of such great players as Lasker, Capablanca, and Fischer.

**Wilson, Fred (ed.),** *A Picture History of Chess* (1981). This handsome volume is more than just a picture book; its copious comments make it a concise and lively history of the game.

## Other Games

**Ainslie, Tom,** *Ainslie's Complete Hoyle* (1975). Since Edward Hoyle first codified the rules of games in 1742, many Hoyles have been published; this is a good one. Rules for cards, dice, and table games of the Western world neatly laid out.

**Bell, R. C.,** *The Boardgame Book* (1979). Written by a distinguished authority in the field of games, this specially designed book can be opened flat while you play its more than eighty games.

**Brady, Maxine,** *The Monopoly Book* (1974). Careful study of its strategies, ploys, and lore will enable the reader to buy up the entire Boardwalk.

**Bright, Greg,** *The Great Maze Book* (1975). Dazzling book of mazes to test the most discerning labyrinthian. For the unusual, see Rick and Glory Brightfield, *Amazing Mazes* (1973).

**Consumer Guide Editions,** *The Complete Book of Wargames* (1980). Complete information and reviews of over 150 of the most popular wargames on the market. See James F. Dunnigan, *The Complete Wargames Handbook* (1980).

**Grunfeld, Frederic V.,** *Games of the World* (1975). Handsomely designed book that treats games on a global scale: how to make them, how to play them.

**Hinch, Derryn,** *The Scrabble Book* (1976). Winning strategies for the world's most popular word game. See Selchow Righter Co., *Official Scrabble Players' Dictionary* (1978).

**Jacoby, Oswald and John R. Crawford,** *The Backgammon Book* (1970). One of the best introductions to the game. See Bruce Becker, *Backgammon for Blood!* (1975).

**Kurzban, Stan and Mel Rosen,** *The Complete Cruciverbalist, or How to Solve and Compose Crossword Puzzles for Fun and Profit* (1981). Helpful and amusing for the old crossword-puzzle hand. Norman Hill's *How to Solve Crossword Puzzles* (1974) is also fun. Of the many dictionaries on the market, many prefer Herbert M. Baus, *The Master Crossword Puzzle Dictionary* (1981). See Michelle Arnot, *What's Gnu?: A History of the Crossword Puzzle* (1981).

**Loyd, Sam,** *Sam Loyd's Cyclopedia of 5,000 Puzzles, Tricks & Conundrums* (1976). Classic collection. See *Best Mathe-*

*matical Puzzles of Sam Loyd* (1959), edited by Martin Gardner.

**New Games Foundation,** *The New Games Book* (1976). Totally original games that are great fun. See *More New Games and Playful Ideas* (1981).

**Rockwell, Anne,** *Games and How to Play Them* (1973). Rules and illustrations for over forty games for children. Other good books on kids' games are Arnold Arnold, *The World Book of Children's Games* (1972), and Brian and Shirley Sutton-Smith, *How to Play with Your Children: And When Not to* (1974).

**Smullyan, Raymond,** *What Is the Name of This Book?: The Riddle of Dracula and Other Logical Puzzles* (1978). "The most original, most profound, and most humorous collection of recreational logic and math problems ever written" (Martin Gardner). See *This Book Needs No Title: A Budget of Living Paradoxes* (1980) and *The Lady or the Tiger? and Other Logic Puzzles* (1982).

**Van Allsburg, Chris,** *Jumanji* (1981). Extraordinary Caldecott medal-winning drawings with their "beautiful simplicity of design, balance, texture and a subtle intelligence beyond the call of illustration" (John Gardner) distinguish this children's book about a boy and a girl and the remarkable board game "Jumanji."

**Wagenvoord, James,** *Hangin' Out: City Kids, City Games* (1974). Twenty games, from ringolevio to skillzies, carefully explained and photo-illustrated. See John Langstaff and Carol Langstaff, *Shimmy-Shimmy-Co-Ca-Pop: A Collection of Children's Street Games and Rhymes* (1973). Iona and Peter Opie's *Children's Games in Street and Playground* (1969) is a fascinating study of what really goes on when kids play.

## Hobbies

**Gossage, Howard and Jerry Mander,** *The Great International Paper Airplane Book*

(1967). No skill required to make the imaginative planes contained in this enjoyable book.

**Holdman, J. J.,** *Naturalist's Guide to Fresh-water Aquarium Fish* (1974). The standard in the field. Over 1,000 pages, numerous color plates; much more than a guide to aquarium maintenance, rather, an in-depth treatment of biology of the fish, breeding, and other aspects of care.

**Jackson, Albert and David Day,** *The Modelmaker's Handbook* (1981). Lucid text and illustrations; handsomely packaged guide to the tricks and techniques of making models — boats, planes, tanks, trains, and other vehicles, as well as figures, buildings, and much more.

**Reader's Digest Crafts and Hobbies** (1980). Expert compendium of thirty-seven traditional crafts with easy-to-understand instruction. Other *Reader's Digest* craft books include *Complete Guide to Needlework* (1979) and *Complete Guide to Sewing* (1980). See *Back to Basics: How to Learn and Enjoy Traditional American Skills* (1981).

**Schleicher, Robert,** *Model Railroading Handbook* (1975). Best introduction available to model railroading.

## Magic

**Christopher, Milbourne,** *The Illustrated History of Magic* (1973). Comprehensive history of the conjurer's art by a respected magician and writer. His other books include *Panorama of Magic* (1962) and *The Magic Book* (1977).

**Gibson, Walter B.,** *The Complete Illustrated Book of Close-up Magic* (1980). One of the best books for beginners. See *The Complete Illustrated Book of Card Magic* (1969) and *Walter Gibson's Big Book of Magic for All Ages* (1980).

**Hugard, Jean,** *The Royal Road to Card Magic* (1949). One of the best of the books by a master magic-explainer. See *The Encyclopedia of Card Tricks* (1937).

**Maskelyne, Neal and David Devant,** *Our Magic* (rev. 1946). Since its publication in 1911 this massive text by a team of great English "deceptionists" has been a standard work. See *Maskelyne on the Performance of Magic* (1981), which emphasizes the "why" rather than the "how" of magic.

**Neil, C. Lang,** *The Modern Conjurer and Drawing Room Entertainer* (1937). Hundreds of instructive photos make this a classic of the art.

## Antique Collecting

**Gash, Jonathan,** *The Judas Pair* (1977). One of a stylish series of English crime novels featuring Lovejoy, an antiques dealer, which are replete with fascinating tidbits about antiquing. Antiques dealer-sleuths also appear in Michael Delving, *No Sign of Life* (1979) and Ty Brett and Barbara Brett, *Promises to Keep* (1981).

**Ketchum, William C., Jr.,** *The Catalogue of American Antiques* (rev. 1979). More selective than Kovel (below), but many more illustrations. See *Collecting American Craft Antiques* (1980).

**Kovel, Ralph and Terry Kovel,** *The Kovel's Antique Price List* (curr. rev.). Over 45,000 price listings. A must for serious collectors. These prolific compilers and writers have also published, among others, *The Kovels' Know Your Antiques* (curr. rev.) and *The Kovels' Know Your Collectibles* (curr. rev.).

**Stillinger, Elizabeth,** *The Antiquers* (1981). Fascinating account of the lives and careers, the deals, the finds, and the collections of the men and women who were responsible for the changing taste in American antiques from 1850 to 1930.

**Theux, Will,** *How to Detect and Collect Antique Furniture* (1978). How to recognize authenticity and quality and avoid deceptive practices, plus a concise history of eighteenth- and nineteenth-century American and English furniture. A useful companion work is Thomas Voss, *Antique American Country Furniture: A Field Guide* (1978).

## Other Collecting

**Chapel, Charles E. (ed.),** *The Gun Collector's Handbook of Current Values* (curr. rev.). Latest market prices of over 3,000 weapons, abundantly illustrated.

**The Colemans,** *The Collectors Encyclopedia of Dolls* (1968). Everything you ever wanted to know about collecting dolls. *The Doll* (1977) with magnificent photographs by H. Landsloff and text by Carl Fox, is a splendid coffee-table book.

**Dance, S. Peter,** *The Collector's Encyclopedia of Shells* (1976). Finely illustrated combination reference and art book. See *The World's Shells: A Guide for Collectors* (1976). R. Tucker Abbott, *American Seashells* (rev. 1974) is a standard work.

**Erbe, Ron,** *American Premium Guide to Baseball Cards: Identification and Values, 1884–1981* (1981). Everything you need to know to spot them and buy and sell. See *Pocket Guide to Baseball Cards, 1960–1981* (1981).

**Haders, Phyllis,** *The Warner Collector's Guide to American Quilts* (1981). One volume in an excellent series of guides for antique collectors. The series includes guides to American toys, longarms, and clocks.

**Jacobs, Flora Gill,** *Dolls' Houses in America: Historic Preservation in Miniature* (1974). Large, illustrated book by the foremost authority, whose other works include *A History of Dolls' Houses* (1965) and *A Book of Dolls and Dolls' Houses* (1967).

**Krause, Chester L. and Clifford Mishler,** *Standard Catalogue of World Coins* (curr. rev.). Every coin in the world issued since the early nineteenth century. For American coins, the bibles are R. S. Yeoman's *Handbook of U.S. Coins* ("Blue Book") and *A Guide to U.S. Coins* ("Red Book"). See *Coins: An Illustrated Survey, 650 B.C. to the Present Day* (1981), published in association with British Museum Publications.

**Patterson, Jerry E.,** *Autographs: A Collector's Guide* (1973). Clear and comprehensive adviser.

**Sutton, Richard John,** *The Stamp Collectors' Encyclopedia* (1972). A valuable tool for every philatelist. See *Linn's World Stamp Almanac: A Handbook for Stamp Collectors* (rev. 1978) and David Lidman and John D. Apfelbaum, *The World of Stamps and Stamp Collecting* (1981).

**Time-Life Editions,** *The Encyclopedia of Collectibles* (1978–1980). Copiously illustrated sixteen-volume set, practical and pleasurable to read.

**Witkin, Lee D. and Barbara London,** *The Photograph Collector's Guide* (1979). Wealth of information and guidance contained in lavishly illustrated format.

## Sleuthing

**Allingham, Margery,** *The Tiger in the Smoke* (1952). Gentlemanly Albert Campion helps out Scotland Yard in this gripping story of a killer loose in fogenshrouded London; one of a long-lived series by a writer with a marvelous talent for evoking place and atmosphere.

**Blake, Nicholas,** *The Corpse in a Snowman* (1941). Blake was the *nom de crime* of poet laureate Cecil Day-Lewis, whose detective novels detailed the exploits of Nigel Strangeways.

**Carr, John Dickson,** *The Three Coffins* (1935). A baffling locked-room mystery for the inimitable Dr. Gideon Fell — a bigger-than-life figure apparently based on the author's mentor, G. K. Chesterton.

**Carvic, Heron,** *Picture Miss Seeton* (1968). Miss Seeton is a fragile, elderly English lady who seems to stumble into crimes and ends up solving them. A delightful series.

**Christie, Agatha,** *Murder at the Vicarage* (1930). One of the earliest mysteries solved by the little old lady of St. Mary Mead, the irrepressible Miss Jane Marple. Her final case was *Sleeping Murder* (1976).

**Creasey, John,** *Introducing the Toff* (1938). Another English gentleman-adventurer, the Hon. Richard Rollison, living in his Mayfair flat with his faithful valet, is featured in this prolific series.

**Queen, Ellery,** *The Adventures of Ellery Queen* (1934). The aristocratic son of Inspector Richard Queen of the N.Y.P.D. uses his amazing powers of deduction to help out dad and others in need.

**Sayers, Dorothy L.,** *Murder Must Advertise* (1933). Droll sendup of the advertising business, featuring the marvelously affected Lord Peter Wimsey, the ultimate gentleman detective of the genre.

**Treat, Lawrence,** *Crime and Puzzlement* (1981). Twenty-four solve-them-yourself picture mysteries that provide more fun than a rainy afternoon of playing "Clue."

**Wheatley, Dennis,** *Murder off Miami* (1936). This unusual book is actually a crime dossier complete with actual clues: it tests your powers of detection. Then you break the sealed section containing the name of the murderer. See *Who Killed Robert Prentice?* (1937).

## Gambling

**Algren, Nelson,** *The Man with the Golden Arm* (1949). Devastating novel of the savage, subterranean world of gamblers, junkies, alcoholics, prostitutes, and thieves, all "so terribly human that their faces, voices, shames, follies and deaths linger in your mind with a strange midnight dignity" (Carl Sandburg). National Book Award winner.

**Ankany, Nesmith C.,** *Poker Strategy: Winning with Game Theory* (1981). A clear and witty treatise by a MIT math professor wonderfully useful for five-card draw for table stakes.

**Dostoevski, Fedor,** *The Gambler* (1867). Brief novel, somewhat reflective of Dostoevski's mania for gambling, about a compulsive gambler. Two modern novels about the gambling compulsion are A. Alvarez, *Hunt* (1978) and James Guetti, *Action* (1972).

**Hoffman, William S., Jr.,** *The Loser* (1968). Memoir of a compulsive gambler, with a fascinating picture of the underworld; "the prose is only a cut above journalism and yet it has a curious power that stems . . . from [the author's] powerfully artistic mind" (Mario Puzo).

**Hutchens, John K. (ed.),** *The Gambler's Bedside Book* (1977). Anthology of more than fifty selections from the gambling literature — autobiography, fiction, profiles of gamblers, and a few how-to pieces —

which gives reader a vivid picture of the many worlds of the gambler.

**Jacoby, Oswald,** *Oswald Jacoby on Poker* (rev. 1981). The classic treatise by the doyen of gambling writers. See *Penny Ante and Up* (1979), about modified poker games.

**Longstreet, Stephen,** *Win or Lose: A Social History of Gambling in America* (1977). Amusing, anecdotal, informal. See Richard Sasuly, *Bookies and Bettors: Two Hundred Years of Gambling* (1982).

**Puzo, Mario,** *Inside Las Vegas* (1977). Engaging, illustrated trip through the mecca of American gambling.

**Richardson, Jack,** *Memoir of a Gambler* (1979). The author, a celebrated playwright, poignantly chronicles his descent into the seamier side of the gambling world, with superb characterizations and insights.

**Scarne, John,** *Scarne's New Complete Guide to Gambling* (rev. 1974). Last word on gambling by a premier authority. See *Scarne on Dice* (1974), *Guide to Casino Gambling* (1978), and *Guide to Modern Poker* (1980).

# FOOD AND WINE

## Cooking

**Adams, Ramon F.,** *Come an' Get It: The Story of the Old Cowboy Cooks* (1952). Colorful tales, true and tall, about the prairie chefs, including recipes.

**Beard, James,** *The New James Beard* (1981). Complete revision of his 1959 classic, *The James Beard Cookbook,* includes over 1,000 recipes by the dean of American food writers. Of his many other books, especially noteworthy are *Delights and Prejudices* (1969) and *Theory and Practice of Good Cooking* (1978). With

Milton Glaser and others he put together *The Cook's Catalog* (rev. 1979), a compendium of 4,000 items.

**Beck, Simone, Louisette Bertholle, and Julia Child,** *Mastering the Art of French Cooking* (1961). Two-volume, well-styled comprehensive cookbook, hailed as a masterpiece. See Mme. Beck's *Simca's Cuisine* (1972) and Mme. Bertholle's *French Cuisine for All* (1980).

**Brillat-Savarin, Jean-Anthelme,** *The Physiology of Taste: or Meditations on Transcendental Gastronomy* (1825, tr.

1944). Unique combination of recipes, aphorisms, reminiscences, history, and philosophy, which raised gastronomy to the level of an art and which "can *still* tell you just about everything you ever wanted to know about food, and a lot more that you didn't know you wanted to know" (M. F. K. Fisher). Another nineteenth-century Gallic classic is Alexandre Dumas, *Dictionary of Cuisine* (1873).

**Child, Julia,** *From Julia Child's Kitchen* (1975). All the glorious dishes she cooks on her TV series. See *Julia Child & Co.* (1978) and *Julia Child & More Co.* (1979).

**Claiborne, Craig,** *The New York Times Cookbook* (1962). With its companion, *The New York Times Cookbook* (1979), it presents thousands of great recipes from the pages of the *Times* by its food editor. See *The New York Times International Cookbook* (1971) and *The New York Times Menu Cookbook* (1966). There are also four volumes of Claiborne's favorite recipes in print.

**Conran, Terence and Caroline Conran,** *The Cook Book* (1980). Big, beautifully illustrated, informative guide to selecting, preparing, cooking, and presenting good food.

**David, Elizabeth,** *Elizabeth David Classics* (1980). Omnibus volume of *Mediterranean Food, French Country Cooking,* and *Summer Cooking* by England's leading cooking expert and "to me probably the greatest food writer we have, a purist and perfectionist, intolerant of mediocrity and totally honest, yet not above breaking with tradition to get at what she feels is the essential nature of a dish" (James Beard).

**Davidson, Alan,** *Mediterranean Seafood* (rev. 1981). Comprehensive guide to the edible sea creatures of the Mediterranean plus recipes. See *North Atlantic Seafood* (1980).

**De Pomiane, Edouard,** *French Cooking in Ten Minutes* (1938). Subtitled *Adapting to the Rhythm of Modern Life,* it is full of

recipes, wit, wisdom, and delightful irreverence.

**Fisher, M. F. K.,** *The Art of Eating* (1954). Collects *How to Cook a Wolf, Consider the Oyster, Serve It Forth, The Gastronomical Me,* and *An Alphabet for Gourmets.* All uncommonly fine books, part autobiography, part meditation, with a few recipes, by a woman who does not consider herself a food writer. W. H. Auden said of her, "I do not know of anyone in the U.S. today who writes better prose." See *With Bold Knife and Fork* (1969) and *As They Were* (1982).

**Franey, Pierre,** *The New York Times 60-Minute Gourmet* (1979). How-to-cook-fast-but-good-(generally French)-food classic. See *More 60-Minute Gourmet* (1981).

**Freeling, Nicolas,** *The Kitchen: A Delicious Account of the Author's Years as a Grand Hotel Cook* (1970). Before achieving success as the creator of the Inspector Van der Valk detective novels, Freeling worked as a chef in Europe. This is a felicitous recollection of that experience.

**Garmey, Jane,** *Great British Cooking: A Well-kept Secret* (1981). This fine book of recipes that cover a wide spectrum of British home cooking is proof that "good English food" is not a contradiction in terms. See Elizabeth Ayrton, *English Provincial Cooking* (1980).

**Gibbons, Euell,** *Stalking the Wild Asparagus* (1962). How to find, cook, and eat wild plants. Full of adventure and appreciation for nature. See *Stalking the Blue-Eyed Scallop* (1964) and *Stalking the Healthful Herbs* (1966).

**Hagen, Uta,** *Love for Cooking* (1976). The noted actress and drama teacher shares her culinary love and recipes in a sound, simple, and helpful volume. Excellent for beginning cooks.

**Hazan, Marcella,** *The Classic Italian Cook Book* (1976). Buona cocina in the best all-round Italian cookbook. See *More Classic Italian Cooking* (1978).

**Heatter, Maida,** *Maida Heatter's Book of Great Desserts* (1974). Scrumptious, fattening recipes by the Julia Child of desserts. See her *Book of Great Cookies* (1977) and *Book of Great Chocolate Desserts* (1980). Her French counterpart is Gaston LeNotre and his *Book of Desserts and Pastries* (1977) and *Book of Ice Cream and Candies* (1979).

**Jaffrey, Madhur,** *An Invitation to Indian Cooking* (1973). Classic dishes — mostly the subtle, spicy cooking of Delhi — carefully worked out for American cooks and American kitchens. See *Madhur Jaffrey's World-of-the-East Vegetarian Cooking* (1981).

**Kennedy, Diana,** *The Cuisine of Mexico* (1972). The first of an outstanding series of Mexican cook books. See *The Tortilla Book* (1975) and *Recipes from the Regional Cooks of Mexico* (1978).

**Kuo, Irene,** *The Key to Chinese Cooking* (1977). There are many books on Chinese cuisine; this simple and elegantly written guide is extraordinary. See Craig Claiborne and Virginia Lee, *The Chinese Cookbook* (1972) and Ken Hom and Harvey Steinman, *Chinese Technique* (1981).

**Lappé, Frances Moore,** *Diet for a Small Planet* (1971). A book with a unique point of view: that of "protein complementarity" — the combination of nonmeat foods that produces high-grade protein nutrition equivalent to, or better than, meat proteins. See *Recipes for a Small Planet* (1973).

**Olney, Richard,** *Simple French Food* (1974). A food writer on basic Gallic fare. See *French Menu Cookbook* (1970). See also Anne Willins, *French Regional Cooking* (1981).

**Pepin, Jacques,** *La Technique: The Fundamental Techniques of Cooking* (1977). French chef and food columnist explains the methods of haute cuisine. See *La Méthod* (1979) and *French Chef Cooks at Home* (1976).

**Pullar, Philippa,** *Consuming Passions* (1971). A social history, both learned and delightful to read, of English eating habits from the Lucullan feasts of the Roman conquerors to today's canned vegetables.

**Robertson, Laurel, et al.,** *Laurel's Kitchen: A Handbook for Vegetarian Cookery and Nutrition* (1976). One of the best and most beautifully produced vegetarian cookbooks. Other good ones include *Tassajara Cookery* (1973) and Sonya Richmond, *International Vegetarian Cookbook* (1965).

**Rombauer, Irma S. and Marion Rombauer Becker,** *The Joy of Cooking* (rev. 1975). Distinguished by its minute clarity, this big cookbook has established itself since it first appeared more than fifty years ago as *the* basic, fundamental cookbook.

**Serecoskey, Susan,** *The Hungarian Cookbook* (1972). The best guide to the most interesting of Eastern European cuisines. See George Lang, *The Cuisine of Hungary* (1971).

**Sokolov, Raymond,** *Fading Feasts: A Compendium of Disappearing American Regional Foods* (1981). Former food editor of the *New York Times,* champion speller, novelist, and literary editor describes an endangered cuisine with wit and affection. See *The Saucier's Apprentice: A Modern Guide to Classic French Sauces for the Home* (1976).

**Time-Life Editors,** *Foods of the World* (1968–71). Beautifully produced series of books employing such writers as Craig Claiborne on classic French cooking, M. F. K. Fisher on provincial French cooking, Nika Hazelton on the cooking of Germany, and Waverly Root on Italian food. See the more recent *The Good Cook* series.

**Toklas, Alice B.,** *The Alice B. Toklas Cookbook* (1954). This book was indeed written by Miss Toklas and it is as much a collection of witty anecdotes about the members of the "charmed circle" of Gertrude Stein as of recipes.

**Tsuji, Shizuo,** *Japanese Cooking: A Simple Art* (1981). This 500-page work is more than just a superb cookbook; it is practically a treatise on the Japanese philosophy of cooking.

**Witty, Helen and Elizabeth Schneider-Colchie,** *Better than Store-Bought* (1979). Great cookbook for making cream cheese, marshmallows, fig newtons, mustard, bouillon cubes, and much more that people used to make themselves.

**Wolfert, Paula,** *Couscous and Other Good Foods from Morocco* (1973). Wonderful collection of savory North African dishes. See *Mediterranean Cooking* (1977).

## Baking

**Braue, John Rahn,** *Uncle John's Original Bread Book* (1961). Written in a homespun style by the son of a German master bread baker, and a great baker in his own right in America, it contains recipes for practically every type of bread imaginable.

**Brown, Edward Espe,** *The Tassajara Bread Book* (1970). Tassajara is the location of a Zen Buddhist practice center in the California mountains. This beautiful book of "natural" bread recipes was produced by members of that community.

**Clayton, Bernard, Jr.,** *The Complete Book of Breads* (1973). Excellent source book for wide range of bread-making techniques. See *The Breads of France* (1978) and *The Complete Book of Pastry* (1981).

**David, Elizabeth,** *English Bread and Yeast Cookery* (1980). Over 200 recipes tried and tested by the English food writer.

**Peck, Paula,** *The Art of Fine Baking* (1970). Clearly written, comprehensive guide to fancy baking. See *The Art of Good Cooking* (1970).

## Eating

**Bemelmans, Ludwig,** *Bemelmans' La Bonne Table: His Lifetime Love Affair with the Art of Dining and in His Own Words and His Own Pictures from Behind the Scenes and at Table* (1964). The subtitle pretty well says it all about this excellent posthumous selection.

**Farb, Peter, and George Armelagos,** *Consuming Passions: The Anthropology of Eating* (1980). Fascinating subject, good survey. See Reay Tannahill, *Food in History* (1973).

**Liebling, A. J.,** *Between Meals: An Appetite for Paris* (1962). Rich, delicious pieces about the pleasures of the Parisian table by the one-time *New Yorker* writer renowned for his wit and appetite.

**Root, Waverly,** *Food* (1980). Leading food writer's essays — authoritative and witty. See *Eating in America* (1976), written with Richard de Rochemont.

**Trillin, Calvin,** *Alice, Let's Eat* (1978). A *New Yorker* correspondent and junk-food gourmand's funny odyssey in search of "something decent to eat." See *American Fried* (1974).

## Wine

**Amerine, Maynard and E. B. Roessler,** *Wines: Their Sensory Evaluation.* Best book on the subject.

**Anderson, Burton,** *Vino* (1980). Guide to the wine and winemakers of Italy, with illustrations, charts, and guides.

**Balzer, Robert L.,** *Wines of California* (1978). Big and beautiful and good. See Robert Thompson and Hugh Johnson, *The California Wine Book* (1976).

**Bespaloff, Alexis (ed.),** *The Fireside Book of Wine: An Anthology for Wine Drinkers* (1977). Admirable selections from a wide range of writers. The perfect accompaniment to a glass of wine. See *The New Signet Book of Wine* (1980).

**Broadbent, Michael,** *The Great Vintage Wine Book* (1981). Compiled by the head of the wine department at Christie's; firsthand descriptions of thousands of wines arranged by group and by vintage year. A unique, monumental work.

**Churchill, Creighton,** *The New World of Wines* (1974). A knowledgeable wine writer's selections from his essays published in *Gourmet* and *Harpers.* See his tourist guide for wine lovers, *The Great Wine Rivers of Europe* (1972).

**Edward Bosqui and Co.,** *Grapes and Grape Vines in California* (1877). First book ever published on California wines and one of the most beautiful wine books ever made.

**Fadiman, Clifton (ed.),** *Dionysus: A Case of Vintage Tales About Wine* (1962). Flavorful collection of literary vintiana. See *The Joys of Wine* (1975).

**Gordon, Manuel Gonzales,** *Sherry: The Noble Wine* (1948). The story of the famous wine of Jerez, Spain.

**Johnson, Hugh,** *The World Atlas of Wine* (1976). Not only a most useful book, but one of the most beautifully illustrated wine books ever published.

**Jones, Idwal,** *The Vineyard* (1942). Novel about winemaking in California's Napa Valley during the first decades of the century. "It makes the people who live in that region not only alive in themselves but a true part of the soil they live on . . . heartening as wine to read" (M. F. K. Fisher).

**Lichine, Alexis,** *Alexis Lichine's New Encyclopedia of Wines & Spirits* (rev. 1981). Comprehensive wine guide covering the history of wine, how it is made, types and evaluations of wines, and more. See *Alex Lichine's Guide to the Wines and Vineyards of France* (rev. 1982).

**Marcus, Irving H.,** *How to Test and Improve Your Wine Judging Ability* (rev. 1974). All the tests, the criteria, how to use the twenty-point scorecard, and much more. See *Lines About Wines* (1971) and *Dictionary of Wine Terms* (rev. 1979).

**Penning-Rowsell, Edmound,** *The International Wine and Food Society's Guide to the Wines of Bordeaux* (1970). Topnotch introduction to the great winemaking region. See the society's *Guide to the Wines of Burgundy* (rev. 1979) by H. W. Yoxall. Another regional guide is *The Wines of Rhone* (1978) by John Livingstone-Learmonth and Melvin Master.

**Quimme, Peter,** *The Signet Book of American Wine* (rev. 1980). Excellent guide to domestic wines. The best little guides to California wines are Charles Olken, *The Connoisseurs' Handbook of California Wines* (1980) and Robert Thompson, *The Pocket Encyclopedia of California Wines* (1980).

**Saintsbury, George,** *Notes on a Cellar-Book* (1920). This wine classic by the eminent literary critic of his day is delightfully quaint, full of genial ferocity, and knowledgeable without being pedantic. Other classics of the British Baroque school of wine writing include H. Warner Allen, *The Romance of Wine* (1935); C. W. Berry, *In Search of Wine* (1935); Ian M. Campbell, *Wayward Tendrils of the Vine* (1948); and Alec Waugh, *In Praise of Wine* (1959).

**Schoonmaker, Frank,** *Frank Schoonmaker's Encyclopedia of Wine* (1964). Masses of information, very well presented.

**Scott, James M.,** *The Man Who Made Wine* (1954). Set in the Médoc district of France, and full of vinous allusions, this warm novel will please the confirmed oenophile.

**Shand, P. Morton,** *Wines and Vineyards of France* (1928, rev. 1964). An architecture critic and wine lover's classic book of French wines.

**Sichel, Peter,** *Wines of Germany* (1980). Revision of Frank Schoonmaker's classic. A good companion is Edmound Penning-Rowsell, *German Wine Atlas* (1977).

**Simon, André L.,** *In the Twilight* (1969). Reflections on his over seventy years as a connoisseur and wine historian. Among his many books are *Bottlescrew Days: Wine Drinking in England During the 18th Century* (1926) and *André Simon's Wines of the World* (rev. 1981), which he edited and which has been revised since his death. He is also author of the classic *Encyclopedia of Gastronomy* (1952).

**Younger, William A.,** *Gods, Men and Wine* (1966). Illustrated history of wine, winemaking, and winedrinking.

PART V

# WORK

# King

**Bengtsson, Frans,** *The Sword Does Not Jest: The Heroic Life of Charles XII of Sweden 1682–1718* (rev. 1960). The enigmatic military genius who died in his thirties. See R. M. Hatton, *Charles XII of Sweden* (1969).

**Blunt, Wilfrid,** *The Dream King: Ludwig II of Bavaria* (1970). Lavishly illustrated biography of the strange and misunderstood "Mad" King Ludwig.

**Brunhoff, Jean de,** *The Story of Babar* (1934). The first of the well-loved children's picture stories of Babar, who reigns over a kingdom of elephants from his capital city of Celesteville. The books poke gentle fun at French bourgeois life.

**Cole, Hubert,** *Christophe, King of Haiti* (1967). The new world's first crowned king. Peter Bourne's *Drums of Destiny* (1947) is a romantic historical novel of the period.

**Fraser, Antonia,** *Royal Charles: Charles II and the Restoration* (1979). The merry monarch and his times in a finely crafted biography.

**Hackett, Francis,** *Francis the First* (1935). Witty, romantic biography of "the first gentleman of France."

**Hibbert, Christopher,** *George IV* (1974–75). Acclaimed two-volume biography of the Hanoverian ruler; vividly describes English society in the 1820s.

**Howarth, David,** *The Desert King: Ibn Saud and His Arabia* (1964). Exciting romantic characterization of the founder of Saudi Arabia. See David Holden and Richard Johns, *The House of Saud: The Rise and Rule of the Most Powerful Dynasty in the Arab World* (1982).

**Hutchison, Harold F.,** *King Henry V* (1967). Skillful portrait of the fifteenth-century Shakespearean hero who conquered Normandy. See H. W. Lewis, *Wife of Henry V* (1957), a novel by a medieval scholar about Catherine of Valois, who was wife to the king for two years.

**Jarry, Alfred,** *Ubu Roi* (1896). Hilarious, irreverent farce about Pere Ubu and his queen, written by the inventor of "pataphysics".

**Kendall, Paul M.,** *Richard III* (1955). Brilliant biography of England's most controversial king. His treachery is the subject of Shakespeare's *Richard III* (1594). See *Louis XI* (1970) and *Warwick the Kingmaker* (1957).

**Mann, Heinrich,** *Henry IV* (1937–39). Henry of Navarre, King of France, 1589–

1610, the first of the Bourbon line, is the subject of this superb, idealized portrait.

**Marlowe, Christopher,** *Edward the Second* (1593). Tragedy about the fourteenth-century English king, his passion for his friend Gaveston, and his assassination. See *Tamburlaine the Great* (1588), a richly poetic drama about the self-proclaimed king of Persia.

**Mitford, Nancy,** *The Sun King* (1966). Delightful impressionistic life of Louis XIV and life at seventeenth-century Versailles. See Mitford's other regal subject in *Frederick the Great* (1970).

**Nicolson, Harold,** *King George V: His Life and Reign* (1952). Urbane biography of Queen Victoria's grandson, who reigned during the empire's waning days.

**Petrie, Charles,** *Philip II of Spain* (1963). One of Sir Charles's first-rate portraits of Spanish royalty. Others are *King Charles III of Spain* (1971) and *Don John of Austria* (1967).

**Scarisbrick, J. J.,** *Henry VIII* (1968). The best scholarly life of the colorful, lusty Tudor king. Carolly Erickson, *Great Harry* (1980) is a fine popular biography.

**Shakespeare, William,** *Richard II* (1595). Dethronement, rebellion, and civil war supply the dramatic action of this study of the young fourteenth-century monarch.

**Slocombe, George,** *William the Conqueror* (1959). Highly readable biography of the leader of the Norman Conquest. See *The White Plume Henry* (1931), about Henry IV.

**Sophocles,** *Oedipus the King* (c. 430 B.C.). The Greek dramatist's masterpiece about the King of Thebes, slayer of his father, husband of his mother. See *Oedipus at Colonus* (c. 406 B.C.).

**Wedgwood, C. V.,** *William the Silent* (1944). Wedgwood calls the Prince of Orange, founder of the Dutch Republic, the "wisest, gentlest and bravest man who

ever led a nation," in an eloquent, scholarly narrative.

**Ziegler, Philip,** *King William IV* (1973). William became king of England in 1830 at age sixty-four and reigned until 1837. "Its condensed yet comprehensive pages make convincing history and are a joy to read" (Elizabeth Longford).

## Queen

**Castelot, André,** *Queen of France* (1957). Vivid life of Marie Antoinette by a noted French scholar. In no biography "has her passion been told with such depth and brilliance, with such force and unimpeachable authenticity" (Frances Winwar). See *Josephine* (1967).

**Chapman, Hester W.,** *The Challenge of Anne Boleyn* (1974). Affectionate biography of one of Henry VIII's six consorts, the mother of Elizabeth I, and victim of execution.

**Fraser, Antonia,** *Mary, Queen of Scots* (1969). Sympathetic account of her tragic life.

**Green, David,** *Queen Anne* (1971). This "wonderful book about one of the most powerful Court dramas of English history" (J. H. Plumb) centers on the last Stuart monarch.

**Kelly, Amy,** *Eleanor of Aquitaine and the Four Kings* (1950). Outstanding popular biography of one of the twelfth century's most fascinating queens — wife of two kings and mother of two others.

**Mahoney, Irene,** *Madame Catherine* (1975). The life of Catherine de Médici, the queen mother of France for fifty years and one of the most maligned figures of the sixteenth century.

**Mattingly, Garrett,** *Catherine of Aragon* (1941). The Spanish princess who was the first wife of Henry VIII, in a simple, scholarly, and skillful biography.

Neale, John, *Queen Elizabeth I* (1934). Best single-volume biography of the incomparable Queen Bess. Mary M. Luke's *Gloriana: The Years of Elizabeth I* (1973) provides an engaging portrait of Elizabeth the woman. *The Queens and the Hive* (1962) by Edith Sitwell is a brilliant fictionalized biography.

Strachey, Lytton, *Queen Victoria* (1921). Surprisingly sympathetic regal portrait (although Victorianism is not spared the biographer's cynical irony): one of the great biographies of the century. Edith Sitwell's *Victoria of England* (1936) is a delicately cynical life history. The best modern biography of the queen as a woman is Elizabeth Longford, *Queen Victoria: Born to Succeed* (1965).

Wells, Evelyn, *Nefertiti* (1964). The queen of ancient Egypt and wife of Akhenaton.

## Emperor

Buchan, John, *Augustus* (1937). The Roman emperor by the Scottish statesman and master storyteller. John William's novel *Augustus* (1972) is a National Book Award winner.

Cronin, Vincent, *Napoleon Bonaparte: An Intimate Biography* (1972). Of the scores of Napoleon biographies, this should be read first: beautifully written and wise, it "makes one see Napoleon the man, as if for the first time" (J. H. Plumb).

Gascoigne, Bamber, *The Great Moghuts* (1971). The first six emperors of Islamic India. Lively story and color photos.

Grousset, Rene, *Conqueror of the World* (1967). A beautifully written life of the Mongol emperor Genghis Khan.

Holland, Cecelia, *Antichrist: A Novel of the Emperor Frederick II* (1970). The life and times of the thirteenth-century Holy Roman Emperor and king of Sicily who attempted to found a Mediterranean empire. Colorful, racy fiction.

Massie, Robert K., *Peter the Great: His Life and World* (1980). Long Pulitzer Prize–winning biography. See also Alex de Jonge, *Fire and Water: A Life of Peter the Great* (1980) and Ian Grey, *Peter the Great* (1960).

Renault, Mary, *Fire from Heaven* (1970). First of an absorbing trilogy of novels tracing the life of Alexander the Great. See *Persian Boy* (1973) and *Funeral Games* (1981). *The Nature of Alexander* (1975) is nonfiction.

Spence, Jonathan, *Emperor of China: Self-Portrait of K'ang-hsi* (1974). The remarkable Manchu dynasty emperor (1661–1722) in his own words.

Vidal, Gore, *Julian* (1964). He was raised a Christian but attempted to restore the old Hellenic gods when he became emperor of Rome in 361 A.D. A skillful paean to paganism.

Whittle, Tyler, *The Last Kaiser: A Biography of William II, German Emperor and King of Prussia* (1977). Good gossipy account of the life of Queen Victoria's grandson, who abdicated in 1918 after a thirty-year reign.

Yourcenar, Marguerite, *Hadrian's Memoirs* (1954). Fictionalized memoirs of the second-century A.D. Roman emperor. A tour de force by the first woman admitted to the French Academy. Stewart Perowne, *Hadrian* (1961) is an excellent biography.

## Empress

Catherine II, Empress of Russia, *Memoirs of Catherine the Great* (1955). Best edition of her remarkable reminiscences. See Zoë Oldenbourg, *Catherine the Great* (1965).

Crankshaw, Edward, *Maria Theresa* (1970). Absorbing biography of the Habsburg empress of Austria and mother of Marie Antoinette.

**Haslip, Joan,** *The Lonely Empress: A Biography of Elizabeth of Austria* (1965). The consort of Franz Joseph was considered the most beautiful woman of the nineteenth century. Haslip wrote of Maximilian and his empress, Carlotta, in *The Crown of Mexico* (1971).

**Masefield, John,** *Basilissa: A Life of Empress Theodora* (1940). This fictional portrait of Theodora, who is usually pictured as ruthless and depraved, as a gentle Christian girl occasioned Vladimir Nabokov's remark: "If this be Byzantium, well, all one can say is that it has been annexed by Ruritania."

**Warner, Marina,** *The Dragon Empress: The Life and Times of Tz'u-hsi, Empress Dowager of China, 1835–1908* (1972). Account of the last decades of the Chinese empire.

## Dictator

**Djilas, Milovan,** *Tito: The Story from Inside* (1980). Concise portrait by a former Tito aide who spent nine years in a Yugoslavian prison. See Fitzroy Maclean, *Josip Broz Tito: A Pictorial Biography* (1980).

**Fermi, Laura,** *Mussolini* (1961). Life of the Fascist leader by a woman who lived in Italy until 1938. Another good popular biography is Christopher Hibbert, *Il Duce* (1962).

**Fischer, Louis,** *The Life of Lenin* (1964). Sturdy biography of the man who has been called the most fascinating political figure of the twentieth century. Winner of National Book Award.

**Fraser, Antonia,** *Cromwell: The Lord Protector* (1973). The Puritan leader who as Lord Protector of the Commonwealth wielded dictatorial power.

**García Márquez, Gabriel,** *The Autumn of the Patriarch* (1976). Imaginative, demanding novel of the corruption that surrounds a Latin American dictator. Other good novels about Latin American dicta-

tors are Francisco Ayala, *Death as a Way of Life* (1964) and Miguel Ángel Asturias, *The President* (1963).

**Grant, Michael,** *Julius Caesar* (1969). Life of the Roman statesman and general whose dictatorship was cut short by assassination. For excellent fictional treatment see Rex Warner, *The Young Caesar* (1958) and *Imperial Caesar* (1961).

**Kinross, Lord,** *Ataturk* (1964). Extremely well written life of the soldier-statesman Mustafa Kemal, founder of the Turkish Republic and one of the most interesting politicians in recent history.

**Toland, John,** *Adolf Hitler* (1976). Long biography of the Nazi dictator. A companion volume is *Hitler: The Pictorial Documentary of His Life* (1978). See also Joachim C. Fest, *Hitler* (1974) and Alan Bullock, *Hitler, A Study in Tyranny* (rev. 1962).

**Ulam, Adam,** *Stalin: The Man and His Era* (1973). Briskly written, detailed account of the Soviet premier's life and times.

**Updike, John,** *The Coup* (1978). Brilliantly executed novel about Colonel Hakim Félix Ellel*ô*, dictator of the emerging African nation of Kush.

## President of the United States

**Adams, John,** *John Adams: A Biography in His Own Words* (1978). Extracts from the second president's diaries, letters, essays, and state papers; a lively picture of the man. The best biography is Page Smith, *John Adams* (1963).

**Adams, John Quincy,** *Diary: American Political, Social and Intellectual Life from Washington to Polk* (1978). Single-volume abridgement by Allan Nevins of the greatest American political diary we have. Full of variety and power, it "bristles with incisive and picturesque records of our social and political history" (Van Wyck Brooks).

**Flexner, James Thomas,** *Washington: The Indispensable Man* (1979). Special Pulitzer Prize Citation winner; the four-volume *George Washington* skillfully distilled into a single, equally outstanding volume.

**Grant, U. S.,** *Personal Memoirs* (1885). The great Union general's great autobiography: "a masterpiece of narrative power, of candor and of historical intelligence" (D. W. Brogan). See William S. McFeely, *Grant: A Biography* (1981).

**James, Marquis,** *Andrew Jackson* (1933–37). Old Hickory, his life and times, vividly depicted in a Pulitzer Prize–winning biography. More scholarly is Robert V. Remini's three-volume biography, the first of which is *Andrew Jackson and the Course of American Empire, 1767–1821* (1977).

**Miller, Merle,** *Plain Speaking: An Oral Biography of Harry S. Truman* (1974). Conversations that vividly recreate the president's refreshing, outspoken personality. Truman's *Memoirs* (1955–56) are candid and captivating as is Margaret Truman's affectionate *Harry S. Truman* (1973).

**Morris, Edmund,** *The Rise of Theodore Roosevelt* (1979). The first volume of a projected two-volume biography is "one of those rare works that is both definitive for the period it covers and fascinating to read for sheer entertainment" (W. A. Swanberg).

**Padover, Saul,** *Jefferson* (1942). The president as a thinker and inspiring force. Compact, well written, it is the best short biography, for the author "has been able to recreate Jefferson as an individual, to give us a sense of the way the man lived and talked and acted and thought" (Henry Steele Commager). The definitive life is Dumas Malone's six-volume *Jefferson and His Times* (1948–81). See Fawn Brodie's provocative *Thomas Jefferson: An Intimate History* (1974).

**Sandburg, Carl,** *Abraham Lincoln* (1954). A one-volume abridgement of the monumental study, it exhibits the touch of poetic genius. This is the apotheosis of the romantic view of the martyred President; the best straightforward biography is Benjamin P. Thomas, *Abraham Lincoln* (1952). See Stefan Lorant's pictorial *Lincoln* (rev. 1958).

**Sorensen, Theodore C.,** *Kennedy* (1965). Clear, tightly written, affectionate biography, covering the years 1953–63, by the President's counsel.

## Governor

**Bailyn, Bernard,** *The Ordeal of Thomas Hutchinson* (1974). Sympathetic picture of the much vilified loyalist governor of Massachusetts at the time of the American Revolution.

**Handlin, Oscar,** *Al Smith and His America* (1958). Brief, highly intelligent look at the popular New York governor who was the Democratic presidential candidate in 1928.

**Morgan, Edward,** *Puritan Dilemma: The Story of John Winthrop, Governor of Massachusetts Bay Colony* (1958). Life and times of the first governor of the seventeenth-century colony. A lively book.

**Warren, Robert Penn,** *All the King's Men* (1946). Inspired by the career of Huey Long, this Pulitzer Prize–winning novel traces the career and character of Willie Stark, demagogic governor of a Southern state.

**Williams, T. Harry,** *Huey Long* (1970). A masterpiece of American biography, it finds behind the buffoon of legend a real person.

## Senator

**Current, Richard,** *Daniel Webster and the Rise of National Conservatism* (1955). Good, brief biography of the great orator who spent twenty years in the U.S. Senate during the critical early years of America.

See Stephen Vincent Benét's folksy modern version of the Faust legend, *The Devil and Daniel Webster* (1937).

**Johannsen, Robert W.,** *Stephen W. Douglas* (1973). The great political leader, famous for his debates with Lincoln and his candidacy for the presidency in 1860, in a magisterial, detailed narrative biography.

**Kirk, Russell,** *John Randolph of Roanoke* (rev. 1964). The distinguished senator from Virginia was perhaps the most spectacular personality ever to sit in Congress.

**Rovere, Richard H.,** *Senator Joe McCarthy* (1959). Respected political journalist's portrait of the witch hunter of the 1950s.

**Schlesinger, Arthur M., Jr.,** *Robert Kennedy and His Times* (1978). Affectionate biography of the former senator from New York, attorney general, and presidential aspirant.

## Mayor

**Fowler, Gene,** *Beau James: The Life and Times of Jimmy Walker* (1949). Gaudy, anecdotal biography of New York's Jazz Age mayor, with generous dollops of Broadway lore and Walker's famous wit.

**LaGuardia, Fiorello,** *The Making of an Insurgent: An Autobiography, 1882–1919* (1948). The early years of the Little Flower, mayor of New York during most of the thirties. See Arthur Mann, *La Guardia* (1959).

**O'Connor, Edwin,** *The Last Hurrah* (1956). Vivid portrait, based on Boston's long-time mayor James M. Curley, of a big-city Irish-American demagogue; roguish, but warm and endearing.

**Royko, Mike,** *Boss: Richard J. Daley of Chicago* (1971). The man, the machine, the city; the incredible story of the last of the backroom Caesars. One of the best books ever written about a city.

**Thomas, Lately,** *The Mayor Who Mastered New York* (1969). Rousing biography of William Gaynor, the honest reform politician who might have been president but for an assassin's bullet.

## Prime Minister of England

**Blake, Robert,** *Disraeli* (1966). Solid, lucidly written account of the life of one of the most colorful Victorians. For a more romantic rendering see André Maurois, *Disraeli* (1928). See also Christopher Hibbert, *Disraeli and His World* (1978).

**Cecil, David Lord,** *Melbourne* (1939–54). Elegant picture of the multifaceted man who taught statecraft to the young Queen Victoria and presided over the rebirth of an empire.

**Gash, Norman,** *Peel* (1977). Shortened, rewritten version of a two-volume biography of Sir Robert Peel, which is not only a "wonderfully thorough portrait of one of the most remarkable statesmen in English history, [but] also . . . a profound and illuminating study of politics between Waterloo and the Reform Bill" (Robert Blake).

**Koss, Stephen,** *Asquith* (1976). Concise and lively biography of the last Liberal P.M. (1908–16).

**Longford, Elizabeth,** *Wellington* (1969). First-rate biography of the Iron Duke. Philip Guedella's *Wellington* (1931) is a highly colorful life history.

**Magnus, Philip,** *Gladstone: A Biography* (1964). The man who was four times prime minister. John Morley's *The Life of William Ewart Gladstone* (1903) is a classic biography.

**Marquand, David,** *Ramsay MacDonald* (1977). Excellent authorized biography of the first Labour prime minister.

**Owen, Frank,** *Tempestuous Journey: Lloyd George, His Life and Times* (1955). Exciting, journalistic narrative of the great Welshman who governed during the First World War.

**Pelling, Henry,** *Winston Churchill* (1974). This 700-page comprehensive work is the "best birth-to-death biography of Churchill that has yet been written" (Peter Stansky). Churchill's *My Early Life* (1930) and *Roving Commission* (1939) are written with frankness and charm.

**Plumb, J. H.,** *Sir Robert Walpole* (1956–61). Magisterial three-volume biography of England's first P.M. by the distinguished historian.

## Revolutionary

**Bely, Andrei,** *St. Petersburg* (1911, tr. 1978). Superb novel about confrontation between a young revolutionary and his conservative father during the unsuccessful Russian revolution of 1905. A complex and richly symbolist masterpiece.

**Cohen, Stephen F.,** *Bukharin and the Bolshevik Revolution* (1980). About the theoretician and revolutionary, who was executed for treason in 1938.

**Conrad, Joseph,** *Under Western Eyes* (1911). Novel, set in Russia and Switzerland, about the revolutionary Razumov and the theme of guilt and atonement.

**Deutscher, Isaac,** *Trotsky* (1954–63). Three-volume biography of the brilliant Russian revolutionary that is sympathetic and authoritative. For a concise study of his political development coupled with a balanced biographical portrait see Robert Wistrich, *Trotsky: Fate of a Revolutionary* (1981). See Trotsky's own *My Life* (1930).

**Djilas, Milovan,** *Memoirs of a Revolutionary* (1973). Intellectual odyssey of former Tito aide, vice-president of Yugoslavia, and jailed critic of the regime.

**Dostoevski, Fedor,** *The Possessed* (1871). Nihilists, socialists, radicals, and the enigmatic Stavrogin move through this, "the

greatest of all novels about the revolutionary" (V. S. Pritchett).

**Fiori, Giuseppe,** *Antonio Gramsci: Life of a Revolutionary* (1971). Portrayal of the leader and theorist of the Italian Communist Party in the thirties, who was imprisoned by Mussolini. See *Selections from the Prison Notebooks of Antonio Gramsci* (1972).

**Guzman, Martín Luís,** *Memoirs of Pancho Villa* (1940). Fascinating recollections of the Mexican revolutionary by a novelist who campaigned with him. See Earl Shorris, *Under the Fifth Sun: A Novel of Pancho Villa* (1980).

**Hawke, David Freeman,** *Paine* (1974). Biography of the English revolutionary theoretician. Howard Fast's *Citizen Tom Paine* (1943) is an engaging biographical novel.

**Herzen, Alexander,** *My Life and Thoughts* (1852–55). Literary masterpiece by the most important revolutionary and intellectual of his time. "In the sensuousness and immediacy with which it transforms lived experience, it is as great a work of art as the finest novels of the 19th century" (Francine du Plessix Gray). The six volumes were masterfully abridged by Dwight Macdonald for a 1973 one-volume edition.

**James, Daniel,** *Ché Guevara* (1969). Balanced account of the life of the Cuban hero.

**Kis, Danilo,** *A Tomb for Boris Davidovich* (1978). Expressive portrait of the modern Russian revolutionary by a gifted Yugoslavian novelist.

**Lacoutoure, Jean,** *Ho Chi Minh: A Political Biography* (1968). A lively biography of the Vietnamese revolutionary leader.

**Lawrence, T. E.,** *The Letters of T.E. Lawrence* (1938). "If you would see the beautiful complexity of this intricate active mind you must look *into* it; and these letters, with *The Seven Pillars of Wisdom,* are the chief means of doing so" (Richard Hughes). See John E. Mack's Pulitzer Prize–winning biography of Lawrence *The Prince of Our Disorder* (1976).

**McLellan, David,** *Karl Marx: His Life and Thoughts* (1974). Personal, intellectual, and political biography of the father of dialectical materialism that provides a lively and fresh picture of the man and a lucid guide to his thinking. See Isaiah Berlin, *Karl Marx: His Life and Environment* (rev. 1978).

**Malraux, André,** *Anti-Memoirs* (1968). Illuminating reflections by the former revolutionary guerrilla in China and Spain, Resistance fighter, novelist, art historian, and French minister of culture under De-Gaulle. See Jean Lacoutoure, *André Malraux* (1976).

**Manach, Jorge,** *Martí, Apostle of Freedom* (1950). Gripping biography of the poet-philosopher who led the first Cuban revolution.

**Masur, Gerhard,** *Simón Bolivar* (rev. 1969). The life of the Liberator, who led the struggles for South American independence. Donald E. Worcester, *Bolivar* (1977) is a good short, popular biography.

**Ridley, Jasper,** *Garibaldi* (1976). Well-written biography of the Italian general and nationalist leader who led revolutions on two continents. See Christopher Hibbert, *Garibaldi and His Enemies* (1966).

**Schram, Stuart,** *Mao Tse-tung* (1967). The long and varied career of the chief theorist of the Chinese Revolution. See Stanley Karnow, *Mao and China* (1972).

## Army Commander

**Chenevix Trench, Charles,** *The Road to Khartoum: A Life of General Charles Gordon* (1979). First-rate biography of the eminent Victorian general, an almost mythical figure.

**Churchill, Winston,** *Marlborough* (1933–38). Gracefully written four-volume biography of the heroic first duke of Marlborough, by his illustrious descendant. A one-volume edition abridged by H. S. Commager was published in 1968.

**Dayan, Moshe,** *Moshe Dayan: The Story of My Life* (1976). The brilliant Israeli general and ardent patriot, by himself.

**Freeman, Douglas Southall,** *R. E. Lee* (1935). Magisterial four-volume biography of the great Confederate hero. *Lee* (1961) is a one-volume abridgement. The end of the story is beautifully told in Charles Bracelen Flood, *Lee: The Last Years* (1981).

**Liddel Hart, B. H.,** *Sherman: Soldier, Realist, American* (1929). Attempt to portray the workings of the mind of the colorful Union commander who was the most original genius of the Civil War. Liddel Hart also edited Sherman's *Memoirs* (1957).

**Loth, David G.,** *The People's General: The Personal Story of Lafayette* (1951). Napoleon, Washington, Robespierre, Benjamin Franklin, and Marie Antoinette all figure in this lively and entertaining account of the Marquis's life.

**Manchester, William,** *American Caesar: Douglas MacArthur, 1880–1964* (1978). Long biography of the controversial general. See MacArthur's *Reminiscences* (1964).

**Mylander, Maureen,** *The Generals* (1974). Excellent study of how American generals got to be American generals.

**Sykes, Christopher,** *Order Wingate* (1959). The story of a military genius who at times seemed slightly mad. "Recommended to anyone interested in the Middle East, Africa, or Burma, anyone who likes lively anecdotes about people, and anyone who finds eccentricity interesting, battle stories exciting, or madmen and geniuses attractive" (Robert St. John).

**Vandiver, Frank E.,** *Black Jack: The Life and Times of John J. Pershing* (1978). Fine biography of the American hero of World War I. See *Mighty Stonewall* (1957), about the Confederate general.

**Young, Desmond,** *Rommel, The Desert Fox* (1951). An English journalist-soldier's admiring portrait of the German general and the Africa campaign. See *The Rommel Papers* (1950), edited by B. H. Liddel Hart.

## Navy Commander

**Allen, William,** *That Bounty Bastard* (1977). Popular attempt to rehabilitate Captain Bligh, commander of the *Bounty*.

**Blond, Georges,** *Admiral Togo* (1960). Lucid biography of Japan's first naval hero, who defeated the Russians in 1904.

**Morison, Samuel Eliot,** *John Paul Jones* (1959). Pulitzer Prize–winning story of the American Revolutionary War naval hero by the eminent sailor-historian. See *"Old Bruin": Commodore Matthew C. Perry 1794–1858* (1967).

**Potter, John Deane,** *Yamamoto: The Man Who Menaced America* (1965). The career of the brilliant Japanese admiral who conceived the surprise attack on Pearl Harbor. See Burke Davis, *Get Yamamoto* (1969).

**Walden, David,** *Nelson* (1978). The hero of the Battle of Trafalgar. *The Life of Nelson* (1813) by poet Robert Southey has been long admired.

## Police Officer

**Daley, Robert,** *Prince of the City: The True Story of a Cop Who Knew Too Much* (1979). Compelling story of an undercover agent investigating police corruption. See *Year of the Dragon* (1981), a novel.

**Freeling, Nicolas,** *The King of the Rainy Country* (1968). The best of the series of novels featuring Inspector Van der Valk of the Amsterdam Police. Two the members of the force, Detectives Grippatra and de Gier, appear in Janwillem van de Wetering's novels, beginning with *Outsider in Amsterdam* (1975).

**McBain, Ed,** *Like Love* (1962). One of a series of novels about the Eighty-seventh Precinct in a city much like Manhattan. The series, written pseudonymously by novelist Evan Hunter, is packed with interesting characters.

**McClure, James,** *Spike Island: Portrait of a British Police Division* (1980). This book about the cops in a tough Liverpool district is also "about ourselves, about the society we have created, and about the precariousness of the bridges we have so painfully created over the chasms of poverty and crime" (P. D. James).

**Simenon, Georges,** *Versus Inspector Maigret* (1960). A superb example of the *roman policier* about the methodical Commissaire Jules Maigret of the Police Judiciare. Subtle, strong on characterization, and redolent of Paris.

**Sjowall, Maj and Per Wahlöö,** *The Laughing Policeman* (1970). Superintendent Martin Beck of the Stockholm Homicide Squad — a uniquely humane detective — is the hero of this Edgar-winning novel and nine other police novels.

**Uhnak, Dorothy,** *Policewoman* (1964). Memoirs of former New York City Transit Police officer's encounters with the realities of justice. See her realistic novels about New York cops, for instance, *The Investigation* (1977).

**Wambaugh, Joseph,** *The Glitter Dome* (1981). The search for the killer of a movie mogul is the center of this fast-paced, gritty novel by an ex-cop who excels in his sharply observed vignettes of the on- and off-duty life of Los Angeles cops. His other novels include *The Blue Knight* (1972) and *The New Centurions* (1970).

**Waugh, Hilary,** *Late Mrs. D* (1962). One of a series of novels about Fred Fellows, chief of police in Stockford, Connecticut.

Wilcox, Colin, *Aftershock* (1975). One of a series of novels about Lieutenant Hastings in San Francisco.

## Scotland Yard

Goddard, Henry, *Memories of a Bow Street Runner* (1959). Artlessly written recollections by an early-nineteenth-century member of the pre–Scotland Yard London police force known as the Bow Street Runners. See John Creasey's history, *The Masters of Bow Street* (1974).

Hill, Reginald, *A Killing Kindness* (1981). One of the series of sophisticated mysteries which feature Detective-Superintendent Dalziel and Sergeant Pascoe.

Hunter, Alan, *Gently with the Innocents* (1970). Introduces to American readers Chief Superintendent George Gently, who has been solving crimes around the Norfolk area in a long-lived series of classic whodunits.

Innes, Michael, *Hamlet, Revenge* (1937). One of the earliest and best of the Detective John Appleby novels, by J. I. M. Stewart under the name of Innes.

Jackson, Richard, *Occupied with Crime* (1967). Inside view of "the Yard" in an autobiographical work by a chief of its Criminal Investigations Department. Harold R. Scott's *Scotland Yard* (1955) is another enthralling memoir.

James, P. D., *Shroud for a Nightingale* (1971). The detached, melancholy Chief Superintendent Adam Dalgleish is the brilliant detective in one of a fine series marked by a concern with contemporary problems.

Lovesey, Peter, *Waxwork* (1978). Sergeant Cribb and Constable Thackeray do their sleuthing in an atmospheric Victorian London.

Marric, J. J., *Gideon's River* (1968). Marric is one of the noms de plume of the prolific John Creasey, and the saturnine Commander George Gideon, devoted family man and Londonophile, is his best creation.

Marsh, Ngaio, *Opening Night* (1951). The hero of Marsh's many novels is the cultured and intelligent Chief Inspector Roderick Alleyn, whose adventures involve the theater, music, ballet, and New Zealand.

Scott, Jack S., *The View from Deacon Hill* (1981). Sergeant Rosher is not of the gentlemanly school of the Yard; he can be tough and do things his own way as he so entertainingly does in this stylish, witty series.

## Private Investigator

Chandler, Raymond, *The Lady in the Lake* (1943). Chandler's unforgettable hard-boiled private eye Philip Marlowe — honest, principled, and for hire in a highly atmospheric Los Angeles — is the hero-adventurer in this novel, rich in incident and character and shot through with wisecracks.

Doyle, Arthur Conan, *The Adventures of Sherlock Holmes* (1892). Despite their puzzles and tricks and their lively melodrama, the stories' imagination and style have made them endure. "These are fairy-tales, as Conan Doyle intimated . . . , and they are among the most amusing of fairy-tales and not among the least distinguished" (Edmund Wilson). See H. R. F. Keating, *Sherlock Holmes: The Man and His World* (1980).

Hammett, Dashiell, *The Big Knockover* (1966). Collection of hard-boiled stories of the Continental op, the nameless operative of San Francisco's Continental Detective Agency, described in one case as "the toughest, hardest, strongest, fastest, sharpest, biggest, wisest, meanest man west of the Mississippi River." Poignant introduction by Lillian Hellman. The Continental op is also featured in *The Red Harvest* (1929) and *The Dain Curse* (1929).

**MacDonald, Ross,** *The Chill* (1964). Lew Archer is a modern knight, a decent, intelligent, merciful, lonely man with an office in Hollywood and a talent for solving complex cases. MacDonald is one of the most artful writers of detective novels.

**Stout, Rex,** *Too Many Cooks* (1938). He likes his orchids rare, his beer cold, his food gourmet and plentiful. He's Stout's brownstone-based, one-seventh-ton, supersleuthing genius of detection — Nero Wolfe. With his rugged, fast-moving aide-de-crime Archie Goodwin they form one of the most delightful teams in the detective genre. See William S. Baring-Gould, *Nero Wolfe of West Thirty-fifth Street: The Life and Times of America's Largest Private Detective* (1969).

## Spy

**Ambler, Eric (ed.),** *To Catch a Spy: An Anthology of Favourite Spy Stories* (1965). First-rate selections by the likes of Buchan, Greene, and Fleming, with a sound introduction to the genre by Ambler. His own novels of espionage include *Epitaph for a Spy* (1938) and *A Coffin for Dimitrios* (1939).

**Buckley, William F., Jr.,** *Saving the Queen* (1976). Introducing the witty, intelligent Blackford Oakes, hero of Buckley's polished and often polemical cold-war novels.

**Donovan, James B.,** *Strangers on a Bridge* (1964). The author was Rudolf Abel's defense attorney in the famous 1957 spy trial and arranged for the Abel-Francis Gary Powers exchange "on a bridge" in 1961. "This is an engrossing and forthright book" (Allan Dulles).

**Fleming, Ian,** *Casino Royale* (1953). The first of the gripping, hilarious James Bond yarns with their wonderfully improbable villains and amorous conquests.

**Golan, Avieger and Danny Pinkas,** *Shula: Code Name the Pearl* (1980). A taut, spellbinding true adventure of a woman spying in Beirut for the Israeli secret service.

**Greene, Graham,** *The Human Factor* (1978). Novel about an English double agent which asks some tough questions about morals, conscience, and good and evil. See *Our Man in Havana* (1958), a somewhat lighter novel about spies.

**Hall, Adam,** *The Scorpion Signal* (1980). One of the best of a series of thrillers about Quiller, who is sent on dangerous missions to a series of exotic places.

**Kipling, Rudyard,** *Kim* (1901). Classic adventure tale of the Irish boy who becomes the Tibetan Lama's companion — and spy for the English. Memorable for its vivid picture of Victorian India.

**Le Carré, John,** *The Honourable School-boy* (1977). One of a series of novels featuring the "breathtakingly ordinary" spy, George Smiley — withdrawn, scholarly, fat and bespectacled; in short, the antithesis of Agent 007. Their detailed topography, shadowing, and relief make them best, and the bleakest, of their kind. A non-Smiley novel, *The Spy Who Came in from the Cold* (1963), is a cold-war classic.

**Maugham, W. Somerset,** *Ashenden; or, the British Agent* (1928). Beautifully crafted stories founded on Maugham's own experiences in the Intelligence Department during World War I.

**Myagkov, Aleksei,** *Inside the KGB* (1977). Swiftly moving account of life inside the KGB in the early seventies, by a Soviet defector. See Vladimir Sakharov, *High Treason* (1981).

**Ostrovsky, Erika,** *Eye of Dawn: The Rise and Fall of Mata Hari* (1978). Lively tale of the famous spy set against the colorful background of Europe in World War I.

**Popov, Dusko,** *Spy/Counterspy* (1974). Activities of an English-Nazi double agent during World War II told by a master spy supposed to be the model for James Bond.

Powers, Thomas, *The Man Who Kept the Secrets* (1979). Story of Richard Helms and the CIA. "A miracle of lucidity, exciting to read, balanced, invigorating" (William F. Buckley, Jr.).

Volkoff, Vladimir, *The Turn-Around* (1981). Gripping tale of espionage á la Le Carré by a Russian-born French writer who knows the business.

## Novelist

Baker, Carlos, *Hemingway: A Life Story* (rev. 1972). Sound, dispassionate telling of the Hemingway story. See *Selected Letters, 1917–1961* (1981).

Bowers, John, *The Colony* (1971). Experiences of a young writer at a summer writers' colony and his own coming of age. Beautifully done.

Burney, Fanny, *The Diary of Fanny Burney* (1940). One-volume edition selected by Joseph W. Cove. At the beginning of her life she is pursued by Doctor Johnson; and at the end, by Sir Walter Scott. See Sarah Kilpatrick, *Fanny Burney* (1981).

Camus, Albert, *Notebook* (1963–65). Started when Camus was 22 and kept up for 15 years, they reveal the artist setting down his feelings, thoughts, and impressions before transmitting them into art. See Herbert Lottman, *Albert Camus* (1979).

Colette, *Earthly Paradise* (1966). Autobiography, drawn from the writings of her lifetime by Robert Phelps. Vivid year-by-year revelation of a long, eager, courageous life. Phelps also assembled a scrapbook of Colletiana, *Les Belle Saisons* (1978) and *Letters from Colette* (1980).

Dostoevski, Fedor, *Dostoevski: A Self-Portrait* (1963). Composite memoirs fashioned from the novelist's letters. The most concise general biography in English is Ronald Hingley, *Dostoyevsky: His Life and Work* (1978). A fascinating series of Dostoevski's notebooks have been published by the University of Chicago, beginning in 1967.

Edgeworth, Maria, *Letters from England, 1813–1844* (1972). Marvelous letters of the Anglo-Irish novelist who inspired Scott and influenced Turgenev. Full of robust intelligence and warmth. See P. H. Newby, *Maria Edgeworth* (1950).

Ellmann, Richard, *James Joyce* (rev. 1982). Judicious and well-written biography of the Irish genius. A triumph of the biographer's art. See the Ellmann-edited *Letters* (1958–66).

Flaubert, Gustave, *The Selected Letters of Gustave Flaubert* (1954). His highly literate letters, edited by Francis Steegmuller: a brilliant self-portrait. See Steegmuller's *Flaubert and Madame Bovary: A Double Portrait* (rev. 1968).

Gaskell, Elizabeth, *Life of Charlotte Brontë* (1857). Classic biography of the Victorian novelist by her friend, a leading novelist of her day. For a beautifully made revision see Margaret Lane, *The Brontë Story: A Reconsideration of Mrs. Gaskell's Biography* (1953). Brontë's superb letters are in *The Letters of the Brontës* (1954), edited by Muriel Spark.

Gide, André, *Journals, 1884–1949* (1939–50). These remarkable books, "a skillful and absorbing mixture of portraits and places, of drawing-room gossip and metaphysical speculation, of remarkable passages of literary criticism and moral scrutiny, of lyrical outbursts and personal revelations, will probably stand as his most enduring work" (Maxwell Geismar). See *If It Die: An Autobiography* (1924).

Glasgow, Ellen, *The Woman Within* (1954). This deeply moving posthumous autobiography of the great regional novelist is "alive with the human anguish and pity of love that was hers. She allowed herself to feel and through feeling came to understand; she has given us a document to be read and cherished" (Leon Edel).

**Goncourt, Edmond De and Jules De Goncourt,** *The Goncourt Journals* (1851–96). The scores of novels they wrote have been forgotten, but their journals live as unrivalled first-hand description of the literary giants of the day, full of sparkling, bitchy miniatures. *Pages from the Goncourt Journals* (1962), edited by Robert Baldick is recommended, as is his biography, *The Goncourts* (1960).

**Green, Henry,** *Pack My Bag* (1939). Collection of reminiscences of the English writer Henry Yorke who, using the pen name of Henry Green, wrote distinctive novels of manners.

**Hart-Davis, Rupert,** *Hugh Walpole* (1952). Delightful biography of the popular English novelist that can be enjoyed even if you never plan to read any of his novels. Somerset Maugham's novel *Cakes and Ale* (1930) is supposedly based on Walpole.

**Hawthorne, Nathaniel,** *The Heart of Hawthorne's Journals* (1929). Edited by Newton Arvin, the journals provide a fascinating light into the mind of the artist. See James Mellow, *Nathaniel Hawthorne in His Times* (1980).

**Howard, Maureen,** *Facts of Life* (1978). Brief, witty autobiographical accounts of three facts of life: culture, money, and sex. "A brilliantly told story. The style is very, very bright; the other characters are wonderfully alive" (Alfred Kazin). Winner of the National Book Critics Circle Award.

**Huxley, Aldous,** *Letters* (1970). A rare mind and a half-century of English literary life illuminated in a bounty of almost 1,000 letters. See *Aldous Huxley: A Biography* (1974) by Sybille Bedford and the recollections of his last years by his wife, Laura Archera Huxley, in *The Timeless Moment* (1968).

**James, Henry,** *Autobiography* (1956). Omnibus volume of the three autobiographical works he wrote in his last years. Together they constitute "the richest, warmest and most luminous of American literary autobiographies" (Newton Arvin). See his *Notebooks* (1947) and Leon Edel's magisterial biography, *Henry James* (1953–72).

**Johnson, Edgar,** *Charles Dickens: His Tragedy and Triumph* (1952). The definitive modern biography. A one-volume readers' edition was published in 1977. See Ivor Brown, *Dickens in His Time* (1963) and Christopher Hibbert, *The Making of Charles Dickens* (1966).

**Lawrence, D. H.,** *Selected Letters* (1950). Whether they are "the best in modern English literature and second only to Keats' in the whole history of English Literature" (Diana Trilling), they are certainly absorbing. A fine introduction by Aldous Huxley enhances the volume, which was edited by Richard Aldington. See Edward Nelha (ed.), *D.H. Lawrence: A Composite Biography* (1958).

**Maurois, André,** *Prometheus: The Life of Balzac* (1966). Engaging telling of one of the great life stories in literature. See his equally vivid biographies of two other nineteenth-century French novelists, Victor Hugo in *Olympio* (1955) and George Sand in *Lélia* (1952).

**Nabokov, Vladimir,** *The Real Life of Sebastian Knight* (1941). Story of a fictitious English novelist of note; a story told by his half-brother and "told with a brilliancy, a delicacy, and a grave and exquisitely venomous humor which makes it a delight to read" (Kay Boyle). *Look at the Harlequins!* (1974) is a pseudoautobiography of a novelist.

**Painter, George D.,** *Proust* (1959–65). Detailed two-volume biography; a monument of erudition. See André Maurois, *The World of Marcel Proust* (1975), a pictorial biography.

**Scott, Sir Walter,** *Journal* (1950). The great romantic novelist was also a superb diarist. This is a selection edited by J. G. Tait. *The Life of Sir Walter Scott* (1837–38) by the novelist's son-in-law, John Gibson Lockhart, is one of the classic English biographies.

**Sinclair, Andrew,** *Scott Fitzgerald* (1962). The whole sad story is "one of the outstanding American literary biographies, a beautifully written book that brings its subject wholly to life" (Jonathan Yardley). The latest facts appear in Matthew J. Bruccoli's admirable *Some Sort of Epic Grandeur* (1981). Not to be missed by Fitzgerald readers are *The Crack-Up* (1945), edited by Edmund Wilson, and Nancy Milford, *Zelda* (1970).

**Stevenson, Robert Louis,** *Letters* (1911). The Scottish writer's letters show the man to be greater than any of his works. See James Pope-Hennessey, *Robert Louis Stevenson* (1974).

**Symons, A. J. A.,** *The Quest for Corvo* (1934). Unusual life history of Frederick Rolfe, the self-styled Baron Corvo — failed priest, paranoiac, and eccentric. This elegantly written "experiment in biography" moves with the excitement of a good detective story. Pamela Hansford Johnson's comic novel, *The Unspeakable Skipton* (1959) is a parody of the Corvo story.

**Trollope, Anthony,** *An Autobiography* (1883). Simple, pleasing, posthumous memoir which outraged his readers by revealing his workmanlike methods of novel writing. Many critics consider it his best book.

**Troyat, Henri,** *Tolstoy* (1965). Tolstoyan treatment of Tolstoy. Panoramic, eminently readable. See Alexandra Tolstoi, *Tolstoi: A Life of My Father* (1953).

**Updike, John,** *Bech: A Book* (1970). Series of sly, funny vignettes about Henry Bech, fictional novelist amidst the New York literary scene. A great satirical tour de force.

**Vidal, Gore,** *Views from a Window: Conversations with Gore Vidal* (1980). Twenty years of interviews with the iconoclastic novelist selected and arranged by subject matter by Robert J. Stanton. A scintillating, provocative treat.

**Waugh, Evelyn,** *The Letters of Evelyn Waugh* (1980). This wide-ranging selection by Mark Amory is filled with the wit, gossip, and perceptions to be expected in the English novelist's correspondence. See *The Diaries of Evelyn Waugh* (1976) and *A Little Learning* (1964), the first volume of a projected three-volume autobiography left unfinished at his death in 1966.

**Wharton, Edith,** *A Backward Glance* (1934). Artfully composed memoirs, reticent about her personal life, always dignified and full of quiet charm. For a look behind these exquisitely well mannered pages see R. W. B. Lewis's Pulitzer Prize–winning biography, *Edith Wharton* (1975), and Cynthia Griffin Wolff's superb study *A Feast of Words* (1977).

**Woolf, Virginia,** *A Writer's Diary* (1954). Extracts from her five-volume diary, selected by her husband, focus on the nature of literary creation. The result is as fascinating as the woman it so clearly reflects. The most moving of her books. See her *Letters* (1975–80), *Moments of Being* (1976) — her unpublished autobiographical writings — and the biography by her nephew, Quentin Bell, *Virginia Woolf* (1972). Phyllis Rose, *Woman of Letters* (1978), is an excellent short literary portrait.

## Short-Story Writer

**Anderson, Sherwood,** *Memoirs* (rev. 1969). An illuminating glimpse into the character of the midwestern storyteller. See *Letters* (1953).

**Babel, Isaac,** *The Lonely Years 1925–1939* (1964). Revealing private correspondence, plus a few unpublished stories, of the Soviet master of the short story, who seems to have disappeared into the gulag in 1939.

**Mansfield, Katherine,** *The Journal of Katherine Mansfield* (1927). A poignant picture of the New Zealand–born writer facing death from tuberculosis. A picture of her literary set, which included D. H. Lawrence, Aldous Huxley, and Virginia Woolf, also emerges. See her *Letters* (1929).

**Maugham, W. Somerset,** *The Summing Up* (1938). "Perhaps the most honest self-evaluation by any author, as it certainly is the most discerning" (Martin S. Day). See *Writer's Notebook* (1949) and Ted Morgan, *Maugham* (1980).

**Migel, Parmenia,** *Titania: The Biography of Isak Dinesen* (1967). A well-conceived life of a singular writer and fascinating personality, the Baronesse Karen Blixen-Frinecke by her close friend. See Frans Lasson (ed.), *The Life and Destiny of Isak Dinesen* (1970), a photobiography.

**O'Connor, Flannery,** *The Habit of Being* (1979). This collection of the letters of the astonishing Georgia novelist and short-story writer reveals her courage, generosity, and intelligence.

**O'Faolain, Sean,** *Vive Moi!* (1964). The Irish writer recalls, in a haunting, enchanting style, how he became an artist and a rebel.

**Paustovsky, Konstantin,** *The Story of a Life* (1964). The first installment of a multivolumed autobiography; simply composed, with dignity of style and the artistry of a master storyteller.

**Steegmuller, Francis,** *Maupassant: A Lion in the Path* (1949). Precise and thoughtful portrayal of the French master of the short-story form.

**Winwar, Frances,** *The Haunted Palace: A Life of Edgar Allan Poe* (1959). While we wait for the great life of this tortured genius to be written, this lush, romantic biography provides genial entertainment.

## Poet

**Atlas, James,** *Delmore Schwartz: The Life of an American Poet* (1977). Judicious biography of the poet, critic, and storyteller who died tragically in New York in 1966. Saul Bellow's Pulitzer Prize–winning novel, *Humboldt's Gift* (1976), presents a fictional portrait of Schwartz.

**Baudelaire, Charles,** *Intimate Journals* (1887, tr. 1949). The tragic poet's comments on love, art, politics, and religion in "tense, abrupt, incisive prose, best of its kind since Pascal" (Cyril Connolly). Translation by Christopher Isherwood, introduction by W. H. Auden. See Enid Starkie, *Baudelaire* (rev. 1958).

**Bogan, Louise,** *What the Woman Lived* (1973). Selected letters, 1920–70, edited by Ruth Limmer, reveal the wisdom and warmth of the poet and critic whose life was devoted to literature. See *Journey Around My Room* (1980), a "mosaic autobiography" also edited by Limmer.

**Byron, Lord,** *Selected Letters* (1953). Excellent selection by Jacques Barzun, full of verve and wisdom, richly reflecting the personality of the charismatic Romantic poet. See *Byron: A Portrait* (1970), a distillation of Leslie Marchand's three-volume biography.

**Carpenter, Humphrey,** *W. H. Auden: A Biography* (1981). Life story of one of the masters of modern poetry. See Stephen Spender (ed.), *W. H. Auden: A Tribute* (1975).

**Chute, Marchette,** *Two Gentlemen: The Lives of George Herbert and Robert Herrick* (1959). Elegantly written lives of the two great, and very different, seventeenth-century English poets serve as a mirror to their age. See Rose Macaulay's historical novel about Herrick, *The Shadow Flies* (1932).

**Cowper, William,** *Selected Letters* (1951). Single-volume selection edited by Mark Van Doren. "Like everything else about him, they are unique. They are so simple that anybody could have written them; but the fact is that nobody has written anything like them. Like a charming companion on a day's ramble he talks delightfully about anything — or nothing" *(Cambridge History of English Literature)*. See Lord David Cecil's biography, *The Stricken Deer* (1930).

**Fitzgerald, Edward,** *Letters* (1979). The Victorian poet and translator of *The Rubaiyat of Omar Khayyam* was one of the greatest letter writers in English literature, his letters having the quality of repose shot through with humor and adumbrations of gentle sorrow.

**Gardner, John,** *The Life and Times of Chaucer* (1977). Biography of the master of Middle English and one of the finest poets in all of literature. See Marchette Chute, *Geoffrey Chaucer of London* (1946).

**Ginsberg, Allen,** *Journals: Early Fifties, Early Sixties* (1977). The poetry of Ginsberg is itself confessional, but these journals contribute additional coloring to the portrait of the artist. See *Indian Journals* (1970) and Jane Kramer's profile of the poet on the road in the sixties, *Allen Ginsberg in America* (1969).

**Gray, Thomas,** *Correspondence* (1935). Of the brilliant and charming letters of the eighteenth-century poet, Cowper remarked: "I once thought Swift's letters the best that could be written; but I like Gray's better." See Lord David Cecil, *Two Quiet Lives: Dorothy Osborne and Thomas Gray* (1948).

**Greene, Graham,** *Lord Rochester's Monkey: Being the Life of John Wilmot, Second Earl of Rochester* (1974). Lively story of the Restoration rake and poet who, after a brief career of violence and several periods of exile from court, died at thirty-three.

**Holmes, Richard,** *Shelley: The Pursuit* (1975). A demythologizing writer's vivid biography of the Romantic lyric poet. See Claire Tomalin, *Shelley and His World* (1980).

**Hopkins, Gerard Manley,** *Journals and Papers* (rev. 1959). These informal jottings

of the English priest and poet have been likened to a workshop littered with the raw material of poetry, giving us more insight into the creative process than a whole library of academic criticism. See Elizabeth Schneider, *The Dragon in the Gate* (1968), a biography.

**Jarrell, Randall,** *The Bat Poet* (1964). Splendid children's book, with illustrations by Maurice Sendak, about a little bat who makes up poems about his animal friends. The poems themselves teach about the nature of poetry.

**Johnson, Samuel,** *The Lives of the Poets* (1779–81). The principal joy of these essays on seventeenth- and eighteenth-century English poets is the display of Dr. Johnson's keen insight and mastery of language.

**Julian, Philippe,** *D'Annunzio* (1973). Popular account of the life and career of the Italian poet, novelist, air force ace, and Fascist theoretician who began his career as a child prodigy and ended it as a cult figure.

**Kaplan, Justin,** *Walt Whitman: A Life* (1980). Vivid, often moving, portrait of the great American poet.

**Keats, John,** *Letters* (1848). Some of the greatest letters in English and a captivating view into the creative mind of the poet who died at twenty-six. See the award-winning biographies, both entitled *John Keats* and both published in 1963, by Walter Jackson Bate and by Aileen Ward.

**Kundera, Milan,** *Life Is Elsewhere* (1974). Ambitious, excellent fictional "portrait of the artist as a young man," about a lyric poet who dies at age twenty. Set in 1948, the year of the Communist takeover of Czechoslovakia.

**Lewis, D. B. Wyndham,** *Francois Villon* (1928). The vagabond-poet colorfully depicted against a fifteenth-century Paris backdrop. See Babette Deutsch's fictional biography, *Rogue's Legacy* (1942). Lewis portrayed another French Renaissance poet in *Ronsard* (1944).

**Lowell, Robert,** *Life Studies* (1959). National Book Award–winning collection of powerful confessional poetry and prose that reads like a novel. See *Day by Day* (1977), autobiographical verse about the poet's struggle with age and death.

**Milosz, Czeslaw,** *Native Realm: A Search for Self-Definition* (1968). Recollections by the Nobel Prize–winning poet, resident in U.S., who writes in Polish. See *Issa Valley* (1981), an autobiographical novel.

**Moore, Thomas,** *Journal of 1818–41* (1964). Peter Quennell edited these gossipy and genial chronicles of English literary life by the Bard of Ireland. See L. A. G. Strong, *The Minstrel Boy: A Portrait of Tom Moore* (1937).

**Origo, Iris,** *Leopardi: A Study in Solitude* (rev. 1954). Illuminating view of the personal life of the great Italian lyric poet and polymath. See *Selected Prose and Poetry* (1966), edited by Origo and John Heath-Stubbs.

**Pasternak, Boris,** *Safe Conduct* (1949). A singular autobiography of isolated sharp impressions and juxtapositions that seem to deny chronology. But you get a feeling of the essence of the young poet's problems as well as his perceptions. Written when the Nobel Prize–winning Soviet poet was forty. See *I Remember: Sketch for an Autobiography* (1959).

**Pound, Ezra,** *Letters* (1950). These letters, from 1907 to 1941, are "the most revealing documents I have read since those of Boswell or Jane Carlyle, but how differently revealing. For where nearly all letters we know are attempts to express personal feelings, to give private news, to entertain, these letters as published contain hardly a paragraph which does not relate in one way or another to one sole theme — the arts" (Katherine Anne Porter). See Peter Ackroyd, *Ezra Pound and His World* (1981), a brief illustrated biography, and Hugh Kenner, *The Pound Era* (1971).

**Quennell, Peter,** *Alexander Pope* (1968). Urbane celebration of the poet, satirist, and literary dictator of the Augustan age, the master of the heroic couplet.

**Rilke, Rainer Maria,** *The Notebooks of Malte Laurids Brigge* (1910). Semiautobiographical novel about a young poet in Paris written in the form of seemingly random journal entries. "A miraculous, perfect work" (Elizabeth Hardwick). Rilke's remarkable *Letters* (1945–48) are an important part of his legacy. See *Letters to a Young Poet* (rev. 1954).

**Sarton, May,** *I Knew a Phoenix: Sketches for an Autobiography* (1959). Evocative, literate memoirs which gracefully illuminate the life of a poet with a generous heart. Her novel, *Mrs. Stevens Hears the Mermaids* (1965), is about a poet.

**Sexton, Anne,** *A Self-Portrait in Letters* (1977). Although her frank confessional poems are her greatest autobiography, these letters, written 1959–74, reveal her thoughts during an agonizing, dramatic period of her life.

**Steegmuller, Francis,** *Cocteau* (1970). The French avant-garde poet, playwright, film maker, novelist, and cartoonist, splendidly captured in a National Book Award–winning biography. See Robert Phelps (ed.), *Professional Secrets: The Autobiography of Jean Cocteau* (1970). Steegmuller also wrote *Appolinaire: Poet Among the Painters* (1963).

**Stevens, Wallace,** *Letters of Wallace Stevens* (1966). Rich collection of letters from 1895 to Stevens's death in 1955, selected by his daughter. Almost an autobiography.

**Thomas, Dylan,** *The Letters of Dylan Thomas* (1966). Marvelous letters, fully reflective of the Welshman's *foudroyant* personality. See Paul Ferris, *Dylan Thomas* (1977), a good biography, and John Malcolm Brinnin, *Dylan Thomas in America* (1955).

**Thompson, Lawrence,** *Robert Frost* (1966–77). Accomplished, very objective, three-volume study by the New England poet's chosen biographer. Winner of Pulitzer Prize. See the one-volume abridgement (1981).

**Trelawny, Edward John,** *Recollections of the Last Days of Shelley and Byron* (1858). A close friend of both poets — he recovered Shelley's drowned body — his remembrances of them are a bit apocryphal, but sparkling and engaging.

**Troyat, Henri,** *Pushkin* (1950). This lively biography of Russia's greatest poet presents a panorama of that nation's life between 1799 and 1837, the span of Pushkin's life.

**Williams, William Carlos,** *Autobiography* (1951). "A book that must become indispensable to any one interested in 20th century American poetry, and especially in the earlier and yeastier period — say up to 1925" (Conrad Aiken). See *Selected Letters* (1957) and Paul Mariani's biography, *William Carlos Williams* (1981).

**Wordsworth, William,** *The Prelude* (1850). This remarkable poem tracing the "Growth of a Poet's Mind" is "the greatest poem about poetry ever written" (C. Day Lewis). The journals of his "exquisite sister" (as Coleridge called her) not only shed light on the poet but are classics in their own right. See *Journals of Dorothy Wordsworth* (1971), edited by Mary Moorman.

**Yeats, William Butler,** *Autobiography* (1936). Ranging over fifty-eight years, from Yeats's earliest memories to his winning of the Nobel Prize, it is a major testament by one of the great poets.

## Literary Critic

**Brooks, Van Wyck,** *An Autobiography* (1965). One-volume edition of his three books of memoirs. "A luminous testament of one of the most dedicated literary careers in our century" (Leon Edel). See Raymond Nelson, *Van Wyck Brooks: A Writer's Life* (1981).

**Howe, M. A. DeWolfe,** *John Jay Chapman and His Letters* (1937). "Chapman was probably the best letter-writer that we have ever had in this country. . . . A personality who does not belong in his time and place and who by contrast makes us aware of the commonness, the provinciality and the timidity of most of his contemporaries" (Edmund Wilson). See his *Selected Writings* (1968) and Richard B. Hovey's *John Jay Chapman: An American Mind* (1959).

**Kazin, Alfred,** *A Walker in the City* (1951). Boyhood and young manhood in Brooklyn: a "singular and beautiful work, a sort of perambulating memoir in lyric form. By turns mournful, violent, and tender, its theme is the immemorial one of the boy in search of the man he must become" (Brendan Gill). Continued in *Starting Out in the Thirties* (1965) and *New York Jew* (1978).

**Nicolson, Sir Harold,** *Sainte-Beuve* (1957). The strange life of an eminent nineteenth-century Frenchman whose name was once synonymous with literary criticism.

**Wilson, Edmund,** *A Prelude* (1967). The great critic's journal of his first trip to Europe in 1908, his college days at Princeton, and his experiences during two years in the army in the First World War. Other autobiographical works include *A Piece of My Mind* (1956) and his notebooks and letters.

## Essayist

**Boswell, James,** *The Life of Samuel Johnson* (1791). "Boswell is the first of biographers. He has no second. Many of the greatest men have written biography. Boswell was one of the smallest men who ever lived and he has beaten them all" (Thomas Babington Macauley). See Walter Jackson Bate's Pulitzer Prize–winning *Samuel Johnson* (1977).

**Bowen, Catherine Drinker,** *Francis Bacon: The Temper of a Man* (1963).

"With her admirable experience as a biographer, her conscientious care as a historian; with her skill at precise delineation, she has seen farther into this difficult and rewarding man than anyone else has" (A. L. Rowse).

**Cecil, Lord David,** *Max: A Biography* (1965). Max Beerbohm, the incomparable one, the cultured satirist of the elegantly mannered prose, memorialized by a sympathetic and urbane biographer. S. N. Behrman's *Portrait of Max* (1960) splendidly illuminates Beerbohm in his later years.

**Chesterton, G. K.,** *Autobiography* (1936). Lively, shrewd, with a mix of high seriousness and wit, by a memorable individualist and felicitous essayist. See Dudley Barker, *G. K. Chesterton: A Biography* (1973).

**Dennis, Nigel,** *Jonathan Swift: A Short Character* (1964). The great satirist delineated in 160 pages. A more spacious biography is John Middleton Murry, *Jonathan Swift* (1954). For a Swiftly-paced fictional characterization see Edith Sitwell, *I Live Under a Black Sun* (1937).

**Emerson, Ralph Waldo,** *The Heart of Emerson's Journals* (1926). Fine abridgement by Bliss Perry of Emerson's diaries, which have a witty terseness not always found in his essays. See Gay Wilson Allen, *Waldo Emerson* (1981).

**Hunt, Leigh,** *Autobiography* (1860). Hunt was at the center of the literary life of his time; he knew Shelley, Keats, Byron, and Dickens, and his autobiography is full of choice, if not totally reliable, bits of gossip about them. See the one-volume abridgement edited by J. E. Morpurgo (1949) and Edmund Blunden's biography, *Leigh Hunt and His Circle* (1930).

**Lamb, Charles,** *Selected Letters* (1956). "Who touches this book touches a man. A man, moreover, who is crusty and fusty enough, punning and cunning enough, tragical and magical enough, to be called, without question, one of the great letter

writers in the history of English literature" (Carlos Baker). See E. V. Lucas, *The Life of Charles Lamb* (rev. 1921).

**Montaigne, Michel De,** *Autobiography* (1935). Autobiographical excerpts from the essays, travels, and letters rearranged in chronological sequence and linked up with explanatory notes by Marvin Lowenthal. An entrancing and useful book. See Donald M. Frame, *Montaigne* (1965).

**Orieux, Jean,** *Voltaire* (1979). Excellent old-fashioned life; "no one has captured so skillfully as Orieux the dramatics of Voltaire and his age, the light and shadow of the emotional surfaces" (Frank E. Manuel).

**Orwell, George,** *Collected Essays, Journals and Letters* (1968). "He always writes here with such burning clarity, such intellectual fervor, such respect for logic as the commonweal of human intelligence" (Alfred Kazin). See Bernard Crick, *George Orwell* (1981).

**Smith, Sydney,** *Selected Letters* (1956). Perfectly delightful letters of the witty English clergyman who contributed down-to-earth critical essays to the *Edinburgh Review,* which he helped found, during the early nineteenth century. See his *Selected Writings* (1956), edited by W. H. Auden and see Hesketh Pearson, *The Smith of Smiths* (1934).

**Thurber, James,** *My Life and Hard Times* (1933). Humorous personal recollections by a master of prose and drawing. See *The Selected Letters of James Thurber* (1981) and Charles S. Holmes, *The Clocks of Columbus: The Literary Career of James Thurber* (1972).

**Twain, Mark,** *The Autobiography of Mark Twain* (1959). Masterly editing of his autobiographical pieces by Charles Neider into a candid, luminous self-portrait. See Justin Kaplan, *Mr. Clemens and Mark Twain* (1966).

**White, E. B.,** *Letters of E. B. White* (1976). These finely penned letters constitute an "involuntary autobiography" of the much admired essayist long associated with the *New Yorker.* See *Essays of E. B. White* (1977).

## Dramatist

**Bakeless, John,** *Christopher Marlowe: The Man and His Time* (1937). Full-blooded biography of the sixteenth-century dramatic and poetic genius whose life ended before age thirty.

**Bingham, Madeline,** *Sheridan: The Track of a Comet* (1972). Life of Richard Brinsley Sheridan recounted in a chatty and spirited style against the colorful background of eighteenth-century England.

**Chekhov, Anton,** *Selected Letters* (1973). The master of both the drama and the short story was also a superb correspondent and these letters, edited by Simon Karlinsky, come as close to an autobiography as anything Chekhov ever wrote. See Ronald Hingley, *A New Life of Anton Chekhov* (1976).

**Chute, Marchette,** *Ben Jonson of Westminster* (1953). Well researched, in-depth portrait of the dramatist and poet, radiant with the spirit of Jacobean England. See *Shakespeare of London* (1949).

**Gorky, Maxim,** *Autobiography* (1913–23). Trilogy comprising *Childhood* (1913), *In the World* (1916), and *My Universities* (1923); rich in fact and insight, it is the Russian writer's most enduring work. As a companion volume, see *Reminiscences* (1919), with its wonderful anecdotes about such literary figures as Tolstoy and Chekhov.

**Hart, Moss,** *Act One* (1959). Zestful autobiography of the collaborator with George S. Kaufman, of "the stage-struck kid who fought his way up from the Bronx," and "the best book on 'show business' as practiced in this country in our time that I have ever read" (S. N. Behrman).

**Hellman, Lillian,** *Three: An Unfinished Woman; Pentimento; Scoundrel Time* (1978). Omnibus volume of eloquent, moving memoirs by an intelligent, caring artist.

**Lahr, John,** *Prick up Your Ears: The Biography of Joe Orton* (1978). Revealing account of the sad life of the English playwright who was bludgeoned to death at age thirty-four. Helpful in understanding the English theater since 1956. See *Up Against the Fourth Wall* (1970), a study of the radical theater of the sixties.

**Lesley, Cole,** *Remembered Laughter: The Life of Noel Coward* (1976). Written by Coward's secretary, companion, and confidant of nearly forty years, the sophisticated playwright-actor appears with all his minor selfishnesses and major generosities. See William Marchant, *The Privilege of His Company: Noel Coward Remembered* (1975).

**Lewis, D. B. Wyndham,** *Molière: The Comic Mask* (1959). Fine introduction to the life and plays of the great French comic dramatist who spent fourteen years as a strolling player in the provinces.

**Meredith, Scott,** *George S. Kaufman and His Friends* (1974). Delightful account of the witty playwright and his circle of clever and waggish cronies. For a detailed biography see Malcolm Goldstein, *George S. Kaufman: His Life, His Theatre* (1979).

**Meyer, Michael,** *Ibsen* (1971). Massive biography of "the father of modern drama." Detailed and scholarly, it will engage anyone seriously interested in the Norwegian playwright.

**O'Casey, Sean,** *Autobiography* (1939–54). Faulted by some for overblown rhetoric, a six-volume, third-person autobiography. "It is a masterpiece of writing. The writing has music, eloquence, passion, bitterness and force" (Brooks Atkinson). *Mirror in My House* (1957) is a two-volume abridgement.

**Pearson, Hesketh,** *Gilbert & Sullivan: A Biography* (1935). Frothy portrait of the

Victorian comic opera geniuses, full of "innocent merriment" guaranteed to delight any Savoyard.

**Schoenbaum, Samuel,** *William Shakespeare: A Compact Documentary Life* (1977). Readers' edition of the author's classic *William Shakespeare: A Documentary Life* (1975), based on all the available evidence. See *William Shakespeare: The Globe and the World* (1979).

**Shaeffer, Louis,** *O'Neill: Son and Playwright* (1968). With its companion, the Pulitzer Prize–winning *O'Neill: Son and Artist* (1973), it is the standard biography of the most autobiographical modern dramatist.

**Sprigge, Elizabeth,** *The Strange Life of August Strindberg* (1949). Noncritical biography of the tormented Swedish dramatist, poet, and novelist, written sympathetically and objectively.

**Weintraub, Stanley (ed.),** *Shaw: An Autobiography* (1969–70). Artfully fashioned from bits and pieces of autobiographical writing into a cohesive, felicitous self-portrait of an astonishing man.

**Wilde, Oscar,** *Letters* (1962). The scintillating wit is seen to perfection here following Wilde's notorious career through his correspondence. See H. Montgomery Hyde, *Oscar Wilde* (1976).

**Williams, Tennessee,** *Memoirs* (1975). Candid revelations of a full life by one of America's foremost modern playwrights.

## Historian

**Adams, Henry,** *The Education of Henry Adams* (1907). Written in the third person, this partial autobiography, subtitled *A Study in 20th-Century Multiplicity,* is really about modern man's search for meaning and is a classic of pessimism. See Ernest Samuels's Pulitzer Prize–winning biography, *Henry Adams* (1948–1964).

**Bradley, David,** *The Chaneysville Incident* (1981). Moving novel about a black historian's search into the eighteenth century for his roots, in a rich blend of fact and fiction.

**Clive, John,** *Macauley: The Making of a Historian* (1973). The brilliant Victorian historian, poet, essayist, and statesman memorialized in a biography of drama and power.

**Durant, Will & Ariel Durant,** *A Dual Autobiography* (1977). Eminently readable and informative. Must reading for anyone who enjoyed their magnum opus, *The Story of Civilization.*

**Froude, James,** *Thomas Carlyle* (1882–84). An authorized biography which honestly portrays the moody Carlyle. This four-volume Victorian classic might be best enjoyed in the one-volume abridgement by John Clubbe (1979). The shrewd and witty letters of the historian's wife shed much light on his character and may well outlive any of his works; see *I Too Am Here: Selections from the Letters of Jane Welsh Carlyle* (1977).

**Gibbon, Edward,** *Autobiography* (1796). Brilliant and candid memoir, principally about how he conceived and wrote his great history of the Roman Empire. See Gavin De Beer, *Gibbon and His World* (1968).

**Mitchell, Joseph,** *Joe Gould's Secret* (1965). Journalist's remembrances of the eccentric Greenwich Village Bohemian, Joe Gould, author of the legendary *Oral History of Our Time.*

**Toynbee, Arnold,** *Experiences* (1969). An informal "postscript" by the distinguished author of the twelve-volume *A Study of History.* See *Acquaintances* (1967) and *Toynbee on Toynbee* (1974).

**Trevelyan, G. M.,** *Autobiography and Other Essays* (1949). The eminent English historian's beautifully written autobiographical sketch accompanied by selected pieces — personal, literary, and historical.

Wilson, Angus, *Anglo-Saxon Attitudes* (1956). The sixty-year-old historian-protagonist of this rich satiric novel finds fraud in academe and in his own relationships.

## Philosopher

Cohen, Morris, R., *A Dreamer's Journey: The Autobiography of Morris Raphael Cohen* (1949). This memoir will take a "permanent place among the classics of immigrant narrative, and one not too far behind the greater classics of intellectual biography. It reveals . . . the sources from which his strength is gathered, it explains why he conspicuously succeeded in writing philosophy that can be read as literature" (Perry Miller). See Leonora Cohen Rosenfield, *Portrait of a Philosopher* (1963).

Franklin, Benjamin, *The Autobiography of Benjamin Franklin* (1791). Written initially to guide his son, it is a lively account of the eventful life of the man David Hume hailed as the first philosopher and great man of letters in the New World. The definitive life is Carl Van Doren's Pulitzer Prize–winning *Benjamin Franklin: A Biography* (1938).

Hollingdale, R. J., *Nietzsche: The Man and His Philosophy* (1965). "Scholarly and attractive study of both the man and his work, it enables us to see Nietzsche against his own background" (Hugh Trevor-Roper). The best critical work is Walter Kaufman, *Nietzsche: Philosopher, Psychologist, Antichrist* (rev. 1968).

James, William, *Selected Letters* (1961). The Harvard philosopher-psychologist is revealed in "pages of exquisite self-questioning, of delightful observation, of sun and of shadow, to which Elizabeth Hardwick has added a beautifully written and penetrating introduction" (Loren Eiseley). See Gay Wilson Allen, *William James* (1967).

Levy, Paul, *Moore: G. E. Moore and the Cambridge Apostles* (1980). Collective biography of the influential Cambridge University philosopher and the exclusive undergraduate society, the Apostles, which included Bertrand Russell, Alfred North Whitehead, and Lytton Strachy.

Malcolm, Norman, *Ludwig Wittgenstein: A Memoir* (1958). The Austrian philosopher, who taught at Cambridge University and was a leading influence on logical positivism, engagingly remembered by one of his students.

Mill, John Stuart, *Autobiography of John Stuart Mill* (1873). Deals with but one part of a life, the life of the mind — but a most remarkable mind. It is as "important a document for the understanding of the nineteenth century as it is for the understanding of Mill himself" (Asa Briggs).

Rousseau, Jean-Jacques, *Confessions* (1782). The first great Romantic autobiography is one of the frankest and most fascinating documents on the life of the eighteenth century.

Russell, Bertrand, *Autobiography* (1967–69). Candid, witty exposition of the personal life of one of the most remarkable figures of our time. *My Philosophical Development* (1960) is his philosophical autobiography, while *Portraits from Memory* (1956) describes his contacts with other well-known people. See Ronald Clark, *The Life of Bertrand Russell* (1975).

Santayana, George, *Persons and Places* (1944–45). This memoir by the Harvard philosopher is "an autobiography with a metaphysical plot; it stands somewhere between Proust's great novel and *The Education of Henry Adams*" (Edmund Wilson).

## Journalist

Crouse, Timothy, *The Boys on the Bus* (1973). Traveling with reporters during the 1972 presidential election, Crouse studied the different styles used by the press and wrote this immensely readable account of how the media covers a campaign.

**Dreiser, Theodore,** *A Book About Myself* (1922). Later republished as *Newspaper Days,* it chronicles the novelist's early unhappy career as a Chicago newspaperman in the 1890s. See W. A. Swanberg, *Dreiser* (1965).

**Fowler, Gene,** *Skyline: A Reporter's Reminiscences of the 1920's* (1961). Colorful recollections of the New York beat of sixty years ago. See *A Solo in Tom-Toms* (1946) and H. Allen Smith, *The Life and Legend of Gene Fowler* (1977).

**Hecht, Ben,** *A Child of the Century* (1954). Thoroughly entertaining and frank autobiography of the journalist, novelist, screenwriter, and coauthor of *The Front Page* (1928). *Gaily, Gaily* (1963) is an evocation of his cub reporter days in Chicago of 1910–15.

**Hough, Henry Beetle,** *Country Editor* (1940). Twenty years as editor of the *Vineyard Gazette* of Martha's Vineyard, recollected in simple and beautiful prose.

**Kendrick, Alexander,** *Prime Time: The Life of Edward R. Murrow* (1969). This biography of a man with a profound commitment to fair-minded reporting "lives up to the Murrow documentary standards: tough, perceptive, fair, full of insight and emotion" (Fred W. Friendly).

**Krock, Arthur,** *Memoirs: Sixty Years on the Firing Line* (1968). The author's long tenure as newspaper correspondent on the international and Washington scene — from TR to LBJ — make this flavorful memoir a "rich and absorbing book" (Arthur M. Schlesinger, Jr.).

**Mencken, H. L.,** *A Choice of Days* (1980). This sampler of his splendid autobiographical classics (*Happy Days, Newspaper Days,* and *Heathen Days*), originally published in the forties, is "an unadulterated, 180-proof delight, the chronicle of a lifelong romance with the printed word" (Justin Kaplan).

**Muggeridge, Malcolm,** *Chronicles of Wasted Time* (1972–73). The English journalist's autobiography is "careless, witty, outrageous, provocative, wise and sometimes silly, [but] never boring, except when carried along on the divine afflatus" (*Times Literature Supplement*). See *Like It Was: The Diaries of Malcolm Muggeridge* (1982).

**Steffens, Lincoln,** *Autobiography* (1931). Classic autobiography, candid and lively, of the great muckraking journalist of the first decades of the century. See Justin Kaplan, *Lincoln Steffens* (1974).

## Foreign Correspondent

**Cameron, James,** *Point of Departure: An Attempt at Autobiography* (1967). Intensely personal, pungent, beautifully told, honest account of recent years in the world's stricken places by a distinguished English foreign correspondent with a rare compassion for the people he writes about. See *An Indian Summer* (1975).

**Duranty, Walter,** *I Write as I Please* (1935). A fascinating period piece: the adventuresome memoirs of a journalist who went to Russia in 1921 as correspondent for the *New York Times* and stayed on fourteen years.

**Farson, Negley,** *The Way of a Transgressor* (1936). The *beau ideal* of cavalier correspondents' books. Not the long view of Duranty or Sheean, but a romantic adventure story of the American journalist's years in Czarist Russia, his spell with the RFC in Egypt, and more. Continued in *A Mirror for Narcissus* (1957).

**Miller, Lee G.,** *The Story of Ernie Pyle* (1950). "This is magnificent biography, as tragic a love story as has been written in our time . . . he wrote himself into the heart of a great army and into the heart of a whole nation with a simpler prose" (Meyer Berger). By a long-time friend and editor of the beloved war correspondent.

**Nevinson, Henry Wood,** *Fires of Life* (1935). Skillful abridgement of three-volume autobiography (1923–28) of a remarkable Englishman — war correspondent, philanthropist, man of letters, and one of the most popular figures of his time. "No better autobiography has been written in English in the last hundred years" (John Masefield).

**Sanders, Marion K.,** *Dorothy Thompson: A Legend in Her Time* (1973). Well-written life of a remarkable woman, one of the most respected journalists of her generation, and wife of Sinclair Lewis.

**Sevareid, Eric,** *Not So Wild a Dream* (1946). Classic memoir of the distinguished journalist as a young reporter during World War II. Beautifully written, it compassionately captures the temper of the times.

**Sheean, Vincent,** *Personal History* (1934). Analytical, cynical account of the between-war years' experiences among the Rif in Morocco, China in the early days of Communism, and Palestine in 1929. "Vastly more appealing than the usual war correspondent's memoirs of things romantically seen and dangers escaped by the breadth of a keen Damascus blade" (Malcolm Cowley).

**Shirer, William L.,** *Twentieth Century Journey* (1976). Illuminating recollections of the noted foreign correspondent best remembered for his dispatches from Germany during the rise of the Third Reich.

**White, Theodore H.,** *In Search of History: A Personal Adventure* (1978). The search for the connection between American power and American purpose by the noted journalist who first won his reputation as a foreign correspondent in Asia and Europe.

## Physicist

**Andrade, E. W. da C.,** *Sir Isaac Newton* (1954). Concise, readable biography of the English scientific genius by a distinguished atomic physicist. Frank E. Man-

uel's *A Portrait of Isaac Newton* (1968) is a psychological study.

**Azbel, Mark Ya,** *Refusenik: Trapped in the Soviet Union* (1981). The plight of a world-renowned Jewish physicist in Russia who was refused permission to leave: a simple, honest, and compassionate book.

**Born, Max,** *My Life: Recollections of a Nobel Laureate* (1979). Memoir by the distinguished contemporary theoretical physicist who died in 1970 at age eighty-seven. See *My Life and My Views* (1968) and the *Born-Einstein Letters* (1971).

**Coulson, Thomas,** *Joseph Henry: His Life and Work* (1950). Sympathetic and restrained story of the dean of early American science.

**Dyson, Freeman,** *Disturbing the Universe* (1979). Written with wit and grace, a scientist's poetic and mystical reflections on the nature of science as well as his insights into the people and ideas of his time.

**Einstein, Albert,** *The World as I See It* (1950). Collection of short essays which mirror the philosophical, political, and social attitudes of an independent and uncompromising thinker. See *Out of My Later Years* (1950) and Helen Dukas and Banesh Hoffmann (eds.), *Albert Einstein: The Human Side* (1979). For biography see Banesh Hoffman, *Albert Einstein: Creator and Rebel* (1972).

**Fermi, Laura,** *Atoms in the Family: My Life with Enrico Fermi* (1954). Informal, entertaining biography of one of the foremost theoretical physicists of his day. See Emilio Segré, *Enrico Fermi: Physicist* (1970).

**Gamow, George,** *My World Line: An Informal Autobiography* (1975). The Russian-American scientist and expert popularizer writes about his life and acquaintances.

**Heisenberg, Werner,** *Physics and Beyond* (1971). The author of the uncertainty principle shares his insights into modern physics and what it was like as a German scientist during the Second World War.

**Millikan, Robert A.,** *Autobiography* (1950). Absorbing memoirs of the American Nobel Prize–winning physicist and president of Cal Tech who discovered cosmic rays. See Robert H. Kargon, *The Rise of Robert Millikan* (1982).

**Moore, Ruth E.,** *Niels Bohr* (1966). The Danish theoretical physicist, who did pioneer work on the theory of nuclear reactions, memoralized in a dramatic biography.

**Planck, Max,** *Scientific Autobiography* (1949). Fascinating memoir by the Nobel Prize–winning physicist who formulated the quantum theory.

**Rukeyser, Muriel,** *Willard Gibbs: American Genius* (1942). Biography by a distinguished poet about the father of physical chemistry, who was born in 1839 and is considered by the author to be one of the towering intellects in American history.

**Segré, Emilio,** *From X-rays to Quarks: Modern Physicists and Their Discoveries* (1980). Anecdotal history from 1895 to the present that captures the drama and excitement of the revolutions in physics, by a Nobel laureate.

**Smith, Alice Kimball and Charles Weiner** **(eds.),** *Robert Oppenheimer: Letters and Recollections* (1980). The frank and often moving writings of the brilliant and controversial physicist who was the scientific leader of the Manhattan Project.

## *Teacher*

**Ashton-Warner, Sylvia,** *Spinster* (1951). Haunting, poetic novel of a teacher of the Maori in an outpost schoolhouse in New Zealand. The author, a distinguished teacher herself, has written *Teacher* (1963) and an autobiography *I Passed This Way* (1979).

**Braithewaite, E. R.,** *To Sir, with Love* (1960). Heartwarming, dramatic account of tribulations that the author, a West Indian black, overcame teaching in a London East End school.

**Chase, Mary Ellen,** *A Goodly Heritage* (1932). With its sequel, *A Goodly Fellowship* (1939), a delightful memoir filled with enthusiasm for teaching, of experiences as an English teacher in settings, from a rural school in Maine to a great university.

**Epstein, Joseph (ed.),** *Masters: Portraits of Great Teachers* (1981). Collection of fine essays on memorable teachers by exceptional students. See Houston Peterson (ed.), *Great Teachers* (1946), which includes first-hand accounts of such teachers as Emerson, William James, and Rodin.

**Erskine, John,** *My Life as a Teacher* (1948). A much-admired professor at Amherst and Columbia, who seems to have led a full and happy life, records his works and days with great gusto. See *The Memory of Certain Persons* (1947).

**Holt, Rackham,** *Mary McLeod Bethune* (1964). This biography of a woman who devoted her life to improving the education of her fellow blacks "gives the reader a nice sense of the stature, strength, earthy wisdom and awesome limitations of this interesting woman" (Lillian Smith).

**Neill, A. S.,** *Neill! Neill! Orange Peel* (1972). The radical educator and founder of Summerhill recounts his long and fascinating career.

**Phelps, William Lyon,** *Autobiography with Letters* (1939). The Yale English professor said that "there is no profession more adventuresome, more exciting, more thrilling than that of teaching"; these warm, anecdotal, spacious reminiscences confirm his words.

**Stuart, Jesse,** *The Thread that Runs So True* (1949). The Kentucky poet-novelist traces his career as a teacher in this eloquent, honest book. Another teacher's memoir by a Kentucky novelist is Harriet Simpson's *Mountain Path* (1936).

**Washington, Booker T.,** *Up from Slavery* (1901). Classic autobiography of the black educator, born a slave in 1856, who founded Tuskegee Institute. See Emma Lee Thornbrough (ed.), *Booker T. Washington* (1969).

# Rogue

**Block, Lawrence,** *Burglars Can't Be Choosers* (1977). The first detective novel of a series featuring Bernie Rhodenbarr, Manhattan's coolest and most literary cat burglar. Others include *The Burglar Who Liked to Quote Kipling* (1979) and *The Burglar Who Studied Spinoza* (1980).

**Dickens, Charles,** *Oliver Twist* (1837–39). At the hands of Fagin and his gang of thieves — the memorable Artful Dodger, Bill Sikes, and Charlie Bates — young Oliver is forced to be a burglar in Dickens's novel of crime and poverty in London.

**Fielding, Henry,** *Jonathan Wild* (1743). Based on the life of the real Jonathan Wild, a famous highwayman of his day, and intended as a political satire of Sir Robert Walpole, this wonderfully odd novel can still be enjoyed by modern readers, for it is "the most dazzling piece of sustained satirical writing in our language" (V. S. Pritchett).

**Gogol, Nikolai,** *Dead Souls* (1842). The hero is Chichikov, an unscrupulous rascal with an ingenious plan to get rich quick by capitalizing on the gullibility and avarice of his neighbors. A great satiric novel.

**Hornung, E. W.,** *The Amateur Cracksman* (1899). Enter Raffles, the debonair, cricket-loving gentleman thief, second in popularity only to Sherlock Holmes in their day. The raffish Robin Hood tradition was continued by Leslie Charteris in his series about the Saint; see *Enter the Saint* (1930).

**Ilf and Petrov,** *Twelve Chairs* (1928). Hilarious novel about Russian trickster Ostap Bender. *Little Golden Calf* (1931) is a sequel.

**Johnston, Alva,** *The Legendary Mizeners* (1953). A gifted reporter's delightful life of Wilson Mizener — celebrated scoundrel, con man, professional gambler, wit, and prodigious liar — whose career lasted from 1890 to 1933.

**Jonson, Ben,** *The Alchemist* (1612). This rollicking comedy about a rogue-swindler-charlatan is one of the best satires on human gullibility.

**McDonald, Gregory,** *Fletch* (1974). Premier adventure of Fletch, a laid-back man of leisure, sometime hard-gunning investigative reporter, and endearing smart-aleck. McDonald's other series — about a remarkable Boston cop–CIA agent — begins with *Flynn* (1977).

**Mann, Thomas,** *The Confessions of Felix Krull, Confidence Man* (1954). Mann's last work of fiction, the first volume of the ironically humorous autobiography of a charming rogue and his many picaresque adventures.

**Parrish, Frank,** *Fire in the Barley* (1978). First of a series of suspense novels about the delightful and highly individual Dan Mallett — poacher, lover, con man, thief — that nicely evoke the English landscape.

**Shaplen, Robert,** *Kreuger: Genius and Swindler* (1960). Classic tale of Ivar Kreuger, the Swedish Match King, who built a financial empire in the twenties, related with zest. Another famous con artist is portrayed in Tom Cullen's *A Playful Panther: The Story of J. Maundy Gregory, Con Man* (1975).

*Till Eulenspiegel* (c. 1520). The original merry prankster; his jolly, ribald adventures are chronicled in many modern versions.

**Trelawny, Edward John,** *Adventures of a Younger Son* (1831). According to this

Cornish charlatan and teller of tall tales, he lived through a series of exotic adventures, including command of a pirate ship, friendship with Shelley and Byron, and service in the Greek rebellion of the 1820s.

## Physician

**Alvarez, Walter,** *Incurable Physician: An Autobiography* (1963). Anecdote-studded memoirs of a columnist-doctor who worked twenty-five years at the Mayo Clinic.

**Ariyoshi, Sawako,** *The Doctor's Wife* (1978). Psychological novel based on life of Hanaoka Seishu, the eighteenth-century Japanese physician who developed the use of anesthesia for surgery a half-century before its use in the West, and his relationships with his wife, mother, and sister.

**Coe, Urling C.,** *Frontier Doctor* (1939). Lusty, straight-shooting autobiography, rich in incident and character, by a physician on the Oregon frontier around the turn of the century.

**Cushing, Harvey,** *Life of Sir William Osler* (1925). The life of the much-loved Canadian physician and teacher in a Pulitzer Prize–winning biography by an eminent Boston surgeon.

**Heisel, Victor,** *An American Doctor's Odyssey* (1936). Medical adventures in forty-five countries.

**Kessell, Joseph,** *The Man with the Miraculous Hands* (1961). Extraordinary story of Dr. Felix Kersten, personal physician to Heinrich Himmler, who used his influence to save thousands of lives.

**Kobler, John,** *Reluctant Surgeon: A Biography of John Hunter* (1960). Story of the eighteenth-century founder of scientific surgery — the Shakespeare of Medicine — his turbulent life set in the world of Covent Garden in all its blowsy magnificence.

**Malinin, Theodore I.,** *Surgery and Life: The Extraordinary Career of Alexis Carrel* (1979). Well-researched and smoothly written account of the volatile career of the French surgeon who worked in America and won the Nobel Prize for Medicine.

**Munthe, Axel,** *The Story of San Michele* (1929). By a Swedish physician — his travels, his meditations, and his villa in Capri, with enough material to furnish writers of short sensational stories with plots for the rest of their lives. One of the most famous books of its day.

**Penfield, Wilder,** *The Torch* (1960). Hippocrates, the Father of Medicine, fictionally depicted in fifth-century B.C. Greece by a noted neurologist. See the author's memoirs, *No Man Alone: A Surgeon's Story* (1977).

**Ross, Ishbel,** *Child of Destiny: The Life Story of the First Woman Doctor* (1949). Popular biography of Dr. Elizabeth Blackwell, the first woman physician of modern times. See Jo Manton, *Elizabeth Garrett Anderson* (1965), about England's first woman doctor.

## Medical Missionary

**Bullard, Roger P.,** *Inuk* (1951). Fascinating recollections of a French Catholic missionary who spent seventeen years working with the Eskimos and came to know them well.

**Dooley, Thomas A.,** *Dr. Tom Dooley's Three Great Books* (1960). Omnibus volume of the compelling books by a medical missionary in Laos. See James Monahan (ed.), *Before I Sleep* (1961), an account of Dooley's last days by people who helped him during his final tragic months.

**Hemenway, Ruth, V.,** *A Memoir of Revolutionary China, 1924–41* (1977). She spent eighteen years in remote areas of prerevolutionary China as a medical missionary.

**Jeal, Tim,** *Livingstone* (1973). Lively biography of the legendary nineteenth-century

English missionary and explorer in Africa.

**Schweitzer, Albert,** *Out of My Life and Thought* (1933). An astounding figure, who was a doctor in Africa, musician, theologian, and writer. *On the Edge of the Primeval Forest* (1931) is about his medical mission. See Norman Cousins, *Dr. Schweitzer of Lambarene* (1960).

## Veterinarian

**Herriot, James,** *All Creatures Great and Small* (1972). Yorkshire animal doctor with a fine literary gift. Continued in *All Things Bright and Beautiful* (1974), *All Things Wise and Wonderful* (1977), and *The Lord God Made Them All* (1981). See *James Herriot's Yorkshire* (1980).

**Klein, Michel,** *For the Love of Animals: The Autobiography of a Veterinary Surgeon* (1979). A Gallic Herriot, who treats exotic as well as domestic pets.

**Lofting, Hugh,** *The Story of Dr. Dolittle* (1920). The eccentric physician's passion for animals leads him to give up his medical practice to become a veterinarian and eventually to "talk to the animals." The first of a delightful series of nonsense stories for children.

**Milts, Milton,** *Only a Gringo Would Die for an Anteater* (1979). Entertaining, sometimes horrifying, tales by the chief vet for the New York City zoos.

**Taylor, David,** *Zoo Vet: Adventures of a Wild Animal Doctor* (1977). Wonderful exotic-animal anecdotes by an English vet enamored of his calling.

## Stage Actor

**Appleton, William Worthen,** *Charles Macklin: An Actor's Life* (1960). Lively biography of the great eighteenth-century English actor-dramatist evokes the colorful era of Drury Lane and Covent Garden.

**Barton, Margaret,** *Garrick* (1949). David Garrick came to London with his friend Samuel Johnson and became one of the foremost players of his time, as well as theater manager, playwright, and Shakespeare revivalist. His leading lady is portrayed in Mary Nash, *The Provoked Wife: The Life and Times of Susannah Cibber* (1977).

**Bevan, Bryan,** *Nell Gwyn* (1970). The seventeenth-century English actress, who achieved enduring fame as the mistress of Charles II.

**Courtney, Marguerite Taylor,** *Laurette* (1955). This intimate, compassionate portrait of Laurette Taylor by her daughter is one of the most captivating modern theatrical biographies.

**Draper, Ruth,** *The Letters of Ruth Draper, 1920–56* (1979). Charming letters woven into a continuous narrative delineating the life of the monologist who "was (with Martha Graham) the greatest individual performer that America has ever given us" (John Gielgud).

**du Maurier, Daphne,** *Gerald: A Portrait* (1935). Clear, cool biography of the famous English actor-producer, Sir Gerald du Maurier, by his daughter. "An original and remarkable performance and, within its limits, one of the best biographies I have read" (J. B. Priestley).

**Fitzsimons, Raymund,** *Edmund Kean: Fire from Heaven* (1976). The tragic life of the greatest Shakespearean actor of the nineteenth century.

**Forbes, Bryan,** *Dame Edith Evans: Ned's Girl* (1978). Affectionate account of a long triumphant career on stage. See *The Despicable Race: A History of the British Acting Traditions* (1981).

**Fowler, Gene,** *Good Night Sweet Prince: The Life & Times of John Barrymore* (1944). Barrymore was a fabulous character and "Gene Fowler, with his word-slinging jargon and his husky-throated sports-writer humor, is the right person to tell this story which . . . contains a most entertaining collection of funny theatrical anecdotes, phantasmagoric binges and . . . 'gorgeous yarns' " (Edmund Wilson).

**Gielgud, John** *Early Stages* (1937). Written while Sir John was in his thirties. *Stage Directions* (1963) is more technical in nature, while *Distinguished Company* (1973) is about performers with whom he has worked. In 1980 he published *Gielgud: An Actor and His Time,* a memoir.

**Hardwicke, Sir Cedric,** *A Victorian in Orbit* (1961). The "irreverent memoirs" of an intelligent actor and first class raconteur. "I have never read a better book of theatrical reminiscences. I doubt very much that there will ever be one" (Edward Wagenknecht).

**Irving, Lawrence,** *Henry Irving: The Actor and His World* (1952). "Irving has been raised by a brilliant biographical engineer from the deep. I can think of no other instance in our literature in which the life of an actor has been so solidly made to replace its echoes" (V. S. Pritchett). See Madelaine Bingham, *Henry Irving and the Victorian Theatre* (1978).

**Jefferson, Joseph,** *Autobiography* (1890). Delightful memoir about his seventy years on the American stage including his experiences as a strolling player in the pioneer West.

**Lahr, John,** *Notes on a Cowardly Lion: A Biography of Bert Lahr* (1970). A son's affectionate life history of his father, the celebrated comic actor.

**LeGallienne, Eva,** *At 33* (1934). A frank, direct, terse autobiography of the English-born American actress, moving force behind repertory theater in the U.S. and translator of Ibsen. Continued in *With a Quiet Heart* (1953).

**Mosel, Tad,** *Leading Lady: The World and Theatre of Katharine Cornell* (1978). Reticent about her personal life, but a rich memoir of her career in the theater. See her own *I Want to Be an Actress* (1939).

**Prideaux, Tom,** *Love or Nothing: The Life and Times of Ellen Terry* (1975). The much-admired English actress, friend of Shaw, and mother of Edward Gordon Craig. See *Ellen Terry's Memoirs* (1932).

**Ruggles, Eleanor,** *Prince of Players: Edwin Booth* (1953). The American Shakespearean actor of the Gilded Age. His letters, edited by Otis Skinner, are in *The Last Tragedian: Booth Tells His Own Story* (1939).

**Skinner, Cornelia Otis,** *Madame Sarah* (1967). The colorful Sarah Bernhardt portrayed by a noted actress and author. See Bernhardt's *Memoirs of My Life* (1907).

**Waters, Ethel,** *His Eye Is on the Sparrow* (1951). Brutally frank account of the author's rise from tough ghetto childhood to Broadway stardom.

## Screen Actor

**Astor, Mary,** *A Life on Film* (1977). Harsh, sad, stimulating memoir to be read with her earlier *My Story* (1959). The autobiography of her contemporary, Bette Davis, *The Lonely Life* (1962) is intelligent and witty.

**Bacall, Lauren,** *Lauren Bacall by Myself* (1979). Candid reminiscences by a vital and captivating woman.

**Bogarde, Dirk,** *A Postillion Struck by Lightning* (1977). Rare among movie memoirists: an author who can write with style and sensitivity. The English actor continues his story in *Snakes & Ladders* (1979).

**Bosworth, Patricia,** *Montgomery Clift* (1978). Unusually well written, sensitive biography of the actor who died in 1966.

**Brooks, Louise,** *Lulu in Hollywood* (1982). Fresh and honest autobiographical essays by a singular woman who was an early screen star.

**Farmer, Frances,** *Will There Really Be a Morning?* (1972). Probably the most astonishing movie-star autobiography ever written; a harrowing self-portrait of a woman who spent years in a mental institution. See William Arnold's autobiography, *Shadowland* (1978).

**Fussell, Betty,** *Mabel* (1982). Remarkable "search for the truth" about Mabel Normand, Hollywood's first I-don't-care girl. A superb biography.

**Gish, Lillian,** *The Movies, Mr. Griffith, and Me* (1969). Her career started with the movies; D. W. Griffith figures largely. See Mrs. D. W. Griffith, *When the Movies Were Young* (1925).

**MacLaine, Shirley,** *Don't Fall off the Mountain* (1970). Warmth and directness pervade these reminiscences of an articulate and perceptive woman. Continued in *You Can Get There from Here* (1975).

**Niven, David,** *The Moon's a Balloon* (1972). Marvelous Hollywood anecdotes charmingly related by the engaging British actor. More of the same in *Bring on the Empty Horses* (1975). His pal Errol Flynn's autobiography, *My Wicked, Wicked Ways* (1959) is a model of the stylish, entertaining Hollywood memoir.

**Palmer, Lilli,** *Change Lobsters and Dance* (1975). Honest, modest memoir, with vivid vignettes of film people, by an international personality who can write.

**Ustinov, Peter,** *Dear Me* (1977). Scintillating memoirs of the actor, playwright, novelist, producer, opera director, and brilliant conversationalist.

## Film Director

**Bjorkman, Stig et al.,** *Bergman on Bergman* (1974). Edited from taped interviews: intense and illuminating.

**Renoir, Jean,** *My Life and My Films* (1974). Simple, relaxed, often stirring recollections by the French director.

**Samuels, Charles, T.,** *Encountering Directors* (1973). Well-conceived, beautifully illustrated collection of interviews with some of the great international directors. See Andrew Sarris, *Interviews with Film Directors* (1967).

**Truffaut, François,** *Hitchcock* (1967). Fascinating interview with Alfred Hitchcock by the admiring French director. See John Russell Taylor, *Hitchcock* (1978), the authorized biography.

## Magician

**Christopher, Milbourne,** *Houdini: The Untold Story* (1969). The standard biography of the great American escape artist. Christopher, himself a magician, declines to reveal his subject's secrets. To find out see Walter B. Gibson, *Houdini's Escapes* (1930) and W. L. Aresham, *Houdini* (1960).

**Davies, Robertson,** *The World of Wonders* (1976). Enchanting tale in which magician Magnus Eisengrim tells his remarkable life story. Part of a trilogy about myth, magic, and illusion which includes *Fifth Business* (1970) and *The Manticore* (1972).

**Fowles, John,** *The Magus* (rev. 1978). Long, exciting novel of magic, eroticism, love, and the quest for meaning. Thoroughly absorbing and startlingly provocative.

**Robert-Houdin, Jean Eugene,** *Memoirs* (1858). Intriguing autobiography of the nineteenth-century French magician called the Father of Modern Conjuring.

**Singer, Isaac Bashevis,** *The Magician of Lublin* (1965). Set in nineteenth-century Poland, the novel tells the story of Yasha Mazur — master magician, skeptic, mind reader, lover, locksmith, hypnotist, tightrope walker, escape artist, and holy man.

## Naturalist

**Andrews, Roy Chapman,** *Under a Lucky Star: A Lifetime of Adventure* (1943). Felicitous autobiography of a former director of American Museum of Natural History.

**Audubon, John James,** *Audubon, by Himself* (1970). Writings of the great naturalist selected by his biographer, Alice Ford. The best introduction to Audubon. An excellent illustrated biography is John Chancellor, *Audubon* (1979).

**Blunt, Wilfrid,** *The Complete Naturalist: The Life of Linnaeus* (1971). Exquisitely made book about the pioneering Swedish botanist who originated the system of taxonomic classification.

**Botting, Douglas,** *Humboldt and the Cosmos* (1973). Breezy, handsomely illustrated biography of Alexander von Humboldt, the Prussian-born naturalist who traveled extensively in South America.

**Carrighar, Sally,** *Home to the Wilderness* (1973). Poignant, deeply felt memoirs of a self-trained observer of nature.

**Darwin, Charles,** *Autobiography* (1887). Darwin modestly and candidly traces the evolution of his own self. See Peter Brent, *Charles Darwin: A Man of Enlarged Curiosity* (1981) and Francis Hitching, *The Neck of the Giraffe* (1982).

**George, Wilma B.,** *Biologist Philosopher: A Study of the Life and Writings of Alfred Russel Wallace* (1964). The great English naturalist and evolution theorist brought vividly to life. See Arnold C. Brackman, *A Delicate Arrangement: The Strange Case of Charles Darwin and Alfred Russel Wallace* (1979).

**Hanley, Wayne,** *Natural History in America* (1977). Biographies and excerpts from the writings of naturalists from Mark Catesby to Rachel Carson. Alan C. Jenkins, *The Naturalists: Pioneers of Natural History* (1978) does for Europe what Hanley does for the U.S.

**Herbst, Josephine,** *New Green World: John Bartram and the Early Naturalists* (1954). Perceptive study of eighteenth-century America's "natural botanist" and wilderness explorer and associates, including his son William, a well known naturalist and writer.

**Hudson, W. H.,** *Far Away and Long Ago* (1918). Written while the naturalist-novelist was almost eighty, this sensuous recollection of his distant youth in Argentina is one of the finest recreations of childhood in English.

**Muir, John,** *The Story of My Boyhood and Youth* (1913). The great naturalist's early experiences from his birth in Scotland through his early life on a Wisconsin farm. See *The Wilderness World of John Muir* (1954), edited by Edwin Way Teale.

**Peattie, Donald Culross,** *Green Laurels: The Lives and Achievements of the Great Naturalists* (1936). Beautifully written survey by a distinguished botanist-philosopher. His own autobiography, *The Road of a Naturalist* (1941) is excellent.

**Seton, Ernest Thompson,** *The Trail of an Artist and Naturalist* (1940). Genial autobiography of the famed naturalist and wildlife illustrator.

**Swift, Hildegarde,** *The Edge of April: A Biography of John Burroughs* (1957). Aimed at young readers, this life of the much-loved, Whitmanesque naturalist, poet, and essayist will delight readers of all ages. See *The Heart of John Burrough's Journals* (1928).

**Tharp, Louise Hall,** *Adventurous Alliance: The Story of the Agassiz Family of Boston* (1950). Jean Louis Rodolphe Agassiz, the Swiss naturalist and teacher who came to Harvard as a lecturer in 1846, became the leading spokesman of his day for the natural sciences and a leading Boston intellectual.

## *Zookeeper*

**Bridges, William,** *Gathering of Animals: The Unconventional History of the New York Zoological Society* (1974). Breezy account of the first seventy-five years of the Bronx Zoo and New York Aquarium.

**Campbell, Sheldon,** *Lifeboats to Ararat* (1978). The social mission of zoos — captive breeding to preserve endangered species — is the theme of this important, lucid, and humorous book.

**Ditmars, Raymond Lee,** *Strange Animals I Have Known* (1931). Fascinating and funny tales by the curator of mammals at the New York Zoological Park for over a quarter-century. See *Thrills of a Naturalist's Quest* (1932).

**Durrell, Gerald,** *A Zoo in My Luggage* (1960). One of the hilarious, wacky accounts of keeping and collecting animals for his private zoo by this unusual English zoologist and talented writer. See also *Island Zoo* (1963) and *Menagerie Manor* (1965).

**Morris, Desmond,** *Animal Days* (1980). Engaging inside-zoo view by the English TV personality who was curator of mammals at the London Zoo. See James Alldis, *Animals as Friends: A Head Keeper Remembers London Zoo* (1974).

## Lawyer

**Auchincloss, Louis,** *The Partners* (1973). The small world of elegantly practiced civil law in Manhattan, by an urbane, tidy observer. Other such legal fictions include *The Great World and Timothy Colt* (1956) and *Powers of Attorney* (1963).

**Faulkner, William,** *Knight's Gambit* (1949). This collection of six masterly whodunits about attorney Gavin Stephens is "the slightest and the pleasantest of all the books that Faulkner has published . . . for those who have never read his work, it perhaps offers the easiest door by which to enter the rich world of his imagination" (Malcolm Cowley).

**Gardner, Erle Stanley,** *The Case of the Velvet Claws* (1933). The novel that introduced America to Perry Mason, the un-

beatable criminal defense attorney who personifies clever courtroom strategy.

**Gilbert, Michael,** *Smallbone Deceased* (1950). English murder mystery with a law-office setting by a master whose knowledge of law provides fascinating glimpses of professional restraints and loyalties.

**Harbaugh, William H.,** *Lawyer's Lawyer: The Life of John W. Davis* (1973). A spacious, admiring biography of "a figure of such dash and elegance that his life reads like a novel fashioned jointly by Henry James and F. Scott Fitzgerald, with a pinch of Allen Drury thrown in for low melodrama in high places" (Richard Kluger).

**Osborne, John Jay, Jr.,** *The Man Who Owned New York* (1981). Behind the doors of a Wall Street law firm; well written, witty novel.

**Rovere, Richard H.,** *Howe and Hummell, Their Time and Scandalous History* (1947). Roisterous history of the New York law firm of shysters, executed with wit and illustrated by Reginald Marsh.

**Tierney, Kevin,** *Darrow* (1979). Written by a professor of law, it is "the best Darrow biography yet, an engrossing portrayal of a man utterly original and all too human" (W. A. Swanberg). See Darrow's own *The Story of My Life* (1932).

**Turow, Scott,** *One-L* (1977). Lively inside account of life in the first year at Harvard Law School.

**Woods, Sara,** *Proceed to Judgement* (1979). One of over thirty whodunits featuring the urbane, quietly brilliant English barrister Antony Maitland. Like Perry Mason, he gets his client acquitted and exposes the real culprit as well.

## Judge

**Bowen, Catherine Drinker,** *The Lion and the Throne: The Life and Times of Sir*

*Edward Coke* (1957). The brilliant, assertive English jurist and his great parliamentary battles in the early seventeenth century. U. S. Supreme Court Justice Oliver Wendell Holmes is the subject of *The Yankee from Olympus* (1944).

**Hyde, H. Montgomery,** *Lord Reading, the Life of Rufus Isaacs, First Marquess of Reading* (1968). Great success story: the Jewish barrister who became Lord Chief Justice, Ambassador in Washington, Viceroy of India, and Foreign Secretary.

**Lyle, John H.,** *The Dry and Lawless Years* (1960). Author's experiences as municipal court judge in Capone's Chicago during Prohibition days.

**Mitgang, Herbert,** *The Man Who Rode the Tiger: The Life and Times of Judge Samuel Seabury* (1963). The man who took on New York City's corrupt Tammany Hall.

**Sonnichsen, C. L.,** *Roy Bean: Law West of the Pecos* (1943). Hilarious chronicle of the exploits of the post–Civil War Texas justice of the peace.

## *Composer*

**Berlioz, Hector,** *Memoirs of Hector Berlioz* (1870). In extravagant prose, the innovative composer reveals himself as a brave, unlucky, lovable man. "Its every chapter is a complete scene in a wonderfully rousing and significant drama" (Harold Clurman). See *Hector Berlioz: A Selection from His Letters* (1966).

**Einstein, Alfred,** *Gluck* (1955). Concise life of the German composer who led the reform of opera in the eighteenth century. See Patricia Howard, *Gluck and the Birth of Modern Opera* (1964).

**Gal, Hans,** *Johannes Brahms: His Work and Personality* (1963). Out of many stories Gal heard from one of Brahms's best friends, he "got to know Brahms like a living person and developed a truly convincing conception of the composer's personality" (Karl Geiringer).

**Gutman, Robert W.,** *Richard Wagner* (1968). The richest and best single-volume biography of the controversial German master. See *The Letters and Diaries* (1979) of his wife, Cosima Wagner.

**Huneker, James,** *Chopin — The Man and His Music* (1900). Classic impressionistic biography of the Franco-Polish piano genius by a leading American music critic of his day. Franz Liszt's *Frederic Chopin* (1852) is less a biography of his friend, more a rhapsody on the theme of Chopin.

**Ives, Charles E.,** *Memos* (1972). Delightful "autobiographical scrapbook of reminiscences" of the American composer who died in 1954.

**Kracauer, Siegfried,** *Orpheus in Paris: Offenbach and the Paris of His Time* (1937). Rich and fascinating portrayal of one of the masters of nineteenth-century light music.

**Lang, Paul Henry,** *George Frideric Handel* (1966). The master of the late baroque in music is the subject of this erudite and lucid portrait.

**Lockspiser, Edward,** *Debussy: His Life and Mind* (1963–65). Two-volume biography, which places the French musical impressionist in the center of the artistic period to which he belonged.

**Mahler, Alma,** *Gustav Mahler: Memories and Letters* (rev. 1970). The composer's widow sheds vivid light on fascinating Vienna in the first decade of this century. See Bruno Walter's heartfelt tribute to his friend, *Gustav Mahler* (1958).

**Mann, Thomas,** *Doctor Faustus* (1947). Fictional biography of the tragic composer Adrian Leverkuehn that joins the Faust theme with Mann's perennial theme of the artist in society, and both to the spirit of music.

**Marek, George R.,** *Gentle Genius: The Story of Felix Mendelssohn* (1972). Intelligent popular biography of the German composer and conductor. Marek's other biographies include *Beethoven* (1969), *Puccini* (1951), *Richard Strauss* (1967), and *Chopin* (1978).

**Mellers, Wilfrid,** *Francois Couperin and the French Classical Tradition* (1951). Called "Le Grand," Couperin was one of the most influential composers of the keyboard and a master clavecinist. Mellers's other studies of composers are *Bach and the Dance of God* (1981) and *Twilight of the Gods: The Music of the Beatles* (1973).

**Mozart, Wolfgang Amadeus,** *The Letters of Wolfgang Amadeus Mozart* (1972). The all-too-human side of genius delightfully revealed. W. J. Turner, *Mozart* (rev. 1966) and Wolfgang Hildesheimer, *Mozart* (1982) are good introductions to the composer's life, while Alfred Einstein's *Mozart* (1946) is an indispensable guide to his work.

**Perényi, Eleanor,** *Liszt: The Artist as Romantic Hero* (1974). Affectionate telling of the flamboyant life of the Hungarian composer and piano virtuoso and his time. See Sacheverell Sitwell, *Liszt* (rev. 1955).

**Robbins, H. C.,** *Haydn: A Documentary Study* (1981). Elegant, illustrated biography drawn from his five-volume work (1976–80).See Karl Geiringer, *Haydn: A Creative Life in Music* (1946).

**Schauffler, Robert,** *Florestan: The Life and Work of Robert Schumann* (1945). Charming biography of the German romantic that captures the essence of the man and the musician. Schauffler's other popular biographies include *Franz Schubert: The Ariel of Music* (1949).

**Schickele, Peter,** *The Definitive Biography of P. D. Q. Bach* (1976). Hilarious, illustrated biography of the last and least of J. S. Bach's sons, composer of the Gross Concerto Pervertimento.

**Seroff, Victor,** *Sergei Prokofiev: A Soviet Tragedy* (1968). Life and works and political fate of the composer in his native Russia from the time of his voluntary return in 1936 to his death in 1953. Seroff, a concert pianist himself, has written other biographies of Russian composers, including *Rachmaninoff* (1950) and *Modeste Mussorgsky* (1969).

**Sheean, Vincent,** *Orpheus at 80* (1958). Affectionate biography of and best popular introduction to Verdi. See *Letters of Giuseppe Verdi* (1972), edited by Charles Osborne, and Frank Walker, *The Man Verdi* (1962).

**Shostakovich, Dmitri,** *Testimony* (1979). These bitter memoirs, smuggled out of the Soviet Union, are one of the most powerful political indictments of the Stalinist era.

**Smyth, Ethyl,** *Impressions that Remained* (1919). Memoirs of the English composer, conductor, militant suffragette, and friend of Brahms and Grieg. Ernest Newman thought it "one of the half-dozen best autobiographies in the English language." Continued in *As Time Went On* (1936) and *What Happened Next* (1940).

**Stendhal,** *The Life of Rossini* (1824, tr. 1970). Delightful contemporary account of the Italian operatic composer by a brilliant writer.

**Stravinsky, Igor,** *Chronicles of My Life* (1936). Autobiography of the great modern composer. See Robert Craft (ed.), *Selected Correspondence, Vol. 1* (1982), *Conversations with Stravinsky* (1959), *Stravinsky: Chronicle of a Friendship* (1972), and *Stravinsky in Pictures and Documents* (1978), with Vera Stravinsky.

**Sullivan, J. W. N.,** *Beethoven: His Spiritual Development* (1927). Provocative, elegantly written analysis of Beethoven's music in relation to his emotional experiences. The best modern biography is Maynard Solomon's *Beethoven* (1977). The standard biography is Alexander Wheelock Thayer, *Life of Beethoven* (rev. 1967). See *Beethoven's Letters* (1972).

**Terry, Charles Sanford,** *Bach: A Biography* (rev. 1953). Well-written biography of the master composer. The standard life is Philipp Spitta, *Johann Sebastian Bach* (1873–80). See Hans David, *J. S. Bach's Musical Offering* (rev. 1967) and, with Arthur Mendel, *A Bach Reader* (rev. 1966), his life in letters and documents.

**Thomson, Virgil,** *Virgil Thomson* (1966). Brisk, forthright autobiography of the American composer.

**Varèse, Louise,** *Varèse: A Looking-Glass Diary* (1972). Based on diaries of his widow, who died in 1965, "covering a half-century of life together and brought into vigor, through a poet's power to relive the past, (it) is a delight" (Virgil Thomson).

**Walker, Frank,** *Hugo Wolf: A Biography* (rev. 1968). Critical biography of the Austrian composer best known for his songs "moves us profoundly by what he tells us about Wolf's personality and behavior, his functioning as an artist, his terrible end, and about the devotion and loyalty of some of the people he became involved with" (B. H. Haggin).

**Wechsberg, Joseph,** *The Waltz Emperor: The Life and Times and Music of the Strauss Family* (1974). Biography of Johann Strauss and his three sons that moves with the grace of a novel.

## Conductor

**Beecham, Thomas,** *A Mingled Chime* (1943). Partial autobiography, from the 1880s to the mid-1920s, of the English conductor's early life, written with generous dollops of his pungent wit.

**Chasins, Abram,** *Leopold Stokowski* (1979). Vivid biography of the colorful English-born American conductor, his years as music's enfant terrible, and his long, full career. See Oliver Daniels, *Stokowski: A Counterpoint of View* (1982).

**Haggin, B. H.,** *The Toscanini Musicians Knew* (1969). Seventeen musicians' reminiscences of the great conductor. Along with *Conversations with Toscanini* (1959), a full picture of his genius emerges.

**Hart, Phillip,** *Conductors: A New Generation* (1979). Miniature portraits of the generation of conductors that has emerged since the sixties, including Muti, Mehta, Levine, and Ozawa.

**Walter, Bruno,** *Theme and Variations* (1946). Written at the end of a long and illustrious conducting career, this autobiography offers a fascinating inside account of the music world of the first three decades of the century. See *Of Music and Musicmaking* (1961).

## Violinist

**Flesch, Carl,** *Memoirs* (1957). The Hungarian violinist and teacher sketches his European contemporaries — principally violin virtuosi — who were active during the first three decades of the century.

**Lochner, Louis Paul,** *Fritz Kreisler* (1950). An authorized collection of Kreisleriana, rich in anecdotes about the long, colorful career of the Austrian-born virtuoso and composer.

**Menuhin, Yehudi,** *Unfinished Journey* (1976). Absorbing memoirs of a gifted musician. A good companion volume is Robin Daniels's *Conversation with Menuhin* (1980).

**Szigeti, Joseph,** *With Strings Attached; Reminiscences and Reflections* (1947). The wise and witty Hungarian-born violinist's musical insights and memories. See *Szigeti and the Violin* (1969).

**Varga, Franz,** *Violins and Violinists* (rev. 1970). History of the instrument and the playing of its exponents from Monteverdi to Isaac Stern. See Margaret Campbell, *The Great Violinists* (1981).

## Pianist

**Graffman, Gary,** *I Really Should Be Practicing* (1981). The American pianist shares his experiences on and off the concert stage in this wry, intelligent memoir.

**Moore, Gerald,** *Am I Too Loud?: A Musical Autobiography* (1962). A frank and delightful book by one of the most successful accompanists of modern times. See *Farewell Recital* (1978).

**Payzant, Geoffrey,** *Glenn Gould: Music and Mind* (1978). Fine portrait of the maverick pianistic genius.

**Rubinstein, Arthur,** *My Young Years* (1973). Charming, gossipy autobiography of the irrepressible Polish-born pianist and supreme raconteur. Continued in *My Many Years* (1980).

**Schnabel, Artur,** *My Life and Music* (1962). Series of lectures which the Austrian pianist delivered to music students shortly before his death in 1951. His off-the-cuff answers to their questions are a special treat.

**Zuckerman, Eugenia,** *Deceptive Cadence* (1980). Novel about the life and loves of a brilliant young pianist that is "one of those rare pieces of contemporary fiction by a musician to be a real *read* — engaging, stylistically strong, witty, and touching" (Leonard Bernstein).

## Prima Donna

**Ardoin, John and Gerald Fitzgerald,** *Callas* (rev. 1982). Judicious assessment of the great diva's career. For gossipy biography, full of juicy tidbits about her sensational off-stage life and loves, see Arianna Stassinopoulos, *Maria Callas* (1981).

**Bushnell, Howard,** *Maria Malibran: A Biography of a Singer* (1980). Admirable biography of the legendary Spanish mezzo of the last century, who died at 26 and was considered one of the most thrilling singers in opera history.

**Glackens, Ira,** *Yankee Diva: Lillian Nordica and the Golden Age of Opera* (1963). Entertaining, affectionate "life and times" of the queen of American opera during the 1880s and 1890s.

**Lehmann, Lilli,** *My Path Through Life* (1914). Autobiography of the great dramatic soprano who later became an outstanding singing teacher. She had a rich emotional life, and her memoir sheds light on a lost musical world.

**Lehmann, Lotte,** *Midway in My Song* (1938). This straightforward and skillful memoir of the German-born soprano is the expression of a high-spirited and endearing personality. She wrote a second autobiography, *My Many Lives* (1948) and a novel, *Eternal Flight* (1938).

## Horn Player

**Armstrong, Louis,** *Satchmo: My Life in New Orleans* (1954). Candid portrait of Storyville in an "unpretentious, rough-hewn, honest-to-badness memoir" (Cleveland Amory).

**Baker, Dorothy,** *Young Man with a Horn* (1938). Hard-boiled standard of the thirties inspired by the music of Bix Biederbecke. For a nonfictional counterpart, see Ralph Berton, *Remembering Bix: A Memoir of the Jazz Age* (1974).

**Gillespie, Dizzy,** *To Be, or Not . . . to Bop* (1979). Memoirs, written with Al Fraser, which provide insight into the early years of bop.

**Marquis, Donald,** *In Search of Buddy Bolden: First Man of Jazz* (1978). Life of the pioneer cornet player delineated in a solidly researched, crisply written volume. Michael Ondaatje's novel, *Coming Through Slaughter* (1976), deals with the Buddy Bolden legend.

**White, E. B.,** *The Trumpet of the Swan* (1970). A little trumpeter swan without a voice learns to express himself by playing the trumpet in a children's book "imbued with the author's sense of the precious heritage represented by wild nature" (John Updike).

## Social Reformer

**Bacon, Margaret Hope,** *Valiant Friend: The Life of Lucretia Mott* (1980). Direct, sympathetic biography of the abolitionist and feminist who at her death in 1880 was called "the most venerated woman in America."

**Day, Dorothy,** *The Long Loneliness* (1952). Powerful, candid, deeply inspiring autobiography of the founder of the Catholic Worker Movement and leader for more than a half-century of countless battles for social justice.

**Gandhi, Mohandas,** *Autobiography: The Story of My Experiments with Truth* (1948). Written while he was in prison in the early twenties, it is "without literary distinction, but it is, nevertheless, great . . . because of the supreme sincerity and humility with which Gandhi reveals his limitations and strengths in his never-ending struggle to approach Absolute Truth or God" (Merle Curti). See Louis Fischer, *The Life of Gandhi* (1950) and Erik H. Erikson, *Gandhi's Truth* (1969).

**Thomas, John L.,** *The Liberator: William Lloyd Garrison* (1963). Dramatic and objective portrayal of the vituperative editor of the *Liberator* and leading abolitionist.

**Tomalin, Claire,** *The Life and Death of Mary Wollstonecraft* (1974). The English author of *A Vindication of the Rights of Women* is the subject of a wise, sympathetic portrait that is "more than a biography; it illuminates the radical world of the 1780s and 1790s as few other books do" (J. H. Plumb).

## Painter

**Bashkirtseff, Marie,** *The Journal of a Young Artist* (1885). The extraordinary life of a young Russian in France, who died at age 24. In its pages, science, art, literature, social questions, love, are treated with all the cynicism of a Machiavelli and the naiveté of an ardent and enthusiastic girl.

**Brooks, Van Wyck,** *John Sloan: A Painter's Life* (1955). Affectionate tribute, by a longtime friend, to one of the most energetic artists of his generation and leader of the Ash Can school.

**Cary, Joyce,** *The Horse's Mouth* (1944). Comic masterpiece about the aging, William Blake-quoting, passionate painter Gulley Jimson, by one of the outstanding humorous writers of the century. It is the concluding novel of a trilogy, the first and second parts of which are *Herself Surprised* (1941) and *To Be a Pilgrim* (1942).

**Delacroix, Eugene,** *Journals* (1893–95). The forty-year chronicle he left is an incomparable revelation of the interior life of the artist and of the nineteenth-century Parisian art world. See the one-volume abridgement by Walter Pach (1948). See also Charles Baudelaire, *Eugene Delacroix, His Life and Work* (1863).

**Gauguin, Paul,** *The Writing of a Savage* (1978). Selected writings, edited by Daniel Guérin, including passages from the French artist's Polynesian literary efforts *Intimate Journal* and *Noa Noa.*

**Gilot, Françoise and Carlton Lake,** *Life with Picasso* (1964). Inside view of the great artist at work by a woman who served a decade as model, mistress, and mother of two of his children.

**Haydon, Benjamin Robert,** *Autobiography and Memoir of Benjamin Robert Haydon, 1786–1846* (1853). One of the most interesting books and pathetically humorous self-revelations in nineteenth-century letters. "As a pictorial artist he was bound to fail; but as a descriptive writer he has left a lasting mark. His journals contain fascinating sketches of some of the most remarkable men and women of his day" (Peter Quennell).

**Hibbard, Howard,** *Michelangelo, Painter, Sculptor, Architect* (1978). "It is unlikely that [this large-format volume] will ever be surpassed as a general survey of its subjects" (John Russell). See *I, Michelangelo, Sculptor* (1962), an "autobiography" made up of his letters arranged by Irving and Jean Stone.

**Kilbracken, Lord,** *Van Maegeren: Master Forger* (1968). Absorbing case history of the Belgian painter who succeeded in duping the experts by imitating the style of Vermeer and was at the center of a celebrated trial in 1945.

**Klee, Paul,** *The Diaries of Paul Klee* (1964). Thoughts on art, metaphysics, and other concerns of the mind by the brilliant Swiss painter. See Werner Haftmann, *The Mind and Work of Paul Klee* (1954).

**Kokoschka, Oskar,** *My Life* (1974). Involved in many of the art movements of the early part of this century, the Austrian expressionist's perceptive memoir traces his development as an artist.

**Leonardo Da Vinci,** *Notebooks* (1955). Astounding notes of the Renaissance genius. The best single book about Leonardo the artist is Sir Kenneth Clark's *Leonardo Da Vinci* (rev. 1952).

**Pissarro, Camille,** *Letters to His Son Lucien* (1943). The honest, impoverished Impressionist wrote these letters (here edited by John Rewald) during the last twenty years of his life. "One of the most fertile of all sources of insights into the nature and state of mind of 19th century French painting" (Clement Greenberg).

**Renoir, Jean,** *Renoir, My Father* (1962). This affectionate memoir "is one of the best-written and most enjoyable books ever devoted to a painter" (Hilton Kramer).

**Rivers, Larry,** *Drawings and Digressions* (1979). Candid recollections of the New York art world skillfully extracted from hours of taped interviews with one of the most important modern American painters. Includes over 300 reproductions of his work.

**Rothenstein, William,** *Men and Memories: Recollections 1872–1938* (1978). One-volume abridgement of an enthralling gallery of prose portraits of such friends as Wilde, Whistler, Shaw, and Degas.

**Schmitt, Gladys,** *Rembrandt* (1961). The merit of this biographical novel is "that she brings this tormented temperament back into vivid life again, whatever the excesses of her fancy or the limitations of her craft" (Maxwell Geismar). See Sir Kenneth Clark's elegantly written and insightful *An Introduction to Rembrandt* (1978).

**Van Gogh, Vincent,** *The Complete Letters of Vincent Van Gogh* (1958). Beautiful three-volume illustrated edition, published by the New York Graphic Society, of an autobiographical classic. The letters are incomparably human and moving. The best one-volume edition is *Van Gogh: A Self-Portrait* (1963), edited by W. H. Auden.

**Weintraub, Stanley,** *Whistler* (1974). Vivid portrait of the colorful, contentious expatriate American painter. Whistler's own *The Gentle Art of Making Enemies* (1890) still makes delicious reading.

**Wolfe, Bertram D.,** *The Fabulous Life of Diego Rivera* (1963). The amazing, often apocryphal, adventures of the larger-than-life Mexican muralist.

## Photographer

**Bourke-White, Margaret,** *Portrait of Myself* (1963). Autobiography containing vivid recollections of her tenure as a war correspondent, her travels around the world, and her successful struggle against Parkinson's disease. See Beatrice Siegel's biography, *An Eye on the World* (1980).

**Gosling, Nigel,** *Nadar* (1977). The pioneering nineteenth-century French photographer; accompanied by his wonderful photographs of the leading artists and writers of the Paris of 1855–70.

**Homer, William Innes,** *Alfred Steiglitz* (1977). Deftly written life of the photographer who played a dominant role in the emergence of the avant-garde in America.

**Jackson, William Henry,** *Time Exposure: The Autobiography of William Henry Jackson* (1940). Written at age ninety-seven, it is as one reviewer put it "as American as 'Swanee River,' or a barrel of Northern Spies in icewater." See Beaumont Newhall and Diana E. Edkins, *William Henry Jackson* (1974).

**Kunhardt, Dorothy Meserve et al.,** *Matthew Brady and His World* (1977). Well-written text and beautifully reproduced photographs make this the best brief assessment of Brady's career.

**Meltzer, Milton,** *Dorothea Lange: A Photographer's Life* (1978). She was most famous for her pictures of the farm poor, taken during the Depression: the life and achievement of a photographer known for her sense of the height of intensity.

**Parks, Gordon,** *A Choice of Weapons* (1966). Evocative memoir of youth by a noted member of *Life*'s award-winning photography team. Continued in *To Smile in Autumn* (1979). See his sensitive autobiographical novel, *The Learning Tree* (1963).

**Steichen, Edward,** *A Life in Photography* (1963). Autobiographical fragments by the pioneer photographer interspersed with seventy years of his photographs. See Carl Sandburg's volume about his brother-in-law, *Steichen the Photographer* (1929).

**Theroux, Paul,** *Picture Palace* (1978). Clever novel about a seventy-year-old world-famous photographer, Maude Pratt.

**Weston, Edward,** *The Flame of Recognition* (1966). Excerpts from Weston's famous daybooks and letters illustrated by his photographs. His philosophies of life and of photography are gracefully related. See Ben Maddow, *Edward Weston: His Life and Photographs* (1979).

## Architect

**Ackerman, James S.,** *Palladio* (1966). Life and times of the sixteenth-century Italian architect whose neoclassical style served as the basis for English Georgian architecture.

**Connely, Willard,** *Louis Sullivan, as He Lived: The Shaping of American Architecture* (1966). The Chicago architect portrayed against the tumultuous beginnings of modern American architecture.

**Ibsen, Henrik,** *The Master Builder* (1892). Powerful play about the architect Solness in which the Norwegian dramatist explores the question of how far an artist may go to achieve and maintain supremacy in his art.

**Summerson, John N.,** *Sir Christopher Wren* (1954). Brief life, authoritative and lively, of the great English architect who designed St. Paul's Cathedral. Summerson's other architects' biographies include *Inigo Jones* (1966) and *John Nash* (rev. 1950).

**Wright, Frank Lloyd,** *Autobiography* (1943). Classic work, provocative and lucid, of the giant of American modern architecture. See Edgar Tafel, *Apprentice to Genius: Years with Frank Lloyd Wright* (1979). Meyer Levin, *The Architect* (1981) is an absorbing fictional account of Wright's life and career.

## Rare Book Dealer

**Ettinghausen, Maurice L.,** *Rare Books and Royal Collectors: Memories of an Antiquarian Bookseller* (1966). Urbane "rambling reminiscences" of a leading scholar-bookman.

**Kraus, H. P.,** *A Rare Book Saga: The Autobiography of H. P. Kraus* (1978). His fifty years as an antiquarian bookseller in New York.

**Magee, David,** *Infinite Riches: The Adventures of a Rare Book Dealer* (1973). An

English bookman's witty and modest recollections of a half-century's career in the trade.

**Randall, David A.,** *A Dukedom Large Enough* (1969). Lively memoirs of the man who headed Scribner's rare book department for over twenty years.

**Rosenbach, A. S. W.,** *Books and Bidders: The Adventures of a Bibliophile* (1928). Recollections of one of the eminent American booksellers of this century. See *Book Hunter's Holidays: Adventures with Books and Manuscripts* (1937). *Rosenbach* (1960), by Edwin Wolf 2d and John F. Fleming, is a superb biography.

## Protestant Clergyman

**Buechner, Frederick,** *The Bebb Trilogy* (1971–74). Comic-grotesque parable about Rev. Leo Bebb of the Church of Holy Love, Inc., of Armadillo, Florida, by a Presbyterian minister-novelist of distinction.

**Commager, Henry Steele,** *Theodore Parker* (1947). Fine biography of the radical New England Unitarian pastor, abolitionist, transcendentalist, and reformer.

**Goldsmith, Oliver,** *The Vicar of Wakefield* (1766). This classic pastoral novel of the fortunes and misfortunes of the kindly vicar and his family remains delightful reading for its picture of country life, its domestic humor, and its gently ironic tone.

**Lewis, Sinclair,** *Elmer Gantry* (1927). Comic nightmare about an ex–football player who becomes a famous evangelist and then leader of a large church. One of Lewis's best novels, its exposure of hysterical evangelism shocked the public.

**McCall, Dan,** *Beecher* (1978). Carefully researched biographical fiction by a scholar-novelist about Henry Ward Beecher, the most idolized minister of the nineteenth century.

**Mano, D. Keith,** *Bishop's Progress* (1962). This novel about the Episcopal bishop of Queens in the hospital is "witty, disturbing, entertaining, grave, full of suspense, and a prolonged meditation on the riddle of faith in our epoch" (R. V. Cassill).

**Richter, Conrad,** *A Simple Honorable Man* (1962). Deeply moving novel of a Lutheran minister in "Dutch" Pennsylvania.

**Thomason, John W.,** *Lone Star Preacher* (1941). This collection of exciting episodes about Rev. Praxiteles Swan, a Texas chaplain during the Civil War, Bible in one hand, sword in the other, is "wonderously clear, memorable and in part stirring" (Allan Nevins).

**Trollope, Anthony,** *The Warden* (1855). In this, the first of the six Barsetshire novels about the clerics and squires of the rural south of England, the warden, the Reverend Mr. Septimus Harding, is one of Trollope's finest creations and "one of the most convincing portraits in English literature of unostentatious goodness" (Martin S. Day). The sequel is *Barchester Towers* (1857).

**Updike, John,** *A Month of Sundays* (1975). Brief, adroit novel about an errant minister's sexual indiscretions remembered during a month's stay at a rest home.

## Catholic Priest

**Bernanos, Georges,** *The Diary of a Country Priest* (1936). Set in rural France, this quiet novel traces the efforts of a saintly young priest to serve the poor, who abuse him, and to discover his own sense of grace.

**Chesterton, G. K.,** *The Innocence of Father Brown* (1911). The first of the popular series of detective stories in which Father Brown is the sleuth. Two modern priest-detective series are those of Father Koesler — see William X. Kienzle, *The Rosary Murders* (1979) — and Father

Dowling — see Ralph McInerney, *Her Death of Cold* (1977).

Farrow, John, *Damian, The Leper* (1937). A Belgian priest and his leper colony at Molokai, Hawaii. Bradford Smith's novel *Molskai* (1963) is about Fr. Damian.

Gerard, John, *Autobiography of a Hunted Priest* (1952). This translation from seventeenth-century Latin of his memoirs of the Tudor underground is as thrilling as a modern spy story.

Greene, Graham, *The Power and the Glory* (1940). In remote Mexico, during an anticlerical purge, the last priest, like a hunted hare, is on the run. Too human for heroism, too humble for martyrdom, the little worldly "whisky priest" is nevertheless impelled toward his squalid Calvary.

Horgan, Paul, *Lamy of Santa Fe* (1975). Pulitzer Prize–winning portrait of the first archbishop of Santa Fe. He was the model for Willa Cather's novel *Death Comes for the Archbishop* (1927).

Keneally, Thomas, *Three Cheers for the Paraclete* (1968). Novel about an Austrailian seminarian's attempt to apply the principles of Christian charity.

Marshall, Bruce, *The World, The Flesh, and Father Smith* (1945). Warm, humorous novel of a Scottish priest whose dream is that his country will return to the ancient faith. Marshall's other novels about priests include *Father Malachy's Miracle* (1931) and *The Bishop* (1970).

Power, Crawford, *The Encounter* (1950). Fr. Cawder discovers his inhumanity to man in this finely crafted, thoughtful first novel.

Powers, J. F., *Morte D'Urban* (1962). National Book Award–winning novel about Fr. Urban of Chicago, rich in characterization, sparkling in dialogue, and full of a wry humor that tempers the pathos. His short stories are collected in *The Prisoner of Grace* (1956), *Prince of Darkness* (1947), and *Look How the Fish Love* (1975).

## Cardinal

Auchincloss, Louis, *Richelieu* (1972). Splendid, illustrated introduction to the French cardinal, chief minister of Louis XIII, and virtual dictator from 1624 to 1642.

Ferguson, Charles, *Naked to Mine Enemies* (1958). Gripping account of the tragic life of Cardinal Wolsey, Lord Chancellor under Henry VIII of England.

Firbank, Ronald, *Concerning the Eccentricities of Cardinal Pirelli* (1926). Camp classic by the "exquisite" English novelist about a cardinal who breaks all the cardinal rules and chases after the choir boys.

O'Faolain, Sean, *Newman's Way: The Odyssey of John Henry Newman* (1952). Urbane, dramatic tracing of the cardinal's journey from the Calvinism of his childhood through the Anglicanism of his youth to the Roman Catholicism of his maturity. See Newman's *Autobiographical Writings* (1957) and *Letters* (1957).

Retz, Paul De Gonde, Cardinal De, *Memoirs* (1717). The fascinating recollections of the extraordinary political cardinal of seventeenth-century France, a man of incomparable verve and genius for intrigue. See J. M. H. Salmon, *Cardinal de Retz: The Anatomy of a Conspirator* (1965).

## Pope

Chamberlin, E. R., *The Bad Popes* (1969). An English historian's lively, illustrated stories of seven popes whose reigns were marked by corruption and dissolution.

Hochhuth, Rolf, *The Deputy* (1964). Controversial, powerful play by the West German dramatist about Pope Pius XII's silence in the face of the Holocaust. See Carlo Falconi, *The Silence of Pius XII* (1970).

Pius II, *Memoirs of a Renaissance Pope* (1959). One-volume abridgement of the only memoir ever left us by a pope; an intimate, uninhibited autobiography by "a gifted Italian humanist of the Quattrocento, a trained diplomatist, an able Pope, and a first-rate observer. No one interested in the Renaissance should miss this book" (Crane Brinton).

**Rolfe, Frederick,** *Hadrian the Seventh* (1904). "Baron Corvo's" autobiographical fantasy that explores with compulsive fascination what might happen if an obscure writer, a failed priest, were suddenly elected pope.

**Royidis, Emmanuel,** *Pope Joan* (1886). Famous Greek satire, a witty and irreverent blend of fantasy and scholarship, about the scandalous legend grounded on substantial fact — that there was a woman pope in the ninth century. Lawrence Durrell's 1960 translation captures the elaborate style of the original.

## Rabbi

**Baker, Leonard,** *Days of Sorrow and Pain: Leo Baeck and the Berlin Jews* (1978). The rabbi who, as leader of Germany's Reform Jews, stayed during the Holocaust to help his people and died in a concentration camp. A study of an era and a man, it won the Pulitzer Prize for History.

**Gordon, Noah,** *The Rabbi* (1965). Rich, caring novel about a modern Reform rabbi.

**Kemelman, Harry,** *Friday the Rabbi Slept Late* (1964). First of a felicitous series of mystery novels in which Rabbi David Small applies his Talmudic detection gifts.

**Knox, Israel,** *Rabbi in America: The Story of Isaac M. Wise* (1957). Concise biography of the father of the American Reform movement, who emigrated from Bohemia in 1846.

**Polner, Murray,** *Rabbi: The American Experience* (1977). Informal, revealing so-

cial history which examines the lives of several contemporary rabbis.

## Inventor

**Bruce, Robert V.,** *Bell: Alexander Graham Bell and the Conquest of Solitude* (1973). The American technological genius, his inventions, and his work with the deaf, vividly recounted. See Dorothy Harley Elu, *Genius at Work* (1982).

**Conot, Robert,** *A Streak of Luck* (1979). A fresh, decidedly nonadulatory, portrait of Edison, the Wizard of Menlo Park.

**Mabee, Carlton T.,** *The American Leonardo: A Life of Samuel F. B. Morse* (1943). Pulitzer Prize–winning biography of a nineteenth-century American renaissance man: painter, promoter of the telegraph, and inventor of the Morse code.

**Mirsky, Jeanette and Allan Nevins,** *The World of Eli Whitney* (1952). Spirited, authoritative account of the great inventor and father of mass production.

**Pupin, Michael,** *From Immigrant to Inventor* (1923). Autobiography of the Serbian immigrant who became an eminent physicist and inventor. Awarded a Pulitzer Prize.

## Prostitute

**Bellocq, E. J.,** *E. J. Bellocq: The Storyville Portraits* (1978). Remarkable photographs of the women who plied their trade in New Orleans bordellos at the turn of the century.

**Brassai,** *The Secret Paris of the 30's* (1976). The famous French photographer's available-light pictures of the dark, seamy side of Paris — the prostitutes, pimps, and other habitués of the night.

**Cleland, John,** *Memoirs of a Woman of Pleasure* (1748). This chronicle of the merry adventures of Fanny Hill long enjoyed an underground reputation as an erotic classic until its republication in the mid-1960s.

**Defoe, Daniel,** *Moll Flanders* (1722). Social novel about the picaresque adventures of Moll Flanders who "during a Life of continued Variety . . . was Twelve Year a Whore."

**Genet, Jean,** *Our Lady of the Flowers* (1964). Obsessive, violent autobiographical novel about the life of a homosexual prostitute in Paris.

**Hyde, H. Montgomery,** *The Cleveland Street Scandal* (1976). The scandal involving a male brothel in London in the 1890s that resulted in a series of celebrated trials and parliamentary debate: "lively, witty and written with exceptional professional competence by a practiced writer" (J. H. Plumb).

**Kimball, Nell,** *Nell Kimball: Her Life as an American Madam, by Herself* (1970). Salty memoirs of a woman of exhaustive memory and distinctive morality, who was a prostitute in post–Civil War St. Louis and a madam in New Orleans until 1917.

**Moravia, Alberto,** *The Woman of Rome* (1947). Sensual novel about a Roman prostitute and about woman as victim.

**Pinzer, Mamie,** *The Mamie Papers* (1977). Written by an ex-prostitute between 1910 and 1922; a vivid, human spirit struggles to find a basis for self-respect.

**Zola, Émile,** *Nana* (1880). Classic novel about the dissipated life of a prostitute in Paris.

## Cowboy

**Abbott, E. C.,** *We Pointed Them North: Recollections of a Cowpuncher* (1939). "This is a beauty. It is the unvarnished, authentic story of Teddy Blue, cowpuncher in the great days of the Texas trail, set down by a skillful writer [Helena Huntington Smith] who has kept herself

out of the picture and yet never let an old man's memories become mere loquacity" (Stephen Vincent Benét).

**Adams, Andy,** *The Log of a Cowboy* (1903). It is uncertain whether this is a memoir or a novel, but it is the classic of the occupation. For an update, see Daniel G. Moore, *The Log of a Twentieth-Century Cowboy* (1965).

**Dobie, J. Frank,** *A Vaquero of the Brush Country* (1929). Based on the reminiscences of a Texas cowboy, it is one of the most authentic and intimate depictions of the range ever — and delightfully written.

**Schaefer, Jack,** *Monte Walsh* (1963). Novel of the Old West about a young man climbing up the cowboy ladder, from trail hand to bronc buster. Its realistic detail makes this one of the few good novels of the true cowboy.

**Siringo, Charles A.,** *A Texas Cowboy, or Fifteen Years on the Hurricane Deck of a Spanish Pony* (1885). The first real cowboy to publish an autobiography. "No record of cowboy life has supplanted his rollicky, reckless, realistic chronicle" (J. Frank Dobie). See *Riata and Spurs* (1927).

## Shepherd

**Austin, Mary,** *The Flock* (1906). Enchanting account of the Basque sheepherders of California.

**Gilfillan, Archer B.,** *Sheep* (1929). These amusing, flavorful tales stem from the author's life as a South Dakota shepherd.

**Outerbridge, David and Julie Thayer,** *The Last Shepherds* (1979). A black-and-white photographic survey of a vanishing way of life — sheepherding in France, Scotland, Italy, and Crete.

**Robertson, Robert B.,** *Of Sheep and Men* (1957). Beguiling, informative account of year spent in sheep-raising country on the northern bank of the river Tweed in Scotland.

**Thorpe, Denis and Alan Dunn,** *The Shepherd's Year* (1979). Striking photographs chronicle the life of an English hill shepherd and his flock.

## Bullfighter

**Collins, Larry and Dominique Lapierre,** *Or I'll Dress You in Mourning* (1968). This account of El Cordobés is "an exciting picaresque adventure . . . and the most complete study of a matador's life that I have ever read, as well as the most detailed, unvarnished, and unromanticized look at the elements that make up a modern bullfighter" (Barnaby Conrad).

**Conrad, Barnaby,** *Matador* (1952). Exciting novel set in Seville by an American with first-hand knowledge of what it is like to be in the bull ring.

**Lea, Tom,** *The Brave Bulls* (1949). Dramatic, impassioned fictional treatment about the life of a Mexican bullfighter. A profound, timeless book.

**Montherlant, Henri De,** *The Bullfighters* (1926). Early novel about arrogance and power by a distinguished French author with some experience fighting bulls.

**Spota, Luis,** *The Wounds of Hunger* (1957). Unflinching novel about a Mexican matador.

## Fisherman

**Bartlett, Kim,** *The Finest Kind* (1977). Vivid journalistic account of the Italian commercial fishermen of Gloucester, Massachusetts.

**Loti, Pierre,** *An Iceland Fisherman* (1886). Impressionistic novel about the fishermen of Brittany. A taut novel about the Breton fishermen who fish by baited lines from *palngriers* is Henri Queffélec's *The Kingdom Under the Sea* (1959).

**Mishima, Yukio,** *The Sound of Waves* (1956). Lyrical tale of a young fisherman in love, set in a small Japanese fishing village.

**Moorhouse, Geoffrey,** *The Boat and a Town* (1979). From his year as a deckhand on a boat out of a small New England fishing village, he has fashioned a remarkable documentary portrait of it and its crew.

**Peffer, Randall S.,** *Watermen* (1979). Evocative portrait of the fishermen who sail their skipjacks off the Eastern Shore of Chesapeake Bay.

## Explorer

**Beaglehole, J. C.,** *The Life of Captain James Cook* (1974). The definitive life of the English discoverer of Hawaii.

**Bishop, Morris,** *Champlain: The Life of Fortitude* (1948). The life of Samuel de Champlain, the Father of Canada, "carefully flavored and beautifully written" (Allan Nevins).

**Bolton, Herbert E.,** *Coronado: Knight of Pueblos and Plains* (1949). Worshipful account of the Spanish explorer and one of the great adventure stories ever — the search for El Dorado.

**Brent, Peter,** *Black Nile: Mungo Park and the Search for the Niger* (1977). The great Scottish explorer's quest for the Niger is the focus of this fine, fast-paced popular biography. See E. W. Bovill, *The Niger Explored* (1968). T. Coraghessan Boyle, *Water Music* (1981) is an imaginative novel about Park.

**Brodie, Fawn M.,** *The Devil Drives: A Life of Sir Richard Burton* (1967). Magnificent biography of one of the most brilliant and turbulent heroes of any era.

**Lytle, Andrew,** *At the Moon's Inn* (1941). Novel, filled with drama and color, based on the life of the sixteenth-century Spaniard, Hernando de Soto, who is generally credited with discovering the Mississippi River.

**Morison, Samuel Eliot,** *Admiral of the Ocean Sea: A Life of Christopher Columbus* (1942). In preparing this Pulitzer Prize–winning biography, Morison sailed Columbus's routes to and from America in a boat of the same size as the explorer's. See *Christopher Columbus, Mariner* (1955) and *The Caribbean as Columbus Saw It* (1965).

**Roditi, Edouard,** *Magellan of the Pacific* (1972). Good popular biography of the sixteenth-century Portugese navigator who commanded the first expedition to circumnavigate the world. See Charles E. Nowell (ed.), *Magellan's Voyage Around the World: Four Contemporary Accounts* (1963).

**Romoli, Kathleen,** *Balboa of Darien, Discoverer of the Pacific* (1953). Solid account of the fascinating career of Vasco Nuñez de Balboa.

**Terrell, John Upton,** *La Salle: The Life and Times of an Explorer* (1968). Smoothly written tale of the Frenchman who explored the Mississippi valley in the seventeenth century. See *Black Robe: The Life of Pierre-Jean De Smet: Missionary, Explorer, Pioneer* (1964), *Journey into Darkness: Cabeza de Vaca's Expedition Across North America 1528–36* (1964), and *Zebulon Pike: The Life and Times of an Adventurer* (1968).

## Traveler

**Adams, Percy G.,** *Travelers and Travel Liars, 1660–1800* (1962). A scholar deals amusingly with travel accounts that in an age of reason told untruths; pseudovoyages that were destined to make the public believe them real. An interesting footnote to seventeenth-century letters.

**Barr, Pat,** *A Curious Life for a Lady: The Story of Isabelle Bird, A Remarkable Victorian Traveller* (1970). This dynamic and intrepid lady began travelling at age forty for her health and wrote a series of best sellers about her adventures. For accounts

of other such curious ladies, see Dorothy Middleton, *Victorian Lady Travellers* (1965) and Leo Hamalian, *Ladies on the Loose: Women Travellers of the 18th and 19th Centuries* (1981).

**Connell, Evan S.,** *A Long Desire* (1979). Exquisite sketches about individuals in history who were inexplicably drawn from their familiar comforts toward a vague goal, a search for unknown lands.

**Fussell, Paul,** *Abroad: British Literary Traveling Between the Wars* (1980). Eloquent, provocative literary and cultural criticism about the English travel writers of the twenties and thirties.

**Hibbert, Christopher,** *The Grand Tour* (1969). Entertaining illustrated account of the Continental tour, which was *de rigeur* for the young English gentleman of the seventeenth through nineteenth centuries.

**Holmes, Burton,** *Burton Holmes: The Man Who Photographed the World, Travelogues 1886–1938* (1977). Beautiful, fascinating book about the inventor of the travelogue, illustrated with many reproductions of his hand-colored glass negatives. See Holmes's autobiography, *The World Is Mine* (1954).

**Newby, Eric,** *A Traveller's Life* (1982). Engaging recollections of the English traveler, soldier, mountaineer, and writer.

**Pomeroy, Earl,** *In Search of The Golden West: The Tourist in Western America* (1957). Sprightly, instructive look at the impact of the Eastern pleasure traveler on the development of the West.

**Reid, J. M.,** *Traveller Extraordinary: The Life of James Bruce of Kinnaird* (1968). The eighteenth-century traveler and his extraordinary journeys to Sudan and Ethiopia.

**Root, Jonathan,** *Halliburton: The Magnificent Myth* (1965). The great adventurer-traveler between the wars, Richard

Halliburton, who was the Lancelot of the Lecture Circuit.

**Sutton, Horace,** *Travelers: The American Tourist from Stagecoach to Space Shuttle* (1980). Witty and honest social history by a respected travel writer.

## Servant

**Gorst, Frederic J.,** *Of Carriages and Kings* (1956). Sparkling reminiscences of a man who rose to the below-stairs aristocracy — royal footman during the reign of Edward VII. Lady Astor's maid, Rosina Harrison, wrote a fascinating memoir, *Rose: My Life in Service* (1975).

**Green, Henry,** *Loving* (1945). Novel, written almost entirely in dialogue, about the servants in an empty Irish castle during the Second World War; clever social comedy, love story, and symbolic tale. Another English conversation novel about servants is Ivy Compton-Burnett, *Bullivant and the Lambs* (1947).

**Huggett, Frank E.,** *Life Below Stairs: Domestic Servants in England from Victorian Times* (1978). The in-service world in a weave of interviews, photographs, and *Punch* cartoons. See Margaret Powell, *Below Stairs* (1970) for a brisk account of service between the wars.

**Travers, P. L.,** *Mary Poppins* (1934). The first book of a series about the stern but endearing English nanny who comes with the East wind to care for the Banks children and leads them on magical adventures. For a charming social history of her profession, see Jonathan Gathorne-Hardy, *The Unnatural History of the Nanny* (1972).

**Wodehouse, P. G.,** *The Inimitable Jeeves* (1924). One of a series of comic novels featuring Jeeves, the redoubtable manservant of Bertie Wooster, both part of a delightful world of English peers and gentlemen untouched by the vicissitudes of twentieth century life. See C. Northcote Parkinson's "biography", *Jeeves* (1981).

## Other Work

**Chesterton, G. K.,** *The Club of Queer Trades* (1905). Story by the master of whimsy about a club which no one can join unless he has invented a brand-new occupation by which he earns a living. A tremendous trifle.

**Dickens, Charles,** *Hard Times* (1854). Moral fable set in industrial Coketown, in and out of Mr. Josiah Bounderby's factory. "Of all Dickens's works it is the one that has all the strength of his genius, together with a strength no other of them can show — that of a completely serious work of art" (F. R. Leavis).

**Hine, Lewis,** *America and Lewis Hine: Photographs 1904–1940* (1977). Social history and art: these images from the Hine retrospective at the Brooklyn Museum of the lives of workers evoke a whole age. A contemporary album of photographs is Bill Owens's *Working* (1977).

**Robertson, Robert,** *Of Whales and Men* (1954). Finely written, inspired study of the industry by a Scottish psychiatrist who signed on as medical officer to a whaling expedition for the Southern Ocean. Packed with adventure, insights, humor, and fascinating facts. See Robert Cushman Murphy, *Logbook for Grace* (1947), an account of a voyage of one of the last Yankee whaleships in the twilight days of sail.

**Smith, Dennis,** *Report from Engine Co. 82* (1972). The lives of firefighters at a busy station in the Bronx. See *Dennis Smith's History of Firefighting in America* (1979) and his incendiary novels *The Final Fire* (1975) and *Glitter and Ash* (1980).

**Sturt, George,** *The Wheelwright's Shop* (1923). An English minor classic that gives real artistic life to the story of a craft, the artisans, and their products.

**Swados, Harvey,** *On the Line* (1957). Skillfully told stories of the lives of eight men who work on an automobile assembly line, by a socially conscious novelist.

**Terkel, Studs,** *Working* (1974). The noted oral historian's casebook of people talking about what they do all day and how they feel about what they do.

**Woodbury, George,** *John Goffe's Mill* (1948). A Harvard anthropologist retired to New Hampshire, built a water mill, and became a miller. This is his unsentimentalized, humorous account of his personal industrial counterrevolution: "the maturely considered, excellently written record of one man who became his own boss

and is glad he did" (Joseph Henry Jackson).

**Wyckoff, Walter,** *The Workers* (1900). The result of the author's long walks around America during which he studied the lives of casual laborers as one of themselves; "few sociological writers could match the lively, flowing, natural style in which he related his discoveries as a worker on the road" (Van Wyck Brooks). See his fascinating *A Day with a Tramp* (1901).

# PART VI

# CULTURE

# LANGUAGE

*The American Heritage Dictionary of the English Language* (rev. 1982). The freshest, most innovative, and most useful dictionary published. Available in a variety of abridged editions.

**Bernstein, Theodore M.,** *The Careful Writer* (1965). Not only a solid work of reference on modern English usage, but also "a delightful 'language reader,' spiced with sly humor, which may be savored in leisurely fashion, a few pages at a time, by the connoisseur in matters of language and taste" (Mario Pei). See *Miss Thistlebottom's Hobgoblins* (1971) and *Dos, Don'ts and Maybes of English Usage* (1977).

**Espy, Willard R.,** *Words at Play* (1973). Felicitously frivolous farrago of wordplay: anagrams to clerihews, acrostics to conundrums. Other works by this amusing word lover include *An Almanac of Words at Play* (1975), *A House of Words* (1981), and *Have a Word on Me* (1981).

**Farb, Peter,** *Word Play* (1973). Subtitled *What Happens when People Talk,* it is an interesting and enjoyable elucidation of structural linguistics.

**Flexner, Stuart Berg,** *I Hear America Talking* (1976). This "illustrated treasury of American words and phrases" is, in the opinion of William Safire, a "masterpiece of cultural history, excitingly laid out and illustrated, infused with the passion and color of the real world of words."

**Fowler, H. W.,** *Modern English Usage* (rev. 1965). Revision by Sir Ernest Gowers of the classic first edition of 1926. "Its slight archaism, its decided perfectionism, its pervasive and disquieting unreality do not prevent it from being the best book of its kind ever written in any European language" (Eric Partridge).

**Funk, Charles E.,** *Hogs on Ice* (1948). The first of a series of four charming books which look at the origins of hundreds of our most commonly used words and phrases. He is not to be confused with another engaging phrase sleuth, Dr. Wilfred Funk, whose etymological pageant of a book is *Word Origins and Their Romantic Stories* (1950).

**Graves, Robert and Alan Hodge,** *The Reader over Your Shoulder* (1943). This "handbook for writers of English prose" analyzes writings by eminent authors and revises them according to the principles elucidated in the book. A fascinating and instructive lesson.

**Howard, Philip,** *Words Fail Me* (1981). Selections from the lively "New Words and New Meanings" column by the author, the language watcher for the *Times* of London. His other, equally humorous, collections are *Weasel Words* (1979) and *New Words for Old* (1977).

**Mencken, H. L.,** *The American Language* (rev. 1936). Brilliant, curious, audacious, informative, high-spirited, this classic study of the American vernacular is a joy to skip about in and to relish. A one-volume abridged and updated edition, by Raven I. McDavid, Jr., was published in 1963.

**Murray, K. M. Elizabeth,** *Caught in the Web of Words: James Murray and the Oxford English Dictionary* (1977). A granddaughter's dramatic biography of the Victorian scholar, the founding editor of the *OED.* "One of the finest biographies of the 20th century" (Anthony Burgess).

**Newman, Edwin,** *Strictly Speaking* (1974). This newsman's witty response to the question Will America be the death of English? is chock-full of hilarious examples of the misuse of our language. See *A Civil Tongue* (1976).

**Nurnberg, Maxwell and Morris Rosenblum,** *All About Words* (1966). One of the best of the many vocabulary-building books. Wonderfully informative and great fun besides.

*The Oxford English Dictionary* (1933). The most comprehensive and most scholarly dictionary of the English language. Through photo reduction, the original thirteen-volume set has been reproduced in a two-volume, 4,000-plus-page compact edition (plus magnifying glass). Several different abridged editions are available.

**Partridge, Eric,** *Eric Partridge in His Own Words* (1981). Amusing and erudite collection of essays about language by one of the leading philologists of his day. See his standard *Origins: A Short Etymological Dictionary of Modern English* (1958) and such entertaining scholarly classics as *Dictionary of Slang and Unconventional English* (1937) and *Shakespeare's Bawdy* (1947).

**Pei, Mario,** *What's in a Word?: Language — Yesterday, Today and Tomorrow* (1968). A medley of essays, sage and sprightly, done in an informal style by the author of *The Story of Language* (rev. 1949) and *The Story of the English Language* (rev. 1967).

**Read, Herbert,** *English Prose Style* (rev. 1952). A classic that is "virtually without competition. The discussions are bright and they are illustrated by fascinating passages from the prose masters" (John Crowe Ransom).

**Reid, Alistair,** *Ounce, Dice, Trice* (1958). Book of original words — funny, beautiful, odd, rude — with marvelous Ben Shahn illustrations. For the whole family.

*Roget's II: The New Thesaurus* (rev. 1980). Compiled by the editors of *The American Heritage Dictionary,* this is one of the best of the heirs to Peter Mark Roget's little book with the long title that was published in 1852: *Thesaurus of English Words and Phrases Classified and Arranged so as to Facilitate the Expression of Ideas and Assist in Literary Composition.* This edition performs that task nobly.

**Safire, William,** *Safire's Political Dictionary* (rev. 1978). Diverting, anecdotal miniessays about the origins of political words by a former pol and present political columnist. His columns about speech have been collected in *On Language* (1980) and *What's the Good Word?* (1982).

**Simon, John,** *Paradigms Lost* (1980). Collects the theater reviewer's mordant magazine columns on the decline of literacy in the Republic. For a corrective to Simon, Newman, and Safire see Jim Quinn, *American Tongue and Cheek* (1981), a decidedly populist and amusing guide to the spoken tongue.

**Strunk, William, Jr., and E. B. White,** *The Elements of Style* (rev. 1972). Brief book on the fundamentals of plain English style that should be on the desk of everyone who deals in words.

**Thorndike, E. L. and Clarence Barnhart,** *Scott, Foresman Beginning Dictionary* (rev. 1976). Great dictionary for young people; lively and superbly designed.

**Watzlawick, Paul,** *How Real Is Real?: Communication and Reality* (1976). The most accessible of the books by a leading communication theorist. How "brute facts" are interpreted; how confusion, misinformation, and communication contribute to the social construction of reality. For anyone interested in language, thought, and linguistics.

**Zinsser, William,** *On Writing Well* (rev. 1981). Useful guide to writing nonfiction: informal, instructive, indispensable.

# BOOKS

**Altick, Richard,** *The Scholar Adventurers* (1950). Stories of scholars unearthing literary documents (Boswell's papers), solving mysteries (the murder of Christopher Marlowe), uncovering forgeries, and such. Full of the excitement of the chase. See *The Cowden Clarkes* (1949), *To Be in England* (1971), and *Lives and Letters: A History of Literary Biography in England and America* (1965).

**Chappell, Warren,** *A Short History of the Printed Word* (1970). Well-written anecdotal history, commencing with the fifteenth century, by an artist-craftsman. The decorated word is superbly treated in John Harthan, *The History of the Illustrated Book: The Western Tradition* (1981).

**Jackson, Holbrook,** *The Fear of Books* (1932). Bibliophobia and condemned books and the reasons why. See *The Printing of Books* (1938) and *The Reading of Books* (1947).

**Painter, George D.,** *William Caxton* (1977). Rich and fascinating biography of England's first printer and publisher, by the award-winning biographer of Proust.

**Perrin, Noel,** *Dr. Bowdler's Legacy* (1969). Good-humored history of expurgated books in England and America.

## Publishing and Bookselling

**Applebaum, Judith and Nancy Evans,** *How to Get Happily Published* (rev. 1982). Complete and candid guide to getting your work in print. See Richard Balkin, *A Writer's Guide to Book Publishing* (1981).

**Beach, Sylvia,** *Shakespeare and Company* (1959). The title is the name of the American bookshop in Paris that the author established in 1919 and that became headquarters for expatriate Americans. She was the first publisher of Joyce's *Ulysses*. "Her reminiscences are literally an index to everybody in the twenties, and she knew them all" (Janet Flanner).

**Berg, A. Scott,** *Max Perkins, Editor of Genius* (1978). Story of the famous Scribner's editor and his relationship with such novelists as Fitzgerald, Hemingway, and Wolfe. See *Editor to Author* (1950), a selection of his letters. Another good book about an editor is Dorothy Cummins, *What Is an Editor?: Saxe Cummins at Work* (1978).

**Henderson, Bill (ed.),** *The Art of Literary Publishing: Editors on Their Craft* (1980). Lively, rewarding anthology of editors, writers, and publishers discussing aspects of the art and business. See *The Publish-It-Yourself Handbook* (rev. 1980).

**Monteilhet, Hubert,** *Murder at the Frankfurt Book Fair* (1976). Bookish mystery by prize-winning French thriller writer. For domestic violence, see Isaac Asimov, *Murder at the ABA* (1976).

**Powell, Anthony,** *What's Become of Waring* (1939). Nutty novel, revolving around an English publishing house, which antedates the author's noted A Dance to the Music of Time series. Another good novel of the publishing world is John Leggett, *Gulliver House* (1979).

**Rogers, W. G.,** *Wise Men Fish Here* (1965). Engaging story of Frances Steloff and New York City's Gotham Book Mart — one of the shrines of bibliophilia.

**Straus, Ralph,** *The Unspeakable Curil* (1928). Robust biographical sketch of the eighteenth-century bookseller and "unspeakable scoundrel," who printed pirated editions of Swift, Addison, Pope, et al. Not to be pirated by Curil was to be slighted.

**Summer, Celia,** *With a Book in My Hand* (1977). Informed with the love of books, this is the memoir of a woman who worked for ten years in Scribner's Book Store in Manhattan.

**Tryon, W. S.,** *Parnassus Corner* (1963). Well-told and interesting life of James T. Fields, "Publisher of the Victorians" and cofounder of the house which published the book you are holding in your hand right now. See James C. Austin, *Fields of the Atlantic Monthly: Letters to an Editor, 1861–1870* (1954).

## Book Collecting

**Goodrum, Charles A.,** *Dewey Decimated* (1977). Urbane whodunit in which the serene world of rare books and libraries is beset by theft and murder. Goodrum is a distinguished librarian with the Library of Congress and author of the magnificent *Treasures of the Library of Congress* (1980).

**Hanff, Helene,** *Eighty-Four Charing Cross Road* (1971). This charming little book is a collection of twenty years of correspondence between the New York author and a London bookseller.

**Jordan-Smith, Paul,** *For the Love of Books* (1934). Subtitled *The Adventures of an Impecunious Collector,* it is spiced with wit, learning, and impetuosity.

**Lewis, Wilmarth S.,** *Collector's Progress* (1951). Spirited recollection by the editor of the Yale edition of Horace Walpole's correspondence of his obsession with the eighteenth-century English author. See *One Man's Education* (1967).

**Newton, A. Edward,** *The Greatest Book in the World* (1925). One of a series of collected essays dealing with the amenities of book collecting. Crammed with curious anecdotes and prejudices and written in a delightfully archaic style.

**Orcutt, William Dana,** *In Quest of the Perfect Book* (1926). Reflections on thirty-five years of collecting and friendship with writers and other book lovers. It is, as one reviewer of the day stated, the very "vital and very human record of a search which has all the fascination for the bookman that the hunt has to the rider of hounds." See *The Magic of the Book* (1930).

**Peters, Jean (ed.),** *Book Collecting: A Modern Guide* (1977). A dozen essays by outstanding contributors make this the new standard work in the field. See *Collectible Books: Some New Paths* (1979).

**Powell, Lawrence Clark,** *Bookmen's Progress* (1968). Selections from numerous books by the former dean of the UCLA Library School and one of the all-time great bibliophiles that brim with his enthusiasm for reading.

**Starrett, Vincent,** *Bookman's Holiday* (1942). These "private satisfactions of an incurable collector" will delight all of like persuasion. The author was a well-known newspaperman and authority on Sherlock Holmes. See *Books Alive* (1940).

**Targ, William,** *Bouillabaisse for Bibliophiles* (1955). Genial anthology of pieces about collecting and collectors. See *Carrousel for Bibliophiles* (1947). Targ was also a publisher and editor of note; his gossipy memoirs are contained in *Indecent Pleasures* (1975).

## Commonplace Books

**Auden, W. H.,** *A Certain World* (1970). In the foreword, the poet states "that this compilation is a sort of autobiography . . . a map of my planet. . . . The bulk of this book will, I hope, make pleasant reading, but there are some entries which will, I trust, disturb a reader as much as they disturb me." One of his most important books.

**Cecil, Lord David,** *Library Looking-Glass* (1977). The selections by the urbane English critic-biographer are mainly unfamiliar, catholic, quiet, and humanistic. See *The Fine Art of Reading* (1957).

**Mayes, Herbert R.,** *An Editor's Treasury* (1968). Huge, eclectic anthology culled from a lifetime of reading by former editor of *McCall's* magazine.

**Origo, Iris,** *The Vagabond Path* (1973). Very personal selections — mostly poems — out of miscellaneous reading of over fifty years by the biographer and Italophile.

**Rosten, Leo,** *Infinite Riches* (1979). The creator of H\*y\*m\*a\*n K\*a\*p\*l\*a\*n has mined the gems of a half-century's reading and displayed them in this thick volume. Richly variegated, they range from the sublime to the absurd.

## Book Lists

**Connolly, Cyril,** *The Modern Movement* (1966). Limiting himself to books from England, France, and America published between 1880 and 1950, the English literary editor selected 100 books with "outstanding originality and richness of texture and with the spark of rebellion alight, books which aspire to be works of art."

**Fadiman, Clifton,** *The Life-time Reading Plan* (1978). A hundred classics introduced in the informal and informative style which has been Fadiman's trademark as one of America's most respected bookpeople.

**Gilbar, Steven,** *The Book Book* (1981). Another "list book" for book lovers by yours truly. More whimsical than the one you are holding, it's a "compendium of lists, quizzes, and trivia about books."

**Kieran, John,** *Books I Love* (1969). The veteran sports and nature writer of two decades ago was a reader of wide range and something of a polymath (he used to be on the old radio show "Information, Please!"). His discussions of his favorite books — all premodern — are full of charm and passion for good reading.

**Raphael, Frederic and Kenneth McLeish,** *The List of Books* (1981). Arranged in forty-four categories, the lists, despite a decidedly Oxbridge tang, are often illuminating and often infuriating.

**Weber, J. Sherwood (ed.),** *Good Reading* (rev. 1978). This reading guide has been around since 1932 and has gone through twenty-one editions. It remains the best one-volume advisor for serious, academic reading.

# LITERATURE

**Beerbohm, Max,** *Seven Men* (1919). The masterpiece of the brilliant satirist and caricaturist. His biographer, Lord David Cecil, said this set of fictional sketches of literary men was "the finest expression of the comic spirit produced by an English writer during this century."

**Brooks, Van Wyck,** *Makers and Finders Series* (1936–52). Vivid, panoramic, often sentimentalized, and a bit thin, but immensely readable historical-biographical survey of American writing from 1800 to 1915. Of the first, chronologically, of the five volumes — *The World of Washington Irving* (1944) — Edmund Wilson wrote that "style, narrative and organization have been brought to a point of perfection seldom reached in our historical and critical writing."

**Connolly, Cyril,** *Enemies of Promise* (1938). "Like all really good books of criticism, it reveals its author's mind as sharply as a good poem or novel; and without being systematic in the great tradition of criticism, it is a work of such resplendent intelligence as to be worth a dozen or more pretentious histories or manuals of contemporary literature" (Alfred Kazin).

**Forster, E. M.,** *Aspects of the Novel* (1927). Classic lectures in which "we discover under his casual and wittily acute guidance, many things about the literary magic which transmutes the dull stuff of He-said and She-said into characters, stories, and intimations of truth" (Jacques Barzun).

**Hazlitt, William,** *Lectures on the English Comic Writers* (1819). In a singular, vigorous style, the great critic assesses the writers of the century before his own. His brilliant essays on his contemporaries appear in *The Spirit of the Age* (1825).

**Highet, Gilbert,** *The Classical Tradition* (1949). Not only is the author of this study on the Greek and Roman influence on Western literature "familiar with the whole body of classical literature, he seems to have read nearly every writer of importance from the Dark Ages down to the Joyce of *Finnegans Wake,* and he talks about them with clarity and sound sense" (Dudley Fitts). See *People, Places and Books* (1953).

**Hyman, Stanley Edgar,** *The Critic's Credentials: Essays and Reviews* (1978). Wide-ranging essays on books and writers by a forthright critic who is always fun to read.

**Lawrence, D. H.,** *Selected Literary Criticism* (1955). His best book reviews and critical essays brought together in a single volume; informal, highly personal, and almost always insightful. See *Studies in Classical American Literature* (1923).

**Lehmann, John,** *The Open Night* (1952). Refreshing, conversational essays by a distinguished British literary editor about writers who died during his lifetime and meant much to him, who include James, Conrad, Woolf, and Proust. His autobiography, *The Whispering Gallery* (1955), paints an illuminating portrait of the English literary-political world of the thirties.

**MacDonald, Dwight** (ed.), *Parodies: An Anthology from Chaucer to Beerbohm and After* (1960). This cornucopia of irreverent poetry and prose is "undoubtedly, the most sense-of-humor-benumbing book ever to appear in a single volume. To adopt Oscar Wilde's epigram, . . . one must have a sense of humor made of stone to read all this funniness without weeping" (D. J. Enright).

**Mudrick, Marvin,** *Nobody Here But Us Chickens* (1981). A "book about people in books," this is a collection of literary and historical portraits by a writer who is erudite, moral, iconoclastic, and wickedly funny. Among his other books of the same brilliance is *Books Are Not Life But Then What Is?* (1979).

**Orwell, George,** *Dickens, Dali and Others* (1946). These studies in popular culture, as Orwell termed them, are "brilliant examples of political anthropology applied to literature by a non-conforming mind" (V. S. Pritchett). For more of this openhearted and open-minded writer see the four-volume *Collected Essays, Journals, and Letters* (1968).

**Pound, Ezra,** *ABC of Reading* (1934). The nature and meaning of literature, illustrated with exhibits meticulously chosen from the classics, "written with a pleasant insolence, in Pound's usual haphazard manner" (Kenneth Burke). See *How to Read* (1931) and *Guide to Kulchur* (rev. 1951).

**Pritchett, V. S.,** *The Living Novel & Later Appreciations* (1964). Critical essays of wit, geniality, and profound good sense by the noted English short-story writer, novelist, and critic. See *The Tale Bearers* (1980) and *The Myth Makers* (1979).

**Saintsbury, George,** *The Collected Essays and Papers* (1923). Pieces about minor nineteenth-century writers by a scholar who, although an old fogey about modern literature, was "the sole English literary English critic of the late-19th early-20th centuries . . . who is really of first-rate stature," said Edmund Wilson, who also called him "the greatest connoisseur of literature that we have ever had in English." He found his *A History of the French Novel* (1917) "one of the most entertaining of books on literature."

**Sheed, Wilfrid,** *The Good Word and Other Words* (1978). Wonderful collection of pieces on literary and other matters by a brilliant commentator and artist with words. See *The Morning After* (1971).

**Sorrentino, Gilbert,** *Mulligan Stew* (1979). Entertaining experimental novel parodying experimental novels. Other satirical novels about writing include Muriel Spark, *Loitering with Intent* (1981) and Geoffrey Wolff, *Inklings* (1978).

**Sutherland, James (ed.),** *The Oxford Book of Literary Anecdotes* (1975). Like his *The Oxford Book of English Talk* (1953), this delightful omnium-gatherum of quips about literary people from the seventh-century poet Caedmon to Dylan Thomas is a perfect bedside book. See Donald Hall (ed.), *The Oxford Book of American Literary Anecdotes* (1981).

**Wilson, Edmund,** *Axel's Castle* (1931). This Marxist critique of the imaginative literature of 1870–1930 is one of many brilliant works by the former dean of American critics. Others include *The Wound and the Bow* (1941) and his anthology of criticism of authors by authors, *The Shock of Recognition* (rev. 1955). His reprinted reviews are always intelligent and witty; see, for example, *The Shores of Light* (1952).

**Woolf, Virginia,** *The Common Reader* (1925). Finely crafted literary essays still make enjoyable and rewarding reading even when their subjects have little relevance today. See *The 2nd Common Reader* (1932).

*Writers at Work: The Paris Review Interviews* (1958–80). Five series have been published to date. Taken from past issues, these lively conversations are the best inside views of the literary life.

# POETRY

**Auden, W. H.,** *The Dyer's Hand and Other Essays* (1962). The poet on other poets. The essays bring to the fore his intelligence, his concern for his craft, and his wit.

**Berke, Roberta,** *A Bound Out of Bounds: A Compass for Recent American and British Poetry* (1981). Sensible and penetrating treatment of recent poetry by an English writer with a sure sense for detecting hype and knowing the "real thing."

**Blackmur, R. P.,** *Language as Gesture* (1952). This classic collection of critical essays, while sometimes oblique, attest to the great intelligence and sensibility of the author.

**Blyth, R. H.,** *Zen in English Literature and Oriental Classics* (1942). Poetry as English Zen is the theme of this remarkable book, which ranges over the great literatures of both the East and the West. A horizon-expanding experience.

**Ciardi, John,** *How Does a Poem Mean?* (rev. 1975). Astute pieces about poetry for the general reader by a poet.

**Fraser, G. S.,** *A Short History of English Poetry* (1981). A distinguished poet and professor surveys thirteen centuries of poetry with wit and freshness. See *The Modern Writer and His World: Innovation in Twentieth Century English Literature* (1964).

**Gibbons, Reginald (ed.),** *The Poet's Work* (1979). Anthology of writings by the great poets of our time on their craft.

**Hall, Donald,** *Remembering Poets* (1978). Poignant memoir of a young poet viewing the poets of the preceding generation at the end of their often anguished lives.

**Hazlitt, William,** *Lectures on the English Poets* (1818). Essays by the magnificent prose stylist of the Romantic age, "one of the keenest and brightest critics that ever lived" (William M. Thackeray). His famous essay, "My First Acquaintance with the Poets," about Wordsworth and Coleridge, is in *The Plain Speaker* (1826).

**Hollander, John,** *Rhyme's Reason: A Guide to English Verse* (1981). A poet and English professor at Yale surveys the schemes, patterns, and forms of English verse, illustrating each variation with an original, witty, self-descriptive example.

**Jarrell, Randall,** *Poetry and the Age* (1953). Jarrell was not only a fine poet, but a critic of wisdom and verve and a corruscating wit when a writer did not meet his exacting standards. Other collections of critical pieces in his inviting, relaxed style are *A Sad Heart at the Supermarket* (1962), *The Third Book of Criticism* (1969), and *Kipling, Auden & Co.* (1980).

**Lowes, John Livingston,** *The Road to Xanadu* (1927). This "study in the ways of the imagination" remains "the finest book on Coleridge's genius and a masterpiece in its own right" (Clifton Fadiman). See *Convention and Revolt in Poetry* (1919).

**Pritchard, William H.** *Lives of the Modern Poets* (1980). Lives of nine early-twentieth-century British and American poets provide prefaces to add reevaluations of their individual achievements. See *Seeing Through Everything: English Writers: 1918–1940* (1977).

**Rexroth, Kenneth,** *American Poetry in the Twentieth Century* (1971). Iconoclastic, gossipy, wide-ranging, vivid review of poetry of this century's first six decades by a poet and social revolutionary.

**Rosenthal, M. L.,** *The Modern Poets: A Critical Introduction* (1960). Fine introduction to modern poetry for the often puzzled general reader by a poet and editor of *Poetry.* See *Poetry and the Common Life* (1974) and *Yeats, Pound, and Eliot* (1978).

**Vendler, Helen,** *Part of Nature, Part of Us: Modern American Poets* (1980). Col-

lection of essays and reviews by the "best poetry reviewer in America" (William H. Pritchard). Winner of National Book Critics Circle Award.

**Zaranka, William (ed.),** *The Brand-X Anthology of Poetry* (1981). Suspiciously reminiscent of a familiar standard poetry anthology, this inspired collection contains over 400 parodies of works of all the major poets, most minor poets, and some insignificant poets. Literary, erudite, and very funny.

# JOURNALISM

## Newspapers

**Beebe, Lucius,** *Comstock Commotion* (1954). Light and lively telling of the story of the *Territorial Enterprise and Virginia City News* — the most famous paper of the Old West — by a one-time Manhattan boulevardier who became co-owner of the paper.

**Churchill, Allen,** *Park Row* (1958). Romanticized, sparkling recreation of turn-of-the-century newspaper days in New York, the good old days of yellow journalism.

**Filler, Louis,** *The Muckrakers* (rev. 1975). The story of the crusading journalists of the first part of the century. For a collection of writings that is practically a treatise on modern investigative journalism, see Jessica Mitford, *Poison Penmanship: The Gentle Art of Muckraking* (1979).

**Fowler, Gene,** *Timber Line: A Story of Bonfils and Tamman* (1933). Highly colored and very readable account of the founders of the *Denver Post.*

**Frayn, Michael,** *Against Entropy* (1967). Hilarious satirical novel of Fleet Street.

**Gies, Joseph,** *The Colonel of Chicago* (1979). Discerning biography of Colonel Robert McCormick, publisher of the *Chi-*

*cago Tribune* for forty years and spokesman for conservatism during his lifetime.

**Hohenberg, John,** *Foreign Correspondence: The Great Reporters and Their Times* (1964). Crisp, capsulized histories of correspondents from the French Revolution to Vietnam by a Columbia journalism professor: for all its scholarly care, it reads like an adventure story.

**Kahn, E. J., Jr.,** *The World of Swope* (1965). Herbert Bayard Swope, that is. Quondam reporter, newspaper editor, politician, dandy, croquet champion, etc. A fascinating 500-page *New Yorker* profile.

**Knightley, Philip,** *The First Casualty* (1975). Splendid history of war correspondence. The first casualty, of course, is the truth.

**Liebling, A. J.,** *The Press* (1961). Caustic, informed, often hilarious; this survey of the omissions, distortions, and downright fiction in our newspapers may be the best book ever written about the American press. His experiences as a young journalist are wittily recollected in *The Wayward Pressman* (1947).

**McAuliffe, Kevin Michael,** *The Great American Newspaper: The Rise and Fall of the Village Voice* (1979). The life and times of New York's famous alternative weekly.

**McKelway, St. Clair,** *Gossip: The Life and Times of Walter Winchell* (1940). Winchell is gone, but as long as gossip-mongering continues this scalpel job on the famous columnist, in the cruelly ironic *New Yorker* style, deserves to be read.

**Morris, Joe Alex,** *A Deadline Every Minute* (1957). Scintillating history of the United Press wire service.

**O'Connor, Richard,** *The Scandalous Mr. Bennett* (1962). Popular biography of James Gordon Bennett, Jr., the owner of the *New York Herald,* the man who sent Stanley to find Livingstone and instigator of some equally fascinating journalistic stunts. Larded with wonderous anecdotes, it is thoroughly entertaining.

**Salisbury, Harrison,** *Without Fear or Favor* (1980). Good, workmanlike history of the *New York Times* by one of its finest writers. A more gossipy inside view can be found in Gay Talese, *The Kingdom and the Power* (1966).

**Swanberg, W. A.,** *Citizen Hearst* (1961). Superb biography of the inimitable William Randolph Hearst. Another newspaper titan is the subject of *Pulitzer* (1967).

**Taylor, A. J. P.,** *Beaverbrook* (1972). The British press lord and kingmaker of twentieth-century English politics sympathetically portrayed by one of the most literary of modern historians.

**Waugh, Evelyn,** *Scoop* (1938). Lively burlesque of the newspaper world in which a nature writer for a London daily, the *Beast,* is sent by mistake to cover a civil war in Africa.

**White, William Allen,** *Autobiography* (1946). White was owner-editor of the Emporia (Ka.) *Gazette,* perhaps the most well-known small newspaper of its day. His posthumous, Pulitzer Prize–winning

autobiography is, as reporting, "reporting of the sort that captures mood and character as well as fact," remarked Richard H. Rovere, "is fit company for any that have been written by an American in this century or the last."

**Wicker, Tom,** *On Press* (1978). A mixture of reminiscences and reflections on journalism by one of America's most respected political correspondents.

## Magazines

**Anson, Robert Sam,** *Gone Crazy and Back Again: The Rise and Fall of the Rolling Stone Generation* (1981). The dramatic rise of *Rolling Stone* and its mercurial publisher, Jann Wenner, and the passing of a generation out of exile in the sixties on to Main Street in the eighties.

**Bainbridge, John,** *Little Wonder: Or, The Reader's Digest and How It Grew* (1946). Good-natured satire done completely in *Digest* format.

**Kramer, Dale,** *Ross and the New Yorker* (1952). Still the best book about the *New Yorker.* Other good ones are Brendan Gill, *Here at the New Yorker* (1975); Jane Grant (Mrs. Harold Ross), *The New Yorker and Me* (1968); E. J. Kahn, Jr., *The New Yorker and Me* (1979); and James Thurber, *The Years with Ross* (1959).

**Swanberg, W. A.,** *Luce and His Empire* (1972). The life and times (and fortunes) of Henry R. Luce, the controversial founder of the Time-Life publishing empire. This lengthy biography won the Pulitzer Prize. For a good history of *Time,* see Robert T. Elson, *Time, Inc.* (1960–73). For an inside look at *Life,* see Dora Jane Hamblin, *That Was the Life* (1977).

**Trillin, Calvin,** *Floater* (1980). A droll behind-the-scenes-of-a-great-weekly-news-magazine novel by a keen-witted journalist. Other amusing magazine fiction include Wilfrid Sheed's novels, *Office Poli-*

*tics* (1966) and *Max Jamison* (1970); Kenneth Fearing's thriller *The Big Clock*

(1946); Leonard Gross, *Mirror* (1981); and Betty Suyker, *Death Scene* (1981).

# ART

**Berger, John,** *About Looking* (1980). Collection of challenging essays by a provocative writer. A fascinating record of the search for meaning within and behind what is looked at. See *Ways of Seeing* (1973), *The Success and Failure of Picasso* (1965), and *A Painter of Our Time* (1958), a novel.

**Berenson, Bernard,** *The Bernard Berenson Treasury* (1962). A sampler of over seventy years of writing by the most celebrated art connoisseur and humanist of our time. See Meryle Secrest, *Being Bernard Berenson* (1979) and Nicky Mariano, *Forty Years with Berenson* (1966).

**Canaday, John,** *What is Art?* (1980). This expansion of the *New York Times* art critic's earlier *The Metropolitan Seminars in Art* may not answer the big question of its title, but it is one of the most lucid, straightforward, profusely illustrated introductions to art and architecture. See *Keys to Art* (1963) and *Mainstreams of Modern Art* (rev. 1981).

**Diamonstein, Barbaralee (ed.),** *The Art World* (1977). This treasury of seventy-five years of *Artnews,* the prestigious magazine of the art world, is not only a fascinating review of the past styles of modern art, but its Milton Glazer–designed format makes it a joy to behold. See *Inside New York's Art World* (1980), *American Architecture Now* (1981), and *Visions and Images: American Photographers on Photography* (1982).

**Flanner, Janet,** *Men and Monuments* (1957). Five *New Yorker* profiles: Matisse, Picasso, Braque, André Malraux, and the acquisitions of paintings by Goering.

**Gombrich, E. H.,** *The Story of Art* (rev. 1978). Comprehensive history of art by the

"most intelligent, the most learned, and the wittiest of English art historians" (Kenneth Clark). Another good introduction is H. W. Janson's *History of Art* (rev. 1977).

**Hughes, Robert,** *The Shock of the New* (1980). Subtitled *Art and the Century of Change,* it is not just another byproduct of a popular PBS television series, but is in its own right one of the best books on twentieth-century modernism. The articulate author, art critic for *Time,* is refreshing and provocative.

**Huxley, Aldous,** *On Art and Artists* (1960). The virtues of these selected essays, in the opinion of Herbert Read, "lies in their lack of pretension, in their sensuous sensibility, . . . in their tolerance and wit."

**Kramer, Hilton,** *The Age of the Avant-Garde* (1973). This is an informative collection of short reviews (interspersed with a few longer essays) which the author, the art news editor of the *New York Times,* wrote between 1956 and 1972.

**Lynes, Russell,** *The Good Old Modern* (1973). Intimate "unofficial biography" of the incomparable Museum of Modern Art in New York.

**Malraux, André,** *The Voices of Silence* (1953). Not an art book exactly, but "a kind of free fantasy on themes from the history of art. A kind of (very-elevated) flea market of the absolute. . . . Certainly one of the most interesting books ever written" (Randall Jarrell). See *Museum Without Walls* (1968).

**Read, Herbert,** *Art and Society* (rev. 1966). This is one of the best books by the noted English art and literary critic, poet, and early champion of art in society. Others include *The Meaning of Art* (rev. 1968), *Art and Alienation* (1967), *Origins of Form in Art* (1965), and *A Letter to a Young Painter* (1962).

**Rosenberg, Harold,** *Art on the Edge* (1975). Collection of pieces by the art critic of the *New Yorker.* Sometimes parochial and negative, they exemplify modern critical journalism at its best. See *The De-Definition of Art* (1972), *The Anxious Object* (1964), and *The Tradition of the New* (1974). For a witty but pointed view of the insular New York world of Rosenberg and abstract expressionism, etc., see Tom Wolfe's *The Painted Word* (1975).

**Ruskin, John,** *The Lamp of Beauty: Writings on Art* (1959). Selected and edited by Dame Joan Evans from the thirty-eight volumes of the great Victorian critic's sometimes empurpled writings, a sampler of his best work.

**Russell, John,** *The Meaning of Modern Art* (1981). Lucid, often lyrical, analysis based on a special series written for the Book of the Month Club in collaboration with the Museum of Modern Art.

**Schapiro, Meyer,** *Modern Art* (1978). Collection of innovative essays by one of America's greatest art historians on such nineteenth- and twentieth-century figures as Cezanne, Van Gogh, and Picasso. Clearly written, they range from the broadest considerations to detailed analysis of particular works of art. See *Romanesque Art* (1976).

**Stein, Leo,** *Appreciation* (1947). Stein referred to his book as "a little debauch in the realm of ideas." It is a rambling, disarming, wise, and iconoclastic series of essays by a most unusual and original man. His passion for ideas and his sensibility as well as his associations with such figures as his famous sister Gertrude and Picasso and Matisse are strikingly portrayed in the autobiographical study *Journey into Self* (1950).

**Steinberg, Leo,** *Other Criteria: Confrontations with Art* (1972). Invigorating collection of essays that call for new approaches to the way we look at art.

**Tomkins, Calvin,** *Merchants and Masterpieces* (1970). Fascinating anecdotal story of the Metropolitan Museum of Art written in celebration of its centenary; a sumptuous pendant volume is Howard Hibbard's copiously illustrated *The Metropolitan Museum of Art* (1980). Tomkins's other fine books about art include *Off the Wall: Robert Rauschenberg and the Art World of Our Time* (1980), *The Bride and the Bachelors: The Heretical Courtship of Modern Art* (1965), and *The Scene* (1976).

**Vasari, Giorgio,** *Lives of the Most Eminent Painters, Sculptors and Architects* (rev. 1568). Sir Kenneth Clark did not exaggerate when he referred to the painter-critic's classic *Lives* as "the most vivid, entertaining and convincing portrait of Italian art at its greatest period." There is not a dull moment in this insider's view of the Renaissance.

**Time-Life Editors,** *Time-Life Library of Art* (1966–70). Outstanding series, unusually well written and handsomely designed, each volume focusing on "the world of" a great artist. It employed the talents of such writers as John Russell, C. V. Wedgewood, Alfred Frankenstein, and James Thomas Flexner for each book.

## Art Dealing and Collecting

**Behrman, S. N.,** *Duveen* (1952). An absorbing, witty portrait of the most spectacular art dealer of the century and the fabulous world he lived in.

**David, Carl,** *Collecting and Care of Fine Art* (1981). Good basic introduction for novice collectors, by an art dealer. See Glen Warner, *Building a Print Collection: A Guide to Buying Original Prints and Photographs* (1981).

**Gimpel, René,** *Diary of an Art Dealer* (1966). Gimpel was an international art dealer during the twenties and thirties when Paris was the cultural cynosure of the West. He knew Monet, Renoir, and Proust. This is "a journal of much the same literary quality and historical value as the Duc de Saint-Simon's classical memoir. . . . The real quality of [the book] resides in its vivid descriptive style and its sudden profound psychological insights" (Edouard Roditi).

**Guggenheim, Peggy,** *Out of this Century* (1946). When first published, this autobiography of the American art collector resident in Venice was considered astonishing due to its recounting of the author's amorous adventures. Today its value lies in its spirited version of the twenties view of life as one long adventure. Later editions, titled *Confessions of an Art Addict,* have been watered down.

**Levy, Julien,** *Memoir of an Art Gallery* (1977). Engaging recollections by New York gallery owner during the thirties who championed the Surrealists; closeup of the avant-garde art world of the time.

**Metropolitan Museum of Art,** *The Chase, The Capture: Collecting at the Metropolitan* (1975). Thomas Hoving and members of the curatorial staff describe the procedures of collecting. Especially interesting is Hoving's tale of how he acquired such masterpieces as the Bury St. Edmunds Cross and the Euphronois Krater.

**Steegmuller, Francis,** *The Two Lives of James Jackson Jarves* (1951). One of America's earliest art collectors, he gathered an impressive array of early Italian paintings during the 1850s. An absorbing portrait of an unusual man.

**Taylor, Francis H.,** *The Taste of Angels* (1948). Vivid, beautifully illustrated history of art collecting from Rameses to Napoleon by the former director of the Metropolitan Museum of Art.

**Tharp, Louise Hall,** *Mrs. Jack* (1965). Fine biography of Isabella Stewart Gardner, art collector and social leader during Boston's carriage days. For the lives and times and tastes of some other adventur-

ous American collectors see Aline B. Saarinen, *The Proud Possessors* (1958).

**Vollard, Ambroise,** *Recollections of a Picture Dealer* (1936). Friend of Cezanne and Renoir, "discoverer" of Picasso, his book is not great literature; it is, as V. S. Pritchett commented, "gossip, and very typical dealer-gossip, and is amusing to open at random."

## Painting and Drawing

**Baudelaire, Charles,** *Art in Paris, 1845–1862* (1981). The French poet's elegant and charming reviews of salons and other exhibitions that show him to be the "father of modern art criticism."

**Bell, Quentin,** *Victorian Artists* (1968). With erudition and charm, anecdotes and fine plates, this series of pieces based on his Slade lectures gives the reader as good a picture as can be had of these minor English painters.

**Clark, Kenneth,** *Looking at Pictures* (1960). Sixteen well-known paintings refreshingly analysed by a judicious and urbane guide. See *The Romantic Rebellion* (1974).

**Cox, Richard,** *The Botticelli Madonna* (1979). A superior mystery novel packed with all sorts of inside information about art critics, dealers, auction houses, and forgers. Other good art world thrillers are Oliver Banks, *The Rembrandt Panel* (1980); Bettz Burr, *Blue Ladies* (1981); Dorothy Salisbury Davis, *Scarlet Night* (1981); Leonard Sanders, *The Second Deadly Sin* (1977); and Clarissa Watson, *The Fourth Stage of Gainsborough Brown* (1977).

**Feiffer, Jules,** *The Great Comic Book Heroes* (1965). Affectionate and informed look at the origins and adventures of the classic superheroes of the comics.

**Flexner, James Thomas,** *American Old Masters* (rev. 1980). Sparkling history (not criticism) of West, Copley, Peale, and

Stuart. See *Nineteenth Century American Painting* (1971), *The Wilder Image: The Painting of American's Native School from Thomas Cole to Winslow Homer* (1962), and *The Light of Distant Skies: American Painting 1760–1835* (1969).

**Goffstein, M. B.,** *An Artist* (1980). Delicate watercolors in a sea of white space distinguish the author-illustrator's joyful celebration of the artist. See *Lives of the Artists* (1981).

**Goncourt, Edmund and Jules Goncourt,** *French XVIII Century Painters* (1856–75). These famous fraternal diarists and novelists were also superb art historians, specializing in eighteenth-century painting — Watteau, Fragonard, and other masters.

**Ivins, William M., Jr.,** *Prints and Visual Communication* (1953). Seminal work on the history and significance of prints as carriers of information as well as works of art. A luminous work. See *Notes on Prints* (1930) and *How Prints Look: Photographs with a Commentary* (1958). An excellent companion is Fritz Eichenberg, *The Art of the Print* (1976).

**James, Henry,** *The Painter's Eye* (1957). James wrote these pieces after going around the art galleries, top hat on his head, gloves in his hand, and precise standards in his mind. The world of Ruskin, Sargent, the Pre-Raphaelites, et al. brought to life with wit and intelligence.

**Lane, Richard,** *Images from the Floating World* (1978). One of the best introductions to the Japanese woodblock print. Written informally and with love.

**Monnier, Genevieve and Bernice Rose,** *Drawing: History of an Art* (1979). The beautiful reproductions make this comprehensive overview of drawing in western art especially valuable. See Theodore E. Stebbins, Jr., *American Master Drawings and Watercolors* (1976).

**O'Hara, Frank,** *Art Chronicles, 1954–1966* (1975). O'Hara was a distinguished poet and a curator of the Museum of Modern Art and right at the center of the New York art world of the fifties and sixties. This volume collects his articles, interviews, and catalog notes and provides a knowing picture of that world.

**Rewald, John,** *The History of Impressionism* (rev. 1973). *The* book on the subject. See *Post-Impressionism from Van Gogh to Gauguin* (rev. 1962).

**Richard H. Childers Productions,** *Air Powered: The Art of The Airbrush* (1980). Broad view of the history and artistry of a new and exciting medium.

## Design

**Arwas, Victor,** *Art Deco* (1980). The most serious and comprehensive book on this style of design. Beautifully illustrated.

**Bayley, Stephen,** *In Good Shape* (1979). Well-designed survey of style in industrial products from 1900 to 1960. Other good books on industrial design include Raymond Loewy, *Industrial Design* (1979) and Jeffrey Meikle, *Twentieth Century Limited* (1979).

**Booth-Clibborn, Edward and Daniele Baroni,** *The Language of Graphics* (1979). Dazzling collection brings together an extraordinary display of graphic design, from the early beginnings to the present day.

**Brown, Erica,** *Interior Views: Design at Its Best* (1980). Large-format, color-photo-filled international overview of modern interior design, comprising interviews with forty famous interior decorators. For do-it-yourself redecoration, see Mary Gilliatt, *The Decorating Book* (1981) and Terence Conran, *The House Book* (1976).

**Fairbanks, Jonathan L. and Elizabeth Bidwell Bates,** *American Furniture, 1620 to the Present* (1981). Solid, luminous, beautiful book that concisely describes and traces the development of American furniture in 1,400 photographs and lucid text.

**Pevsner, Nikolaus,** *Pioneers of Modern Design* (rev. 1964). Traces the emergence of modernism from William Morris to Walter Gropius. A classic by the eminent German-born English art historian. See *The Sources of Modern Architecture and Design* (1968).

**Praz, Mario,** *The House of Life* (1964). The author was a devoted connoisseur and collector of Empire and Regency furnishings as well as a literary critic of some note. This, ostensibly a tour of his collection in his Roman flat, is really a frame for a series of remarkable portraits of the people he met in the course of his life. See *An Illustrated History of Furnishing from the Renaissance to the Twentieth Century* (1965).

**Rice, Brian and Tony Evans,** *The English Sunrise* (1972). Radiant little book of dazzling photographs of English objects, old and new, with a sunrise motif.

## Fashion

**Batterberry, Michael and Ariane Batterberry,** *Mirror, Mirror* (1977). Comprehensive social history of fashion done in lively, anecdotal style. See Geoffrey Squire, *Dress and Society, 1560–1970* (1974).

**Dior, Christian,** *Christian Dior and I* (1957). Inside view of the famous couturier's house. The *Times* of London wrote that "in its detailing of craftsmanship, it is as fascinating as Cezanne's analysis would have been of what Proust called his 'little sensation.' " Other interesting books on French designers are Pierre Balmain, *My Years and Seasons* (1965); Diana De Marley, *Worth: Father of Fashion* (1980); Paul Poiret, *King of Fashion* (1931); and Elsa Schiaparelli, *Shocking Life* (1954).

**Fraser, Kennedy,** *The Fashionable Mind* (1981). Reflections on a decade of fashion by the fashion critic of the *New Yorker*.

**Lurie, Alison,** *The Language of Clothes* (1981). A novelist and scholar looks at the secrets people reveal by the way they choose to dress. "A delightful book about a subject everyone is obsessed with — especially those who claim they aren't" (Tom Wolfe). Just why styles change is taken up in Quentin Bell, *On Human Finery* (rev. 1977).

**Penn, Irving and Diana Vreeland,** *Inventive Paris Clothes, 1909–1939* (1978). This beautifully conceived photographic essay was a spinoff of a show at the Metropolitan Museum of Art.

## Photography

**Adams, Ansel,** *The Camera* (1980). Inaugural volume of the New Ansel Adams Photography series, a rewriting of the earlier, influential five-volume Basic Photography Books by the great camera artist and technician.

**Buckland, Gail,** *Fox Talbot and the Invention of Photography* (1980). This biography of the great Victorian inventor is "at once learned, readable and wise, and where appropriate . . . it achieves an eloquence rarely to be found in a work containing so much original research" (Hilton Kramer). See *The Magic Image* (1975) and *First Photographs: People, Places, and Phenomena as Captured for the First Time by the Camera* (1980).

**Coleman, A. D.,** *Light Readings* (1979). Collects pieces from the preceding decade by a leading photography critic, full of insight and pungent independent judgment.

**Eastman Kodak Company,** *The Joy of Photography* (1979). Guidance on developing a personal style, detailed technical information for implementing it and 100 specific ideas for taking more creative 35mm photographs. See *More Joy of Photography* (1981).

**Galloway, David,** *A Family Album* (1978). This imaginative, moving novel is "an icy, brilliant piece of writing based on attentive scrutiny of snapshots" (A. D. Coleman).

**Goldberg, Vicki (ed.),** *Photography in Print: Writings from 1816 to the Present* (1981). Enjoyable anthology of varied writings. Another well-selected compendium is Nathan Lyons (ed.), *Photographers on Photography* (1966).

**Hirsch, Julia,** *Family Photographs: Content, Meaning, and Effect* (1981). Provocative look at how family photographs, both candid and formal, reveal our beliefs and values. See Michael Lesy, *Time Frames: The Meaning of Family Pictures* (1981).

**Maddow, Ben,** *Faces: A Narrative History of the Portrait in Photography* (1977). Monumental volume; photographs selected by Constance Sullivan.

**Malcolm, Janet,** *Diana & Nikon: Essays on the Aesthetic of Photography* (1980). Superb collection of writings by the photography critic of the *New Yorker.*

**Newhall, Beaumont,** *The History of Photography* (1964). Basic chronological history of the medium. See *Photography: Essays and Images: Illustrated Readings in the History of Photography* (1981), *The Daguerreotype in America* (1962), and *Airborne Photography* (1971).

**Scharf, Aaron,** *Pioneers of Photography* (1976). Utilizing their photographs, and excerpts from their letters and journals as well, Scharf has put together an enthralling story of photography's early days. See *Art and Photography* (1968).

**Sontag, Susan,** *On Photography* (1977). National Book Critics Circle Award–winning essays that consider the relationship of photography to art, to conscience, and to knowledge. Other interesting aesthetic studies are Roland Barthes, *Camera Lucida: Reflections on Photography* (1981); John Berger and Jean Mohr, *Another Way of Telling* (1982); and Marine Vaizey, *The Artist as Photographer* (1982).

**Szarckowski, John,** *Looking at Photographs* (1973). The head of the photography section of the Museum of Modern Art has written brief essays on each of 100

pictures. The result is the best short introduction extant to photography. See *Mirrors and Windows: American Photography Since 1960* (1978) and *American Landscapes* (1981).

**Time-Life Editors,** *Life Library of Photography* (1970–72). This outstanding series is the best there is on the subject. Comprehensive, authoritative, and splendidly designed.

## *Architecture*

**Alexander, Christopher et al.,** *A Pattern Language: Towns, Buildings, Construction* (1977). Two hundred fifty-three patterns to make private and public spaces more habitable and graceful; "simply a great book — a bracing adventure in architectural thought, a lift for the spirit, an inspiration for practical work" (Stewart Brand).

**Allen, Edward,** *How Buildings Work* (1980). Good, clear account of the physical principles of building. With his own fine drawings.

**Andrews, Wayne,** *Architecture, Ambition, and America* (rev. 1979). Not about buildings, but about architecture as fine art and about taste in America, by an historian who is a romantic, passionate lover of architecture. It is witty and larded with his fine illustrations. See *American Gothic: Its Origins, Its Trials, Its Triumphs* (1975).

**Banham, Rayner,** *The Age of the Masters: A Personal View of Modern Architecture* (rev. 1975). By an English architectural historian and critic, an entertaining and enlightening essay on the state of the art, amply illustrated. See *Design by Choice: Ideas in Architecture* (1981).

**Betjeman, John,** *Ghastly Good Taste; or a Depressing Story of the Rise and Fall of English Architecture* (1971). Reissue of the original 1933 edition (plus author's current notes) of his tongue-in-cheek account of British buildings from the Middle Ages onward. See *A Pictorial History of English*

*Architecture* (1972). The best guide is J. M. Richards, *The National Trust Book of English Architecture* (1981).

**Goldberger, Paul,** *The City Observed: A Guide to the Architecture of New York* (1979). You don't have to love the Big Apple to love this book. By the architecture critic of the *New York Times* and one of the best writers in the field today. See *The Skyscraper* (1981).

**Heyer, Paul,** *Architects on Architecture* (rev. 1978). The design approach, ideas and major work of some forty leading American architects whose work represents influential direction in U. S. architecture today.

**Huxtable, Ada Louise,** *Kicked a Building Lately?* (1977). Incisive, finely-written pieces by a Pulitzer Prize–winning architectural critic. See *Will They Ever Finish Bruckner Boulevard?* (1970).

**Jencks, Charles A.,** *The Language of Post-Modern Architecture* (1977). Provocative, irreverent look at the new directions in architecture, beyond the modern movement.

**Lancaster, Clay,** *Architectural Follies in America: or Hammer, Saw-tooth and Nail* (1960). Fifty wonderful, amazing examples of folly architecture.

**Lancaster, Osbert,** *Here of All Places* (1958). Slim little book of masterly pen-and-ink drawings, with comments, that provide a wry tour through architecture.

**Macauley, David,** *Great Moments in Architecture* (1978). Portfolio of captioned drawings that delightfully spoof architecture with a donnish whimsy. The author-illustrator's "children's" books are fascinating, informative, and stylishly drawn; see, for example, *City* (1974) and *Unbuilding* (1980).

**McHarg, Ian,** *Design by Nature* (1969). Impassioned, vividly written book on designing cities with nature and with open spaces in order to avoid urban blight and destruction of our landscape.

**Mumford, Lewis,** *Sticks and Stones* (rev. 1976). Classic analysis of American architecture from its eighteenth-century beginnings to the present day by the preeminent architectural critic of our day. See *The City in History* (1961).

**Nevins, Deborah, and Robert A. M. Stern,** *The Architect's Eye* (1979). Beautiful large book of American architectural drawings. Remarkable insight into the history of this art form and into American architecture.

**Pevsner, Nikolaus,** *An Outline of European Architecture* (rev. 1960). Probably the best introduction to the subject. A superbly informative and eloquent narrative.

**Pouillon, Fernand,** *The Stones of the Abbey* (1970). In language that is brisk and finely tooled, this novel by a French architect recreates the building of the Abbey of Le Thoronet in Provence, one of the masterpieces of twelfth-century art. A superbly illustrated companion is David Macauley's Caldecott Medal winner *Cathedral: The Story of Its Construction* (1980).

**Rand, Ayn,** *The Fountainhead* (1943). The long-popular polemical novel of "objectivism" about an architect of skyscraper-size conceit who sticks to his principles. No matter how you feel about Rand's philosophy, there is no doubting that her book is a real melodramatic page-turner. For an interesting novel about an architect who sells out, see Robert Herrick, *The Common Lot* (1904).

**Riseboro, Bill,** *The Story of Western Architecture* (1979). Brief, lucid, informative. With the author's own sketches. A good introduction to architecture.

**Roth, Leland M.,** *A Concise History of American Architecture* (1977). With over 300 illustrations and an easy writing style, it is the best general survey in print.

Rudofsky, Bernard, *Architecture Without Architects: A Short Introduction to Nonpedigreed Architecture* (rev. 1964). Exhilarating survey of "vernacular" architecture. See *The Prodigious Builders* (1977).

Salvadori, Mario, *Why Buildings Stand Up: The Strength of Architecture* (1981). Easy-to-understand explanation of the methods and problems involved in erecting a structure that does not fall down.

Smith, G. E. Kidder, *A Pictorial History of Architecture in America* (1976). A beautifully produced volume written by an architect and critic who toured the U.S. for almost ten years taking photographs. A striking achievement. See his three-volume field guide, *The Architecture of the United States: An Illustrated Guide to Notable Buildings Open to the Public* (1981).

Summerson, John W., *Heavenly Mansions, and Other Essays on Architecture* (1950). The foremost English architectural critic of his generation talks about architecture in an attractive blending of learning and wit.

Thorndike, Joseph J., Jr., (ed.), *Three Centuries of Notable American Architects* (1981). With essays by notable architectural historians and critics, this handsome volume surveys the lives and work of America's master builders from Charles Bulfinch and Thomas Jefferson to today's leading architects.

Wolfe, Tom, *From Bauhaus to Our House* (1981). The dean of the new journalism takes on modern architecture: a cranky, often wrongheaded, but always amusing, polemic. A more telling critique, by an architect, is Peter Blake, *Form Follows Fiasco: Why Modern Architecture Hasn't Worked* (1977).

Wright, Frank Lloyd, *Writings and Buildings* (1960). Representative selection covering seventy years of the great architect's words and works. Contains an abundance of photographs, drawings, and plans. See *The Future of Architecture* (1953) and *The Natural House* (1970).

# MUSIC

## Classical

Barzun, Jacques (ed.), *The Pleasures of Music* (1951). Diverting and varied selection of great writing about music, from Cellini to Shaw, collected by an eminent educator and critic.

Battcock, Gregory (ed.), *Breaking the Sound Barrier: A Critical Anthology of the New Music* (1981). For the listener who wants to understand what is happening on the leading edge of modern music, the twenty-seven incisive pieces gathered here are most instructive.

Berlioz, Hector, *Evenings with the Orchestra* (1956). First published in 1852 — here translated and edited by Jacques Barzun — and aimed at a large audience, it is "full of knowledge, penetration, good sense, individual wit, justifiable exasperation, understanding exaggeration, emotion and rhetoric of every kind" (Randall Jarrell).

Bernstein, Leonard, *The Unanswered Question* (1977). Bernstein is as gifted a writer and speaker as he is conductor and composer, as these trenchant and lively talks delivered at Harvard demonstrate. His earlier books, *The Joy of Music* (1959) and *The Infinite Variety of Music* (1966), are equally enjoyable.

Biancolli, Louis and Herbert F. Peyser, *Masters of the Orchestra* (1954). Sketches of the great composers that brilliantly capture the essence of each.

**Bowen, Catherine Drinker,** *Free Artist* (1939). Fascinating story of Anton and Nicholas Rubinstein, teachers of Tchaikovsky, by a woman who is not only a fine biographer, but an accomplished musician as well. See her book about Tchaikovsky and his patroness, *Beloved Friend* (1937).

**Casals, Pablo,** *Conversations with Casals* (1957). Transcription of a series of talks recorded by J. M. Corredor. The celebrated Spanish cellist's intelligence and warmth shine through and make absorbing reading for any lover of music.

**Copland, Aaron,** *Copland on Music* (1963). Anthology of three decades of the popular American composer's writings. He has written several other books as well, among which is *What to Listen for in Music* (1957), a helpful and clear introduction to music appreciation.

**Craft, Robert,** *Current Convictions: Views and Reviews* (1977). Intelligent, erudite selections of the author's pieces for the *New York Review of Books* that illuminate and stimulate. See *Prejudices in Disguise* (1974).

**Debussy, Claude,** *Debussy on Music: The Critical Writings of the Great French Composer* (1977). Selection of short, witty articles, written pseudonymously as "Monsieur Croche" before the First World War. They display his penetrating insight into music and musicians and his mastery of the caustic Gallic epigram.

**Downes, Olin,** *Olin Downes on Music* (1951). The *New York Times* music critic during the first quarter of the century, Downes was once described as the last of the music reviewers to enjoy music. This selection from his writings makes "delightful reading — he wrote passionately from the heart and with no mean gift of understanding" (Virgil Thomson).

**Einstein, Alfred,** *Essays on Music* (1956). Posthumous collection of engaging and accessible selections by a prominent musicologist.

**Fay, Amy,** *Music-study in Germany* (1881). In a series of casual and lively letters, a young American pianist recounts the experience of studying piano with such teachers as Lizst, Tausig, and Kullak.

**Gal, Hans,** *The Musician's World* (1966). A personal selection of letters by more than fifty composers, from Lasso to Schoenberg.

**Gold, Arthur and Robert Fitzdale,** *Misia: The Life of Misia Sert* (1980). The authors, a celebrated piano duo, have drawn a fascinating portrait of the Polish-born pianist who was at the center of the Parisian art world of her day, knew everyone, and was the inspiration of other musicians.

**Haggin, B. H.,** *Music Observed* (1964). Collection of thirty-five years' writings by a brilliantly perceptive, opinionated critic. See *A Decade of Music* (1973) and *New Listeners' Guide to Classical Music* (rev. 1978).

**Hanslick, Eduard,** *Vienna's Golden Years, 1850–1900* (1951). The Austrian capital was the hub of the nineteenth-century musical world, and Hanslick was its most powerful critic. This collection of his reviews, although slightly outmoded in style, are interesting and charming and still bristle with the excitement of the times.

**Harding, James,** *The Ox on the Roof* (1972). Classical music life of Paris during the 1920s vividly brought to life.

**Hindemith, Paul,** *The Composer's World: Horizons and Limitations* (1952). Intellectually stimulating Harvard lectures by one of the giants of modern music — happily free of technical jargon and presented in a pleasant writing style.

**Holt, John,** *Never Too Late* (1978). The author, a highly regarded critic of education, decided in middle age to become a cellist. This book eloquently relates how he conquered his fear of failure.

Hughes, Gervase, *Sidelights on a Century of Music* (1971). Unusual essays about the out-of-the-way corners of nineteenth-century music, such as the byproducts of famous composers and sketches of the overshadowed composers. Distinctive and enjoyable reading. See *Composers of Operetta* (1962) and *Dvorak* (1967).

Kolodin, Irving (ed.), *The Critical Composer* (1940). Instructive excerpts from the critical writings of composers. *The Composer as Listener* (1958) is a sequel. Kolodin's nontechnical critical writings are in *The Musical Life* (1958) and *In Quest of Music* (1980).

Lang, Paul Henry, *Music in Western Civilization* (1941). The authoritative one-volume history. "He has the imaginative power that can transfer erudition into a history of vivid, meaningful immediacy" (Howard Taubman).

Laski, Audrey, *The Dominant Fifth* (1969). Elegant, profound novel about the members of an English string quartet.

Newman, Ernest, *From the World of Music* (1957). Selection of critical essays, which appeared in the *London Sunday Times* over thirty years, by "the wisest and most readable of critics" (Harold C. Schoenberg). Because they deal with timeless subjects, they remain fresh and witty. See *More Essays from the World of Music* (1958).

Piatigorsky, Gregor, *Cellist* (1965). The Russian virtuoso's admirable memoir, full of intelligent and humorous comments on music and musicians.

Porter, Andrew, *Music of Three Seasons: 1974–1977* (1978). Collection of pieces by the *New Yorker* reviewer: lucid, informal, provocative, and generous in spirit. See *Music of Three More Seasons: 1977–1980* (1981).

Previn, Andre (ed.), *The Orchestra* (1980). Musicians talk candidly about playing in the orchestra. An informative, absorbing "oral history."

Rosen, Charles, *The Classical Style* (1973). Luminous study of the style epitomized by Mozart, Haydn, and Beethoven. Requires ability to read music. See *Sonata Forms* (1980).

Schoenberg, Harold C., *The Great Conductors* (1967). With *The Great Pianists* (1963) and *The Lives of the Great Composers* (rev. 1981), a provocative and entertaining trilogy by the Pulitzer Prize–winning critic of the *New York Times*. The best of his writings, plus an autobiographical essay, are gathered in *Facing the Music* (1981).

Schumann, Robert, *On Music and Musicians* (1946). The nineteenth-century German composer was as fine an artist with words as he was with music. The pieces collected here preserve the charm and the passion of the man.

Shaw, George Bernard, *Shaw on Music* (1955). The best of his writings on music, edited by Eric Bentley. The Shavian wit at its most sparkling. The complete musical criticism in three volumes, edited by Dan H. Laurence, was published as *Shaw's Music* (1981).

Slonimsky, Nicolas, *Lexicon of Musical Invective* (1953). Hilarious anthology of critical vituperation since the days of Beethoven.

Thomson, Virgil, *Virgil Thomson Reader* (1981). Collects the reviews and articles by the composer who has been called "the most knowledgeable and (in the best sense of the phrase) serious-minded music critic this country has ever produced" (Alfred Frankenstein). Winner of National Book Critics Circle Award.

Tovey, Donald Francis, *The Main Stream of Music* (1949). Of this collection of essays by the scholar-pianist, once hailed as "the most learned musician who ever lived," Roger Sessions said: "This book is never for a moment tiresome, almost always stimulating, and for the most part sheer delight." For a biography of this

## Opera

wise and witty man see Mary Grierson, *Donald Francis Tovey* (1952).

**Barnard, Robert,** *Death on the High C's* (1979). Grand Guignol meets grand opera in one of the best of the backstage opera mysteries, a subgenre which includes Fred G. Jarvis, *Murder at the Met* (1971) and Chelsea Quinn Yarbro, *Music when Sweet Voices Die* (1979). A sub-subgenre is opera mysteries by divas; it includes Queena Mario, *Murder in the Opera House* (1934) and Helen Traubel, *The Metropolitan Opera Murders* (1951).

**Bing, Rudolph,** *5,000 Nights at the Opera* (1972). Recollections by the outspoken general manager of the Metropolitan Opera for over twenty years. It is "as absorbing and sometimes as incredible as the man himself" (Irving Kolodin). See *A Knight at the Opera* (1981).

**Cain, James M.,** *Serenade* (1937). "Tough guy" novel about a down-and-out baritone by one of the best of the boys in the back room. Other opera novels are Nancy Freedman, *Prima Donna* (1981) and Mac-Donald Harris, *Herma* (1981).

**Chaliapin, Feodor,** *Pages from My Life* (1927). Colorful memoir of Volga peasant who became, with the gift of a dark, splendid bass voice, the great singing actor of the early decades of the century. See *Man and Mask* (1932) and *Chaliapin* (1968), his autobiography as told to Maxim Gorky.

**Curtiss, Mina,** *Bizet and His World* (1958). Objective documentary biography — really a sort of montage — of the French composer. Perhaps of greater literary and social interest than purely musical interest, it beautifully divulges the inner life of the artist. A must for all *Carmen* lovers.

**Davenport, Marcia,** *Of Lena Geyer* (1936). This fictional life of a great opera singer makes rewarding reading because its author, the daughter of Alma Gluck and stepdaughter of Efram Zimbalist, knew the musical world. Her memoirs, *Too Strong for Fantasy* (1967), deal in a large part with music, especially her passion for Mozart and Toscanini.

**Gatti-Casazza, Giulio,** *Memories of the Opera* (1941). Recollections of the autocratic manager of the Metropolitan Opera Company for over twenty-five years before his retirement in 1934. Illuminates the fabulous era of the "diamond Horseshoe."

**Hartmann, Rudolf,** *Opera* (1977). Sumptuous volume by former director of the Munich Opera that explains, with the aid of over 300 photographs, how an opera production comes into being. See *Richard Strauss: The Staging of His Operas and Ballets* (1982).

**Hetherington, John,** *Melba* (1968). Affectionate biography of the great Australian soprano, Nellie Melba, toast of Covent Garden during the decades around the turn of the century. See Joseph Wechsberg, *Red Plush and Black Velvet: The Story of Melba and Her Times* (1961).

**Higgins, John,** *The Making of an Opera* (1978). Copiously illustrated look at Peter Hall's mounting of *Don Giovanni* at Glyndebourne in 1977, from its casting to its critical reception.

**Kerman, Joseph,** *Opera as Drama* (1956). He believes that "music here does not nicely decorate what the playwright or librettist has designed. The music creates a drama they never suspected." "A passionate, argumentative, brilliantly written book" (Alfred Frankenstein).

**Knapp, J. Merrill,** *The Magic of Opera* (1973). Survey of all aspects of opera. Authoritative, interesting.

**Kobbe, Gustav,** *The New Kobbe's Opera Book* (rev. 1976). For serious opera-goers who desire to have a book with alphabetically listed summaries of operatic works, it is a toss-up between this classic compendium and *The New Milton Cross Complete*

*Stories of the Great Operas* (1955) and its 1980 supplement.

**Kolodin, Irving,** *The Opera Omnibus: Four Centuries of Critical Give and Take* (1976). Fascinating compendium of critical hosannas and pans.

**Lang, Paul Henry,** *Critic at the Opera* (1971). Well-written, often brilliant, informal essays by eminent American musicologist, critic, and opera coach.

**Massenet, Jules,** *My Recollections* (1919). Amiable memoirs of the French composer of *Manon* and *Thaïs.* Like his music, it is sometimes sentimental but full of charm and grace.

**Mordden, Ethan,** *Opera in the Twentieth Century* (1978). Fine introduction to the modern repertoire, with history, analyses, and synopses. See *The Splendid Art of Opera* (1980).

**Newman, Ernest,** *The Wagner Operas* (1949). The great Wagner authority and long-time music critic for the *London Sunday Times* "surveys the masterpieces of Wagner from *The Flying Dutchman* to *Parsifal,* and does so with the same unfailing comprehension, generosity and wisdom" (Vincent Sheean).

**Osborne, Charles,** *The Complete Operas of Mozart* (1978). Concise treatment of all of Mozart's works for the stage. See *The Complete Operas of Verdi* (1970) and *The Complete Operas of Puccini* (1982).

**Rosenthal, Harold and John Warrack (eds.),** *The Concise Oxford Dictionary of the Opera* (rev. 1979). The standard reference. Thorough and fun for the buff to browse.

**Sheean, Vincent,** *First and Last Love* (1956). With great charm, he relates his personal history as a listener of music, and especially of opera. He knew many of the great musicians and ably recreates their personalities and performances. See *Oscar Hammerstein I: The Life and Exploits of an Impresario* (1956).

## Jazz

**Balliett, Whitney,** *Night Creatures* (1981). Collection of superb pieces from the *New Yorker* by its knowledgeable jazz correspondent. See *Improvising* (1978).

**Bechet, Sidney,** *Treat It Gentle* (1960). Stylized memoir by the New Orleans–born clarinetist that "traces the plight of an American artist — perceptive asides on black/white and American/European relationships are scattered throughout — with gumption and generosity" (Gary Giddins).

**Blesh, Rudi and Harriet Janis,** *They All Played Ragtime* (1950). Zestful, detailed study of the early jazz style of ragtime and the people who played it.

**Feather, Leonard,** *The Pleasures of Jazz* (1977). Series of interviews with some leading performers on their lives, their music, and their contemporaries. See *The Passion For Jazz* (1980).

**Giddins, Gary,** *Riding on a Blue Note* (1981). This jazz chronicle collects pieces from the *Village Voice* by one of the most reflective and talented contemporary jazz critics.

**Handy, W. C.,** *Father of the Blues* (1941). Edited by Arna Bontemps, the value of these memoirs is not literary, but historical — the picture of the early days of the blues and jazz in the South.

**Holiday, Billie,** *Lady Sings the Blues* (1956). The great singer wrote this tough, bitter autobiography with William Dufty. Somewhat sensational, but an unsentimental and gripping story. See Alexis De-Veaux, *Don't Explain: A Song of Billie Holiday* (1980), a prose poem.

**Holmes, John Clellon,** *The Horn* (1958). One of the best of the few good jazz novels, about the last sad days of a black sax player. A similar musician plays lead in John Williams's *Night Song* (1962).

Jones, Le Roi, *Blues People* (1963). Passionate study of black music in the context of white America by the angry poet-jazz critic known today as Imaru Baraka. See *Black Music* (1968).

Lomax, Alan, *Mister Jelly Roll* (1950). Subtitled *The Fortunes of Jelly Roll Morton, New Orleans Creole and 'Inventor of Jazz'*, it is based on conversations Morton had with folklorist Lomax while making recordings for the Library of Congress. "It is a curiously tragic story in many ways, partaking almost of the quality of legend. Yet it is an enormously fascinating one, too" (Joseph Henry Jackson).

Mezzrow, Mezz, *Really the Blues* (1946). Enthralling glimpse into the "hep" world of jazz and drugs in New York in the twenties and thirties by a white clarinetist. Written with novelist Bernard Wolfe in the hipster patois of the times, it is vigorous and unique.

Russell, Ross, *Bird Lives* (1973). This story of Charlie "Yardbird" Parker is "one of the few jazz books that deserve to be called literature, a monument to match the gargantuan figure . . . who, like Wagner, was so heavy that a generation of artists drove themselves to despair trying not to sound like him" (Grover Sales). See *Jazz Style in Kansas City and the Southwest* (1971).

Skvorecky, Josef, *The Bass Saxophone* (1979). Two novellas by a Czech writer now living in the West, suffused with his passion for jazz.

Williams, Martin, *Where's the Melody: A Listener's Introduction to Jazz* (1966). A seasoned jazz critic and historian's lively guide for the new listener covers just what jazz performers do with a popular melody as they improvise, and much more. See *The Jazz Tradition* (1970).

Wilmer, Valerie, *As Serious as Your Life* (1980). Informative, well-written story of avant-garde jazz from the late fifties to the present day. See *Jazz People* (1972).

Young, Al, *Bodies & Soul: Musical Memoirs* (1981). A novelist's fine recollections of music he listened to on records in his youth. "Easily one of the best books about the jazz experience ever to see print. More than that, it's one of the best, and perhaps the most hopeful books about black life in America to be published in years" (Grover Sales).

## Blues

Albertson, Chris, *Bessie* (1973). Well-researched biography of Bessie Smith, the great blues singer who died tragically in 1937, that separates the myth from the woman.

Charters, Samuel, *Country Blues* (1959). Vividly traces the origins of this vital American folk art form and the musicians who contributed to its development. Two good studies of the country blues as performed today are Paul Oliver, *Conversation with the Blues* (1965) and William Ferris, *Blues from the Delta* (1978).

Guralnick, Peter, *Feel Like Going Home: Portraits in Blues and Rock and Roll* (1971). Remarkable profiles of leading blues artists. See *Lost Highway: Journeys and Arrivals of American Musicians* (1979); *Nighthawk Blues* (1980) is a novel about a rediscovered blues singer.

Keil, Charles, *Urban Blues* (1965). Illuminating study of the blues singer as ghetto culture hero.

Palmer, Robert, *Deep Blues* (1981). *New York Times* pop-music critic charts the development of the Delta blues through the experiences of some of its most renowned performers.

## Rock and Roll

Carson, Tom, *Twisted Kicks* (1981). This story of a seventies rock singer on the lam in Virginia is probably the best rock novel yet. Another amusing novel is Laurence Gonzales, *Jambeaux* (1979).

**Christgau, Robert,** *Christgau's Record Guide: Rock Albums of the Seventies* (1981). Wonderful compilation of capsule reviews of 3,000 albums. Highly provocative. See *Any Old Way You Choose It* (1974).

**Cohn, Nik,** *Rock from the Beginning* (1969). Excellent history that, despite some inaccuracies, remains thought-provoking. More recent and more wide-ranging is Michael Bane, *White Boy Singin' the Blues* (1982).

**Friedman, Myra,** *Buried Alive* (1973). A friend's deeply felt biography of Janis Joplin, who died pathetically in 1970. Captures the furious rock world of the sixties.

**Gillett, Charlie,** *The Sound of the City: The Rise of Rock and Roll* (1972). Exhilarating account of rock from 1940 to 1970, richly detailed, it is particularly good on the racism in the early days of the industry. See *Making Tracks: Atlantic Records and the Growth of a Multi-Billion Dollar Industry* (1974) and (with Stephen Najut) *Rock Almanac* (1978).

**Goldman, Albert,** *Elvis* (1981). Morbidly riveting, provocative biography that concludes that "the life of King Elvis consisted of nothing but ritualized routine."

**Goldrosen, John,** *Buddy Holly: His Life and Music* (1975). Admirable biography of the great Texas rocker who so greatly influenced the sound and style of rock and roll. This is the real Buddy Holly story.

**Hebridge, Dick,** *Subculture: The Meaning of Style* (1979). Lively study of British youth subcultures, including Mods, Rockers, Skinheads, and Punks. Necessary to an understanding of English rock.

**Heilbut, Tony,** *The Gospel Sound: Good News and Bad Times* (1971). Not rock and roll exactly, but an integral source; an important book that offers a lively excursion into the gospel world and portraits of its dominant figures.

**Henderson, David,** *'Scuse Me While I Kiss the Sky: The Life of Jimi Hendrix* (1978,

rev. 1981). Penetrating account of the brief, brilliant career of the psychedelic pyrotechnician of the guitar; "a major book with tremendous musical insight and lots of facts — for once a black writer deals with a black musician" (Robert Christgau).

**Lydon, Michael,** *Rock Folk* (1971). Collection of superb profiles of the musical personalities that shaped sixties rock.

**Marcus, Greil,** *Mystery Train: Images of America in Rock and Roll Music* (rev. 1982). Perceptive cultural study of this musical form. Perhaps the best book there is about rock and roll. Marcus edited *Stranded* (1980), an amusing and provocative volume in which writers tell which one rock album they would take with them to the mythical desert island.

**Marsh, Dave and Kevin Stein,** *The Book of Rock Lists* (1981). A list book that is imaginative, informative, provocative, and great fun to skip around in. Marsh edited *The Rolling Stone Record Guide* (1979) and wrote *Born to Run: The Bruce Springsteen Story* (1979).

**Miller, Jim (ed.),** *The Rolling Stone Illustrated History of Rock and Roll Music* (rev. 1980). Handsome, large-format anthology of pieces by top rock writers that relate the music's history from 1950 to 1980. See *Shooting Stars: The Rolling Stone Book of Portraits* (1973), edited by Anne Liebovitz, and *The Rolling Stone Interviews: Talking with the Legends of Rock and Roll, 1967–1980* (1981).

**Norman, Philip,** *Shout: The Beatles in Their Generation* (1981). The definitive Beatle book: well-researched, comprehensive, a mine of information, by an experienced Beatle-watcher who can write. See Nicholas Schaffner, *The Beatles Forever* (1977).

**Parsons, Tony and Julie Burchill,** *The Boy Looked at Johnny: The Obituary of Rock and Roll* (1980). A scathing, fascinating indictment of the sorry state of rock and roll in the seventies by two British critics known as the Scourges of the rock industry. See Parsons's trashy rock novel, *Platinum Logic* (1981).

**Peelaert, Guy and Nik Cohn,** *Rock Dreams* (1973). Gallery of astounding paintings by Peelaert depicting rock fantasies. A unique, bizarre work.

**Shepard, Sam,** *The Tooth of Crime* (1974). Confrontation between a king of rock and roll and a challenger. "A splendid violent artifact, it broods on and wrestles with the quest not simply to be known but to be known inexhaustibly, magically, cosmically; the exaltation and tragedy of fame" (Richard Gilman).

**Stokes, Geoffrey,** *Star-Making Machinery: The Odyssey of an Album* (1976). In tracing the production of a Commander Cody album, Stokes has written the best book on the business of rock. See *The Beatles* (1981).

## Country Music

**Flippo, Chet,** *Your Cheatin' Heart: A Biography of Hank Williams* (1981). Interpretative psychobiography of the short and sad life of a singer done in by booze, drugs, and fast city women.

**Hall, Tom T.,** *The Storyteller's Nashville* (1979). Sharply observed and amusing look at the country music scene by talented singer-songwriter and storyteller. See *The Laughing Man of Wood Coves* (1982).

**Hemphill, Paul,** *The Nashville Sound: Bright Lights and Country Music* (1970). Not the music, but the atmosphere of Opryland, about how the music business works, is the subject of this delightful impressionistic portrait of the country scene.

**Lynn, Loretta,** *Coal Miner's Daughter* (1976). Despite its unpolished literary style, the unpretentiousness and simple eloquence of its author makes for absorbing and touching reading.

**Malone, Bill C.,** *Country Music U.S.A.: A Fifty Year History* (1968). The best history. See *Stars of Country Music: Uncle Dave Macon to Johnny Rodriguez* (1975).

**Porterfield, Nolan,** *Jimmie Rodgers* (1979). This "life and times of America's Blues Yodeler" attempts to sort the facts from the legend of the father of country music.

**Tosches, Nick,** *Country: The Biggest Music in America* (1977). A raucous, comprehensive, offbeat history done with wit and style. See *Hellfire: The Jerry Lee Lewis Story* (1982).

**Townsend, Charles R.,** *San Antonio Rose: The Life and Times of Bob Wills* (1976). Sympathetic, carefully researched story of the father of Texas swing and the Texas Playboys' fifty-year career.

**Wynette, Tammy,** *Stand by Your Man* (1979). A "frank" autobiography, bordering on exposé, by one of the reigning queens of country music. A country camp classic.

## Popular Music

**Balliett, Whitney,** *American Singers* (1979). Dozen gracefully limned portraits of great vocalists by the discerning jazz critic of the *New Yorker*.

**Ewan, David,** *The Life and Death of Tin Pan Alley* (1964). Engaging history of the golden age of American popular music — the 1830s to the 1930s. See *A Journey to Greatness: The Life of George Gershwin* (1956).

**Howard, John Tasker,** *Stephen Foster* (1934). The short, sad life of the prolific song writer whose melodies linger on.

**Pleasants, Henry,** *The Great American Popular Singers* (rev. 1981). Not pop profiles, but intelligent, extremely informative, and rewarding essays on the great singers from Jolson to Streisand, Garland to Sinatra, Johnny Cash to Ray Charles.

Wilder, Alec, *American Popular Song: The Great Innovators 1900–1950* (1972). First authoritative, fully analytical study of the development of American popular song, with separate chapters on Kern, Berlin, Gershwin, Rodgers, Porter, and Arlen. Knowledgeable yet engagingly informal.

# DANCE

Balanchine, George, *Complete Stories of the Great Ballets* (rev. 1977). The stories, but also a history and a guide, by the great choreographer. An essential *vade mecum* for the balletomane.

Bland, Alexander, *The Royal Ballet* (1981). Beautifully illustrated celebration of the first fifty years of the eminent British company which began as the Sadler's Wells Ballet.

Brahms, Caryl and S. J. Simon, *A Bullet in the Ballet* (1938). Scotland Yard Inspector Adam Quill attempts to solve a murder in a hilarious mystery full of fantastic comic characters and ballet allusions. See *Murder à la Stroganoff* (1938) and *Six Curtains for Natasha* (1946).

Buckle, Richard, *Buckle at the Ballet* (1980). Selected criticism by the former dance critic of the *Times* of London and ballet historian. His other writings include two fine biographies, *Nijinsky* (1972) and *Diaghilev* (1979).

Clarke, Mary and Clement Crisp, *Ballet Art* (1978). Beautiful album of reproductions of paintings from the Renaissance to the present. Clarke and Crisp are also the authors of *Ballet: An Illustrated History* (1973) and *The Ballet Goer's Guide* (1981).

Cohen, Selma Jeanne (ed.), *Doris Humphrey: An Artist First* (1973). Cohen edited Humphrey's unpublished autobiography and added her own study to make an engaging book. Humphrey was a very good writer, as further evidenced in *The Art of Making Dances* (rev. 1962). See Eleanor King's memoir of the Humphrey-Weidman era, *Transformations* (1978).

Croce, Arlene, *Afterimages* (1977). The *New Yorker* dance critic's rare gift for lucidly describing dance movement is shown to perfection here, in "the most readable chronicle of theatrical dancing in the United States from 1966 to 1977, which is the most prolific epoch of the art in America" (Lincoln Kirstein). See *Going to the Dance* (1982).

De Mille, Agnes, *Dance to the Piper* (1952). Memoirs of the ballerina and choreographer, creator of *Rodeo* and the ballets in *Carousel* and *Oklahoma*. "No other choreographer has written so penetratingly on this difficult subject, explaining not only her own methods and back stage experiences but telling about the conditions under which all of us work. . . . [She] writes with such wit and intensity that her life, her successes, her failures, grip the reader" (Ruth Page). See *And Promenade Home* (1958) and *The Book of the Dance* (1963).

Denby, Edwin, *Looking at the Dance* (rev. 1968). Selected writings by a former critic of the *New York Herald Tribune*. "Probably the best book of dance criticism ever written . . . he has shown that one can write on dance with the easy tension and cultivated tone that people write on the other arts. He never talks down. He knows the value of dance like a carpenter knows the value of wood" (Clive Barnes). See *Dancers, Buildings and People in the Street* (1965).

Fokine, Michel, *Memoirs of a Ballet Master* (1951). Interesting reminiscences of the Russian dancer-choreographer who helped bring ballet into the modern age and created ballets for Diaghilev.

**Gautier, Theophile,** *The Romantic Ballet: As Seen by Theophile Gautier* (1972). Notices of all the principal romantic ballets given at Paris during the years 1837–48, by the French writer considered to be the best dance critic ever.

**Godden, Rumer,** *Candles for St. Jude* (1948). Of this novel about a day in a London ballet school, Anthony Tudor wrote that the author had "filled her small novel with emotions, incidents and people that have for the most part the ring of authenticity."

**Haggin, B. H.,** *Ballet Chronicle* (1971). Writings covering over a quarter of a century of ballet in New York, particularly about Balanchine, and handsomely embellished by over 250 photographs. Irving Howe described Haggin as a "contentious sometimes cranky writer . . . but also a powerful critic: honest, impassioned, utterly devoted to his calling . . . and in control of a virile writing style." See *Discovering Balanchine* (1982).

**Haskell, Arnold,** *Balletomania: Then and Now* (1977). Reprint and update of 1939 edition by British ballet expert that "tells more about his enthusiasm for Pavlova, Karsavina, Boronova and others than it does about the specifics of their dancing, but his unmalicious gossip and sensitive speculations about ballet are always illuminating" (Deborah Jowitt). His collaborations with photographer Baron are noteworthy; see *Baron's Ballet Finale* (1959).

**Jowitt, Deborah,** *Dance Beat* (1977). Selected "views and reviews," 1967–76, from the *Village Voice* by a fine writer with a dance and choreography background.

**Kahn, Albert E.,** *Days with Ulanova* (1962). Remarkable photo and prose portrait of the Russian ballerina, Galina Ulanova, taken just before her retirement.

**Karsavina, Tamara,** *Theatre Street* (1931). Warm, entertaining account of the prima ballerina's education in Imperial Petersburg. "One of the most delightful and novel books ever written for the theatre" (J. M. Barrie).

**Kendall, Elizabeth,** *Where She Danced* (1979). Elegantly designed book which traces the roots of American modern dance, with emphasis on feminist and social factors. The sketches of the extraordinary personalities of the time, such as Duncan and St. Denis, make fine reading.

**Kerensky, Oleg,** *Anna Pavlova* (1973). This biography of the great Russian dancer is "not only a most readable and engrossing book; it also makes one reassess Pavlova's influence and power" (Clive Barnes).

**Kirstein, Lincoln,** *Movement and Metaphor* (1970). Four centuries of ballet examined in keen analysis of fifty ballets and in hundreds of illustrations. By one of the founders of the New York City Ballet.

**Krementz, Jill,** *A Very Young Dancer* (1976). This black-and-white photoessay about the leading child ballerina for Balanchine's annual New York City Center Ballet production of *The Nutcracker* is "quite the best ballet book ever written for children" (Clive Barnes).

**McDonagh, Don,** *Martha Graham* (1973). Engrossing unauthorized biography of one of the monuments of modern dance. Her genius for innovation can be seen in her *Notebooks* (1973). The remarkable photo studies of a Graham dance in the process of creation can be seen in Leroy Leatherman, *Martha Graham* (1966).

**Makarova, Natalia,** *A Dance Autobiography* (1979). Sensitive and stimulating memoirs of the Russian emigré ballerina.

**Martin, John,** *Ruth Page* (1977). Biography of the renowned choreographer and founder of the Chicago Opera Ballet. See John Martin's *Book of the Dance* (rev. 1964).

**Massine, Leonide,** *My Life in Ballet* (1968). In a dry style, the internationally famous Russian-born dancer-choreographer captures a colorful era of ballet.

**Mazo, Joseph H.,** *Prime Movers* (1977). Lively, carefully researched story of the makers of modern dance in America. *Dance Is a Contact Sport* (1975) is a revealing behind-the-scenes view of the New York City Ballet.

**Nijinska, Bronislava,** *Early Memories* (1981). The sister of Nijinsky and one of the most important neoclassical choreographers of the twentieth century reflects on her long career and relationship with her brother.

**Nijinsky, Romola,** *Nijinsky* (1934). Eloquent and dramatic intimate biography of her husband, the brilliant premier danseur of Diaghilev's ballet company, whose life ended in madness. Lincoln Kirstein's handsome *Nijinsky Dancing* (1975) includes many striking photographs of the dancer in different roles.

**Reynolds, Nancy,** *Repertory in Review: 40 Years of the New York City Ballet* (1977). Comprising photographs, programs, newspaper reviews, interviews, and comments by the author, a former dancer with the company, it is a festive commemoration of the Balanchine epoch.

**St. Denis, Ruth,** *An Unfinished Life* (1939). Candid, informative, if too long, autobiography of one of the pioneers of dance and cofounder of the Denishawn Company. See Suzanne Shelton, *Divine Dancer: A Biography of Ruth St. Denis* (1981).

**Seroff, Victor,** *The Real Isadora* (1971). The now-legendary Isadora Duncan's life by a friend and confidant of her later years. It corrects the apocryphal accounts in her own autobiography, *My Story* (1926–27) and renders the astonishing tale of her tempestuous times.

**Shawn, Ted,** *One Thousand and One Night Stands* (1960). Informal, articulate memoir by the Father of American Dance and the man most responsible for liberating male dancing from effeminacy. See Walter Terry's biography, *Ted Shawn* (1976).

**Siegel, Marcia B.,** *The Shapes of Change: Images of American Dance* (1979). A penetrating look at American dancing and choreography by one of our most gifted critics. Her critical pieces are gathered in *At the Vanishing Point* (1972) and *Watching the Dance Go By* (1977).

**Sokolova, Lydia,** *Dancing for Diaghilev* (1960). Richard Buckle edited these remembrances by the thoroughly Russianized British dancer born Hilda Munnings. Her vivid personality and recollections of the Ballet Russe make this enjoyable reading.

**Sorrell, Walter,** *Dance in Its Time* (1981). Probably the best basic introduction to dance. See *The Dancer's Image* (1971).

**Stewart, Edward,** *Ballerina* (1978). Enjoyable light novel about two friends who become dance rivals, with plenty of good inside stuff about the ballet world. Other popular novels about dance are James Lipton, *Mirrors* (1981) and Monique Raphel High, *Encore* (1981).

**Taper, Bernard,** *Balanchine* (1964). Extension of admiring *New Yorker* profile of the great Russian-born choreographer that remains the best account of his early days and his work in this country into the sixties.

**Terry, Walter,** *I Was There* (1978). Forty years of reviews by the dean of American dance critics. They are not high literary achievements but offer an interesting, and even nostalgic, look at ballet history. See *Great Male Dancers of the Ballet* (1979), *The Dance in America* (rev. 1972), *Alicia and Her Ballet Nacional de Cuba* (1981), and *How to Look at Dance* (1982).

**Vaughan, David,** *Frederick Ashton and His Ballets* (1977). Fine text and remarkable photographs unite in picture of the life and work of the famous British choreographer and former director of the Royal Ballet.

**Van Vechten, Carl,** *The Dance Writings of Carl Van Vechten* (1976). He was an accomplished novelist who was assistant music critic of the *New York Times* early in the century and the first professional dance critic in America. These reviews of the performances of such figures as Nijinsky, Pavlova, and Duncan are fresh

with the thrill of discovery and often quite eloquent. See *The Dance Photography of Carl Van Vechten* (1981).

**Wigman, Mary,** *The Mary Wigman Book* (1975). Selections from the writings of the woman considered to be the originator of modern dance in Germany. They prove her to be insightful and humanistic. *The Language of the Dance* (1967) is also provocative.

# THEATER

## Drama

**Artaud, Antonin,** *Antonin Artaud: Selected Writings* (1976). Essays, poems, letters, as well as excerpts from the books of the immensely influential originator of the Theatre of Cruelty, including the manifesto *The Theatre and Its Double* (1938). See Martin Esslin, *Antonin Artaud* (1977) and Eric Sellin, *The Dramatic Concepts of Antonin Artaud* (1969).

**Atkinson, Brooks,** *The Lively Years* (1973). Brief, lucid discussions of the outstanding plays of 1920–73 by the respected one-time *New York Times* drama critic. Ornamented with delightful Hirschfeld caricatures. See *Broadway* (1970).

**Beerbohm, Max,** *A Selection from "Around Theatres"* (1960). Witty sampler of newspaper essays of the twenties penned by the brilliant and finely mannered English man of letters.

**Bentley, Eric,** *What Is Theatre?* (1968). A query in chronicle form by one of the most insightful of theater scholars. See *The Life of the Drama* (1964).

**Brett, Simon,** *Cast, in Order of Disappearance* (1975). The first of the Charles Paris mysteries, those witty and ingenious tales about the small-time British actor turned amateur sleuth. Brett conveys inside knowledge of show business. Another thespian-detective series — written by

Anne Morice — features Tess Crichton; see *The Man in Her Death* (1981).

**Brockett, Oscar G. and Robert R. Findlay,** *Century of Innovation* (1973). The most comprehensive history of European and American theater drama after 1870. Brockett's *History of the Theatre* (1974) is a good one-volume history.

**Brook, Peter,** *The Empty Space* (1968). Rambling, provocative lectures by the celebrated experimental English director who asks all the basic questions.

**Brown, John Mason,** *Dramatis Personae* (1963). Selected writings from a drama critic who was known for his urbanity and enthusiastic affection for the theater.

**Brustein, Robert,** *Seasons of Discontent* (1965). Reflections on theater and society by a tough-minded, passionate critic. Other pertinent and challenging works are *The Theatre of Revolt* (1964), *The Culture Watch* (1975), and *Critical Moments* (1980).

**Bulgakov, Mikhail,** *Black Snow* (1968). Light *roman à clef,* first published in 1926, that provides an entertaining backstage glimpse of the Moscow Art Theatre of the twenties.

**Chaikin, Joseph,** *The Presence of an Actor* (1972). In these *Notes on the Open Theatre, Disguises, Acting and Repression*

the founder of the experimental Open Theatre sets forth his theories, production notes, and some autobiography.

**Clurman, Harold,** *All People Are Famous* (1974). Clurman was one of the founders of the Group Theatre in the thirites and a highly respected director and critic. These memoirs, "rich, vibrant and rough-textured, read like an affectionate postscript to the history of cultural modernism" (Irving Howe). See *The Fervent Years: The Story of the Group Theatre and the Thirties* (1945), *The Divine Pastime* (1974), *The Naked Image* (1966), and *Lies Like Truth* (1958).

**Cole, Toby and Helen Krich Chinoy (eds.),** *Actors on Acting* (1950). Carefully selected theories, techniques, and practices of the great actors of all time, as told in their own words. See *Directors on Directing* (1963) and Cole's *Playwrights on Playwriting* (1960).

**Crawford, Cheryl,** *One Naked Individual* (1977). Fascinating memoir of fifty years in the theater as producer and cofounder of the Group Theatre, the Actor's Studio, and the American Repertory Company.

**Esslin, Martin,** *The Theatre of the Absurd* (rev. 1969). Seminal work of the modern drama by one of the most profound scholars of the theater. See *An Anatomy of Drama* (1977), *Reflections* (1969), and *Meditations* (1982).

**Gascoigne, Bamber,** *The Heyday* (1973). Nostalgic novel by a theater scholar which "recreates the atmosphere of a touring company with loving precision and should charm all those who enjoy old posters, old photographs, and old biographies of the Edwardian Idyll" (Margaret Drabble). His well-written history, *World Theatre* (1968), is very good.

**Gilman, Richard,** *Common and Uncommon Masks* (1971). His critical writings of the sixties, on such diverse subjects as Ibsen and Beckett to Mostel and Redford. See *The Making of Modern Drama* (1974).

**Grotowski, Jerzy,** *Towards a Poor Theatre* (1969). The founder of the influential Polish Laboratory Theatre discusses his methods and theories.

**Guthrie, Tyrone,** *A Life in the Theatre* (1961). Reading the renowned director's autobiography is "the same as spending an evening with a superlative mind; it should appeal to anyone who delights in cultivation, fair comment, distinction, and enlightenment" (Faubion Bowers).

**Hagen, Uta,** *Respect for Acting* (1973). "Simple, lucid and sympathetic statement of actors' problems in the theatre and basic tenets for their training wrought from the personal experience of a fine actress and teacher of acting" (Harold Clurman).

**Hazlitt, William,** *A View of the English Stage* (1818). Brilliant and beautifully written reviews of the London theater. His magnificent collections of essays about Elizabethan drama are *The Characters of Shakespeare's Plays* (1817) and *Lectures on the Dramatic Literature of the Reign of Queen Elizabeth* (1820).

**James, Henry,** *The Scenic Art* (1947). These notes on acting and the drama culled from the novelist's newspaper reviews, 1872–1901, constitute a "valuable, indeed a delightful addition to the meager library of enduring theatre criticism in the English language" (Harold Clurman).

**Kauffmann, Stanley,** *Persons of the Drama* (1976). He is better known for his movie criticism, but his comments on the theater will interest anyone interested in American drama.

**Kerr, Walter,** *Journey to the Center of the Theatre* (1979). Reviews from the *New York Times* during the seventies. See *Tragedy and Comedy* (1967).

**Marsh, Ngaio,** *Vintage Murder* (1937). Suddenly, a jeroboam of champagne crashed down at the cast party bashing in the famous producer's head. Inspector Alleyn must find the murder in this felicitous mystery set in the author's native New Zealand. Other good backstage mysteries include Marsh's *Night at the Vulcan* (1951); Joyce Harrington, *No One Knows My Name* (1980); and Kay Nolte Smith, *Catching Fire* (1982).

**Nathan, George Jean,** *The Magic Mirror* (1960). Memorial volume of selected writings on the theater from 1917 to the forties by the legendary drama critic and editor. They show off his knowledgeable, sophisticated, pungent — and, when riled, vitriolic — style.

**Robins, Elizabeth,** *Theatre and Friendship* (1932). Collection of letters recording an unusual type of friendship, between Henry James, then a man of fifty and already a figure in literary circles, and Elizabeth Robins, a young American actress who was presenting Ibsen's plays to Londoners in the nineties. See *Ibsen and the Actress* (1928).

**Shaw, George Bernard,** *Shaw on the Theatre* (1958). Bewitching salmagundi of sixty years' worth of letters, reviews, and speeches. See the marvelous letters, exchanged with Ellen Terry, collected in *A Correspondence* (1931).

**Shurtleff, Michael,** *Audition* (1978). Candid advice of a Broadway casting director on "everything an actor needs to know to get the part."

**Simon, John,** *Singularities* (1975). Brief essays written during the late sixties–early seventies about the drama. Often cranky, truculent, even brutal when his finely tuned esthetic sense is violated, they are nonetheless provocative and vital and make for good guilty-pleasure reading. A companion volume, *Uneasy Stages* (1975), contains his theater reviews for the same period.

**Spolin, Viola,** *Improvisation for the Theater* (rev. 1973). Excellent introduction to improvisation by the originator of Theater Games.

**Stanislavsky, Konstantin,** *My Life in Art* (1924). Autobiography of the influential Russian who was the director of the Moscow Art Theatre for forty years, contemporary of Chekhov, and creator of the acting system which evolved into the "Method." His theories are laid out in *An Actor Prepares* (1936) and *Building a Character* (1950). See David Magarshack's biography, *Stanislavsky: A Life* (1951).

**Tynan, Kenneth,** *Curtains* (1960). Masterly *New Yorker* profiles that entrance by dint of his rare blend of sensitivity, wit, insider's knowledge of theater, and limpid prose style. See *The Sound of One Hand Clapping* (1975) and *Show People* (1980).

**Webster, Margaret,** *Don't Put Your Daughter on the Stage* (1972). Lively memoir of the Anglo-American director-producer, best known for her productions of Shakespeare, which she wrote about in *Shakespeare Without Tears* (1942). See *The Same Only Different: Five Generations of a Great Theatre Family* (1969).

## Musical Theater

**Bordman, Gerald,** *American Musical Theatre* (1978). A broad-scoped historical "chronicle" of the musical. A treasurehouse of information and illustrations. See *American Operetta: From H.M.S. Pinafore to Sweeney Todd* (1981), *Jerome Kern* (1980), and *Vincent Youmans* (1982).

**Dietz, Howard,** *Dancing in the Dark* (1974). These wonderfully anecdotal "words by Howard Dietz," the great Broadway lyricist of the twenties and thirties, are "the cherries jubilee of theatrical autobiographies" (Howard Taubman).

**Eels, George,** *The Life that He Led* (1967). Detailed, sympathetic biography of Cole Porter. See the sumptuous Bea Feitler–designed bouquet to the composer, *Cole* (1971), edited by Robert Kimball.

**Fordin, Hugh,** *Getting to Know Him* (1977). Absorbing biography of Oscar Hammerstein II, richly detailed not only with regard to the life of the gifted lyricist, but to the musical stage as well.

**Hibbert, Christopher,** *Gilbert & Sullivan and Their Victorian World* (1976). Affectionate look at the lives and times of the great comic-opera composer and librettist. The extremely well written text by a fine popular historian is accompanied by hundreds of wonderful period illustrations.

**Lerner, Alan Jay,** *On the Street Where I Live* (1978). The composer of *My Fair Lady* and *Camelot* shares his experiences in a witty, articulate memoir.

**Marx, Samuel and Jan Clayton,** *Rodgers & Hart: Bewitched, Bothered and Bedeviled* (1976). Anecdotal account of the collaboration of Richard Rodgers and Lorenz Hart and the twenty-eight musical comedies they wrote together. See Doro-

thy Hart (ed.), *Thou Swell, Thou Witty: The Life and Lyrics of Lorenz Hart* (1977).

**Priestley, J. B.,** *Lost Empires* (1965). Pre–World War I English music hall circuit is the background for this colorful and lively novel. *The Good Companions* (1929) is also set in this quaint milieu. Peter Leslie, *A Hard Act to Follow: A Music Hall Review* (1978) is an affectionate celebration.

**Rodgers, Richard,** *Musical Stages* (1975). Not just another and-then-I-wrote memoir, but a thoughtful, brisk account of the composer's life and backstage world.

**Sanders, Ronald,** *The Days Grow Short* (1980). Genial popular biography of the German-born composer, Kurt Weill, most famous for *The Threepenny Opera,* on which he collaborated with Bertolt Brecht, and for the musicals he composed in America.

# FILM

**Agee, James,** *Agee on Film* (1958). Probably the greatest *writer* to review films (for *Time* and the *Nation*), he was a brilliant and honest critic. This collection is a classic on the small shelf of great film books.

**Anger, Kenneth,** *Hollywood Babylon* (1975). Republication of the underground classic of the fifties that portrays the decadent film world of the twenties and thirties and that has been described as "a delicious box of poisoned bonbons." Adored by movie lovers for its general sleaziness and the fact that it is utterly without redeeming social value.

**Brownlow, Kevin,** *The Parade's Gone By* (1968). The awesomely knowledgeable film historian's work on the silent film. It is beautifully done as are his *The War, the West and the Wilderness* (1979) and the opulently illustrated *Hollywood: The Pioneers* (1980).

**Croce, Arlene,** *The Fred Astaire and Ginger Rogers Book* (1972). Elegantly produced, stylishly written, wonderfully illustrated, lovingly inspired toast to the couple "who danced their way into the hearts of millions." The best book on Astaire is *Starring Fred Astaire* (1974), by Stanley Green and Burt Goldblatt.

**Crowther, Bosley,** *Hollywood Rajah: The Life and Times of Louis B. Mayer* (1960). The former *New York Times* film reviewer traces the rise of an obscure immigrant from junk peddler to friend of presidents. In doing so he has written a story "more colorful, more fascinating than any Hollywood movie — the growth of M-G-M" (Arthur Knight). See *The Lion's Share* (1957).

**Dunne, John Gregory,** *The Studio* (1969). After spending a year hanging out at 20th-Century-Fox, the journalist-novelist produced this breezy and informative backlot look at how movies are made.

**Everson, William K.,** *A Pictorial History of the Western Film* (1969). One of the best books on the genre by an influential and devoted film historian. See *The Bad Guys: A Pictorial History of the Movie Villian* (1968). *The Detective in Film* (1972), and *Classics of the Horror Film* (1974).

**Farber, Manny,** *Movies* (1971). Originally published as *Negative Space,* it is a collection of serious and stimulating essays by a critic with fresh perspectives.

**Fitzgerald, F. Scott,** *The Last Tycoon* (1941). Last, unfinished novel about the wunderkind producer Monroe Stahr, written while Fitzgerald was working as a screenwriter in Hollywood. Masterfully captures the essence of the Hollywood of its time.

**French, Philip,** *The Movie Moguls* (1971). Well written, fascinating look at the legendary Jewish immigrants — Lasky, Schenk, Goldwyn, Mayer, et al. — who were the powers behind the early Hollywood.

**Halliwell, Leslie,** *The Filmgoer's Companion* (rev. 1978). Indispensable reference tool for the serious film buff. Admired for the "lapidary concision" of its alphabetical entries, this exhaustive 800-page volume makes irresistible browsing. See his superb *Halliwell's Film Guide* (1979).

**Herman, Gary,** *The Book of Hollywood Quotes* (1980). Dandy collection of gems. Ultimate bedside book — as tempting as popcorn.

**Isherwood, Christopher,** *Prater Violet* (1945). This British "Hollywood novel," presented as autobiography, serves as a parable of the dilemma of the intellectual on the threshold of World War II and is "one of the best short novels in English written in this century" (Stanley Kauffmann).

**Johnson, Dorris and Ellen Leventhal (eds.),** *The Letters of Nunnally Johnson* (1981). A "Pepys's diary" of Hollywood at work and play in its most dazzling years.

**Kael, Pauline,** *When the Lights Go Down* (1980). Periodic collection of the provocative, pungent, passionate reviews by the *New Yorker* film critic. Her other books are *I Lost It at the Movies* (1965), *Kiss, Kiss, Bang, Bang* (1968), *Going Steady* (1970), *Deeper Into the Movies* (1973), *Reeling* (1976), and *5001 Nights at the Movies* (1982).

**Kaminsky, Stuart,** *Murder on the Yellow Brick Road* (1977). One of the felicitous Toby Peters mysteries, each of which deals with an actual Hollywood figure of the forties. His nonfiction study, *American Film Genres* (1975), is illuminating. See *Basic Filmmaking* (1981).

**Kauffmann, Stanley,** *Before My Eyes* (1980). Reviews and essays by one of the most incisive and readable contemporary film critics. Earlier collections are *A World on Film* (1966), *Figures of Light* (1972), and *Living Images* (1975). He co-edited *American Film Criticism: From the Beginnings to Citizen Kane* (1972), which contains reviews of significant films from the times they first appeared.

**Kerr, Walter,** *The Silent Clowns* (1975). Lively, caring essays by the eminent drama critic on the great comedians of the silent screen, including Chaplin, Keaton, and Lloyd.

**Korda, Michael,** *Charmed Lives: A Family Chronicle* (1979). The public and private lives of the three Korda brothers, especially of the larger-than-life Alexander, who as a producer dominated the British film industry during the 1950s.

**Lambert, Gavin,** *GWTW: The Making of Gone With the Wind* (1973). Brief, enthralling book which brings to life the creation of the legendary 1939 pop classic. See *On Cukor* (1972), the fine Hollywood novel *Inside Daisy Clover* (1963), and the short-story collection, *The Slide Area* (1959).

**McCarthy, Todd and Charles Flynn (eds.),** *Kings of the Bs* (1976). Delightful anthology of film history and criticism about the moviemakers working within the Hollywood system who turn out low-budget exploitation films. See Robin Cross, *The Big Book of B Movies* (1982).

**MacDonald, Dwight,** *Dwight MacDonald on Movies* (1969). Brings together the reviews and pieces which he did for *Esquire.* He had wit and style and his "nose for the inflated or the grandiose is as sharp as a unicorn grazing in a field of balloons" (Andrew Sinclair).

**Maltin, Leonard (ed.),** *TV Movies: 1982–83* (1982). This (or its rival, Steven H. Scheuer, *Movies on TV*) has thumbnail sketches of over 10,000 movies and is not only useful to the old-movie fan but great fun to dip into.

**Pratt, George C.,** *Spellbound in Darkness: A History of the Silent Film* (rev. 1973). Collection of writings that in some ways works better than the usual narrative history in describing the pretalkies era.

**Rhode, Eric,** *A History of the Cinema* (1976). The best introduction to the movies. See *Tower of Babel: Speculations on the Cinema* (1966).

**Rosenberg, Bernard and Harvey Silverstein,** *The Real Tinsel* (1970) Interviews with movie old-timers provide a delightful record of the early Hollywood days.

**Ross, Lillian,** *Picture* (1952). Behind-the-scenes account of the making of *The Red Badge of Courage,* written by a sharply observant reporter and which reads like a novel. Other literary story-of-a-film books include Jean Cocteau, *Diary of a Film* (1951); Dore Schary, *The Case History of a Movie* (1950); and Jessamyn West, *To See the Dream* (1957).

**Sarris, Andrew,** *Confessions of a Cultist: On the Cinema, 1955–1969* (1970). Collection of reviews and essays, mainly from the *Village Voice,* by an erudite defender of the cinema as art. Later collections are *The Primal Screen* (1973) and *Politics and Cinema* (1978).

**Sennett, Ted,** *Hollywood Musicals* (1981). Coffee-table book that fills the eye and stirs the memory in its history of fifty years of the musical film. The beautifully reproduced stills are matched by an intelligent text. See Stanley Green, *Encyclopedia of the Musical Film* (1981).

**Simon, John,** *Reverse Angle: American Film, 1970–1980* (1981). A decade's reviews by the acerbic, opinionated critic. Earlier collections are *Private Screenings* (1967) and *Movies into Film* (1971).

**Thomas, Frank and Ollie Johnston,** *Disney Animation: The Illusion of Life* (1981). Splendid large-format production by two of Disney's chief animators. Intended for everyone to enjoy — from Disney buff to serious artist — it is the most complete book on animation ever.

**Thomson, David,** *A Biographical Dictionary of Film* (rev. 1981). Entertaining "personal, opinionated and obsessive" biographical dictionary by an intelligent English theoretician. See *America in the Dark* (1976) and *Overexposures: The Crisis in American Filmmaking* (1981).

**Warshow, Robert,** *The Immediate Experience* (1962). Collects major pieces by the distinctive critic of American pop culture and movies who died in 1955 at age thirty-seven. He was "impressively acute in dealing with the run-of-the-mill motion picture, the half-mythic entertainments that are the true scriptures of our time" (Leslie Fiedler). Other critics who died in their thirties leaving a body of perceptive reviews are Otis Ferguson, *The Film Criticism of Otis Ferguson* (1971) and Michael Winnington, *Film Criticism and Caricature* (1976).

**West, Nathanael,** *The Day of the Locust* (1939). Not only the finest novel to come out of Hollywood, but surely one of the best of all modern American novels. Its theme and parable are universal, its satire scorching, its humanity immense — a brilliant, scathing, altogether unforgettable book.

**Wilson, Harry Leon,** *Merton of the Movies* (1922). Classic novel of Hollywood's early days. Still funny after all these years.

**Wood, Michael,** *America in the Movies* (1975). Spirited, well-written look at the images of America conveyed by its moving picture industry.

# TELEVISION

**Arlen, Michael,** *The Camera Age* (1981). Collection of essays by the TV critic of the *New Yorker,* who, as John Updike remarked, "writes like a waterbug skates and his commentaries, ostensibly on television, are in truth among the best prose poems being written on life, love, war and the state of the nation." See *The View from Highway 1* (1976), *Living-Room War* (1969), and *Thirty Seconds* (1980).

**Compton, D. G.,** *The Unsleeping Eye* (1974). In the closing years of the twentieth century the bored populace turns to TV broadcasts of the last moments of dying people. A sobering novel by one of the best British science-fiction writers.

**Deandrea, William L.,** *Killed in the Ratings* (1978). Inaugural appearance of Matt Cobb, chief troubleshooter and investigator for the "Network," in a series of stylish mysteries with authentic TV backgrounds. See *Killed in the Act* (1981).

**Friendly, Fred W.,** *Due to Circumstances Beyond Our Control* (1967). Memoir and reflections on television by a former president of CBS.

**Gans, Herbert J.,** *Deciding What's News* (1979). Solid introduction to news broadcasting and its effect on our lives. See *Pop-ular Culture & High Culture: An Analysis and Evaluation of Taste* (1975).

**Greenfield, Jeff,** *Television: The First Fifty Years* (1977). Informative, handsomely illustrated, breezy history of the medium to date. Another good survey is Harry Castleman and Walter J. Podrazik, *Watching TV: Four Decades of American Television* (1981).

**James, Clive,** *The Crystal Bucket* (1981). Witty, perspicacious selections from the columns of the TV critic of the *London Observer.*

**Newcomb, Horace,** *TV: The Most Popular Art* (1974). General introduction to the television industry. See *Television: The Critical View* (rev. 1979).

**Williams, Martin,** *TV: The Casual Art* (1981). Provocative pieces by an amusing and perceptive writer who periodically reviews TV for the *Village Voice,* the *National Review,* and others.

**Winn, Marie,** *The Plug-In Drug: Television, Children, and the Family* (1977). Challenging study about television as a sociopolitical instrument and its powerful effect on American culture. The most provocative antitelevision polemic is Jerry Mander, *Form Arguments for the Elimination of Television* (1978).

# FOLK CULTURE

**Afanas'ev, Aleksandr,** *Russian Fairy Tales* (1945). Fullblooded, magical tales collected by Afanas'ev, the Russian counterpart to the brothers Grimm, and admirably translated by Norbert Guterman.

**Berlant, Anthony and Mary Hunt Kahlenberg,** *Walk in Beauty: The Navaho and Their Blankets* (1977). Extraordinary illustrations of the expressive Navaho weavings form the body of this beautiful, large-format volume.

**Bettelheim, Bruno,** *The Uses of Enchantment: The Meaning and Importance of Fairy Tales* (1975). Brilliant, moving revelation of their importance and how they educate, support, and liberate the emotions of children, according to the noted child psychologist.

**Black, Mary and Jean Lipman,** *American Folk Painting* (1966). Resplendent illustrations accompanied by solid, well-written text combine to make this an inviting work. See Lipman's (and Tom Armstrong's) *American Folk Painters of Three Centuries* (1980).

**Botkin, Ben A. (ed.),** *A Treasury of American Folklore* (1944). "A monumental tome, a Behemoth, a Paul Bunyan, among books, nearly one thousand closely packed but easy to read pages" (John Lomax). An abridged, paperback edition was published in 1980. See *A Treasury of Southern Folklore* (1949).

**Briggs, Katharine,** *British Folktales* (1977). Wonderful anthology of stories collected throughout the island by the eminent folklorist and Boswell of the faeries.

**Calvino, Italo,** *Italian Folktales* (1980). Masterly retelling by one of Italy's finest contemporary novelists. A classic of its kind.

**Colum, Padraic,** *A Treasury of Irish Folklore* (rev. 1969). Of this lavish volume, edited by the Irish poet and storyteller, Frank O'Connor said: "to my mind, this is the best collection of folklore which ever appeared in any language, because it is folklore set back into the rural life from which it sprang."

**Cooper, Patricia and Norma Bradley Buferd,** *The Quilters: Women and Domestic Art* (1977). Fine, small book of interviews with old women of Texas and New Mexico, enhanced with affecting photographs of them and their houses and quilts.

**Courlander, Harold,** *A Treasury of African Folklore* (1974). Oral literature, traditions, myth, legends, epics, tales, recollections, wisdom, sayings, and humor of sub-Sahara Africa. A rich feast for the reader. See *The Drum and the Hoe: Life and Lore of the Haitian People* (1960).

**Dance, Daryl Cumber,** *Shuckin' and Jivin': Folklore from Contemporary Black Americans* (1978). Superb anthology of over 500 bits and pieces.

**De Angelo, Jaime,** *Indian Tales* (1953). The writer has fashioned the story of one family out of myriad American Indian folktales. "It brings to mind *The Wind in the Willows,* although it is more often frankly funny than that masterpiece. It is a book that causes the reader to laugh aloud or exclaim his delight" (Oliver LaFarge). See *Coyote Man and Old Doctor Loon* (1973).

*Folk Traditions in Japanese Art* (1978). Splendid photo-and-text art book of the finest quality that captures the richness and charm of Japanese folk art.

**Fowke, Edith,** *Folktales of French Canada* (1980). Delightful gathering of Canadian Francophone traditional stories. See *Folklore of Canada* (1977) and (with Joe Glazer), *Songs of Work & Freedom* (1960).

**Grimm, Jacob and William Grimm,** *Grimm's Tales for Young and Old* (1978). The complete stories translated in a straightforward and engaging manner by Ralph Manheim. A more poetic translation is *The Juniper Tree and Other Tales* (1973), translated by Lore Segal and illustrated by Maurice Sendak, plus several retellings by Randall Jarrell.

**Guthrie, Woody,** *Bound for Glory* (1943). The wayfarings of the Oklahoma folk singer and writer, written "in a kind of dialect, as the poems of Burns were written, a language that has the exact speed and timbre of colloquial speech and yet is nervous and alive with metaphor and simile, and musical, too, in a balladlike way" (Clifton Fadiman). See *Seeds of Man* (1976) and *Born to Win* (1965). See Joe Klein's fine biography, *Woody Guthrie* (1980).

**Hughes, Langston and Arna Bontemps,** *The Book of Negro Folklore* (1958). Zesty, entertaining compilation, from Br'er Rabbit to Jesse B. Simple.

**Johnson, Ethel,** *The Maid of the North: Feminist Folk Tales from Around the World* (1981). Good corrective to tales in which women counted on their beauty or rescue by a man.

**Lomax, John A.,** *Adventures of a Ballad Hunter* (1947). Memoir of the great collector of living folksongs. "His is the saltiest, singingest autobiography of our time; its character and color, its dialect and melody, come straight from the heart of our people" (Edward Weeks).

**Marriott, Alice,** *Maria: The Potter of San Ildefonso* (1948). Detailed and personal account of the life of Maria Martinez, who crafted splendid blackware pottery until her death in her nineties. A beautiful, large-format book of her work is Susan Peterson, *The Living Tradition of Maria Martinez* (1978).

**Panyella, August (ed.),** *Folk Art of the Americas* (1981). Dazzling big book with over 1,000 photos offering a country-by-country guide to our hemisphere's rich folk tradition.

**Roberts, Moss,** *Chinese Fairy Tales and Fantasies* (1979). Entrancing collection, ably translated by Roberts.

**Siddiqui, Ashraf and Marilyn Lerch,** *Toontomy Pie and Other Tales from Pakistan* (1962). Lively retelling based on Mrs. Steel's famous *Tales from the Punjab* (1894).

**Wolkstein, Diane,** *The Magic Orange Tree, and Other Haitian Folktales* (1979). Personally gathered by the author in Haiti, the tales are fraught with vitality, wisdom, and humor. Philip Sherlock's *West Indian Folk Tales* (1956) will delight any lover of Caribbean folklore.

# PART VII

TIME

# NATURE OF TIME

**Aldiss, Brian,** *Cryptozoic!* (1968). A world where time runs backward with interesting consequences for the principle of cause and effect. Another time-reversal novel is Philip K. Dick, *Counter-Clock World* (1967).

**Ballard, J. G.,** *Chronopolis and Other Stories* (1971). The title story is about a city where time-enslaved citizens have destroyed all the clocks. Many of the other stories by this imaginative British writer deal with the nature of time.

**Bowman, Peter,** *Beach Red* (1945). World War II novel that describes the landing on a Pacific island, with one line to the second, one chapter to the minute. An interesting literary curiosity.

**Calder, Ritchie,** *The Living Clocks* (1971). Brisk popular explanation of biochronometry; it unfolds the dramatic researches that have made "living clocks," which govern the behavior of all life, a central concern of those seeking to understand the total environment.

**Gribbin, John,** *Timewarps* (1979). The ways in which people have thought about time, the state of present scientific knowledge, and the possibilities of such phenomena as parallel universes, time travel, and reincarnation.

**Hoyle, Fred,** *October the First Is Too Late* (1966). Fascinating novel by the astronomer-science-fiction writer about an earth where different countries and cultures exist at different times. Another novel which treats the nature of time is Gordon R. Dickson, *Time Storm* (1977).

**MacDonald, John D.,** *The Girl, The Gold Watch, & Everything* (1962). Comic fantasy about a watch that seems to freeze time.

**Park, David,** *The Image of Eternity* (1981). The "roots of time in the physical world" are the subject of this well-researched and vivid study by a physics professor.

**Priestley, J. B.,** *Man and Time* (1964). Fascinating discussion of the mythology, philosophy, and science of time, accompanied by varied and handsome illustrations. See L. R. B. Elton and H. Messel, *Time and Man* (1979).

**Proust, Marcel,** *Remembrance of Things Past* (1913–27). This wonderful unfinished novel — the longest ever written — is the "magisterially executed conception of a master-mind in which art erects its monument to dead loves using for material only thought and the passage of time" (Cyril Connolly). Excellent companions are Howard Moss, *The Magic Lantern of*

*Marcel Proust* (1963) and Roger Shattuck, *Proust's Binoculars* (1963).

**Thurber, James,** *Thirteen Clocks* (1950). A multitiered fairy tale about a captured beautiful princess, her handsome rescuer-prince, and a duke so cruel and cold that time has frozen around him.

**Vonnegut, Kurt,** *Slaughterhouse Five, or the Children's Crusade* (1969). Middle-class optometrist Billy Pilgrim, survivor of the bombing of Dresden, has become "unstuck in time," living alternately in the past, the future, on earth, and on the planet Tralfamadore.

**Williamson, Jack,** *The Legion of Time* (1952). Wide-ranging "space opera" of swashbuckling adventure through time and space. Other time sagas include Poul Anderson, *The Guardians of Time* (1960); Isaac Asimov, *The End of Eternity* (1955); J. Barrington Bayley, *The Fall of Chronopolis* (1974); and Keith Laumer, *Dinosaur Beach* (1971).

**Woolf, Virginia,** *To the Lighthouse* (1927). Sensitive and fluid novel, ostensibly about a vacation on an island in the Hebrides, that shows the obsession with rendering the concept of passage of time, which dominated the author's later works.

# TIME TRAVEL

**Brunner, John,** *Quicksand* (1967). Woman from future utopia comes to modern-day England. Other novels about visitors from the future are Robert Silverberg *The Masks of Time* (1968) and Michael Moorcock's Dancers at the End of Time series, the first novel of which is *An Alien Heat* (1972).

**DeCamp, L. Sprague,** *Lest Darkness Fall* (1941). Inadvertent time traveler tries to prevent the fall of Rome by introducing modern technology. Other change-the-past novels include Manly Wade Wellmann, *Twice in Time* (1940), set in Leonardo's Florence, and Brian Aldiss, *Frankenstein Unbound* (1973), set in Mary Shelley's time.

**Edmondson, G. C.,** *The Ship that Sailed the Time Stream* (1965). Navy ship is accidentally hurled back in time a thousand years in an amusing parody of time travel stories. *Sail the Century Sea* (1981) is a sequel.

**Harrison, Harry,** *The Technicolor Time Machine* (1967). Intriguing future where "shooting on location" for historical movies is done in the past, right on the spot! Other comic treatments of time travel are

Keith Laumer, *The Great Time Machine Hoax* (1964) and Bob Shaw, *Who Goes Here* (1977).

**Kipling, Rudyard,** *Puck of Pook's Hill* (1906). Kipling's much-loved Downs country of England is seen at different historical periods as figures from the past visit the juvenile protagonists. Two English classics about children going back in time are E. Nesbit, *The Story of the Amulet* (1906) and Hilda Lewis, *The Ship that Flew* (1939).

**Moorcock, Michael,** *Behold the Man* (1970). Award-winning novel in which the hero travels back to check the truth of the story of Christ, changes place with him, and is crucified.

**Moore, Ward,** *Bring the Jubilee* (1953). In an alternate world which evolved because the Confederacy won the Civil War, a time traveler goes back to Gettysburg, meddles in history, and, oops, destroys that world and brings our own into existence.

**Pearce, Philippa,** *Tom's Midnight Garden* (1958). Beautiful children's story about Tom's garden, which takes him to the late nineteenth century when the grandfather clock strikes thirteen. Modern masterpiece of English children's literature.

**Saberhagen, Fred (ed.),** *A Spadeful of Spacetime* (1980). Anthology of fine stories about time travel done without benefit of machine. See Robert Silverberg (ed.), *Trips in Time* (1977).

**Silverberg, Robert,** *Up the Line* (1969). Amusing farce set in a future when time travel is a popular recreation, wherein the ineptness of a "time courier" threatens to wink the world out of existence. Other good novels about time paradox are David Gerrold, *The Man Who Folded*

*Himself* (1973) and Wilson Tucker, *The Lincoln Hunters* (1957).

**Tucker, Wilson,** *The Year of the Quiet Sun* (1970). A government sends a team to 2000 A.D. in order to anticipate problems of the future. Man traveling to the future is the theme of James Blish, *Midsummer Century* (1972); L. P. Davies, *Genesis Two* (1970); Rex Gordon, *First Through Time* (1962); and Christopher Priest, *The Perfect Lover* (1977).

**Wells, H. G.,** *The Time Machine* (1895). Classic about a trip to the future where the time traveler encounters the Morlocks and the Eloi.

# SEGMENTS OF TIME

## *Century*

**Aston, Margaret,** *The Fifteenth Century* (1967). The century of the plague, the invention of the printing press, the fall of Constantinople, the discovery of the New World, and other events, surveyed (with the aid of over 200 beautiful illustrations) by a noted English historian.

**Briggs, Asa (ed.),** *The Nineteenth Century* (1971). Large, handsome, coffee-table volume of essays by prominent English scholars about the main trends of the century, documented with hundreds of fine color plates of period art works and photographs. Completely, and without ever being dull, captures the essence of the era.

**Sainte-Beauve, Charles A.,** *Portraits of the Eighteenth Century* (1836–39). Luminous portraits of French historical and literary personalities by the great nineteenth-century French literary critic and man of letters. Called from *Critiques et Portraits Literains.*

**Time-Life Editors,** *This Fabulous Century* (1969–70). Nostalgia-brimming eight-volume series that, decade by decade,

recreates in words and pictures American life during the first seventy years of the twentieth century.

**Trevor-Roper, Hugh,** *The Crisis of the Seventeenth Century* (1968). By one of the best modern writers of history, a collection of lively and provocative essays about the crisis in society, government, and ideas that occurred in Europe between the Reformation and the mid-seventeenth century. See Maurice Ashley, *The Golden Century: Europe 1598–1715* (1969).

## *Decade*

**Allen, Frederick Lewis,** *Only Yesterday* (1931). Informal history of the flappers, blind pigs, the Teapot Dome scandal, and other events that made the twenties roar.

**Cowley, Malcolm,** *Exile's Return: A Literary Odyssey of the 1920's* (rev. 1951). "The irreplaceable account of the most dramatic episode in American literary history, the story of the so-called 'expatriates' after the First World War and the how-and-why of their going abroad and coming home again. Malcolm Cowley was the man who saw and lived it all"

(Van Wyck Brooks). A unique and eloquent book. See *The Dream of Golden Mountains: Remembering the 1930's* (1980).

**Davidson, Sara,** *Loose Change: Three Women of the 60s* (1976). Intensely personal and novelistic weaving of the stories of three young women and their experiences at most of the watersheds of the turbulent decade.

**Stone, I. F.,** *The Haunted Fifties* (1961). Selections from *I.F. Stone's Weekly,* the author's Washington-based newspaper. Its pungent, readable style and radical point of view earned it a reputation as the intellectual and moral tonic of the capital. The columns remain exemplars of good journalism.

**Wilson, Edmund,** *The Twenties* (1975). Made up of his notebooks and diaries of the period, it provides "perhaps the largest authentic document of the time, the observations of one of the principal actors in the American twenties. . . . Nowhere have we had a picture less varnished and so rich in focused detail" (Leon Edel). See *The Thirties* (1980).

## Historical Year

**Angle, Paul M.,** *Crossroads, 1913* (1963). Interesting account of what the author believes was a transitional year — it would have changed American life radically even if World War I had not ensued. Another chronicle of that fateful year is Virginia Cowles, *1913: An End and a Beginning* (1968).

**Davidson, Marshall B.,** *The Horizon History of the World in 1776* (1975). Vivid panorama of what transpired during America's revolutionary year.

**Fisher, John,** *1815: An End and a Beginning* (1963). Month-by-month review of the major events of the year that saw the Battle of New Orleans, Napoleon's escape from Elba, and Lord Byron's wedding day.

**Sloat, Warren,** *1929: America Before the Crash* (1979). Reconstruction of a pivotal year in twentieth-century America and the figures who shaped the years leading to the crash.

## Country Year

**Borland, Hal,** *Book of Days: 12 Months of the Year* (1979). Three hundred sixty-five "outdoor editorials," one for each day of the year, from the author's column, which appeared for years on the editorial page of the *New York Times.* Wonderful reminders of the richness of nature.

**Fairbrother, Nan,** *An English Year* (1954). Leisurely, personal accounts from the journal that a young London woman kept while living in an old country house where she and her two small children found refuge while her husband was serving in the R.A.F. during the war.

**Holden, Edith,** *The Country Diary of an Edwardian Lady, 1906: A Facsimile Reproduction of a Naturalist's Diary* (1977). The changing seasons of 1906 in Warwickshire in words and drawings. Charming and beautiful.

**Peattie, Donald Culross,** *An Almanac for Moderns* (1935). Of these short essays for each day of the year, Mark Van Doren remarked that it was not merely "the best book of its kind that I have read in years; it is one of the best books I ever read. I suspect it of being a classic." *A Book of Hours* (1937) is a pendant.

**Teale, Edwin Way,** *A Walk Through the Year* (1978). A year of days at his New England farm, culled from his journal of over twenty years. Inspired by Thoreau's proposal: "It would be pleasant to write the history of one hillside for one year."

## Day

**Carrighar, Sally,** *One Day on Beetle Rock* (1944). Focuses on nine very different wild creatures throughout a single day and unfolds a vast, interlocking drama of adventure and survival. A modern nature classic. See *One Day on Teton Marsh* (1947).

**Joyce, James,** *Ulysses* (1922). This comic-epic masterpiece — generally acknowledged as the greatest twentieth-century novel written in English — may be about many things; it is certainly about two things: Dublin and the events of one day, June 16, 1904, since celebrated by all good Joyceans as Bloomsday. Among the best reading guides to this monument are Gilbert Stuart, *James Joyce's Ulysses* (rev. 1952); Robert Martin Adams, *Surface and Symbol* (1962); and A. Walton Litz, *The Art of James Joyce* (1961).

**Prange, Gordon W.,** *At Dawn We Slept: The Untold Story of Pearl Harbor* (1981). The last word on the events of December 7, 1941 — a day of infamy. For a different view see John Toland, *Infamy: Pearl Harbor and Its Aftermath* (1982).

**Ryan, Cornelius,** *The Longest Day* (1959). Masterful reconstruction of June 6, 1944, D-day, from various personal points of view.

**Solzhenitsyn, Aleksandr,** *One Day in the Life of Ivan Denisovich* (1963). Utterly authentic, this novel by the Russian Nobel laureate treats one day of an inmate in one of Stalin's forced labor camps.

## Night

**Deverson, H. J. (ed.),** *Journey into Night* (1966). Fat, felicitous anthology of the night in words and pictures. The editor is English, and he has made many of his selections from refreshingly unfamilar authors.

**Restif De La Bretonne, Nicholas-Edme,** *Les Nuits de Paris; or the Nocturnal Spectator* (1964). Selections written during the French Revolution and containing his observations made during prowls around the underbelly of Paris at night. Fascinating picture of eighteenth-century Parisian life by the Rousseau of the Gutter.

**Sendak, Maurice,** *In the Night Kitchen* (1970). A little boy's fantastic journey into the "night kitchen" and his adventures among the merry bakers and huge kitchen implements. See the brilliantly drawn *Where the Wild Things Are* (1963), in which little Max, sent to his room without supper, dreams of big monsters who acclaim him their king.

**Shakespeare, William,** *A Midsummer Night's Dream* (c. 1594). Comic masterpiece of fantasy and dream, love and fairies, set in an enchanted forest one midsummer night.

**Wallace, David Rains,** *The Dark Range: A Naturalist's Night Studies* (1978). How do animals spend their secret nights? The author's flashlight backpacking over five years in the Yolla Bolly mountains of Northern California, condensed vividly into one night-long adventure, tells all. See Louis Milne and Margery Milne, *The World of Night* (1956).

# THE PAST

**Bettmann, Otto L.,** *The Bettmann Archives Picture History of the World* (1978). Wonderous pictorial collage. The story of Western civilization in 4,500 miniature captioned pictures.

**Brinton, Crane et al.,** *A History of Civilization* (rev. 1976). In three volumes, its simple style and wealth of pictures and maps make it one of the most readable surveys.

**Clark, Kenneth,** *Civilisation* (1970). Book based on his celebrated BBC TV series. Fresh, genial personal view of European history from the fall of Rome to the present.

**Durant, Will and Ariel Durant,** *The Story of Civilization* (1935–1975). Of this eleven-volume set, Clifton Fadiman wrote: "Its style is always readable and at its best brilliant, for the authors are masters of the neat phrase and the vivid detail."

**McNeill, William H.,** *The Rise of the West: A History of the Human Community* (1963). This long, crowded, and concentrated winner of the National Book Award is "not only the most learned and the most intelligent, it is also the most stimulating and fascinating book that has ever set out to recount and explain the whole history of mankind" (H. R. Trevor-Roper).

**Mumford, Lewis,** *Technics and Civilization* (1934). A brilliant account of the development of machine civilization, "might perhaps be classed as one of the prophetic books" (Herbert Read). Part of a four-volume study, The Renewal of Life, which also includes *The Condition of Man* (1944), *The Conduct of Life* (1951), and *The Culture of Cities* (1938).

**Thomas, Hugh,** *A History of the World* (1978). Combines breadth, detail, and a thematic, rather than chronological, approach. "He is no Gibbon, but he is a mine of fascinating information that makes him rather fun to read" (C. Vann Woodward). Differs from McNeill in focusing on political history; McNeill is more interested in the nonpolitical aspects.

**Time-Life Editors,** *Great Ages of Man* (1965–71). Twelve-volume series, each volume written by a distinguished scholar, such as C. M. Bowra on classical Greece and Moses Hadas on imperial Rome, and richly illustrated and designed.

*The Times Atlas of World History* (1978). Attractive, lucid depiction of the broad historical movements in the world, as charted by a panel of distinguished scholars for Hammond and the London *Times*.

**Toynbee, Arnold,** *A Study of History* (1934–61). Monumental twelve-volume work considered to be "an immortal masterpiece" (Randall Jarrell).

**Trager, James (ed.),** *The People's Chronology* (1979). A fascinating 1,200-page year-by-year record of human events from prehistory to the present. A less comprehensive, though somewhat clearer, volume is Bernard Grun, *The Timetables of History: A Horizontal Linkage of People and Events* (1979).

## The Distant Past

**Burl, Aubrey,** *The Stone Circles of the British Isles* (1976). Lively writing about a fascinating subject, with emphasis on Stonehenge and Avebury, that clearly sets forth all the theories. Attractively illustrated. See *Rings of Stone* (1980). See also John Fowles (t), Barry Brukoff (p), *The Enigma of Stonehenge* (1980).

**Ceram, C. W.,** *Gods, Graves, and Scholars* (rev. 1972). This enthusiastic, fluent "story of archaeology" has become the classic popular introduction to the subject. See *The First American: A Story of North American Archaeology* (1972).

**Chang, Kwang-Chih,** *Shang Civilization* (1980). Origins of Chinese civilization as pieced together from archaeological evidence. For earlier history, see *The Archaeology of Ancient China* (1963).

**Clark, Grahame,** *World Prehistory* (rev. 1972). Authoritative and wide-ranging survey of a complex subject.

**Cottrell, Leonard,** *The Bull of Minos* (1958). Popular account of excavations of Schliemann, Evans, and Ventrus at Knossos, the capital of the priest-kings of Crete in about the second millennium B.C. Reads like a detective story.

**Fagan, Brian M.,** *Return to Babylon: Tombs, Archaeologists, and Monuments in Mesopotamia* (1979). Informative, up-to-date, and compelling reading. See *Elusive Treasure: The Story of Early Archaeologists in the Americas* (1977).

**Hawkes, Jacquetta (ed.),** *The World of the Past* (1963). Superb two-volume sampler of first-hand reports by archaeologists who can write as well as dig. Among Hawkes's other books are *The Atlas of Early Man* (1976) and *Prehistory and the Beginnings of Civilization* (1963), written with Sir Leonard Woolley.

**Herm, Gerhard,** *The Celts* (1976). Brisk narrative tracing the history of the Celtic-speaking peoples of Europe. See Barry Cuncliffe, *The Celtic World* (1979).

*The Horizon Book of Lost Worlds* (1962). Sumptuously illustrated guide to the most notable ancient civilizations, including the Mesopotamian, Etruscan, and Mayan.

**Kramer, Samuel Noah,** *The Sumerians* (1963). Urbane account of their history, culture, and character. See *History Begins at Sumer* (1959).

**Kubie, Nora Benjamin,** *The Road to Nineveh* (1964). Story of the adventures and excavations of Sir Austin Henry Layard that "recaptures in enthralling detail the daring, courage, persistence, and above all, the youthful exuberance of this extraordinary man. . . . Like her subject, Mrs. Kubie writes with a youthful zest" (Leonard Cottrell).

**Kurten, Bjorn,** *Dance of the Tiger* (1980). Lyrical and evocative novel by a leading paleontologist about the meeting between Cro-magnon and Neanderthal humans. The same prehistoric meeting is brilliantly rendered in William Golding, *The Inheritors* (1955).

**Leroi-Gourkan, Andre,** *Treasures of Prehistoric Art* (1967). Learned text and fine color plates have made this the standard work on paleolithic art. Aimed more for the general reader is Thomas George E. Powell, *Prehistoric Art* (1966).

**Macqueen, J. G.,** *The Hittites and Their Contemporaries in Asia Minor* (1975). Graphic and elegant reconstruction of an interesting and mysterious people.

**Piggott, Stuart,** *The Druids* (1968). Entertaining and handsomely illustrated look at the fact and fiction about the ancient British and Gaulish order of priests who appear in Irish and Welsh legend as sorcerers and prophets. See *Ancient Europe: A Survey* (1965).

**Renault, Mary,** *The King Must Die* (1958). Archaeologically exact reconstruction of the legend of Theseus and the Minotaur of ancient Crete is "one of the most remarkable historical novels of modern times" (Orville Prescott). Continued in *The Bull from the Sea* (1962). Cottrell makes a good companion.

**Struever, Stuart and Felicia Antoinette Hilton,** *Koster: Americans in Search of Their Prehistoric Past* (1979). Vivid you-are-there account of the ten-year dig in farmer Koster's Illinois cornfield, which unearthed a village from about 6500 B.C. For other American excavations, see Josleen Wilson, *The Passionate Amateur's Guide to Archaeology in the U.S.* (1981).

**Time-Life Editors,** *The Emergence of Man* (1972–75). Splendidly executed thirteen-volume series tracing man's development to civilization.

**Treece, Henry,** *The Dark Island* (1952). First of a cycle of novels of Britain from earliest Bronze Age to the first century. Often melodramatic, but with the poet's deft descriptive touch. The other novels are *Great Captains* (1956), *Golden Strangers* (1957), and *Red Queen, White Queen* (1958).

**Woolley, Sir Leonard,** *Excavation at Ur* (1957). His own account of his famous excavation at Ur in Iraq. See *History, Unearthed* (1958).

## Ancient Egypt

**Brackman, Arnold,** *The Search for the Gold of Tutankhamen* (1976). Graceful account of the excavation of the famous tomb in the Valley of the Kings. See Thomas Hoving, *Tutankhamen: The Untold Story* (1978).

**Cottrell, Leonard,** *Lady of the Two Lands: Five Queens of Ancient Egypt* (1967). The few facts that are known plus interesting speculations add up to fascinating reading. Among the other books on ancient Egypt by this deft writer are *Life Under the Pharaohs* (1960) and *Land of the Pharaohs* (1960).

**Fagan, Brian M.,** *The Rape of the Nile: Tomb Robbers, Tourists, and Archaeologists* (1975). Intriguing tales of grave robbers and desecrators.

**Gedge, Pauline,** *Child of the Morning* (1970). Novel of Hatshepsut, the only woman pharaoh, that richly conveys the sense of place and past. Another good fictional recreation is Sandra Adelson, *Wrap Her in Light: A Novel of Ankhesenamon* (1981). Two outstanding novels for young readers are Eloise Jarvis McGraw, *Mara, Daughter of the Nile* (1953) and Lucille Morrison, *The Last Queen of Egypt* (1937).

**Greener, Leslie,** *The Discovery of Egypt* (1966). Diverting history of Egyptology in a lively mix of anecdote, straight narrative, and pictures.

**Hawkes, Jacquetta,** *King of Two Lands* (1966). Novel of the pharaoh Akhenaten, religious reformer and husband of Nefertiti. A brilliant reconstruction of the period.

**Hoffman, Michael A.,** *Egypt Before the Pharaohs: The Prehistoric Foundations of Egyptian Civilization* (1979). Lively, up-to-date general survey of prehistoric Egypt told through the achievements of the archaeologists whose discoveries brought the information to light.

**Mertz, Barbara,** *Red Land, Black Land* (1967). Daily life under the pharaohs. A sound and witty description. See *Temples, Tombs and Hieroglyphs* (1964).

**Michalowski, Kamierz,** *The Art of Ancient Egypt* (1969). Comprehensive, lavishly illustrated history of the fine arts of the epoch. See Arpag Mekhitarian, *Egyptian Painting* (1978).

**Romer, John,** *Valley of the Kings* (1981). A man who has devoted his life to preserving the royal tombs of the pharaohs near Thebes from further destruction tells of the men who built them and the men who studied them. "Years of research into travel books, scientific literature, and the unpublished notes of archaeologists themselves have created a book that is bound to become a classic of Egyptology" (Brian Fagan).

**Wilson, John A.,** *Culture of Ancient Egypt* (1951). Not a history, but "an interpretation." "Undoubtedly the most significant, stimulating, and provocative contribution on Egyptian history and culture . . . in recent years" (Samuel Noah Kramer). The best "straight" history is George Steindorff and Keith Steele, *When Egypt Ruled the East* (rev. 1957).

## Classical Greece

**Auden, W. H. (ed.),** *The Portable Greek Reader* (1948). Highlights of Greek thought and literature in a balanced one-volume collection, with a good brief introduction by the poet. See C. Maurice Bowra, *Landmarks in Greek Literature* (1966).

**Bowra, C. Maurice,** *The Greek Experience* (1958). Lucid analysis of Greek culture and life. Another scholar's enjoyable survey is H. D. F. Kitto, *The Greeks* (rev. 1964).

**Bryher,** *Gate to the Sea* (1958). Poetic recreation of the story of the courageous Greeks who chose exile rather than bar-

barian dominance in fourth-century-B.C. Paestum.

**Coolidge, Olivia E.,** *The King of Men* (1966). This retelling of the story of Agamemnon is one of her fine novels for children about ancient Greece. See *Marathon Looks at the Sea* (1967) and *The Maid of Athens* (1969).

**Finley, M. I.,** *The Ancient Greeks* (1963). Lively trip through the history, life, and thought of the times. See *Aspects of Antiquity* (1968) and *The World of Odysseus* (rev. 1965).

**Graves, Robert,** *Hercules, My Shipmate* (1945). Rich, ribald yarn about Jason and the Argonauts. See *Homer's Daughter* (1955).

**Hamilton, Edith,** *The Greek Way* (1930). Her learning is matched by her gift for clarification. This book occupies a permanent place in the minds of all who love ancient Greece. See *Echo of Greece* (1957).

*The Horizon Book of Ancient Greece* (1965). Beautiful color plates and genial text capture the glory that was Greece.

**MacKendrick, Paul,** *The Greek Stones Speak* (rev. 1981). Lucid story of archaeology in Greek lands.

**Plutarch,** *Parallel Lives* (c. 110). Series of short character studies of famous Greek and Roman soldiers and statesmen written during the Roman Age by a Greek who wished to show that his forebears' exploits were equal to those of the Romans. Dramatic and full of fascinating anecdotes.

**Renault, Mary,** *The Last of the Wine* (1956). Superb portrayal of Athens in the days of the third Peloponnesian War, as narrated by a disciple of Socrates. Her other absorbing novels of the period include *The Mask of Apollo* (1966) and *The Praise Singer* (1978).

**Robertson, Martin,** *A Shorter History of Greek Art* (1981). Condensation of his authoritative two-volume *A History of Greek Art* (1975).

**Scully, Vincent,** *The Earth, The Temple, and the Gods* (rev. 1980). Refreshing study of Greek sacred architecture, organized by deity rather than by chronology or area. See also Arnold Walter Lawrence, *Greek Architecture* (rev. 1975).

**Treece, Henry,** *Amber Princess* (1963). Engaging melodramatic romance of that tragic heroine of Greek mythology, Electra. See *The Eagle Kings* (1965), about Oedipus, and *Jason* (1961), about the quest for the Golden Fleece. Other mythological figures are given fictional treatment in Ursule Molinaro, *The Autobiography of Cassandra, Princess and Prophetess* (1979) and Miranda Seymour, *Medea* (1982).

**Vidal, Gore,** *Creation* (1981). Fictional memoirs of one Cyrus Spitama, half-Greek diplomat, who knew everyone, including the Buddha and Confucius. A vivid mosaic of men and society in the fifth century B.C.

**Warner, Rex,** *Men of Athens: The Story of Fifth Century Athens* (1972). Admirable, evocative coffee-table volume of short essays on the giants of the time — the playwrights and Pericles and Socrates. Exquisite photographs. See *The Stories of the Greeks* (1967), a vivid and racy retelling of the Hellenic myths.

## Imperial Rome

**Andreae, Bernard,** *The Art of Rome* (1978). Splendid large-format pictorial survey. Authoritative and delightful.

**Arnott, Peter D.,** *The Romans and Their World* (1970). An entertaining view of Roman life at three different points in its thousand-year history. See F. R. Cowell, *Everyday Life in Ancient Rome* (1961).

**Brauer, George C.,** *The Young Emperors, Rome A.D. 193–244* (1967). Colorful recounting of the years when Rome was ruled by a group of young and irresponsible rulers. Moves with the excitement of a good popular novel.

**Bryher,** *Roman Wall* (1954). Third-century Switzerland during the waning days of Roman civilization is the setting of this fine novel. See also her novel about the Punic Wars, *The Coin of Carthage* (1963).

**Cuncliffe, Barry,** *Rome and Her People* (1978). Over a thousand beautiful photographs. The grandeur of Rome. See *Rome and the Barbarians* (1975) and *Fishbourne: A Roman Palace and Its Gardens* (1971).

**Duggan, Alfred,** *Three's Company* (1958). Clever novel about Lepidus, a member, with Mark Antony and Octavius, of the Second Triumvirate in the last half of the first century B.C. See *Winter Quarters* (1956).

**Gibbon, Edward,** *The History of the Decline and Fall of the Roman Empire* (1776–88). Although most of the information has been superseded by later scholarship, it is, according to the third edition of *The Concise Cambridge History of English Literature,* "not only the greatest historical work in the English language, it is perhaps the greatest piece of literary achievement in any language."

**Grant, Michael,** *A History of Rome* (1978). From its beginnings to the sixth century. Grant is a prolific and excellent popularizer of Roman history. See *The Climax of Rome* (1968) and *The World of Rome* (1961).

**Graves, Robert,** *I, Claudius* (1934). Fascinating "autobiography" of the unusual emperor; "a good book singular enough to be immortal" (Randall Jarrell). Its sequel is *Claudius the God* (1934).

**Highet, Gilbert,** *Poets in a Landscape* (1957). Part anthology of the great Latin poets, part biography, part literary gossip, part architectural promenade in photographs add up to "an exceptionally interesting and illuminating book, a genuine labor of love, the product of taste and scholarship combined" (Peter Quennell).

**Livy,** *The Early History of Rome* (c. first century A.D.). Moralistic glorification of the good old days that was aimed at the historian's fellow citizens of a decadent Rome. Its gleaming rhetorical style and colorful narrative have made it last.

**Petersen, Nis,** *The Street of Sandal-makers* (1931). Vivid, Rabelaisian novel, set during the reign of Marcus Aurelius, that depicts a cross-section of life in the capital.

**Petronius Arbiter,** *The Satyricon* (c. first century A.D.). Adventures of a trio of irreverent friends that give an unmatched view of everyday life in Nero's Rome. The William Arrowsmith translation (1960) renders it into a fresh and vigorous colloquial American idiom.

**Suetonius,** *The Twelve Caesars* (c. first century A.D. tr. Robert Graves 1957). Wonderful gossipy portraits of the first twelve emperors, from Caesar to Domitian, by the emperor Hadrian's private secretary.

**Sutcliff, Rosemary,** *The Eagle of the Ninth* (1954). One of her best historical novels for children, this is the first of a sequence set in Roman Britain. The series dovetails with another about the Saxon era. Together they create a memorable panorama of early England.

**Tacitus, Cornelius,** *Annals of Imperial Rome* (c. second century A.D.). Events in the empire from the death of Augustus to 68 A.D. His superb powers of description and psychological insight, mastery of the innuendo and epigram, and fine lapidary style make it the most brilliant history written in Latin. The chronicle is continued to the year 96 in his *History.*

## Byzantium

**Diehl, Charles,** *Byzantine Portraits* (1927). Vivid Suetonius-like portraits make up "this extraordinarily colorful and interesting book by a brilliant and witty writer" (Conrad Aiken).

**Graves, Robert,** *Count Belisarius* (1938). Fictional contemporary chronicle written by the servant of the wife of Belisarius, principally about the latter's relationship with the Emperor Justinian and Empress Theodora. Graves's primary source was the scandalous court chronicle, *Secret History,* appended to *The History of the Wars* (c. 560) by the lascivious Procopius, one-time private secretary to Belisarius.

**Jenkins, Romilly,** *Byzantium: The Imperial Centuries, A.D. 610–1071* (1967). "Throughout this long and immensely complicated story, Mr. Jenkins writes clearly, vigorously, and with immense gusto" (Rex Warner). The standard history for the entire 1,200 years of the empire is Georgije Ostrogorski, *History of the Byzantine State* (1958), an uncommonly clear and elegant short account.

**Kitzinger, Ernst,** *Byzantine Art in the Making* (1977). Handsomely designed survey of the period; lucid and well illustrated. Another first-rate overview is David T. Rice, *Byzantine Art* (rev. 1968).

**Runciman, Sir Steven,** *Byzantine Style and Civilization* (1975). Knowledgeable, sympathetic portrait by one of England's most eloquent historians. See *The Byzantine Theocracy* (1977) and *The Last Byzantine Renaissance* (1970).

its destruction by the Spaniards written by the son of an Incan princess and a conquistador. It possesses a nostalgic charm and remains a "considerable work of literature, an enthralling, and at times, genuinely tragic story, of a sensitive man who felt himself the heir to two distinct races and cultural traditions" (J. H. Parry). The 1966 translation by Harold Livermore is the best.

**Prescott, William Hickling,** *History of the Conquest of Peru* (1847). Classic account of Pizarro's conquest of the Incas by "one of the very few historians whose works have successfully withstood a century of criticism, and which still interest and enchant us by the beauty, as well as the masculine strength, of their style" (Samuel Eliot Morison). The best modern history is John Hemming, *The Conquest of the Incas* (1970).

**Thompson, J. Eric S.,** *The Rise and Fall of Maya Civilization* (1967), Brief, fascinating chronicle of the "Greeks" of American Indians. See *Maya History and Religion* (1971). Robert L. Brunhouse's *In Search of the Maya* (1973) and *Pursuit of the Ancient Maya* (1975) recount the early archaeologists' quest for artifacts of Mayan civilization.

**Von Hagen, Victor W.,** *The Ancient Sun Kingdoms of the Americas* (1961). Each of the three great Indian civilizations — the Maya, the Incas, and the Aztecs — in a lively, popular portrayal.

## Pre-Columbian America

**Caso, Alfonso,** *The Aztecs: People of the Sun* (1959). The best short introduction to the Indian tribe that dominated Mexico for centuries. The classic history is George Vaillant's *The Aztecs of Mexico* (rev. 1962). For meticulously researched novels see Gary Jennings, *Aztec* (1980) and Daniel Peters, *The Luck of Huemac* (1981).

**Garcilaso de la Vega,** *Royal Commentaries* (1609). Account of the Inca empire and

## American History

**Boorstin, Daniel,** *The Americans: The Colonial Experience* (1958). The first of an award-winning trio of books that reinterpret American social history in a fresh and arresting manner. Stimulating reading. The others are *The Americans: The National Experience* (1965) and *The Americans: The Democratic Experience* (1973).

**Burns, James MacGregor,** *The American Experiement, Vol. 1: The Vineyard of Lib-*

*erty* (1982). The Pulitzer Prize–winning biographer's first of projected three-volume popular history of the U.S.

**Morison, Samuel Eliot,** *The Oxford History of the American People* (1965). Robust, expert, highly personal overview, "embellished with a literary grace and fluency unexcelled among contemporary American historians" (Daniel Boorstin). For more detail see the projected nine-volume *Oxford History of the United States* under the editorship of C. Vann Woodward, beginning with Robert Middlekauff, *The Glorious Cause: The American Revolution, 1763–1789* (1982).

**Nevins, Allan and Henry Steele Commager,** *A Short History of the United States* (rev. 1976). Standard one-volume history by two of America's greatest historians.

**Smith, Page,** *A New Age Now Begins* (1976). The first of a multivolume panoramic "people's history." For a view of history from the perspective of the exploited see Howard Zinn, *A People's History of the United States* (1980).

## Middle Ages in Europe

**Adams, Henry,** *Mont-Saint-Michel and Chartres* (1904). Historical "study in 13th-century unity" that uses the great cathedral at Mont-Saint-Michel and the Virgin of Chartres as symbolic pivot points. Written in an elevated literary style. In the same tradition is Allan Temko, *Notre Dame of Paris* (1956).

**Barraclough, Geoffrey,** *The Crucible of Europe: The Ninth and Tenth Centuries in European History* (1976). Best short summary in English of the political origins of the major states of western Europe. See *The Medieval Papacy* (1968).

**Bengtsson, Frans G.,** *The Long Ships* (1954). Colorful saga of the Viking age. "One of the funniest, most knowing and most delightful historical novels I ever read" (Randall Jarrell). See *The Red*

*Orme* (1941). Fine novels for young readers, each the first of a series, are Erik Haugaard, *Hakon of Rogen's Saga* (1963) and Henry Treece, *Vikings' Dawn* (1956).

**Bloch, Marc,** *Feudal Society* (1939, tr. 1960). Hailed as a masterpiece of historical writing and the best introduction to the subject.

**Burnett, Virgil,** *Towers at the Edge of the World* (1981). Mock-medieval fables about a French hilltop town; rich in eroticism, mysticism, and wit.

**Calvino, Italo,** *The Nonexistent Knight* (1952). Fabulous tale of chivalry in the days of Charlemagne, by the great Italian fabulist.

**Deuchler, Florens,** *Gothic Art* (1973). Good, concise introduction to the style of art and architecture which dominated western Europe between the twelfth and fifteenth centuries.

**Douglas, D.C.,** *The Norman Achievement* (1969). Narrative, rich and smooth-flowing, about the Norman impact on Europe. Continued in *The Norman Fate* (1976).

**Druon, Maurice,** The Accursed King Series (1956–62). Vivid recreation of the fourteenth century, brimming with power and intensity, delineated in six novels on "the accursed kings" of medieval France.

**Fowler, Kenneth,** *The Age of Plantagenet and Valois* (1967). This beautifully designed book about the struggle for supremacy between 1328 and 1498 is "one of the best books that I have found on historical themes, both for texts and exceptionally fine illustrations" (J. H. Plumb).

**Froissart, Jean,** *Chronicles* (1373–90). Classic contemporary history of the fourteenth century, full of feudal pageantry and vivid narrative.

**Gardner, John,** *Grendel* (1971). Retelling of the Old English epic, set on the Danish island of Seeland, from Grendel's point of view. "Absolutely marvelous: witty, intelligent, delightful, so totally a work of the imagination that it creates its own world while touching upon our memories of myth and verse" (Peter S. Prescott).

**Graham-Campbell, James,** *The Viking World* (1980). Wide-ranging, authoritative, handsomely illustrated introduction to the great northern sea adventurers.

**Holland, Cecelia,** *The Firedrake* (1966). The first of several medieval novels by an author who breathes life into a bygone era with her lean prose. See *Ghost on the Steppe* (1970), *Until the Sun Falls* (1969), and *Rakovy* (1967).

*The Horizon Book of the Middle Ages* (1968). Beautifully executed picture survey with brief lively essays by noted scholars. Another large-format feast of illustration is The National Geographic Society, *The Age of Chivalry* (1969).

**Huizinga, Johan,** *The Waning of the Middle Ages* (1924). Imposing, varied, and lively assemblage of strange facts and keen comments about medieval France and the Netherlands. See *Erasmus and the Age of the Reformation* (1957).

**Johnson, Eyvind,** *The Days of his Grace* (1960). Powerful political novel about the struggle for freedom by young Italians from the harsh regime of Charlemagne; by the winner of 1974 Nobel Prize.

**Kunstler, Gustav (ed.),** *Romanesque Art in Europe* (1969). An excellent introduction to the subject with fine illustrations. See Meyer Schapiro, *Romanesque Art* (1976).

**Lea, Henry Charles,** *The Inquisition in the Middle Ages* (1961). One-volume abridgement of the American scholar's monumental 1887 history. "Lea, an admirable readable writer, deserved to be included in the short list of historians who are also classics" (Van Wyck Brooks).

**Le Roy Ladurie, Emmanuel,** *Montaillou: The Promised Land of Error* (1978). Everyday life in a medieval village in the Pyrenees, based on contemporary documents. These people live. See *Carnival in Romans* (1979).

**Marks, Claude,** *Pilgrims, Heretics and Lovers: A Medieval Journey* (1975). Spirited account of medieval life in the Midi — the troubador country of France, where langue d'oc was spoken.

**Moss, H. St. L. B.,** *The Birth of the Middle Ages, 395–814* (1935). Absorbing account of the four centuries from the death of the Emperor Theodosius to the death of Charlemagne. Compact, clear, popular.

**Norwich, John Julius,** *The Other Conquest* (1967). The Norman conquest of Sicily in the twelfth century. The author's "style is usually elegant and smooth; and he has an infectious enthusiasm for his subject" (Sir Steven Runciman). *Kingdom in the Sun* (1971) continues the history. See *A History of Venice* (1982), about the Venetian empire between the fifth and eighteenth centuries.

**Oldenbourg, Zoë,** *The World Is Not Enough* (1948). The crusades supply the background for this imaginative novel and its sequel, *The Cornerstone* (1954). See *Cities of the Flesh* (1963), *Destiny of Fire* (1962), and *The Heirs of the Kingdom* (1970).

**Power, Eileen,** *Medieval Women* (1976). Very readable lectures by a fine medievalist about the different types of women of the age — peasant, nun, lady of the court, and others. See *Medieval People* (rev. 1963).

**Runciman, Sir Steven,** *A History of the Crusades* (1951–54). Vast amount of complex data summarized with great clarity, assurance, and style. *The First Crusade* (1981) is a one-volume illustrated condensation. See *The Sicilian Vespers: A History of the Medieval World in the Later 13th Century* (1958).

**Taylor, Henry Osborn,** *The Medieval Mind* (1911). Stylish history of the development of thought and emotion in the Middle Ages. "Thanks to his active sympathy with the efforts and the passions and desires of men, one could not imagine a day when it would not open to sensitive readers a world of enchantment" (Van Wyck Brooks).

**Les Très Riches Heures de Jean, Duke de Berry** (1969). Magnificent facsimile edition of the most beautiful illuminated manuscript in the world. Its captivating illustrations of medieval life are exquisite.

**Trevor-Roper, H. R.,** *The Rise of Christian Europe* (1965). Lively and provocative study of the 1,500 years of European history from the Roman Empire onward. "One of the most brilliant works of historiography to be published in English in this century" *(Times Literary Supplement).*

**Tuchman, Barbara W.,** *A Distant Mirror: The Calamitous 14th Century* (1978). The Pulitzer Prize–winning historian follows the career of one feudal lord of France. An exciting and illuminating picture of the Middle Ages.

**Undset, Sigrid,** *The Master of Hestviken* (1928–30). The Norwegian Nobel Prize–winner's tetralogy comprises *The Axe* (1928), *The Snake Pit* (1929), *In the Wilderness* (1929), and *The Son Avenger* (1930). A Götterdämmerung which portrays the medieval world with startling richness and fullness.

**Vidal, Gore,** *A Search for the King* (1950). Novel based on the twelfth-century legend of the search by Blondel for King Richard the Lion-Hearted.

**White, Lynn,** *Medieval Technology and Social Change* (1962). In a work that is humorous and scholarly, the author surveys the social changes brought about by technical innovation. See Jean Gimpel, *The Medieval Machine: The Industrial Revolution of the Middle Ages* (1976).

**Williams, Jay,** *The Siege* (1955). Hugely entertaining and historically aware novel set in thirteenth-century France when Pope Innocent III sent the crusaders against the Albigensian heretics. See *Tomorrow's Fire* (1964). These times are also the focus of Hannah Closs's trilogy that begins with *High on the Mountains* (1959).

## Middle Ages in England

**Andrews, Prudence,** *The Constant Star* (1964). Dramatic portrayal of the inhabitants of a Gloucestershire peasant community caught up in Tyler's Rebellion.

**Bennett, H. S.,** *Life on the English Manor* (1937). Richly detailed picture of everyday life of the peasant, 1150–1400. See William Stearns Davis, *Life on a Medieval Barony: A Picture of a Typical Feudal Community in the 13th Century* (1923).

**Bryant, Arthur,** *The Age of Chivalry* (1964). The High Middle Ages, 1272–1381, by England's most readable historian. "There is not a dull moment in this splendid book. . . . The remote century comes vividly alive" (C. V. Wedgwood). His *Makers of England* (1962) traces England's past from prehistory to 1272, and his *The Medieval Foundation of England* (1967) is a wonderfully rousing tale.

**Bryher,** *Ruan* (1960). This novel of the Celts of the sixth century, and also *The January Tale* (1966) and *The 14th of October* (1952), both set in the eleventh century, obtain their distinctive haunting flavor from the author's masterly use of unobtrusive details. They "are among the classics of our time" (Horace Gregory).

**Chaucer, Geoffrey,** *The Canterbury Tales* (1387–1400). "He paints an immortal picture of Catholic medieval England, drawn with all the warts left in, and painted in colors as fresh and lively as though applied only yesterday" (Clifton Fadiman).

**Coulton, G. C.,** *Medieval Panorama: The English Scene from Conquest to Reformation* (1955). Superb survey of the period by an outstanding English medievalist. See *Chaucer and His World* (1950) and *Medieval Village, Manor, and Monastery* (1960).

**Duckett, Eleanor,** *Alfred the Great* (1956). Portrait of an enlightened king in a dark age who truly deserved to be called great. A sprightly biography of a Saxon successor two centuries later is Frank Barlow, *Edward the Confessor* (1970).

**Duggan, Alfred,** *Conscience of the King* (1951). Agreeable, unvarnished novel about the founding of the west Saxon kingdom. Duggan has carved out a niche in writing about pre-Norman Britain. See *The Cunning of the Dove* (1962).

**Ford, Ford Madox,** *Ladies Whose Bright Eyes* (1919). This delightful half-satire half-historical romance about a twentieth-century Englishman projected back into the fourteenth century distills the essence of the period.

**Gies, Joseph and Francis Gies,** *Life in a Medieval Castle* (1974). Daily life at a castle in Monmouthshire, its damsels, pageants, knights, and other features. See John Burke, *Life in the Castle in Medieval England* (1978).

**Golding, William,** *The Spire* (1964). Richly textured novel about a dean who believes a great spire should be added to his cathedral when reason dictates against it. A moral drama of great intelligence, beauty, and lasting significance.

**Gray, Elizabeth Janet,** *Adam of the Road* (1942). The merry adventures of a minstrel boy on the road between Winchester and London in Chaucerian England are related in this Newberry Award–winning novel for young people. The times are also vividly rendered in Barbara Leonice Picard, *Ransom for a Knight* (1956).

**Greenberg, Joanne,** *The King's Person* (1963). The massacre of the Jews of York in 1190 is the climax of a first novel which weaves a vivid tapestry of medieval life.

**Hartley, Dorothy,** *Lost Country Life* (1979). How sixteenth-century country folk lived, worked, threshed, thatched, rolled, fleeced, milled corn, and brewed mead. Fine contemporary illustrations.

**Holland, Cecelia,** *The Earl* (1971). Novel of Henry II's struggle for power in twelfth-century England that catches the feeling of the age superbly. See *The Kings in Winter* (1968).

**Morris, John,** *The Age of Arthur* (1973). Superb history of the British Isles from 300 to 650, which demythologizes much of the romance, but finds too a fascinating reality.

**Muntz, Hope,** *The Golden Warrior* (1950). Brilliantly rendered novel of Harold and William and the Norman Conquest. "Her accounts of the battles of Stamford Bridge and Hastings are little masterpieces in themselves" (Orville Prescott).

**Nye, Robert,** *Falstaff* (1976). The most beloved comic figure in English literature decides that history hasn't done him justice — it's time for him to tell the whole unbuttoned story his way. Irascible and still lecherous at 81, Falstaff spins out these outrageously bawdy memoirs as an antidote to legend and in the process recreates his own. A marvelous tour de force.

**Rush, Philip,** *The Minstrel Knight* (1956). Swiftly paced retelling of an Anglo-Norman family history poem that takes place in the time of King John by a fine English children's author who has written several Middle Ages stories set near Canterbury. See *A Face of Stone* (1973) and *That Fool of a Priest* (1970).

**Simon, Edith,** *Golden Hand* (1952). The last half of the fourteenth century during the reign of Richard II in a novel remarkable for its homely depiction of ordinary life.

**Stewart, Mary,** *The Crystal Cave* (1970). The first of the Merlin Trilogy, set in fifth-century Britain, adheres to the spirit of the legend of King Arthur but makes the great sorcerer very human. Popular fiction at its best. The sequels are *The Hollow Hills* (1973) and *The Last Enchantment* (1979).

White, T. H., *The Once and Future King* (1958). Much-loved collection of his four King Arthur fantasies, which formed the basis for the musical *Camelot*.

## The Renaissance in Europe

Boccaccio, Giovanni, *The Decameron* (c. 1350). Lusty stories of adventure and love that are informed with a modern objectivity and realism.

Braudel, Fernand, *The Mediterranean* (1972). This masterpiece of historical scholarship brings to life, in all their complexity, the economics, politics, and personalities of the Mediterranean world in the second half of the sixteenth century at the very moment when it began to lose its primacy.

Cellini, Benevenuto, *Autobiography* (1730). Wonderfully frank adventures by the great Italian sculptor and "wicked superman." Goethe wrote that it brought the whole sixteenth century to life and that one learns more from him than from historians.

Cronin, Vincent, *The Florentine Renaissance* (1967). The whole story told with engaging informality. Continued in *The Flowering of the Renaissance* (1969).

Gadol, Joan, *Leon Battista Alberti: Universal Man of the Early Renaissance* (1970). Intellectual portrait of the great art theorist, humanist, architect, cartographer, and mathematician.

Ginsburg, Carl, *The Cheese and the Worms: The Cosmos of a 16th Century Miller* (1980). From the records of a heresy trial, the author has reconstructed the world view of a man who was burned as a heretic.

Hale, John R., *Renaissance Exploration* (1972). Brief, stimulating study of that great wave of new-world exploration. See Boies Penrose, *Travel and Discovery in the Renaissance, 1420–1620* (1952).

Hartt, Frederick, *History of Italian Renaissance Art: Painting, Sculpture and Architecture* (1969). Best overview of the subject, and one of the few to discuss all three art forms together. See Manfred Wundram, *Art of the Renaissance* (1972).

*The Horizon Book of the Renaissance* (1961). Extraordinary giant volume printed on heavy paper with a wealth of gorgeous illustrations and splendid historical essays.

Kleist, Heinrich Von, *Michael Kohlhaas* (1808). Outstanding novella set around sixteenth-century Brandenburg.

Lewis, Janet, *The Wife of Martin Guerre* (1941). This novel, based on a true story of circumstantial evidence, has been likened to a stately procession across a sixteenth-century tapestry of provincial France.

Mallett, Michael, *The Borgias: The Rise and Fall of a Renaissance Dynasty* (1977). The story of the remarkable Italian family influential in church, government, and the arts from the fourteenth to the sixteenth century. Maria Bellonsi's *The Life and Times of Lucrezia Borgia* (1939) is about one of its most fascinating members.

Merimee, Prosper, *Chronicles of Charles IX* (1829). Short novel focusing on the Massacre of St. Bartholomew that is laden with cool irony and incomparable scenes.

Montaigne, Michel de, *Essays* (1580–88). Moral insight and balanced skepticism in personal essays by the creator of the genre. Enduring masterpieces and an absorbing glimpse into one of the great minds of the Renaissance.

Origo, Iris, *The World of San Bernardino* (1963). Splendidly illustrated, beautifully made book about the most popular preacher of his day and the society in which he moved. See *The Merchant of Prato* (1957).

Rabelais, François, *Gargantua and Pantagruel* (1533–35). "All the richness of Renaissance Europe is preserved in his book. Learning, skepticism, earthy vitality, and narrative power immortalized the work of this friar turned doctor into writer" (Lawrence Clark Powell). A marvelous witty companion volume is Albert Jay Nock, *A Journey into Rabelais's France* (1934).

**Roeder, Ralph,** *The Man of the Renaissance* (1933). In heightened prose he tells the history of a remarkable era through the biographies of four famous Italians: Machiavelli, Savonarola, Castiglione, and Arentino. See *Catherine de Medici and the Lost Revolution* (1937).

**Schevill, Ferdinand,** *The Medici* (1949). Classic account of the great Florentine family. For an evocative novel about the subtle and sometimes ruthless world of the Medici see Arvin Upton, *Lorenzino* (1977).

**Shellabarger, Samuel,** *Captain from Castille* (1945). Outstanding example of the romantic costume novel, it is set in sixteenth-century Spain and Mexico during its conquest by Cortez. See *Prince of Foxes* (1947) and *The King's Cavalier* (1950).

**Timmermans, Felix,** *Droll Peter* (1930). Delightful novel about Peter Breughel, the sixteenth-century Flemish painter.

**Van Passen, Pierre,** *Crown of Fire: The Life and Times of Girolamo Savonarola* (1960). Stirring biography of the martyred fifteenth-century Florentine monk and fiery sermonizer. He figures prominently in George Eliot, *Romola* (1863).

## Tudor England

**Burgess, Anthony,** *Nothing Like the Sun* (1965). This sparkling tour de force, a fictional reconstruction of Shakespeare's love life, is "an Elizabethan novel, unsurpassed for idiosyncratic pith and flavor since the first part of Virginia Woolf's *Orlando*" (Stanley Kauffmann).

**Chapman, Hester,** *Two Tudor Portraits* (1975). In polished prose, she tells the story of two strange minor figures: Henry Howard, Earl of Surrey, and Lady Katherine Grey. See *The Last Tudor King: A Study of Edward VI* (1959); *Lady Jane Grey* (1963), a novel about the nine-day queen; *The Thistle and the Rose* (1971), about the sisters of Henry VIII; and *Ann Boleyn* (1974).

**Haydn, Hiram,** *The Portable Elizabethan Reader* (1946). Superb one-volume anthology of the great literary period.

**Jones, Gwyn,** *Garland of Bays* (1938). Rich, long novel based on the life of Robert Green, poet and playwright and contemporary of Shakespeare.

**Lacey, Robert,** *Sir Walter Ralegh* (1974). Highly dramatic, entertaining biography of an extraordinary man. See *The Life and Times of Henry VIII* (1974) and *Robert, Earl of Essex: An Elizabethan Icarus* (1971).

**Mattingly, Garret,** *The Armada* (1959). "A masterpiece of historical writing which retells a great story better than it has ever been told before, with more drama and color and literary fire" (Orville Prescott). See David Howarth, *The Voyage of the Armada: The Spanish Story* (1981). For a provocative imagining of our world had the Spanish Armada been victorious see Keith Roberts, *Pavane* (1968).

**Prescott, H. F. M.,** *The Man on a Donkey* (1952). In this fictional life of the Prioress of Marrick the author "has brought the crowded years to life as though she had lived in them herself" (Marchette Chute). She is also the author of the fine biography of Mary I, *Mary Tudor* (rev. 1953).

**Rowse, A. L.,** *The Elizabethan Renaissance* (1972). Everyday life under the long reign of Queen Bess. See *The Expansion of Elizabethan England* (1955) and *Elizabethans and America* (1959).

**Smith, Lacey Baldwin,** *The Elizabethan World* (1966). Fresh popular survey of the age. See *Elizabeth Tudor: Portrait of a Queen* (1975) and *Henry VIII: The Mask* *of Royalty* (1971), an admirable study of the king's old age.

**Unwin, Rayner,** *The Defeat of John Hawkins: A Biography of His Third Slaving Voyage* (1961). Crisp reconstruction of life aboard an Elizabethan ship on the Spanish Main. A true adventure with the immediacy of fiction.

**Urquhart, Sir Thomas,** *The Life and Death of the Admirable Crichton* (1652). A fantastic (and unreliable) biographer portrays the ill-fated Mirror of Perfection — the sixteenth-century Renaissance man from Scotland of legendary gifts, who died at 22.

**Williams, Neville,** *Henry VIII and His Court* (1971). Blend of eloquent narrative with superb illustrations which "brings alive that strange mixture of medieval barbarism and Renaissance sophistication that surrounded Henry VIII" (J. H. Plumb). See *The Sea Dogs: Privateers, Plunder and Piracy in the Elizabethan Age* (1975), *All the Queen's Men* (1972), and *The Cardinal and the Secretary* (1975), about Wolsey and Thomas Cromwell.

## Seventeenth Century in Europe

**Clark, George Norman,** *The Seventeenth Century* (1929). Graphic survey of the times, in lucent and pithy prose. See *War and Society in the Seventeenth Century* (1958).

**Lewis, Janet,** *The Trial of Soren Quist* (1947). An actual case of murder, in a sensitive retelling that evokes the period with a striking economy of detail rare in historical novels. See The *Ghost of Monsieur Scarron* (1959).

**Lewis, W. H.,** *The Splendid Century* (1953). First-rate stylish social history of life in the France of Louis XIV. See *Assault on Olympus: The Rise of the House of Granmont Between 1604–1678* (1957).

**Manzoni, Alessandro,** *The Betrothed* (1826). Peasants, brigands, plague, love,

religion; they are all here in this great panoramic romance, "the only Italian novel that can be compared with the great European novels of the 19th century" (V. S. Pritchett).

**Saint-Simon, Duc de,** *Memoirs* (1839). This record of court life under Louis XIV is almost compulsively readable, for "no writer of memoirs has ever approached him in vividness, originality, and irregular power" (George Saintsbury). The best abridgement is *Saint-Simon at Versailles* (1959), selected and translated by Lucy Norton. An elegant fictional portrait of Saint-Simon is Louis Auchincloss, *The Cat and the King* (1981).

**Sainte-Beauve, Charles A.,** *Portraits of the Seventeenth Century* (1836–39). Sensitive portraits of the great French personalities of the times by the distinguished critic.

**Sévigné, Marquise de,** *Letters* (1806). Classic letters of the sensitive, perceptive mistress of one of the finest salons of the age which "form a vivid record of a brilliant, educated, fastidious, proud, gay, brave, and sociable aristocracy, a monument of 'polite life' which is peculiar to France and scarcely likely to be repeated in our own times" (Richard Aldington).

**Singer, Isaac Bashevis,** *Satan in Goray* (1955). This novel about the fervor that grips a Polish hamlet in the wake of Sabbatai Zevi's claim to be the messiah, "beautifully written by one of the masters of Yiddish prose, and beautifully translated, is folk material transmuted into literature" (Meyer Levin).

**Steegmuller, Francis,** *The Grand Mademoiselle* (1955). She was the "granddaughter of Henry IV, niece of many crowned heads, 1st cousin of Louis XIV, 'Fille de France' in the fullness of the term, left voluminous if incomplete memoirs, of no commanding literary value. Out of that amorphous mass, Steegmuller has extracted a clear, swift-moving narrative" (Albert Guerard).

Thomas, Gwyn, *A Wolf at Dusk* (1959). The Welsh novelist's witty and elegant recreation of the decline and fall of Don Juan Tenorio, legendary Spanish gallant and swordsman.

## Seventeenth Century in England

Ashley, Maurice, *Life in Stuart England* (1964). Fine introduction to the social life of the seventeenth century. See *The Stuarts in Love* (1964) and *The Glorious Revolution of 1688* (1967). Another lively social history is Elizabeth Burton, *The Pageant of Stuart England* (1962).

Aubrey, John, *Brief Lives* (1813). Written by a seventeenth-century antiquarian, these gossipy sketches of notables of that and the preceding centuries have been plundered for their picturesque detail by later historians. See Anthony Powell, *John Aubrey and His Friends* (rev. 1963).

Bredvold, Louis I., *The Intellectual Milieu of John Dryden: Studies in Some Aspects of Seventeenth Century Thought* (1934). The life of the poet is the thread that ties together this interesting study of philosophical and religious thought after the Restoration.

Bridenbaugh, Carl, *Vexed and Troubled Englishmen, 1590–1642* (1968). Why did sixty thousand people leave England for America? Here is a portrait of the society that forced the emigration, a vivid picture of what it was like to live in England during the early seventeenth century "written as few American historians do, with clarity and grace" (J. H. Plumb).

Bryant, Arthur, *Restoration England* (1960). Skillful blend of vivid narrative, anecdotal history, and personal profiles by one of England's most literary historians. See *England of Charles II* (1934).

Bryher, *The Player's Boy* (1953). Novel set during the decline of Elizabethan glory into the darkness of James I's reign and "written with the intensity and sharpness of a dramatic poem" (Horace Gregory).

Evelyn, John, *Diary* (1818). These records of the life of a proper English gentleman are not as racy as his contemporary Pepys's, but have a special charm all their own. The one-volume abridgement by E. S. DeBeer (1960) is recommended. See John Bowle, *John Evelyn and His World: A Biography* (1981).

Grierson, H. J. C. and G. Bullough (eds.), *The Oxford Book of Seventeenth Century Verse* (1934). The standard anthology.

Hill, Christopher, *The Century of Revolution: 1603–1714* (rev. 1980). During this century a modern state began to take shape and England became the greatest power in the world. A classic by a master of Balliol who has written many books about the social implications of puritanism. See *Change and Continuity in Seventeenth Century England* (1975) and *The World Turned Upside Down: Radical Ideas During the English Revolution* (1972).

Macauley, Thomas Babington, *The History of England* (1855). Despite the comprehensive of the title, it begins in 1685 and ends twelve years later. "His energetic and persuasive style, his adroit manipulation of illustrative facts, and artful alternation between generalization and detail, combine to make this one of the most readable of extended histories" (David Daiches).

Osborne, Dorothy, *Letters to Sir William Temple* (1888). Delightful letters to her future husband, the statesman and author. Full of good sense, humor, and penetration. Temple's *Memoirs* (1691) also make fascinating reading. See Lord David Cecil, *Two Quiet Lives: Dorothy Osborne and Thomas Gray* (1948).

Pepys, Samuel, *Diary* (1825). This secret diary — probably the most famous in the world — is refreshingly candid and shows Pepys to be a keen, close observer of the world around him. There are several good one-volume abridgements. See Richard Ollard, *Pepys* (1974).

**Powys, Llewelyn (ed.),** *The Life and Times of Anthony Wood* (1961). Abridgement of Andrew Clark's biography of Wood that was published in the 1890s. It provides a life of the seemingly unpleasant antiquarian and a racy chronicle of his times, 1632–1695.

**Trease, Geoffrey,** *Silver Guard* (1948). Civil War novel for young readers in which a family defends its home against Cavalier attacks. Other good children's novels about the Roundhead-Cavalier battles are Rosemary Sutcliff, *Simon* (1953); Hester Burton, *Kate Rider* (1975); and Ronald Welch, *For the King* (1962).

**Trevelyan, G. M.,** *England Under the Stuarts* (1906). Its beguiling style has made this a classic. The best up-to-date history is Barry Coward, *The Stuart Age: A History of England 1603–1714* (1980).

**Waldstein, Baron,** *The Diary of Baron Waldstein: A Traveler in Elizabethan England* (1981). Waldstein spent the summer of 1600 as a tourist in England during which he kept a diary in Latin. This translation, annotated and illustrated, provides a splendid glimpse of the country at the close of the Elizabethan Age.

**Wedgwood, C. V.,** *A Coffin for King Charles: The Trial and Execution of Charles I* (1964). Eloquent account by the historian of whom J. H. Plumb said "her scholarship is comprehensive, her narrative is crisp, her style elegant and her insight into men and events profound." See *Truth and Opinion* (1960) and *Seventeenth Century English Literature* (1950).

## Eighteenth Century in Europe

**Berlin, Isaiah (ed.),** *The Age of Enlightenment* (1956). Selections, with commentary, from the writings of Berkeley, Locke, Hume, and other philosophers of the rational and humanistic age animated by the belief that science's achievements

could be translated into philosophical terms. For further exegesis see Peter Gay's award-winning *The Enlightenment: An Interpretation* (1966–69).

**Calvino, Italo,** *The Baron in the Trees* (1977). Strange fantasy-allegory of a twelve-year-old boy who climbs a tree and never returns to the ground. Perhaps a satire on the age of Voltaire; but certainly enthralling reading.

**Casanova, Giacomo,** *Memoirs* (1826–38). Much more than the famous love life of an extraordinary man, an encyclopedia of the manners and morals of the mid-eighteenth century as well "as the best-stocked menagerie of human beings that any one writer has ever packed into the enclosure of a single book" (Stefan Zweig). Willard R. Trask's National Book Award–winning translation (1967) is outstanding.

**Soehner, Halldor and Arno Schonberger,** *The Rococo Age* (1960). First-rate introduction to the art and civilization of the century.

**Wilson, Arthur M.,** *Diderot* (1972). National Book Award–winning biography of the French encyclopedist and man of letters. A long but always elegant and vivid portrait.

## Eighteenth Century in England

**Addison, Joseph and Sir Richard Steele,** *The Spectator* (1711–12). Graceful and witty series of essays which provide a splendid picture of London coffeehouse life under Queen Anne.

**Amory, Thomas,** *The Life of John Buncle* (1770). This eccentric novel mixes theological discussions and descriptions of beautiful young ladies with great gusto.

**Boswell, James,** *Boswell's London Journal 1763–4* (1950). Discovered in the 1920s, these wonderfully frank journals, full of uninhibted charm, provide an unparalleled picture of the young would-be man of letters on the make in Georgian London. For highlights from the first six journals see Mark Harris (ed.), *The Heart of Boswell* (1981).

**Chesterfield, Lord,** *Letters to His Son* (1774). Letters by the statesman to his illegitimate son, Philip Stanhope, full of affectionate, didactic, rather overworldly advice. Dr. Johnson wrote that "they teach the morals of a whore, and the manners of a dancing master." Elegant portrait of the eighteenth-century gentleman. See Samuel Shellabarger, *Lord Chesterfield and His World* (1951).

**Cibber, Colley,** *Apology for His Life* (1740). Memoirs brimming with the color of post-Restoration England by a leading actor of his day, later poet laureate.

**Falkner, J. Meade,** *Moonfleet* (1893). Enthralling tale of smugglers, hidden treasure, and the curse of the Black Mohunes, set in the 1750s when smuggling was rampant over all of the south coast of England. It "will have a permanent place among the minor *genre* pieces of our literature" (V. S. Pritchett).

**Fielding, Henry,** *Joseph Andrews* (1742). Hazlitt said of this entertaining novel: "I should be at a loss where to find in any authentic documents of the same period so satisfactory an account of the general state of society, and of moral, political, and religious feeling in the reign of George II as we meet with [here]." Pat Rogers's intimate biography, *Henry Fielding,* renders a lively picture of the times.

**Garfield, Leon,** *Drummer Boy* (1970). One of a series of outstanding historical novels for young readers that are set in eighteenth-century England. See *Devil in the Fog* (1966) and *Smith* (1967).

**Hibbert, Christopher,** *King Mob* (1958). Deftly told story of Lord George Gordon and the London riots of 1780 — the factual counterpart of Dickens's *Barnaby Rudge.* Other books on the eighteenth century by this engaging historical

popularizer are *Wolfe at Quebec* (1960) and *The Personal History of Samuel Johnson* (1972).

**Hickey, William,** *The Prodigal Rake* (1913–25). This Hogarthian autobiography of a fascinating man with a weakness for claret and ladies is "one of the most entertaining memoirs of the eighteenth century. It rivals in sheer lust for life Boswell's *London Journal*" (J. H. Plumb). The 1962 readers' edition edited by Peter Quennell is recommended.

**Kronenberger, Louis,** *Kings and Desperate Men: Life in the Eighteenth Century* (1942). Swiftly moving social chronicle of the age written in a witty, conversational style. See *Marlborough's Duchess* (1958) and *Eighteenth Century Miscellany* (1936).

**Lucas, F. L.,** *The Art of Living: Four Eighteenth Century Minds* (1959). Hume, Burke, Horace Walpole, and Benjamin Franklin are the subjects of these elegant essays.

**Marshall, Dorothy,** *English People in the Eighteenth Century* (1957). Profusely and tastefully illustrated introduction to the society of the times. See Derek Jarrett, *England in the Age of Hogarth* (1974) and M. Dorothy George, *London Life in the Eighteenth Century* (1925).

**Montagu, Lady Mary Wortley,** *Letters* (1771). The manners of one of the most colorful ages of English life are radiantly reflected in these letters of an amusing and intelligent bluestocking. See Robert Hasbland, *Life of Lady Mary Wortey Montagu* (1957).

**Plumb, J. H.,** *Georgian Delights* (1980). Delightful pieces by the leading modern authority on eighteenth-century England. See *Chatham* (1953), *Men and Centuries* (1963), and *The First Four Georges* (1975).

**Quennell, Peter,** *Caroline of England* (1939). He uses the life of the consort of George II as an occasion for "an Augustan portrait" of such early Hanoverians as

Pope, Swift, and Walpole. "Rarely does a biography proceed with such perfect ease, and the reader is kept perpetually entertained with a series of vivid pictures" (A. J. P. Taylor). See *Four Portraits: Studies of the Eigtheenth Century* (1965).

**Saintsbury, George,** *The Peace of the Augustans: Survey of 18th Century Literature as a Place of Rest and Refreshment* (1916). A study by the great scholar and critic and one of the best English writers of his time that is marked by his "easy handling of biography and history, his expert analysis of the technique of writing, his unexpected and witty allusions, his warm and luminous glow and his inexhaustible curiosity" (Edmund Wilson).

**Sheridan, Richard Brinsley,** *The Rivals* (1775). Brilliant, polished comedy with its delightfully complicated plot and the memorable Mrs. Malaprop satirically reflect the manners of George III's England. See *The School for Scandal* (1777).

**Thackeray, William Makepeace,** *The History of Henry Esmond* (1852). The Victorian novelist's attempt at a historical novel carefully reproduces the life, speech, and manners of society during the reign of Queen Anne.

**Walpole, Horace,** *Correspondence* (1937–80). These zestful, humor-filled letters, strangely by a man described by one contemporary as "affected, frivolous, fanatical, and over-fastidious," survive as a real contribution to literature and have made Walpole the "prince of letter writers."

**Woodforde, James,** *The Diary of a Country Parson, 1758–1803* (1924). The humorous, kindly curate kept a diary for forty-five years. It is an enchanting illumination of village life in Oxford, Somerset, and Norfolk during the eighteenth century.

## Discovery of America

**Davies, Nigel,** *Voyagers to the New World* (1979). Lucid account of "trans-oceanic contacts between the Old World and the New before Columbus," including the most current theories.

**Day, A. Grove,** *Coronado's Quest* (1940). First-rate popular account of the Spanish explorer's "discovery" of the southwestern states in pursuit of his dream of gold.

**DeVoto, Bernard,** *The Course of Empire* (1952). History of the exploration of North America during the 300 years ending in 1805; hailed at its publication as "the best written book about the West since Parkman" (Henry Steele Commager). Winner of National Book Award.

**Morison, Samuel Eliot,** *The Great Explorers: The European Discovery of America* (1978). One-volume abridgement of the scholar-sailor's fine two-volume work covering the years 500 to 1616. His own seamanship gives a practical cast to the writing.

**Severin, Timothy,** *Explorers of the Mississippi* (1967). DeSoto and La Salle are but two of the explorers treated in this vivid history of 300 years of discovery.

## Colonial America

**Alberts, Robert C.,** *The Most Extraordinary Adventures of Major Robert Stobo* (1965). Story of a spy for Washington behind French lines, who was captured and made a dramatic escape. "Combines a fascinating style with a scrupulous regard for fact and forms an exciting adventure story as well as a revealing vantage point from which to survey the French and Indian War and its times" (J. T. Flexner).

*The American Heritage History of the Thirteen Colonies* (1967). Lavishly illustrated large-format history with text by outstanding scholars.

**Breen, T. H.,** *Puritans and Adventurers: Change and Persistence in Early America* (1981). Engaging essays about the many ways in which the English colonists arranged themselves socially.

**Bridenbaugh, Carl,** *Jamestown 1544–1699* (1980). Brief, comprehensive, and vivid account of the earliest permanent English settlement in the New World. See *Early Americans* (1981). *Cities in the Wilderness: The First Century of Urban Life in America, 1625–1742* (1938), and *The Colonial Craftsman* (1950).

**Crevecoeur, J. Hector St. John de,** *Letters from an American Farmer* (1782). Series of essays by the French settler in the colony of New York about the customs and manners of the time. See *Sketches of Eighteenth Century America* (1925) and *Crevecoeur's Eighteenth-Century Travels in Pennsylvania and New York* (1961).

**Forbes, Esther,** *Paul Revere and the World He Lived In* (1942). Nonfictional picture of colonial Boston by a historical novelist which "takes at once a high and lasting place in American literature" (Carl Van Doren) and won a Pulitzer Prize. *Paradise* (1937) is a long, rich novel about seventeenth-century Massachusetts.

**Gebler, Ernest,** *The Plymouth Adventure* (1950). Chronicle novel of the voyage of the *Mayflower* in 1620.

**Gordon, Caroline,** *Green Centuries* (1941). The southern frontier is the setting for this "distinguished, vivid, and continuously readable novel which lights up an essential part of the American past" (Stephen Vincent Benét).

**Morison, Samuel Eliot,** *Builders of the Bay Colony* (rev. 1958). Sympathetic portrait of the early English settlement rendered in a charming conversational style. For a fictional depiction, see Anya Seton, *The Winthrop Woman* (1958).

**Roberts, Kenneth,** *Northwest Passage* (1937). Gripping, sometimes melodramatic narrative about Captain Robert Rogers and his Rangers. "The hunger and desire of the nation just about to break westward into the untrodden lands . . . are [here] as they have not been in our fiction before" (Bernard De Voto).

**Rowse, A. L.** *Elizabethans and Americans* (1959). Entertaining, witty view of the age that paved the way for the settlement of British America by a scholar who "has the Elizabethan sense of wonder and adventure, and the Elizabethan ability to communicate this sense in racy and stirring language" (Henry Steele Commager).

**Sewall, Samuel,** *Diary* (1878–82). Written between 1674 and 1729, it is an engrossing account of the life of Boston Puritans by the American Pepys.

**Smith, Bradford,** *Captain John Smith, His Life and Legend* (1953). Exciting biography of the English explorer and his adventures in Jamestown. See *Bradford of Plymouth* (1951).

**Starkey, Marion L.** *The Devil in Massachusetts: A Modern Inquiry into the Salem Witch Trials* (1949). "How this terrible hysteria swelled and in less than a year was dead Miss Starkey tells with a passion and veracity that will hold any reader spellbound" (Esther Forbes). See Ann Petry, *Tituba of Salem Village* (1965) and Arthur Miller, *The Crucible* (1953).

**Wertenbaker, Thomas J.,** *The Golden Age of Colonial Culture* (1949). Gracefully written brief survey of the arts in eighteenth-century America by distinguished scholar of the period. See *Torchbearer of the Revolution: The Story of Bacon's Rebellion* (1940).

**Wright, Louis B.,** *The Cultural Life of the American Colonies, 1607–1763* (1957). To all his books the author brings a lucid, attractive literary style and the rich background of a man who has devoted years of study to colonial history. See *The Dream of Prosperity in Colonial America* (1965), *The Atlantic Frontier* (1948), and *Culture on the Moving Frontier* (1955).

## American Independence

**Bowen, Catherine Drinker,** *Miracle at Philadelphia: The Story of the Constitu-*

tional Convention, May to September 1787 (1966). In this day-by-day account "she has brought to the retelling both imagination and art, and the result is the most readable of all accounts of the Philadelphia Convention" (Henry Steele Commager). See *John Adams and the American Revolution* (1950) and *The Most Dangerous Man in America: Scenes From the Life of Benjamin Franklin* (1974).

**Fehrenbach, T. R.,** *Greatness to Spare: The Heroic Sacrifice of the Men Who Signed the Declaration of Independence* (1968). Biographies of the forty-two signers.

**Malone, Dumas,** *The Story of the Declaration of Independence* (1954). Pictorial history of the great document, the era, and the signers with an illuminating text and hundreds of illustrations selected by the Library of Congress.

**Van Doren, Carl,** *The Great Rehearsal* (1948). In the author's story of the making and ratifying of the constitution, "told from the records themselves, with an effectiveness which no one has matched in comparable space, [he] has made both the action and the issues come alive" (Dumas Malone).

**Wills, Garry,** *Inventing America: Jefferson's Declaration of Independence* (1978). Historical and intellectual history which attempts to un-Locke the mysteries of the Declaration's genesis. Winner of National Book Critics Circle Award. See *Explaining America: The Federalist* (1981).

## Nineteenth Century in Europe

**Barzun, Jacques,** *Berlioz and the Romantic Century* (rev. 1969). Of this prodigious and fascinating book, W. H. Auden remarked that "in order to understand the 19th century, it is essential to understand Berlioz, and in order to understand Berlioz, it is essential to read Prof. Barzun."

**Chateaubriand, Francois René de,** *Memoirs* (1848–50). "It is a masterpiece not only as an example of the genre but also as an expression of the 19th-century spiritual quest and its permanent malaise, the *mal du siecle*" (Neal Oxenhandler). See André Maurois, *Chateaubriand: Poet, Statesman, Lover* (1940).

**Hobsawn, E. J.,** *The Age of Revolution, 1789–1848* (1962). With its companion volume, *The Age of Capitalism, 1848–1875* (1975), a searching history of revolutionary fervor and the flowering of free enterprise.

**Schultze, Jurgen,** *Art of Nineteenth Century Europe* (1972). Well-illustrated, lucid survey.

**Taylor, A. J. P.,** *Bismarck* (1955). The topography of the life of the Iron Chancellor. Brief, lively, epigrammatic. See *The Habsburg Monarchy, 1809–1918* (rev. 1948).

## Nineteenth Century in England

**Auden, W. H. and Norman Holmes Pearson,** *Romantic Poets* (1957). Marvelous anthology, with trenchant introductory essay. Part of the Poets of the English Language series. See *Victorian and Edwardian Poets* (1957).

**Austen, Jane,** *Emma* (1816). Set in a world the author made uniquely her own — the world of country gentry in Regency England — the novel centers upon a supremely self-assured young lady, determined to arrange her life and the lives of all around her into a pattern dictated by her romantic fancy. A perfect novel. David Cecil, *A Portrait of Jane Austen* (1979) conveys an admirable feeling for the life of the period.

**Briggs, Asa,** *Victorian People* (1955). Lively trip through society at the high noon of the Victorian reign. See *Victorian Cities* (1965) and *The Age of Improvement* (1959).

**Bryant, Arthur,** *The Years of Endurance* (1942). The first of the noted historian's trilogy about England during the Napoleonic Wars, 1793–1822, written in the style of the Leisurely Gentleman school of Gibbon and Trevelyan. The other volumes are *The Years of Victoria* (1945) and *The Age of Elegance* (1951).

**Burton, Hester,** *Time of Trial* (1964). Exciting novel for young adults about a bookseller's family during the early part of the century. See *Castor's Army* (1963).

**Cameron, Julia Margaret,** *Victorian Photographs of Famous Men and Fair Women* (rev. 1973). Collection of noble photographs by the pioneer camera artist; introduced by Virginia Woolf. A "masterpiece of its kind" (Hilton Kramer).

**Cole, Hubert,** *Beau Brummell* (1977). Dandy life of the great fop and a delightful view of life and manners during the Regency. Other dandy portraits are T. A. J. Burnett, *The Rise and Fall of a Regency Dandy: The Life and Times of Srope Berdmore Davies* (1982); Willard Connely, *Count D'Orsay: The Dandy of Dandies* (1952); *The Reminiscences and Recollections of Captain Gronow* (1964); and E. R. P. Vincent, *Ugo Foscolo: An Italian in Regency England* (1953). See Ellen Moers, *The Dandy* (1960).

**Dangerfield, George,** *Victoria's Heir: The Education of a Prince* (1941). Princely biography of Albert, Queen Victoria's consort, pungently portrays midcentury politics and history.

**Fowles, John,** *The French Lieutenant's Woman* (1969). Rich, gifted novel, which in the story of one triangle of lovers pictures an entire generation trapped in its own time.

**Gaunt, William,** *The Pre-Raphaelite Tragedy* (1975). Lively look at a fascinating group of painters. For a memoir of its personalities see Violet Hunt, *The Wife of Rossetti* (1932). For illustrations see Christopher Wood, *The Pre-Raphaelites* (1981).

**Greville, Charles,** *The Great World* (1963). The Greville Memoirs, a great gossipy eight-volume portrait of the years 1814–1860 by a man who seemed to know everyone, skillfully edited by Louis Kronenberger into one inviting volume. Greville's vignettes of Lord Melbourne and the Duke of Wellington are memorable.

**Hibbert, Christopher,** *The Horizon Book of Daily Life in Victorian England* (1975). Nicely done illustrated survey of social manners of the day.

**Hudson, Derek,** *Munby, Man of Two Worlds: The Life and Diaries of Arthur J. Munby, 1828–1910* (1972). "An authentic life story which is not only deeply moving in human terms, but which provides the psychologist with a classic story of sublimated sexual perversion, and the sociologist with a horribly vivid picture of life below stairs in a Victorian household" (Richard Crossman).

**Johnson, Diane,** *The True History of the First Mrs. Meredith and Other Lesser Lives* (1972). Fine, sympathetic biography of the daughter of Thomas Love Peacock, wife of George Meredith, that highlights the difficulties for an intelligent woman in Victorian England.

**LeGallienne, Richard,** *The Romantic 90's* (1925). Absorbing memoirs, rich in insight and incident, of the literary circle of the decade — Meredith, Swinburne, Tennyson, Wilde, and their cohort.

**Peacock, Thomas Love,** *Nightmare Abbey* (1818). The most entertaining of his novels, almost devoid of plot, that levels shots at almost every passing craze and idea of his day, and especially at such romantic figures as Coleridge, Byron, and Shelley.

**Praed, W. M.** *Selected Poetry* (1954). The rhyming banter of the poet who died at age thirty-six in 1839 satirizes with wit and elegance both contemporary politics and well-bred society.

**Priestley, J. B.,** *The Prince of Pleasure and His Regency 1811–20* (1969). Felicitous account of the decade preceding the Prince Regent's coronation as George IV by one of the most charming of writers in a splendidly illustrated volume. See *Victoria's Heyday* (1972).

**Raverat, Gwendolyn,** *Period Piece: A Cambridge Childhood* (1952). Sparkling reminiscences by an English artist, a granddaughter of Charles Darwin, that evoke Victorian manners with drollness and charm.

**Strachey, Lytton,** *Eminent Victorians* (1918). Brilliantly compresses four important lives — those of Cardinal Manning, Florence Nightingale, the great educator Thomas Arnold, and General "Chinese" Gordon — into inconoclastic sketches that crackle with epigram and sardonic wit. This book transformed the art of biography.

**Thackeray, William Makepeace,** *Vanity Fair* (1847–48). This "novel without a hero" is a Victorian masterpiece, with unforgettable characters and scenes, and is a telling social satire of early nineteenth-century British society.

**Woodham-Smith, Cecil,** *Florence Nightingale, 1820–1900* (1951). This gracefully written biography is a "first-class contribution to social history for it gives an extraordinary insight into the strengths and weaknesses of the British and their Empire in the 19th century" (Anthony West). See her biography, *Queen Victoria: Her Life and Times* (1972).

**Young, George M.,** *Victorian England: A Portrait of an Age* (rev. 1964). Detailed study; the "standard work, and a model of how such things should be done" (David Daiches). He edited *Early Victorian England* (1934).

## American Expansion

*The American Heritage History of the Making of the Nation* (1968). Beautifully illustrated account of the years between the inaugurations of Washington and Lincoln. See *The American Heritage Book of the Pioneer Spirit* (1959).

**Bartlett, Richard,** *New Country* (1974). Social history of the American frontier from 1776 to 1890. See Alexander B. Adams, *The Disputed Lands: A History of the American West* (1981).

**Bemis, Samuel Flagg,** *John Quincy Adams and the Union* (1956). This portrait of the sixth president during the years 1824–28 "in the depths of its insights and the restrained passions of its presentation is one of the great biographical studies of our time" (George Dangerfield). Preceded by the Pulitzer Prize–winning *John Quincy Adams and the Foundation of American Foreign Policy* (1951).

**Berger, Thomas,** *Little Big Man* (1964). Adventure novel, rich in comedy and tragedy, in the form of the memoir of Jack Crabb, 111-year-old frontiersman. "Berger took a familiar literary mode, the tall tale, and freshened it with a freshet of imagination" (Stanley Kauffmann).

**Billington, Ray A.,** *Westward Expansion* (rev. 1974). History based on Frederick Jackson Turner's epoch-making theory of the significance of the frontier in shaping American genius. See *Land of Savagery, Land of Promise: The European Image of the American Frontier in the Nineteenth Century* (1981).

**Crockett, David,** *Autobiography* (1834). The great American folk hero, bear hunter, and "coonskin Congressman" wrote these memoirs of life on the frontier a few years before he died heroically at the Alamo.

**Dangerfield, George,** *The Era of Good Feeling* (1952). America during Monroe's terms, 1817–25 — the transition from Jeffersonian to Jacksonian democracy. A dramatic and delightful history. Winner of the Pulitzer and Bancroft Prizes.

**DeVoto, Bernard,** *Year of Decision: 1846* (1943). Monumental, rich mosaic of the settling of the far west capsulized dramatically into one year. See *Across the Wide Missouri* (1947), awarded the Pulitzer Prize for History.

**Goetzmann, William H.,** *Exploration and Empire* (1966). Pulitzer Prize–winning account of "the explorer and the scientist in the winning of the American West." Lucid and refreshingly unpretentious.

**Guthrie, A. B., Jr.,** *The Way West* (1949). The covered-wagon days of the 1840s are the subject of this Pulitzer Prize–winning novel, which weds historical fact with fine characterization.

**Hassrick, Peter,** *The Way West* (1977). Beautiful reproductions of the best of the frontier painters: Remington, Russell, et al.

**Havighurst, Walter,** *Wilderness for Sale: The Story of the First Western Land Rush* (1956). Colorful story of the settlement of the old Northwest (around Ohio). See *Land of Promise: The Story of the Northwest Territory* (1947).

**Jahoda, Gloria,** *The Trail of Tears* (1975). Vivid, often outraged and sarcastic account of the forced march of thousands of Indians of the eastern U.S. to the western Indian territory in 1830.

**Johnson, Dorothy M.,** *Indian Country* (1953). Life in the country of the Plains Indians during the early days of white settlers, mostly told from woman's point of view. "The world's best Western stories including the magnificent 'A Man Called Horse'" (Scott Meredith). See *Hanging Tree* (1957).

**Johnson, Gerald White,** *America's Silver Age* (1939). Focuses on Henry Clay, Daniel Webster, and John C. Calhoun during the first half of the century. "It gets beneath the surface of events. It is full of ideas. It is alive and interesting. It is written with force and pungency" (Allan Nevins).

**Kirkland, Caroline,** *New Home; or Life in the Clearing* (1839). These amusing sketches of life on a frontier settlement in Michigan written by a New York City–born minister's wife "remain one of the most vivid and intimate records of the new faraway communities" (Daniel Boorstin).

**Lewis, Meriwether and William Clark,** *Journals of the Lewis and Clark Expedition* (1953). One-volume abridgement by Bernard De Voto of the chronicle of the expedition's twenty-eight months in wilderness where no white men had ever set foot. It remains captivating.

**Mahood, Ruth I.,** *Photographer of the Southwest, Adam Clark Vroman, 1856–1916* (1961). Handsome volume of photographs of life on the frontier by pioneer camera artist. See Freeman Tilden, *Following the Frontier with F. Jay Haynes, Pioneer Photographer of the Old West* (1964) and Joel Snyder, *American Frontiers: The Photographs of Timothy H. O'Sullivan, 1867–74* (1981).

**Nevins, Allan,** *The Ordeal of the Union* (1947–60). Monumental, almost Tolstoyan, eight-volume narrative history of the years 1847–1865 — from the Mexican War through the death of Lincoln — told in crisp style. See *The Ordeal of the Union: Selected Chapters* (1973).

**Nye, Russell Blaine,** *The Cultural Life of the New Nation, 1776–1830* (1961). Upbeat survey, well written and informative, of the development of key ideas and institutions during the first half-century of nationhood. Continued in *Society and Culture in America, 1830–1860* (1974).

**Parkman, Francis,** *The Oregon Trail* (1847). Classic memoir of the great historian's trek to Wyoming, during which he lived with a tribe of Sioux Indians.

**Phillips, David R.,** *The West: An American Experience* (1973). Collection of old glass wet-plate negatives taken by pioneer photographers on the frontier.

**Roberts, Elizabeth Madox,** *The Great Meadow* (1930). Outstanding historical novel about the settling of Kentucky by emigrants from Virginia.

**Royce, Sarah Eleanor,** *Frontier Lady: Recollections of the Gold Rush and Early California* (1932). Graphic, moving reminiscences, with a classic quality about them, by the mother of the eminent Harvard philosopher.

**Schlesinger, Arthur M., Jr.,** *The Age of Jackson* (1945). Pulitzer Prize–winning history of one of the most interesting periods of our national life — "crisply written, full of pungent comment and quotation, and abounding in vivid thumbnail sketches of important figures . . . [it is] a remarkable piece of analytical history" (Allan Nevins).

**Stegner, Wallace E.,** *The Gathering of Zion: The Story of the Mormon Trail* (1964). Skillful interweaving of diarists' accounts with historical data produces a dramatic account of the Mormon migration westward between the mob attack at Nauvoo in 1845 and the completion of the Union Pacific Railroad in 1869.

**Straight, Michael,** *Carrington: A Novel of the West* (1960). Tale of the Fetterman massacre in Wyoming in 1866 and the Army officer held responsible. "Restores to the West its true dimensions and the historic men. It's lasting fiction which will be read for years to come" (Walter Havighurst).

**Time-Life Editors,** *The Old West* (1973–79). Spirited pictorial presentation in twenty-six volumes. A dazzling series, redolent of leather and the open range.

**Turner, Frederick,** *Beyond Geography: The Western Spirit Against the Wilderness* (1980). Imaginative and fresh view of what the author perceives as the conflict between the myths of the Indian and a vanishing European culture. Beautifully written, more poetry than history.

**Van Every, Dale,** *American Frontier series* (1962–64). Dramatic narrative by a historian-novelist beginning with *Forth to*

*the Wilderness* (1962), followed by *A Company of Heroes* (1963), *Ark of Empire* (1963), and *The Final Challenge* (1964).

**Vidal, Gore,** *Burr* (1973). The early days of the republic are brought to life in this fictional portrait of Aaron Burr — his confrontations with Jefferson, his duel with Hamilton, his trial for treason. See *1876* (1976).

## Reconstruction and Industrial America

**Brodie, Fawn M.,** *Thaddeus Stevens: Scourge of the South* (1960). Vivid portrait of the demagogic congressman who was the chief architect of Reconstruction and the leader in the impeachment of Andrew Johnson. See Ralph Korngold, *Thaddeus Stevens* (1955).

**Handlin, Oscar,** *The Uprooted* (rev. 1973). Epic story of the atomization and alienation of the urban immigrant. A Pulitzer Prize–winning classic by the foremost authority on American immigration history. See *The Americans* (1963).

**Josephson, Matthew,** *The Robber Barons: The Great American Capitalists, 1861–1901* (1934). Gould, Fisk, Hill, and other captains of industry in a muckraking study which "still remains a standard popular work, novelistically provocative if not invariably just" (Justin Kaplan).

**Leech, Margaret,** *In the Days of McKinley* (1960). Four decades — 1861–1901 — seen by a Pulitzer Prize–winning historian.

**McCullough, David,** *The Great Bridge* (1972). Clear, dramatic history of the engineering of the Brooklyn Bridge that is "an engrossing piece of social history, a latitudinal view of the politics and business practices and daily life of the two or three decades after the ending of the Civil War" (Justin Kaplan).

**Maddow, Ben,** *A Sunday Between Wars: The Course of American Life from 1865–*

*1917* (1979). History in letters, diaries, and unpublished memoirs of anonymous people — housewives, union organizers, Indians — the often unheard, often eloquent voices.

**Morgan, H. Wayne,** *From Hayes to McKinley* (1969). Richly painted picture of the Gilded Age — between the Civil War and Progressivism (1877–96). See *The Gilded Age* (rev. 1970).

**Rawls, Walton (ed.),** *The Great Book of Currier & Ives' America* (1979). Huge (15 inches high and almost a foot in width) collection of high-quality reproductions of prints by America's best-loved printmakers. Beautifully reflects nineteenth-century living. As a corrective to this rosy picture see Otto L. Bettmann, *The Good Old Days — They Were Terrible* (1974).

**Schurz, Carl,** *The Reminiscences of Carl Schurz* (1961). One-volume abridgement of a three-volume memoir, published 1907–08, by a German emigrant who became a Civil War general, U.S. ambassador, senator, and cabinet member. His classically pure prose gives an unsurpassed picture of political and cultural life in America in the 1850s and 1860s.

**Twain, Mark,** *The Adventures of Huckleberry Finn* (1885). Perhaps the greatest American novel, a "hymn to the strange, puzzled, but still beautiful youth of our nation" (Clifton Fadiman).

**Wallace, Anthony F. C.,** *Rockdale: The Growth of an American Village in the Early Industrial Revolution* (1979). Brilliant, fluid epic of one mill town near Philadelphia, which serves as a microcosm of the age.

## The Twentieth Century

**Berlin, Isaiah,** *Personal Impressions* (1980). A distinguished British scholar shares his impressions of important figures whom he knew personally — Churchill and FDR, among others.

**Cary, Joyce,** *A Fearful Joy* (1949). In chronicling the life of Tabitha Baskett this warm, humorous novel presents "a panorama of English culture and history for a fifty-year period beginning with the *fin de siècle* 1890s and going through every *ism* and trend almost to midcentury" (Martin S. Day). A modern-day *Moll Flanders.*

**Drucker, Peter F.,** *Adventures of a Bystander* (1979). Provocative and amusing recollections of a man who knew many of the shapers of modern history, from Freud to Luce, and his intelligent opinions of them and the times.

**Eisenstadt, Alfred,** *Witness to Our Times* (rev. 1968). The finest work over the past four decades by the man Luce called "the father of photojournalism." He captures the makers and events of contemporary history.

**Kennan, George,** *Memoirs* (1967–72). Pulitzer Prize–winning intellectual biography that covers the years 1925–63. "May well be not only a most excellent memoir but the single most valuable political book written by an American in the twentieth century — because of its instructiveness" (John Lukacs). Another memoir by a U.S. diplomat is Charles E. Bohlen's *Witness to History, 1929–1969* (1973).

**Koestler, Arthur,** *Arrow in the Blue: An Autobiography* (1952). Remarkable mix of self-analysis, political examination, and lively chronicling that, with its sequel, *The Invisible Writing* (1954) is "one of the great 20th-century autobiographies. . . . There is little of this lousy century that he didn't experience, from a Berlin Communist cell group that included Wilhelm Reich to death row behind the Franco lines in civil-war Spain" (John Leonard).

**Lippmann, Walter,** *Public Persons* (1976). Selection of profiles of personalities of his times (1910–67) by the political journalist who "had the odd habit of thinking before he wrote, rather than letting his pen run wild all over the page. That is why this is a book of such carefully polished gems" (James Reston). See Ronald Steel, *Walter*

*Lippmann and the American Century* (1980).

**Nicolson, Harold,** *Diaries and Letters, 1930–1964* (1981). One-volume edition, condensed by Stanley Olson, of urbane insights into life during the middle decades of the century.

**Wilson, Edmund,** *Letters on Literature and Politics, 1912–72* (1977). Collection of letters by the preeminent literary critic of mid-twentieth-century America, it is "for anyone interested in literature or the literary life in America these past sixty years, . . . simply a treasure, a feast" (Irving Howe).

**Woolf, Leonard,** *Autobiography* (1960–69). Hailed as "one of the great intellectual autobiographies of our century" (Leon Edel), these memoirs of the English political writer and husband of Virginia Woolf were "written as a valediction to a civilization determined on suicide" (V. S. Pritchett).

## Edwardian England

**Dangerfield, George,** *The Strange Death of Liberal England* (1935). Classic account of the Edwardian era by a Pulitzer Prize–winning historian who writes lucid prose.

**Forster, E. M.,** *Howards End* (1910). Forster stated that the novel is a "hunt for a home." It is a key book of the Edwardian period for "he (pretty well alone) had his eye on the spiritual inadequacy and mental lethargy of a period which was stuffed with received ideas" (V. S. Pritchett).

**Goodall, John S.,** *An Edwardian Summer* (1976). One of a series of delightful post-card-size picture-books, by a contemporary English artist, of delicate watercolors filled with period detail and no words. See *An Edwardian Holiday* (1980) and *Edwardian Entertainments* (1982).

**Hibbert, Christopher,** *The Royal Victorians: King Edward VII, His Family and Friends* (1976). The life and times of the king who gave his name to an era depicted "with gentle irony and impressive understanding. His book is unremittingly interesting" (Paul Fussell). See Gordon Brook-Shepherd, *Uncle of Europe: The Social and Diplomatic Life of Edward VII* (1976).

**Jenkins, Roy,** *Asquith: Portrait of a Man and an Era* (1965). The story of the prime minister by a contemporary politician. "As the inside story of British politics between 1906 and the end of 1916, this book is a masterpiece" (D. W. Brogan).

**Morrell, Lady Ottoline,** *Memoirs of Lady Ottoline Morrell: A Study in Friendship, 1873–1915* (1964). From the diaries of one of the great hostesses of this century. "No one has conveyed more clearly, in terms of a group of artists and intellectuals, the inner turmoil of that time . . . a significant and valuable record of an era still close to us, and of one of its remarkable personalities" (Leon Edel). See *Ottoline at Garsington: Memoirs of Lady Ottoline Morrell, 1915–1918* (1975).

**Nowell-Smith, Simon (ed.),** *Edwardian England, 1901–1914* (1964). Superb collection of pieces by such experts as John Betjeman, John Russell, and Edmund Blunden that covers all aspects of the period. For a lively survey in pictures and text see J. B. Priestley, *The Edwardians* (1970).

## Pre–World War I

**Camusso, Lorenzo (ed.),** *La Belle Epoque: 1900–1914* (1978). Fifteen euphoric years of European history in photographs.

**Crankshaw, Edward,** *The Fall of the House of Habsburg, 1898–1918* (rev. 1976). The last days of the Austro-Hungarian Empire, viewed from Vienna.

**Doctorow, E. L.,** *Ragtime* (1975). Original, imaginative novel set in America at the beginning of the century. Its characters: three remarkable families whose lives become entwined with such figures as Henry Ford, Emma Goldman, Harry Houdini, J. P. Morgan, and Emiliano Zapata. Winner of the National Book Critics Circle Award.

**Lord, Walter,** *The Good Years: From 1900 to the First World War* (1960). An amusing panorama of the times presented with gusto and ironic nostalgia.

**Tuchman, Barbara W.,** *The Proud Tower: A Portrait of the World Before the War 1890–1914* (1966). The Pulitzer Prize–winning historian "paints the scene for us with a masterly brush: a scene glittering and brilliant, sumptuous and outrageous" (Henry Steele Commager).

## Between the Wars

**Ford, Ford Madox,** *Parade's End* (1924–28). Monumental novel divided into four books that celebrates the end of an era, the destruction of the comfortable, predictable society that vanished during World War I.

**Graves, Robert and Alan Hodge,** *The Long Week-end: A Social History of Great Britain 1918–1939* (1940). Breathless, witty survey of the interwar period not only includes every imaginable surface aspect of the era, from current plays being seen in London to the latest dance fads imported from America, but also the influences at work in politics, science, and the church.

**Hemingway, Ernest,** *The Sun Also Rises* (1926). The novelist's masterpiece about "the lost generation" wherein "the post-war disillusionment and the post-war liberation are united in the physical enjoyment of living and the pains of love" (Cyril Connolly).

**Mencken, H. L.,** *A Carnival of Buncombe* (1956). Superb selection of articles on politics, 1920–36, and "just about as refreshing political writing as this country has ever known. It has the peculiar timelessness of all genuinely great clowning" (Eric F. Goldman).

**Nicolson, Harold,** *Some People* (1927). Stories about a French snob, a Ronald Firbank esthete, a phony expert on foreign affairs, an English lord and his valet — types that the author has known, who are "as funny and as well observed as anything in Max Beerbohm or Evelyn Waugh" (Edmund Wilson).

**Salomon, Erich,** *Portrait of an Age* (1967). The faces of statesmen, politicians, and social and cultural leaders of 1928–43 captured by the German Father of the Candid Camera.

**Smith, Gene,** *When the Cheering Stopped: The Last Years of Woodrow Wilson* (1964). The drama of Wilson's last days is one of the urgent stories of modern history and Smith "has written it with a verve that holds our interest and a feeling that commands our sympathy" (Allan Nevins).

**Taylor, A. J. P.,** *English History, 1914–1945* (1965). Lively narrative by a first-rate historian. See *The Origins of the Second World War* (1962) and *From Saravejo to Potsdam* (1966).

**Waugh, Evelyn,** *A Handful of Dust* (1934). Scathing novel of the well-mannered death struggles of the upper classes — an irrepressibly amusing picture of society politely blowing its own brains out with a defiant smile. In *Vile Bodies* (1930), he satirically dissects Mayfair of the twenties, when the Bright Young Things exercised their inventive minds at a madcap pace.

**Wheeler-Bennett, John,** *Knaves, Fools and Heroes in Europe Between the Wars* (1975). An English gentleman-scholar, intimate with those who made history, takes an urbane, stylish view of the times. See *Friends, Enemies and Sovereigns* (1977). With Lord Longford he edited *The History Makers: Leaders and Statesmen of the Twentieth Century* (1973).

## The Depression

**Algren, Nelson,** *Somebody in Boots* (1935). In his first novel, the Chicago realist explores relentlessly the social reality of the hobo world of the 1930s.

**Baigell, Matthew,** *The American Scene* (1974). Large-format view of the Great Depression through the eyes of such painters as Thomas Hart Benton, Grant Wood, and Ben Shahn.

**Caldwell, Erskine and Margaret Bourke-White,** *You Have Seen Their Faces* (1937). Classic text-picture book wherein a great writer and a great photographer act as one.

**Cantwell, Robert,** *The Land of Plenty* (1934). A strike by Pacific Northwest lumber mill workers as a microcosm of Depression America; it is "still a powerful and edifying work" (Harvey Swados).

**Conroy, Jack,** *The Disinherited* (1933). The story of the making of a young American revolutionary and an ode to the parents who sacrificed so that he could go to school. A moving proletarian novel.

**Kromer, Tom,** *Waiting for Nothing* (1935), Honest, unvarnished novel written on scraps of paper as its author "bummed across the country in boxcars and afoot, it is a . . . cry from the lower depths" (Harvey Swados).

**Stryker, Emerson and Nancy Wood,** *In This Proud Land: America 1935–43 as Seen in the FSA Photographs* (1975). Beautiful album of striking photographs of common citizens.

**Swados, Harvey,** *The American Writer and the Great Depression* (1966). "So far as the written word can ever serve to give people some inkling of an experience they have not shared, this is the book that shows what the Depression was like" (Granville Hicks).

**Terkel, Studs,** *Hard Times* (1970). This marvelous "oral history of the Great Depression" gives "the human dimensions of the most traumatic experience in our 20th century history . . . and with a depth, variety and vividness I've found in no other book!" (Dwight MacDonald).

**Wilson, Edmund,** *The American Jitters: A Year of the Slump* (1932). Straight reporting during 1931 by an acute observer and writer. "A dazzling panorama of an epoch in our history" (Arthur M. Schlesinger, Jr.).

## Postwar Years

**Alther, Lisa,** *Kinflicks* (1976). Ambitious novel, full of humor and candor, about a sixties Candide, Ginny Babcock Ellis, and her adventures as cheerleader, college coed, antiwar activist, militant lesbian, communard, farmer, and housewife.

**Clark, Ronald W.,** *The Greatest Power on Earth: The International Race for Nuclear Supremacy* (1981). In a lively narrative a superb science popularizer offers a fresh view of this century's most awesome drama: the international interplay of science, politics, and technology in the discovery and development of nuclear fission.

**Cooke, Alistair,** *Generation on Trial: U.S.A. vs. Alger Hiss* (rev. 1952). Absorbing narrative, which reads like a mystery novel and is "not only the finest report on a much-reported case but one of the most vivid and literate descriptions of an American political event that has ever been written" (Richard H. Rovere).

**Davidson, Sara,** *Real Property* (1980). Collection of personal pieces on the seventies; "not many writers can cover the ground Sara Davidson does here with anything like her grace, energy and humor" (Jane Howard).

**Didion, Joan,** *Slouching Towards Bethlehem* (1968). One of the best artifacts of the sixties, it is a collection of essays full of bizarre detail. The title piece may be the best short work on the decade. See her essays of the seventies, *The White Album* (1979).

**Goldman, Eric,** *The Crucial Decade — and After: America 1945–1960* (1961). A punchy, witty, swift-moving flashback of the Truman-Eisenhower years.

**Halberstam, David,** *The Best and the Brightest* (1972). Gracefully written study of the decision-making process of the sixties, which drew the U.S. deeper into the Vietnam War.

**Hoagland, Edward,** *Walking the Dead Diamond River* (1973). Collection of honest, tough-minded essays on contemporary American life, the New England wilderness, assassinations, dogs, jury duty, mountain lions, meat markets, power, and fame; about women's liberation and city life. Other collections of his fine personal essays are *The Courage of Turtles* (1970), *Red Wolves, Black Bears* (1976), and *The Tugman's Passage* (1982).

**McNally, Dennis,** *Desolate Angel: Jack Kerouac, the Beat Generation, and America* (1979). More than a biography, it is a vivid reconstruction of the Beat milieu.

**McNeill, Don,** *Moving Through Here* (1970). Selection of McNeill's weekly columns for the *Village Voice,* 1967–68, chronicling East Village life from the Summer of Love to the bloody Grand Central "Yip-In."

**Mailer, Norman,** *The Armies of the Night* (1968). Treating in novelistic style the 1967 peace march on the Pentagon, this Pulitzer Prize–winning book, one of the author's best, tells us much about what we were like in the sixties. See *Miami and the Siege of Chicago* (1968).

**Piercy, Marge,** *Small Changes* (1973). Novel about radicals and the counterculture of the sixties that captures the argot and aspirations of that generation. *Vida* (1979) is about the underground of the seventies, while *Braided Lives* (1981) is a spacious feminist novel of the fifties.

**Raines, Howell,** *My Soul Is Rested* (1977). Oral history of the civil-rights movement of the late fifties and early sixties. A moving work.

**Schlesinger, Arthur M., Jr.,** *A Thousand Days: John Fitzgerald Kennedy in the White House* (1965). Informative, personal memoir of the short-lived administration by a personal admirer of the president. Winner of Pulitzer Prize.

**Stone, I. F.,** *In a Time of Torment* (1967). Great reporting by the distinguished independent journalist from the sixties, with emphasis on the then-dominating issues of Vietnam and race. See *The Truman Era* (1953).

**Stone, Robert,** *Dog Soldiers* (1974). National Book Award–winning novel that gives magnificent, indelible artistic expression to the dark side of the American dream in the savage seventies.

**Updike, John,** *Rabbit, Run* (1960). Harry "Rabbit" Angstrom is a twenty-six-year-old salesman, a husband, and a father attempting to figure out what he should do. This is a rich novel that explores the rootlessness of contemporary America. The effect of the immense social changes of the sixties and seventies on Rabbit is examined in *Rabbit Redux* (1971) and *Rabbit Is Rich* (1981).

**White, Theodore H.,** *The Making of the President, 1960* (1961). The first of an award-winning series of dramatically rendered presidential election reports by one of America's best journalists. For an unorthodox and driving view of an election campaign, see gonzo journalist Hunter S. Thompson's *Fear and Loathing: On the Campaign Trail '72* (1973).

**Willis, Ellen,** *Beginning to See the Light* (1981). With intellectual vigor and affecting honesty and wit, this gathering of Willis's essays from the seventies on politics, feminism, mass culture, and other phenomena helps define the decade.

**Wolfe, Tom,** *The Electric Kool-Aid Acid Test* (1968). The father of the "new journalism" limns an unforgettable picture of the psychedelic era in this report about Ken Kesey and the Merry Pranksters. The best of his short pieces are in *A Tom Wolfe Reader* (1982).

# THE FUTURE

**Aldiss, Brian,** *Greybeard* (1964). Hopeful novel of post–World War III earth in a twenty-first century rendered sterile by nuclear holocaust.

**Bass, T. J.,** *Half Past Human* (1971). The far future, when humans live in underground utopias. Full of fascinating biophysical detail. See *The Godwhale* (1974).

**Bester, Alfred,** *The Stars My Destination* (1957). Science-fiction classic of adventure in the twenty-fifth century when teleportation is common; *The Count of Monte Cristo* of the future.

**Brunner, John,** *The Sheep Look Up* (1972). One of the bleakest dystopias ever imagined in science fiction literature. See *Stand on Zanzibar* (1968).

**Burgess, Anthony,** *A Clockwork Orange* (1963). Fascinating Swiftian picture of a violent England written in an intriguing special patois. See *The Wanting Seed* (1963).

**Carr, Terry (ed.),** *Dream's Edge: Science Fiction Stories About the Future of Planet Earth* (1980). Excellent, wide-ranging collection of stories about what life will be like within the next hundred years.

**Christopher, John,** *The White Mountain* (1967). Opening novel of a crisply written trilogy for young readers set in post-apocalypse England: three boys fighting an alien race who view humanity with contempt. A second "juvenile" trilogy begins with *The Prince in Waiting* (1970).

**Clarke, Arthur C.,** *Childhood's End* (1953). A visionary, humanistic novel of a utopian earth by the leading English science fiction writer. See *Imperial Earth* (1976).

**Crowley, John,** *Engine Summer* (1979). This novel's projection of postdoomsday civilization is wonderfully exciting and imaginative. See *Beasts* (1976).

**Harrison, Harry,** *The Year 2000* (1970). Anthology of science-fiction writers' non-fiction projections of what life on earth will be like at the turn of the century. Harrison's novel, *Make Room, Make Room* (1966) is set in New York City when man has run out of living and agricultural space.

**Hoban, Russell,** *Riddley Walker* (1981). Haunting novel of postdoomsday England, reverted to primitivism. A bold, verbally imaginative work of art.

**Huxley, Aldous,** *Brave New World* (1932). Classic novel of a soulless, streamlined Eden — a brilliant and terrifying evocation of the future. See *Brave New World Revisited* (1958).

**Lee, Tanith,** *Night's Master* (1978). First of a projected six-volume Flat Earth series, a heroic fantasy spanning thousands of years in which the forces of good and evil do battle with each other. One of the best, and certainly the sexiest, of contemporary fantasies.

**Lem, Stanislaw,** *The Star Diaries* (1976). Fictional remembrances of Ijon Tichy, peripatetic astronaut-philosopher, that tell us much about how we live today. More in *Memories of a Space Traveler* (1982). See *Tales of Pirx the Pilot* (1980) and *Return from the Stars* (1980).

**Lessing, Doris,** *Shikasta* (1979). First of a cycle of novels called Canopus in Argos: Archives that encompasses millions of years of earth's evolution and uses several conflicting styles and manners to do it.

**Merle, Robert,** *Malevil* (1974). A cheerful doomsday novel where survivors set about rebuilding civilization.

**O'Neill, Gerard K.,** *2081: A Hopeful View of the Human Future* (1981). Fictionalized narrative by Princeton physicist-futurologist about future technology and space colonies. Fascinating and happily optimistic.

**Orwell, George,** *Nineteen Eighty-Four* (1949). Novel of a totalitarian future which points to "the danger of a society of automators who will have lost every trace of individuality, of love, of critical thought, and yet who will not be aware of it because of 'doublethink' " (Erich Fromm).

**Percy, Walker,** *Love in the Ruins: The Adventures of a Bad Catholic at a Time near the End of the Earth* (1971). A remarkably original, thoughtful, and funny novel.

**Piserchia, Doris,** *Earth in Twilight* (1981). The future here is devoid of human life, but strange quasihumans roam the earth. A grim projection, told with deadpan humor. Other far future novels are *A Billion Days of Earth* (1978) and *Earthchild* (1977).

**Toffler, Alvin,** *The Third Wave* (1980). Popular predictions of the changes society will go through in the immediate future. Be prepared for "future shock."

**Vance, Jack,** *The Dying Earth* (1950). Rich romantic fantasy set in the final days of our planet when sorcery reigns.

**Vidal, Gore,** *Messiah* (1954). Compelling novel about a new California cult and the prophet of a worldwide religion based on the worship of death. See *Kalki* (1978).

**Vonnegut, Kurt,** *Player Piano* (1952). Sharp-eyed satire about a failed revolution against automation in a machine-run world. Vonnegut's first, and one of his best, novels. See *The Sirens of Titan* (1959).

**Wolfe, Gene,** *The Shadow of the Torturer* (1980). Inaugural volume of the Book of the New Sun series about Severin the torturer. It blends the lyric extravagance of fantasy and the keen edge of science fiction, and its future is so distant that it seems like the ancient past. Already acclaimed a masterpiece.

**Zamiatin, Eugene,** *We* (1924). The joys of unfreedom in a regimented future by a powerful Russian novelist to whom Orwell acknowledged his debt.

# INDEXES

# Author Index

# Subject Index